W9-CQP-842

AA

THE VISITOR'S GUIDE TO
BRITAIN

AA

THE VISITOR'S GUIDE TO

BRITAIN

Edited and with an Introduction by
ESMOND WRIGHT

Webb&Bower

MICHAEL JOSEPH

The publishers would like to thank Mary Tamplin
for her work in researching the material for the
gazetteer section of this book

Frontispiece: Salisbury Cathedral

First published in Great Britain 1987 by
Webb & Bower (Publishers) Limited
9 Colleton Crescent, Exeter, Devon EX2 4BY
in association with The Automobile Association,
Fanum House, Basingstoke and Michael Joseph Limited
27 Wright's Lane, London W8 5SL

Designed by Ron Pickless

Production by Nick Facer

British Library Cataloguing in Publication Data
Wright, Esmond
AA visitors guide to Britain.
1. Great Britain—Description and travel
—1971– —Guide-books
I. Title
914.1'04858   DA650

Webb & Bower ISBN 0–86350–111–7

AA ISBN 0–86145–356–5

AA reference 59336

Typeset in Great Britain by Keyspools Ltd.,
Golborne, Lancashire

Printed and bound in Great Britain
by Purnell Book Production Ltd., Paulton, Bristol

CONTENTS

HOW TO USE THIS BOOK

Places open to the public

Places of interest, such as stately homes, castles, etc, that are open to the public, are indicated, where known, either by the letters 'OACT', meaning 'open at certain times'; or 'NT', standing for National Trust'; or 'AM', standing for Ancient Monument (i.e. one under the care of the Department of the Environment).

The National Grid

This system of map reference divides the country into a series of 100km squares, each identified by two letters of the alphabet – for example, **SX, SY, NT, NU, TL, TM**. These large areas are shown on the maps by heavy blue lines and each square so formed contains the appropriate letters, printed in blue on the atlas pages at the end of this book. Each of these large squares is divided into 10 smaller squares of 10km, marked on the atlas by fainter blue lines and numbered 0–9 around the edges of the map. To find **Canterbury** for example, with a map reference **6 TR15**, turn to page 6 of the atlas, then find the large square (marked out by heavy blue lines) containing the letters 'TR'. Next, look along the bottom edge of the map for the **number 1**, and along the side of the map for the **number 5**. Where these two lines cross is the bottom left-hand corner of the 10km square in which **Canterbury** will be found. The National Grid system is common to most modern British atlases, of whatever scale, so that it is possible to find any place on any atlas by looking up the National Grid Number.

FOREWORD

Henry James's famous list of those features of England that he missed in his own country and that led him into permanent exile – he lived for forty years in Rye and became a British citizen – gives one clue to Britain's appeal to the visitor. He writes 'What is America?... no sovereign, no court, no aristocracy, no country gentlemen, no palaces, no castles, nor manors, nor old country-houses, no parsonages, nor thatched cottages, no ivied ruins; no cathedrals, nor abbeys, nor little Norman churches ... no Oxford, nor Eton ... no Epsom, nor Ascot....'

Henry James's list gives, however, only one man's view. There are other even more famous lines, those of Shakespeare in Richard II, that give a clue to British history, or to the myths that are its legacy:

> 'This royal throne of Kings, this sceptr'd isle,
> This earth of majesty, this seat of Mars,
> This other Eden, demi-Paradise,
> This fortress built by Nature for herself
> Against infection and the hand of War,
> This happy breed of men, this little world,
> This precious stone set in a silver sea,
> Which serves it in the office of a wall,
> Or as a moat defensive to a house
> Against the envy of less happier lands.
> This blessed plot, this earth, this realm,
>   this England.'

To understand Britain, one must start not just with history and its visible evidence in castles, cathedrals and palaces, but with that particular blend of rock and water, geology and landscape out of which its history has grown. An island, yes. But only in and after Shakespeare's day did British seapower – or at first and more accurately English seapower – ensure that it was a fortress 'against the envy of less happier lands.' It was made so less by nature than by Tudor ships and captains, by the courage and skill of Raleigh and Grenville, Drake and Frobisher in the days of the first Elizabeth, by Nelson's qualities two centuries later, and by those of its airmen in 1940. Until then, as it is now again, it was at the mercy of the elements. Of these some were basic: the sea, and the lines between highland and lowland, and between chalk and clay. Ever since, some 10,000 years ago, the Atlantic flood cut Britain off from the European mainland, the seas have been for her as much a highway as a moat. When roads were no more than worn but muddy tracks, the coastal waters were the main trade and transport routes. Until Tudor times the Channel was not a political, cultural, religious or linguistic boundary; from the time when written records began, Britain's story is totally enmeshed with that of Europe; it was – as originally it probably had been anyway – 'part of the main'. In the 12th and 13th centuries English kings ruled over much of what is now France, and French rulers made counter-claims of their own. Not until the 16th century did English kings abandon some French territory, not until 1802 did they abandon the title in all formal documents of 'Kings of England and France'.

The Irish seas were even more a highway; an ocean on whose shores lived peoples with common traditions who, originally speaking a single language, only gradually became distinct: Irish, Scots (originally from Ireland), Welsh, Bretons and Cornish – linguistically linked but never politically united. From them would seem to have come the first inhabitants of what is now 'England'. And it was invaded by successive waves of peoples: by Celts; by the Romans; by Angles, Saxons and Jutes; by the Danes and the Norsemen (the Vikings); and then, in 1066 at Hastings, by the Normans and their allies, while another Danish invasion was taking place further north.

Invasion did not cease with the Norman conquest. For at least a century the king and his liegemen were uncertain which side of the Channel was 'home' for them. Henry II had to invade the country three times before he was recognized as king in 1154. When King John died in 1216, a French army was in 'England', and both Henry III and the French Dauphin, the future Louis VIII, could claim the throne. During the Angevin period, England was part of France, and vice versa; England was also in religious terms a fief of Rome, and Latin was the international language of the Church. Thus the country had been after 55 BC so much a distant outlying flank of a great common market, and of a religious, cultural and Latin-speaking empire, that our recent arguments over 'joining' the European Economic Community have seemed to many totally unhistoric. Indeed not since 1066 has England had a native English dynasty on the throne. It has been ruled by Normans and Danes and French, by Welsh, by Scots, by Dutch and by Hanoverians. Some have come as invaders, some by legitimate succession, some by invitation; all have rapidly been absorbed and 'naturalized'.

Nevertheless, the Channel did during the pre-Tudor period assure some decades – and, though rarely, some centuries – of freedom from invasion. After the accession of Alfred to the Kingdom of Wessex in 871 there was a gradual, if interrupted, movement towards political unity, notably by the absorption of the other major English kingdoms of Mercia and Northumbria until, by the time Henry III was safely on the throne, one can speak of an England with something like its present frontiers; with Wales along Offa's Dyke, and with Scotland along the line of the Tweed, the Cheviot Hills and the Roman Wall.

There is another frontier. Quite as important as the Channel, at once linking yet cutting us off from the mainland of Europe, is the line between highland and lowland, and the line between light soils and heavy clay. On the land below 600 feet there has been large-scale arable farming, especially on the heavy clay of the English Midlands. The higher land is for dairy farming and for sheep grazing – or at least for forests and for peat. Throughout British history, the line between the two – however imprecise the boundary – has been a key to the story. To the Romans, the civil area was that of the south-east lowlands, with London at its centre; the rest was for the military. There were two sharp frontier lines, one stretching from the Northumbrian fells to the Solway, where Hadrian's Wall was built, and another, a line of earthworks, farther north as an outer defence. The Celtic areas – Wales, Cumbria and Scotland – lay beyond the 'highland line'. Both inside Wales – in the line between 'Welsh' Wales (where Welsh is still a widely spoken – and widely sung – language) and 'English' Wales (mainly Glamorgan) – and inside Scotland, the line between highland and lowland is clear.

The Anglo-Saxon invaders, whatever their motives and their hunger for booty, became arable farmers, reclaiming the lowlands from the dense forest and working the heavy clay; the natives fell back into their fastnesses before them. And even inside the smaller regions the land would determine its history. Along the seventy miles of Roman Wall the history of the Western Cumbrian end, where there are mountain ranges, is more bloodthirsty than that of the gentler granary towards Wallsend.

This is a universal theme: the distinction between highland and lowland, mountain and river valley. The mountain sheep might be sweeter but the valley sheep are fatter; and in the words of Thomas Love Peacock* highland reivers have always 'deemed it meeter to carry off the latter'.

From this series of invasions and these clashes of race and region came into being the 'True-Born Englishman'. As Defoe said of him: ' "True-born Englishman"? Picts, Romans, Gauls, Greeks, Lombards, Irish –

Auxiliaries or slaves of every nation –
All these their barb'rous offspring left behind,
The dregs of armies, they of all mankind;
Blended with Britons who before were here,
Of which the Welsh have blessed the character,
From this amphibious ill-born mob began
That vain ill-natured thing, an Englishman.'

* Thomas Love Peacock, 'The Misfortunes of Elphin' II (1829).

ANCIENT BRITAIN

In prehistoric terms, Britain's is a recent history. Even so, her human history appears to go back some 400,000 years to Paleolithic times. During this period, on at least four occasions an ice-sheet spread south, lowering the sea-level as it did so and making Britain a western promontory of Europe. At times, in these glacial advances, there was no 'Scotland' or 'Wales' at all, and no 'England' north of the Wash. In the warmer intervals, *homo erectus* appears – as parts of a skull and some flint tools found at Swanscombe in Kent testify. The technique of carbon-dating proved that 'Piltdown Man' was a hoax, and it seems likely that the second oldest human fossil in Britain is the so-called Red Lady of Paviland, found in the Gower Peninsula of Wales, and dated c 16,500 BC. Paleolithic man was a cave-dweller, using unpolished stone tools, ignorant of pottery and weaving, and no domestic animals. There is no evidence that he warred with other men.

The ice moved back for the fourth and final time about 8000 BC. In the following great thaw birch and mosses gave way to pine, and gradually to oak, beech and ash. Grassland gave way to forest, reindeer and bison to boar, elk and deer. The seas moved in, and the land bridge with Normandy disappeared. With the final surfacing and thawing of the island of Britain, a continuous 'British' history begins.

The rocks that give the British Isles their geological skeleton confirm this origin. They link it with a vanished continent now submerged under the Atlantic; and in this sense the western mountains – of Snowdonia, of the Lake District and of Wester Ross – are the peaks of the lost continent of Atlantis, to poets the drowned land of Lyonnesse. It can be no accident that these are the regions rich in legends and tales of magic, from which later the Arthurian legends and fairy tales came. The land was now heavily forested, with mainly conifers in the north, oak and elm, ash and alder

further south. Its aboriginal people were nomads, hunting and food-gathering in small family groups, camping alongside rivers and lakes but in winter for the most part still cave-dwellers. They struggled for food and survival against wild boar and wolves, elk and deer, using bows or flint-tipped spears and harpoons, living on eggs, roots and berries, and meat when they were lucky or skilful.

Invaders, from the Continent or by sea, even from the Levant, came early. They sought the tin and copper of Cornwall and the gold ornaments of Ireland; for traders from the Mediterranean these were the Tin Islands. They brought knowledge of agriculture, of grain-growing and of the domestication of animals, of the hoe and the spade, of cloth-weaving and of the making of clay pots; and they were traders as well as boat-builders and sailors. Settled life, tillage and pasturage and mixed farming began. It is this that constitutes the Neolithic Revolution. These early farmers were ancestor worshippers, burying the dead with their possessions around them in communal graves or long barrows; and worshippers too, it seems, of that magic that each spring brought rebirth and renewal of life. Apart from this, we know nothing of their religion. Two of their great legacies, Stonehenge and Avebury, are seen by some as sepulchres – but empty of human remains – and by others as temples of sun-worshippers. Stonehenge in its stark majesty is evidence of considerable knowledge of architecture and geometry. Some estimates suggest that to build either Stonehenge or Silbury Hill would require the labour of 1000 men for at least ten years. These Stone Age men were short and dark, in England and through Europe – for they lived in Southern France, Northern Spain, West Wales and the Highlands of Scotland. Numbers grew, nomadism declined, and cultivation developed.

Between 1000 and 500 BC came the successive small-scale invasions of the tall, blue-eyed Celts or Gaels, or Goidels, from what is now France and originally probably from eastern Europe. Their strength was their knowledge of the working of bronze, more durable than copper, easy to smelt, savage as weapons. They were tribal and bloodthirsty, addicted not only to headhunting but to cannibalism, when they were not more interested in treasuring their captured heads as souvenirs. They seem to have been vain, boastful and especially proud of their long, fair moustaches. They drove the earlier peoples into the west; they built permanent villages and especially hill-forts, mainly in the south east and south west; and they may have spread over one fifth of the whole country.

Prehistoric periods	
Paleolithic (Old Stone Age)	c 450 000 – 8000 BC
Mesolithic (Middle Stone Age)	c 8000 – 4000 BC
Neolithic (New Stone Age)	c 4000 – 2000BC
Bronze Age	c 2000 – 700 BC
Iron Age	c 700 BC – AD 43

Their language survives in two forms: Goidelic in Ireland, some parts of the Western Isles, Highlands of Scotland and Isle of Man; Brythonic in Brittany and in Wales.

Alongside the Celts, and later in time, were other invaders, themselves driven out of their own lands: the Belgae (to Julius Caesar the bravest of all the tribes) who dominated Essex and reached as far as Salisbury and Dorset; the Brigantes of the Yorkshire Dales; and the Iceni of Norfolk.

Perversely, it was one of the smallest and most recent of the invading groups, the Cymri or Brythons, representing an Iron Age culture, who ultimately gave their name to the whole island. And with the name comes the beginning of real archaeological evidence: bronze helmets and golden torques and bracelets, amber cups and engraved hand-mirrors. For they were skilled workers in gold, tin and iron. With chariots and wheels, swords and ploughs, they broke their enemies – and the soil. They traded with the Phoenicians – Pytheas of Marseilles (c 330 BC) noted the large corn crops they exported – and the Long Ships Rock off Land's End refers to the long ships of the Phoenicians. On the hilltops they built great earthwork castles: Maiden Castle in Dorset, Old Sarum near Salisbury, Caer y Twr in Anglesey, Gwynedd, Hambledon Hill and Hod Hill in Dorset, Bredon Hill in the Malvern Hills, Uffington with its White Horse in Oxfordshire, and Dun of Downpatrick in Ulster. We know of some 2400 hill-forts in Britain.

Their lives were tribal, and their religion Druidical, with faith in the immortality of the soul (in barrows the dead are surrounded with food and weapons) but with a clear addiction to human sacrifice. They used and developed Stonehenge. Just as they had driven the Gaels westward, to the Highlands and to Ireland (the Welsh word for Irish is *Gwyddel*), so they in turn were to be pushed west later; and one form of their name survives in 'Britain', another in 'Cymri' (the Welsh name for Wales) and 'Cumbria'.

Places to Visit

British Museum of Natural History, S Kensington, London; flint tools from 200,000 BC, or before, are on display. *Kirkdale*, Yorkshire. Paleolithic cave paintings.
Cheddar Caves and Museum, Cheddar Gorge; the *Wookey Hole Caves* near Wells, both in Somerset. The *British Museum*, London, and the *Oxford University Museum*. The Red Lady of Paviland is in *Oxford Museum*.
Museum of Sussex Archaeology, Lewes. *Maes Howe*, near Kirkwall in Orkney, for Britain's finest megalithic tomb and *Skara Brae* for a Stone Age Village. *Yeavering Bell*, in the Cheviots, for an Iron Age hill-fort. As well as Stonehenge and Silbury Hill, see the chambered tombs of *West Kennet*, west of Marlborough in Wiltshire; *Brane Tomb* near St Just and *Chun Quoit* near Penzance, in Cornwall; *Hetty Pegler's Tump* near Stroud in Gloucestershire; a number of sites on St Mary's Island in the Scilly Islands; *Parc Cwm* in the Gower Peninsula to the west of Swansea; or *La Hougue Bie* on Jersey.

Note: Megalithic tombs are known by different names in different regions: chambered tombs, tumuli, tumps (in Gloucestershire), quoits (in Cornwall), dolmens or cromlechs (Wales and the West of England), cairns (Scotland).

In County Armagh *Navan Fort* – the 'Stonehenge of Ulster' was the royal residence of Ulster's pre-Christian Kings and, known as Emain Macha, was the site of the tales associated with Deirdre of the Sorrows and Cuchulain. Its fort is probably at least 3000 years old.

Further Reading

A H A Hogg, *A Guide to the Hill-Forts of Britain* (Paladin)
Peter Clayton, *Archaeological Sites of Britain* (Weidenfeld & Nicolson)

Stonehenge, Avebury (inset left) and Silbury Hill (inset right)

Two of the few legacies of Stone Age man, Stonehenge and Avebury, are seen by some as sepulchres – but empty of human remains – and by others as the temples of sun-worshippers. Stonehenge in its stark majesty is evidence of considerable knowledge of architecture and geometry. Some estimates suggest that to build either Stonehenge or Silbury Hill would require the labour of 1000 men for at least ten years.

ROMAN BRITAIN

The first Roman invasions of Britannia, to them just outside the 'known' world, were designed to curb the support the Celtic tribes were giving to Armorican and German tribes opposing Rome in Gaul. Caius Julius Caesar, Governor of Cisalpine and Transalpine Gaul, did not stay long, and both in 55 BC (when he had two legions – some 10,000 men – with him) and 54 BC (when he brought five legions and 2,000 cavalry) his ships were almost wrecked as they lay in harbour. If *veni, vidi, vici* 'I came, I saw, I conquered', is true, it should be added also that *abui*, 'I vanished'. It was not until the reign of the Emperor Claudius (acceded AD 41) that Roman legions, and for sixteen days the Emperor in person, came – and stayed. By AD 78, after a generation of resistance led by Druid priests, Wales was under Roman sway, with garrisons at Chester and Caerleon near Newport. For the rest, Rome controlled the south east, but supported three client states: to the north the Brigantes (Midlands, Yorkshire, Northumbria), the Iceni (Norfolk) and the Belgae of West Sussex.

In AD 79 the Roman governor Agricola, applying a new policy of direct military control, reached the Tyne-Solway line, and in the following year that of Forth and Clyde. By 84 30,000 Caledonians had been defeated at Mons Graupius in the Grampians, but after Agricola's recall in 85, it was the Tyne-Solway that became the definitive frontier line. And we begin now to have near-continuous written evidence, in part because Agricola was wise or lucky enough to have as son-in-law the historian Tacitus. Hadrian built his Wall, begun in 122, from Tyne to Solway; especially striking is the middle section at Housesteads (*Vercovicium*), with its protective ditch and *vallum* and its regular mile-stations, noteworthy too are the auxiliary forts, as at Chesterholm (*Vindolanda*), Corbridge, (*Corstopitum*), and Hardknott

(*Mediobogdum*) in the Lake District. The Wall ends in the west at Bowness on Solway. For the thirty miles beyond it to St Bees, its flank on the Solway Firth is protected against sea-borne threats by three forts comparable to those of the Wall: at Beckfoot, south of Silloth, at Maryport, where a hoard of altars has been found, and at Moresby, just north of Whitehaven. It was known until Tudor times not as the Roman Wall, but as the Picts Wall, since it was designed to keep them out, or at least to discourage raiding parties. In 142, Antoninus Pius also had a turf wall built forty miles to the north, from the Forth to the Clyde, but it did not last more than some twenty years. Its ditch is still clearly visible, one mile east of Bonnybridge.

The impact of Rome was permanent. The Romans built 5000 miles of splendid paved and raised roads, some, 2000 years later, transformed into motorways and still in use, many to be buried under later developments – Ermine Street, Stane Street, Watling Street, the Fosse Way, and Dere Street (from Corbridge running north), to give them their Saxon names. The roads often ignored the grain of the land, and were built with a superb disregard both for the terrain and for labour costs. They built towns, modelled on their own, originally on or near the sites of legionary fortresses, and sometimes inhabited by retired legionaries: like *Camulodunum* (Colchester), where Claudius, in AD 43, received the formal surrender of the native chiefs, *Lindum* (Lincoln), *Nervia Glevensium* (Gloucester), *Eboracum* (York), HQ of the illustrious ninth legion and later of the sixth, *Venta Belgarum* (Winchester), *Isca Silurum* (Caerleon) in Gwent, HQ of the second legion for three centuries, *Deva* (Chester), HQ of the twentieth legion, *Verulamium* (St Albans), London – and many more. The 'Chesters' the Saxon invaders called them – which later invaders would destroy or bypass.

These Roman towns are still the natural centres of their regions. They were impressive and almost uniform examples of town-planning, with defensive walls, a central forum, shops with the owners living above, a basilica for the administration of justice, a temple or temples for worship and, not least, the public baths, of which those at Bath are the best surviving example. The Roman emphasis on cleanliness, sanitation – and on underfloor heating – was remarkable. At its best, a Roman villa, with its tessellated pavements of mosaics (*tesserae*) and its *hypocaust*, its underfloor hot air ducts, was both elegant and comfortable. Apart from the Wall, some of the most striking examples of Roman building date from the 3rd century, when the Empire was threatened by Saxon raids from across the North Sea. The forts of the so-called Saxon shore – from the Wash to Spithead – indicate the awesome skill of the Romans as military builders and architects. But even they proved unavailing. As foreign threats mounted, so native breakaway movements also surfaced – in 286 Carausius, commander of the British fleet, declared himself an independent emperor of Britain and North Gaul; and in 350 Magentius and in 383 Magnus Maximus each tried, and failed, to usurp power. In 410 the legions were finally recalled for home defence, and Britain was told – as 1500 years later it would have to tell each of its own former colonies – to look to its own defences. The price of empire was now too high. And then, as later, there were few votes of thanks. Nor was there any declaration of independence, no ringing sentiments, no secession of rebellious states, no proclamation of emancipation, no salute to the flag as the trumpets sounded farewell.

The power of the Roman Empire rested on its splendid army, of which one-tenth of its total forces were kept in Britain, and almost all the surviving evidence of the Roman presence is

military. But the Romans gave equal justice to all citizens and the empire was infinitely mixed in race. If many of the auxiliaries were natives, the legionaries were drawn from the whole of the known world. *Arbeia*, the fort at South Shields, was garrisoned in the 3rd century by a cohort of Gauls, in the 4th by a unit of boatmen from the Tigris delta, who must have found it a bleak posting; at Housesteads there was a cohort of Tungrians from Belgium. Africans and Greeks, Spaniards, Germans and Danubians all served in Britain; many married local girls: many retired here. To be able to say *Civus Romanus sum* – I am a Roman citizen – was a proud passport.

Places to Visit
Roman forts of the Saxon shoreline worth visiting are: *Brancaster*, Norfolk; *Burgh Castle*, Dover; *Richborough*, Kent; *Pevensey*, East Sussex; *Portchester*, Hampshire. As a preliminary visit to Hadrian's Wall, see the *Museum of the University of Newcastle-upon-Tyne*. The major Roman collection is in the *British Museum*, London. Other major museums with plenty of interest on the Roman period are at *Chester* (Grosvenor Museum), *Cirencester* (Corinium Museum), *Colchester, Canterbury, Bath, St Albans* and note recent excavations at *York*. For a Brigantes site see *Stanwick Park* near Richmond, North Yorkshire, and *Isurium* at Aldborough, near Ripon, North Yorkshire.

Further Reading
Anthony R Birley, *Life in Roman Britain* (Batsford)

Hadrian's Wall

Anthony R Birley, *The People of Roman Britain* (Batsford)
Levin Birley, *Vindolanda: A Roman Frontier Post on Hadrian's Wall* (Chesterholm Museum, Hexham). An account of the rich finding in 1972 of Hadrianic Roman textiles, leatherwork, and, most astonishing of all, wooden writing tablets. One of the richest collections ever found in Western Europe.
Keith Branigan, *Roman Britain* (Reader's Digest)
Rena Gardiner, *The Country of Hadrian's Wall* (National Trust)
Rudyard Kipling, *Puck of Pook's Hill*
Malcolm Todd, *Roman Britain 55 BC–AD 400* (Fontana)
Margeurite Yourcenar, *Memoirs of Hadrian* (Secker & Warburg 1955)

WHO WAS KING ARTHUR?

In the fifth century, a military leader whom the Welsh chronicler, Nennius, called Artorius (? c 480–c 540), led a small but mobile force of cavalrymen in defence, originally, of south-west England against the invading and heathen Saxons. He was presumably a Christian, and his name suggests a Romano-British origin. He was not a king but a *dux bellorum*, a professional soldier who appears to have won twelve battles in locations ranging from southern Scotland to Somerset. Given the surviving Roman roads, given that helmeted horsemen wearing armour could relatively easily destroy less experienced infantry equipped only with swords and spears, his movements, his victories and his reputation all become explicable. Some authorities, like Arthur Duggan, however, argue that Arthur's strength depended on his large and strong horses, carefully imported from the Continent, and that military decline coincided with the failure to keep up the breed, and soon there were only the insular horses, smaller and less formidable.

Literacy was the privilege of the monastic communities; for the rest, it was oral tradition that mattered, the legacy of bards and storytellers. As chroniclers like William of Malmesbury (in his *Gesta Regum Britanniae*, written c 1125) and Geoffrey of Monmouth (he wrote his *Historia Regum Britanniae* in 1137), or poets like Chrétien de Troyes told, reflected on and embroidered the legend of Arthur, so later kings exploited it. Henry II called his grandson, born in 1187, Arthur – but his death (murdered by his uncle King John?) prevented his accession. Henry, however, also had Glastonbury Abbey restored, since according to the legend Arthur and his queen, Guinevere, were buried there; and it was there, on a hill surrounded by marshes, almost an island, that two skeletons were found in 1190, the male one being a strikingly tall man with a damaged skull, on whose leaden cross were inscribed the words: *Hic jacet sepultus Rex Arthurius in Insula Avalonia* (here lies buried King Arthur in the Isle of Avalon).

In 1344 Edward III vowed to restore Arthur's Round Table, and in 1348 founded the Order of the Garter in succession to Arthur's knighthood. In 1485 Henry Tudor, a cautious Welshman succeeding to the throne as Henry VII and quick to seize on a Celtic legend, named his first-born son Arthur; but the boy died, and it was his younger brother who succeeded as Henry VIII. In 1485 with the printing press just invented, came Sir Thomas Malory's *Morte d'Arthur*. Malory places Arthur's court in Winchester, and not in Camelot. The Round Table at least survives in the castle there; it was probably constructed in the 14th century and was given its Tudor rose and its Tudor colours, green and white, by Henry VIII. Legends live by repetition, and this many layered Arthurian story, which clearly has a firm historic root, and a rich array of characters (Guinevere, Lancelot, Galahad, Merlin, Tristram and Iseult) has become, thanks to Tennyson and Wagner, familiar across the world. It is the central myth in British history.

Places to Visit
Tintagel, Cornwall. Arthur's reputed birthplace.

Glastonbury, Somerset. Glastonbury was one of the holy places of the Celtic church, visited by St Patrick and St David.
Carlisle, the Roman *Luguvalium*.
Winchester Castle, where Arthur's court allegedly broke up.
South Cadbury, near Yeovil, and reputed to be the site of Camelot.
Arthur's Seat, Edinburgh.
Bamburgh, the possible site of Sir Lancelot's castle of Joyous Gard.
Hartfell, near Carlisle. Merlin's last sanctuary?
Bardsey Island, where Merlin is buried?

Further Reading
Geoffrey Ashe, Ed, *The Quest for Arthur's Britain* (Pall Mall Press)
Neil Fairbairn, *A Traveller's Guide to the Kingdoms of Arthur* (Evans Bros)
Mary Stewart, *The Crystal Cave* (for Merlin), *The Hollow Hills* (for Arthur's youth), *The Last Enchantment* (all Coronet). A splendid, fictionalized telling of the story.

Tintagel Castle ruins

DARK AGES

The centuries that followed the withdrawal of the Roman legions are Britain's Dark Ages, and the prosperous Roman way of life was all but forgotten; indeed even before 410 many villagers still lived primitive lives, untouched by Roman civilization, with plague a too-frequent visitor. In the 4th century there was a serious drop in population and roads and building went unrepaired. In the 5th and 6th centuries attacks by Picts from Scotland, and Scots from Ireland, devastated the north and north west; the Franks and those Germanic tribes whom contemporary historians called Angles, Saxons and Jutes, and others simply Vandals, devastated the eastern coasts. Many of these incomers stayed, of course, to settle and to intermarry. By the 9th and 10th centuries, indeed, the Saxons were building fortifications of their own or using Iron Age hill-forts or old Roman sites or earthworks to protect themselves in turn from Viking raiders from northern Europe, who swept inland, wrecked Lindisfarne, raided northern coasts, and sailed round Scotland, to attack and settle from Shetland southwards via the Western Isles to Cumbria and the Isle of Man. From the 9th century the Norse Lords of Man (the present Queen's title on the Island is still 'Lord of Man') held regular open assemblies on Tynwald Hill to pass and proclaim laws – the precursor of the House of Keys, the Manx Parliament.

Yet through these troubled times there was some slow progress, like the making of the massive wheeled four- or eight-ox plough to tackle the heavier clay soils, and the water-mill for grinding corn. By the 8th century towns were developing again, often on the sites of old Roman cities, like Rochester, Winchester and Chichester. Some of them – Oxford and Shaftesbury for example – were new creations of Alfred of Wessex; and with them came trade. But, for the majority, life was nasty, brutish and short; and petty kingdoms warred savagely with each other.

England did not yet exist; it was a heptarchy; a collection of the seven small kingdoms of Kent, Essex, Sussex, East Anglia, Mercia, Wessex and Northumbria, of which the last three were the most important. Oswy of Northumbria controlled as far north as Aberdeen, but at Nechtansmere in 685 'English' rule over Scotland was permanently halted. Offa of Mercia in the 8th century, and Alfred of Wessex in the 9th were the two greatest English kings in the six centuries from 410 to 1066. These 'kings' often began as native regional warlords – or even, in the very early days, veteran officers of the Roman army – to resist barbarian invaders. One of these in Wales, 'Vortigern' or 'Chief Lord' was probably the ancestor of the later kings of Powys. Another was Ambrosius or Aurelianus, probably the real leader on whom the Arthur legends are based. Some of them even invited in some Saxons to hold back Pictish and Scottish invaders, only to become subject to blackmail and loss of territory to their 'allies'. Some built defensive earthworks, like Offa's Dyke which served later as a border between Mercia and Wales, or like Devil's Dyke in Cambridgeshire, a high earthwork that seems to have been built as a defence by the Anglo-Saxons as they, for their part, retreated before the Romano-British. Nevertheless, in the century before the Norman Conquest there was an almost united England, and Athelstan of Wessex (reigned 925–940) could with some justice call himself *Rex Anglorum, curegulus totius Britanniae*, 'King of the English and Lord of the whole of Britain'.

In the midst of this confusion, there was one stable bastion, the Church. It is usually said that St Augustine brought Christianity to England. It came in fact to the north of England from Ireland, through Iona off the island of Mull on the Scottish coast, under the leadership of St Columba, and through Lindisfarne off the Northumbrian coast under Aidan's direction (Aidan preached in Gaelic and King Oswald interpreted for him); and in Wales through the dedication of St David; and there were even earlier Christian converts – St Alban in the 4th century was one of the first English martyrs. With Christianity came churches and abbeys, monasteries and cathedrals, so many of them surviving as picturesque ruins that the list is endless and any choice inevitably personal. What is clear is that 'England' was in religion and education and through the Latin language of its churchmen, drawing inspiration from Europe. The conversion of a mainly barbaric and heathen group of peoples took at least three centuries. Guthrun, king of the Danelaw, the Danish territories in eastern England, agreed to be converted as part of the settlement with King Alfred (the Treaty of Wedmore 878); Northumbria was not fully Christian until the 9th century or even later. The conversion in England was accompanied by a cultural awakening, sometimes called the Northumbrian Renaissance (when the kingdom of Northumbria stretched from the Vale of York to the Scottish lowlands) but usually associated with the name of the Venerable Bede (died 737) the historian/scientist/theologian. He lived in his abbeys at Jarrow and Wearmouth, and left among many writings his famous *Ecclesiastical History of the English Nation*. We know also of other now historic figures; St Augustine of Canterbury, St Columba of Iona, St Wilfrid of York, the ascetic St Cuthbert of Melrose and Lindisfarne (whose body was moved by the monks to Durham after the Danish raiders destroyed his monastery in 793), St Dunstan in Glastonbury (later Archbishop of Canterbury), St Patrick in Ireland, St David in Wales and other monk historians like Gildas or Nennius; all are evidence of a considerable

Devil's Dyke, Cambridgeshire

population able to read the Gospels in the Latin tongue.

At Whitby Abbey in 664 a solemn conclave decided that the Christian Church in Northumbria (and so ultimately in the whole island) should follow the customs of Roman, not Celtic, Christianity. Roman Christianity was episcopal, urban and imperial, and rested firmly on Roman law and the legacy of the secular organization; Irish Christianity was tribal, monastic and loosely organized; simpler, but perhaps more an individualist faith. The church of the tribe gave way to the church of the empire. England became again part of a Roman Europe. The chief adviser of the Emperor Charlemagne (crowned 800), formally the first Emperor of the revived, Holy, Roman Empire, was Alcuin, a monk from York.

But England was still a fragmented country – it was that division that made possible the Norman conquest, like the Roman ten centuries before. When William the Conqueror, claiming the throne as Edward the Confessor's great-nephew, landed at Pevensey Bay in 1066, Harold Godwinson, the Saxon king who had been crowned only months before, had just returned from resisting an incursion into Northumbria of yet another claimant, Harold Hardrada, King of Norway. Harold Godwinson, killed at Hastings in 1066, was the last truly English king of England.

The immediate effect of the Norman Conquest was revolutionary. An alien army of a few thousand knights had seized a country with a population of over a million. The Duke of Normandy and his court were French speaking, even though he used native lords and prelates as his instruments. All who fought against him had their lands confiscated; a rebellion in 1069 was ruthlessly suppressed; after a second, in the northern counties in 1070, not a house remained standing on the road from York to Durham. In his tax-survey, written against many parts of Yorkshire is the single word 'waste'. Some took to the country, the fens and the forests, like Hereward the Wake. At the end of his reign in 1087 there were only two English landowners left, and only one English bishop. The lands reclaimed went to the King, and from him either to the Church or to some 170 of his immediate supporters. Half of it went to ten men, the great barons. The borders to north and west in particular had to be secure. The prince-bishop of Durham, and the Earls of Chester, Shrewsbury and Hereford ruled what later would be called palatinates, the last three enjoined to keep the 'marches' against Wales. Castles were built in the earldoms, at Cardiff and Monmouth. But most of those rewarded found their gifts of land scattered nationwide; there would be no other 'imperia' in the King's single 'imperium'. He had the whole country mapped and minutely surveyed, so that he would know 'about this land, and how it was peopled, and with what sort of men'. The structures of state and shire were sharper now. The Domesday Book, 1086–7, solidified the English kingdom and its new social order. It also mentions the existence of forty-nine castles.

Places to Visit
For Celtic Christianity: *Iona*; *Holy Island* (Lindisfarne), where, cut off from the mainland twice a day by the incoming sea,

'With the ebb and flow, its style
Changes from continent to isle;'

The simple monastic cells on the windswept and romantic headland of *Tintagel*, Cornwall.

For Roman Christianity: the 7th-century monastic church of *St Paul's* at Jarrow, now the chancel of the present church, where there has been continuous worship for almost 1300 years; *St Laurence's* at Bradford-on-Avon in Wiltshire; and not least *St Andrews* at Greensted, Essex, the sole surviving pre-Conquest wooden parish church.

·RUNNYMEDE

Runnymede on the Thames near Windsor is, thrice over, an Anglo-American memorial.

Here, on 15 June 1215, on the level grasslands along the river, King John agreed to terms imposed on him by the feudal barons. The King could not write, but he made his mark. The Great Charter has sixty-three clauses. Feudal exactions were to be limited, and no taxes were to be levied by the King against his feudal tenants, except by the consent of the Commune Concilium, to which the archbishops, bishops and greater barons were to be summoned individually, and other tenants-in-chief by a general writ sent to the sheriff (to this, the first 'Parliament', representatives of the cities and boroughs were to be added in 1265 and in 1295 and thereafter; from 1341 the members sat in two distinct houses). This was the beginning of government by consent. It was the beginning too of due process of law, a basic principle in American law as in English. 'To none will we sell, to none will we deny or delay right or justice'. No man could be punished except by due process of law, and after a trial by a jury of his peers. The great Charter was the work of the

Magna Carta memorial

barons, who sought to limit the King's exactions not for the nation but for themselves; but in their selfishness they spoke, however indirectly, for the people, and for the eight centuries of ordered government that began, at least as a principle to be aspired to, at Runnymede. They protected not only themselves but the Church and the people of towns and counties.

Without the Charter it is possible that a completely monarchical and arbitrary despotism would have grown up in England, as it did in France. It is in the Magna Carta that parliamentary – and in the end, limited – monarchy is born; in essence this document is, in primitive feudal form, the only British Constitution that exists.

The Magna Carta Memorial at Runnymede, a small temple, was erected in 1957 by the American Bar Association. Here too, on Cooper's Hill above Runnymede, is a memorial to the 20,000 RAF and British Commonwealth airmen killed in World War II who have no known grave. And here too, in tribute to his dedication to 'the survival and success of liberty', is a simple memorial erected in 1965 to President John F Kennedy. It stands on an acre of English ground given in perpetuity to the people of the United States. It is built of Portland stone, cut from the same quarry as that for St Paul's Cathedral. The inscription on it quotes part of President Kennedy's Inaugural Address of January 1961.

John F Kennedy memorial

FEUDAL ENGLAND

During the 300 years after the Norman Conquest England was ruled by Normans and Plantagenets, some of whom had extensive territories in France, and all of whom claimed to be rulers of part of it – and at intervals of parts also of Scotland and Wales. When Henry II (r 1154–89) married the runaway divorced queen of Louis of France, Eleanor of Aquitaine, he became ruler of half of France. But wherever the anointed and crowned King of England went, the king's justice (and for a time his Witenagemot, or counsel of wise men, part-brains trust, part-Civil Service and tax collecting arm, part-court) went with him, promising and often providing reasonably equal justice for all. This was especially so with Henry II, the Lawgiver-King, who trained non-feudal officials, raised a professional non-feudal army, relied on local juries to assess the value of personal property, and sent royal judges on regular circuit. The king's army was largely composed of the feudal levies provided by his immediate retainers, who were usually titled and honoured. Under feudal law they were the king's liegemen, and their own retainers in turn pledged fealty to them and rendered them service – in the army, in road maintenance or on the land – in return for protection and security. Feudalism was a legal as well as a landed system, an intricate interlinked chain of mutual obligations and mutual services. And it involved the king himself. As Henry de Bracton, the 13th-century judge, put it, 'The King is under no man, but he is under God and the Law'. Everyone else was his 'subject', though the greatest among them had small devoted armies of tenants-in-chief and tenants of their own. The palatine earls, as at Chester and Shrewsbury, had courts of almost regal scale. And at Bridgnorth, Robert de Belleme, the son of the Earl of Shrewsbury, housed a thousand knights and retainers in his castle.

Nevertheless the feudal 'system' was only as strong as the stability at the top ensured. Some 'over-mighty subjects' with private armies became greater than their superiors. Perhaps the greatest of these was Richard Neville, Earl of Warwick and Salisbury, 'Warwick the Kingmaker', chief minister of Edward IV, who had great estates in South Wales, Gloucestershire, Warwickshire, Oxfordshire, Wiltshire, Hampshire and the North Riding of Yorkshire (now North Yorkshire), and with still-surviving castles at Warwick, Raby, Middleham and Barnard Castle. The 'over-mighty subject' was especially menacing in periods of contested or uncertain succession, eg the reign of Stephen and Matilda (1135–1154), during which 375 castles were built, dubbed 'adulterine' castles because they were built without royal approval, or periods of weak or juvenile kingship, eg the reign of Henry III. At such times the French kings, with interests of their own in England, aided and abetted one side or the other, as did Ireland. There were one hundred years of war with France.

The feudal age was, in other words, an age of violence and disputed succession. Seven times kings were driven from their thrones; one was killed in battle (Richard III), one died of disease contracted in battle (Henry V), and four were murdered (Edward II, Richard II, Henry VI and Edward V). Simon de Montfort, Henry 'Hotspur' Percy and Warwick the Kingmaker all died in battle against their king.

The violence spread, and there were periodical popular risings, such as the Peasants Revolt of 1381, in the reign of Richard II, the rising of the Lollards in the reign of Henry V, and Jack Cade's rebellion of 1450. Few such protests were romantic – except the legend, somewhat Arthurian, of Robin Hood of Sherwood Forest. Famine and plague were regular visitors too. The Black Deaths of 1349, 1361 and 1369

halved the population. Hence wages increased, rents and prices were lowered, and economic disaster ensued.

Of these ages of turbulence, the castle is the symbol. Eighty-six of them were built in the reigns of William I and his son William II (Rufus). They were built of timber and earth in the motte-and-bailey style and although none of these timbered structures has survived, their mottes often have, when square stone keeps gradually replaced timber ones. With peace the keep was relegated to storehouse and the bailey became more important. Stone castles became more and more impregnable; parapeted and crenellated, with towers, turrets and barbicans.

With few exceptions however, early Norman domestic building is usually a mixture of stone and timber, as

Tomb of Richard Beauchamp, Earl of Warwick, St Mary's Church, Warwick

evidenced in the halls, churches and barns that survive. The style can be seen at its best in the 12th-century tithe barn at Harmondsworth, Middlesex or the Great Hall at Berkeley Castle in Gloucestershire (1340s, replacing an

earlier hall) and the splendid surviving Great Hall of Penshurst Place in Kent with its open timber roof and central hearth, built in the 14th century, the property of the Sidney family – illustrious as poets, explorers and soldiers for some six centuries.

The reign of Edward I saw a more splendid development, especially on the Welsh marches, of fortress-castles. A number of towers now replaced the single square or round keep. By contrast, the Scottish Borders are dotted with some 200 keeps, more simple than the crenellated forests of stone further south, though a few later ones like Forres are impressive, even daunting in their scale. And some of the castles – the Hermitage at Liddesdale in the Scottish borders, or Dunstanburgh on the Northumbrian coast – often built in lonely glens or on open windswept moors – are now grim and haunting in their stark isolation.

The castles are evidence of feudal power, their ruins the evidence of the artillery and cannon power that made them anachronisms – and in doing so brought to birth a more truly national justice, based on law and, slowly, on equality of all subjects, mighty or vassal, before the nationwide power of king and parliament. Equally striking, and again now mainly ruins, are the

monasteries and, happily some of them still in use, cathedrals and churches. The cathedrals, now (since Henry VIII's day) Protestant, were of course when built expressions of the Catholic faith, and are part of the religious conviction that held Europe united for more than a thousand years. Secular ruler and ruled alike believed that the only hope of salvation lay in the prayers and services of those ordained by God. God or the devil might appear in visions or in miracles, in storm or plague; and the refuge, the Church, was open to all. Belief in Christ and membership of his Church was, in medieval times, all but universal. Church buildings, especially cathedrals, towered above the wooden or earthen huts or barns of the people; their interiors, with their paintings and embroideries, their ribbed vaulting and pillars, their soaring arches and light flooding in through stained glass windows, their altar-pieces and reredos, brought a warmth and colour all too rare outside; the ritual, the music and not least the familiar language of the prayers brought comfort and grace to a humdrum, hard and primitive world.

Even more central to the lives of the people were the abbeys and monasteries. Many of these – the

Hermitage Castle, Borders

Benedictine in particular – preceded the Conqueror's coming. Westminster Abbey was consecrated in 1065, a few days before its founder, Edward the Confessor, died. The abbeys and especially the monasteries and convents of the 'regular' clergy, the monks and nuns, were the guardians and cultivators of what culture survived, of records, manuscripts and music. They were centres of husbandry and pastoral skills; they provided the social services of their day; schools, hospitals and libraries. The greatest of them were very wealthy – so much so that they would in the end be dispossessed – and their abbots and bishops, not least because of their literacy and their role as international scholars, became advisers, secretaries and treasurers to kings, keepers of writs and records, powerful men in the king's Council. (The sole modern survivors are the twenty-four Bishops, the Lords Spiritual, who still sit in the House of Lords, and who – now as in the past – advise on secular as well as spiritual topics.)

After 1066, it was not just a Benedictine revival. A house of Augustinian canons was established at

17

Conwy Castle, North Wales

Colchester in the last decade of the 11th century; there were over 200 by the end of the next century. In 1128 the first Cistercian house in England was founded at Waverley in Sussex. Enjoined to lives of austerity and silence, and wearing undyed woollen tunics, the 'white monks' moved to the more desolate lands to north and west. By 1150 there were twenty Cistercian monasteries in Yorkshire alone, and twenty more elsewhere. They cleared the land, drained marshes and planted trees, built roads and bridges – and not least were the greatest shepherds of the Middle Ages. The ruins of Fountains (founded 1132) and Rievaulx (founded 1131) in Yorkshire, show the scale of their work, as do Whitby and Tintern, Valle Crucis in Clwyd and Abbey Dore in Hereford; Wensleydale cheese is still a tribute to the labour of one of the smallest, yet most private and appealing of their houses, at Jervaulx in the Yorkshire Dales. And they were cathedral builders too: Canterbury, Durham and Ely, Norwich and Winchester, Coventry and Carlisle, St Albans, Westminster, Peterborough and Bury St Edmunds all began as monastic churches.

The abbeys and monasteries reflected the need for order in contrast to the turbulence of the world outside:

no less than 115 arose in the nineteen troubled years of Stephen's reign, 113 during the reign of Henry II. Some 500 monastic buildings were built in the 12th century. Revenues, however, slumped as a consequence of the Black Death, villages were deserted, churches ruined. Despite ruthless taxation by Pope and King, abbeys and cathedrals became overwealthy, the mendicant and Franciscan friars perhaps apart, and church building dropped sharply. 'The hungry sheep looked up', wrote Milton savagely, 'and were not fed'. The Dissolution of the monasteries was due, however, to other factors; in part the result of the new royal supremacy over all the Church in England, and of Henry VIII's break with Rome and with Roman Catholicism. He became head of a reformed, episcopal, Protestant Church, its Prayer Book written by Archbishop Cranmer and in English, and Erastian in spirit; the cathedrals, churches and monasteries and their resources, plate, vestments and lands, were acquired and sold to the highest bidder.

Places to Visit
Norman Architecture
Castles:
Chepstow on the Wye; *Ludlow*, Shropshire, with a 100ft high keep; *Windsor Castle*, Edward I's lavish pride, the most expensive single building raised by any medieval English king; *Warwick Castle*, for the scale of its preservation – well maintained by the Beauchamps for some nine centuries; the *White Tower*, oldest medieval structure in the Tower of London; *Richmond* in Yorkshire, *Lancaster Castle* and *Durham Castle* (now part of the University), all three designed to guard the north; *Colchester Castle* and *Arundel Castle* (much restored) in West Sussex, homes for some eight centuries of the Duke of Norfolk, still the senior peer in the realm. For sheer physical beauty *Leeds Castle* in Kent, for long the home of the Fairfaxes who later moved to Denton in Yorkshire and who, in the 18th century, owned the Northern Neck of Virginia; and one of whom gave the young George Washington his first job as surveyor while another,

with his wife, became the young man's best and most admired friends – and then became his enemies as Loyalists. The other fortress-castles to see are: *Conwy*; *Caernarvon*; *Harlech*; and *Beaumaris* on Anglesey, which took fifty years and 2000 labourers to build in the 14th century.

Castles particularly associated with William I are *Lincoln Castle*, *Ludgershall*, and *Bamburgh*.

Castles particularly associated with William Rufus are *Newcastle*, *Carlisle*, *Rochester*; and *Westminster Hall*.

Church buildings:
Any brief comments must inevitably be personal. In antiquity, *Durham* clearly has primacy, Norman, probably indeed the greatest Romanesque church in Europe, it has a commanding position on its bluff above the Wear – 'half church of God, half fortress gainst the Scot' in Sir Walter Scott's phrase. Both Cuthbert and Bede are interred here. In some ways *Peterborough* is its nearest Norman rival. For external grace and an uncluttered interior, visit *Salisbury*, the only surviving 13th-century cathedral; for internal beauty of tracery, *Wells* or *Exeter*; *York* for its stained glass; *Winchester* or *Norwich* for their cloisters. 12th-century *St David's* in Wales is the smallest cathedral city in Britain. In Scotland *Iona* is known as the cradle of Christianity in the north, while for an atmospheric setting, there is *St Andrews* in Fife, on its headland above the cold grey sea.
Architecture of the 12th and 13th centuries includes: *Haltwhistle Church*, Northumbria; *Finchale Priory*, Durham; *Lanercost Priory*, Cumbria, an Augustinian house dating from 1169, one of Edward I's bases for attacks on Scotland; *Fountains* and *Rievaulx Abbeys*, North Yorkshire, both Cistercian; *Littleshall Abbey*, Shropshire; *Penshurst Place*, Kent; *Haddon Hall*, Derbyshire; *Bradley Manor*, near Newton Abbot, Devon.

ROBIN HOOD

The English, like the Americans, make folk heroes out of strange material. Rhymes about Robin Hood are mentioned as early as the 14th century in Langland's *Piers Plowman*. Before that, the only historical references are to a Robert Hood, fugitive, in the reign of Henry III, and to a Robert Hood, valet, in the reign of Edward III almost a century later. The first complete ballad is 'Lytell Geste of Robyn Hode' by Wynkyn de Worde, at the end of the 15th century. He was an outlaw, living off the king's deer in Nottingham Forest (or in the West Riding of Yorkshire) – deer could only lawfully be killed by the king – but befriending the poor and never harming husbandmen or farmers. Clearly, if he has any historic roots, he is a Saxon yeoman of the 12th or 13th centuries, opposing the advance of foreign Normans; not an enemy of the king, but of the king's evil servants and greedy sheriffs, bishops or abbots. By the 15th century, the legend of Robin Hood and those of other historical outlaws like Hereward the Wake, who had surrendered at Ely to William the Conqueror in 1071, or William Wallace in Scotland, were fully entrenched in English lore. Tudor historians even give him a noble birth, as Earl of Huntingdon. To many, however, he was the people's hero, unlike King Arthur, the symbol of aristocratic chivalry.

For good kings in distress, he could be a useful ally of the rulers – as he was for Richard the Lionheart back from the Crusades, to whose memory Robin Hood had been loyal against 'bad' King John. And the legend was still there in the tales of King Charles in the oak – or in the Green Man who has given his name to many a village pub.

Historically, we are among 'ifs' and 'might-have-beens'. Robin Hood might have been a foster brother to Richard the Lionheart (and Sir Edward Coke, the first Lord Chief Justice of England, says in his *Institutes* that Robin Hood lived in Richard's reign). Or a leader of the followers of Simon de Montfort, outlawed after the battle of Evesham in 1265.

Or a supporter of Thomas, Earl of Lancaster in his insurrection in 1322 against Edward II.

Or a supporter (even son-in-law) of Jack Cade, leader of a rebellion against Henry VI in 1450, during the Wars of the Roses.

The strongest evidence points to a real Robin Hood, living in the reign of Richard I, and helping Richard to regain control of Nottingham Castle which was, certainly, besieged by the Earls of Chester and Huntingdon. That some important people accept part of the legend can be attested by the fact that many members of the family of the Earls of Huntingdon include, among their christian or given names, the name of Robin Hood, and that one brother of the 12th Earl was christened Edward Plantagenet Robin Hood Hastings.

Places to Visit
Nottingham Castle
Sherwood Forest
Kirklees in Yorkshire

MACBETH

Shakespeare's tragedy is a tale – but its principal character is real. He ruled Scotland for seventeen years, as a soldier, a Scottish patriot and a great king; but, partly as a result of the Norse invasions, and those, three centuries later, of Edward I, all the real evidence has gone; only the legends remain. On them, Shakespeare drew lavishly, and he made of them a tale of ruddy gore, with Macbeth a giant but a villain.

Macbeth was elected King of Scotland in 1040, on Duncan's death. The Scotland of Duncan and his predecessors had been a land of private and civil wars, ready to fall to Cnut (Canute) the Danish leader, just as (almost all) England had done. Macbeth was of royal blood, Mormaer of Moray and King of Aelsan (but *not* 'thane of Glamis') as well as Duncan's battle commander and close heir; he did not need to murder Duncan to take control, and at that time in any event thrones were elective, as well as successive. It seems clear that Duncan was killed in battle at Bothgouanan, near Elgin. Macbeth ruled for seventeen years (1040–1057), and they were – for once – years of peace and prosperity. (He himself went on pilgrimage to Rome in 1050, perhaps in remorse for Duncan's death?) This did not prevent, and that prosperity may even have attracted, the English invasion of 1054, led by Siward, Earl of Northumbria. Macbeth was defeated at Dunsinane, near Perth, and retired northwards, to reign another three years. He was defeated and killed at Lumphanan in Aberdeenshire (*not* Birnam nor Dunsinane), August 1057, by Malcolm Canmore, Duncan's son, who at least inherited a prosperous and a united Scotland.

Shakespeare's play is theatre, not history. It drew on Holinshed's *Chronicles* printed in 1577, and it gives a brilliant but false portrayal of a great leader, as part of the propaganda of a unifying Tudor England. It helped to portray Scotland as a land of civil war, in which ruthless usurpers could readily seize power. The Tudor myth-makers exploited the legends of Arthur and of Merlin; they were prompt to blacken the legends of one of Scotland's greatest kings, just as they blackened the name of Richard III.

Places to Visit
Macbeth's Hillock, near Nairn, where he met the three weird sisters; and *Cawdor Castle* (built 1450s, seat of the Campbells, privately inhabited) nearby.

For 'medieval atmosphere' and haunted houses: *Glamis* – the birthplace of the Queen Mother; *Blair Atholl*; *Craigievar*; *Crathes*; *Fraser*; *Fyvie*; and *Drum*.

19

THE TUDORS

The first of the dynasty, Henry VII, was prudent, mean and shrewd. He had won the throne by conquest but his grandfather had married Catherine de Valois, widow of Henry V. He himself married Elizabeth of York, to heal the wounds. His second son, Henry, became his successor as Henry VIII, tall and handsome, highly cultured, in prospect a true Renaissance prince who became a tyrant, and broke the power of the Church of Rome over England and Wales. With him, and with the printing of journals and books, we enter fully recorded history; legends give way to records. His daughter Mary reigned as a Catholic. On her death her half-sister Elizabeth succeeded, to reign from 1558 to 1603. She was immensely skilful. In a period remarkable for long and sanguinary wars, when threatened by French and Scottish intrigues and open Spanish invasion on behalf of Philip of Spain, who had married Mary, she kept the peace; and she made her name and country respected abroad, without waste of blood or treasure. Her diplomacy had always a touch of coquetry, but her authority at home was absolute, yet with no loss of popular affection as Shakespeare, Spenser and a host of writers testified. 'When she smiled,' wrote Sir John Harrington, in his *Nugae Antiquae*,

'It was pure sunshine, that everyone did choose to bask in, if they could: but anon came a storm from a sudden gathering of clouds, and thunder fell in wondrous manner on all alike.'

Her own prose was equally matchless: 'Though God has raised me high, yet this I count the glory of my crown: that I have reigned with your loves.'

With the Tudors the feudal age came to an end. Their secularism, their emphasis on national sovereignty, their merger of Wales with England in administration, the end of all rival imperialisms, whether baronial or spiritual – and, not least, the first colonies overseas, with foreign trade and exotic products – bred a new middle-class world of commerce, markets and towns. Castles deteriorated or were transformed into country houses, some of them still fortified, their money coming less from tenants than from trade in wool. Merchant adventurers risked ships and capital overseas, and often offered up hallelujahs in charity, chapels and tombs, churches and colleges. War itself – and that was all but unending from 1066 onwards, both foreign and civil – had brought fortunes, and not only to kings. Men won land and fame and royal recognition, plunder if they could move it, cash from relatives and friends of their prisoners. The Black Prince made £20,000 out of three prisoners taken at Poitiers, and the Earl of Warwick made £8000 for the ransom of the Archbishop of Sens at the same battle. The money went into land, into great houses and manors, and effigies and brasses for their churches and chantries or collegiate churches, where masses would be said for the soul of the donor. And 15th century Caister Castle, near Great Yarmouth, now ruined but with a still-standing 90ft high tower, was built by Sir John Fastolf (Shakespeare's Falstaff) out of his booty in the French Wars. His treasure (buried there?) has never been found.

Queen Elizabeth was personally interested in and concerned about America. She supported her seamen, notably Drake's voyage around the world, Frobisher's voyage in search of a North-West Passage, and the first Virginia voyage led by Raleigh's cousin, Sir Richard Grenville. She was captivated by John Dee, mathematician, cosmographer, and astrologer, who devoted much thought to the overriding problem of a water route to the riches of the East free of Spanish or Portuguese interference; and she made provision for Richard Hakluyt, geographer and foremost propagandist of English colonization. Spenser, Marlowe and Raleigh all reflect this interest in America, and a whole succession of literary men went as officials to Virginia.

This was in a sense the end of English history as such. When Elizabeth, the last of the Tudors, died in 1603, the heir was the Stuart James VI of Scotland, the son of Mary, Queen of Scots. Thereafter 'Jamey the Saxt' became also James I of England. This union of the Crowns led, 104 years later, to a union of the Parliaments and a United Kingdom. And this is also the beginning of Anglo-American history.

Places to Visit
(in approximate historical order)
St Mary Radcliffe's, Bristol: the hexagonal north porch and its intricate carved doorway, legacy of the wealth of its merchant princes of the 15th century; *Cabot Tower*, Bristol.
St Patrick's, Patrington, Yorkshire: . Decorated style, built on the profits of Humber wool trade; early 14th century
Caister Castle, Great Yarmouth: Sir John Fastolf, and the Paston family.
Haddon Hall, Derbyshire: much is 16th century, but the hall is late 14th century; home of the Vernons.
Markenfield Hall, Yorkshire: 14th-century moated and fortified manor house, with second floor hall reached by outer stair; centre of plots against Elizabeth.
Stokesay Castle, Shropshire: fortified manor house of Ludlow wool merchant, 14th century, with towers and curtain wall.
Tattershall Castle, Lincolnshire: its five-storey brick tower only remaining evidence of defence; built by Lord Cromwell, Henry VI's treasurer who made his money in the wars with France.
Chantry chapels: at Warwick, Beauchamp chapel at *St Mary's*; *Dennington* (Suffolk); *Eton* and

Tattershall Castle

gentlemen and esquires rather than nobility, *see* among others:

Brympton d'Evercy, three miles from Yeovil, in its warm Ham Hill stone, mid-15th century in original building, a west front dated c 1520, the whole developed – still in the same golden stone – in 1690, with a parapet and ten bays and six dormer windows; home of the Sydenhams until 1697, and ever since 1731 of the Fane family.

Montacute, two miles away, is almost entirely Elizabethan, and more commanding. It owed its creation to the wealthy lawyer Sir Edward Phelips (Speaker of the House of Commons 1604, later Master of the Rolls) who had acquired the small priory nearby after the dissolution of the monasteries in 1539. Its designer was a skilled Somerset stonemason, who was also responsible for the building of Wadham College, Oxford.

Burton Agnes, in Humberside: also a late Elizabethan house, built 1601–10 by Sir Henry Griffith – with the original Old Hall standing, rather perversely, alongside it – with, inside its red-brick cover, an 1170 stone house still intact. It is rare to have two such buildings of distinctly different styles, cheek by jowl together. And the Elizabethan house is unusual, with its bay and bow windows rising the full three storeys; the top floor Long Gallery has splendid views down to the sea.

Hever Castle, Kent, home of Anne Boleyn, who met Henry VIII here; restored by Lord Astor.

Sutton Place, near Guildford. First English 'manor' built without defences, little changed externally. Built for Richard Weston, one of Henry VIII's courtiers and, more recently, home of Paul Getty. Strongly Renaissance in style.

Further Reading

John, Duke of Bedford, with George Mikes, *How to Run a Stately Home* (Deutsch)

Bence-Jones, Mark and Hugh Montgomery-Massingberd, *The British Aristocracy* (Constable)

Diane Phipps, *Affordable Splendour* (Weidenfeld)

Lawrence Stone, *The Crisis of the Aristocracy* 1558–1641 (Oxford University Press)

Winchester Colleges; *New College*, *Merton* and *Christ Church*, Oxford; and *King's College*, Cambridge. And *The Tower of London*. The 'beefeaters' originated in Henry VIII's personal guard, uniformed in red.

They were 'buffetiers' because their duties included guarding the King's plate.

For Elizabethan domestic architecture, houses rather than castellated mansions, homes for

MARY, QUEEN OF SCOTS

She was strikingly tall and beautiful, a skilled musician who wrote poetry and spoke at least three languages fluently. She is also a tragic figure, whose story in many respects makes personal the tortuous relations between two countries and religions with whose destiny her own life was so involved. She claimed the throne of England through her grandmother, Margaret Tudor (daughter of Henry VII), who had married James IV of Scotland. English Catholics did not acknowledge Henry VIII's divorce from his first wife, Katherine of Aragon, and thus denied the legitimacy of Elizabeth. Mary's father, James V of Scotland, had married as his second wife Mary of Guise, who built up a strong Catholic and French party in Scotland, and their daughter Mary, herself a queen when she was a week old, was educated in France, and married Francis I of France when she was seventeen; he only reigned for one year. After his death in 1560 (two years after Elizabeth's accession in England) she returned as a beautiful young widow to Scotland in 1561 (one year after John Knox's return from Geneva, the Protestant centre of Europe), to become thereafter a potential enemy to Elizabeth. Scottish Presbyterians, critical of the compromise religious settlement of Elizabeth and especially of the system of church government by bishops, themselves attacked Mary; their religious leader was John Knox; their military-political leader was Mary's half-brother, the Protestant Earl of Moray, who fled to England in 1565. Scotland was thus itself a divided country.

To win over English Catholics, Mary married her younger cousin Henry Stewart, Lord Darnley, a Catholic and himself a grandson of Margaret Tudor and claimant to the English throne, and thus abandoned any nominal friendship with Elizabeth. In 1566 Mary's son James was born; 'The Queen of Scots is lighter of a fair son, and I am but a barren stock', said Elizabeth Tudor. Darnley and his supporters killed Mary's secretary and chief adviser David Rizzio, in Holyrood Palace. Darnley himself was murdered in 1567, and Mary then married the Earl of Bothwell, a strong military leader but generally believed

to be Darnley's murderer. Her forces were defeated at Carberry Hill (in fact more accurately they simply drifted away) in 1567, and at Langside in 1568, by the Regent Moray. She was imprisoned on an island in Loch Leven by the Scottish lords, during which time she abdicated in favour of her son James, who at one-and-a-half years of age, was proclaimed King James VI of Scotland. She then crossed the Solway and took refuge in England, appealing to Elizabeth for sanctuary. This posed a difficulty to the Queen, for clearly the objective of France was to ensure the control of England and Scotland under Mary Queen of Scots; they commanded the Channel, had one foot in Calais, and the other in Edinburgh. Mary was imprisoned. There were a number of 'Papist' plots, though there is no certainty of Mary's personal involvement in any of them.

In one respect she was as a prisoner more powerful than she would have been at large. The defence of a beautiful but captive princess threw a halo over the cause of the Old Faith, young knights vowed to defend her, abetted by the recently formed Society of Jesus, with its vow of total dedication to Rome. And in 1588 Philip of Spain, who had married Mary Tudor (Mary I 1553–8) Elizabeth's Catholic half-sister and predecessor, readied an armada with which to invade England, and also claimed the throne of his dead wife. The existence of Mary Queen of Scots, whether or not she was personally a party to any conspiracy, clearly constituted a danger to Elizabeth, who had her imprisoned in a number of castles, and finally at Fotheringhay Castle near Oundle (no longer standing). Elizabeth, here as elsewhere, acted with caution. In September 1586 Mary was tried at Fotheringhay before forty-six commissioners, who included the Archbishop of Canterbury, the Lord Chancellor, and Lord Burghley, the High Treasurer. In October she was found guilty, under an Act of 1585, for 'the Security of the Queen's Person' and sentenced to death. Elizabeth signed the warrant after four months' agonizing, but claimed not to have given orders for its delivery, and punished her officials, Burghley and Davison, who carried out her orders.

Mary was executed in February 1587. She was buried in Peterborough, but the body was removed in 1612 to Henry VII's chapel at Westminster, where her son, James VI and I of England, erected a sumptuous tomb.

Places to Visit
Mary was imprisoned in *Carlisle Castle*, in *Tutbury Castle* in Staffordshire, and in *Wingfield Manor*, near Matlock as well as *Coventry*, *Chatsworth* in Derbyshire, *Sheffield*, *Buxton*, *Chartley* and *Fotheringhay*, but the best preserved of her prisons is *Bolton Castle* in Wensleydale, North Yorkshire. *Linlithgow*, her birthplace, is now in splendid ruins.

Further Reading
John Bossy, *The English Catholic Community* (Darton, Longman and Todd)
Antonia Fraser, *Mary, Queen of Scots* (Weidenfeld)
Elizabeth Jenkins, *Elizabeth the Great* (Gollancz)
Elizabeth Jenkins, *Elizabeth and Leicester* (Gollancz)
Sir Walter Scott, *Kenilworth*.
And for the trial of the 'False Duessa' Spenser's *Faerie Queene*, Book V Canto IX.

A posthumous portrait of Mary, Queen of Scots

SIR WALTER RALEIGH

Poet and historian, explorer and statesman, soldier, sailor, and strikingly handsome courtier, Raleigh touched nothing that he did not adorn – and yet he lost his life to the executioner's axe in the Tower of London. Born in a still-standing small thatch-roofed house at Hayes Barton near Sidmouth, Devon, and educated at Oriel College, Oxford, he soldiered in the Huguenot cause in France and Ireland, where he showed courage and dash. He was a protégé of Leicester at court, and became a favourite of the Queen. He was knighted in 1584, and became an MP for Devon in 1585. From the start he mixed thought and action. Although he never visited the North American continent himself, he planned and financed the expedition led by Sir Richard Grenville (of Bideford, Devon) which discovered Roanoke Island in 1584 and the colony he named Virginia, in honour of the Virgin Queen. In 1585–7 he fitted out two more expeditions to explore the coast north of Florida; no settlements followed, and the unsuccessful colonists brought only potatoes and tobacco back; then exotic and the first of their kind, Raleigh planted them in his Youghal garden. He planted people too – on his Irish estates; he became a friend of the poet Spenser, another admirer of his *Faerie Queene*. In 1592 he planned an expedition to seize Spanish treasure ships. In 1595 he searched for gold in Guiana, explored the coast of Trinidad and sailed up the Orinoco in an abortive quest for the gold of El Dorado. In 1596 he published *The Discovery of Guiana*. He served in expeditions against Cadiz in 1596 and the Azores in 1597. His secret marriage to Elizabeth ('Bessie') Throckmorton, one of the Queen's maids of honour, however, angered the Queen when she discovered it, and he could never count on her total support thereafter. He was supplanted by Essex, and Cecil became a critic.

On James's accession, Raleigh was sent to the Tower charged with treason, for which there was no evidence. While awaiting execution, he wrote a moving letter of farewell to his wife: 'Your mourning cannot avail me that am but dust'. He was then pardoned, but condemned to perpetual imprisonment in the Tower, where he

wrote his *History of the World*. Its first and only volume (1300 folio pages) reaches the second Roman war of Macedonia. He wrote a number of other books, including *A Discourse on War*. In 1616 – by which time he was sixty-four – the King, who was short of money, released him, on condition that he lead another expedition to the mines of Guiana, but on condition also that there would be no fighting with the Spaniards. There was no gold, and he did fight the Spaniards, and he lost his only son in the course of it. He returned in his ship *Destiny* to Devon, where he had built Sherborne Castle, much enlarged later. He was executed at Whitehall on the continuing, and still unproven, charge of treason.

Raleigh was not alone. His half-brother was Sir Humphrey Gilbert, of Compton Castle, whose expeditions he helped to plan, and who, with royal patents to discover and occupy heathen lands, took possession of Newfoundland for the Queen, and spent all his resources doing so, including four out of five of his ships. On his return from Newfoundland, Gilbert went down with his last ship, the *Squirrel* of only eight tons burden. Sir Martin Frobisher dreamed of a north-west passage to Cathay, fought against the Spanish Armada, and died of wounds in battle. Sir Francis Drake, like his kinsman and fellow-explorer John Hawkins, in family origin a poor boy, beginning as an apprentice, was to die on the Spanish Main. And Drake was like all of them, an adventurer, but with his own not other people's money, a patriot and something of a pirate-king; he too was knighted, for his discoveries and his mapping of new worlds, and his quest for God as well as gold. The age of Elizabeth was rich in scholar-heroes, and it was their courage and their seamanship that kept the island and 'Gloriana' herself virginal, Protestant and safe.

Places to visit

Hayes Barton, for Raleigh's home. *Sherborne Castle* (open to the public). The old castle is in ruins but the new castle built by Raleigh remains, as do the gardens which he planned and which Capability Brown also worked on. *White Hart Inn*, High Street, Salisbury, where he was arrested. *The*

Raleigh Walk, Tower of London. *St Margaret's*, Westminster, where Raleigh's headless body is interred. His widow had his head embalmed and enclosed in a red leather bag and she carried it with her wherever she went until she died, aged eighty-two, in 1647. The head may be in the Nicholas Chapel of West Horsley Place, in Surrey.
Plymouth Hoe
Science Museum, South Kensington, for models of Tudor ships.
Buckland Abbey, Devon (for Drake).

Further Reading
J B Brebner, *The Explorers of North America* (Black & Co)
Richard Hakluyt, *Principal Navigations, Voyages and Discoveries of the English Nation* (Everyman edition)
D B Quinn, *England and the Discovery of America* (Allen & Unwin)
Raleigh, *The Discovery of Guiana*, (Hakluyt Society, 1848, 1929)
A L Rowse, *The Elizabethans and America* (Macmillan)

Sherborne Castle

THE STUARTS

The accession of James VI of Scotland, Mary Queen of Scots only son, to the English throne in 1603 as James I (note that his predecessor was Elizabeth I of England, and thus the present Queen is strictly Elizabeth II of England but Elizabeth I of Scotland, or of Great Britain) brought about the unity of the crowns, and – for the first time, and unbroken since – the union of the countries (and in 1707 a union of the Parliaments). He succeeded as of right, as the great-grandson of James IV's English wife, the Princess Margaret. The formal title of the realm is 'The United Kingdom of Great Britain and Northern Ireland'.

By the terms of the Act of Union of 1707, and of the Revolution Settlement of 1689, when William of Orange and his English-born Queen Mary came by invitation to the thrones of England and Scotland (and James VII and II, a Catholic, went into exile), Scotland retained, and still retains three distinct constitutional characteristics. Its own legal system (with its own Faculty of Advocates in Edinburgh) is rooted in Roman law and not the common law of England; and it retains its distinct system of legal hearings and enquiries by the Procurator Fiscal and his officers. Secondly, it keeps its own educational system; its schools are more comprehensive in their recruitment than were the English, at least until recently, but they are more strongly academies (as they are still so called) in curricula.

Thirdly, and not unrelated to its educational system, Scotland is distinct in religion, in that its established Church is not Episcopalian but Presbyterian, governed by its own congregations, its head, the Moderator, elected annually (and changing annually) from among its leading ordained clergy. The annual Assembly of the Kirk, meeting each May in Edinburgh, is the nearest to a Parliament that the Scots have. The sovereign, who changes her religion from Anglican to Presbyterian when she crosses the border, appoints each year a High Commissioner, a layman, as her representative in the Assembly, but however eminent the royal representative may be, he or she sits one step below the Moderator in any meeting of the Kirk. It is a democratic, egalitarian and at times contentious Church. And, as James VI himself recognized, and feared: 'No bishop, no King'.

James brought as his legacy from Scotland, to which he was determined never to return and to which in fact he paid only one visit, an equal determination to steer a middle way, and to maintain Elizabeth's compromise religious settlement. He was glad to escape from the Scots Calvinists, for they disliked the Episcopacy he now accepted – he had formally announced Episcopacy in Scotland in 1600. He respected his mother's faith but could not possibly condone the continuing Catholic plots against the Throne or Parliament (witness the 'Gunpowder Plot' of 1605), and warred in Scotland against the Catholic lairds in the north in 1591–1594. In both countries some great families stayed firmly Catholic, like Elizabeth Throckmorton's (Lady Raleigh's) family in Coughton Court in Warwickshire, where the east wing of the house was destroyed in 1688 by an anti-Catholic mob, where the white chemise worn by Mary Queen of Scots is still cherished, and where indeed a list can be seen of other recusant families, a great nexus of Catholic kinship of marriages and intermarriages that is itself a piece of English (and indeed European) history: Catesby, Petre, Sheldon, Stonor, Acton, Plowden, Tresham (at Rushton Triangular Lodge near Kettering), Stapleton, Stourton. A not dissimilar tale could be told of the Howard family – the leading Catholic peers – and of the Arundells of Trerice near Newquay in Cornwall. And some of these families – like Loyalists in the War of American Independence – were themselves divided, father from son, brother from brother, often by conviction, sometimes by shrewd and prudent calculation. Despite James's skill, both his countries were at his death bitterly split along religious lines. His governing by favourites lost him support. Although he was well read and well educated he was ungainly and unwise – 'the wisest fool in Christendom'.

The reign of Charles I (1625–1649), who for eleven years ruled without summoning Parliament and who imposed arbitrary taxation and encouraged Archbishop Laud's efforts to Anglicize the Scottish Church, led to four years of Civil War, his defeat at Naseby in 1645 and his surrender to a Scottish force at Newark in 1646. Captivity first at Holmby House near Northampton, then in Carisbrooke Castle on the Isle of Wight, led to the 'trial' at Westminster of 'the tyrant,

Castle Howard, North Yorkshire

Greenwich on the River Thames

traitor and murderer, Charles Stuart'. On 30 January, 1649 the King was executed in front of Whitehall Palace; Charles the Tyrant to some, Charles the Martyr to others, brave and composed to the end. 'He nothing common did, or mean, upon that memorable scene' wrote Marvell. And Montrose vowed, 'I'll sing thy obsequies with trumpet sounds, And write thy epitaph with blood and wounds'

The Cromwellian Protectorate lasted eleven years, and seemed likely to ensure only military despotism. Charles II was restored to the throne in 1660; whatever his high Anglicanism (he died in 1685 admitting his Catholicism on his death-bed) he was at least determined 'not to go on his travels again'. His marriage to the Portuguese Catherine of Braganza was happy but childless, and he had some ten or more illegitimate children, the descendants of whom constitute part of today's aristocracy. Nevertheless the first half of the reign was both anti-Catholic and anti-Puritan. If after 1670, by the secret treaty of Dover, he became in some measure a pensioner of France, the country was prosperous, the navy and merchant marine strong, science and the arts encouraged, the Royal Society founded and the Royal Observatory built at Greenwich. The reign of Charles II was also the age of

Wren. The king was shrewd and intelligent behind an agreeable front. He was, said Defoe, 'an exact knower of mankind', who had 'a world of wit and not a grain of ill-nature in him'.

His brother James, who succeeded him, was an avowed Catholic. When a son was born to him, by his second wife Mary of Modena, with every likelihood of a reversion of the country to Catholicism, the Whig nobles invited the Protestant William of Orange (James's nephew) and his wife Mary (James's daughter by a first marriage) to become King and Queen. On William's death, Anne, James's other daughter, succeeded, ensuring a continuing Protestant succession. And by the Act of Settlement of 1701, all future rulers were required by law to be Protestant in faith. But the son whose birth in 1688 triggered off the 'Glorious Revolution', attempted an invasion of Scotland in 1715 (with French aid) as 'The Old Pretender' – he only stayed six weeks, landing at Peterhead and sailing away from Montrose; he lived the rest of his life in permanent exile in Rome, where he died in 1766. By the time of his death his own son, 'Bonnie Prince Charlie', had also attempted, again with French help, an invasion of Scotland and got as far as Derby in 1745. He was defeated at Culloden in 1746, the last battle fought on British soil. He too

returned to Rome, to dream of what might have been, to brood, and to drink his worries away. With his defeat and permanent exile, the German Hanoverians (from 1714 onwards) were firmly on the English throne. And by that time the country was governed by a Parliament, however unrepresentative it might be, and was more prosperous than it had ever been.

Places to Visit

Banqueting House, Whitehall. All that survives of Whitehall Palace (burnt 1698), built by Inigo Jones, and from which Charles I stepped to his execution.

Knole, near Sevenoaks, Kent. Home of the Sackvilles since 1603.

Hatfield House, built 1612, home of the Cecils.

Audley End, Saffron Walden, Essex. Much altered by Vanbrugh in the 18th century.

And, in Yorkshire:

Castle Howard, home of the Howard family. Filmed in 'Brideshead Revisited'.

Harewood House, near Leeds. Home of the Lascelles.

Nostell Priory, near Wakefield. Home of the Winns.

Wentworth Woodhouse, home of the Rockinghams.

ANGLO-AMERICAN HISTORY

The roots of the first age of Anglo-American history lay firmly in English (East Anglia and the West Country), in Lowland Scots and in Ulster soil: they were fed by hunger for God and for Mammon. In Elizabeth's reign, especially after the removal of the threat of a Catholic succession, merchant adventurers organized in limited companies were sailing from Bristol, Whitehaven and London, and the south coast ports. They behaved as much like pirates and privateers as explorers, raiding Spanish Caribbean ports and despoiling cargoes of precious metals. By the time of the Armada, as later in Cromwell's naval struggles in the Channel against the Dutch, or when France abetted Catholic rulers or pretenders (1688, 1715, 1719, 1745, 1798, 1805), they were patriots also. They saw their enemies as Rome, the Inquisition, episcopacy and obscurantism. The result was that a number of commercial and religious foundations were planted in Ulster and in North America; trade, mercantilism, smuggling, piracy, and freedom of worship and freedom of expression were intermingled. Historians like Max Weber and R H Tawney have made much of the thesis of 'Religion, and the rise of capitalism'. But Benjamin Franklin put it all more pithily when he created his own *alter ego, Poor Richard*: 'The sleeping fox catches no poultry'; 'then plough deep, while sluggards sleep, and you shall have corn to sell and to keep'.

This 'first British Empire' was well-knit: the North American colonies stayed on the coast and in the Tidewater — it took 150 years for the settlers to penetrate and settle 150 miles inland. To Britain went their staples, tobacco and sugar, furs and timber; from it came industrial goods, coaches and carpets, fine damask for the ladies and ornaments for drawing rooms. And to Britain, to its schools, to the Inns of Court and the University of Edinburgh, rather than Oxford and Cambridge, came their sons for education. Along the James and Potomac Rivers Georgian houses were built, modelled on what their owners could remember of their own England (Westover, Shirley and Mount Vernon, to cite three); the first college in the South, William and Mary, was built from plans drawn by Christopher Wren.

American political independence did not, however, bring economic independence, not for some half-century at least. The new state still exported its raw materials, and still imported not only luxuries but the capital and skills it needed. Indeed much of the cattle country of Texas was financed in the late 19th century from Edinburgh and Dundee. It was the twenty-five years of Britain's war with revolutionary and Napoleonic France that gave America a tremendous opportunity and total freedom. A 'second' British Empire came into being after 1815, with territories in South Africa, East and West Africa, and India and ports on the Indian Ocean and South China Seas, not to mention Australia, an 'invention' when 'criminals' could no longer be transported to America. All was the legacy of British seapower.

By the end of the 19th century the main direction of the Atlantic flow of goods was increasingly easterly: the goods in demand in office and home and factory were, more and more, American: telephones, cameras, phonographs, electric streetcars, cars and typewriters, elevators ('lifts') and machine tools of all kinds. The higher the standard of living rose in Britain, as it did steadily, the more grew the demand for American goods: by the mid-20th century even the transatlantic traffic of people and freight was increasingly in planes, not ships, more often supplied by American airlines than by British.

The 'third' (20th-century) British Empire steadily became the 'Commonwealth of Nations', as former colonies acquired political (if very rarely economic) independence. It was, like contemporary North America, steadily urbanized. To it came waves of ex-colonial peoples, giving its cities problems of housing, racial mixture and urban 'blight', disturbingly similar to those of the US. The British citizen is not, yet, as mobile as the American. The slogan still tends, in crises, to be not Horace Greeley's 'Go West, young man, and grow up with the country' but 'Emigrate', as for centuries now Scots and Irish in particular have done. The legacy remains, however, an Anglo-American bond in language, history and culture, to which there is no parallel. Caleb Whiteford, Franklin's Scots-born neighbour in Craven Street through his London years, was present when in Paris in November 1782, the preliminary treaty of peace was signed ending the War of Independence. No matter, he said, 'We will all speak English'. We all do nowadays even if increasingly with an American accent.

Franklin's house in Craven Street off The Strand, London

WINSTON CHURCHILL

AND THE ANGLO-AMERICAN MARRIAGES

In his address to congress after Pearl Harbour 1941, Winston Churchill reminded his audience that if his father had been an American and his mother English, rather than the other way round, he might have got to Congress on his own. His origins are a reminder of the number of Anglo-American marriages of the late 19th century. One of them was more American than British: William Waldorf Astor, whose father had moved to England in 1890 and become a British citizen, married Nancy Langhorne, one of three very attractive Virginian girls. The Astor family lived in Hever Castle, bought by the Astors in 1903, originally the home of Henry VIII and Anne Boleyn, Queen Elizabeth I's mother. Both the Astor husband and wife became in turn MPs for Plymouth, Lady Astor being the first woman to sit in the House of Commons – not, it should be said, that she won any approval from Winston Churchill. Her home at Cliveden on the Thames became a famous assembly point for the politically influential in the years before and after World War II.

Jennie Jerome was the daughter of a wealthy New York stockbroker, who was a cousin of James Roosevelt, father of FDR. She met and married Randolph Churchill in April 1874, when Anglo-American marriages were still rare; but they did not remain so – Randolph's brother, the 8th Duke of Marlborough, also married an American, and his son, the 9th Duke, married two. Two other Dukes, Roxburghe and Manchester, also married Americans. President John F Kennedy's sister Kathleen married Lord Hartington in 1944; Prime Minister Macmillan's mother hailed from Spencer, Indiana; Lord Curzon of Kedleston married Mary Leiter, a Chicago millionaire's daughter, in 1895; Joseph Chamberlain married an American; and, most dramatically of all, an American socialite, Wallis Simpson, married a king.

It might be added that it was chance not design that led to Winston Spencer Churchill's birthplace being Blenheim Palace; his parents were on a family visit there when the happy event took place. His mother, to whom he was devoted, was a brilliant personality. On Randolph's death in 1895, she became the centre of a rather giddy circle. In 1900 she remarried, to George Cornwallis-West, who was only two weeks older than her son, Winston. They divorced in 1912, and then, aged sixty-four, she married Montague Porch, who at forty-one was three years younger than Winston, Jenny Jerome died in 1921.

Churchill's career is familiar: Sandhurst and the army, the Boer War and thereafter politics: for some ten years a backbencher, at times a Liberal, at others Conservative, always and proudly an Imperialist. But he was also, and equally proudly, Anglo-American. In the years of his wartime Prime Ministership and indeed for the year before, he wrote a long letter every fourth day for five years to his friend, President Franklin Roosevelt. The Anglo-American relationship may or may not be special. It is certainly unique. And for our days, it rests on the total support of each country for the other, and on the special friendship and mutual respect of two great men.

Places to Visit
Bladon Church, near Woodstock and Blenheim, where Churchill is buried. *Blenheim Palace*, built for the first Duke of Marlborough by architect Sir John Vanbrugh between 1705 and 1722.
Chartwell, near Westerham, Kent. Churchill's home for forty years, and where he built the wall and the garden. *Cliveden*, now an American college campus. It was sold to the Astors by the Duke of Westminster (to Queen Victoria's vast displeasure). *Hever Castle*, Kent, where there is a 'trace-your-origins' service.

Let Henry James have the last word. Writing to his brother William, 29 October 1888, he said:

'I can't look at the English-American world, or feel about them, any more, save as a big Anglo-Saxon total, destined to such an amount of melting together that an insistence on their differences becomes more and more idle and pedantic; and that melting together will come the faster the more one takes it for granted and treats the life of the two countries as continuous or more or less convertible, or at any rate as simply different chapters of the same general subject.'

Monument to Winston Churchill in Parliament Square, London

A

ABERFORD
W Yorkshire *15 SE43*
Near the brewery town of Tadcaster is the village of Aberford. The entrance to Parlington Hall has a Triumphal Arch built by Sir Thomas Gascoigne in 1783 to celebrate the end of the War of Independence. An inscription, which reads 'Liberty in North America Triumphant 1783', gave great offence to a visiting Prince Regent – later George IV.

ABERYSTWYTH
Dyfed *7 SN58*
Aberystwyth stands on a prehistoric site at the mouths of the Rheidol and Ystwyth rivers. The town's importance began in the 13th century with the building of the castle, later destroyed by Cromwell. The ruins remain on the seafront, the precincts laid out as public gardens. Opposite stands a Victorian Gothic building, the nucleus of the University of Wales, whose campus on Penglais Hill includes the National Library of Wales. This houses the finest existing collection of Welsh manuscripts and books, as well as maps, prints and portraits relating to Wales. Many are

in Welsh – one of the five Celtic languages, and spoken in this part of Britain since the 6th century. The collection contains the manuscripts of the 12th-century Black Book of Carmarthen, the White Book of Roderick, and the Book of Taliesin. Part of the collection deals with Welsh migration to America, indeed the Library's interior was refurbished by Welshmen in America. Readers' tickets are obtainable from the Library. The university has produced many talented scholars, particularly of the Welsh language and literature.

The funicular railway on Constitution Hill is a further reminder of Aberystwyth's Victorian heritage.

ABINGDON
Oxfordshire *4 SU49*
The town grew up around its abbey, founded in 676, on the banks of the Thames. The 15th-century abbey gatehouse still survives, and the granary contains a reconstruction of an Elizabethan theatre where performances are given in the summer. Stones from the ruined abbey were used in the 19th century to build an artificial ruin.

St Helen's Church contains a medieval Lady Chapel on the ceiling of which is painted a 'Tree of Jesse'; a representation of Christ's genealogy often illustrated in medieval stained glass and painting. The County Hall in the market place is attributed to a design by Christopher Wren or one of his masons, and now houses the town's museum. The school is said to have two masts from the *Mayflower*

built into it. The Crown and Thistle pub was a temporary home for John Ruskin following his appointment as the first Slade Professor of Art at Oxford in 1869.

ACTON BURNELL
Shropshire *9 SJ50*
Burnell Castle (AM) is one of England's oldest fortified manor houses and the first meeting of an English parliament to include commoners is said to have been held here by Edward I in 1283. The parish church of St Mary contains some fine 14th-century brasses, and a memorial to Sir Richard Lee and his wife. Lee was an ancestor of Robert E Lee, and the resemblance between the two is striking.

ALDBURY
Hertfordshire *11 SP91*
Since Aldbury was already called 'old fort' by the Saxons, its history is obviously long. The manor house, church, thatched cottages and beamed almshouses overlook a village green where stocks and whipping post still stand near the pond. A monument to canal pioneer the 3rd Duke of Bridgewater looks down over Ashridge Park (NT) designed by Capability Brown and Humphry Repton.

ALDEBURGH
Suffolk *12 TM45*
A flourishing town, which grew up after the prosperous medieval centre of Slaughden was partially destroyed by the sea, Aldeburgh took over its role as a fishing and shipbuilding port. Drake's ship the *Pelican*, later to be renamed the *Golden Hind*, was built here and local men sailed with him. The area is a setting in 'The Village' and 'The Borough', poems by the Reverend George Crabbe, who was born here in 1754 and later lived at Slaughden. Aldeburgh church has a commemorative bust to him. Wilkie Collins' novel *No Name* is also set locally. Benjamin Britten also lived here. His opera *Peter Grimes* (1945) was based on a character in Crabbe's 'The Borough' (1810) which dealt with the harsh lives of the working people of Aldeburgh. Britten used the 16th-century Moot Hall as the setting. The annual Aldeburgh Music Festival, originally organized by Britten, is held nearby at **Snape**. Elizabeth Garrett Anderson, the first woman mayor, and one of the first women doctors, lived at Alde House.

Aberystwyth

Aldeburgh

ALDERBURY
Wiltshire *3 SU12*
The village contains the remains of
Ivychurch, a 12th-century Augustinian
priory (founded by King Stephen).
Alderbury House, an 18th-century
residence, is said to have been built of
materials from the old bell-tower of
Salisbury Cathedral after it was
replaced in 1789. Alderbury claims its
Green Dragon Inn as the model used
by Dickens for the Blue Dragon in
Martin Chuzzlewit, which Dickens
wrote while staying nearby at Marie's
Grange. The Grange was built in 1835
by the architect Augustus Welby Pugin
for himself and his young bride. Pugin
helped in the design of the new Houses
of Parliament.
  The surrounding area also contains
several points of interest. 2 miles SE
Eyre's Folly or 'the Pepperbox', a
slate-roofed 6-sided structure built in
1606, is set in 73 acres of downland
(NT). 2 miles south is Trafalgar
House, built in 1753, and renamed in
1814 when it was given to Lord
Nelson's family by a grateful nation.
Its Ganges room is panelled with
timbers from the man o' war of the
same name which fought with Nelson's
fleet at the Battle of Copenhagen.

ALDERSHOT
Hampshire *4 SU85*
Possibly the most famous military
centre in Britain, Aldershot is very
much an army town, with a number of
service museums such as the Airborne
Forces Museum and the Royal Corps
of Transport Museum. 'Home' of the
British Army it has many associations
with North America, while Canada
has long-standing connections with
Aldershot, a main centre for the

Canadian military in both World
Wars. In 1945 her Army received the
freedom of the Borough. There are
some Canadian graves in the military
cemetery, and several of the town's
military museums contain items
relating to America.

ALFORD
Lincolnshire *16 TF47*
This small Georgian town close to the
coast of the Pilgrim country, has a 5-
sailed windmill in full working order,
and holds a weekly craft market.
Alford was the birthplace of Anne
Hutchinson who emigrated to
Massachusetts in 1634. She was
banished to Rhode Island for her
religious principles; her society was
known as the Antinomians. John
Smith went to school here and Tom
Paine also lived here for a while.
  One mile east is Bilsby. In 1656,
Archbishop Lamb suspended the vicar
of Bilsby, the Reverend John
Wheelwright, who then emigrated to
America. However, he was among
Anne Hutchinson's Antinomians, who
were banished from Massachusetts.
Wheelwright was a founder of Exeter,
New Hampshire. He was a
contemporary of Cromwell at
Cambridge, and returned to England
during the Commonwealth.
  Three miles south, Willoughby was
the birthplace of Captain John Smith,
the famous Elizabethan navigator of
the world, and the founder of
Jamestown, Virginia – the first
permanent English settlement in North
America. Born the son of a tenant
farmer on Lord Willoughby
D'Eresby's estate, Smith was
apprenticed to a **King's Lynn** merchant
before he ran away to sea.

In 1635, Sir Henry Vane left Belleau
4 miles north west of Alford to become
Governor of Massachusetts.

ALLOWAY
Strathclyde *22 NS31*
Scotland's national poet, Robert
Burns, was born here on 25 January
1759, still celebrated as Burns' Night.
The thatched cottage has been
preserved as a museum (OACT). The
Brig o' Doon mentioned in 'Tam o'
Shanter' spans the river. A monument
in the nearby gardens was erected by
Boswell's son in 1820 (OACT). South
of Alloway is Mt Oliphant farm where
Burns moved at the age of 6; his first
education was at Alloway School.

ALNMOUTH
Northumberland *24 NU21*
Established as a shipbuilding centre
and a port in the 13th century,
Alnmouth prospered until the River
Aln changed its course during a storm
in 1806. Now the quiet town lies in the
centre of the Northumberland
Heritage Coast, a 56-mile stretch of
impressive coastline. The town has one
of the oldest golf courses in England,
laid out in 1869. In 1778 Alnmouth was
bombarded by John Paul Jones.

ALNWICK
Northumberland *24 NU11*
The main market town on the River
Aln, and an excellent centre for
touring the Border country. Alnwick
Castle (OACT), built on a 12th-
century site and principal seat of the
historic Percy family, stood as a ruin
for 200 years following the Borders
warfare, and was restored in the 18th
and 19th centuries by the Dukes of
Northumberland. The Percy lion
emblem is displayed on the Tenantry
Column at the southern entrance to
the town. This was erected by 1000
grateful tenants after their rents had
been reduced.
  Sir Hugh Smithson, father of the
founder of the Smithsonian Institute in
Washington, lived in Alnwick.
Smithson married into the Percy family
and claimed their title. Sir David
Smith, formerly a lieutenant in the
Northumberland Fusiliers, surveyor-
general of Upper Canada in the 1790's
and Speaker of the house of Assembly,
is buried in Alnwick Church.
  Warkworth, a medieval castle a few
miles south east is also associated with
the Percies and was mentioned in
Shakespeare's *Henry IV*.

ABERDEEN
Grampian *28 NJ90*

Aberdeen received its first royal charter in the 12th century and was a thriving port by the 13th – but in 1336 much of it was burned to the ground by Edward III of England. The rebuilt areas of 'New Aberdeen' gradually merged with the remains of the old town, though the original cobbled streets and pink granite houses of the latter still exist as an easily identifiable nucleus.

The beginnings of modern Aberdeen came with the building of Union Street, opened in 1805, running broad and straight from the 17th-century Mercat Cross. Large numbers of neo-classical buildings were erected in the local, mica-flecked grey granite, and the city gradually assumed the face so often described as 'austere' – despite the many thousands of roses that bloom in its parks each year. Today it is a major commercial centre, involved in engineering, shipbuilding, papermaking and the production of granite and chemicals; it is also the largest fishing port in Scotland, and has gained a new importance with the coming of the North Sea oil industry – its position and seafaring traditions making it an ideal base for the servicing of drilling rigs and production platforms. Oil has made a significant contribution to the life of the city. It is also an important university and cathedral city, however, with a wealth of fine old buildings that make its history a living part of the 20th century.

Aberdeen has strong American links. Following the War of Independence American churchmen were unwilling to sign the Oath of Allegiance to the British Crown. Many turned to Scotland and the Episcopal Kirk centred on Aberdeen. Near the site of the Marischal College three Scottish bishops consecrated Samuel Seabury in a secret ceremony. He was the first Anglican bishop to owe no allegiance to the Crown. St Andrew's Cathedral in Aberdeen is regarded as the mother church of the Episcopal Communion in America. Another American link surrounds the story of the Scotsman Peter Williamson who, in the 18th century was kidnapped from Aberdeen and sold as a labourer in Philadelphia. Eventually Williamson became a farmer, but was ruined when captured by Indians. He returned to Scotland, wrote a book describing his experiences, and took successful legal action against his original captors. He finally settled in Edinburgh where he was known as 'Indian Peter'. Eric

Marischal College

Linklater, best known for his *Don Juan in America* (1943), was a student and lecturer in Aberdeen.

PLACES TO SEE

The Harbour has brought wealth to the city ever since the 13th century. Even today the trawling industry is important, and vast catches of fish are handled here – but in the 19th century the old docks also saw the launching of the famous clippers, the fast sailing ships that played such an important part in the expansion of trade with the Far East and Australia.

Shiprow runs up from the harbour and is possibly the oldest street in Aberdeen. It contains the 16th-century Provost Ross's House (NTS) which has been restored and is now a Maritime Museum.

Castlegate, nearby, is the oldest part of New Aberdeen. The castle has long since disappeared, but the area has been regarded as the centre of the city for the past 600 years. The Mercat Cross (erected in 1686) is the finest burgh cross existing in Scotland today – a circular edifice of red sandstone with a pillar supporting a white unicorn.

King's College, dating back to 1494, is the old part of the university; its splendid tower is

surmounted by a crown honouring James IV who aided the founding.

Marischal College was founded in 1593 as a Protestant alternative to King's College; the two merged in 1860 to become the University of Aberdeen. Attached to Marischal is Aberdeen's important anthropological museum. General Hugh Mercer, who fell at the Battle of Princeton in 1777, was founder of Mercersburg, Pennsylvania and studied at the College.

James Dun's House holds a children's museum whose displays include Victorian toys and treasures from Scottish history; there are also opportunities for children to participate in various activities.

Provost Skene's House, a 16th-century building in Flourmill Lane, contains a folk museum on the top floor, and its chapel has interesting religious paintings on the ceiling.

The Art Gallery has paintings by Hogarth, Degas, Renoir and Augustus John. John Singer Sargent is among its American artists. It also includes sculptures by Henry Moore, Barbara Hepworth and Epstein. The gallery was formerly a school, which the young Lord Byron attended.

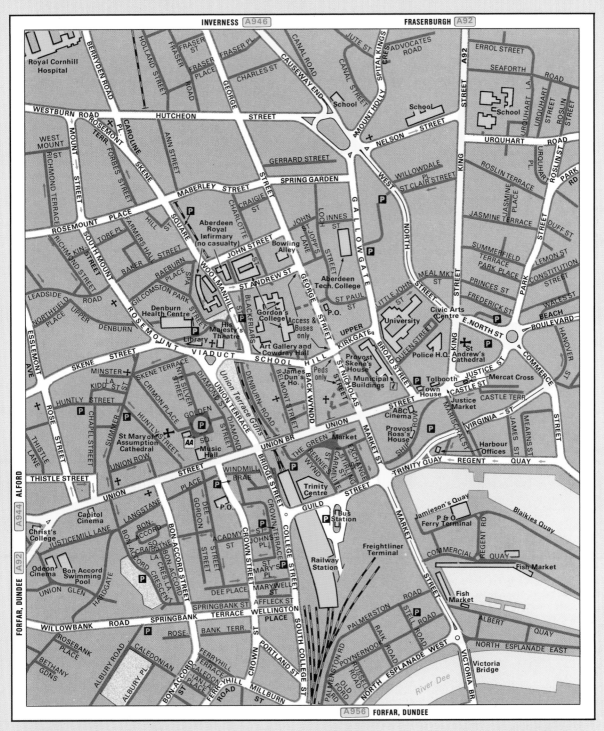

St Machar's Cathedral is one of the three cathedrals in the city – the others being St Mary's (Roman Catholic) and St Andrew's (Episcopalian). It was founded in the 12th century but the present building dates mainly from the 15th. Partly castellated, it was fortified against attacks by the English on the seaward side and the Celtic Highlanders from the mountains.

St Nicholas' Kirk is one of the finest examples of ecclesiastical architecture in Scotland; it is also noted for having 48 bells – the largest carillon in Britain.

The Golf Links represent a bridge between the old and the new; the game has been played here since the 17th century, and the course – both literally and metaphorically – spans the distance between the city and the 'resort' on the wide beaches between the Rivers Don and Dee.

ALTHORP
Northamptonshire *10 SP66*
Althorp Hall (OACT) has been the
home of the Princess of Wales' family,
the Spencers, since 1508. The house
has an extensive picture gallery which
includes portraits by Gainsborough
and Reynolds.

The surrounding area has several
associations with the Washington
family. Lawrence Washington lived in
a stone house in Little Brington's main
street after selling Sulgrave Manor.
His younger brother Robert, lived in
Great Brington, and later his widow,
Anne, lived a few miles north at East
Haddon. The parish church in Great
Brington contains Washington family
tombs, and pews they once occupied.

ALTON
Hampshire *4 SU73*
An old cloth-making and brewery
town which the Roundheads captured
from the Cavaliers during the Civil
War. The fight ended in the church of
St Lawrence, where the Royalist
leader, Colonel Boles, was killed. No 1
Amery Street was the Tudor home of
Edmund Spenser when he came from
Ireland in 1590 with Sir Walter
Raleigh, in order to publish *The Faerie
Queene*. Cardinal Newman stayed in
Alton while an undergraduate at
Oxford, and John Murray, a native of
Alton, founded the Universalist
Church of the USA. A tablet in the
parish church commemorates him. Sir
Compton Mackenzie, the writer, lived
in the neighbouring village of Beech,
while nearby **Chawton** was the last
home of Jane Austen.

AMBLESIDE
Cumbria *18 NY30*
A well-known Lake District centre,
famous for its walking and climbing
facilities and its annual sheepdog
trials. Another event takes place each
July when children process through
the streets carrying rushes and flowers
to the parish church, a tradition dating
from medieval times when rushes
where used to carpet churches. This
part of the Lake District has many
literary associations. Matthew Arnold
lived at Fox House. Charlotte Brontë
used to visit her friend the writer
Harriet Martineau at her home in
Ambleside. William Wordsworth and
his sister Dorothy would often walk to
the post office in Ambleside when they
lived at Dove Cottage, 12 miles away
at **Grasmere**. Ambleside's church of St
Mary contains a memorial window
presented by American admirers of

Ancient water mill, Ambleside

Wordsworth. Bridge House (NT), a
stone summerhouse, set over a stream,
houses the National Trust Information
Centre. A lane behind the Salutation
Hotel leads to 70ft-high Stock Gill Force.

AMERSHAM
Buckinghamshire *5 SU99*
The broad High Street of this growing
country town is lined with cobbled
courtyards leading to ancient inns and
thatched cottages. A stream flows
through the Mill Stream House, a
public house. A monument on a
nearby hillside commemorates the
Lollards, extremist followers of the
religious reformer John Wyclif. They
were burned at the stake during the
turbulent 15th and 16th centuries.

Amersham has several associations
with America, in particular with
William Penn. Bury Farm was the
home of Isaac Pennington and his wife,
after they left Chalfont St Peter in
1669. William Penn's first wife was
Gulielma Springett, Mrs Pennington's
daughter. Thomas Hooker, founder of
Hartford, Connecticut was married in
Amersham parish church.

AMMANFORD
Powys *7 SN61*
Ammanford grew up rapidly in the late
19th century due to its location on an
anthracite coalfield. Nevertheless, the
area preserves much beautiful scenery
and rural landscape. The Reverend
John Jenkins, later Archdruid of
Wales, had a school here early this
century, that produced many
prominent men. The building is now
the English Congregational Chapel.

George Borrow stayed at

Brynamman 5 miles east of
Ammanford. Dr Richard Price was
educated at Garnant, near
Glannaman. Price was a philosopher
and friend of Benjamin Franklin and
his pamphlets on the American war
caused his name to be linked with the
objectives of American independence.
He died in 1791. The roads over the
Black Mountains afford striking views.

AMPTHILL
Bedfordshire *11 TL03*
Ampthill's connections with royalty
began after Agincourt, when Sir John
Cornwall built a castle here for his
bride, Henry IV's sister. Katherine of
Aragon, the first of Henry VIII's six
wives, stayed here while Henry
arranged to divorce her. The castle fell
into ruin in the 17th century, its
original site is marked by a cross with
an inscription to Katherine of Aragon
written by Horace Walpole. Charles II
gave the Great Park to Lord
Ashburnham who built Ampthill Park
House in 1694 – it was formerly a
Cheshire home. 1 mile north stand the
ruins of 17th-century Houghton House
(AM), John Bunyan's inspiration for
'House Beautiful' in *The Pilgrim's
Progress*. Ampthill's parish church
contains the tomb of General Richard
Nicolls (1624–72), believed to have
been born here too. In 1664 Nicolls
was sent to conquer the New
Netherlands which he did and then
renamed New York in honour of his
patron the Duke of York, later James
II. A plaque to the left of the altar tells
the story of Nicolls' death in the naval
battle of Sole Bay. The cannonball
which killed him is embedded in the
monument, which also displays the
'stars and stripes'.

ANDOVER
Hampshire *4 SU34*
A town of antiquity – and there are
remains of Iron Age encampments on
the surrounding hills – that has taken
on a new lease of life as one of
London's overspill towns. Andover
boasts several inns that were
patronized by royalty. James II stayed
at the Angel the night before his
abdication in favour of William of
Orange. Charles I and later George III
stayed at the Star and Garter.

In 1643 numerous people left
Andover for the New World and
founded Andover, Massachusetts.
Nearby Red Rice Estate, a Georgian
house dating from 1740, was used
before 'D' Day as an HQ by General
Eisenhower and General Bedell Smith.

PILGRIM COUNTRY

In a general sense the Pilgrim Fathers (who were distinctly English) came from the east, from a region stretching from South Yorkshire southwest to Nottingham and southeast to Lincolnshire and the Fens, from the flat, cold and empty lands looking east and south as far as Essex. It is Cromwell's and Pym's country too, and it has 'intellectual headquarters' they are in Cambridge, at Emmanuel College, which was founded in 1583 and which John Harvard attended, at Peterhouse College, where Brewster matriculated, and Caius (pron 'keys') and Christ's Colleges, where John Robinson was a Fellow. Only one member of the first Harvard Board of Overseers went to Oxford: John Davenport, who went to Merton College. Almost all the rest were Cambridge men. The two great Pilgrim leaders, William Brewster and William Bradford, came from neighbouring villages – Scrooby in Nottinghamshire, where there is a prominent pub on the Great North Road called The Pilgrim Fathers, and Austerfield, just inside South Yorkshire. Forty miles east of Scrooby is Boston, from which the very first Pilgrims sought to escape to Holland. And if one adds that strong Pilgrim contingents also came from the southwest of England, it is striking that these two regions were, on the whole, opposed to the King in the Civil War.

The Society of Mayflower Descendants erected a plaque in St Helena's Church, Austerfield, in 1955, 339 years after the sailing of the *Mayflower*, to William Bradford, who is described as 'the first American citizen of the English race who bore rule by the free choice of his brethren'. He became Governor of Plymouth Colony in April 1621.

Brewster, son of the village bailiff and postmaster, is similarly commemorated in St Wilfred's, Scrooby, an unusual fourteenth-century church.

The Pilgrims, or Separatists, wanted a church purified, after Henry VIII's break with Rome, even of any remaining Catholic features, especially bishops; a man – and it was a masculine Church – should commune directly with his God, and he should be able to read and preach the Word and need no one to intercede for him; in church and, in the end, in state he should be made self-governing. As such, the Puritans were disloyal to the King and to the new carefully contrived Anglican establishment of the late Tudor and early Stuart years. The Reformation and the economic depression of the 1620s had bitten deep in eastern England.

The *Mayflower* leaving Plymouth for America

Places to Visit

Billericay, Essex, where *Christopher Martin*, 'Governor' of the *Mayflower*, and Treasurer and Victualler of the expedition, worshipped and was married.

Bristol: Cabot Tower on Brandon Hill; St Mary Redcliffe Church; and No 1 Great George Street, home for thirty years of Mayor *Henry Cruger*, the only man to have been both an MP (for Bristol 1774–80, 1784–90) and a Senator (in NY State).

Dedham in Essex, from which a number of Puritans came, including *Edmund Sherman*, the progenitor of General William Tecumseh Sherman, *John Dwight*, *John Page* and *John Rogers*.

Droitwich, Worcestershire, where *Edward Winslow* was baptized in St Peter's Church.

Duxbury Hall near Wigan and Chorley in Lancashire, for *Miles Standish* – he gave the name Duxbury to his estate in New England.

Gainsborough, Lincolnshire. Home of pastor *John Robinson*.

Groton Manor, near Sudbury in Suffolk, where *John Winthrop*, the first Governor of the Colony of Massachusetts Bay, was brought up, and spent his first forty years.

London; the Pilgrim Fathers' Memorial Church, Southwark, is the oldest Congregationalist house of worship in England, first built in 1616, much rebuilt. In Southwark Cathedral, *John Harvard* was baptized, and there is a commemorative Harvard Chapel. Not far away, in St Sepulchre's, Holborn Viaduct, is the tomb of *Captain John Smith*, 'sometime Governor of Virginia and Admiral of New England'; and downriver in St George's at Gravesend, lies buried – though not in her original grave – *Pocahontas*.

Plymouth, The Barbican, from where the *Mayflower* sailed, and the Guildhall.

Further Reading

Vernon Heaton, *The Mayflower* (Webb & Bower, 1980)

D B Quinn, *England and the Discovery of America 1481–1620* (Allen and Unwin, 1974).

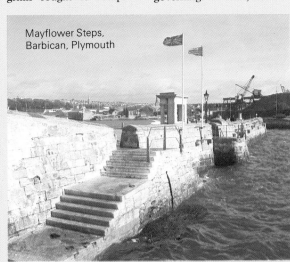

Mayflower Steps, Barbican, Plymouth

ANGLESEY, ISLE OF
Gwynedd   *13 SH47*

Anglesey is a popular holiday area, with attractive contrasts of scenery, the coastline ranging from cliffs with rocky bays to wide, smooth beaches. The visitor can see many ancient monuments, such as the passage grave of Bryn-Celli-Ddu (AM), the best example of its kind in Britain. Another fascinating site is Din Lligwy, where the remains of a pre-Roman settlement were discovered. Other places of interest include Plas Newydd (NT), the beautiful 18th-century house of the Marquesses of Anglesey. A column at Llanfair PG which can be climbed for fine views of the island commemorates a Marquis known as 'One-Leg', who is remembered for his contributions in the Battle of Waterloo, where he received the wound from which he earned his nickname. Beaumaris Castle (AM) is a magnificent fortress of concentric design. The famous South Stack lighthouse stands on a rocky islet off Holy Island, and the village with one of the longest names in the world, Llanfairpwllgwyngyllgogerychwyrndrobwllllantysiliogogogoch – usually shortened to Llanfair PG! – is in the south east of the island. Apparently, the name was 'invented', or at least extended, by a local businessman during the 19th century; not surprisingly most tourists are incapable of pronouncing it. Moelfre on the north coast was the birthplace of Goronwy Owen, the Welsh poet and earlier settler of Brunswick

South Stack off Holy Island, Anglesey

County, Virginia. It was off here that the *Royal Charter* was wrecked in a storm in 1859. 460 lives were lost and bullion and valuables worth over £400,000 from Australia were later recovered. The story was used by Dickens in *The Uncommercial Traveller*.

APPLEBY-IN-WESTMORLAND
Cumbria   *18 NY61*

Appleby lies at the foot of the Pennines in the Eden Valley, an area rich in both natural beauty and historical interest. Each June the country's largest horse fair is held here, when gypsies come from all over Britain to buy and sell horses. The town is dominated by the castle, restored in 1653 by Lady Anne Clifford, Countess of Dorset, Pembroke and Montgomery, a noted opponent of Cromwell. She built and restored many of the town's buildings. At each end of the Boroughgate stand crosses bearing Lady Anne's motto, 'Retain your loyalty, preserve your rights'.

Lawrence and Augustine Washington, half-brothers of George by his father's first marriage, were educated at the old Grammar School. Richard Pearson, who was defeated by John Paul Jones off **Flamborough**, also went to the school. Portraits of all three famous pupils can be seen in the present school library, together with that of John Robinson, who was Secretary to Lord North's Government.

ARDELEY
Hertfordshire   *11 TL32*

A deceptively 'olde worlde' English village with a green surrounded by white-walled thatched cottages; deceptive because it was all rebuilt in 1917 by the lord of the manor. Nevertheless Ardeley has a long history. In medieval times the village supplied malt to the Dean and Chapter of St Paul's Cathedral, who in turn provided funds to build the parish church of St Lawrence.

Ardeley was the birthplace and ancestral home of Charles Chauncy who emigrated to America in 1637, and later became the president of Harvard College. He was a great-grandfather of Charles Chauncy, the founder of the New England Unitarian Movement.

ARISAIG
Highland   *25 NM68*

At Arisaig the Road to the Isles meets the sea, with Rhum, Eigg and Muck

clearly visible across the bay and the mountains of Skye beyond. To the north of the village stretch smooth expanses of silver-white sand and to its south lies Borrodale Beach, scene of Bonnie Prince Charlie's landing in 1745 and his flight the following year; the cave in which he hid before his escape is near Arisaig House.

ARRAN, ISLE OF
Strathclyde   *21 NR93*

Arran is famous for its association with Robert the Bruce, who landed at Lochranza ('the loch of safe anchorage') in 1306 and later sheltered in King's Caves near Blackwater. The island is roughly 20 miles long by 10 miles wide, and from Goat Fell in the north (its highest point at 2866ft) there are magnificent views of the Clyde, the Western Isles and the coast of Ireland. The Isle of Arran Heritage Museum (OACT) is at Brodick, on the east coast, the most important village. Its 15th-century castle (NTS) (OACT) – traditional home of the Hamilton family – overlooks Brodick Bay.

ARUNDEL
W Sussex   *5 TQ00*

Sited where the Arun cuts through the Sussex Downs, Arundel is dominated by its castle above which flies the flag of the Duke of Norfolk, head of England's leading Catholic family. Flanked by the late 14th-century church of St Nicholas (unique in being three-quarters Protestant and a quarter Roman Catholic) and the Roman Catholic cathedral of St Philip Neri, the castle (OACT) was built by Roger Montgomery, Earl of Shrewsbury, after the Norman Conquest. It was largely destroyed by Cromwellian troops in 1643. Sir William Springett was killed here during the siege. The castle was rebuilt in the 18th century. Inside there are several interesting collections of furniture and armour, as well as pictures by Gainsborough, Van Dyke and Reynolds. From the castle one may enter the chancel of the parish church which became the Roman Catholic Fitzalan Chapel when Henry VIII sold the castle to the family. The wall which previously separated the Catholic chapel from the Protestant church has now been removed. Of interest in the town is the William Potter Museum of Curiosity (OACT). William Potter was an eccentric Victorian taxidermist who specialized in arranging stuffed animals in tableaux of nursery rhymes.

Arundel Castle

ASHBOURNE
Derbyshire *15 SK14*
Surrounded by hills rising to 600ft, Ashbourne is an attractive tourist centre on the edge of the Peak District National Park. It is famous for the free-for-all, no-holds-barred football match waged there over a 3-mile pitch each Shrove Tuesday – sometimes lasting well into Ash Wednesday. Fine old buildings abound in the town – Church Street has a 16th-century grammar school, 17th-century almshouses and a Georgian mansion visited by Dr Johnson and Boswell. The church of St Oswald – substantially 13th- and 14th-century, with a 212ft spire – is one of the finest in the country.

· ASHBY-DE-LA-ZOUCH
Leicestershire *10 SK31*
Originally a Danish settlement, Ashby acquired its full name with the arrival of the Breton family of La Souche in the 12th century. The town became a spa in the 19th century, but contains Elizabethan half-timbered houses as well as bow-fronted Georgian shops. Behind the main street are the ruins of the 15th-century castle. Nearby the Tournament field was the setting for the pageant in Scott's *Ivanoe*.

ASHWELL
Hertfordshire *11 TL23*
Ash trees surround the springs at the source of the Rhee, giving the village its name. It owes its spacious planning to the Romans, though the first settlement here was probably an Iron Age hill-fort, the Arbury Banks, controlling the ancient Icknield Way. The tower of the mainly 14th-century church of St Mary rises to 176ft, tipped with a small 'Hertfordshire spike', and on the south wall beneath it is a carving of old St Paul's. A Latin inscription in the tower testifies to the plague, 14th-century killer of a third of the village population, as do the graves of victims outside. The restored Town House (OACT), probably once used for tithe-gathering, contains a museum of village history and rural life.

AUCHINLECK
Strathclyde *22 NS52*
The Second Keep 3 miles west of this mining village was the Boswell family home until 1772, when the father of James Boswell built Auchinleck House, designed partly by the Adam brothers. It was here that the American scholar Chauncy B Tinker discovered the *London Journal* which describes Boswell's first meeting with Samuel Johnson; Boswell was buried in Auchinleck church in 1795.

AUDLEY END HOUSE
Essex *11 TL53*
Audley End House (AM) was built in 1630 for Thomas Howard, Earl of Suffolk and Lord High Treasurer. Built on the site of a Benedictine Abbey, the house was originally much larger. Its Jacobean exterior was carefully preserved when it was restored by Robert Adam who is also responsible for the fine 18th-century interiors. The house hosted several famous people including Sir Philip Sidney and Pepys. During World War II the old grammar school was used as an HQ by the 65th Fighter Wing of the US Army Air Force – the sports complex is now a memorial. Another memorial is in the parish church.

AUSTERFIELD
S Yorkshire *15 SK69*
William Bradford, a Pilgrim Father, author of the *History of Plimouth Plantation*, log keeper of the *Mayflower*, and a major Governor of Plymouth, New England for 30 years, was born at Austerfield Manor. He was baptized in the Norman church, in which the north aisle was restored by the Society of Mayflower Descendants in 1897. The manor house was almost certainly used for separatist religious meetings; many pilgrims came from the surrounding area. William Butten, also a native of Austerfield, was one of these.

Two miles west is Harworth, birthplace of pilgrims Thomas Morton and George Thornton. Serlby Hall, near Bawtry, was the home of General Robert Monkton, second-in-command to Wolfe at Quebec.

· AVEBURY
Wiltshire *3 SU06*
The 28 acres of the village of Avebury, but not the fine Elizabethan Manor (OACT), lie within a late Neolithic circle of vast standing stones or sarsens – the largest weighing some 60 tons – which is in turn surrounded by earthworks. Inside the large circle are two smaller, incomplete rings, the stones in all three having been carefully selected from the nearby Marlborough Downs. It has been suggested that the tall, narrow stones represent men and the more diamond-shaped ones women, and that the whole thing was an open air temple for fertility rites, but we have no real knowledge of its significance. Many of the stones are missing, destroyed because of medieval superstition or broken up for use in local buildings. The Alexander Keiller Museum (AM) (NT), in what was formerly the manor coach-house, contains objects excavated in the village and also at Windmill Hill, Silbury Hill and West Kennet Long Barrow. The 50ft-wide avenue of megaliths which apparently ran out past West Kennet to Overbury

Stone circles, Avebury

Hill seems to indicate that the Avebury circles were part of a larger scheme, involving a number of these ancient religious sites. The approximate date of this complex of stones, 1500 BC, makes it contemporary with parts of Stonehenge, 18 miles to the south.

AVIEMORE
Highland   *26 NH81*
Aviemore's position on the edge of a 600-acre nature reserve enhanced its importance as the heart of Britain's winter sports area in the 1960s when a massive leisure complex was built. The concrete plaza contains shops, restaurants, hotels, a theatre and concert hall as well as many sports facilities, including ice-rinks, a swimming pool and a dry ski-slope. Though the design is modern, the materials used were wood and granite, blending well with Aviemore's setting at the foot of Craigellachie, traditional gathering place of the Clan Grant.

AXMINSTER
Devon   *3 SY29*
Built on high ground above the River Axe and centred round a tree-shaded green, the busy streets of this small

market town are still rich in Georgian and Victorian buildings and it has several fine coaching inns. Its name is synonymous with the manufacture of fine carpets, though the factory opened by Thomas Whitty in the 18th century – based on his close study of Turkish methods – was in production for only 80 years before being sold out to a Wilton weaver. The industry did not return to the town until 1937.

AYLESBURY
Buckinghamshire   *10 SP81*
Aylesbury is now a busy modern town at the junction of six main roads, but its centre recalls more leisurely days. Narrow Tudor alleys run between four squares – St Mary's, Market, Temple and Kingsbury. St Mary's Square has old terraces of houses on three sides and the ancient church, with its distinctive 'Aylesbury' font, on the fourth. The cattle market is still in use, reached through the arches under the old Town Hall, and in Market Square stands a statue of John Hampden, famous for his opposition to Charles I's demands for ship money. The King's Head Hotel (NT) was founded in 1386 and has a medieval gateway

and fine 15th-century stained glass. The County Museum in Church Street is set in dignified 18th-century buildings that were originally a monastery guesthouse.

Six miles northwest lies Quainton, an exceptionally attractive village, with a large green and many thatched cottages. Many imposing monuments and medieval brasses embellish the interior of the church. The Quainton Railway Centre (OACT) has one of the country's most comprehensive collections of items relating to standard-gauge railways.

Sir James Clark Ross, the Arctic explorer, is buried in the church at Aston Abbotts 5 miles north of Aylesbury and there is a commemorative window. He discovered the north magnetic pole in 1829. He also searched unsuccessfully in the Canadian Arctic for the ill-fated Franklin expedition, lost in 1847–48.

Nether Winchendon House (OACT) lies 7 miles south west of Aylesbury.

AYOT ST LAWRENCE
Hertfordshire   *11 TL11*
George Bernard Shaw chose this village as his home when he saw the epitaph of a local woman who died at the age of 70 years. It reads 'Her Time was Short'. Shaw lived here from 1906 till his death in 1950, aged 94. His ashes and those of his wife were scattered in the garden at Shaw's Corner. The house, originally a rectory, now belongs to the National Trust and is preserved as it was in Shaw's lifetime, and contains many mementoes of Shaw and his contemporaries. The summerhouse where Shaw worked can also be seen. The village has two churches, the earlier 14th-century one is in ruins; its 18th-century replacement was commissioned by Sir Lionel Lyden, its Grecian façade built by Nicholas Revett. Lullington Silk farm, which produces the silk for royal vestments, is open to the public in the summer.

AYR
Strathclyde   *22 NS32*
Ayr, a fishing harbour, port and major resort, is best known for its associations with Robert Burns who was born at **Alloway**. He was baptized in the Auld Kirk at Ayr. The Tam o'Shanter Inn which Burns knew as a brewhouse is now a museum containing many relics of the poet. A statue of Burns stands in the town square.

B

BABWORTH
Nottinghamshire   *15 SE68*
The Reverend Richard Clyfton was
rector here from 1586–1606; he was
the only Puritan preacher in the area
and attracted a large congregation,
among them William Brewster.
Clyfton later became pastor of the
Pilgrim group at **Scrooby**,
accompanying them to the
Netherlands where he died before the
migration to the New World. The
parish church contains items relating
to the Pilgrims.

BAGSHOT
Surrey   *5 SU96*
The road through Bagshot was once
the coaching route from London to
Exeter; the town was a point where
horses were changed. Bagshot Heath
and Bisley Common were once
notorious for highwaymen. Bagshot
Park (1879) belonged to Prince Arthur
of Connaught, who was Governor-
General of Canada 1911–16. It is now
the Museum of the Royal Army
Chaplains' Department (OACT by
written permission) and contains many
items relating to North America.
  Sandhurst, a few miles to the west, is
most famous as the home of the Royal
Military Academy, built by French
prisoners of war during the
Napoleonic Wars. The first cadets
arrived in 1812, and the Museum has
items relating especially to India, but
also to America and Ireland.

BAKEWELL
Derbyshire   *15 SK26*
The rich brown stone of Bakewell is
set against woodland at the foot of the
Peak District hills. The church is on
high ground, its spire a landmark for
miles, and has a famous Saxon cross
(AM) in the churchyard. One of the
oldest packhorse bridges in the
country crosses the Wye here. The
early settlement grew up around 12
springs – their water now analyzed as
iron bearing and at a temperature of
15°C. Though most of them have run
dry they are not forgotten, for their
sites are decorated each July in the
ancient ritual of well-dressing. Of

interest are Old House Museum
(OACT) and Magpie Mine a 19th-
century lead mine, the town's oldest
building and now a museum, and Bath
House, still fed by warm springs.
Lambton, the setting of Mr Darcy's
residence in *Pride and Prejudice*, is said
to be based on Bakewell; Jane Austen
stayed at the Rutland Arms Hotel
while writing it. The prototype
Bakewell tart is said to have been made
when an inept chef at the same hotel
misunderstood a recipe!

BALA
Gwynedd   *13 SH93*
Set amid the Welsh mountains, Bala
makes a convenient break in any tour
of Wales. Its main feature is Bala Lake
to which many legends are attached,
and is the only home of the Gwyniad –
a kind of white-scaled salmon. Unlike
many Welsh towns, Bala has remained
relatively untouched by centuries of
feuding. Previously it was known for
its stocking industry. George III
insisted on wearing Bala stockings
when he suffered from rheumatism.
But more recently Bala became an
important centre of Welsh
Nonconformism. In the forefront of
last century's revivalist movement was
Carmarthen-born Thomas Charles,
who settled in Bala at the end of the
18th century after graduating from
Jesus College, Oxford. He held several
curacies within the Anglican Church,
but his increasing dissatisfaction
finally caused him to join the

Methodist movement. Charles set up
Sunday schools which were novel in
that adults attended as well as
children. These were especially
popular amongst the Welsh hill
farmers and Welsh Bibles were printed
and distributed. In 1804 Charles
founded the British and Foreign Bible
Society which is dedicated to
'providing a Bible for all the people of
the world'. He was prompted to do
this when Mary Jones, a 16-year-old
from Llanfihangel-Y-Pennant over 20
miles away journeyed barefoot to Bala
with her savings in order to buy a Bible
– only to find they were sold out.
  Charles died in 1814, but his work
was continued by his grandson David
who, with Dr Lewis Edwards, founded
the Calvinistic Methodist College in
the hills above Bala in 1837. At the
height of the Methodist revival crowds
of 20,000 were recorded at 'sessions' at
Bala Green. A statue of Charles stands
in front of the Methodist church. He is
buried at Llanycil, known as the
Westminster Abbey of Wales.

BALERNO
Lothian   *23 NT16*
In Balerno stands Malleny House
(NTS), built in the early 17th century
and famous for its rose shrubberies
and fine old 'doocot' – a pigeon house
with 915 nesting boxes, originally
designed to provide a supply of fresh
meat during the winter. During World
War II there was an American airbase
4 miles west at Kirknewton.

Bala

BALLANTRAE
Strathclyde *17 NX08*

Robert Louis Stevenson took the name of this small resort for his novel *The Master of Ballantrae*. This was Kennedy country, and many of their castles are in evidence, such as the ruined Ardstinchar Castle, visited by Stevenson in 1876, and further up the valley, Knockdolian and Kirkhill Castles. Just south of Ballantrae are the beautiful gardens of Glenapp Castle. Nearby a small mid-19th-century church has been restored in memory of the Hon Elsie Mackay, lost flying the Atlantic in 1928. 7 miles north east on the beautiful coast road is Kennedy's Pass.

BALMORAL
Grampian *27 NO29*

Balmoral Castle was known in the 15th century as Bouchmorale – Gaelic for 'majestic dwelling'. Queen Victoria and Prince Albert bought it in 1853 and rebuilt it as a castle mansion in Scottish Baronial style. It is still used by the Royal Family as a summer residence. Crathie Church, just to the east, was built in 1895 and is the Royal Family's place of worship when at Balmoral. The church contains many mementoes of Queen Victoria and the Royal Family.

BALQUHIDDER
Central *22 NN52*

Best known as the burial place of Robert MacGregor, the brigand 'Rob Roy' immortalized in Scott's novel,

Rob Roy's grave, Balquhidder

Balquhidder is beautifully situated at the eastern end of Loch Voil. Rob Roy died at his home nearby at Inverlochlaraig in 1734. His wife Mary and two sons Coll and Robert (Robin Oig of Robert Louis Stevenson's *Kidnapped*), are buried beside him in the churchyard of the ruined kirk. The present church also commemorates the dead outlaw and contains an autographed scroll and inscribed bronze plaque presented in 1975 by members of the Clan MacGregor Society of America.

BAMBURGH
Northumberland *24 NU13*

Bamburgh Castle (OACT), a border stronghold that was once the seat of the Kings of Northumbria, stands on a crag above the North Sea; objects of interest include its weapon collection, fine tapestries and paintings, and a cradle which belonged to Queen Anne. The Grace Darling Museum (OACT) is opposite St Aidan's Church – her burial place – and the exhibits include the boat in which she and her father in 1838 rescued the survivors from the wrecked steamship *Forfarshire*. The Farne Islands (NT), 4½ miles offshore, were the home of St Aidan and St Cuthbert in the 7th century. Now they are an important breeding ground for young seabirds, and have been designated an Area of Outstanding Natural Beauty.

BANBURY
Oxfordshire *10 SP44*

Best known for its cakes and its cross of nursery rhyme fame, Banbury dates from Saxon times, though few pre-17th-century buildings survive. This is largely due to a peculiar trait of demolition among Banbury's inhabitants. In the 17th century they petitioned Parliament to pull down their great castle so that the stone could be used to repair damage caused to the town by two Civil War sieges. In the 18th century they blew up a church rather than restore it. The original Banbury Cross was destroyed too, in an upsurge of Puritanism 300 years ago. The present cross dates only from 1859. The 'fine lady' of the rhyme is believed to have been a member of the Fiennes family, who still live nearby at Broughton Castle. The ride to the cross was probably a May Morning ceremony.

In 1685 Benjamin Franklin's father, Josiah, moved from Banbury with his wife and four children to America. Benjamin was born in Boston in 1706.

Nearby Wroxton Abbey was the home of Lord North, the Prime Minister, whose Intolerable Acts of 1774 prompted the American Revolution. The abbey is now the English campus of the Fairleigh Dickinson University of New Jersey. 5½ miles further west, over the Warwickshire border, is Compton Wynyates, home of the Marquess of Northampton. The house was seized from this Royalist family and used as a garrison for Cromwellian troops in the Civil War. At Greatworth, 6 miles north east of Banbury, George Washington's ancestor, Lawrence, came to marry Amy Pargiter, his second wife.

BANGOR
Gwynedd *13 SH57*

The name of this cathedral and university town derives from a protective fence that surrounded a local monastery. The town's bishopric was established during the 6th century and is the oldest in Britain – older than that of Canterbury. The 12th-century Cathedral of St Deiniol was considerably restored in the 1860s by Sir Gilbert Scott, architect of the Albert Memorial in London. Near the cathedral is Gardd yr Esgob, a garden containing all the trees, shrubs and plants mentioned in the Bible which can survive in the Welsh climate – they are laid out in the order they appear in Scripture. The Museum and Art Gallery here includes traditional Welsh costume and furniture and also contains a few items relating to America, including a collection which belonged to Dr Griffith Evans, a veterinary surgeon who visited American field hospitals in the Civil War, where he met Abraham Lincoln. The original Penrhyn Castle (NT), 1 mile east, was built in the 12th century, but the present castle is 19th century. It contains a large collection of dolls, stuffed animals and birds, and a slate bed weighing four tons; the grounds contain a wide range of exotic plants and a display of railway relics.

BANNOCKBURN
Central *22 NS89*

The National Trust owns the 58-acre battlefield, at the heart of Scottish conflicts over the centuries. Here, in 1314, Robert the Bruce triumphed over an English army three times larger than his own. A rotunda with panels describing the course of the battle encircles the Borestone in which the shaft of Bruce's (and Scotland's) Standard is said to have been set.

Stirling Castle, the prize of the battle, can be seen from Bannockburn. Sir Walter Scott describes the conflict in *Lord of the Isles*. A statue of Bruce mounted on horseback by C d'O Pilkington Jackson was unveiled by the Queen in 1964. In the vicinity is also the site of the Battle of Sauchieburn, where James III was defeated and fatally wounded in 1488. Prince Charles Edward made Bannockburn House, 1½ miles south east, his headquarters in 1746.

BARDON MILL
Northumberland *19 NY76*
At *Vindolanda* (Chesterholm) 1¼ miles north west of Bardon Mill, can be seen the remains of a Roman fort and settlement of the 3rd and 4th centuries AD. Museums contain the results of various excavations, and there are replicas of Hadrian's turf and stone walls. The only Roman milestone still to stand in its original position (AM) is situated at Chesterholm.

BARDSEY ISLAND
Gwynedd *13 SH12*
Bardsey Island, off the beautiful Lleyn Peninsula, is now a bird observatory; previously it was a place of pilgrimage. Early Celts built a monastery here and Bardsey became known as the Island of Twenty Thousand Saints. It is also said that the Welsh wizard, Merlin, lies here in an enchanted sleep, with the golden throne of Britain, awaiting the return of King Arthur.

BARKHAM
Berkshire *4 SU76*
The processional crucifix for the parish bears an inscription to Edward Ball, reputedly an ancestor of George Washington. The Ball family were previously Lords of the Manor. A Colonel William Ball emigrated to Virginia in 1630. Ball's granddaughter, Mary, returned to Barkham after the death of her father. On a visit to Cheshire Mary met and married Augustine Washington and became mother of the first American President.

BARLASTON
Staffordshire *14 SJ83*
At Barlaston, in the Wedgwood Museum and Visitor Centre (OACT) is an exhibition of ceramics dating from the 18th century to the present day and including a comprehensive collection of the works of Josiah Wedgwood. Traditional skills are displayed in the demonstration area.

BARNARD CASTLE
Co Durham *19 NZ01*
On a clifftop 80ft above the Tees stand the ruins of Barnard (originally 'Bernard's') Castle (AM), built by Bernard Balliol in the 12th century on the site of an earlier family stronghold. The Balliols gained power in the 13th century, when John Balliol was crowned King of Scotland – a member of the same family later founded Balliol College in Oxford. *Master Humphrey's Clock* (1840) in which *The Old Curiosity Shop* and *Barnaby Rudge* appeared, may have been inspired by a clockmaker's shop in the town. Dickens and his illustrator Hablôt Browne stayed at the King's Head Inn while they were investigating abuses in cheap boarding-schools for background to Dotheboys Hall of Dickens' *Nicholas Nickleby*, the original of which was at Bowes nearby. The Bowes Museum, built by a prominent local family in the 19th century, resembles a French Renaissance château. Set in its own parkland, the museum contains some 10,000 exhibits, including paintings. The beautiful ruins of the 12th-century Egglestone Abbey (AM) stand close to the town. Halfway between Barnard Castle and Bishop Auckland is Cockfield, home of Jeremiah Dixon of the Mason-Dixon line.

BARNSTAPLE
Devon *2 SX53*
Barnstaple was an established borough, minting its own coins, as early as the 10th century. The town prospered as a harbour and wool town in the 18th century – its finest buildings date from this period – but it suffered from the silting of the Taw estuary and from the development of road and rail transport in the 19th century. Queen Anne's walk, an 18th-century colonnade, was the town's exchange; the merchants' money table, the Tome Stone, is still there and Barnstaple still holds a lively market. The medieval St Anne's Chapel once housed the grammar school where the poet John Gay (1685–1732), author of *The Beggar's Opera*, was educated. The building is now a local museum (OACT).

Barnstaple has several New World connections. John Otis, an ancestor of the well-known American family, was born here in 1581. The Reverend Nathaniel Mather was vicar here from 1656–62. Barnstaple, Devon also maintains links with Barnstaple,

Bowes Museum, Barnard Castle

Massachusetts, off which the Mayflower Compact was signed. More recently a connection has grown with the Kennedy family. The 200-year-old organ in the parish church was restored and dedicated to J F Kennedy, who was born in Barnstaple, Massachusetts.

BARRINGTON COURT
Somerset *3 ST31*
Barrington Court (NT) 3 miles north east of Ilminster, is a handsome Tudor mansion of yellow Ham stone with impressive spiral chimneys. The interior was restored in the 1920s. The National Trust tenant (Colonel A A Lyle, a member of the famous sugar-manufacturing family) exercised enormous ingenuity and acquired carved beams from Italy, linenfold panelling from demolished houses – and even a 16th-century Norfolk shop front from King's Lynn, which was converted into a screen. He also re-created an appropriate setting for the house – a beautiful garden (which contains an unusual 10-faced sundial) and a park ornamented with horse-chestnut trees.

BASILDON
Essex *6 TQ68*
Basildon New Town was designated as a London overspill town in 1949. The district has an area of 42 sq miles, and is one of the largest in England, incorporating the towns of Basildon, Billericay and Wickford plus intervening villages. Before the coming of the railway in the 19th century Basildon was a very small village; the original cottages clustered around Holy Cross Church which still survives. Billericay's Mayflower Hall has memorials to Christopher Martin, the unpopular Governor of the

Mayflower and treasurer of the expedition, and to three fellow travellers. The timber-framed house opposite the parish church was the meeting place for the Essex Pilgrim Fathers before leaving for London. Christopher Martin was born nearby in Great Burstead. He was married in the church of St Mary Magdalen which contains the grave of George FitzGeorge, illegitimate son of George IV.

BATTLE
E Sussex 6 TQ71

William the Conqueror swore that he would build a church if he won the Battle of Hastings, and he fulfilled that promise, setting the high altar at the spot where Harold fell. Nothing remains of that original building now, and in 1903 Harold's Stone was erected where the altar once stood. Benedictine monks replaced this church with St Martin's Abbey, the remains of which (OACT) are now incorporated into a school. Battle Historical Society Museum (OACT) in Langton House has many relics of the Battle of Hastings, including a half-size replica of the Bayeux Tapestry.

St Martin's Abbey with the battlefield in the foreground

BATH
Avon 3 ST76

'I really believe I shall always be talking of Bath . . . I do like it so very much. Oh! who can ever be tired of Bath?'

Jane Austen, *Northanger Abbey*

An elegant city of well-preserved Georgian buildings in the mellow local stone, Bath has its origins in the 1st-century Roman Spa of *Aquae Sulis* ('waters of Sul' – a Celtic goddess.) In fact its origins may be even older, and legend attributes the discovery of the springs to Bladud, a Celtic prince who is thought to have lived about 860 BC.

Since Roman times the value of the warm mineral springs has always been recognized, but the popularity of the place increased dramatically in the 18th century after Dr William Oliver – of Bath Oliver biscuit fame – opened a bath for the treatment of gout.

The building of Georgian Bath was largely due to the enterprise of a local postmaster, Ralph Allen, and the stone came from his quarries on Coombe Down. As the fine new buildings went up, the élite, led by the fashionable dandy Beau Nash, flocked to 'take the waters', and the social importance of being seen at the balls and assemblies of Bath is reflected in the pages of Smollett, Fielding, Jane Austen and Dickens. Bath is used as a setting for many plays including Sheridan's *The Rivals* and the American Booth Tarkington's *Monsieur Beaucaire*. Although few people now come for health reasons, the Bath Festival of Music and Drama, held in May/June each year, attracts performers of international standing and thousands of visitors from all over the world.

PLACES TO SEE

No 1, Royal Crescent has been restored by the Bath Preservation Society and furnished in period.

The Circus, Queen Square and Royal Crescent are fine examples of the replanned city's architecture. The formal pattern of squares, terraces and crescents and spacious thoroughfares lined with elegant houses, has never been bettered. The famous Circus and Queen Square were designed by John Wood the Elder, as was Prior Park on Coombe Down, the home of his patron, Ralph Allen. His son, John Wood the Younger, was responsible for the Palladian splendour of the Royal Crescent, the first terrace ever built to this design, and one of the finest examples of its kind in Europe. Major John André lived at No 22 as did Thomas Pownall, Governor of Massachusetts (1751–60). Sir Edward Parry was born at No 27 in 1790. He led 4 expeditions to the Arctic between 1819 and 1827. Parry Strait and Parry Sound, Ontario are named after him.

Pulteney Bridge

Roman Baths

The Roman Baths stand at the
centre of the city, their remains
shown to full advantage by means
of skilful reconstruction; finds
unearthed during the excavations
are displayed in the adjoining
museum.

The Pump Room still has two
sedan chairs used by its 18th-
century patrons. In these gracious
surroundings modern visitors can
partake of tea and coffee to the
strains of music by the Pump Room
Ensemble.

Bath Abbey is sometimes called
The Lantern of the West because of
the enormous clear glass windows
of the nave and choir. Bath owed its
abbey to the energy of Oliver King,
Bishop of Bath and Wells, who had
a dream in which angels climbed up
and down ladders to heaven and a
voice exhorted a 'king to restore the
church', which he did, between
1495 and 1503. His dream is carved
in stone in the abbey. There are a
number of memorials to Americans
in the abbey. Thomas Pownall is
buried here, as is Senator William
Bingham, after whom Binghamton,
NY is named. He died in 1804 and
his memorial is by Flaxman.

The Assembly Rooms (NT), near
The Circus, were completed in 1771
by John Wood the Younger. Badly
damaged during World War II,
these classically proportioned
rooms have now been faithfully
restored to their original elegance.
In the basement is one of the
world's finest museums of costume
– based on the collection of Mrs
Doris Langley Moore.

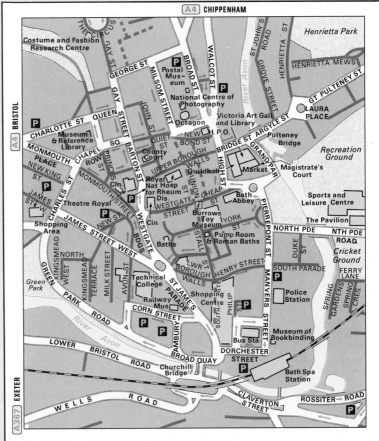

The Carriage Museum is housed in
stables and coach-houses behind
the Circus; the 30 carriages are
displayed with all their accessories
and trips can be taken in them
during the summer.

Burrows Toy Museum contains
exhibits covering 200 years of
children's amusements.

Pulteney Bridge, based on the Ponte
Vecchio ('old bridge') at Florence,
is the only work of Robert Adam in
Bath. The bridge, its three arches
supporting a wide street lined on
both sides by shops, is unique of its
kind in Britain. At the western end,
over the library, is the **Victoria Art
Gallery** whose collections include
one of antique watches.

**The Holbourne of Menstrie
Museum** in Sydney Gardens, has
outstanding collections of porcelain
and glass.

Claverton Manor (OACT), $2\frac{1}{2}$
miles east of Bath, houses the
American Museum in Britain which

covers American life from the
17th–19th centuries. This is an
important collection of materials
relating to American domestic life
and also has good holdings of
American primitive paintings.
There is a replica of George
Washington's garden at Mount
Vernon. The original was planted
1784–5, many of the plants coming
from friends of his near Bath.

The Camden Works Museum
preserves and displays a Victorian
family business (J B Bowler) almost
exactly as it would have been in its
founder's day. Bowler's was a firm
of engineers and brass founders,
with a profitable sideline in bottled
mineral waters.

The Octagon on Milsom Street,
formerly a private chapel, houses
the museum of the Royal
Photographic Society.

The Guildhall contains a superb
18th-century banqueting hall
(OACT) with three beautiful
chandeliers.

Beaulieu Abbey

BEACONSFIELD
Buckinghamshire *5 SU99*
Beaconsfield's old inns, timbered cottages and creeper-clad 17th-century houses preserve the town's elegance. The surrounding area was once thickly wooded, and the haunt of highwaymen. Sword cuts on the staircase of the George Inn were supposedly made by the highwayman Claude Duval while fighting off Bow Street Runners. Edmund Burke, the 18th-century politician and writer, was born in Beaconsfield, and G K Chesterton lived here for many years. Between 1912 and 1915 Robert Frost the American poet, lived at The Bungalow in Reynolds Road. His first two books were published while he was here.

BEAMINSTER
Dorset *3 ST40*
The small town of Beaminster stands in an area of outstanding natural beauty and was much loved by Thomas Hardy, who made it 'Emminster' in his novel, *Tess of the D'Urbervilles*. The picturesque River Brit runs along beside the main street, the little square is edged by 18th-century houses of golden Ham stone, and the church's richly ornamented Tudor tower is one of the best in Dorset. Rolling hills surround the town, and 800ft-high Toller Down offers fine views of the area. Two basically Tudor houses stand near Beaminster – Mapperton Manor (gardens OACT) to the south east, and Parnham House (OACT) to the south. Beaminster was the childhood home of Samuel Hearne who, in 1769–70, explored the Coppermine River for the Hudson's Bay Company, in whose employ he spent most of his life.

BEAULIEU
Hampshire *4 SU30*
Beaulieu Abbey (AM) was founded in 1204. Most of it has been demolished; of the remaining parts the refectory has been rebuilt as the parish church, the lay dormitory is a restaurant, and the Domus building contains an exhibition on monastic life. Palace House was once the abbey gatehouse, but today, after being extended and refurbished in the 19th century, it is the family home of Lord Montagu. The National Motor Museum contains a large library and over 250 veteran and vintage cars, motorcycles and bicycles, including American examples. Exhibits range from the first petrol-driven car of 1895 to Donald

Campbell's 'Bluebird'. Visitors can take monorail or veteran bus rides in the grounds, and there is a model railway. Steam fairs are sometimes held here too.

BEAWORTHY
Devon *2 SX49*
A rather isolated parish to the north west of Dartmoor, Beaworthy was the birthplace of John Maverick, ancestor of Samuel Maverick whose name lives on in everyday language. Maverick became Vicar of Beaworthy after graduating from Exeter College, Oxford. He married in 1600, and gradually became attracted to the dissenting Puritan movement – the parish records contain no record of his children's baptism. Maverick subsequently joined a group of Puritans from the West Country who emigrated from Plymouth to found Dorchester, Massachusetts in 1629/30. Two centuries later Samuel Maverick gained notoriety when his cattle were left unbranded on his Texas ranch.

BEDFORD
Bedfordshire *11 TL04*
The county town of Bedford has existed since Saxon times and is now a thriving commercial and industrial centre on the Great Ouse. On St Peter's Green stands a statue of John Bunyan, who lived in the town from 1655 until his death in 1688, and wrote *The Pilgrim's Progress* while incarcerated in Bedford jail for his Nonconformism. There is a John Bunyan Library, and the Bunyan Meeting House (OACT) is now a museum. Bunyan was a tinker until his conversion. He was born at Horrowden, a village near Elstow,

now on the outskirts of Bedford. It was in Elstow that Bunyan spent his childhood; the 16th-century Moot Hall (OACT) there now houses an exhibition of rural life in Bunyan's time.

BELVOIR
Leicestershire *10 SK83*
Looking across the Vale of Belvoir (pronounced 'Beever') towards the Leicestershire wolds, the castle (OACT) stands on a ridge surrounded by dense woodland. In the 16th century the original 11th-century fortress was given to the Manners family, who later became Dukes of Rutland. Its present mock-medieval appearance is largely the early 19th-century work of James Wyatt. The interior is famous for its Gobelin tapestries and for its paintings which include works by Van Dyck, Gainsborough and Holbein. It also

Belvoir Castle

houses the Regimental Museum of the 17th and 21st Lancers. The grounds – particularly the water-gardens – are splendid, and regular demonstrations of jousting and mock battles are held. This is fox-hunting country, and the famous Belvoir foxhound was bred here in the 18th century.

BEN NEVIS
Highland *26 NN17*
At 4406ft, Ben Nevis is Britain's highest mountain. The 2000ft-high vertical cliffs of its north face can be tackled only by skilled climbers, but the gentler southern slope from the wooded valley of Glen Nevis offers a route to the summit that has actually been twice negotiated by car early this century.

BERKELEY
Gloucestershire *3 ST69*
This small Georgian town stands at the centre of the Vale of Berkeley, a 15-mile stretch of flat land on the east bank of the Severn. It is dominated by its 12th-century castle (OACT), set in Elizabethan terraced gardens and deer park, the home of the Berkeley family for 800 years. Here the barons gathered before they set out to witness the signing of Magna Carta in 1215, and here Edward II was murdered in 1327. The castle has been the home of the Berkeleys since 1153; the family is closely associated with colonial Virginia. There is an Elizabethan garden and an ancient bowling green in the grounds. The parish church has a fine rose window and its east window is dedicated to Edward Jenner, pioneer in the field of smallpox vaccination; there is also a Jenner Museum in the town, housed in his original home.

BERKHAMSTED
Hertfordshire *5 SP90*
It was here that William the Conqueror accepted the throne of England from the Saxon leaders in 1066, and soon afterwards work started on the castle (AM) – of which only earthworks and a moat now remain. The church of St Peter has a window dedicated to the 18th-century poet, William Cowper, whose father was its rector. Novelist Graham Greene was born in Berkhamsted where his father was headmaster of the public school. The Grand Union Canal (built in the 19th century to link London and Birmingham) passes through the town, and Berkhamsted Common (NT) lies to the north.

BERRY POMEROY
Devon *2 SX86*
In a wooded valley to the north east of the village stand the impressive ruins of Berry Pomeroy Castle (AM), founded by Ralph de Pomeroy in the late 13th century and destroyed during the Civil Wars of the 17th century. A wishing tree in the grounds is supposed to grant the requests of anyone walking round it backwards three times. The village itself is tiny, but it has a fine church of red Devon stone, built 500 years ago on Norman foundations by the Pomeroy family – whose coat of arms adorns the porch. In the church is a 42ft long screen with fine tracings of saints.

BERWICK-UPON-TWEED
Northumberland *24 NT95*
Berwick-upon-Tweed, the most northerly town in England, changed hands 13 times in the border struggles between England and Scotland before surrendering to the English Crown in 1482. The Elizabethan town walls (AM) – built as a defence against gunpowder – are ten feet thick in places, and the 1-mile walk around their tops from Meg's Mound gives a fine view of the river, shipyards, salmon fisheries, quay and shore. Several of the houses on the quay are Georgian, as is the Town Hall, and the parish church (one of the few built during the period of the Commonwealth) dates from the 17th century, though it was extended in the 19th with stone from the castle ruins. The town has three bridges – the Royal Tweed road bridge of 1928, the 1850 Royal Border Bridge which carries the railway, and the 15-arch stone bridge built in 1611 on the orders of James I to link Berwick to Tweedmouth on the other side of the estuary. The Museum of the King's Own Scottish Borderers is housed in a barracks designed by Vanbrugh.

BETWS-Y-COED
Gwynedd *13 SH75*
Three rivers, the Conwy, Llugwy and Lledr, foam over rocks between beautiful wooded slopes to meet in Betws-y-Coed – a popular touring centre since Victorian times. Its most famous sight is the Swallow Falls, on the Llugwy 2 miles west of the town, where a railed footpath gives fine views of the spectacular series of cascades. The Conwy Falls and Fairy Glen Ravine are also well worth seeing. In the town a picturesque 15th-century stone bridge, the Pont-y-Pair

(or 'Bridge of the Cauldron'), crosses the Llugwy, with the strange Miners' Bridge – sloping from one bank to the other – further west; the Conwy is spanned by Thomas Telford's iron Waterloo Bridge (built in the year of the battle). Cyffty Lead Mine Trail in nearby Gwydyr Forest takes walkers round the old mine buildings. The Conwy Valley Railways Museum covers the whole railway scene, with special reference to North Wales.

BEWDLEY
Hereford & Worcester *9 SO77*
With an intermediate station on the preserved Severn Valley Railway, Bewdley is an extremely attractive old town, the three-arched Telford bridge over the Severn leading into Load Street with its many fine Georgian houses. A museum (OACT) in the Old Shambles illustrates traditional local trades, including the making of rope and charcoal-burning; occasional demonstrations are given by craftsmen. Not far away is the West Midlands Safari Park, on the A456 Kidderminster road, a popular pleasure park with animal reserves and many other attractions.

BIDDENDEN
Kent *6 TQ83*
On the green at Biddenden stands a village sign depicting the Biddenden Maids – Siamese twins Eliza and Mary Chulkhurst, reputedly born joined at shoulder and hip some time in the 12th century. They lived for 34 years, and bequeathed 20 acres of land to provide an annual 'dole' for the poor; this, in the traditional form of bread and cheese, is still given to pensioners on Easter Monday, and commemorative biscuits showing the Maids are distributed to onlookers. Many of the half-timbered cottages of Biddenden have been converted into antique shops or eating-places to cater for visitors, and the weavers' houses and shops in High Street have now been declared Ancient Monuments. A fine medieval Cloth Hall survives, as do original pavements of Bethersden marble, which used to be quarried near here.

BIDEFORD
Devon *2 SS42*
A pleasant town whose 24-arch bridge spans the Torridge estuary. In 1573 Sir Richard Grenville, who was born in nearby Appledore, secured a market charter for the town from Queen Elizabeth I. Bideford became the

principal port of North Devon, and by 1700 drew most of its wealth from tobacco trade with the New World. The grave of an American Indian, christened Christian Rawley and brought from Roanoke by Grenville, can be seen in Bideford churchyard. Charles Kingsley wrote *Westward Ho!* (1855) when staying here in 1854. A statue at the north end of the promenade commemorates Kingsley.

BIGGAR
Strathclyde *23 NT03*
Each July, the 'Fleming Queen' is crowned here in a ceremony commemorating Mary Fleming, one of the 'four Marys' who were ladies-in-waiting to Mary Queen of Scots, the others being Mary Seton, Mary Beaton and Mary Livingstone. The Gladstone Court Museum – named after the family of the Victorian Prime Minister, who came from the area – contains, among other items of interest, a street of recreated 19th-century shops. Greenhill Covenanters' House (OACT) contains relics of Covenanters. 6 miles east, Broughton was the home of John Buchan's grandparents. He and his sister, Anna, often spent the summer here.

BIGGLESWADE
Bedfordshire *11 TL14*
The Shuttleworth Collection of Historic Aeroplanes and Cars, situated 2 miles west of Biggleswade at Old Warden Aerodrome, contains a wide range of methods of transport with regular flying dates. Swiss Garden (OACT), also at Old Warden, has many rare plants.

At Southill, 3 miles west of Biggleswade, Admiral John Byng lies buried in the village church. He was a governor of Newfoundland. In 1756 he failed to raise the French siege of Minorca, was unjustly court-martialled and sentenced to death. In March 1757 he gave the signal for his own execution by firing squad on board the *Monarch* at Portsmouth.

BIGNOR
W Sussex *5 SU91*
The 4½-acre site of Bignor Roman Villa (OACT) – first excavated in 1811, after a section of floor depicting a dancing girl was discovered during farm work – contains some of the finest mosaics in the country. The buildings, set round a large courtyard, seem to have been the home of a rich man, and they were probably occupied from the 2nd to 4th centuries AD. The

results of various digs are shown in the site museum.

BIRKENHEAD
Merseyside *14 SJ38*
Prior to 1847, only a hamlet existed here, with only 106 inhabitants in 1810. The adventurous Laird family were at the heart of Birkenhead's development. The family company built the *Sirius*, the first steamship to cross the Atlantic from Europe to America in 1832. The CSS *Alabama* was launched in Birkenhead in 1862. There is a statue of John Laird in Hamilton Square. Nathaniel Hawthorne lived here at Rock Park when he was US Consul at Liverpool. The Williamson Art Gallery and Museum has an extensive collection of English watercolours and ceramics.

BIRMINGHAM
W Midlands *10 SP08*
Birmingham, second only to London in size, and a city since 1899, is traditionally the home of small industries – anything from coins and guns to steam locomotives were made here. This rich industrial heritage is admirably displayed in Birmingham's excellent Museum of Science and Industry.

Originally smiths of all kinds were attracted by the availability of fuel from the mines of north Warwickshire, and settled in different parts of the city. Around St Paul's Church, for example, was the old silversmith's

quarter. Nowadays the principal industry is the supply of components for the motor industry. The university was founded in 1900, and in 1966 the College of Advanced Technology in Aston also received university status.

There are two cathedrals – St Philip's built as the parish church in 1711, which has four superb Pre-Raphaelite windows by Sir Edward Burne-Jones, who was christened here, and the Roman Catholic St Chad's. The Victorian centre of Birmingham was Victoria Square, where the neo-classical Council House, with its clock tower emulating Big Ben, dominates the scene. The Town Hall, modelled on a classical Roman temple, houses a fine organ on which Mendelssohn gave several concerts, and is the home of the Birmingham Symphony Orchestra. Part of the Council House is used for the Art Gallery, which has an important collection of modern sculpture and Pre-Raphaelite paintings, as well as the interesting Pinto Gallery of wooden bygones.

Birmingham is said to have more miles of waterways than Venice, though much of this intricate network of canals is hidden and neglected. Gas Street Basin and James Brindley Walk, however, have been restored and parts of the canals are now lively once more.

The city is proud of its progressive attitudes – symbolized perhaps by the Rotunda in the Bull Ring, the Central Library, an arrangement of ziggurat-like buildings around a quadrangle,

Gas Street Basin, Birmingham

and the road interchange system at Gravelly Hill, popularly known as Spaghetti Junction. Birmingham is now well established as an international exhibition centre, with the building of the massive new complex – complete with its own railway station – 8 miles east of the city centre.

Washington Irving lived in Easy Row and Aston Hall (at Aston University) was his model for Bracebridge Hall. Joseph Priestley, who discovered oxygen, is commemorated in the Unitarian Church on Broad Street. Bishop Francis Asbury, a Methodist, who travelled over 275,000 miles preaching in America, lived in West Bromwich as a boy. At Sheldon, near Birmingham Airport, is a memorial to Thomas Bray who became responsible for the Society for the Propagation of the Gospel when he started a mission to Maryland in 1699.

BISHOP BURTON
Humberside *16 SE93*
For centuries this attractive village belonged to the Archbishops of York, and one of their palaces is said to have stood in a nearby field called Knight Garth. The parish church contains a bust of John Wesley, carved from an elm under which he preached when he came to the village. His visit is also commemorated by an open-air service on the green each July.

BISHOP'S CASTLE
Shropshire *8 SO38*
The original castle – now just a few stones – was built in 1127. The town stands on the edge of the Clun Forest, 500ft above sea-level and surrounded by hills, the highest rising to 1500ft. It has three Tudor houses – the Old Hall, the Old Market Hall and the Old House on Crutches, with its overhanging upper storey supported on posts. The Town Hall is one of the smallest in England and contains two silver maces hallmarked 1607. The Three Tuns Inn dates from 1642 and beer is made on the premises.

BLACKBURN
Lancashire *14 SD62*
The old and new merge in Blackburn – the old mills crowding round the canal locks and the clear-cut lines of the new multi-storey buildings rising above them. The town has been involved in the manufacture of textiles ever since Flemish weavers settled here in the 14th century (though it has now

diversified into brewing, engineering and the making of electrical equipment) and the Lewis Textile Machinery Museum traces the development of the industry. It includes a model of the spinning jenny, for its inventor – James Hargreaves – was a Blackburn weaver.

About 15 miles north is Accrington, an industrial town engaged in textiles, brick making and engineering. The Haworth Art Gallery (OACT) there contains the largest collection of Tiffany glass in Europe.

BLACKNESS
Central *23 NT08*
The ruined 15th-century castle (AM) – often called Ship Castle because of its shape – was one of the four left fortified in Scotland after it was merged with England by the Act of Union in 1707; it has been a prison for Covenanters in the 17th century, a powder magazine in the 19th – and a youth hostel in the 20th! 1 mile south is Binns (NTS), built in 1478 and converted into a mansion in the 17th century.

BLACKPOOL
Lancashire *14 SD33*
Blackpool is perhaps best known for its 'Golden Mile' of funfair attractions on the South Shore and the 518ft-high tower, with its ballroom, zoo, circus and aquarium. Trams, the last of their kind in England, run along the front, and the famous illuminated decorations attract many visitors each autumn. The beach stretches for 6 miles, and there are three piers with all the usual attractions – but the town also offers theatres, gardens, horse-trials, dog shows and dance festivals.

BLAENAU FFESTINIOG
Gwynedd *13 SH74*
The narrow-gauge Ffestiniog Railway – which originally used horses to pull its wagons – was built to carry the slate from here to **Porthmadog**, a thriving slate-exporting centre. However, at the turn of the century other roofing materials were introduced and the slate mines became unprofitable. Now they have taken on a new lease of life as a tourist attraction, for both the award-winning Llechwedd Slate Caverns and Gloddfa Ganol Slate Mine give a fascinating glimpse of the old days of slate mining. The Ffestiniog Railway has been re-opened, too; the final section of line was restored in 1982.

BLAIR DRUMMOND
Central *22 NS79*
The Safari Park at Blair Drummond (OACT) features a wide variety of animals in their natural surroundings. It includes a Pets' Corner and such attractions as Boat Safari and Astra Glide. There are picnic and amusement areas. Benjamin Franklin stayed here as a guest of Lord Kames; the trees he planted during his stay here still stand.

BLAIRGOWRIE
Tayside *27 NO14*
The little town of Blairgowrie lies at the centre of a prosperous soft-fruit-growing area, and it is also popular for angling and as a tourist centre. The River Ericht is spanned here by the 19th-century Brig o'Blair which links the town to Rattray; 2 miles further north it flows through a steep gorge, above which stands 17th-century Craighall, the mansion which may be the original of Tully-Veolan in Scott's *Waverley*. Meickleour, 4 miles south of the town, is notable for a magnificent beech hedge – over 200 years old, 600 yds long and 90 ft high – at modern Meickleour House.

BLAKENEY
Norfolk *12 TG04*
This village on the estuary of the River Glaven used to be a busy port and is now a popular boating centre. The church of St Nicholas has a second tower which was used as a beacon for sailors. The marshy flats which extend north west towards Blakeney Point are rich in plant and insect life, and a ferry service sometimes runs to the 1000-acre Nature Reserve and bird sanctuary at the Point.

BLANDFORD FORUM
Dorset *3 ST80*
Blandford Forum was a very old settlement, but a fire in 1731 destroyed it almost completely, leaving a mere 50 or so houses standing. The rebuilt town has the classical proportions of Georgian architecture – the Corn Exchange being a fine example. The only major buildings to survive were the Old House, Dale House and Ryves Almshouses, all 17th century, 5 miles north west of the town is Child Okeford, a prosperous farming settlement, with thatched cottages, Georgian houses, and an impressive manor house. Here on the slopes of Hambledon Hill in 1759 General Wolfe trained his troops before his attack on Quebec.

Chettle, 5 miles north east of Blandford Forum, is associated with the Protestant missionary to the Canadian Indians, John West, chaplain to the 1820 Red River settlement. In 1823 he came back to England. He died at nearby Farnham where he had been born. There is a memorial in the church at Chettle recalling his work.

BLANTYRE
Strathclyde   *22 NS65*
Blantyre is chiefly famous for its connection with explorer David Livingstone, born in 1813 in Shuttle Row. His birthplace has been restored and houses a museum, and there is a Livingstone Memorial Church which bears his statue on the tower, which also contains relics of H M Stanley.

BLICKLING
Norfolk   *12 TG12*
Early 17th-century Blickling Hall (NT) is a fine example of Jacobean architecture; it stands in formal gardens laid out by Repton and pleasant parkland where a crescent-shaped lake has been enlarged to stretch almost a mile. The pyramid-shaped mausoleum was designed by the Italian architect Bonomi in 1793 for the Earl and Countess of Buckingham. The State Rooms of the house have magnificent furniture and pictures, and the library contains the finest collection of pre-16th-century books in England. The estate was once owned by the Boleyn family, and Anne was born and spent her childhood in an earlier house on the same site. The church of St Andrew (originally Early English, but much restored in the 19th

century) has a typically East Anglian octagonal font and contains a memorial to Anne Boleyn.

BLYTH
Nottinghamshire   *15 SK68*
Blyth was a staging point on the old London to York road in Georgian days and still has three coaching inns, the Angel being the oldest. The church of Sts Mary and Martin was part of an 11th-century Benedictine Priory and its nave is a particularly interesting example of early Norman work. Facing the village green is an ancient stone building with a 700-year-old doorway; now a private residence, it was founded in the 12th century as a leper hospital.

The early pilgrim Francis Cooke was born here. 3 miles north east of Blyth is **Scrooby**, home of William Brewster and the Reverend Clyfton's Separatist congregation. 2 miles further north is **Austerfield**.

BOAT OF GARTEN
Highland   *27 NH91*
This village on the River Spey gets its name from the ferry that served it before the bridge was built. The Strathspey Railway Association operates steam locomotives between Boat of Garten and **Aviemore** (OACT). Ospreys – once believed extinct in Britain – now breed round Loch Garten; there is an RSPB observation point on the loch.

BODIAM
E Sussex   *6 TQ72*
At the edge of the village of Bodiam the romantic silhouette of its castle (NT) is reflected among the water-

lilies of a moat designed to look like a lake. It was built in the 14th century, when the Rother was navigable as far as Bodiam and the French seemed set on hostilities. This attack did not materialize, but the castle was wrecked in the Civil War. The building remains a shell, but the exterior was restored early this century by Lord Curzon of Kedleston, who married an American; he gave Bodiam to the nation, considering it, with its towers, moat and swans, 'the most fairy of English castles'.

BODMIN
Cornwall   *1 SX06*
Bodmin, set on the steep south-western edge of the moor, was once Cornwall's largest town and is the only one in the area mentioned in the Domesday Book. St Petroc is said to have founded a monastery here in the 6th century; he was the patron saint of the 12th-century Augustinian priory, and his name lives on in 15th-century St Petroc's – the largest parish church in the county. At one time the town was renowned for holy wells believed to cure eye complaints, and one, St Guron's can be seen near the church.

BODMIN MOOR
Cornwall   *1 SX17*
The rocky slopes of Bodmin Moor – designated an area of outstanding natural beauty – extend for about 12 square miles, and few roads cross their wild solitude. The plateau on the moor stands about 800 ft high, and from this rise steep granite tors – the tallest being Brown Willy (1375ft) and Rough Tor (1312ft).

BOGNOR REGIS
W Sussex   *5 SZ99*
Much of the architecture of Bognor Regis dates from the 18th century when it was a watering-place favoured by the aristocracy. It originated, however, as a Saxon fishing village. Its attractions for today's visitor include good seafishing, five miles of sand and shingle beaches, bathing and a pier. Hotham House is a Georgian mansion surrounded by woodland and gardens; its amenities include a small zoo. In Felpham, now a suburb of Bognor, is Blake's House, where the poet, William Blake, lived and composed 'Jerusalem'.

Blickling Hall

Rough Tor, Bodmin Moor

BOLDRE
Hampshire *4 SZ39*
Boldre's most famous vicar was William Gilpin, the 18th-century British travel writer. Robert Southey married his second wife here. The parish church contains memorials to the American pilots who worshipped here during the war. They were based at Walhampton House, then used as a resthouse. Walhampton was the birthplace of Sir Harry Burrard (1755–1813) who served in North America during the 1776 Revolution, and then later under Cornwallis from 1781 to 1782.

BOLTON
Gtr Manchester *14 SD70*
The town is traditionally connected with cotton, and two inventions that changed the course of the textile industry were made here in the 18th century. Arkwright's water frame and Crompton's spinning mule are among items displayed at Tonge Moor Textile Museum. Crompton's experiments were carried out while he was living at Hall i' th' Wood (OACT), a 15th-century half-timbered manor house which now contains a folk museum. Smithill's Hall (OACT), another fine half-timbered house, dates back to the previous century. The Old Man and Scythe Inn is housed in a building that has its origin in the 13th century; in 1641 Cromwell lodged Lord Derby there the night before his execution. The Civic Centre of 1873 houses a museum, aquarium and art gallery which contains a good collection of American works including some by Thomas Moran, a Bolton man who died in California and specialized in American landscapes. Bolton public

library has a large collection of Walt Whitman manuscripts.

BOLTON ABBEY
N Yorkshire *15 SE05*
The remains of 12th-century Bolton Abbey (in fact a priory) stand on the bank of the River Wharfe against a background of woods, meadows and waterfalls – the setting made famous by Landseer's painting 'Bolton Abbey in Olden Time'. The nave still stands, having been used as a parish church since about 1170, and a gatehouse to the west has been incorporated into Bolton Hall, a 19th-century mansion. There are beautiful walks beside the river to the Strid, where the water surges under limestone ledges ('strid' being the Old English word for 'turmoil'), or on to 15th-century Barden Tower, which stands above a humpbacked bridge.

BO'NESS
Central *23 NS98*
The Roman fortification known as the Antonine Wall had its eastern end at Bo'ness (Borrowstounness); a facsimile of a distance slab excavated in 1868 has been set up at the east end of the town, the original being on display in Edinburgh's National Museum of Antiquities. Bo'ness was an important port in the 19th century (until the development of Grangemouth a few miles away), but is now involved in industry. Kinneil Museum, housed in the renovated 17th-century stable block of Kinneil House (AM), traces the growth of the town's industry and also has an extensive display of local pottery. Kinneil House itself has interesting 16th- and 17th-century wall paintings,

and in 1764 James Watt experimented with his steam engine in its park. The grounds are now open to the public, and Bo'ness car hill climb takes place here.

BOSCASTLE
Cornwall *1 SX09*
Picturesque Boscastle is set in a glen where the Rivers Jordan and Valency converge before meeting the sea – which they do with dramatic effects when rivers are high and tides strong. The small harbour (NT) is protected by cliffs on either side, and behind it the long, broad road which forms the main part of the village rises through steep woodland. The Museum of Witchcraft and Black Magic (OACT) has eerie but fascinating displays from all parts of the south-west peninsula. 1 mile east of the village stands the isolated church of St Juliot – its restoration in 1870 having been supervised by novelist Thomas Hardy – then still a practising architect.

BOSHAM
W Sussex *4 SU80*
Bosham, a yachting centre also popular with artists, occupies a small peninsula on **Chichester** harbour – and the high, stepped doors of houses near the quay are an eloquent reminder of the town's vulnerability to the tides. Legend claims that King Cnut tried to turn back the waves at Bosham, and also that his daughter is buried here; certainly a Saxon stone coffin containing the bones of a young child was found in the church about 100 years ago. The church is depicted in the Bayeux Tapestry, for Harold Godwin (later to become King Harold) attended mass here before sailing for France in 1064 to enter into the negotiations with William of Normandy that were to culminate in the Battle of Hastings.

BOSTON
Lincolnshire *16 TF34*
In medieval times Boston was a major port for Continental trade. Its decline resulted from the increasing importance of the western ports for New World trade, and from natural silting of the Wash. Nevertheless, Boston still operates as a minor port. Many fine buildings still stand as reminders of the early prosperity of the town. Among these are the 15th-century Guildhall, Blackfriars Theatre (a 13th-century friary), as well as many former merchants' homes and warehouses. Most important, however, is St Botolph's Church, built

between 1309 and 1460. (The name Boston is thought to be a corruption of Botolph's town). The interior of the church has many interesting features, and its 272ft octagonal tower is one of the tallest in the country, commanding views of the surrounding countryside as far away as Lincoln. Known as the 'Boston Stump' it was rebuilt by Americans following World War II.

Since the early 17th century Boston has maintained close links with North America and Boston, Massachusetts was founded by Pilgrims from the town. In 1607 several of the Pilgrim Fathers were captured in Boston while fleeing the country, and imprisoned. John Cotton of the First Church of Boston was vicar of St Botolph's before leaving for America. Throughout the town are reminders of these American links. One of the windows of the church commemorates John Cotton and Anne Bradstreet, the first American woman poet. Bosses in the ceiling of the church remember John Cotton, the *Mayflower*, and Boston, Massachusetts. The cells where the Pilgrims were held can be seen in the Guildhall, and next door in Fydell house, built in 1726 by William Fydell, mayor of Boston, is an American Room especially reserved for visitors from Boston, USA.

In 1636 the Reverend Whiting and his family left Skirbeck on the outskirts of Boston. 6 miles south west of the town is Swineshead home of Herbert Pelham who emigrated to Massachusetts in 1638. 1 mile north east are the slight remains of the abbey where King John took refuge after losing his baggage in the waters of the Wash in 1216.

BOTHWELL
Strathclyde *22 NS75*
Bothwell Castle (AM) is ruined now, but its remains are impressive. It was the home of the Douglas family, built in the 13th and 15th centuries and one of the finest of Scottish strongholds. The Battle of Bothwell Brig, in which the Covenanters were defeated, was fought near here in 1679 and is commemorated by a monument. The Collegiate Church dates back to the 14th century and has a magnficent pointed barrel vault. Sir Walter Scott wrote *Young Lochinvar* in the town.

BOURNEMOUTH
Dorset *3 SZ09*
Bournemouth was 'discovered' by Victorian society in the mid-19th century when an eminent physician –

Bournemouth Pier

one Dr Granville – recommended its mild, sunny climate to those in delicate health. Until 1811 the area had been completely undeveloped, a tract of wild commonland between Christchurch and Poole through which the stream of Bourne wound its way to the sea. Then a local squire, Lewis Tregonwell, built himself a summer home where the Royal Exeter Hotel now stands, and in 1837 another local landowner, Sir George Tapps, saw the potential of the area and began to establish a resort to the east of Tregonwell's house. His investment was the beginning of a massive expansion; in the second 50 years of the last century the town's population grew from 695 to 59,000, as rich gentlemen built villas among the pines of the river valley and speculators erected hotels on the clifftops.

The popularity of 'The Queen of the South' continues for few resorts can rival its 6 miles of sheltered sandy beaches, or the magnificence of the 100ft-high cliffs, split dramatically by wooded chines. The town does not rely solely on its natural advantages to tempt the holiday-maker, however: lifts and walks connect the beaches with street-level, where, behind the promenades and gardens, is a modern town with excellent facilities.

Parks and gardens cover 2000 acres, one-sixth of the area of Bournemouth. The valley of the Bourne has been landscaped into Lower, Central and Upper Gardens, ablaze with flowering trees and shrubs in the early summer.

Robert Louis Stevenson lived for 3 years in Bournemouth; the site of his house is now a public garden. Mary Shelley, second wife of Percy Bysshe Shelley and author of *Frankenstein*, is buried along with her husband's heart in St Peter's churchyard. A memorial window inside the church commemorates John Keble, author of the *Christian Year*, after whom Keble College, Oxford is named. He died in Bournemouth in 1866.

BOWNESS-ON-WINDERMERE
Cumbria *18 SD49*
On the east bank of Lake Windermere, Bowness has become a popular centre for watersports. A ferry runs to Belle Isle (OACT), where England's first completely round house (OACT) was built in 1774. St Martin's Church is 15th century; inside, a piece of 14th-century glass brought from **Cartmel Priory** shows the Washington arms combined with the crest of the Lawrence family. This is perhaps the reason why the christian name Lawrence was so popular among the Washingtons. The church also contains an ancient font, chained books, Breeches Bible and an unusual equestrian statue of Saint Martin.

BOX HILL
Surrey *5 TQ15*
Box Hill (NT), 590ft high, takes its name from the box trees which once were so common here. Many were cut down in the 18th century to be used for engraving. There are beautiful views over the North Downs, and Box Hill has been designated an area of outstanding natural beauty. It has been a popular picnic site since at least the 17th century, when the diarist John Evelyn sang its praises, and Jane Austen in *Emma* (1816) chose Box Hill as a setting for an important outing.

BOSTON

The Boston 'Stump', the 272-foot high steeple originally built in the fifteenth century, still crowns St Botolph's, one of the largest parish churches in England. Along with Scrooby and Austerfield, this is the centre of the Puritan faith that led pioneers to settle in New England. Boston was the birthplace of John Foxe, whose *Book of Martyrs* was a basic Puritan text.

It was from Boston, England, in 1607 that the Pilgrim Fathers first attempted to flee religious persecution. They were arrested on board ship and the cells where they were imprisoned in the Guildhall in Boston, before trial in Lincoln, can still be seen today.

A more successful expedition set out from Boston in 1633, in the *Griffin*, landing at the already eponymous colony in New England. The settlers included the Recorder and an alderman of Boston, both of whom became Governors of Massachusetts, and they were led by John Cotton, Vicar of St Botolph's who became a famous Congregationalist leader in the New World. Cotton had resigned his living in 1633 after frequent protests at his over-eloquent Puritanism; his five-hour harangues from the pulpit and his persistent catechizing of his unworthy flock drove him into a voluntary exile that was perhaps welcome to his exhausted congregation. He became, in the word of the day, a 'teacher' at the First Church of the new Boston.

The prosperity which had enabled Boston to raise this great church of St Botolph's came from its eminence as a port. In the thirteenth century Boston paid an amount in tax on merchants' goods second only to London, and merchants from the Hanseatic ports and other Continental towns had houses here. Unfortu-nately, the silting up of the river led to a slow decline which only ended with the building of a new dock downstream in 1882.

A few buildings survive, other than St Botolph's, to testify to Boston's medieval importance. There is the Guildhall, the old Guild of the Blessed Virgin Mary, which is now a delightfully old-fashioned museum, and there is Shodfriars Hall, a half-timbered structure elaborately and imaginatively rebuilt in a Hanseatic style in the 1870s by the younger Gilbert Scott. However, Boston's architectural glories are chiefly eighteenth century and some of the Georgian buildings are very unusual; such as the great warehouses between South Square and the river, and an extraordinary early brick terrace at the end of the High Street which has a hipped roof, tiny doors and giant pilasters. But the grandest building is undoubtedly Fydell House, built by a three-times Mayor of Boston in 1726. This now contains an American Room, opened by Ambassador Kennedy in 1938, and is owned by the Boston Preservation Trust.

The Boston 'Stump'

BRADFORD
W Yorkshire *15 SE13*
Bradford was an early centre for the wool trade, but the Industrial Revolution brought it real prosperity. In 1966 the Institute of Technology was given university status. The Cartwright Memorial Hall in Lister Park houses the Art Gallery and Museum, and there is another museum in Bolling Hall (OACT). The Hall, which has a medieval tower, is an amalgam of architectural styles. The house was once the home of the Bollings. Robert Bolling, aged 14, sailed to Virginia and later he married Jane Rolfe, granddaughter of Princess Pocahontas. President Woodrow Wilson's wife, Edith Bolling, was descended from this couple, and Bolling Hall was her ancestral home. 5 miles south east, at Gildersome, the pilgrim John Reyner was born and further south east, Morley was the birthplace of Asquith, in 1852. Asquith was Liberal Prime Minister between 1908 and 1916. Also south east of Bradford, Birstall Smithies, on the outskirts of Batley, was the birthplace of Joseph Priestley, who was to 'discover' oxygen and other gases. Charlotte Brontë was a visitor to Oakwell Hall, which she later used as 'Fieldhead' in her novel *Shirley*.

At Eccleshill is the interesting Moorside Mills industrial museum with exhibits on textiles and transport. The composer Delius and author J B Priestley were both born here. At the age of 22, Delius went to work in Florida. He was encouraged in his musical talents by an organist from Brooklyn and returned home to devote himself to composing.

BRADFORD-ON-AVON
Wiltshire *3 ST86*
The bridge (AM) at Bradford-on-Avon has two medieval arches and a chapel – originally provided for pilgrims travelling between **Malmesbury** and **Glastonbury**, but used as the town lock-up in the 17th century. The buildings in the steep winding streets, from medieval cottages to the Georgian mansions of the wealthy cloth-makers, are of Bath stone. The Saxon church in Church Street, lost for centuries among the surrounding buildings but rediscovered in the 19th century, was founded by St Adelin in the 8th century and is one of the finest remaining Saxon buildings in the country. A 14th-century Tithe Barn (AM) stands in Barton Farm Country Park, near the river.

Just south of Bradford-on-Avon is the former house of Henry Shrapnel who, at the turn of the 18th-century, developed the shrapnel shell. He served in the Royal Artillery in Newfoundland 1780–84, and his son settled in Orillia, Ontario.

BRAEMAR
Grampian *27 NO19*
Of all the Highland Gatherings, that held at Braemar in September each year – with traditional music, dancing, and games culminating in the tossing of the caber – is possibly the most famous, perhaps because it is attended by the Royal Family. Nearby, Braemar Castle (OACT) overlooks the River Dee. Built by the 2nd Earl of Mar in 1628, it was burned down in 1682 and purchased by the Farquharsons who then rebuilt it.

Braemar Castle

BRAINTREE
Essex *12 TL72*
Braintree and Bocking, now merged, are traditionally textile-producing towns. The woollen industry has thrived here since the 14th century but is now superseded by silk production, introduced by Courtaulds in 1880; the making of metal windowframes also dates from the 19th century. Modern buildings such as the Town Hall blend happily with centuries-old houses that reflect the town's long history. Excavations have indicated that there was a Roman settlement here, at the junction of two ancient cross-country routes.

Two of the Pilgrim Fathers came from Braintree: they were John Bridge and John Carver, who was involved in the organization of the voyage. Nathaniel Rogers, pastor of Ipswich, Massachusetts, was a curate in Bocking, where the church had a stained glass window commemorating emigrants to America. 1 mile north west, Panfield was the home of Edward Bangs, another Pilgrim to Plymouth, Massachusetts.

BRANDON and the BRECKLAND
Suffolk *12 TL78*
Brandon is largely built on flint and there has been a flint-knapping industry here since prehistoric times, and primitive tools have been excavated here and at **Grimes Graves** (AM), 3 miles north east of the town. Breckland is a 300-square-mile stretch of rough heathland shared between Norfolk and Suffolk. 'Brecks' are pieces of land long ago broken up for cultivation but then allowed to become wild again.

BRAND'S HATCH
Kent *6 TQ56*
The famous motor-racing circuit at Brand's Hatch lies in a natural amphitheatre, with spectator stands on the slopes beside the track. Important events held here include the British Grand Prix.

BRECON
Powys *8 SO02*
One of the oldest Welsh market towns, receiving its charter in 1246, Brecon now serves as an administrative centre for the surrounding **Brecon Beacons** (National Park). Most of the town dates from the 18th and 19th centuries, but important remnants of its earlier history can be seen in the ruined Norman castle, and in St John's Church, previously the church of a Benedictine abbey, and since 1923 a cathedral. Brecon has two museums; the Brecknock Museum concentrates on local history and folklore, while the Regimental Museum of the South Wales Borderers deals with military history and contains items relating to the Battle of Bemis Heights (Saratoga) in 1777. Brecon was the birthplace of Dr Thomas Coke in 1747, who was the founder of the American Methodist Episcopal Church. In 1784 he went to Baltimore, Maryland as Superintendent of the Methodist Societies in America. There he was associated with John Wesley in the ordination of ministers. The

Methodist Chapel in the centre of Brecon is particularly beautiful. Also among Brecon's famous residents was Sarah Siddons the 18th-century actress whose birthplace, now the Siddons Arms, is in the centre of the town.

Three miles west is Gaer, a ruined fortress where, in the 1st century, the Romans built the largest of their Welsh auxiliary forts.

BRECON BEACONS
Powys *8 SO02*
Bonfires once flared on the summits of the Beacons to alert people to important happenings in the days of less easy communications. This 500-square-mile area of wild, hilly country is a National Park. The highest of the red sandstone peaks are Cribin (2608ft), Corn-Du (2863ft) and Pen-y-Fan (2907ft).

BREDON
Hereford & Worcester *9 SO93*
The 14th-century spire of St Giles' Church rises to 160ft, a landmark for miles, and the church contains the magnificent canopied tomb of Sir Giles Reed, whose family built the Reed almshouses in the main street. The Tithe Barn (NT), carefully restored after a fire in 1980, is 14th century and one of the largest in England. 3 miles north east, Bredon Hill, described by A E Housman in *A Shropshire Lad*, is reputed to offer views of 14 counties and is topped by ancient earthworks and a Gothic folly.

North, the manor house at Bredon's Norton was bought in 1585 by the merchant venturer Thomas Copley, a founder of Virginia. Later, the house was adapted as a guesthouse for Americans. Sir Walter Raleigh is known to have stayed at Bredon's Norton. 3 miles north is Eckington, where Pilgrim George Soule was born.

BREDWARDINE
Hereford & Worcester *8 SO34*
Bredwardine – 'the place on the slope of a hill' – stands where a fine, six-arched, 18th-century bridge crosses the Wye. The Norman church, extended – and curved slightly to the north – in the 14th century, has the original font, hewn from a single block of stone, and two medieval effigies of knights. This was the parish of the mid-Victorian diarist Francis Kilvert. On the other side of the hill, behind the village, lies Arthur's Stone, the famous Neolithic long barrow.

BRENTWOOD
Essex *6 TQ69*
Although most of its buildings are modern, Brentwood is an old town built at a crossroads. The White Hart Hotel is a coaching inn which dates from the late 15th century.

Nathaniel Ward, a rector of Stondon Massey, 6 miles north of Brentwood, is buried at Shenfield on the Billericay road. He bequeathed 500 acres to Harvard College before leaving for America where he founded Ward, Massachusetts. North west at Greensted (-Juxta-Ongar) is England's oldest wooden church, part of it dating from Saxon times. 5 miles south of Brentwood, Cranham Hall was the home of the wife of James Oglethorpe, founder of Georgia. This pioneer and friend of the Wesleys is buried at Cranham church.

BRIDGEND
Mid Glamorgan *8 SS97*
For centuries Bridgend, lying in the valley where the Rivers Ogmore, Garw and Llynfi meet, was the market town for this part of the Vale of Glamorgan; now it is also an industrial centre. Three castles once dominated the area – the ruined Norman New Castle (AM) on the wooded hill above Bridgend, Coity Castle (AM) to the north east, and Ogmore Castle (AM) to the south west.

North, Llangeinor was the birthplace of Doctor Richard Price in 1723. In 1776 he published a pamphlet *Observations on the Nature of Civil Liberty*, in which he defended the American colonists' right to freedom. In 1778 the Congress pronounced Price an honorary American citizen.

BRIDGNORTH
Shropshire *9 SO79*
The old market town of Bridgnorth is divided into Low Town and High Town by a red sandstone cliff, the two parts linked by steps and by the Castle Hill Cliff Railway. Caves in the sandstone were used as dwellings until Victorian times, and one – the Hermitage (AM) – is said to have housed Ethelred, brother of King Athelstan, in the 10th century. The tower, sole remnant of the castle, leans 17 degrees from the perpendicular because it was undermined during the Civil War. Bishop Percy's House (1580) is the most ancient building in Bridgnorth; it was the birthplace in the 18th century of Thomas Percy, who became Bishop of Dromore. St Mary Magdalene's Church, Italianate in style, was designed by the engineer Thomas Telford.

In summer, the Severn Valley Railway runs from here to **Kidderminster**. Midway between the two is Alveley, where the church contains glass from the ruined chapel of Coton Hall, 1½ miles north east. The Hall was associated with the famous Lee family for 500 years. It contains a number of family portraits and can be visited by prior arrangement. Colonel Richard Lee, a Cavalier and Privy Councillor, went to Virginia in 1641 as secretary to Sir William Berkely. From him, the Civil War general Robert E Lee was descended. West of Bridgnorth is Upton Cresset.

Brecon Cathedral

BRIDGWATER
Somerset *3 ST33*

Bridgwater, now an industrial centre, was a busy port until Bristol overshadowed it. A tidal bore comes up the River Parrett twice a day; the times are posted on the bridge. The 14th-century church of St Mary is noted for its fine Jacobean screenwork, and from its tower the rebel Duke of Monmouth is said to have surveyed the field before the Battle of Sedgemoor in 1685. One of Cromwell's admirals, Robert Blake, was born here, and his house contains relics of the famous Confederate ship the *Alabama*. In Huntworth, 3 miles east of Bridgwater, Sir John Popham was born in 1531. Popham was an adviser to Elizabeth I and ordered the exploration of the coast of Maine and founded the short-lived settlement of Popham on the Kennebec River in Maine. His brother George built the *Virginia* of Sagadohock, the first European ship constructed in America (**see** Wellington). Coleridge had associations with Bridgwater, preaching at the Unitarian chapel. He lived north west at **Nether Stowey**.

Three miles north west of Bridgwater at Cannington lived Edward Pierce who tried to fashion a community living the life of English gentlemen on the prairies of Saskatchewan. By the time he died in 1888 there was a flourishing community of 150 at the Canadian Cannington Manor but without his energies and will, it fell to pieces and now all that remains of his vision in Saskatchewan is a park with the community church and four of its buildings.

BRIDLINGTON
Humberside *16 TA16*

Bridlington is a popular resort, its fine sandy beaches sheltered by **Flamborough Head** and offering good bathing, angling and sailing. The Bayle Gate (built 1388) – serving at various times as courtroom, school, sailors' prison and barracks, is now a museum. Sewerby Hall (OACT), a Georgian mansion north east of the town, also has a museum (which includes relics of Amy Johnson) and an Art Gallery, and its grounds contain a small zoo.

William Strickland of Boynton 3 miles west of Bridlington sailed to America with Sebastian Cabot in 1497, and was the first Englishman to set foot on American soil; he also brought turkeys to Europe. The east window of Boynton church contains the

Strickland coat-of-arms, which incorporate a turkey. The lectern too has a turkey carved on it.

In 1657 Robert Fowler, a Quaker from Bridlington, built a ship, believing it to be God's will that he should. It was then sailed to London where a group of Quakers had been praying for such a vessel. The *Woodhouse*, as the ship was called, then made the voyage across the Atlantic without navigational aids and arrived at Long Island, only 2 miles from the Pilgrims' intended haven.

BRIGHTON
E Sussex *5 TQ30*

Most popular of all the seaside towns of the south east, Brighton began life as Brighthelmstone – an unpretentious little fishing village. Its metamorphosis began in 1754 when Dr Richard Russell took up residence there and prescribed sea-air, sea-water and sea-bathing as the remedy for all ailments. In 1783 the Prince of Wales, later George IV, paid a visit and decided to build a villa here – designed by Henry Holland but later transformed into an Indian extravaganza by John Nash.

Fashionable London flocked to Brighton, and elegant squares and terraces were built – largely around the Steyne – to accommodate the new patrons. In Victorian times, the railways brought trippers in ever-increasing numbers – the famous *Brighton Belle*, which ran until the late

Brighton Palace Pier

1960s, could do the journey from London in 55 minutes – and the town acquired a rather risqué reputation as an illicit weekend resort. Today, the town is a popular conference venue, and the vast modern marina, with moorings for more than 2000 craft, has given the seafront a new lease of life. The Kemp Town racecourse was the setting of the climax of Graham Greene's novel of underworld life, *Brighton Rock*. The University of Sussex, designed by Sir Basil Spence in the 1960s, stands next to Stanmer Park on the Brighton Road, and the influx of students and of foreign visitors to the many language schools, has made its own contribution to this cosmopolitan resort.

William Goffe, born 4 miles north of Brighton and son of a rector of Stanmer, was married to Edward Whalley's daughter – and was involved in the execution of Charles I. At the Restoration he emigrated with his father-in-law, and died at Hadley, Massachusetts, in 1679.

BRISTOL
Avon *3 ST57*

Bristol grew up round a natural harbour on the River Avon, and for several centuries its wharfage continued to grow, originally involved in the export of wool, but diversifying its interests in the 16th century with the formation of the Society of Merchant Venturers. In the 17th century the city became involved in the slave trade, and its abolition in the 19th century was a financial blow; the wine trade, however, continued to thrive and many of Britain's largest importers, such as Harvey's, are based at Bristol.

The city is rich in old buildings, and particularly in churches. The cathedral began life as the church of a 12th-century Augustinian abbey, becoming a cathedral in 1542. St Mary Redcliffe, the 'fairest, goodliest, and most famous parish church in England', as Queen Elizabeth I described it, is a graceful church which dates back to the 13th century, its 285ft spire a noted landmark. The 14th-century church of St John the Baptist, built over a vaulted medieval gateway, the ruined Temple Church, with its leaning tower, the Lord Mayor's Chapel, the only one to be owned by a City Corporation, and the ecclesiastical museum in St Nicholas' Church are also of interest. One of the most picturesque corners of the city is the quaintly named Christmas Steps, a narrow alley with many antique shops and antiquarian booksellers. Bristol boasts the oldest theatre – the Bristol Old Vic – in the country.

The University was opened in 1925 on the Clifton side of the city where the Regency crescents and Georgian terraces include Royal York Crescent, possibly the longest of its kind in Europe. Bristol Zoo is housed on Clifton Down.

Bristol played a major part in North American discovery. In 1497 John and Sebastian Cabot sailed from Bristol in the *Matthew* and claimed Newfoundland for Henry VII. The Sheriff of Bristol at the time was Richard Amerycke and it is suggested that the continent was named after him and not Amerigo Vespucci.

Martin Pring was financed from Bristol. His 1603 expedition sailed into Massachusetts Bay and he named his landfall Whitson Harbour after a Bristol alderman. The Pilgrim Fathers, also financed in Bristol, renamed the same spot Plymouth Harbour. In St Stephen's Church there is a memorial to Pring. While charting Hudson Bay seeking the North-West Passage to the east, Captain Thomas James discovered James Bay. This was in 1631, again financed in Bristol. Soon the city was the centre for colonizing the new lands. Between 1654 and 1679 around 10,000 people sailed to the American colonies. Many of their names are recorded in two books called *Servants to Foreign Plantations*. Bristol's many American connections include the Pilgrim Francis Eaton, who was born here, and Hannah Callowhill, a Bristol woman who was William Penn's second wife, married at Quaker's Friars in 1696. James Logan, Penn's secretary, was a Bristol schoolmaster. He became Chief Justice and Governor of Pennsylvania. Penn received territorial grants in America from Charles II. This was in settlement of the King's debt to Admiral Sir William Penn, the Quaker's father. The Admiral's tomb and armour are in the church of St Mary Redcliffe. An American, Henry Cruger of New York, was MP and Mayor of Bristol in the late 18th century and worked alongside another Bristol MP, Edmund Burke, in the attempt to retain the colonies for England.

John and Charles Wesley, who were in Georgia in 1736, came to Bristol 3 years later. Their religious revival led to the foundation of Methodism. They built the first Wesleyan Chapel in Broadmead, Bristol, the oldest

SS *Great Britain*

Methodist Chapel in the world, and in it, in 1784, ordained Richard Whatcoat and Thomas Vasey to serve as presbyters in America. The importance of Bristol to American trade was recognized in 1792 when the second American Consulate in England was established at 37 Queen's Square with Elias van der Horst as Consul. The first woman to graduate as a doctor in America was Elizabeth Blackwell who was born in Bristol in 1821. In 1857 she set up the New York Infirmary, staffed by women. The engineer Isambard Kingdom Brunel, closely associated with Bristol, established the first steam transatlantic liner service in the 1830's. One of his huge ships, the *Great Eastern* laid the first successful transatlantic cable. The iron-built *Great Britain* (1843) is in the City Docks, having been built, along with the *Great Western*, in Bristol.

Monuments include a window to the Cabots and the Amerycke Brass in St Mary Redcliffe and the Cabot Tower erected on Brandon Hill in 1897. The painting 'The Departure of Cabot' by Ernest Board is in the City Art Gallery, which also holds the finest collection of American portraiture of the revolutionary period outside the United States. These include Washington and Lafayette and are mainly pastels done by members of the Sharples family who made two long visits to America.

During World War II Clifton College was Headquarters for the United States Army during preparations for the invasion of Europe. The heritage of trade with America, continuous since the early 16th century, is maintained today in space research.

One mile south west of Bristol, Long Ashton was the birthplace of Sir Ferdinando Gorges, also buried there, who founded two Plymouth companies to help settle the New World. In 1639 he was named proprietor of Maine. Richard Amerycke was Lord of Long Ashton Manor.

The execution of the Duke of Buckingham in 1521 meant that Thornbury 'castle', 10 miles north of Bristol, and one of the most imposing Tudor buildings in the west of England, was never completed. It now accommodates one of the best restaurants in Britain. To the south west is the village of Elberton, birthplace of Joseph Sturge, a Quaker who travelled in America with John Greenleaf Whittier. Sturge was at the fore of the anti-slavery movement.

BRIXHAM
Devon *2 SX95*
Brixham falls into two parts – the old village on the slopes of a hill, and the fishing village half a mile below. The shingle beach of St Mary's Bay is popular with holidaymakers, and many artists have painted the picturesque harbour. Brixham Museum at Bolton Cross includes displays of shipbuilding. HM Coastguard National Museum is also here. A fine replica of Sir Francis Drake's ship the *Golden Hind* is preserved at Brixham Quay. 4 miles west on the beautiful wooded bank of the river Dart estuary stands Greenway House which, in the 16th century belonged to Otho Gilbert of **Compton Castle**. His second son was Sir Humphrey Gilbert, born here in 1539, the explorer and half-brother of Sir Walter Raleigh.

BROADHEMBURY
Devon *2 ST10*
Almost all the houses in this charming Devon village are thatched, and the walls of some are made of 'cob' – the traditional mixture of clay, straw and animal hair. By the square stands the 13th-century church of St Andrew, with a 100ft-high tower and a memorial to Augustus Toplady – vicar here for the last ten years of his life – who wrote the hymn, 'Rock of Ages'.

BROADSTAIRS
Kent *6 TR36*
Several miles of sheltered, sandy bays made this resort popular in the Regency period, and it remains so today. To the north stand the chalk cliffs and lighthouse of the North Foreland, with wide views over the Thames Estuary. Bleak House (OACT) is now a Dickens Museum: it contains early editions of his books, pictures, photographs and some personal items. Nearby Dickens House (OACT) (which also contains a museum) was immortalized as the home of Betsy Trotwood in *David Copperfield*, written while the author was living in Broadstairs. In June each year a Dickens Festival is held, when the townsfolk throng the streets in appropriate dress.

BROADS, THE
Norfolk *12*
In a roughly triangular area between Lowestoft, Sea Palling and Norwich, over 30 Broads are joined by streams and rivers to create 200 miles of navigable waterways. Once thought to be the result of glacial action, the Broads are now accepted as the aftermath of centuries of widespread diggings for turf or peat. The five major ones are Wroxham, Barton, Hickling, Ormesby and Filby, and the chief rivers are the Bure, Yare and Waveney. Yachts and motor cruisers can be hired, and villages such as Potter Heigham and Wroxham cater for the needs of the holidaymakers.

BROADWAY
Hereford & Worcester *10 SP03*
Broadway was described by Henry James as 'the perfection of the old English rural tradition', and is generally regarded as one of the most beautiful of Cotswold villages. For Americans the village holds particular interest as the home for several years of an intimate circle of American artists and writers, and some notable English contemporaries. In 1884 Francis Davis Millet moved with his family to Broadway. Millet was an historical painter, and the rural atmosphere of Broadway was an ideal location for his scenes of 17th-century English life. Here he was able to combine his work with another interest, the preservation of ancient buildings – part of the arts and crafts movement rapidly growing in popularity under the guidance of William Morris. Millet successfully renovated three houses in Broadway:

Farnham House, Russell House and later Pershore Grange. Rapidly a society of expatriate artists grew up around the Millets, starting with Edwin Austin Abbey, the illustrator who arrived in 1885 and stayed at Russell House for 4 years. Abbey had been sent to England by *Harpers Weekly* of New York in order to capture the English lifestyle though his illustrations. He remained in England growing in importance as an illustrator and eventually, at the age of 40, he took up painting. With encouragement from another Broadway artist, John Singer Sargent, whose 'Carnation, Lily, Lily Rose' was painted in the garden at Russell House, Abbey became a successful historical painter. He specialized in large highly detailed pictures and murals. Other visitors included writer Henry James, Pre-Raphaelite painter Edward Burne-Jones, landscapist Alfred Parsons, Edmund Gosse, an English literary historian and critic, and Mary Anderson the American actress who was a model in many works of the Broadway artists.

BRUTON
Somerset *3 ST63*
Bruton is historically a textile town, and one of the first fulling mills in England was built nearby in 1290. The River Brue is crossed here by an ancient and exceptionally narrow packhorse bridge, known locally as Bruton Bow. Near the bridge stands a section of wall which, with the three-storey dovecote in a field above the town, is all that remains of the 12th-century priory. King's Grammar School dates from the 16th century and was attended by R D Blackmore, author of *Lorna Doone*. Hugh Sexey's Hospital, founded in 1638 by a former stableboy who rose to become auditor to Elizabeth I, has been converted into homes for old people. The mainly 16th-century church has a 12th-century chancel, two towers and a fine tie-beam roof.

BUCKDEN
Cambridgeshire *11 TL16*
Buckden's High Street was once part of the road from London to the north, and it is still flanked by two old coaching inns, the 16th-century Lion and the 17th-century George. The brick-and-timber cottages of the village are dominated by the remains of Buckden Palace (OACT), used by the Bishops of Lincoln from the 15th century until 1836. In the church which

adjoins the Palace, Laurence Sterne, author of *Tristram Shandy*, was ordained in 1736.

BUCKFASTLEIGH
Devon *2 SX76*
Buckfastleigh Station is the northern terminus of the preserved Dart Valley Railway (OACT), a steam service operated by enthusiasts. It runs to Totnes and back. At the station locomotives in process of restoration are on show and there is a picnic area. One mile north of the village is Buckfast Abbey, the work of a succession of teams of French Benedictine monks between 1906 and 1932. Built of limestone, with modern stained glass designed and made by the monks, the Abbey stands on the site of an original medieval monastery and incorporates the Gothic mansion that replaced it.

BUCKHAVEN AND METHIL
Fife *23 NT39*
Buckhaven and Methil were seaside villages that became mining towns in the 19th century. In 1891 they united to form Scotland's major coalport, and now, with the dwindling importance of the coal trade, the town is becoming increasingly involved in the production of North Sea oil. It still, however, has many quaint corners and the stepped streets are typical of old Fife villages. Local fishermen brought the church in sections from St Andrews and re-erected it. A few miles east is Largo, birthplace of Alexander Selkirk, whose adventures formed the basis for Defoe's *Robinson Crusoe*. A statue of Selkirk as the castaway stands in the village.

BUCKLAND ABBEY
Devon *2 SX46*
Originally a Cistercian abbey before the Dissolution, Buckland Abbey near Tavistock, was bought in 1581 by Sir Francis Drake from the Grenville family. Drake himself was born at Crowndale Farm, 1 mile south west of Tavistock, in 1540. Buckland Abbey now contains a museum of Drake relics and local antiquities.

BUCKLERS HARD
Hampshire *4 SU40*
Today, pleasure-craft are the only boats at Bucklers Hard, but it was an important shipyard in the 18th and 19th centuries and built three of the ships that fought at Trafalgar – including Nelson's *Agamemnon*. Relics of the era are contained in the

Buckland Abbey

Maritime Museum, but to visit the village itself is to step back in time: the shipbuilders' cottages still face one another across the wide green that runs down to the River Beaulieu, while New Forest ponies graze with no fear of traffic, for there are no through roads and vehicles have to be left in a nearby car park. The hotel was once the house of Nelson's master-shipwright, and next to it stands an unusual chapel – a single consecrated room in a cottage.

BUDLEIGH SALTERTON
Devon   *2 SY08*
Discreetly prosperous, the town has changed little since it was developed as a resort in the early 19th century. Its chief attractions are the safe bathing and the magnificent views from its red cliffs. An 18th-century thatched house, complete with smugglers' cellar and lookout tower, holds the Fairlynch Arts Centre and Museum (OACT). The Victorian painter Sir John Millais lived for some time in the 'Octagon', a house on South Parade. Here he painted 'The Boyhood of Raleigh'. Sir Walter Raleigh was born at Hayes Barton near East Budleigh a couple of miles inland in 1552. Raleigh led expeditions to the Americas, exploring what is now Guiana. In 1587 he tried to establish the 'Virginia' colony near Roanoke Island. Following this he returned to his family home adding a porch and smoking room so that the house formed an 'E' shape in honour of Queen Elizabeth. Hayes Barton is not open to the public. In the reign of

James I Raleigh was imprisoned in the Tower of London. He was accused of treason and executed in 1618. East Budleigh was also the original home of the ancestors of James Bryant Conant the American scientist and President of Harvard University.

BUNGAY
Suffolk   *12 TM38*
It is an indication of Bungay's long history that its civic head still holds the office of Town Reeve. Originally it was a market town, but printing and leatherworking were introduced in the 18th century, and today its position on the River Waveney also makes it a popular yachting centre. Only the foundations of the castle (AM) – originally 12th century – remain; they show an unfinished mineshaft that was intended to destroy the castle after Hugh Bigod's rebellion against Henry II. St Mary's Church had its bells melted by a fire that swept that part of the town in 1688, and the Bungay Stone (near the north porch) is said to be a Druid Cross 2000 years old. Earsham Otter Trust (OACT), 1½ miles out of the town has one of the largest collections of otters in the world. 7 miles south east is Wissett, where John Lawrence, an ancestor of Abbott Lawrence and an early settler of Groton, Massachusetts, lived.

BURFORD
Oxfordshire   *10 SP21*
Burford's narrow, three-arched bridge over the River Windrush is built of old Cotswold stone, as are the picturesque

houses and inns that line its wide, climbing main street. The church of St John the Baptist, with its impressive spire, is one of the largest in Oxfordshire. The Grammar School, the Crown Inn and the Bear Inn are virtually unchanged since the 15th century, and the Priory, though largely rebuilt in the early 19th century, still bears the arms of William Lenthall, who, as Speaker of the Long Parliament, defied Charles I. The Cotswold Wildlife Park (OACT) lies south of the town in Bradwell Grove Estate.

BURGHCLERE
Hampshire   *4 SU46*
Two groups of almshouses and the Sandham Chapel (NT) were built at Burghclere in 1926 in memory of Henry William Sandham, a hero of World War I. The walls of the chapel are completely covered with frescoes by another soldier, artist Stanley Spencer, and they depict his reaction to his experiences of that war.

BURNHAM-ON-SEA
Somerset   *3 ST34*
A 19th-century curate built a lighthouse at Burnham-on-Sea and exacted tolls from passing ships to finance two wells which were to establish the town as a spa. The venture failed, but Burnham, with its 7 miles of sandy beach and its fine views across Bridgwater Bay, became popular with holidaymakers – and the wooden 'lighthouse on legs' is still a tourist attraction. The medieval church of St Andrew contains a 17th-century marble reredos designed by Inigo Jones and carved by Grinling Gibbons; originally made for the chapel of Whitehall palace, it passed to Hampton Court and Westminster Abbey before coming to rest here in the 19th century. The tower of the church tilts three feet from the vertical – the subsidence being due to its sandy foundations.

BURNHAM THORPE and BURNHAM MARKET
Norfolk   *12 TF84*
Lord Nelson was born in Burnham Thorpe in 1758, at Parsonage House (now demolished). He was a son of the rector. The church contains the font at which he was christened and also a lectern made from the timbers of the *Victory*. The church at Burnham Market, an attractive little town, has unusual carvings of Biblical scenes on its battlement tower.

BURTON AGNES
Humberside *16 TA16*

The sleepy village of Burton Agnes is one of the most attractive in the Wolds. The main attraction to visitors is Burton Agnes Hall (OACT), built by Sir Henry Griffith more than 380 years ago and still owned by his family. It stands among smooth lawns and clipped yews, its red brick mellowed by time, and its semi-octagonal plan echoed in the octagonal towers of the gatehouse (built slightly later). The interior is splendidly furnished and has a fine collection of Impressionist paintings, including works by Renoir, Pissarro, Manet, Gauguin and Sickert, as well as drawings by Augustus John and other 20th-century masters. The Norman church, containing a fine alabaster tomb, stands next to the hall, and nearby is a restored Norman manor house (AM).

BURTON-UPON-TRENT
Staffordshire *10 SK22*

Legend has it that in the 13th century, at a time when Burton was involved in cloth-making, the Abbot realized the suitability of local water for brewing. Today the streets are permeated by its smell and the famous name of Bass is met at every turn, for the family gave the town some of its finest buildings, including the Town Hall. The Bass Museum traces the history of the brewing industry, and has many fascinating exhibits including a 1920s Daimler shaped like a bottle.

BURWASH
E Sussex *6 TQ62*

Burwash was the centre of the iron industry 300 years ago, when most of the country's ore came from the Weald. It is an outstandingly attractive village with several ironmasters' houses surviving; one of these is Bateman's (NT) a fine Restoration building where Rudyard Kipling lived from 1902 until his death in 1936. Here he wrote the poem 'If' and *Puck of Pook's Hill* in which the Sussex countryside is described. His American wife gave Bateman's to the National Trust on condition that his study should be kept as the writer left it.

St Bartholomew's Church has a Norman tower, 15th-century octagonal font, and one of the oldest iron graveslabs in Sussex. 7 miles west is the village of Heathfield, well known for cannon-making in the days of the Sussex iron industry. Robert Hunt, chaplain to the Virginia expedition of 1607 was vicar here. Jamestown,

Virginia, has a monument to his work. Heathfield Park is a William and Mary period house with late Victorian alterations. The grounds contain the 55ft Gibraltar Tower, built in honour of General Eliott, who bought the Park with the prize money gained in Havana, and later commanded at the seige of Gibraltar in 1779–83. Hawkhurst, 7 miles east of Burwash is the area's largest village, formerly a centre of smuggling and of the iron and cloth industries. Some of the original mills survive, including Furnace Mill which once belonged to William Penn.

BURY
Gtr Manchester *14 SD81*

A statue of Sir Robert Peel, 19th-century prime minister and founder of the police force, stands in the market square of Bury, his birthplace. John Kay, who invented the flying shuttle in 1733, revolutionizing weaving methods, was born 2 miles north. The Museum and Art Gallery has exhibits found in the locality going as far back as the Bronze Age, and some fine paintings, whilst the Transport Museum (OACT) specializes in the steam era of the railways. The town's traditional role in the manufacture of yarn has expanded to take in the printing of textiles and its industries now also include engineering and papermaking.

BURY ST EDMUNDS
Suffolk *12 TL86*

Bury St Edmunds, the county town of West Suffolk, is named after the last king of East Anglia, who died at the hands of the Danes in AD 870 and whose bones were interred in the monastery here some 30 years later. The town became a place of pilgrimage, and the remains of the abbey founded in the 11th century show it to have been an imposing edifice. Both the parish church of St James, given cathedral status in 1914, and nearby St Mary's were originally 15th century and the latter contains a magnificent hammerbeam roof and the grave of Mary Tudor, sister of Henry VIII. John Winthrop the younger was educated at the Grammar School. The Atheneum, the centre of social life in Regency times, stands on the town's spacious square; Dickens is known to have given readings here, and he used the Angel Hotel as the setting for *Pickwick Papers*. Moyses Hall, perhaps once the home of a Jewish merchant, is a 12th-century building of

flint and stone with a vaulted ground floor. It houses a museum of local and natural history and of archaeological items. Angel Corner (NT), a Queen Anne mansion, contains the Gershom-Parkington collection of clocks and watches. The Norton Bird Gardens, on the A1088 (off A45) contain foreign birds and waterfowl.

Four miles north west of Bury St Edmunds, Hengrave Hall was built in the early 16th century by Sir Thomas Kitson. His sister Margaret married John Washington and was the mother of Lawrence, purchaser of **Sulgrave**. It was at this stage in the family genealogy that the link between the Washingtons and the Spencers and thus Winston Churchill and the Princess of Wales occurred. A window at Hengrave depicts the Washington coat-of-arms.

• BUXTON
Derbyshire *15 SK07*

The waters of Buxton – charged with nitrogen and carbon dioxide, and bubbling up at a constant 28°C – were popular in Roman times, but it was the 5th Duke of Devonshire who established the spa in this small Peak District market town as a fashionable rival to Bath at the end of the 18th century, building the magnificent crescent opposite St Anne's Well (OACT), which houses a micrarium. The Devonshire Royal Hospital was opened in 1859, its 156ft dome among the largest in the world. Today one can swim in an indoor spa-water pool at the Pavilion, which is set in 23 acres of public gardens. The magnificent Edwardian opera house has recently been restored as a theatre. The 19th-century folly on Grin Low (1450ft) offers a splendid viewpoint and beneath it, Poole's Cavern in Buxton Country Park, is interesting to visit.

BYLAND ABBEY
N Yorkshire *15 SE57*

In 1177 Cistercian monks settled here and established a community that was to last until the Dissolution. The site (AM) has been excavated, and the plan of the church and monastic buildings can be seen, as can well-preserved green and yellow glazed floor tiles. Most of the great west front of the abbey stands, topped by a single turret and the broken circle of a rose window 26ft in diameter.

CADBURY CASTLE
Somerset *3 ST62*
There is a powerful tradition that this was the site of Camelot, King Arthur's stronghold, but there is no positive proof. The castle (AM), of which only the earthworks survive, crowns a hill above the village of South Cadbury. Excavations have uncovered traces of cultures from Neolithic to Anglo Saxon times. North east of the village, Cadbury House is a fine example of Elizabethan architecture.

CAERLEON
Gwent *8 ST39*
Four miles upriver from Newport, Caerleon has associations with King Arthur, and is thought to be the 'Carlion' of Malory's romance, *Le Morte d'Arthur*, written in 1485. Caerleon was *Isca Silurum*, headquarters of the Second Augustan Legion from AD 75 to the 4th century. The fort covered $51\frac{1}{2}$ acres, and its ramparts can still be identified today. Finds from the site can be seen at the Legionary Museum, including carved stone heads, coins, pottery, domestic items, glassware and a number of old weapons. You can also view the remains of one of the few Roman barrack blocks (AM) to survive in Britain. Until it was excavated, the Roman amphitheatre (AM) was popularly held to be King Arthur's Round Table. Tennyson stayed here, at the Hanbury Arms, while researching for his poetic work *Idylls of the King*.

CAERNARVON (Also *Caernarfon*)
Gwynedd *13 SH46*
The name means 'Fort on the Shore'. The Romans were the first to build a fort here, and finds from the excavations can be seen at the site museum. The castle (AM) built by Edward I in the 13th–14th centuries is one of the most popular tourist attractions in Wales, especially since the Investiture of Charles, Prince of Wales in 1969. The first English-born Prince of Wales, the son of Edward I, was proclaimed here, and he is said to have been born in the Eagle Tower in 1284. It was here, too, that Edward I issued the Statute of Wales, bringing the country under the sovereignty of the Kings of England. Opposite the castle balcony stands a statue of Lloyd George. Also in Caernarvon Castle, the regimental museum of the Royal Welch Fusiliers testifies to their role when, as the 23rd Foot, they defended the British position at Yorktown – unsuccessfully – in 1781.

CAERPHILLY
Mid Glamorgan *8 ST18*
Famous for its castle (AM) (the second largest in Britain after Windsor), Caerphilly was equally renowned for its cheese, which is still made, but not in any quantity in the town itself. Work began on the castle in 1268, under the direction of Gilbert de Clare, Lord of Glamorgan. It was only half-completed in 1270, when Llwelyn ap Gruffydd arrived in force and demolished it. Building had to start all over again, and on its completion, the castle, with its 320yd-long curtain wall and intricate system of defences, was virtually impregnable until Cromwellian times. As a result of Cromwell's destruction, it has a leaning tower, more steeply inclined than that of Pisa.

CAERWENT
Gwent *3 ST49*
The Roman walls (AM) survive as evidence that, 1800 years ago under the name of *Venta Silurum*, this was the second largest civilian settlement in South-West Britain (the biggest was Bath). The population of about 2000 enjoyed all modern Roman amenities – including an amphitheatre for their entertainment. Less enjoyable were the incursions of raiders from Ireland along the shores of the Severn. One of their victims was the future St Patrick, who was kidnapped from 'somewhere near to the sea', and quite possibly from Caerwent itself. The present town lies within the Roman walls, and in the porch of the 13th-century church is an interesting mosaic. The double lychgate is a memorial to Thomas Walker – involved in the building of the Severn Tunnel and the Manchester Ship Canal.

CAIRNGORMS
Highland/Grampian *26/27 NH90*
The Cairngorms, which extend between Speyside and Braemar, are the highest mountain massif in the British Isles. Several of the granite peaks are over 4000ft high and the tallest is exceeded only by Ben Nevis, Britain's highest mountain. In the 600-acre Cairngorm National Nature Reserve, golden eagles, capercaillie (a large species of grouse), ptarmigan, wild cats and deer are all to be found. Access may be restricted in the grouse-shooting and deer-stalking seasons. **Aviemore**, Grantown-on-Spey and Carrbridge are the main ski resorts, and in the **Glen More** Forest Park there are fine walks, particularly around Loch Morlich. Cairngorm stones, translucent, yellowish quartz crystals, are found in the granite.

CAISTER-ON-SEA
Norfolk *12 TG51*
In ancient times, before nature redesigned the coastline, Caister was a Roman port. Caister Castle (OACT) was built in 1432 by Sir John Fastolf, the model for Falstaff in Shakespeare's play *Henry IV*. In real life he had command of the archers at Agincourt. In the castle grounds is a fascinating motor museum and the treewalk from Battersea funfair was re-erected here in the 1970s.

CALDY ISLAND
Dyfed *7 SR19*
Best reached from Tenby, Caldy Island still has the atmosphere of being a storm-battered triumph of human settlement. The present occupants are a colony of Trappist Cistercian monks, but the island was first settled by the Benedictines. The church and parts of the monastery date from the 12th to 16th centuries. Whilst only men may visit the monastery itself, the other religious buildings are open to all members of the public. Perfume, made by the monks from flowers and herbs, is on sale.

CALLANDER
Central *22 NN60*
Callander describes itself as 'the natural gateway to the Highlands' though its appearance is more suggestive of a Lowland town. It is the Tannochbrae of the television series, 'Dr Finlay's Casebook', and there are some very pleasant houses built in the Regency style, especially in the main street and square. Several beauty spots are within walking distance – such as the Falls of Bracklinn and Ben Ledi. 1 mile west of the town is the interesting Kilmahog Woollen Mill (OACT), famous for its handwoven blankets and tweed.

CAMBRIDGE
Cambridgeshire   11 TL45

'We were walking the whole time – out of one College into another . . . I felt I could live and die in them and never wish to speak again.'

Mary Lamb, *Letters*

The unforgettable sight of Cambridge is the view across the River Cam and the Backs to the stately Gothic chapel of King's College. The town itself contains much new building, often at variance with the character of the old. Although overshadowed by the university, the town, too, is very ancient and has its origins in Celtic settlements around a ford on the Cam. The Romans built a bridge and established an outpost here, at the meeting point of a network of roads and navigable waterways. The town has always been a flourishing regional centre, and of recent years the university's scientific activities have encouraged the foundation in Cambridge of several research-based industries.

The university grew from small beginnings at the start of the 13th century, when a group of students, in trouble with the authorities at Oxford, came to Cambridge in 1209. There were no colleges as such at this period; the students were attached to the schools of cathedrals and monasteries, and lodged where they could in the town. The first college, Peterhouse, was founded in 1281 by the Bishop of Ely, and by 1284 was established in its own buildings. Over the next few hundred years, most of the other colleges were established – though there are a number of modern foundations, such as Churchill, Darwin and New Hall. New Hall (1954) is the most recent of the three women's colleges: Girton and Newnham date from the 19th century. Nowadays, after some debate, almost all the colleges have opted for co-education and admit both men and women as undergraduates.

More than 100 early New England settlers attended Cambridge University. Many were at Emmanuel College, founded in 1584 by Sir Walter Mildmay to help propagate Puritan doctrine. John Harvard studied here and it was through his benefactions that Harvard College was founded. Emmanuel College chapel was designed by Wren. In 1884 a series of windows celebrating the tercentenary of the foundation were put in. One depicts John Harvard. Other Emmanuel students include John Cotton, Thomas Hooker, Nathaniel

King's College Chapel

Rogers, Thomas Shepherd, Samuel Stone and Samuel Whiting. From Christ's College came Ralph Cudworth, Sir Walter Mildmay, Ezekiel Rogers and John Smyth. Nicholas Ferrar was at Clare College, John Eliot and Francis Higginson were at Jesus College, Roger Williams at Pembroke. William Brewster and John Norton were at Peterhouse. Norton emigrated to America in 1635, became pastor at Ipswich and Boston and instigated the persecution of the Quakers. John Singleton Copley the younger, Charles Chauncy, Thomas Pownall and John Winthrop the elder were all at Trinity. The first American student to study at a British university was John Stone, Harvard class 1653, who was at Pembroke College in 1654. Edward Braddock of Corpus Christi commanded the British forces against the French in North America in 1775. George Washington served under him as a volunteer officer. Braddock was killed in battle and is buried near Braddock, Pennsylvania, named after him. There are many portraits of early Americans in their respective colleges.

Downing College was founded in 1800 with funds left by Sir George Downing, 3rd baronet, who had made a large fortune in America. His grandfather had married Lucy, Governor John Winthrop's sister and gave his name to Downing Street, London. He was the second man to graduate from Harvard College and headed the movement to offer the crown to Cromwell. George Long, Fellow of Trinity College, became Professor of Ancient Languages at the

University of Virginia, where he taught Edgar Allan Poe. Oliver Wendell Holmes, the American writer, descended through his mother from Thomas Dudley and Simon Bradstreet, both governors of Massachusetts, was an honorary doctor of both Oxford and Cambridge universities.

PLACES TO SEE

King's College Founded by Henry VI. Only the chapel was completed in his lifetime.

Queens' College Founded at different times by two queens, Margaret, wife of Henry VI, and Elizabeth, wife of Edward IV. The 'Mathematical' bridge, built in 1749 without the aid of nails, and on geometric principles, was one of the curiosities of Cambridge. The present structure is a replica.

Pembroke College The chapel is the first of Christopher Wren's designs ever to be completed. Not far from the college is **Hobson's Conduit**, named after a mayor of the city who had run a livery stable, and inspired the saying 'Hobson's Choice' because he refused to allow his customers to choose their own horses.

Trinity College Three medieval colleges were incorporated into Trinity by Henry VIII. The Great Court has a magnificent Renaissance fountain, and the library, designed by Wren, has carvings by Grinling Gibbons.

Magdalene College Samuel Pepys was one of the famous alumni of Magdalene, and his diaries, together with his bookcases and the desk at which he worked, are preserved in the Pepys Library.

St John's College like Queens', has a famous bridge, modelled on the Bridge of Sighs at Venice.

St Benet's Church is the oldest building in the county, believed to date from the reign of King Cnut.

Holy Sepulchre One of only five round churches remaining in England, it was founded in 1130 by the Knights Templar on the model of the Church of the Holy Sepulchre at Jerusalem. Succeeding centuries have added to the original Romanesque structure.

Fitzwilliam Museum Egyptian, Greek and Roman antiquities, oriental porcelain and ceramics are among the objects bequeathed by

the 7th Viscount Fitzwilliam as the nucleus of this outstanding collection of treasures.

The Cambridge and County Folk Museum displays local crafts, agriculture and industry.

Scott Polar Research Institute Arctic and Antarctic exhibitions with information on current scientific exploration.

University Botanic Gardens cover acres of ground, filled with fine botanical specimens.

Willingham The 14th-century church has a magnificent angel roof.

St Ives An interesting market town with ancient bridge where a rare medieval chapel can be seen.

Godmanchester One of the most picturesque of the riverside towns on the Ouse.

Hinchingbrooke House (OACT), on the edge of Huntingdon is a Tudor mansion associated with the Cromwell family.

Brampton Pepys House (OACT), was the home of the diarist's parents.

Buckden Remains of the palace where Katherine of Aragon was imprisoned.

St Neots Attractive old market town.

Bourn Postmill (OACT) Dating from 1636, this is possibly the oldest working windmill in the country.

Grantchester A charming village immortalized by the poet Rupert Brooke.

Madingley 2 miles west of Cambridge on the road to St Neots was the site of an American Airforce base in World War II. There is also the largest American military cemetery in Britain.

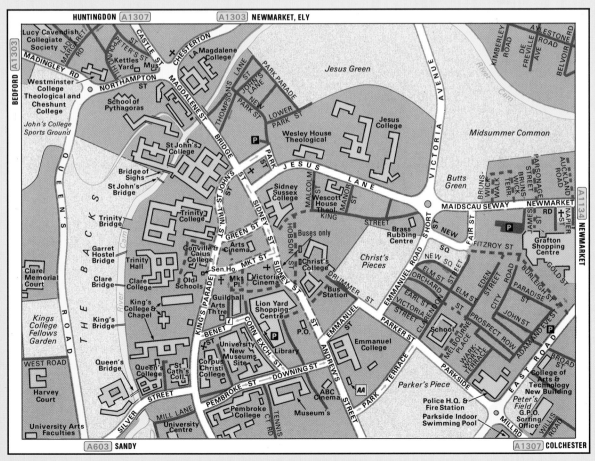

59

CALSTOCK
Cornwall *2 SX46*
Near this small village beside the
Tamar is Cotehele House (NT) one of
the finest Tudor manor houses in the
country. The main part of the house
was built between 1485 and 1539 by
Richard Edgcumbe, a supporter of
Henry VIII. The house and its gardens
remained in the Edgcumbe family's
possession until 1947, and the interior
decoration and furnishings are superb.
The great hall, with its collection of
armour, its fantastic roof, the
tapestries that hang from its walls, and
its hunting trophies is very impressive.
Cotehele Mill has been restored and
can be visited, as can the picturesque
quay with its small museum and
Tamar sailing barge.

CAMBER
E Sussex *6 TQ91*
The seashore here, where the English
Channel retreats a $\frac{1}{2}$ mile at low tide, is
a splendid place for dunes, marram
grass, relics of World War II coastal
defences, and acres and acres of sand,
best walked late on a fine winter's
afternoon, into the setting sun.
Dunkirk was one of several films made
on location here. Camber Castle (AM),
on the far side of Rye harbour, was
built by Henry VIII as an artillery fort.
It is laid out in the shape of a Tudor
rose, and stood originally on the shore,
as a defence against invasion from
France. The sea has gradually receded
and it is now about a mile inland.

CAMBERLEY
Surrey *4 SU86*
Camberley is deep in the heart of Sir
John Betjeman's Joan Hunter-Dunn
country – where, if the late Poet
Laureate is to be believed, love-sick
subalterns once played tennis with
girls named Pam and Joan. The Staff
College was originated by the
underrated Duke of York in 1799, and
the Royal Military College at nearby
Sandhurst was also his brainchild.
Sandhurst used to be known as 'Hell-
over-the-Hill' by the nearby public
school at Wellington; and cadets were
once a wild bunch. The National
Army Museum is at Sandhurst.
   Francis Brett Harte, American
author of *The Luck of Roaring Camp*,
editor of *The Californian* and
Overland Monthly, and US Consul in
Glasgow 1880–85, died at The Red
House in Camberley (1902) and is
buried in St Peter's Churchyard,
Frimley.

CAMBO
Northumberland *19 NZ08*
Cambo was built as a model village in
1740 and is almost unspoiled. The
beautiful stately home of Wallington
Hall (NT), a 17th-century mansion
about a mile away, was built by Sir
William Blackett, a Newcastle
merchant. Sir William's descendant,
Sir Walter Blackett, dedicated 40 years
of his life to improving the house and
the 13,000 acres of land. A team of
craftsmen from Italy carried out some
magnificent plasterwork – notably on
the ceilings of the hall and staircases.
In the grounds the landscaper
Capability Brown began his
professional career. Nearly a century
later, under the benevolent rule of
Pauline, Lady Trevelyan, a picture
gallery was created. The walls are
decorated with Pre-Raphaelite
portrayals of the story of
Northumberland, and the gallery
contains works by Cranach, Reynolds
and Gainsborough among others.

CAMBORNE-REDRUTH
Cornwall *1 SW64*
At Pool, between Camborne and
Redruth, there is a winding engine of
1887 and a pumping engine built in
1892 (NT). Camborne and Redruth
were at the centre of Cornwall's tin
and copper mining industries (in 1856,
the county's output of copper ore
amounted to 209,000 tons or £2
million of revenue). Nowadays,
employment comes from light
industry. Camborne was the birthplace
in 1771 of the inventor Richard
Trevithick, who in 1801 built the first
passenger steam vehicle.

CAMPBELTOWN
Strathclyde *21 NR72*
Kintyre is a long tongue of land
reaching from the Highlands towards
Northern Ireland, and protecting the
Isle of Arran against the Atlantic
westerlies. On the east coast of
Kintyre, not far from the tip, is
Campbeltown, its main centre. The
excellent anchorage encouraged the
growth of a herring fishing fleet; coal
was discovered; other industries were
established. At the end of the 19th
century, about 650 fishing boats were
based there, and the town has 30
distilleries producing the celebrated
Campbeltown malt whisky. Now it is
tourism that keeps the town alive. The
museum is worth a visit; facilities for
sea angling, sailing, and so on are
good, and the golf course at nearby
Machrihanish is famous. In a cave on

Davaar Island at the mouth of
Campbeltown Loch an artist named
Archibald MacKinnon painted the
Crucifixion. Lit by a shaft of daylight
that pierces a hole in the rock, the
effect is dramatic. Flora Macdonald
sailed to America from Campbeltown
in 1774.

CAPESTHORNE
Cheshire *15 SJ87*
The old hall (OACT), home of an
important Cheshire family, the
Bromley-Davenports, was much
altered and enlarged, first by Blore in
1837 and later, in 1867 by Salvin in a
flamboyant Victorian style. Among its
collections are many American items.
Not far away, Redesmere is a
charming wooded lake.

CARDIFF
S Glamorgan *8 ST17*
In 1955 Cardiff was created the official
capital of Wales. The other contenders
for the title, Machynlleth and
Caernarvon had stronger historical
claims, but Cardiff had better
communications, was more accessible
to London and, thanks to its docks,
was a more flourishing centre of trade
and industry.
   Welsh speakers prefer to call the city
Caerdydd, meaning 'seat of Dydd'.
The identity of Dydd is uncertain, but
he was probably a Roman commander
– the genesis of Cardiff was a Roman
fort, built in what are now the castle
grounds in AD 75. After the Norman
conquest, Robert Fitzhamon built a
motte and bailey castle in 1093, and
this was replaced by a stone keep in the
12th century, the remains of which,
restored in the 19th century by the
Marquess of Bute, can be seen in the
castle grounds.
   In the Tudor period, the inhabitants
of Cardiff were notorious pirates,
preying on shipping in the Bristol
Channel, with the connivance of the
city officials who grew rich on the
proceeds. Seafaring continued to be an
occupation even after piracy had been
suppressed, but it did not become
important to the city until the coal and
iron ore of South Wales began to be
exploited during the Industrial
Revolution. It was the 2nd Marquess
of Bute, whose family had acquired
land in Cardiff, who saw the potential
of this trade and in 1839 built the city's
first dock – Bute West, later much
extended.
   This was the foundation of the city's
prosperity and by the outbreak of
World War I Cardiff was the world's

premier port for the export of coal. In 1898 the Bute family sold Cathays Park to the city corporation, and this became the site for an impressive complex of public buildings comprising the City Hall, the Law Courts, the National Museum of Wales, County Hall, the University of Wales Registry, the University of South Wales, the Welsh Office, the Temple of Peace and Health and the Welsh National War Memorial. All were built between 1905 and 1938. More recent landmarks are the

Cardiff Castle

National Rugby Stadium at Cardiff Arms Park, which, with seating for 50,000 people, is an expression of the Welsh passion for rugby, and the National Sports Centre. Sir Thomas Button, who searched the Canadian Arctic for the North-West Passage early in the 17th century, was born at St Nicholas, 2 miles west of Cardiff.

CARDIGAN
Dyfed *7 SN14*
Cardigan is a delightful town that used to be a prosperous seaport until the River Teifi silted up. It is a town steeped in the culture of Wales. The first national Eisteddfod was held here in 1177. The castle was built by the Welsh in an attempt to safeguard their

independence. The fact that it is now in ruins is the price the town had to pay for its support of Charles I. In 1645, Parliament – determined to exact a penalty – turned its guns upon it. Nowadays the most imposing architectural feature is the bridge over the river, which dates from the 17th century. The Wildlife Park halfway between Cardigan and Cilgerran, specializes in European animals.

CARDINGTON
Bedfordshire *11 TL04*
Cardington itself is an attractive little village that owes much to the brewing family of Whitbread (Samuel Whitbread, who founded the firm, was born there in 1720). On the edge of it are giant airship sheds which housed the R100 and the R101, which crashed at Beauvais in France on her maiden flight. Only 6 of her 54 passengers and crew survived. Nowadays, the premises are occupied by the Royal Aircraft Establishment and are devoted to research. In St Mary's Church is a rare Wedgwood font, donated by Harriet Whitbread and several memorials to the family.

CAREW
Dyfed *7 SN00*
Carew, which nestles in a creek about halfway between Tenby and Pembroke, is most picturesque. The 14th-century church has an intricately carved 11th-century Celtic cross (AM) 14ft high, outside. Carew Castle (AM) is early Norman, though its more important association is with Rhys ap Thomas, who was one of those who welcomed Henry Tudor when he landed – and fought on his side at the Battle of Bosworth. The name of the village comes from Thomas Carew who was born in Kent. For several generations, the Carews were keepers of the castle, and the family tombs can be seen in the church. Downstream is one of the few working tidal mills in Britain today. It was restored in 1972.

CARLISLE
Cumbria *18 NY45*
Originally *Luguvalium*, a prosperous Roman settlement, Carlisle was later raided successively by Picts, Vikings and Scots. William II began work on the castle, which was later to house the imprisoned Mary Queen of Scots. Queen Mary's Tower contains the museum of the former Border Regiment. During the Jacobite rebellion of 1745, Bonnie Prince Charlie made his proclamation at

Carlisle Cross. The city's cathedral is one of the smallest in England, but is nevertheless beautiful. Sir Walter Scott married Margaret Charlotte Charpentier (known as Charlotte Carpenter) in the cathedral in 1797. The house in Castle Street where Charlotte lived with a companion, can still be seen. The poet Longfellow was a friend of Robert Ferguson of Morton, Carlisle, and was his guest here.

President Woodrow Wilson visited the cathedral in 1918 and was made a Freeman of the City. Janet Woodrow, the President's mother, was born and lived in Annetwell Street and in Warwick Road. Her father was a pastor of the Lowther Street Congregational Church. The church bears a memorial tablet.

The City Museum and Art Gallery has a good exhibition on the Lake District, a collection of Pre-Raphaelite paintings and a unique William Rothenstein collection.

CARMARTHEN
Dyfed *7 SN42*
Carmarthen can rightly claim to be one of the oldest towns in Wales. It probably began its life as a Celtic hill-fort, but this was obliterated by the Romans who built a wooden fort here in AD 75. This was the most westerly of their large forts, but few traces remain – though the discovery of an amphitheatre with a seating capacity of 5000 suggests that there must have been a fairly sizeable garrison. Later the Normans built a castle here. The ruins (AM) can still be seen, but much of the site is now occupied by County Hall. Of the Augustinian Priory little but the site remains. It was here that the oldest known manuscript in Welsh was written – the *Black Book of Carmarthen*, now in the National Library of Wales in Aberystwyth. Among other legends, it tells the story of Merlin, King Arthur's wizard, who is said to have been born here. Carmarthen's Welsh name is *Caerfryddin*, 'the city of Merlin'. A carefully preserved stump of an oak tree bore the prophecy 'When Merlin's oak shall tumble down, Then shall fall Carmarthen town', its remains now in the foyer of St Peter's Civic Hall. On the River Tywi the ancient craft of coracle fishing is still practised.

CARNFORTH
Lancashire *18 SD47*
The village is the home of the
Steamtown Railway Museum where
the famous *Flying Scotsman* is one of
the most popular exhibits. **Leighton
Hall** (OACT) lies 3 miles to the north.
While 1 mile north of Carnforth, the
tower of the restored 15th-century
church at Warton bears the
Washington arms. The family lived
here for many generations, between
leaving Washington and moving to
Sulgrave. Thomas, the last
Washington of Warton, was parson
here from 1799 to 1823. Robert Kitson
lived at Warton in the 15th century.
His daughter Margaret married John
Washington, while his son Thomas
was the father-in-law of Sir John
Spencer of **Althorp**, from whom both
the Princess of Wales and Winston
Churchill descended. Robert Kitson is
therefore a link in the genealogy of
George Washington, and these
important Britons.

Three miles north west of Warton is
the village of Silverdale where Mrs
Gaskell lived and was visited by
Charlotte Brontë.

CARTMEL
Cumbria *18 SD37*
Cartmel used to be a centre of faith
and scholarship. The priory and its
church of Sts Mary and Michael were
established in the 12th century. King
Henry VIII dissolved the former: after
it had fallen into disuse, local builders
helped themselves to the stones until
only the impressive gatehouse (NT)
survived. The church remained and it
has the atmosphere of a cathedral. The
treasure of the church is a first edition
of Spenser's *The Faerie Queene*. A
number of people who failed to beat
the tide on their journeys between
Lancashire and the Lake District
across the treacherous sands of
Morecambe Bay are buried in the
graveyard. 1 mile north the church at
Cartmel Fell contains a rare pre-
Reformation carved figure of Christ.

CASTLE COMBE
Wiltshire *3 ST87*
The houses here are of honey-coloured
Cotswold stone, there is a medieval
market cross, a three-arched bridge
over the stream which runs through
the village, and the church (its tower a
gift from the 'clothiers of the district')
have survived the ravages of well-
meaning but ill-conceived Victorian
restoration. Hardly any traffic passes
along the street. Castle Combe is held

to be the prettiest village in England.
(In 1962, the word 'probably' was
deleted and the village became
officially so.) Drama came to Castle
Combe in 1966, when the film makers
turned it into what cinema audiences
may have mistaken for a seaport for
the filming of *Dr Doolittle*.

CASTLE DONINGTON
Leicestershire *10 SK42*
The 'castle' was Norman: built by
Baron Haulton, hereditary Constable
of Cheshire, in the 12th century. In
1595, it was virtually demolished, and
another residence built in the park 2
miles away. Nowadays, there are some
charming houses in the town,
including the Hall, which was designed
by Wilkins – who also designed the
National Gallery in London. When
visiting the 13th–14th-century church,
notice the pulpit: the inside of it is
made from memorial slabs to children
which were removed from the floor.
Among the tombs is a fine brass to
Robert de Staunton and his wife. Car
enthusiasts will enjoy the Donington
Collection of historic racing cars, and
there is a nearby racing circuit.

Three miles north east on the
outskirts of Long Eaton is Sawley,
where John Clifford was born in 1836.
Clifford began working in a local lace
factory when only 10 years old. Later,
he went to the General Baptist
Academy in Leicester, and in 1858
became the minister of the Praed Street
Chapel, London. He was known as a
popular evangelist and social reformer,
and became the first president of the
Baptist World Alliance.

CASTLE HEDINGHAM
Essex *12 TL73*
Miraculously the Tudor and, indeed,
the medieval atmosphere of the village
survives. Above it broods the massive
keep, once a stronghold of the Earls of
Oxford, who established a vineyard
here in Norman times.

The Castle (AM) was admirably
sited to control the trade route along
the Colne valley. For the next 500
years, the de Veres were lords of the
manor with only one setback. That
was in 1215 when King John took the
castle from Robert de Vere. However,
the king later relented. Not long
afterwards, he granted Castle
Hedingham a Market Charter.
Matilda, wife of King Stephen, died
here in 1151. Queen Elizabeth I was
the last sovereign to enjoy the de
Veres' hospitality. Afterwards, for no
apparent reason, the 17th Earl of

Oxford pulled part of the castle down.
The stones were used to build a
Georgian house by Robert Ashurst,
who had bought the ruin from the 18th
(and last) Earl of Oxford's widow.

The village, clustered round the
Norman church, has some lovely
houses and pretty little streets. The
Colne Valley Railway and Museum,
on the A604 Great Yeldham road is
worth visiting.

John Winthrop, later Governor of
Massachusetts, married Margaret
Tyndal in the neighbouring village of
Great Maplestead. The Winthrop
family home was in Groton, east of
Sudbury. Little Maplestead has a 14th-
century round church of the Knights
Hospitaller; there are only 4 others
like it in England.

CASTLE HOWARD
N Yorkshire *16 SE77*
To some people, this may be better
known as 'Brideshead', for it was at
Castle Howard (OACT) that much of
the TV version of Evelyn Waugh's
Brideshead Revisited was filmed. It
was built for Charles Howard, 3rd
Earl of Carlisle, to replace
Henderskelfe Castle, which was
burned down in 1639. Sir John
Vanbrugh was chosen as architect;
very much a Renaissance man, he was
also a gifted playwright and as captain
of marines, a man of action. With
assistance from Nicholas Hawksmoor
(Wren's clerk of works), he designed
this tremendous castle and then went
on to conceive Blenheim. The interior
of the house – which isn't really a
castle at all – matches the grandeur of
the exterior. In the 1000-acre grounds,
there are two lakes, the Temple of the
Four Winds and the Mausoleum,
which is as big as a Wren church in
London. Castle Howard cost £78,000
and took 37 years to complete
(1700–37). It is still owned by the
Howard family.

The Canadian artist, Scott Medd,
repainted the Dome Mural at Castle
Howard in 1962–63.

CASTLE KENNEDY
Dumfries & Galloway *17 NX16*
The name of the castle is Lochinch. It
was built in 1867, and is the home of
the Earl of Stair. Situated on a
peninsula that juts out between White
and Black Lochs, the present building
replaced Castle Kennedy which was
destroyed by a fire in 1716, and *this*
was the seat of the Kennedy family.
The plan of the grounds (OACT) was
inspired by the gardens of Versailles.

CANTERBURY

Kent   6 TR15

Dominating the narrow streets and ancient buildings, the incomparable cathedral, setting for many dramatic events in past centuries, stands at the heart of a city that still retains its ancient character. Parts of Canterbury are still enclosed within the medieval city walls, about half of which, built on medieval foundations, remains, as does the keep of the castle, which has defied periodic attempts over the centuries to demolish it.

Settlements existed here at the time of the Roman invasion, and the Romans built their regional centre, *Durovernum*, on this site. A well-preserved Roman tessellated pavement can be seen beneath one of the shops in the Longmarket shopping precinct.

When St Augustine arrived in 597, he founded his cathedral here in 602, and thus the city became the centre of the Anglican Church. The present cathedral was founded by the Normans in 1070, but the nave had to be rebuilt in the 14th century, and the central tower (called Bell Harry), which is such a feature of Canterbury,

was added in 1500. The earliest Norman work is to be found in the splendid crypt, but the majority of the cathedral, in particular the nave, completed early in the 15th century, is a glorious expression of Gothic architecture. Despite the ravages of World War II, some magnificent stained glass remains. There is an American Trust for Canterbury Cathedral. In 1947 a considerable donation was made by a New York businessman towards the cost of repairs resulting from war damage.

The most famous event that took place here was the murder of Archbishop Thomas Becket in 1170 by Henry II's knights. Becket was immediately proclaimed a martyr and his shrine drew innumerable pilgrims to Canterbury, such as those immortalized by Chaucer in *Canterbury Tales*, until the reign of Henry VIII when it was destroyed. Many former archbishops are interred here, some in tombs of great splendour, as are Edward, the Black Prince, and Henry IV and his queen.

Adjoining the cathedral was once a Benedictine monastery, the cloisters of which remain. Nearby, around Green Court, parts of the monastery are incorporated in the buildings of King's School, one of the oldest and foremost of English public schools.

Although the cathedral is the focal point of interest, there are several other historic churches, including St Martin's, said to be the oldest church in England still in use. It is believed to predate the arrival of St Augustine. A little way outside Canterbury, the new buildings of the University of Kent are also of interest.

Two Pilgrims came from Canterbury: James Chilton, a tailor, and Robert Cushman, a woolcomber. Chilton, born in 1583, was the 24th signatory of the Mayflower Compact and his wife was apparently the first passenger to step ashore at Plymouth Rock. Cushman (1578–1628) was involved in the business arrangements for the *Mayflower* expedition and was appointed Governor of the second ship, the *Speedwell*. He was unable to

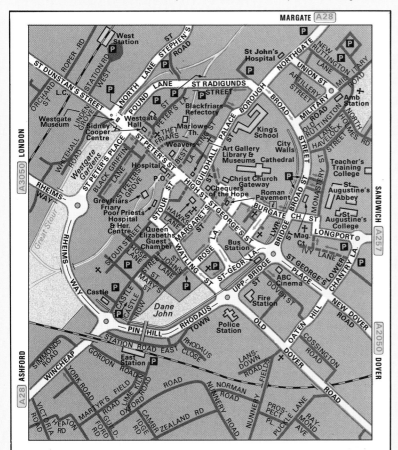

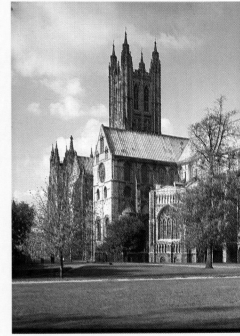

Canterbury Cathedral

sail and eventually reached the New World in 1621. His son, Thomas, was baptized in St Andrew's Church. Thomas's wife, who died in 1699, was the last of the original Pilgrims to survive.

EISTEDDFOD

Half a mile over the Severn Bridge, with London 120 miles behind, the sign is unmistakeable: *Croeso I Cymru* – Welcome to Wales. In the distance, the mountains of Monmouth. In the foreground appear two posts, whitewashed and neat as flagpoles, joined by a crossbar. The latter, as symbols, matter more than any mountains – the game of Rugby. It is the Welsh national game, or even its sacrament, some say its Holy Grail, as well as the occasion for the singing of the finest male voice choirs in the world. The singing of 'Land of my Fathers' at Cardiff Arms Park is an essential experience. Rugby began, however, outside Wales: at Rugby School in the last century, when William Webb Ellis picked up the ball and ran with it, breaking the soccer code. Rugby is a game for hooligans played by gentlemen, whereas soccer seems to have become a game for gentlemen, with supporters' clubs to which hooligans are attached. In neither form do players need, or at least they do not wear, the thick protective padding required in the wild American variant of the game. The American game is thoroughly professionalized – mercenary, and especially favoured by University alumni. But in Wales Rugby is at once classless and democratic. It is not played for money but for honour and glory. In Wales it demands total dedicated ruthlessness. A tiny boy calls out:

'Who are you for then, Mister?'
'Nobody,' he replied, 'I'm neutral.'
'Neutral? What's that?'
'I'm not supporting anybody.'
'Oh, don't be ridiculous, man!'

The visitor to Wales, struck by bilingual highway signs, may feel himself in a foreign country for the only time during his tour of Britain. One in four of the Welsh people speak Welsh, especially around Merioneth and Caernarvon; it is a required language in the schools, and some 6000 people speak Welsh only. Welsh Nationalism, unlike Scottish, is rooted in the campaign to preserve the language as the evidence and vehicle of Welsh identity. If the annual General Assembly of the Presbyterian Kirk sitting for a week in Edinburgh has been for generations Scotland's Parliament and its assertion of its distinctiveness, with speeches, hymns and much talk of church organization, the national Eisteddfod – a festival each August, of poetry, dance and song – is Wales' equivalent

Caernafon Castle

(the singing of the exiles' hymn, 'Once again in dear old Wales' is particularly moving.)

Administered since Henry VIII's day as part of the UK, Wales is distinct and picturesque. It has countless splendid chapels, six cathedrals, five university colleges, three national parks, castles and broad sweeps of coastline; the boast is that is has one hundred castles and one hundred golf courses, and more than one hundred pits. Its soils are thin, its moorlands high, but its rocks rich in minerals. The Romans mined gold in Dyfed, lead in Clwyd, copper in Gwynedd, iron and coal in Gwent. In the nineteenth century the coal and iron of south and southeast Wales and the slate of the north west were massively

Snowdonia from Portmadog

exploited.

If its most famous names are those of politicians like David Lloyd George (born in fact in Manchester) or

Aneurin Bevan of Ebbw Vale, its real heroes are its rugby forwards. And when it wins it celebrates – unlike Scotland – less with alcohol than with song. Inside every Welshman, they say, there is an orator or a singer.

Wales has played a special part in American history – at once popular and democratic. Its impact on Pennsylvania, on Delaware – originally the 'Welsh Tract', on settlements on the Peedee River in South Carolina, and on Ohio is part of American history. When the Pennsylvania Railroad Company built its railway through an area settled by Welsh Quakers, one of its directors George Roberts, himself a Welshman, dotted the stations on his line with Welsh names. Thus, moving out of Philadelphia, one passes through Merion, Narberth, Wynnewood, Ardmore, Haverford, Bryn Mawr, Radnor, St David's and Berwyn.

Of the fifty-six signers of the Declaration of Independence, no less than seventeen were Welsh, or of Welsh descent. One of these was Francis Lewis, born in Newport, Gwent, whose brother-in-law was a vicar of St Woollo's Church, Newport, now a cathedral. Thomas Jefferson claimed his family originated in Snowdonia, and his father's farm was called Snowdon. Richard Price's tract *Observations on the Nature of Civil Liberty* appeared five months before the Declaration was signed. So important was his pamphlet in shaping American opinion that in 1778 Congress resolved to consider him a citizen of the United States, and in 1781 Yale awarded him an honorary doctorate. The importance of Welsh liberalism in shaping American thought was important in 1776. It has influenced the Baptists and Methodism too. The Welsh impact has been strong in democratic ideas, in liberalism of spirit and in education – as evidenced in Brown University's origins, as well as in Yale.

The docks at Milford Haven

Indeed, the traffic has not been in one direction only. The port of Milford Haven was developed by Samuel Starbuck and other religious dissidents from America in 1793. The group originated in East Anglia and moved to New England. They moved on to Nantucket and set up a whaling station in Nova Scotia. The War of Independence posed problems to them and they moved back across the Atlantic to the south-west corner of Wales, to build a port to which their whale oil could be sent. Milford Haven was planned on the pattern of New York, with straight streets parallel to the waterfront and three streets at right angles to them.

In the nineteenth century over one hundred thousand Welsh people emigrated to the US, compared with four and a half million Irish, six hundred thousand Scots and some two and a half million English, with distinctive Welsh communities in Tennessee – and Patagonia. These two states became closely interlinked, economically, in the late nineteenth century. Of this the tinplate industry is perhaps the best example. The industry was almost totally Welsh – of the seventy-seven tinplate works in Britain in 1875, no less than fifty-seven were located in South Wales, and most of the tinplate they produced were exported to the United States. But in 1890 the McKinley tariff in the US hit all the imported tinplate and almost destroyed the prosperity of Cardiff and Swansea. The jobs the Welsh tinplate workers lost in South Wales were available to them in the US, however, and many of them moved as a result.

Further Reading

Alan Conway, *The Welsh in America* (University of Wales Press, Cardiff 1961)

A H Dodd, *The Character of Early Welsh Emigration to the United States* (University of Wales Press, Cardiff 1957)

D O Thomas, *Richard Price and America* (Pub by the author, Aberystwyth 1975)

David Williams, *John Evans and the Legend of Madoc* (University of Wales Press, Cardiff 1963)

David Williams, *Wales and America* (University of Wales Press, Cardiff 1975)

Gareth Williams, *The Eagle and the Dragon* (Pub by the Welsh Sub-Committee of the British Bicentennial Liaison Committee 1976)

Glanmor Williams, *A Prospect of Paradise* (BBC Wales Annual Radio Lecture 1976)

Gwyn A Williams, 'Morgan John Rhees and his Beula' (*Welsh History Review* Vol 3 No 4, Dec 1967, University of Wales Press)

CASTLETON
Derbyshire *15 SK18*

Peveril Castle (AM), the scene of Sir Walter Scott's *Peveril of the Peak*, stands on high ground above the village, which was given to William Peveril by William I. The keep was added a century later by Henry II. Much of the castle has been capably restored: it's certainly worth the walk to see it. In Castleton itself and in the vicinity are some of the country's most famous caverns: the villagers used to seek sanctuary in them when raiders came. A secret passage connects one of them, Devil's Cavern, with the castle. The Blue John Cavern, where the attractive blue stone is mined, Peak, Treak Cliff and Speedwell Caverns (OACT) are all fascinating to visit.

CAWDOR
Highland *26 NH85*

Shakespeare set King Duncan's murder at Cawdor Castle, though it is more likely that Macbeth killed him in battle near Elgin. Cawdor Castle is a high walled, medieval fortress and certainly looks a suitable setting. Still the home of the Earls of Cawdor, the family treasures include some exceptionally fine tapestries.

Cerne Abbas giant

CERNE ABBAS
Dorset *3 ST60*

The Cerne Abbas giant (NT) can be seen from afar, a 180ft-long fertility figure carved on the hillside during the Roman occupation, probably representing Hercules, with elements of a local deity added. At the foot of Giant's Hill, the site of a Benedictine abbey (987–1539) forms the heart of an unusually beautiful village in which thatched cottages happily coexist with one or two Tudor buildings. Of the abbey, only the gatehouse and the

church survive. In the grounds of the latter (admirably restored in the 1960s) there is a wishing well named after St Augustine, who is said to have brought Christianity to Dorset.

CHALFONT ST GILES
Buckinghamshire *5 SU99*

An attractive village to which Milton came in the year of the plague, 1665. Old, lonely and blind, he still managed to complete his masterpiece *Paradise Lost* and to write *Paradise Regained*. The former earned him £5. His cottage is now a museum (OACT). The Chiltern Open Air Museum (OACT) has old buildings and other artefacts relating to life in the Chilterns in days gone by. There is a nature trail in the 25-acre park.

CHARLECOTE
Warwickshire *10 SP25*

Charlecote Park (NT), 4 miles from **Stratford-upon-Avon**, has been the home of the Lucy family since the 13th century. The present Elizabethan house was built in 1558 and enlarged during the 19th century. The octagonal tower gatehouse, however, has remained unaltered, and is now used as a museum. Shakespeare is said to have been brought before Sir Thomas Lucy after he'd been caught poaching in the grounds, and satirized him as Justice Shallow in *Henry IV* (Part 2) and *The Merry Wives of Windsor*. Herds of fallow and red deer still roam the parkland. The house contains portraits by Gainsborough and Kneller.

CHARMOUTH
Dorset *3 SY39*

Jane Austen liked Charmouth for its peaceful atmosphere. The village, which used to be a fashionable stopping place for coaches, has many attractive old houses and enjoys fine views over Lyme Bay. Katherine of Aragon stayed at the Queen's Arms soon after arriving in England and in 1651, Charles II came here in disguise, seeking a boat that would take him to France. Black Ven, not far away, is where Mary Anning made the discovery of the fossilized ichthyosaurus, now in the Natural History Museum. Fossil-hunting is still a popular pastime on the attractive beach just south of the village, and the cliffs around Charmouth offer some excellent walks.

CHARTWELL
Kent *5 TQ45*

Winston Churchill bought Chartwell

(NT) in 1922, and lived here for 40 years. He made a number of alterations and added a new wing. Everything has been left just as it was, and every room is filled with family belongings and relics of Churchill. Among the many paintings at Chartwell are Monet's famous study of 'London Bridge' and works by Lavery, Sargent and William Nicholson. Churchill's own paintings hang in the house and in his studio, a cottage in the gardens.

To celebrate their Golden Wedding, Sir Winston and Lady Churchill planted 32 species of yellow roses, and their family gave them an album of paintings of the roses, the illustrations by distinguished painters such as Ivon Hitchens and John Nash. The former vegetable garden is of particular interest since the wall around it was built by Winston Churchill.

CHATSWORTH
Derbyshire *15 SK27*

The principal seat of the Duke and Duchess of Devonshire in the lovely setting of Derbyshire's Peak District, Chatsworth (OACT), is one of the great houses of England. The estate was originally acquired by Sir William

Chatsworth

Cavendish, who married that indefatigable builder, Bess of Hardwick who later became Countess of Shrewsbury. Of this particular one of her houses nothing remains. The present Baroque mansion was begun by her great-great-grandson, the 1st Duke of Devonshire, and its construction was not quite complete when the 6th Duke inherited the title. Its stately rooms contain innumerable treasures, but the outstanding works of art are the paintings, which include works by Rembrandt, Frans Hals, Murillo, Veronese, Van Dyck and Lely. In 1760 Capability Brown was brought in to landscape the grounds, to splendid effect. Many of its most triumphant features, however, were wrought by Joseph Paxton – as, for example, the magnificent Emperor Fountain that throws its jets of water 260ft into the air. From 1916–21 the then Duke of Devonshire was Governor-General of Canada.

CHAWTON
Hampshire *4 SU73*
Anyone passing through Chawton in a hurry might be forgiven if he failed to notice the modest brick house which stands on the village street. But this was Jane Austen's home for the last 8 years of her life, and it was here that she wrote or completed her six great novels, working at a small fireside table in the living room. The house is, of course, a museum, but one of those that give the impression, despite the memorabilia, of still being a family home. Chawton House, which her brother inherited, still belongs to descendants of the family; it stands just outside the village, and is not open to the public.

CHEDDAR
Somerset *3 ST45*
The Cheddar Gorge consists of nearly a mile of dramatic limestone cliffs that rise almost vertically to 450ft. The best view from the top is to be had by climbing 'Jacob's Ladder' at the south end. In the gorge itself, two caves, Cox's and Gough's, are profuse in stalagmites and stalactites. In the town, there's a car museum.

Cheddar cheese, once a local farm product, is these days made on a commercial scale. The village of Cheddar has a fine market cross and an interesting church.

North of Cheddar is Wrington, where the philosopher John Locke (1632–1704) was born at his uncle's house, which he later inherited. There

Cheddar Gorge

is a commemorative plaque on the churchyard wall. Between Cheddar and Wrington is Burrington, where Augustus Montagu Toplady sheltered in the Gorge, and was inspired to write the hymn 'Rock of Ages, cleft for me'.

CHEDWORTH
Gloucestershire *10 SP01*
Surrounded by superb countryside, Chedworth is a village of stone houses set in the hills to the west of the Fosse Way. The church is a mixture of Norman and Perpendicular. North of the village is a Roman villa (NT) sited in 6½ acres of woodland. Discovered in 1864, it probably conveys the best impression, anywhere in Britain, of life as it was lived in Romano-British times. The mosaic pavements and the bathhouse have been excellently preserved.

CHELMSFORD
Essex *6 TL70*
Chelmsford, the county town of Essex, is an important link between London and the East coast, as well as being the centre of local government. There has been a livestock market here since about the year 1200, however few old buildings survive. The 15th-century church of Sts Mary, Peter and Cedd

was promoted to the status of cathedral in 1914. Its 15th-century tower is crowned by an 18th-century lantern and spire, and the south porch is a fine example of Perpendicular flush-work. Among the oddities is a figure of St Peter in the dress of a modern fisherman holding a Yale key in his hand.

From 1626–9 the Reverend Thomas Hooker, founder of Hartford, Connecticut, was a lecturer at the church where he gave evangelical addresses on holy and market days. The south porch of the cathedral is almost entirely dedicated to USAAF men based in Chelmsford during the war; there is also a memorial to them. At Boreham 3 miles north east, the airmen are commemorated by a stone memorial. Chelmsford was the birthplace of Sir Walter Mildmay, who founded Emmanuel College, Cambridge as a stronghold of Puritanism. He is quoted as saying to Elizabeth I, 'I have set an acorn which, when it becomes an oak, God alone knows what will be the fruit thereof.' Many of the most influential Separatist leaders and settlers of America were graduates of the college.

In 1899, Guglielmo Marconi set up the world's first radio factory at Chelmsford and in February 1920 the first radio programmes (music, news, talks) were broadcast from the town. This was two years before the foundation of the British Broadcasting Company (which, in 1927, became the British Broadcasting Corporation). In Oaklands Park, the Chelmsford and Essex Museum has much of local historical interest.

Springfield, on the outskirts of the town, was the birthplace of the Pynchons. William Pynchon emigrated with John Winthrop in 1630, and was eventually to found Springfield Massachusetts. Pynchon's opposition to Calvinism offended the colonists and in 1652 he returned to England. 4 miles east at Little Baddow, Thomas Hooker conducted a school assisted by John Eliot, 'Apostle to the Indians'.

CHELTENHAM
Gloucestershire *9 SO92*
Three hundred years ago, Cheltenham was just an ordinary Cotswold village. In 1715, however, somebody diascovered a mineral spring, from having noticed (they say) the drinking habits of an unusually healthy flock of pigeons. The story may be apocryphal: nevertheless, Cheltenham has seen fit to include a pigeon on its crest. By the

end of 1783, a retired privateer named Captain Henry Skillicorne had set up the first pump room, and 50 years later the town was established as a fasionable spa. George III, who had a great liking for these watering places, was a frequent visitor. When the Duke of Wellington came here for the cure in 1816, the spa's popularity increased dramatically, and the town was virtually rebuilt in a most pleasing blend of Regency and classical styles.

It soon became clear that the waters of Cheltenham were particularly salubrious for military officers and colonial administrators, whose livers had been ruined by excessively long service in the tropics and thus the town became a byword for its conservative attitudes. Nowadays, you can take the waters at the Town Hall as well as the Pump Room. Their beneficial effects are believed to be due to the presence of magnesium and sodium sulphates and sodium bicarbonate. The Pittville Pump Room (OACT, named after Sir Joseph Pitt, MP) was inspired by the colonnade of a temple in Athens and is a masterpiece of the Greek Revival style. The Promenade, Lansdown Place and Montpellier Parade are among the most impressive Regency achievements, and Montpellier Walk, ornamented with caryatids, is a most elegant shopping precinct. Gustav Holst, the composer, was born here, and the Holst Museum contains memorabilia. The Art Gallery and Museum has collections of ceramics, furniture and paintings.

Cheltenham College for Boys, on the Bath road, was built between 1841 and 1843 as a public school for the sons of Indian Army Officers. The even more famous Cheltenham Ladies' College was founded by Miss Beale, a forceful Victorian champion of education for girls. The Festival of Music is held in July and the Festival of Literature in October.

Just south of Cheltenham is Leckhampton where there is a memorial to Colonel Henry Norwood, treasurer of the Virginia Colony.

CHEQUERS
Buckinghamshire   *4 SP80*
Chequers Court was originally a 13th-century manor house, which was rebuilt in the 15th century. The sister of Lady Jane Grey was put under house arrest here by Elizabeth I, after she had married without obtaining the Queen's consent: her husband died in prison. In 1917, it was presented to the nation by Lord Lee of Fareham – as a

Pittville Pump Room, Cheltenham

country retreat for Prime Ministers. Understandably, it is not open to the public.

CHESIL BANK
Dorset   *3 SY58*
This 18-mile natural breakwater, which separates the English Channel from the Fleet (an elongated lake) between Portland and Abbotsbury, is the product of thousands of years of labour by the sea, the tides, and the storms – which threw up masses and masses of pebbles. The process of time has succeeded in grading them: at the Portland end, they average $3\frac{1}{2}$ inches in diameter, declining little by little until, at Abbotsbury, they are just under one inch in diameter. Many and most various things have been washed up on the bank, but the merman, reported in the 18th century, should not be taken seriously. The 95-ton sloop, thrown over Chesil Bank by a gale in 1824, and dumped in the Fleet, is a fact.

CHESSINGTON ZOO
Gtr London   *5 TQ16*
Zoos have to be commercial to survive, but Chessington, which was established in 1931, has the welfare of its animal occupants as its first consideration. Set in spacious surroundings, the enclosures give them as much freedom as is compatible with public safety.

CHESTERFIELD
Derbyshire   *15 SK37*
Chesterfield is mostly known for its church of St Mary and All Saints, which has a crooked octagonal spire. The fault is believed to have been caused by changing temperatures

distorting the lead that covers its wooden frame. The church was built in the 14th century and is a good example of ecclesiastical architecture of that period. Among many fine monuments are those of the Foljambe family. Apart from the church, most of Chesterfield's interesting buildings are modern, but a Heritage Centre has been set up in the medieval timber-framed Peacock Inn.

On the northern outskirts of the town at Old Whittington is Revolution House, where, in 1688, the Earl of Devonshire and his fellow conspirators plotted to depose James II and put William of Orange on the throne. The house is now a museum. 4 miles south east of Chesterfield, at Sutton Scarsdale, is Sutton Hall, which supplied the 18th-century interiors for the Philadelphia Museum of Art. At Bolsover, 7 miles east of Chesterfield, Peter Fidler, the explorer of the Canadian West, was born. There are plaques at Sutton Mill Farm and the Castle Inn.

• CHEVIOTS
Borders   *24 NT71*
The Cheviots, an impressive range of bleak, rounded hills, extend for 35 miles, occupying 200 square miles of Northumberland (including the northern part of the Northumberland National Park) and, in Scotland, 100 square miles of the Borders. The density of population is estimated at one person per 350 acres; there are rather more sheep. The walking is superb – though the country is wild, recalling the centuries of Border raids between Scotland and England, and visitors should be adequately equipped.

CHESTER
Cheshire *14 SJ46*

One of the most important Roman military bases in the country, Chester was the headquarters of the famous 20th Legion, known as *Valeria Victrix*. Its Latin name, *Deva*, meaning 'holy place', honoured the goddess of the River Dee which, until it gradually silted up, was the source of Chester's wealth and importance throughout the medieval period, when the city conducted a flourishing trade with Ireland, Scotland and parts of Europe.

Architecturally, Chester owes much to the Victorians, who greatly admired the black and white 'magpie' buildings which make the centre of Chester almost dazzling to look at, and so they built more of them, often in a more elaborate and exuberant style than the originals, and restored others. They also restored the Rows, a unique feature of the city. The Rows are raised, covered galleries, with shops at first-floor level and another tier of shops underneath at street level. They completely line Eastgate Street on both sides, and part of Bridge Street. Their origin is unknown, but the first mention of them is in the 13th-century documents, and they are peculiar to Chester, there being no record of anything similar in any other English town. Among the interesting buildings in the Rows are the 17th-century Bishop Lloyd's House, carved with heraldic beasts and panels depicting Biblical scenes. George Lloyd was Bishop of Chester 1604–15. His eldest daughter married twice. Thomas Yale, her first husband, was grandfather of Elihu Yale, from whom Yale University takes its name. Her second husband, Theophilus Eaton of Stony Stratford, went to Boston in 1637 and founded New Haven in 1639. He was Governor of New Haven until his death in 1658.

There is an inscription on a neighbouring house, 'God's Providence is Mine Inheritance', which was a thanksgiving from the inhabitants for their escape from plague during a disastrous outbreak of the disease in the Civil War. In the Town Hall Assembly Rooms are portraits of the Grosvenor family. The Duke of Westminster, present representative of the family, owns Grosvenor Square in London where the American Embassy is situated. The family had an option on 12,000 acres in East Florida, lost in the War of Independence. Also in the Town Hall is a Thomas Lawrence portrait of Richard Philpot, Sheriff in 1831.

Another feature of Chester is its exceptionally well-preserved city walls, which completely enclose the old centre. A walkway along the top of them allows visitors to make the tour of the whole city. The Eastgate, surmounted by an ornate, gaily painted clock, erected to commemorate Queen Victoria's Jubilee, is still, as it was in medieval times, the main entrance to Chester. Tolls on trade passing through any of the four original gates helped, in the old days, to pay for repairs to the walls.

PLACES TO SEE

Roman Amphitheatre and Garden One of the largest yet excavated in Britain, the amphitheatre could seat 7000 spectators. In the Roman Garden are the remains of a hypocaust.

Grosvenor Museum Models illustrating life in a Roman fort and remains excavated in and around Chester are displayed here.

Chester Heritage Centre This was the first Heritage Centre in the country. A short film shows conservation work in the city.

British Heritage Exhibition Here can be seen a fascinating reconstruction of The Rows as they were in Victorian times.

St Werburgh's Cathedral Heavily restored in the 19th century, the cathedral has its origin in the Anglo Saxon abbey of St Werburgh. The choir stalls are beautifully and intricately carved. In the south transept are flags of the Cheshire Regiment, two of which flew at Bunker Hill in 1775. One was used to wrap Wolfe's body after victory at the Plains of Abraham. In the cathedral are memorials to George Clarke, Lieutenant-Governor of New York, who retired to Chester and died in 1760, and to exiled Loyalist Frederick Phillips who died in Chester in 1785.

King Charles Tower From here, King Charles I watched the defeat of his troops at Rowton Moor. A small exhibition on Chester's part in the Civil War is housed here.

Cheshire Military Museum Housed in Chester Castle is the museum of the Cheshire Regiment. The castle was entirely rebuilt in the 18th century as a barracks and administrative centre. It is regarded as a masterpiece of the Classical Revival. The Cheshire Regiment served in America throughout the Revolution.

Chester Zoo Just outside the city, the zoo has 110 acres of natural enclosures and parts can be toured by waterbus.

Remains of a hypocaust in the Roman Garden

CHICHESTER
W Sussex *4 SU80*
A Roman fort existed here before Chichester became a capital of the South Saxons, given by their King Aella to his son Cissa, whence Cissa's Ceaster, the origin of the name. It has always been a peaceful place, the city centre still more or less confined within the lines of the Roman walls, parts of which have been incorporated into the gardens of the Bishop's Palace.

Four main roads, North, South, East and West Streets divide the centre into tidy quadrants, and meet at the market cross, which is Chichester's most prominent landmark, built by Bishop Story in 1501; the octagonal cross has a central tower supported on open arcades; the carvings are superb.

The south-east quadrant is also divided into four segments, by charming streets known as the Pallants – again called north, south, east and west – which form a complete Georgian townscape in miniature. Pallant House, at the crossroads, is an elegant Queen Anne mansion which has now been restored and opened as an art gallery.

Although many of Chichester's finest buildings are 18th century, the period when the city prospered from shipping and the corn trade, some more ancient houses survive around the cathedral, and near St Martin's Square, a unique almshouse, founded in the 13th century as a hospital. It is England's only example of such a building still in use. Originally, hospital and chapel, divided by a beautiful carved screen, were housed in the same building, so that the sick could benefit from religious services. The infirmary has now been converted to flats for eight old ladies, but the character of the building is unchanged.

Chichester Cathedral, founded in the 11th century, was largely rebuilt after a fire at the end of the 12th century, and its spire collapsed in 1861 in a violent storm, but was rebuilt by Sir Gilbert Scott. Inside, treasures range from 12th-century stone carvings to John Piper's vividly coloured altar tapestry and windows by Marc Chagall.

The Festival Theatre, one of the most prestigious provincial theatres in the country, opened in 1962 under the direction of Sir Laurence (now Lord) Olivier.

$3\frac{1}{2}$ miles north east the parish church at Boxgrove was once part of Bolgrove Priory. Its architecture is some of the finest early English work in the country. The splendid chantry was built to house the tomb of the De le Warrs, who originated in Isfield. Thomas West, 12th Baron De la Warr (1577–1618) was Governor of Virginia in 1609, and did a great deal to ensure the survival of the colony. A later generation of the family produced John West, Governor of New England and New Jersey in 1737.

◂ CHILHAM
Kent *6 TR05*
When you can see Chilham through the crowds of people that go there, you can only stand and marvel; so much beauty, and so unspoiled. The village is built around a square, with the church at one end. Behind it, the Queen Anne rectory makes a nice contrast with the half-timbered Tudor and Jacobean houses nearby. In Chilham Castle grounds (OACT) a falconer gives demonstrations at certain times in summer. Sir Dudley Digges built the castle and was buried in the church in 1639. He was greatly interested in the colonization schemes of his time and helped to send Henry Hudson on his exploration in the north west. Cape Digges and Digges Island in Arctic Canada are named after him. His son, Edward, settled in Virginia where he became Governor.

CHILTERNS, THE
Buckinghamshire *4 SU79*
Rightly described as an Area of Outstanding Natural Beauty, the Chilterns run in an arc from Goring in the Thames Valley to a point near Hitchin in Hertfordshire. Although the woodlands are not as extensive as they once were, the hills are noted for their beech trees. The name of the county may well be derived from the old word for beech tree, *buccan*. One of the highest points is Coombe Hill (853ft). Admirable walks are available. Around the High Wycombe area, the old rural craft of chairmaking once flourished. Traditional Windsor chairs are made of beechwood, with ash and elm used for the bow and seat.

◂ CHIPPING CAMPDEN
Gloucestershire *10 SP13*
The word 'chipping' is Old English for 'market' or 'trading centre'. Chipping Camden's speciality in the 15th and 16th centuries was wool. The fleece was brought to the 14th-century Woolstapler's Hall, which is now a museum. Many prosperous-looking stone houses have survived to lend character to this attractive old market town, and the Market Hall (NT) is a fine Jacobean building. Near Chipping Campden is the house Burnt Norton which gives title and inspiration to the first of T S Eliot's *Four Quartets*.

CHIRK
Clwyd *14 SJ23*
The small village of Chirk is the gateway to the beautiful Ceiriog Vale. The castle (NT) is a fine border stronghold with four massive drum towers around its courtyard. It was begun in 1310 on a fortress given to Roger Mortimer, a local baron who helped overthrow Llywelyn the Last (the last Welsh Prince of Wales) during the wars with Edward I. The castle had a succession of owners including Thomas Seymour, husband of Queen Catherine Parr, and Robert Dudley, Earl of Leicester, but it has been occupied by the Myddleton family since 1595. Thomas Myddleton was a businessman, Lord Mayor of London and an original shareholder in the East India Company; he was also responsible for the publication of the first pocket Bible in Welsh in 1630. Over the years the castle has been much altered; it contains a notable collection of Restoration furniture and portraits. Its magnificent 18th-century wrought iron gates are the work of Robert and John Davies of Croes Foel near **Wrexham**, whose work adorns many churches and great houses in the border country. The Shropshire Union Canal is carried close to Chirk on an impressive aqueduct built by Thomas Telford; it passes through the Vale of Ceiriog to **Llangollen**.

Nearby at Glyn Ceiriog, a beautifully situated village $5\frac{1}{2}$ miles west, The Hughes Institute has a tablet to Thomas Jefferson commemorating his Welsh ancestry. There are other memorials to many Welsh poets and to George Borrow.

CHORLEY
Lancashire *14 SD51*
Chorley, an industrial town, was the birthplace in 1819 of Henry Tate. Having made his fortune from sugar, he used some of his wealth to endow the Tate Gallery in London. Ten minutes' walk from the town centre Astley Hall, an exquisite Renaissance structure, stands beside a lake and has collections of furniture, pottery and paintings. Chorley was almost certainly the birthplace of Captain Miles Standish, military commander of the *Mayflower*. However, records of his birth are inconclusive and he

claimed to be descended from another, wealthier, branch of the Standish family (**see** Wigan).

CHRISTCHURCH
Dorset   *3 SZ19*
The River Stour which forms a boundary between the two, has, perhaps, saved Christchurch from being engulfed by its neighbour **Bournemouth**. Both the Avon and Stour meet here – hence the town's original name of Twynham. The name Christchurch comes from a story about the building of the church. The townspeople had decided on St Catherine's Hill for the site, but every night their building materials were removed and when a beam that had been cut too short was mysteriously lengthened, they decided that Christ himself had intervened, built their church on the new site and renamed their town. The priory church has a magnificent Norman turret on the north transept. The Red House Museum contains interesting exhibits from the excavations at Hengistbury Head. Between Christchurch and Bournemouth is Tuckonia (OACT), which has scale models of famous buildings.

CHYSAUSTER
Cornwall   *1 SW43*
Chysauster (AM) is one of the few Iron Age settlements where not only the outlines of the houses but also a clearly identifiable village street can be seen. The village, set high on a hillside, seems to have been inhabited between 100 BC and AD 300. The village was not fortified, but the house walls were massive, probably as a defence against the weather. Each of the houses opened on to a central courtyard, and each had its own terraced garden. A short distance away were tin mines, suggesting that the inhabitants were miners.

• CIRENCESTER
Gloucestershire   *3 SP00*
In Roman times Cirencester was the second most important city in Britain, after London, and the many relics of its Romano-British heritage are displayed in the Corinium Museum – *Corinium Dobunnorum* was the town's Roman name. There is also an amphitheatre just outside the town. Cirencester's fortunes declined in the Anglo Saxon period, but in the Middle Ages it became wealthy again when the wool trade came to the Cotswolds, and as one of England's largest wool

Cirencester House from the tower of the parish church

markets, justified its claim to be the 'Capital of the Cotswolds'. Its magnificent parish church, much enlarged in the 15th and 16th centuries, is nearly as big as a cathedral. From the market place, the three-storey porch, with its superb fan-vaulting, and the soaring tower, are a beautiful sight. Inside are many monuments and brasses to the wool merchants. The peal of 12 bells is the oldest in the country, there is a valuable collection of silver, and beautiful stained glass in the east and west windows. Ciren-cester House is not open, but the park, with its avenue of chestnut trees, is.

John Masefield (1878–1967) lived at Pinbury Park near Sapperton, west of Cirencester, during World War II.

CISSBURY
W Sussex   *5 TQ10*
An Iron Age fort, on the downs just to the north of Worthing, Cissbury (NT) was occupied from the 5th century BC until the middle of the 1st century AD. It is an enormous fortress, and it has been estimated that 60,000 tons of chalk were needed to construct the ramparts.

CLEOBURY MORTIMER
Shropshire   *9 SO67*
Locals claim this attractive old place to be the birthplace of William Langland, one of the great English medieval poets, who wrote his masterpiece, *Piers Plowman* in the 14th century. No

evidence has been found, but one of the east windows in the church is dedicated to the poet. Appropriately it shows Piers dreaming his dreams. The wooden church spire has an interesting twist to it, and has defied all efforts to straighten it.

CLIVEDEN
Buckinghamshire   *5 SU98*
Cliveden House (NT) is flanked on one side by the Thames, on the other three by woodland. Built in 1851, it is the third house of its name to be erected on the site. Home of the Astor family, it was famous for 'the Cliveden Set', which – aided by Dawson of *The Times* – thought it knew what was best for Britain in the 1930s. Nancy, Lady Astor, was a political hostess of great influence, and Britain's first woman MP, representing Plymouth from 1919 until after World War II. Cliveden House was given to the National Trust in 1942 by Lord Astor, son of William Waldorf Astor of New York, with the condition that it be used to promote Anglo-American friendship. It is now used by Stanford University as a study centre. The House was also the site of the Canadian Red Cross Memorial Hospital. 50,000 Canadian wounded were treated in hospitals erected here in two world wars. There is also a cemetery. The Canadian government gave the hospital to Britain in 1946 but it is no longer used.

CLOUDS HILL
Dorset *3 SY89*
This cottage (NT) a mile north of Bovington Camp in Dorset, was rebuilt by T E Lawrence (of Arabia) in 1923, who lived in it when he was serving with the Royal Tank Corps. In a letter, he described it as 'very quiet, very lonely, very bare' and listed the contents as 'a bed, a bicycle, three chairs, 100 books'. He seldom slept here, but used it as a retreat. It was from Clouds Hill that, at 11.30am on 13 May 1935, he set off on his motorbike for the village of Moreton; on his return he swerved to avoid two errand boys, was thrown off, and died at eight o'clock on the following Sunday.

CLOVELLY
Devon *1 SS32*
Possibly the prettiest coastal village in Britain, it occupies one cobbled street that runs down a steep, wooded slope to the shore. Sleds towed by donkeys were used for carrying loads, as the motor car has not been allowed to intrude. Clovelly was restored by Christine Hamlyn (the Hamlyns were lords of the manor) in the early 1920s.

Clovelly

CLYDEBANK
Strathclyde *22 NS56*
In 1871, Clydebank amounted to no more than a farm. Later that year, James and George Thomas moved in and began to establish a shipyard. In 1882, the American firm of Singers built a sewing-machine factory and the last traces of rural life were swept away. In 1899, John Brown and Co from Sheffield acquired the shipyard. Among the famous vessels built there were the *Lusitania*, *Queen Mary*, *Queen Elizabeth*, and the *QE2*.

COBHAM
Kent *6 TQ66*
Cobham Hall, (OACT holidays), now a girls' school, is one of the largest historic houses in Kent. The village is chiefly famous for its church, which contains an unrivalled collection of memorial brasses to members of the Cobham family. Owletts (NT) is a charming Jacobean house nearby, and the Leather Bottle, an interesting old public house, was featured by Dickens in his comic masterpiece, *The Pickwick Papers*.

COCKERMOUTH
Cumbria *18 NY13*
A fine 18th-century house on Main Street was the birthplace (NT) of the poet William Wordsworth in 1770, and is now a museum devoted to his life and works. The town is a very old one, and an excellent centre for touring the Lake District.

COCKLEY CLEY
Norfolk *12 TF70*
Here can be seen a full-scale reconstruction (OACT) of an Iceni encampment – showing how the tribe of Queen Boudicca lived 2000-odd years ago. A museum in one of the old cottages fills in some of the details.

COLCHESTER
Essex *12 TM02*
When the Emperor Claudius received the surrender of the British kings here in AD 43, Colchester had been an inhabited site for something like 1000 years. It was at that period named *Camulodunum*, and was the capital of Cunobelin (Shakespeare's Cymbeline), ruler of south-east England and the most powerful man in pre-Roman Britain.

The Roman city, the first they founded in Britain, was sacked by Boudicca and the Iceni, but after her defeat, it was eventually rebuilt as a walled city and became one of the most important centres of Roman administration. Parts of the walls may still be seen, and the arch of the Balkerne gate remains, which marked the entrance of the Roman road from London. The many Roman remains are the nucleus of the museum contained in the massive keep of the Norman castle, built in about 1085 on the vaults of the Roman Temple of Claudius. In the medieval period, Colchester was a centre of the cloth industry and many Flemish refugees settled here in the 17th and 18th centuries, in the area around West Stockwell Street known as the Dutch Quarter. This has been restored, but much of the town centre is now a modern shopping precinct. After the decline of the wool trade, Colchester developed an engineering industry. In the 1960s the University of Essex was established in Wivenhoe Park, its four stark concrete towers already a local landmark. As a fishing and trading port, Colchester is no longer significant, but its oysters were famous even in the Roman period.

Several early Pilgrims came from Colchester, which has connections with Thomas Beach. 5½ miles east of Colchester, the splendid Perpendicular church at Great Bromley, with its buttressed and pinnacled tower, has a memorial window to early emigrants to America.

COLYFORD
Devon *3 SY29*
Colyford is the birthplace (c 1559) of Sir Thomas Gates, who sailed with Drake in punitive actions against the Spanish in 1585; on this voyage he visited the ailing Roanoke settlement. Later he became involved with two of the New World companies, sailing with Sir George Somers (of nearby **Lyme Regis**) to Bermuda where they were wrecked. Relieved by Lord De la Warr, Gates returned to England to sail once more for the Virginia colony, where he was Governor from 1611–14. Known as 'Honest' Tom Gates, he was well respected, and left the colony in a sound economic state. Just to the north, Colyton has connections with the Pole family, and was the home of Lady Jane Grey's father.

Beer, a pretty coastal village beside Seaton on the Roman Road from Lyme Regis to Exeter, 2 miles south of Colyford, was once notorious for smugglers. The Bovey House Hotel there dates from Tudor times – its secret hiding places a legacy of smuggling. A splendid cliff walk via Beer Head, a 400ft chalk cliff, leads to Branscombe, 3 miles along the coast.

COMPTON BEAUCHAMP
Oxfordshire *4 SU28*
A mile or two to the south of the village lies a megalithic long barrow named Wayland's Smithy (AM). In Norse legend, Wayland was the blacksmith of the gods, and manufactured swords and armour that rendered their users invincible. Using coins left for the purpose he also, according to local legend, shod horses that were left there overnight.

COMPTON CASTLE
Devon   *2 SX86*
Compton Castle (NT) is Devon's most impressive fortified manor house, and has been the home of the Gilbert family and their descendants for 600 years. Sir Humphrey Gilbert (1539–83) founded the Newfoundland Colony in 1583, but was lost in the Atlantic returning to England. He was the half-brother of Sir Walter Raleigh and together they played a major part in colonial expansion during the reign of Elizabeth I. A generation later, Raleigh Gilbert founded Sagatohoe County, Maine in 1607. Compton is in the parish of Marldon, and the parish church contains many memorials to the Gilberts.

Ipplepen, a neighbouring village, was the birthplace of Christopher Avery, a local weaver who sailed to Massachusetts with John Winthrop. His descendants remember him as a typical 'puritan, magistrate and Indian fighter'; however, Avery favoured the established Church of England, and a greater freedom for the population of Massachusetts.

CONISTON
Cumbria   *18 SD39*
The village, which lies beside Coniston Water, is dominated by the summit of the Old Man of Coniston, 2627ft above sea-level. John Ruskin, the 19th-century writer, lived on the east side of the lake in a house called Brantwood (OACT) which contains many relics and pictures. Coniston Water has been used for attempts to break the World Water Speed Record – sometimes with tragic results. Donald Campbell was killed here in 1967, when his jet-powered boat *Bluebird* went out of control at over 300mph.

CONWY
Gwynedd   *13 SH77*
This was the third of Edward I's great castles (AM), built on a rocky site defended by both river and sea. With its massive battlemented walls and eight commanding drum towers, it is one of the best preserved of all the medieval castles. The old town, situated at the mouth of the Afon Conwy, is still surrounded by medieval walls. Among the few ancient houses that survive are Aberconwy (NT) a 14th-century house used for exhibitions of the life of the town, and Plas Mawr, one of the finest extant examples of an Elizabethan town house. The Conwy estuary is spanned by three bridges, the most impressive

Coniston Water from Brantwood

being Telford's great suspension bridge, built in 1826. On the picturesque quayside is Britain's 'smallest house' (OACT), a Victorian fisherman's cottage.

The Canadian painter Robert Harris came from Caerhun on the western slopes of the Conwy valley. His parents emigrated to Canada in 1856. He and his brother, an architect, are particularly associated with Prince Edward Island.

COOKHAM
Berkshire   *4 SU88*
This very pretty Thames-side village has been immortalized in the works of Stanley Spencer, one of the greatest modern British painters. Some of the best of his works can be seen in the small art gallery. The old ceremony of swan-upping takes place near Cookham and swan-upping on the Thames is the theme of one of the best known of Spencer's paintings.

CORBRIDGE
Northumberland   *19 NY96*
Half a mile away lies the Roman camp at *Corstopitum*, the ancestor, perhaps, of this very pleasant, stone-built market town, where the road still crosses the Tyne on a bridge built in 1674 (the only bridge to survive the

great Tyne flood of 1771). The Roman camp (AM) was initially a cavalry depot, then in AD 140 it was modified to serve as a base for operations against Scotland; there is an excellent museum on the site. Of the old buildings in the town, the pele tower of Low House and the fortified vicarage, reminders of fierce border raids, are particularly interesting. At Newton, 3 miles to the east, the Hunday National Tractor and Farm Museum has, among other items, more than 250 tractors and engines.

CORFE CASTLE
Dorset   *3 SY98*
One of the most impressive ruins in southern England, Corfe Castle (NT) was the work of William I. Earlier, at a hunting lodge on the site, the Saxon King Edward ('The Martyr') was murdered in 978. His stepmother wished to seize the throne for her 11-year-old son Ethelred (the Unready). King John added to the saga of villainy when he used the Norman castle as his treasure-house and prison. The final infamy came in the Civil War – when, after the Roundhead forces had failed to reduce the castle, a member of the garrison turned traitor and let them in. Corfe Castle Museum contains many items of local interest.

CORWEN
Clwyd *13 SJ04*
The wooded scenery of the beautiful
Dee valley surrounds this small town
overlooked by the Berwyn Mountains.
It was here that the foundations of the
first Welsh National Eisteddfod were
laid in 1789, when the first public event
was held at the Owain Glyndwr Hotel.
This is the heart of Glyndwr (Owen
Glendower) country. His estates were
nearby, and a groove in the lintel of the
church door was supposedly made by
a dagger flung by him in a fit of rage.

In the parish church 5 miles north
east at Bryneglwys is the Yale Chapel.
The ancestral home and birthplace of
Elihu Yale's father is 2 miles north east
of the village at Plas-yn-Yale.

COSFORD
Shropshire *9 SJ70*
Cosford Airfield has a fascinating
Aerospace Museum. The array of
aircraft includes the World War II
Spitfire, Mosquito, Messerschmitt, and
V1 and V2 rockets. The British
Airways collection and a Moon Buggy
reflect less bloodthirsty achievements.

▲ COTSWOLDS
Gloucestershire *3, 10*
The Cotswold hills extend from near
Bath in Avon across to north
Oxfordshire and part of
Northamptonshire. At first, their
wooded slopes descend steeply to the
Severn Vale. Later, however, they
seem to shake off the trees as they roll
towards the Midland plain. Near
Cheltenham Spa, and, again, on the
high ground above Broadway, they
reach heights of over 1000ft.

Drystone walls, towns and villages
built exclusively either from silver-grey
or yellowish limestone (all of it
quarried locally), characterize the
Cotswolds. Although the wool
industry has gone into a decline sheep
continue to roam the hills, and the
manufacture of cloth has survived in
the area around Stroud.

COUGHTON COURT
Warwickshire *10 SP06*
Built in the 16th century and
approached by way of a majestic stone
gatehouse, Coughton Court (NT) was,
for many years, the home of the
Throckmorton family. One of the
most anxious moments in the history
of this formidable house occurred on 5
November 1605, when the wives of
several gunpowder plot conspirators
waited anxiously for news of their
husbands. Before the year was over,

most of them had become widows. But
the dramas, so far as Coughton Court
was concerned, were not yet ended.
During the Civil War, it was occupied
by Roundhead forces, bombarded by
the Royalists, and finally abandoned in
flames. When James II left the country,
the house was pillaged. In the 18th and
19th centuries it was remodelled.

↘ COVENTRY
W Midlands *10 SP37*
Coventry began in the 7th century,
when an Anglo Saxon convent was
erected somewhere near the present
city centre. Four centuries later,
Leofric, Earl of Mercia, built a
Benedictine abbey, and the town began
to grow. The story of his wife, Lady
Godiva, riding naked through the
streets, with only her long hair to
preserve her modesty, first came into
circulation in 1235.

The 19th century, that great age of
innovation, brought the manufacture
of sewing machines and cycles to the
city – and then came the motor car. In
1898, the Daimler Company produced
Britain's first horseless carriage in
Coventry. From then onward,
Coventry was a strong magnet,
attracting labour from all over Britain.
The Museum of British Road
Transport tells Coventry's part in the
history of transport. The Herbert Art
Gallery and Museum has collections of
social history, art and archaeology.

On a terrible night in November
1940, German bombers blew the heart
out of the city. The church of St
Michael – which, in 1918, had been
promoted to the status of cathedral –
was almost totally destroyed. Only the
medieval tower and the spire survived.
Work on building the new cathedral
began in 1951, when Basil Spence (later
Sir Basil) won an open architectural
competition for his striking modern
design which incorporates the ruin of
the old. Perhaps the best-known
feature is the altar tapestry by Graham
Sutherland, but there is much else
about the building that is equally
distinguished, in particular the
beautiful modern stained glass.
Canadians gave over £30,000 towards
building the new Coventry Cathedral.
Canadian spruce was used for the roof.

The phrase 'sent to Coventry'
originated in 1647. It referred to a
group of Royalists who had been
captured by Parliamentary forces in
the Midlands, and were imprisoned in
Coventry's Church of St John. They
had, to put it another way, been
banned from society.

Coventry has 3 main American
connections. John Davenport, the first
minister in New Haven, Connecticut,
was born here in 1597, emigrating in
1637. Henry Sewall, father of Judge
Samuel Sewall, was a native of
Coventry and emigrated to America in
1661. Samuel Sewall was educated at
Harvard College and became Judge of
the Supreme Court of Massachusetts.
Known as the 'last of the Puritans',
Sewall helped to establish an Indian
Meeting House. He was also the
author of the first anti-slavery tract to
be published in America, and a
journal describing the Massachusetts
colony as it was then. In 1689 Sewall
made a visit to Coventry, staying at the
King's Head, now demolished. On his
return to America he was to preside at
the notorious witch trials in Salem.

Theophilus Eaton was the son of the
vicar of Holy Trinity Church, now
Coventry Cathedral.

COXWOLD
N Yorkshire *15 SE57*
One of the most idyllic villages in this
part of Yorkshire, Coxwold's broad
main street is lined by warm-toned,
stone cottages, set back behind the
wide green verges so often found in
rural Yorkshire. In the 18th century,
the village was fortunate to have as its
clergyman the eccentric and writer
Laurence Sterne, whose comic
masterpiece, *The Life and Opinions of
Tristram Shandy* had been published
just before his appointment to
Coxwold. He named his house Shandy
Hall (OACT) and it now belongs to
the Sterne Trust who have preserved
and renovated both it and the garden.

CRAIGIEVAR CASTLE
Grampian *27 NJ51*
With its profusion of turrets and
conical roofs, Craigievar (NTS) is the
perfect example of a Scottish Baronial
building. It is a tower-house, six
storeys high and its internal decoration
has changed as little as its exterior
since 1626 when the building was
finished. All the rooms are decorated
in the Renaissance manner and the
ceiling of the Great Hall is particularly
magnificent.

CRAIL
Fife *24 NO60*
A picturesque fishing port of crow-
stepped red-tiled houses that used to
be the haunt of smugglers, Crail is now
more popular with artists and tourists.
The town was exporting salt fish to
Europe as early as the 9th century, and

Robert the Bruce gave it a royal charter in 1310 – conceding that its inhabitants might trade on the Sabbath. 200 years later, John Knox made plain his views on the matter, preaching from the pulpit of the parish church. A large blue stone at the gateway to the church is said to have been thrown by the devil from the Isle of May, 5 miles away. The church was founded in the 12th century and contains one of the town's two ancient Pictish crosses.

CRANBORNE CHASE
Dorset & Wiltshire *3 ST91*
The Chase, which covers 100 square miles, used to be a hunting forest, often visited by King John, to hunt fallow deer. In time, the forest laws, instead of keeping poachers out, allowed the Chase to become a haven for all kinds of miscreants, until in 1830 Parliament passed a special Act to bring it under the control of the law. Cranborne itself, once the centre of the Chase Court, is now a picturesque village, its attractive houses grouped around a village green. The gardens (OACT) of Cranborne House were laid out in the 17th century by the 1st Earl of Salisbury.

CRASTER
Northumberland *24 NU22*
Craster Tower is the home of the Craster family, who built the village's harbour in memory of a brother who had been killed in Tibet. 1½ miles north, on high cliffs overlooking the North Sea, are the ruins of the 14th-century Dunstanburgh Castle (AM, NT), parts of which were built by John of Gaunt, Duke of Lancaster. It was dismantled after the Wars of the Roses and the ruins feature in several of J M W Turner's paintings. Embleton, 2½ miles north west, and Craster, are associated with Viscount Grey of Falloden, the statesman and naturalist. Embleton was the birthplace of W T Stead, opposer of the Boer War, and of prostitution. Stead died aboard the *Titanic*, and was the first crusading journalist to have a commemorative statue erected to him in America.

Just south of Craster is Howick Hall, home of the Greys. The fourth Earl Grey died in 1917. He was Governor-General of Canada in 1904–11. He was a man of vigour and sometimes eccentric vision. One idea he had was to put up a new, even bigger, Statue of Liberty in Quebec. This was never done. Canada's Grey

Cup recalls his name. His grave is in the churchyard at Howick.

CREDITON
Devon *2 SS80*
Crediton used to be the cathedral city of Devon in Saxon times until Exeter took over its position. Tradition says that St Boniface, who brought Christianity to the Germans, was born there in the 7th century.

Creedy Park between Sandford and Crediton, was the ancestral home of Sir John Davie, one-time town clerk of Groton, Connecticut, and a Harvard graduate. The family held a baronetcy, conferred for their contribution to the Exeter cloth trade. In 1707 Davie came to take over his inheritance; the house, now rebuilt, is still the home of the Creedy family.

CREWKERNE
Somerset *3 ST40*
A pleasant little town with traditions stretching back to Anglo Saxon times, when it had the right of minting coins. In later centuries, it became associated with the flax-weaving and sail-making industries. The sails for HMS *Victory* were made here – and those for several Americas Cup contenders. The 15th-century church has fine stained glass. Clapton Court Gardens are 2½ miles south west.

CRICCIETH
Gwynedd *13 SH53*
A very pleasant and unspoiled little resort, with the Lleyn peninsula providing shelter from north-westerlies, and Snowdonia supplying a

dramatic backdrop to the north. The Welsh royal line of Llywelyn had already built a castle (AM) before the arrival of Edward I: the English king merely had to strengthen it, but over the centuries it crumbled into ruins. David Lloyd George, who lived nearby at **Llanystumdwy**, married a Criccieth girl.

CROMARTY
Highland *30 NH76*
Cromarty is a small seaport on the Black Isle – serving Easter Ross and guarding the entrance to the Firth of Cromarty. Much of the town is now devoted to North Sea oil. Hugh Miller, the geologist, was born here in 1802. The cottage (NTS) in which he was born contains a collection of geological specimens. 7 miles west of Cromarty is Balblair, the home of the Rosses, who included Colonel George Ross, a signatory of the Declaration of Independence.

CROMER
Norfolk *12 TG24*
Like so many resorts, Cromer was a small fishing village until the 19th century, when the railways brought sea fever to Britain. You can still see the original cottages clustered around the church of Sts Peter and Paul – the tower of which, 160ft high, is the tallest in the county, and there are several fine Victorian hotels, a pier, and a small zoo. A former Cromer lifeboat coxswain, Henry Blogg, saved so many lives that the lifeboat is named after him. Crabs are a popular local delicacy.

Cromer

CROMFORD
Derbyshire *15 SK25*
It was here, in this stone built
Derbyshire village, that Richard
Arkwright built, in 1771, the world's
first mechanized textile factory. The
original mill survives, a rather grim-
looking place that appears to have
been designed along the lines of a
fortress. The Arkwright Society is
undertaking renovations of the mill,
warehouses and watercourses. The
church and some of the cottages were
built for his workers.

CRUDEN BAY
Grampian *28 NK13*
Before World War II, Cruden Bay was
notable for its huge hotel and its
championship golf course. The golf
course remains. The pipeline from the
Forties North Sea oil field comes
ashore here. The 1697 Bishop's Bridge
spans Cruden Water – and the ruins of
Slains Castle are 'built upon the
margin of the sea, so that the walls of
one of the towers seem only a
continuation of a perpendicular rock,
the foot of which is beaten by the
waves'. So wrote Dr Johnson, who
was much impressed by the castle,
which was given by Robert the Bruce
to the Earl of Errol in the early 14th
century. Dr Johnson was equally
impressed by the Buller's of Buchan, a
vast amphitheatre, gouged out by the
sea, 'which no man can see with
indifference who has either sense of
danger or delight in rarity'.

CULLODEN
Highland *26 NH74*
A sad place this: a windswept ridge of
moorland (NTS) with a plantation of
trees where cairns commemorate 1200
Highlanders who were slain in 40
minutes by the Duke of Cumberland's
forces at the Battle of Culloden on 16
April 1746.

CULROSS
Fife *23 NS98*
A beautifully restored 16th- and 17th-
century small Scottish town, once
famous for its baking plates ('girdles')
and its trade in coal and salt. Culross
Palace (AM) is small as palaces go, but
it was large enough to merit a visit
from James VI (James I of England).
The Study (home of the National
Trust for Scotland's representative),
the Nunnery, Parley Hill House and
the Manse are among other buildings
that should be seen. The delightful
snuffmaker's house bears the
inscription: 'Who would have thocht

it, noses would have bocht it'. The
choir of the old abbey (AM) is used as
the parish church.

CULZEAN CASTLE
Strathclyde *22 NS20*
The castle (NTS) was built in the 1780s
by Robert Adam for the 10th Earl of
Cassillis. Built around an earlier
Kennedy stronghold, it is one of the
finest Adam houses in Scotland. Set in
a 565-acre park, the castle overlooks
Culzean Bay. In 1945 a suite was
presented to General Dwight D
Eisenhower by the people of Scotland
in gratitude for his role as Supreme
Commander of the Allied Forces.
Eisenhower stayed here during his
Presidency.

CYFARTHFA
Mid Glamorgan *8 SO00*
Cyfarthfa ironworks was founded in
1765. 30 years later, the management
was taken over by an ironmaster
named Robert Thompson Crawshay.
Crawshay was a remarkable man. He
built a church with an impossibly
Gothic tower, and then carried
Victorian Gothic to the wildest
extremes in the creation of his home,
Cyfarthfa Castle. He was also an
excellent photographer, who
summoned his daughters with the blast
of a whistle whenever he needed
models. You can see his work in the
castle's museum. The epitaph on his
gravestone, 'God Forgive Me',
suggests that he was not above self-
criticism.

CYNWYL ELFED
Dyfed *7 SN32*
Set in a lovely wooded valley where the
Rivers Duad and Nant Coch (it means
'red stream') meet, the village is a sheer
delight – very neat and trim and
artlessly pleasing to the eye. A number
of Roman relics have been dug up in
the vicinity – including a golden figure
of the goddess Diana. In a farmhouse
called Y Gangell about a mile away,
the Rev D H Elved Lewis was born.
This grand old man lived to be 94 and
became one of the most famous writers
of Welsh hymns. A museum in the
house honours his memory.

DALKEITH
Lothian *24 NT36*
An old mill and market town on the
banks of the River Esk, Dalkeith serves
the mining and agricultural districts
south east of Edinburgh. Dalkeith
Palace – now occupied by a computer
firm – originally a 12th-century
building, was remodelled in about
1700 by Vanbrugh for Anne, Duchess
of Buccleuch. Widow of the rebel
Duke of Monmouth, she was the
Duchess of Scott's *Lay of the Last
Minstrel*. The grounds (OACT) of the
palace contain a beautiful Adam
bridge and an orangery. The ruins of
12th-century Newbattle Abbey are just
south of the town.

DANBY
N Yorkshire *20 NZ70*
A stone village at the head of Danby
Dale in the lovely Esk Valley, Danby's
main street leads from the wooded
river up on to Danby Low Moor.
Danby Lodge, a former shooting
lodge, is the information centre for the
North York Moors National Park.
The Eskdale railway line passes
between the village and the restored
Saxon church of St Hilda where Canon
Atkinson, author of the classic *Forty
Years in a Moorland Parish*, was
buried in 1900.

DARLINGTON
Co Durham *20 NZ21*
This busy industrial town on the River
Skerne was first a Saxon settlement,
growing into a market and later a
textile town. Then came the Stockton
and Darlington railway. The world's
first public passenger train, hauled by
Stephenson's Locomotion No 1 (1825),
ran from Darlington, and was financed
by the Quaker businessman, Edward
Pease. This and six other locomotives
can be seen at the Darlington Railway
Museum which is housed in the North
Road Railway Station. The poet Ralph
Hodgson was born here in 1871. He
later visited America and Japan.

DARTINGTON HALL
Devon *2 SX76*
Since 1925 this fine 14th-century quadrangular manor house by the River Dart has been an innovative centre for education. It has a progressive school, a college of arts and music, and units for adult education and young people. It is also a centre for practical research into rural industries. The Trust which controls the hall was set up by the Americans Mr and Mrs Leonard Elmhirst, and runs farms and forests, a textile mill, shops, engineering, horticultural and glass making companies.

DARTMOOR
Devon *2 SX58*
The 'moor' often conveys a feeling of ill-omen, of high moorland, broken by jagged granite tors; of mist-shrouded blanket bog where unwary travellers are sucked to oblivion. Whether this impression comes from the landscape itself, from the grim prison at **Princetown**, from the Sherlock Holmes adventure related in *The Hound of the Baskervilles*, or from all three is hard to tell. In 1951 Dartmoor was made a National Park, covering 365 square miles. Its boundaries are, roughly speaking, Okehampton in the north, Ivybridge in the south, Tavistock in the west and Bovey Tracey in the east. Most of the land is over 1000ft above sea-level and the highest points are High Willhays (2038ft) and Yes Tor (2030ft). Fourteen rivers rise on Dartmoor, among them the Teign, the Bovey and the Dart. Some of the most beautiful scenery is to be found in the wooded river valleys – for example around Dartmeet, where the waters of the East and West Dart join. Here and at Postbridge are fine examples of the ancient clapper bridges – rough slabs of granite supported on boulders, many of which date back to medieval times and beyond, when tin was extensively mined here. Human settlement dates back to the Bronze Age, and the area is rich in prehistoric monuments and remains; probably the best-known village site is at Grimspound. Tin-mining flourished throughout the medieval and Tudor periods, when the tinners virtually ruled the moor, with stannary towns at **Plympton**, **Tavistock**, Ashburton and Chagford, and their own 'parliament', held in the open on Crockern Tor for more than 400 years – from 1305 to 1749. Nowadays, apart from the tourists and the 'wild' ponies (which in

Flore Wharf, Daventry

fact all have owners and are rounded up in the autumn 'pony drift'), the only business is that carried on by the army who use large parts of the moor as a firing range. Among the most famous beauty spots are Lydford Gorge (NT); the ancient Wistman's Wood, where gnarled oak trees shelter a nature reserve; Yarner Wood, also a nature reserve in oak woodland; Dunsford Nature Reserve on the River Teign, and, finally, that famous village **Widecombe-in-the-Moor**.

DARTMOUTH
Devon *2 SX85*
Dartmouth has been an important harbour since Roman times. Many historic naval expeditions sailed from here, including Edward III's fleet which sailed from Dartmouth to assist in the siege of Calais in 1347. Three centuries later in 1620, the Pilgrim ships *Mayflower* and *Speedwell* paid an unscheduled call at Dartmouth for repairs. Many passengers were so discouraged by the problems that the captain, Christopher Martin, confined them to quarters to prevent desertion. After a week, the ships were able to sail on to Plymouth. A plaque commemorating the Pilgrims is at the entrance to Bayard's Cove, where one of Henry VIII's defensive castles also stands. A waterside path leading to the

sea passes St Petrox Church, rebuilt in the Gothic style in 1641–2. Nathaniel Hawthorne's mother was a member of St Petrox's parish. Alongside the church are the remains of Dartmouth Castle, a 15th-century cliff castle, which faces Kingswear Castle. The two castles were built so that a thick chain could be stretched across the estuary to hold off enemy ships in time of war. Other notable features of Dartmouth include the Butterwalk, a row of 17th-century houses on granite pillars with carved overhanging storeys; the Castle Hotel – mostly 19th century – incorporates a 17th-century coaching inn; the local Maritime Museum; Agincourt House, which dates from 1380; the Customs House, built in 1739; and beside the river is the first effective steam engine, invented by Dartmouth-born inventor Thomas Newcomen (1663–1729). Overlooking the town stands the Britannia Royal Naval College, which has trained naval cadets since 1905.

Chaucer spent some time in Dartmouth and possibly used a local man as the model for the shipman in the *Canterbury Tales*. Flora Thompson, the author of *Lark Rise to Candleford*, lived for many years in Dartmouth. Nearby Greenway House was the birthplace of Sir Humphrey Gilbert. From 1942–4 Slapton Sands further down the coast was used as a training ground for American soldiers. In 1944 they finally embarked from Dartmouth for France.

A car ferry regularly crosses the River Dart and there are frequent boating trips along the beautiful estuary.

Dartmouth owed much of its wealth to the Newfoundland fish trade and John Davis from Sandridge Farm just north on the Dart River was active in exploring that coast. He led 3 expeditions in the attempt to open up a North-West Passage and explored the area of Davis Strait. He was christened in Stoke Gabriel parish church and was killed at sea in 1605.

DAVENTRY
Northamptonshire *10 SP56*
Daventry has a long history. Just east of the town the earthworks of Borough Hill are the remains of an Iron Age fort. There are magnificent views despite the many radio masts of Daventry broadcasting station. During the Civil War Charles I is alleged to have stayed at the Wheatsheaf Inn while his soldiers camped outside the town before the Battle of Naseby. John

Washington lived here before going to America. Daventry has a pleasant market place and an 18th-century Moot Hall.

Four miles south the church in the beautiful park of Fawsley House has stained glass containing the heraldic shields of the Washingtons. These are said to have come from **Sulgrave** when part of the manor house was pulled down. Flore, 5 miles south east of Daventry, was the birthplace of John Adams who followed George Washington as President of the United States. His ancestors are said to have lived in the thatched Adams Cottage.

DAWLISH
Devon *2 SX97*
This seaside town, between the Exe and Teign estuaries, is like Lyme Regis but in a lower key. Jane Austen liked both; Dickens made Dawlish the birthplace of Nicholas Nickleby, hero of his novel of the same name. The town is set slightly back from the sea, and the elegant Regency houses on the Strand were built, unusually, facing inland. Also unusual is the fact that the main railway line runs between the town and sands on its lovely route between Exeter and Newton Abbot. It was here that Brunel tried out his experimental atmospheric railway. Dawlish's deep red cliffs, sandy beaches and colourful, luxuriant vegetation attract as many visitors as anywhere in Devon. The town's main feature is the Lawn, landscaped gardens created in 1803 round Dawlish Water. On the sand-dune peninsula of Dawlish Warren are a national wildfowl reserve, holiday camps and caravan sites.

DEAL
Kent *6 TR35*
Deal's past importance as a Channel port is recalled by the many ships visible from the seafront as they hug the coast, avoiding the Goodwin Sands 5 miles offshore. A plaque on the front commemorates the place where Julius Caesar is said to have landed in Britain in 55 BC. The Time Ball Tower previously informed shipping of Greenwich Mean Time. The town has many narrow old streets, giving character to the former smuggling stronghold. Deal Castle (AM 1540), one of a chain built by Henry VIII to guard against Catholic invasion, was designed like a Tudor rose to give it maximum defensive power. Walmer Castle (AM), Deal's twin, also dates from the 16th century and is the official

residence of the Warden of the Cinque Ports, an important group of five ports in the medieval period. Now the sea has receded and only Dover is now important. The Wardenship is honorary.

William Penn sailed for America in 1682 after writing his *Last Farewell to England* here.

DEAN, FOREST OF
Gloucestershire *9 SO61*
These 27,000 acres of largely wild woodland, lying between the Severn and the Wye, are a reminder of the days when England was largely afforested. Since Roman times, the area has housed a wide variety of rural industries and many survive today – iron-making, charcoal-burning, stone-quarrying, and coal-mining. Traces of the Roman occupation of the area abound; there are temple ruins at Camp Hill and remains of paved Roman roads at Blakeney and Little Dean. Ancient rights peculiar to the area still remain, bearing testimony to its independent nature. They range from the Foresters' right to graze sheep, to 'pannage' – the right for pigs to forage for acorns from the many mature oaks which, with birch, beech and holly (some holly trees in Speech House Wood are over 300 years old), form the backbone of the forest.

DEDHAM
Essex *12 TM03*
The area around Dedham, now designated as an area of outstanding natural beauty, has many connections with the artist John Constable. His father owned a water-mill in Dedham, which stood on the banks of the Stour on the site of the present Victorian replacement. The parish church also features in many of Constable's paintings. The artist attended Dedham grammar school. Opposite the beautiful church is Sherman's Hall, a house which derives its name from the Dedham family, ancestors of both Roger Sherman, a signatory to the Declaration of Independence, and of William Sherman, the Civil War General. The churchyard contains tombs of the family. It was the Reverend John Sherman who emigrated to America in 1634, following several of the original settlers who left the village in 1631. The Victorian artist Sir Alfred Munnings, President of the Royal Academy, lived in Castle House where some of his works are on display (OACT).

DENBIGH
Clwyd *13 SJ06*
The ancient market town contains many buildings of historical interest. Denbigh Castle, built by the Earl of Lincoln in 1282, featured in many battles during the conflicts between England and Wales. It was finally ruined by Parliamentary troops in 1660, but eight towers and the gatehouse still stand. Leicester's Folly is the ruined wall of an unfinished church begun in 1579 by Dudley, Earl of Leicester, to replace St Asaph's as the cathedral after the Reformation. Below the castle once stood the cottage where H M Stanley the explorer was born. He was born John Rowlands in 1841, of a poor family. When his father died Stanley went to the workhouse at St Asaph from where he ran away to sea. He eventually went to New Orleans where he was befriended and adopted by a merchant called Henry Stanley, from whom Rowlands took his name. Stanley became an American citizen and was sent by the editor of the *New York Herald* to find David Livingstone in Africa. It was he who pronounced the immortal greeting 'Dr Livingstone, I presume.' Stanley later returned to England and became an MP.

• DERBY
Derbyshire *10 SK33*
This ancient county town on the River Derwent officially became England's newest city in 1977. Originally a Roman camp, Derby had 6 churches at the time of the Norman Conquest. It was here that Bonnie Prince Charlie gave up his march to London with 17,000 troops. Its cathedral, built in Henry VII's reign, was rebuilt, except for its 178ft pinnacled tower, in 1725 by James Gibb. Inside you can see the tomb of Bess of Hardwick, Countess of Shrewsbury, who died in 1607.

The industrial revolution resulted in great expansion in Derby. Porcelain was first made here in 1756 by William Duesbury. The right to use the Crown insignia was granted by George III: Queen Victoria later allowed the company to add Royal to the title. Royal Crown Derby is still produced. In 1908 Rolls-Royce opened its car-manufacturing works here. There is a monument to Sir Henry Royce in the Arboretum – the largest of many urban parks, which also has a plaque stone. Rolls-Royce aero engines are among the many exhibits in the Industrial Museum, housed in an 18th-century silk mill.

DEVIL'S BRIDGE
Dyfed *8 SN77*

Devil's Bridge is one of the most
popular Welsh tourist attractions. Set
in the splendid Welsh hill country are a
series of dramatic waterfalls – most
spectacular are the 300ft Mynach Falls
falling from the River Mynach to meet
the Rheidol. The village has 3 bridges
built above each other; the earliest and
lowest of these is the stone Devil's
Bridge, probably 12th century.
According to legend, the bridge came
into being when an old woman whose
cow was stranded on the opposite side
of the gorge bargained with the Devil.
The narrow-gauge railway from
Devil's Bridge to Aberystwyth is the
last outpost of steam on British Rail.

Four miles away is Ponterwyd
where writer George Borrow stayed on
his journey through Wales in 1854,
recorded in *Wild Wales*.

DEVIZES
Wiltshire *3 SU06*

An old market town on the edge of
Salisbury Plain, set in rich agricultural
country near the source of the
Wiltshire Avon, Devizes had a
Norman castle, built by the Bishop of
Salisbury on the boundary between
manors, so giving the town its name.
The original castle was destroyed by
Cromwell: the present one is 19th
century. The town has some fine old
houses and inns, including the Bear

The longest flight of locks in Britain, Devizes.

Devil's Bridge

Hotel which enjoyed such a high
reputation in the 18th century that the
landlord put posts across the Plain
from Salisbury to guide fashionable
travellers.

From Caen Hill, Devizes, the Kennet
and Avon Canal descends 230ft, by
means of 29 of Rennie's locks – the
longest flight in Britain.

DIDCOT
Oxfordshire *4 SU59*

The Great Western Railway put
Didcot, until then a quiet, thatched
village with a handsome 15th-century
church, on the map. Today the Great
Western Society (OACT) is a poignant
reminder of the glories of 'God's
Wonderful Railway'. Its painstakingly
restored collection of steam
locomotives, rolling stock and other
railway memorabilia is overlooked by
the 20th-century power station, a
landmark from all over the Berkshire
Downs.

DINGWALL
Highland *26 NH55*

Macbeth, in real life, is said to have
ruled Ross-shire from here before he
captured the Scottish throne from King
Duncan in 1040. Of the castle, ruined
since 1700, only traces remain. Once a
Royal Burgh and the county town of
Ross and Cromarty, Dingwall lies near
the mouth of the River Conon and is a

popular Highland holiday centre. The
harbour was built by Thomas Telford.

DISLEY
Gtr Manchester *15 SJ98*

Lyme Park (NT), former ancestral
home of the Leghs, an influential
family of Cheshire landowners, lies in
1300 acres of deer park high on the
edge of the Derbyshire moors. The
quadrangular Elizabethan mansion
with its 18th-century Palladian front, is
one of the finest in England. Many of
the rooms have elaborate decorations
and carvings in the Jacobean style. The
Peak Forest Canal passes near Disley.

DISS
Norfolk *12 TM17*

Narrow, twisting streets lead
enticingly off the triangular market
place, at the top of which stands the
15th- and 16th-century St Mary's
Church, where John Skelton, poet and
tutor to Henry VIII, was once rector.
The town has an attractive Victorian
Shambles, and a wealth of Georgian
and earlier buildings. The 18th-century
Lacon's Maltings and the ancient
timbered Dolphin and Greyhound Inns
represent both ends of the brewing
process.

Five miles west is Redgrave, where
Sir John Holt, who inspired abolition
by declaring free a Virginian slave
brought to Britain, is buried.

THE SCOTTISH LEGACY

Alexander McDougall, born in Islay, was a major-general in the War of Independence, a leader of the 'Sons of Liberty', and the first American to be imprisoned for his speeches in favour of Separation from Britain. General Hugh Mercer was 'out' with Prince Charlie as a surgeon in the '45; after emigrating to America he met a young colonel named George Washington and became one of his closest friends; Mercer's death at the battle of Princeton was one of the first personal tragedies that the War brought to the American Commander-in-Chief. Arthur St Clair, one of Washington's generals, came from Thurso. Fort Moultrie in Charleston Harbour is named after William Moultrie, the son of a Scots physician who held it against Sir Peter Parker, and whose accurate shooting, in the words of an old song, 'propelled him – Sir Peter Parker – along on his bumpus'.

American Independence owes a great deal not only to the Scots generals but to ano-

ther Scot active at sea, John Paul Jones, the first Commodore of the American Navy. The son of a gardener, he was born at Kirkbean, down on the Solway; he went to sea when he was a boy and later took a job on a slave ship dealing in human cargoes, and in the course of it he attacked and killed one of the crew. He emigrated to America for the good of his health, to save himself perhaps from the gallows, and he added the surname Jones to the original John Paul. When the War broke out he became a captain in the tiny American fleet. His most spectacular victory was in a French ship, based on the French port of Brest – France by this time was an ally of the United States – the *Bonhomme Richard*, a one-decked twelve-pounder, with which he engaged the British *Serapis*, a two-decked eighteen-pounder. He ran the *Richard* alongside, lashed her to the *Serapis* stem to stern, and forced the British to strike colours after a three-hour fight. Better remembered

down on the Solway, however, is a raid he carried out on his own home town and the stealing of the Earl of Selkirk's silverware. He went on, having helped America to win her freedom, to serve Catherine the Great of Russia, and ended his days in beggarly fashion in Paris. Nevertheless he too is an American hero.

Scots have played a notable part in American life. It was George Rogers Clark, whose family came from south-west Scotland, who opened up the areas now known as Michigan and Illinois; Scots like Sam Houston helped to free Texas from Mexico, and one of his henchmen was Jim Bowie, killed at the Alamo. From the Gorbals of Glasgow came Allan Pinkerton, who organized the Secret Service Division of the US Army in 1861, and who got Lincoln safely from Chicago to Washington to take up the Presidency when almost everyone thought he would be killed passing through Maryland. Pinkerton founded the first great

detective agency in America, although his sons made it primarily an industrial protection agency which was often used to thwart strike action by labour unions.

In one of these ugly industrial towns perhaps the best known name of all occurs. It was in the great steel city of Pittsburgh – for which Washington had fought it out with French and Indians 130 years before – that Andrew Carnegie of Dunfermline (where Robert the Bruce is buried) built his industrial empire. He was a weaver's son who went to America in 1849 when he was fourteen; his hand-loom weaver father was broken by the slump of the 1840s. He had nothing to give to America – except hard work and enterprise and skill; he was hard-headed but kind-hearted. By the age of thirty, he was earning 50,000 dollars. He amassed a huge fortune, and was at one moment – in 1901 when he sold his company to US Steel for $400 million – the richest man in the world. Part of his success was due to hard work and quickness. Part was due to chance – as in his meeting with Tom Scott of the Pennsylvania railway, who made him his assistant. Part was his quick realization of the value of money; when he got, as a boy, his first dividend payment from the ten shares he owned, he said, 'Eureka, here's the goose that lays the golden eggs.' The Radical Chartist of Dunfermline soon became an American Republican Conservative. On his death in 1919 he gave it all away – $350 million of it – in benefactions, not least to Dunfermline, to the Universities of Scotland, and to ensure that every town in Scotland had a public library. The scale of the generosity, and the size of the endowment, have ensured an easy access to books – and indeed the Government aid to book-buying in Scotland has as a

Action between *HMS Serapis* and *Bonhomme Richard* by William Elliott

The birthplace of Andrew Carnegie in Dunfermline, Scotland

result never needed to be so generous as it is in England. Carnegie in fact made philanthropy a Big Business. And what he did, many other American industrialists have gone on doing – Rockefeller and Ford, Harkness and Guggenheim to name only the more conspicuous. Indeed to attempt to catalogue the Scottish contribution to America is to engage on an endless quest, for it is a mark of pride in America to be able to claim Scottish blood, or to invent it.

The Scots constitute the third largest ethnic group in Canada, and one in every second New Zealander has Scottish blood. In the US they were – according to an American Census Bureau Report in 1979 – the best educated and the best paid of all US immigrants – and have provided one in four of the Presidents, one in three of the Secretaries of State and one in two of the Secretaries of the Treasury.

The return of the wanderer is not only a romantic pilgrimage, to the tune of the Eriskay Love Lilt or the Skye Boat Song, but, as with Carnegie, the wish to end his days in his native land as Laird of

Skibo, in his carefully restored castle (and carefully built waterfall) on the Dornoch Firth in Sutherland. One of the striking features of the years since the end of World War II has been the growth of American industrial interest in Scotland. Over two dozen firms have set up plants in Scotland, which now has its own 'Silicon Glen'. Partly it was due to the danger that American firms might lose sales from the British shortage of dollars, partly to the Scottish reputation for good craftsmanship, partly no doubt to sentiment. Today these companies still employ some 25,000 workers; in Dundee, in the Vale of Leven, in Livingston, Hillington and Greenock; producing cash registers and trucks, domestic appliances and clocks, electric shavers and typewriters and microchip devices of all kinds. And it is of course a two-way traffic, for Harris and Border tweed and whisky in great quantities go the other way, aided these days by ease and frequency of travel. The relatively cheaper American industrial methods, too, are influencing Scot-

land: more mechanization, better lighting, new ways of handling employees. Before long there will have to be a third Baseball League, the Scottish, in addition to the American and the National.

The ties, then, between Scotland and America are ties of trade and traffic, as well as ties of language and race, and of a shared belief in the place of the individual in society. They wed Calvinist ethics and the gospel of work, via the radical Chartism of Carnegie's Dunfermline, to American business opportunities, the machine and skill of invention, and its exploitation. When in 1941, Harry Hopkins, President Roosevelt's special agent, was looking around Britain and judging the War effort, his last engagement was in Glasgow, and Tom Johnston, Mr Churchill's Secretary of State for Scotland, gave a small and very private dinner party for him in the North British Station Hotel in Glasgow which the Prime Minister, Mr Churchill, attended. Mr Johnston had discovered that Mr Hopkins' grandmother had come from Auchterarder. He asked him

to say a few words. What he said was:

In the language of the old book to which my grandmother from Autcherarder, and no doubt your grandmother too, Mr Chairman, paid so much attention, that,' and here Hopkins paused and looked straight down the table at Churchill, 'Wheresoever thou goest we go, and where thou lodgest we lodge, thy people shall be our people, thy God our God, even unto the end.'

He sat down in dead silence. Mr Churchill's eyes welled up in tears. Here was the first news that the United States was throwing its weight in with the Allied side. There is a lot to be said in America, as in the old country, for having a Scottish grandmother.

One Scotswoman makes a dramatic appearance in American history. Fanny Wright (1795–1852) was born in Dundee to a wealthy father but orphaned at three. She saw the US as her dream of Utopia, and founded the commune of Nashoba in Tennessee, where slaves would work and, through their products, secure their freedom. Nashoba's failure was in part the result of the scandals caused by her avowal of free love. She was bitterly attacked as 'the high priestess of infidelity'. Her attacks on the capitalist system led to a crusading, notorious and erratic career, and a totally unsuccessful marriage. She was indeed one of America's first feminists, whose triumph perhaps was the First Women's Rights Convention at Seneca Falls in 1848. Mercy Otis Warren and Abigail Adams would have been proud of her, but – disappointed?

Further Reading

Joseph Frazier Wall, *Andrew Carnegie* (OUP 1970).

DITCHLEY PARK
Oxfordshire *10 SP32*
This classical 18th-century mansion
(OACT) was built for the Lee family,
next to Wychwood Forest, a former
Royal hunting ground and now a
nature reserve; the house is therefore
the ancestral home of General Robert
E Lee who signed the surrender of the
South in the American Civil War.
Ditchley was designed by James Gibbs,
architect of Oxford's Radcliffe
Camera. The interior design is mainly
by William Kent, and the parkland by
Capability Brown. Sir Henry Lee, an
occupant during the Civil War appears
in Sir Walter Scott's novel *Woodstock*
(1826), set during this period. In
wartime Ditchley Park was Sir
Winston Churchill's weekend HQ; it is
now used as an Anglo-American
conference centre.

DOBWALLS
Cornwall *1 SX26*
You can enjoy a taste of America here:
at the Forest Railroad Park (OACT)
you can ride on a miniature railway
modelled on the Denver and Rio
Grande's Cumbres Pass route and on
the Union Pacific's Sherman Hill route.
The miniature-scale locomotives climb
the steepest gradients on any miniature
railway system in Britain.

The Thorburn museum and gallery
displays the work of the great local
bird painter (1860–1935).

DOLAUCOTHI
Dyfed *8 SN64*
The Romans mined for gold here, in
the 2577 acres of the Dolaucothi Estate
(NT), exploiting the Ogofau
goldmines, originally worked by the
Celts. Water for the mines was
brought from the Cothi and Annell
rivers by a 7-mile-long aqueduct,
channelled along the hillsides. The
Romans had departed by the middle of
the 2nd century AD but the mines were
reworked as recently as 1939.

DOLGELLAU
Gwynedd *13 SH71*
A compact, slate-built market town in
the Mawddach Valley, Dolgellau lies
at the foot of the impressive Cader
Idris (2927ft). There is a handsome
seven-arched 17th-century bridge
across the River Wnion and Maesgwm
Visitor Centre 6 miles to the north
recounts the story of the local
goldmines, worked from 1844 until the
middle of the 20th century, and which
provided the gold for the wedding
rings of both Queen Elizabeth II and

Dorchester High Street

the present Princess of Wales.
Dolgellau is a well-positioned base
from which to explore the Snowdonia
National Park.

DOLLAR
Central *23 NS99*
Dollar is known for its Academy,
designed in 1818 by William Playfair,
architect of the Royal Scottish
Academy and the National Gallery.
The beautiful Dollar Glen (NTS) runs
between the Burn of Sorrow, flowing
through Windy Pass, and the Burn of
Care, on the slopes of the 2111ft King's
Seat. Of ruined Castle Campbell
(AM), on a crag in Dollar Glen, you
can still see a 15th-century tower and a
16th-century wing.

DONCASTER
S Yorkshire *15 SE50*
Charles Dickens watched the 110th St
Leger from the 18th-century Italianate
grandstand at the Town Moor
racecourse. However, Doncaster's past
as a Roman town and a farming centre
for the neighbourhood rural lowlands
is largely obscured by its present
industrialized status. Nevertheless,
there are some fine Georgian buildings,
in particular the 18th-century mansion
house, and some 19th-century
churches. Doncaster was the home
town of John Carver, a well-known
Massachusetts pilgrim. 2 miles away,
Sprotborough has a fine parish church
where Francis Washington is buried. 6
miles east south east is Finningley,
where Martin Frobisher, the first
explorer of the American far north,
lived in the manor house. Finningley
was the site of a large RAF aerodrome
during World War II. 7½ miles south of

Doncaster is **Austerfield**, home of
William Bradford.

The Thelluson Chapel of the Parish
Church at Adwick le Street contains
the alabaster tomb of James
Washington, collateral ancestor of
George. A carved crest of stars and
stripes is on the side of the tomb, and
the church registers contain records of
the family. At Adwick upon Dearne,
6½ miles west of Doncaster, the
Washington Arms appear on the pulpit
in the parish church.

DORCHESTER
Dorset *5 SY69*
Dorchester is still the busy market
town of Thomas Hardy's *The Mayor
of Casterbridge*. The lines of its main
streets were laid out by the Romans
and there is an excavated Roman
house in Colliton Park, and the
County Museum contains many items
relating to Roman and pre-Roman
times. In Colliton Walk there is a
statue of Hardy, who was born near
Dorchester at Higher Bockhampton.
Hardy's Cottage has been preserved by
the National Trust. Hardy spent his
later years at Max Gate, just outside
Dorchester – he had trained as an
architect and designed the house
himself. The Dorset County Museum
also has a room reconstructed as
Hardy's study.

In 1685, Dorchester hosted the
Bloody Assizes at which Judge
Jeffreys presided. His courtroom was
allegedly in the Antelope Hotel. The
trial resulted in 74 people being
hanged, and many more were
transported to the colonies. The
famous trial of the Tolpuddle martyrs
took place in the Shire Hall in 1834,

which is now a TUC memorial. The early trade unionists were transported to Australia but following a reprieve 4 years later, five of the six families involved emigrated to Ontario, where their descendants still live.

Maumbury Rings, a Stone Age circle, adapted by the Romans for use as an amphitheatre, seated 10,000. As late as 1767, the site was used for public executions or 'hanging fairs'.

Dorchester has a number of American connections. The Reverend John White, founder of Dorchester, Massachusetts, was born here. White raised money and procured a charter from Charles I for a group of 140 emigrants who made up the Massachusetts Bay Colony of New England. They were instructed to build a church upon landing; the Church of Dorchester, Mass, is still known as the daughter of John White. The group sailed in 1630, in the *Mary and John*. White is buried in St Peter's Church where the Massachusetts State flag flies. Another early settler John Endicott was probably born in Dorchester. The Dorset Military Museum has a display of Major John André, hanged as a British spy at Tappan in 1780. West of Dorchester at Kingston Russell, John Rothrop Motley, the historian and American ambassador, lived in the manor house.

DORKING
Surrey *4 TQ14*
This small market town was settled by Saxons and raided by Danes; the Roman road Stane Street runs through the town and forms a crossroads with the old Pilgrim Way, which ran along the Downs to Canterbury. Local shop owner William Mullins left Dorking with his family to sail in the *Mayflower*. Mullins's daughter, Priscilla, made famous by Longfellow, was courted by the ship's cooper John Alden, his rival being Miles Standish. Alden was the last surviving signatory to the *Mayflower* Compact.

Dickens stayed at the White Horse Inn in Dorking, and it is thought that this was the model for the Marquis of Granby Inn of *The Pickwick Papers*. Disraeli wrote part of *Coningsby* (1844) at Deepdene, and dedicated it to the owner, Henry Hope. The house is no longer there, but the wooded terrace behind it is owned by the National Trust. The writers Gissing and Meredith, lived in Dorking, Meredith is buried in the town cemetery.

One mile north the hotel at Burford Bridge is where Lord Nelson finally separated from Lady Nelson in 1800, following his affair with Lady Hamilton. It was here 18 years later that Keats completed 'Endymion'. Near the hotel stepping stones cross the River Mole to **Box Hill**.

DORNIE
Highland *25 NG82*
A crofting village in a beautiful mountain setting where Lochs Long and Duich meet. Eilean Donan Castle (OACT) is strikingly situated just south of the village on a small island where the two lochs meet a third – Loch Alsh. A 13th-century fortress of the Mackenzies, the castle was destroyed in 1719 by the English warships in their assault on the occupying Spanish Jacobites. It was restored in 1932.

DORNOCH
Highland *30 NH78*
This Royal Burgh and former county town of Sutherland was the site of Britain's last recorded judicial execution for witchcraft. The town's cathedral is a notable landmark, built originally in 1224. The golf course was first used in the early 17th century.

DOVEDALE
Derbyshire & Staffordshire *15 SK15*
The Twelve Apostles, Jacob's Ladder, Lion Rock, Dovedale Castle, Lover's Leap, Viator's Bridge, Tissington Spires: Dovedale's rocks have weathered into strange shapes. There are caves, too, notably Dove Holes and Reynard's Cavern. Dovedale itself is a lovely, twisting limestone gorge in the gentler south of the Peak District National Park, beloved of fishermen since Izaak Walton's day.

• DOVER
Kent *6 TR34*
At the end of the beautiful North Downs, famous for its white cliffs, Dover is an ancient port linking Britain with the Continent. It was once the walled Roman town of *Dubris*, and the start of the Roman road, Watling Street. Later it was the chief of the Cinque ports, which, in return for special privileges, were expected to supply ships for the Royal fleet. The Kentish town is dominated by its castle (OACT), a largely Norman construction built on a Roman site, and incorporating the Roman *pharos* – the oldest stone lighthouse in Britain.

Dover Castle

A tunnel system under the castle walls was dug during the Napoleonic wars, and used as air-raid shelters in the last war. Near the castle is the restored Saxon church of St Mary in Castra; St Edmund's Chapel near the Municipal Library is a rare surviving 12th-century wayside chapel. The Roman Painted House (OACT) is famous for its wall paintings.

Dover has had many literary visitors passing through on their way to the Continent. Byron spent his last two days in England here, waiting for a favourable wind which would enable him to sail to Europe, away from his creditors. Fenimore Cooper, author of *Last of the Mohicans* (1826), and another American, N P Willis, the journalist and poet, spoke highly of the comforts of Dover. In 1852, Wilkie Collins stayed with Dickens in Camden Close. Henry James had lodgings in Marine Parade, where he began *The Bostonians*.

Dover is famous for two historic channel crossings – the first by Captain Matthew Webb, who in 1875 became the first cross-channel swimmer. In 1905 Louis Bleriot landed here after making the first flight across the Channel. An aeroplane-shaped granite memorial marks the site where he landed in North Fall Meadow.

The Dover Patrol Monument in St Margaret's Bay commemorates the joint naval organizations of British and American destroyers against German mines and submarines during World War II. President Woodrow Wilson, the first American President to visit Britain while in office, landed here in 1918. On William Penn's instructions Dover, Delaware, was laid out following the plan of Dover.

DOWNE
Kent   *5 TQ46*
Downe House was the home of Charles Darwin, author of *The Origins of Species*, the theory of evolution by natural selection. Darwin's granddaughter, Gwen Raverat, recaptures family holidays here during the 1890s in *Period Piece* (1952). The house is now owned by the Royal College of Surgeons and is preserved as a museum.

DREWSTEIGNTON
Devon   *2 SX79*
Drewsteignton sits on a ridge above the Teign gorge and on the edge of the Dartmoor National Park. The yellow-lichened 15th-century tower of Holy Trinity Church overlooks the granite

and thatch houses clustered round the attractive village square.

One mile south west of the village is Castle Drogo (NT). Completed in 1930 and designed by Sir Edwin Lutyens, this extravagantly towered and battlemented building is built on a 900ft-high granite rock with extensive views of Dartmoor.

Two miles further south west in the upper reaches of the Teign valley lies Chagford, one of Devon's medieval stannary towns. Middlecourt Manor there was associated with John Endecott, the first official Governor of Massachusetts. His son and father both lived there. In 1628 Endecott led a group of emigrants from **Weymouth**, Dorset to Salem, Massachusetts, taking over the Governorship from Roger Conant, another Devon man. A list preserved in Chagford shows the contributions sent by parishioners to America in 1652 for the propagation of the Gospel.

At Dunsford, 5 miles east of Drewsteignton, there is a memorial to Bishop Francis Fulford of Montreal (1830–60) in the parish church. The Tudor house of Great Fulford is 2 miles north west of Dunsford.

DROITWICH
Hereford & Worcester   *9 SO96*
Droitwich stands on an agricultural plain by the River Severn and overlies a substantial bed of rock salt. It was the Romans who discovered this natural resource which was Droitwich's earliest wealth. Later the market town was developed into an elegant spa by the 19th-century businessman John Corbett. He built the original St Andrew's Brine Baths and, more flamboyantly, a château nearby at Dodderhill. This he designed in the style of Francis I. It is now the Château Impney Hotel. Some half-timbered buildings survive in the town, which also has several interesting churches. St Andrew's and St Peter's are both medieval. The former has a chapel to St Richard de Wych, Droitwich's patron saint (the more recent church of the Sacred Heart and St Catherine is known for its striking mosaics depicting the life of Sir Richard). In St Peter's the Pilgrim Father, Edward Winslow, was baptized in 1595. Winslow, a printer, was born in Careswell, now a suburb of Droitwich. Edward was the eldest of five sons and three daughters. He sailed with one of his brothers in the *Mayflower*, and was followed soon by three others. He is the only member of

the Mayflower Company of whom a contemporary portrait survives; this hangs in Plymouth, Massachusetts.

Droitwich lies in an area rich in magnificent country houses. Salwarpe Court, 2 miles south west, and Westwood Park, 2 miles north west, are both Elizabethan. To the west are 18th-century Ombersley Court, and the grounds of Witley Court, with their elegant classical fountains (the latter house was destroyed by fire earlier this century).

DRUMNADROCHIT
Highland   *26 NH52*
On the west bank of Loch Ness, the village is a centre for monster-spotting. Here you can see the official Loch Ness Monster Exhibition. Urquhart Castle (AM), one of Scotland's grandest ruins, overlooks Loch Ness from Strone Point.

DRYBURGH ABBEY
Borders   *24 NT53*
The ruins of this 12th-century abbey church (AM) stand quietly now amid lawns and trees beside the River Tweed. It was not always so: three times in the 14th century and again in the 16th the abbey was plundered and burned, victim of the constant border raids and skirmishes between England and Scotland. The cloisters have survived well, but except for the transept, little remains of the church itself. Sir Walter Scott is buried here. The abbey also contains the tomb of Field Marshal Haig, Commander-in-Chief of the British Army in World War I.

DUDLEY
W Midlands   *9 SO99*
Countryside and industry coexist in Dudley, former capital of the Black Country, and an iron town since the Middle Ages. The solid ruins of the castle (AM), built largely in the 13th and 14th centuries, with walls 8ft thick in places, stand on a wooded hill. Dudley Zoo lies in the castle grounds and below are the remains of a Norman priory. Underneath Castle Hill runs the Dudley Canal, its 1¾-mile tunnel recently reopened and now offering trips on the *Electra*, the world's first electric narrow boat. At the Tipton end of the tunnel is the Black Country Museum, an open air village.

DUMBARTON
Strathclyde   *22 NS37*
Formerly Dunbreaton – Fort of the

Britons – the centre of the ancient kingdom of Strathclyde, and now a Royal Burgh, the town is commanded by one of Britain's oldest strongholds, Dumbarton Rock, rising 240ft above the Rivers Clyde and Leven. The remains of the castle (AM) perched on the Rock include the Wallace Tower (he was imprisoned here in 1305).

Alexandria, 3 miles north near the southern end of Loch Lomond, was connected with the Smollett family. Tobias Smollett, who wrote *Humphry Clinker* and *Roderick Random*, spent much of his childhood here. As a young man Smollett became a ship's surgeon on the HMS *Cumberland*. He was at the siege of Cartagena in 1741 and returning via Jamaica he met and married Nancy Lascelles, the daughter of a planter.

- **DUMFRIES**
Dumfries & Galloway *18 NX97*
Sir Walter Scott's 'Queen of the South' is a prosperous and handsome county town and market centre; with old sandstone buildings and large parks. The town's focal point is the Midsteeple, the municipal building dating from about 1707. On its walls are an ell measurement and a table of distances that includes Huntingdon – for the 18th-century cattle drovers made long journeys. Dumfries Burgh Museum and Camera Obscura (1835–6) occupy an old windmill. The stone Old Bridge replaced the wooded one erected by the Lady Devorgilla, wife of John of Balliol, founder of Balliol College, Oxford. Here you can see the old Bridge House Museum, and downstream, the Caul, an 18th-century weir where salmon leap. The remains of the collegiate church of Lincluden College (AM) stand on the west side of the river. Burns House (OACT) is where the poet lived until his death in 1796. His Mausoleum is in St Michael's Churchyard.

DUNDRENNAN
Dumfries & Galloway *17 NX74*
Defeated at the Battle of Langside in 1568, and destined shortly after to be imprisoned in England, Mary Queen of Scots spent her last night on Scottish soil at Dundrennan Abbey (AM). This Cistercian foundation is now a ruin, thanks to the resourceful local villagers who used much of the abbey stone to build their own homes. Mary sailed from Port Mary, 2 miles south, for England to seek help from Elizabeth I who instead imprisoned her.

DUNDEE
Tayside *27 NO33*

Scotland's fourth largest city stands on the banks of the Tay, backed by the Sidlaw Hills. Dundee has been known since the 19th century for its jams – Mrs Keiller began making marmalade in 1797; for jute – its carpet industry still flourishes; and journalism – the ever-popular comics *Beano* and *Dandy* are published here. Since 1881 it has been a university city, and its royal charter dates back to the 12th century, at which time it had a castle and a monastery. A plaque on Castlehill marks the site of the castle, and commemorates William Wallace, who began his rebellion against the English by killing the son of Dundee's constable. Of the old town walls, all that remains is Cowgate Port (Wishart Ark). The Old Steeple, sole relic of St Mary's Church, typifies the fate of many of the city's old buildings: since Dundee was a strategic point in the defence of Central Scotland, it was fought over by English and Scots for more than 300 years. Much of what survived the many battles was in its turn pulled down to make way for industrial expansion.

A natural deep-water harbour on the Firth of Tay has made Dundee an all-cargo port, and an expanding base for the offshore oil industry. Its shipyards built the *Terra Nova* for Shackleton and the *Discovery* for Scott; they still do work on ships destined for voyages in polar regions.

The toll bridge across the Tay, opened in 1966, is one of the longest ($1\frac{1}{2}$ miles) river bridges in Britain, and links Dundee with Fife and southern Scotland. The railway bridge, on the main line between Edinburgh and Aberdeen, was opened in 1887 to

replace the one that collapsed in the 1879 disaster, made notorious by Dundee's self-styled poet, William McGonagall.

Dudhope Castle, now used as offices, was the home of the hereditary constable of Dundee, and was rebuilt in the 16th century when this office passed to the Graham family, by John Graham of Claverhouse, the 'Bonnie Dundee' made famous by Sir Walter Scott. On the opposite side of the city, the ruined Mains of Fintry Castle was also a Graham stronghold.

PLACES TO SEE
The Albert Institute houses the Central Museum and Art Gallery; among the exhibits to do with the city's maritime traditions is a rare astrolabe of 1555.

Barrack Street Museum covers the natural history of the lowlands and highlands.

Camperdown House Formerly the residence of the Duncans the house is now the centre for leisure activities (including a wildlife reserve) in the surrounding park.

HMS Unicorn Lying in the Victoria Dock, this early 19th-century wooden warship has been renovated as a floating museum.

Broughty Castle (OACT) Four miles east of the city, this 15th-century castle was rebuilt as a 19th-century estuary fort, has displays relating to the whaling industry, arms and armour, and natural history.

Central Dundee

DUNFERMLINE
Fife *23 NT08*
A royal burgh and ancient capital of Scotland, in the Kingdom of Fife, Dunfermline was the home of Scotland's kings from Malcolm III in the 11th century until the Union of the Crowns in 1603. Dunfermline Abbey (AM), in Pittencrieff Park, was founded in 1072 by Queen Margaret, wife of Malcolm Canmore. Robert Bruce is buried here and there is a shrine to Margaret, who was canonized in the 13th century. Pends Archway links the abbey to ruined Dunfermline Palace (AM). Malcolm Canmore's Tower, built in the 11th century, stands in the grounds of Pittencrieff House, now a museum.

Pittencrieff Glen, which has fine views of the abbey and the Forth Estuary, was given to Dunfermline by Andrew Carnegie, the millionaire philanthropist born here in 1835, who gave away nine-tenths of his massive fortune. He believed that the rich should distribute surplus wealth for the general good, the theme of his book *The Gospel of Wealth* (1889). He left Scotland for America with his family when he was 13. His endowments for libraries and educational foundations are vast. His birthplace and a museum overlook the park and are open to visitors.

DUNKELD
Tayside *27 NO04*
Birnam Hill (1324ft), Craig Vinean (1247ft), the wooded Craigiebarns (1106ft) and Newtyle (996ft) – each offer differing aspects of this attractive cathedral town set in the wooded Tay Valley. The lawn-surrounded cathedral ruins (AM) date from the 14th and 15th centuries. The cathedral was despoiled in 1689 at the Battle of Dunkeld. The National Trust for Scotland's Visitor Centre is in the converted 'Little Houses' which were rebuilt after the battle. At the Loch of Lowes Nature Reserve, a variety of wildlife can be observed.

DUNSTER
Somerset *2 SS94*
In this medieval, timbered village the Norman castle (NT) sits on a wooded, pyramid-shaped hill at one end of the village, and at the other end is Conygar Hill Tower (1775), a noted landmark for Bristol Channel shipping. The former Priory Dovecote (OACT), the distinctive eight-sided yarn market and the packhorse bridge (AM) across the River Avill provide a cross-section of English architectural styles between the 12th and 18th centuries.

DUNWICH
Suffolk *12 TM47*
In medieval times Dunwich was a prosperous port with its own charter, granted by King John, and rights over all wrecks on its shore, in return for payment of 5000 eels annually. It boasted nine churches in 1326 when three of them, together with 400 houses, were swept away by a storm. Over the years more of Dunwich has succumbed to the sea. However, the remains of the 13th-century Greyfriars monastery and the ruined chapel of the 12th-century leper hospital indicate the town's former architectural standing.

Dunwich was the birthplace of Sir George Downing of Harvard and Cambridge University, after whom Downing Street in London was named. Downing was the nephew of John Winthrop, Governor of Massachusetts. The town attracted several literary figures during the 19th century, among them, Jerome K Jerome and Henry James.

Dunwich Heath (NT) offers views of the coastal marshland, Minsmere Bird Reserve, and of Sizewell atomic power station.

DURDLE DOOR
Dorset *3 SY88*
West of the famous Lulworth Cove lie two bays, divided by a limestone headland in which the sea has cut an arch – Durdle Door. This is one of the most beautiful parts of the Dorset coast. There is sheltered bathing and a 5-mile footpath along the chalk cliffs.

DYMCHURCH
Kent *6 TR12*
This old smuggling port on the edge of Romney Marsh is now a holiday village with miles of beach, chalets and caravans. The famous Romney Hythe and Dymchurch miniature steam railway passes through here en route to Dungeness. It was for centuries the headquarters of the 'Lords of the Level', local governors of this part of Romney Marsh, who met in New Hall. A restored Martello tower (AM) is now a museum.

Durdle Door

DURHAM
Co Durham *20 NZ24*

Built on a wooded rock, lapped on three sides by the River Wear, Durham is one of the most splendidly sited of English cities. Dominating the sandstone outcrop, the dramatic outlines of cathedral and castle stand as a reminder of the great medieval strongholds of the Norman invaders. Durham was the only English city to be ruled as County Palatine by a Prince-Bishop, with his own army and privileges. The bishops retained this status, in name at least, until it was revoked by Act of Parliament in 1836.

The cathedral's defensive position, with the border country to the north as a second line of defence, was originally colonized by Saxon monks, particularly those driven from Holy Island by the Vikings. Their monastery grew into a cultural and religious centre and was the shrine of the two great Saxon saints of the North: Cuthbert, whose coffin, the story goes, rooted itself to this spot; and the Venerable Bede, whose bones were stolen from Jarrow by Durham's Sacrist. These ecclesiastical treasures ensured that Durham prospered on pilgrims' money.

The Saxon monastery has long vanished, but the tombs of St Cuthbert and Bede were housed by the Normans in the cathedral they built. It is a magnificent building, uniting strength and size with grace. The whole of its main structure was built between 1093 and 1133; its great central tower being rebuilt in 1470. Particularly striking are the huge decorated pillars; the first successful execution on a grand scale of ribbed vaulting; and the evocative 12th-century sanctuary knocker which gave fugitives the right of sanctuary once they had seized hold of it. Sadly, all the ancient woodwork, save for Prior Castell's four-faced 15th-century clock, was destroyed by the 3000 Scotsmen that Cromwell imprisoned here after the Battle of Dunbar. The Normans set Durham Castle (OACT) beside the cathedral and it proved to be the only northern castle never to fall to the Scots. Inhabited ever since the Prince-Bishops made it their palace over 900 years ago, the castle today, with its 19th-century keep, is part of the university. The challenge of expanding the university from its fortified setting, enhanced by the 18th-century houses in North and South Bailey, has exercised the minds of such modern architects as Ove Arup, who designed one of the bridges.

The city itself grew compactly around the fortified rock. Its downhill

Durham Cathedral

streets and steep winding alleys known as vennels, form one of the best townscapes in Britain, running past the 17th-century Bishop Cosin's House and the old grammar school, to the three old bridges across the Wear – Elvet, Prebends and Framwellgate. The 19th-century town hall was designed by the same architect who was responsible for the late-lamented Great Hall at Euston Station in London, and contains the relics of 'Lord' Tom Thumb, a tiny Polish violinist, just one metre tall, who died in 1837 aged 98.

Outside the city is the old Durham racecourse. Each year for one day this becomes the site for the world-famous Durham Miners' Gala with brass bands from all over the country. Also, 4 miles west is Ushaw College, which succeeded Douai, in France, as a training college for Catholic priests.

PLACES TO SEE
Durham Cathedral Tomb of the Venerable Bede, the great early English historian whose remains were brought from Jarrow in 1020. In the Monks' Dormitory Museum is the coffin of St Cuthbert and other cathedral treasures. In College Green, the cathedral close, are the Norman stables and monks' prison. In the cathedral cloisters there is a plaque commemorating John Washington, Prior of Durham, an early member of the first President's family. The Cathedral Museum contains two Washington seals.

Durham Castle (OACT) Two chapels, one 11th century, and the other 16th century with beautifully carved choir stalls. The outstanding features of the castle are Bishop Cosin's magnificent three-storey Black Staircase and the 15th-century kitchens. Bishop Cosin's Library, in Palace Green, contains portraits and original furnishings. Sir Walter Scott held a banquet to honour the Duke of Wellington in the Castle Hall in 1827, and he used the ballad 'Durham Garland' as the basis of his novel *Guy Mannering*.

Durham Heritage Centre The 17th-century church of St Mary-le-Bow now houses displays of the history and conservation of the city.

Saddler Street Nos 43–4 have restored their original 18th-century frontage, thought to have been a theatre box-office.

Archaeology Museum Reached by a riverside path, the museum is housed in an old fulling mill.

Durham Light Infantry Museum and Arts Centre As well as the history of the famous regiment, the building houses an Arts Centre.

Gulbenkian Museum of Oriental Art Unique in Britain – being the only museum devoted to this subject. Collections of Egyptian, Chinese, Japanese and Tibetan art, and jade, ceramics and sculpture.

E

EAST BERGHOLT
Suffolk *12 TM03*
John Constable was born here in 1776, the son of a local miller. The fortunes of East Bergholt flourished between the 13th and 16th centuries with the success of the wool trade – many of the village's fine old buildings date from this period. The village and surrounding landscape were made famous through the artist's paintings. Particularly well known is his picture of Flatford Mill, just a mile from East Bergholt on the River Stour. Constable worked here for a year before going to London to study art. Adjacent is Willy Lott's white cottage which often featured in Constable's work. Constable's family home no longer stands, but a plaque marks its former site. The parish church has memorials to both the artist and his wife, Maria. His parents are buried in the graveyard, as is Willy Lott.

The journalist and author Randolph Churchill lived here until his death in 1968. The grounds of his home have been relandscaped as Stour Gardens. 2½ miles north is Little Wenham Hall (AM), an example of very early English brickwork.

EASTBOURNE
Sussex *5 TV69*
One of the sunniest resorts in England, Eastbourne owes much to the Victorians who laid out many parks and gardens and built the pier. In the early 19th century, fortifications against the French included the Redoubt, transformed into a model village, aquarium, grotto and Services museum. The Royal Sussex Regimental Museum contains items relating to campaigns in India and to the Regiment's experiences in North America, where they fought at Bunker Hill, White Plains, Quebec and Louisbourg, and suffered heavy losses at Fort William Henry under Colonel Munro (who figures in James Fenimore Cooper's book *The Last of the Mohicans*). There is a model reconstruction of the Battle of Quebec. There is a museum of the RNLI, and housed in the Wish Tower, which incorporates a Martello tower, is the

Coastal Defence Museum. In the Towner Gallery are works of 19th- and 20th-century British painters and sculptors. Beachy Head, at nearly 600ft above sea-level, is one of the highest cliffs on the south coast. There are magnificent views from its top, from the **Isle of Wight** in the west to Dungeness in the east, and the beam of the lighthouse at its foot sweeps 16 miles across the English Channel.

Lord Willingdon, appointed Governor-General of Canada in 1926, lived north of Eastbourne at Ratton Hall, since destroyed. There is a bust in the Town Hall

EAST COKER
Somerset *3 ST51*
The home of T S Eliot's ancestor Andrew, who emigrated to America in the 1660s. The ashes of the American-born poet and Nobel Prize winner are buried, as he requested, in the Parish Church. There is a commemorative plaque inside the church. The second section of the *Four Quartets* (1944) was named after the village. East Coker was also the birthplace of the buccaneer and explorer William Dampier (1652–1715). Soon after he was orphaned at the age of 16, Dampier undertook his first voyage to Newfoundland, later sailing to the Gulf of Mexico and the East Indies. He explored the Australian and New Guinea coasts, and was navigator of the ship that rescued Alexander Selkirk, the real-life Robinson Crusoe. Dampier made important early contributions to the study of natural phenomena. Two of his works, *A New Voyage Round the World* (1697) and *A Discourse of the Winds*, are particularly noteworthy. East Coker's parish church contains an impressive monument to Dampier.

EAST DEREHAM
Norfolk *12 TF91*
East Dereham owes its origins to Saint Withburga who founded a nunnery here in the 7th century. The unusual town sign at the entrance to the market place depicts two does which, according to legend, came to the nunnery to give their milk during a famine, in answer to Withburga's prayers. St Nicholas' Church stands on the site of the nunnery, and William Cowper, the 18th-century poet is buried here. The parents of the author George Borrow (1803–81) lived in East Dereham. He was born in Dumpling Green, a suburb of Dereham, and spent much of his childhood there.

2½ miles north east is Swanton Morley, which has ancestral links with Abraham Lincoln. The remains of the home now belong to the National Trust. The Angel Inn was the home of Richard Lincoln in the 16th century. The pilgrim, Henry Ainsworth, was baptized here.

EAST GRINSTEAD
W Sussex *5 TQ33*
The old market centre of the town, which received its charter in 1221, still contains Tudor buildings. Sackville College (OACT), an early Jacobean almshouse founded by the 2nd Earl of Dorset in 1609, is still in use, retaining much of its original character. The Queen Victoria Hospital here treated more American airmen than any other British hospital during World War II. Many Canadian servicemen were also treated. The hospital was particularly noted for plastic surgery. A section of the hospital, opened by the Queen, was paid for by donations from 'grateful friends in America'. President Kennedy visited the town, attending Mass in the Roman Catholic church. Standen (NT), off the B2110 south of the town is a late Victorian house with decorations by William Morris.

Six miles west of East Grinstead is Wakehurst Place (NT, Gardens open all year), headquarters of the Canadian Armed Forces 1942–3.

EAST LINTON
Lothian *24 NT57*
Preston Mill (NTS), with its attractive pantiled roof, is the oldest working water-driven meal mill in Scotland, and dates from the 16th century. Also of interest is Phantassie Doo'cot (NT) which once housed 500 birds. Originally, it stood in the grounds of Phantassie mansion where the engineer John Rennie was born. Ruined Hailes Castle (AM), where Bothwell fled with Mary Queen of Scots, lies a mile away, and south of it rises Traprain Law, where a famous hoard of Roman silver was found.

EASTWOOD
Nottinghamshire *15 SK44*
A hilltop mining town, whose grimness and array of pit-head machinery contrast with the beauty of the surrounding farmland. This was the birthplace of D H Lawrence (1885–1930), the inspiration for much of whose work derived from this area. Lawrence was born at 8A Victoria Street, and lived at 28 Gardens Road, the 'Bottoms' of *Sons and Lovers*; the

Preston Mill, East Lynton

house has been restored. Eastwood is the 'Bestwood' of *Sons and Lovers* (1913), 'Woodhouse' in *The Lost Girl* (1920), and 'Beldover' in *Women in Love* (1920). Many local places feature in Lawrence's works, and he described the view from his house in Walker Street as 'the country of my heart'.

EBBW VALE
Gwent *8 SO10*
First coal-mining, then the steel industry have been the mainstays of Ebbw Vale. The town made the rails for the historic Stockton to Darlington railway, and was one of the first places to use the Bessemer process of converting iron to steel. Its name is forever linked with that of the great Labour politician Aneurin Bevan who was its MP for 31 years, from 1929 to 1960.

In neighbouring Brynmawr to the north east, the community was organized as a social experiment by Quakers. The American town and famous women's college take their name from here.

ECCLEFECHAN
Dumfries & Galloway *18 NY17*
Arched House (NTS), so called because it was built over a pond, was the birthplace in 1795 of the scholar Thomas Carlyle. His statue is a prominent sight in the village, and he is buried in the churchyard.

EGHAM
Surrey *5 TQ07*
At nearby Runnymede, King John was obliged to sign Magna Carta in 1215. The monument that marks what is thought to be the historic site was erected by the American Bar

Association. A plot of land opposite Magna Carta Island was given to the United States in 1963 and here stands the John F Kennedy memorial. The Runnymede Memorial is inscribed with the names of more than 20,000 Commonwealth World War II airmen who have no known grave. Over 3000 are from the Royal Canadian Airforce.

At Wraysbury, just north of Egham, William Pynchon, founder of Springfield, Massachusetts, is buried in the parish church.

ELLESMERE
Shropshire *9 SJ33*
This pleasant little market town lies at the heart of Shropshire's lake district, a tranquil region of nine lakes in the north west of the county. Some, such as Cole, Blake and Kettle Meres are small, wooded and more or less untouched by the 20th century; others, such as White Mere and The Mere, are used for sailing and other leisure activities; Crose Mere and Sweet Mere are well known for their bird life.

ELLISLAND FARM
Dumfries & Galloway *18 NX98*
Robert Burns, Scotland's national poet, lived in this Nithdale farmhouse from 1788 to 1791. It was here that he composed many of his poems, including the famous 'Tam O'Shanter'.

ELY
Cambridgeshire *11 TL58*
According to the Venerable Bede, Ely's name derives from the abundance of eels in the surrounding fens – these were an important part of the diet of the Saxon population of the area. Previously Ely was an island. It was here that Hereward the Wake held out

against the Normans until 1071, when they succeeded in building a road across the marshes. Begun in 1083, on the site of a 7th-century Benedictine monastery, the magnificent cathedral dominates the fenland. Notable are the octagonal lantern tower and the choir stalls, which are carved underneath, both designed by Alan de Walsingham; also the fine painted ceiling. Oliver Cromwell and his family lived in the old vicarage for 10 years when Cromwell was a tithe collector for the cathedral. The fens around Ely were drained in the 17th and 18th centuries with the help of the Dutch engineer, Cornelius Vermuyden. The intention was to grow flax enabling the British cloth industry to compete successfully with their Dutch rivals. Fearful of increased trade between Holland and North American colonies, a Royal Commission of 1622 recommended tight control of trade and manufacturing industry in the colonies. By 1660 the theoretical justification for the colonial policy of mercantilism had been established; the enforcement of this policy spelled the beginnings of the tensions which brought about the American Revolutionary war. South east of Ely, at Isleham, the church bell commemorates the Peyton family and its American connections.

EPPING FOREST
Essex *5 TL40*
A welcome 6000-acre tract of beautiful woodland on the outer edge of London, Epping Forest was once part of a royal hunting ground used by Saxon, Norman and Tudor monarchs. The woodland was bought for public use in 1882 and is famous for its hornbeams – a hardwood tree native only to south-east England. Queen Elizabeth's hunting lodge, a timbered Tudor building, is at Chingford on the edge of the forest; it contains a museum of the area.

EPSOM
Surrey *5 TQ20*
Horse-racing has been an established sport on Epsom Downs since the 18th century. It is here that the Derby is run, the most famous of English flat races, named after the Earl of Derby in 1780; the Oaks, named after his country seat, had been instituted in 1779. The town was, in the past, well known for medicinal springs; Epsom Salts can still be purchased.

EDINBURGH

Lothian *23 NT27*

The Athens of the North
'Edinburgh . . . a lyric, brief, bright,
clear and vital as a flash of lightning.' –
Charlotte Brontë *Letters*

Holyroodhouse

Before the border between England
and Scotland was finally settled,
Edinburgh was part of Northumbria.
Edwin, King of Northumbria, built the
earliest fortress, which gives the city its
name – 'Edwin's Burgh' – in the 6th
century. The English King Edward I
later took the castle and fortified it,
and Robert the Bruce destroyed all but
St Margaret's Chapel in 1313. Edward
I captured it again, but the Scots finally
retook it in 1341.

The old town, clustered in narrow,
winding streets around the base of
Castle Rock, was confined within the
boundaries of the defensive King's
Wall, built in 1450 by James II, and
unable to spread outwards, the
buildings grew upwards in a maze of
tenements, sometimes as much as 14
storeys high. Characteristic old
buildings of this period may still be
seen on the Royal Mile and around the
Grassmarket. Eventually, the city
outgrew these limits and extended
towards Greyfriars Church and the
area where the university now stands,
but the threat of conflict with the
English still kept the city within
narrow limits until the 17th century.
By the mid 18th century however, the
loch, which lay at the foot of the castle
where the railway stations and Princes
Street Gardens are today, was drained,
and increased shipping trade on the
Firth of Forth brought the prosperity
that resulted in the building of the
New Town.

The regular layout of the wide
streets, crescents and gardens of the
Georgian development was mainly the
work of James Craig but Robert
Adam, Thomas Hamilton and Charles
Cockerell were also instrumental in
giving a new look to the city. Princes
Street, named after the sons of George
III, is the main east-west thoroughfare,
with buildings on one side only, and
open on the south to Princes Street
Gardens with their famous floral clock
installed in 1903.

Edinburgh won its nickname of the
'Athens of the North' in the 18th and
early 19th centuries, when it was the
home of many distinguished men of
letters such as James Boswell, the
philosopher David Hume, Sir Walter
Scott and Thomas Carlyle. 39 Castle
Street was Scott's favourite Edinburgh
residence. Kenneth Grahame, author

of *The Wind in the Willows* also lived
in Castle Street. Sir Arthur Conan
Doyle was born in the city, and Robert
Louis Stevenson lived here from
1857–79.

The university, founded in 1582,
expanded greatly in the 18th century.
Many of Scotland's academics and
artists studied at the university and art
school, among them James Blair,
founder of William and Mary College,
and James Geddes of Iowa State
University.

In the 19th century, body-snatchers
Burke and Hare terrorized Edinburgh
when they murdered people in the
streets to supply the university with
human bodies for dissection.

St Mary's Cathedral is the seat of
the Scottish Episcopal Church and has
associations with Samuel Seabury, first
bishop of the American Episcopalian
Church. There is a chapel to him in
Old St Paul's on the Royal Mile.

The National Portrait Gallery and
the National Museum of Antiquities
include portraits of many well-known
Scots associated with the Americas.
The art collections in the city are
excellent.

Since 1947, the Edinburgh
International Festival, held in August/
September every year, contributes to
the city's cultural life with an excellent
range of theatrical productions,
concerts, exhibitions and a host of
avant-garde 'Fringe' activities.

In addition to its historical and
cultural importance Edinburgh is
naturally also the legal and
administrative centre of Scotland.
Here are housed the Supreme Courts
of Justice, the Scottish Office, and, if

devolutionists have their way, the
Scottish Assembly.

Edinburgh's Gaelic name is Dun
Eidean and Dunedin, Florida was
named by James Somerville and J O
Douglas, native of the Scottish capital.
Dunedin's Presbyterian church and
pipe band flourish.

**PLACES TO SEE: Old City
Edinburgh Castle** Built on the
commanding heights of a volcanic
rock, the castle is a magnificent
spectacle. The oldest part is St
Margaret's Chapel, dedicated to
the saintly queen of Scotland, sister
of the Atheling, who married
Malcolm III in 1109. The Great
Hall dates from the reign of James
IV and has a fine collection of
armoury. In the Old Royal Palace
are displayed the Scottish crown
jewels. Mons Meg, the massive
cannon forged in the 15th century,
stands at the chapel door. The
Military Tattoo is held every year
on Castle Esplanade. The Scottish
United Services Museum contains
material relating to Scottish
regiments in North America and
has a section on John Paul Jones,
the Scotsman who became 'father
of the American navy'.

Greyfriars Church In 1638 the
National Covenant began in
Greyfriars churchyard.
Covenanters signed it in opposition
to Charles I's imposition of the
Anglican faith on Scotland. The
Protestant faith united most
sections of Scottish society at this
time and reminders abound in the

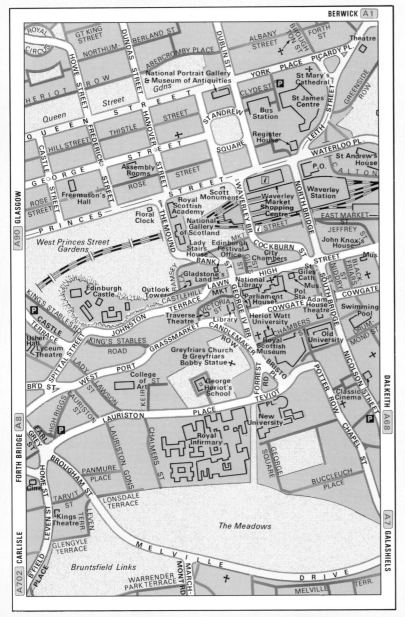

minister until his death in 1572 and was buried in the original graveyard.

John Knox's House A 15th-century house with a magnificent 16th-century painted ceiling.

The Museum of Childhood A rich collection of toys, books and games of all periods.

Canongate Tolbooth Once a prison, it is now used for exhibitions and a permanent display of Highland dress.

Huntly House A reconstructed 16th-century town house, containing the city's local history museum and collections of silver, glass and pottery.

Palace of Holyroodhouse Reconstructed by the architect Sir William Bruce for Charles II, though there are older apartments associated with Mary Queen of Scots who lived here for 6 years. Rizzio, her secretary, was murdered here. The Palace is now the Queen's official residence in Scotland. The ruined Abbey of Holyrood stands beside the Palace.

PLACES TO SEE: New City
National Gallery of Scotland Paintings by Scottish artists and the great European masters.

National Museum of Antiquities of Scotland and the **National Portrait Gallery** are both in Queen Street.

Scott Memorial Characters from his works fill 64 niches on this memorial erected by George Kemp in 1844.

Charlotte Square No 7 in this gem of Georgian architecture was designed by Robert Adam. The rooms have been furnished in period and in the basement is a display about the building of the New Town. Joseph Lister, the medical pioneer, lived at No 9 Charlotte Square, and Field Marshal Haig at No 24. Alexander Graham Bell was born in South Charlotte Street, off the square.

Royal Botanic Gardens Situated some distance from the city centre, noted for displays of rhododendrons.

The Scottish National Gallery of Modern Art is at Belford Road, Dean'.

Edinburgh Zoo Animals are housed in 80 acres of grounds. This is one of Europe's finest zoos.

---

city. A prison in the churchyard held 1200 Covenanters in 1670.

Outlook Tower Fine views of the city from the top of this tower and a fascinating Camera Obscura.

Gladstone's Land Restored 17th-century merchant's house.

Lady Stair's House Off Lawnmarket, the house (1622) has exhibitions about Burns, Scott and Stevenson.

St Giles Cathedral Outside the west door is the 'Heart of Midlothian', marking the site of the Old

Tolbooth prison, and outside the east door, the old Mercat Cross. Here in 1513 the people were told of the death of James IV and 10,000 Scots at the Battle of Flodden. In 1745 Bonnie Prince Charlie proclaimed his exiled father king from the same spot. Nearby, Parliament House was where the Act of Union between Scotland and England was agreed in 1707. Sir Walter Scott's *Heart of Midlothian* was in part based on the Porteous riots of 1736 when the prison was stormed. St Giles has a fine 15th-century steeple; its showpiece is the Thistle Chapel. John Knox was

EPWORTH
Humberside *16 SE70*
The small town of Epworth lies in the arable land of the Isle of Axholme, which was drained by Cornelius Vermuyden and his Dutch engineers in the early 17th century; a century later it became the birthplace of Methodism. The founder of Methodism, John Wesley, was born in 1703, the 15th of 19 children. They were born in the Old Rectory, where their father Samuel was rector. The original building was destroyed by a mob which disagreed with the Reverend Wesley's political views. The Old Rectory, which contains many items relating to the family, is now owned by the World Methodist Council; much of the restoration was financed by American Methodists, who owe their foundation to the inspiration of John Wesley, who founded the first Methodist chapel in New York. The brothers travelled extensively in Britain, and also in America. Although founders of Methodism, the brothers remained high churchmen and members of the Church of England throughout their lives. Samuel Wesley's tombstone is in the churchyard; John once preached from it having been banned from the church (another of his early pulpits was Epworth's market cross). The font where the Wesleys were baptized is in the church. Epworth's large Methodist church was built in 1889.

ESHER
Surrey *5 TQ16*
In the heart of London's commuter belt, Esher is surrounded by common and heathland and manages to preserve a village green and several 18th-century houses. A 15th-century gateway known as Wolsey's Tower is all that is left of the mansion to which Cardinal Wolsey retired when he fell from Henry VIII's favour. Thomas Hooker, who founded Hartford, Connecticut, was rector here, and the writer George Meredith lived in Esher for several years. Claremont House, now a school, was originally a Vanbrugh house, rebuilt in 1709 for Clive of India, and later lived in by Prince Leopold of Belgium and the exiled French Imperial family. The grounds, known as Claremont Landscape Gardens (NT), were laid out by Capability Brown, Charles Bridgeman and William Kent. North of the town is Sandown Park racecourse.

ETON
Berkshire *5 SU97*
Linked to Windsor by an old bridge over the Thames, the ancient town of Eton has become synonymous with England's second oldest public school, round which the life of the town revolves. The college (parts OACT) founded by Henry VI in 1440, stands at the end of the long main street. Lower School, dating from 1443, and still in use, and the chapel, similar to that of King's College, Cambridge, also founded by Henry VI, are the original buildings. The adjacent quadrangle recently became more famous through the film *Chariots of Fire*. Other parts of the college, such as Lupton's Tower, the cloisters and Upper School, where various scholars, among them Shelley and Gladstone, have carved their names on the desks and the panelling, can also be seen when not being used by the school. Many of England's writers and politicians were Eton educated. Among the writers were Henry Fielding, Horace Walpole, Thomas Gray and Robert Bridges, and more recently, Aldous Huxley, Cyril Connolly and Eric Blair (George Orwell). Etonians have spread their influence throughout the world; several were important in the early history of colonial America. James Oglethorpe, founder of Georgia, Sir Humphrey Gilbert, General Howe, William Pitt, Arthur Lee, Horne Tooke and Thomas Lynch, a signer of the Declaration of Independence.

EVESHAM
Hereford & Worcester *9 SP04*
The town lies on the River Avon, at the centre of the fertile Vale named after it, a region of orchards. Evesham has many interesting old buildings, including the Round House, also known as Booth Hall, a charming half-timbered structure that stands in the market place and was formerly an inn. In the Abbey Gardens are, besides the ruined abbey, two churches, St Nicholas and All Saints, and a lovely 16th-century bell tower. The Almonry (OACT), a 14th-century building connected with the abbey, houses a museum of local history. In the church at Aston Somerville, 6 miles south, there is a window to Sir Francis Bond Head, governor of Upper Canada in 1836, put up by his son George who was rector here.

EXMOOR
Somerset/Devon *2 SS74*
From the coast at Combe Martin to the Brendon Hills, 265 square miles of moorland have been designated a National Park. Of the many rivers crossing Exmoor, the Barle and the Exe are most important. The ancient packhorse bridge Tarr Steps (AM, NT) crosses the Barle south west of Winsford Hill. Red deer and ponies still roam the moor. Bampton in Devon holds a pony fair in October. The Doone Valley is the setting for R D Blackmore's *Lorna Doone*. The coastline in the north is dramatic, especially around **Lynmouth.**

EXMOUTH
Devon *2 SY08*
Exmouth is the oldest of Devon's seaside resorts. The Country Life Museum at Sandy Bay has hundreds of exhibits and many farm animals. A La Ronde (OACT) on the northern edge of the town is a unique 16-sided house designed by the Misses Parminster in 1798 and contains many curiosities, including a shell gallery.

Whitbourne in Newfoundland takes its name from 16th-century Sir Richard Whitbourne, born in Exmouth.

EYAM
Derbyshire *15 SK27*
This is the plague village, whose rector, William Mompesson, persuaded his parishioners to isolate themselves when plague struck in 1665 and so prevent the disease reaching other communities. More than 80 per cent of the villagers died. A memorial service is held at the end of August every year in a nearby dell called Cucklet Church where Mompesson held open-air services in the plague year. In the churchyard, where his wife, a plague victim, is buried, there is an unusual 18th-century sundial which tells world-time. Eyam is one of several Derbyshire villages which take part in well-dressing ceremonies.

EYNSFORD
Kent *6 TQ56*
Around this little village is grouped a trio of interesting ancient buildings. The oldest is Lullingstone Roman Villa (AM), which has a fine tessellated pavement. 12th-century Eynsford Castle (AM) is ruined, but Lullingstone Castle (OACT) is still inhabited by descendants of the Peche family who owned the estate in the 14th century. There is a fine Tudor gatehouse, and the 'castle' (a Tudor manor house remodelled in the 18th century) has impressive State Rooms.

EXETER
Devon   *2 SX99*

Founded in about AD 50 by the Romans on a Celtic site, Exeter has a long history, though most of the physical evidence was destroyed in an air raid in 1942. Parts of the Roman Walls, much strengthened in the Norman period, still stand. In Anglo Saxon times Exeter flourished, but was sacked several times by the Danes, and was eventually, in 1068, captured by the Normans. William I promptly built a castle, of the distinctive local red sandstone, and the ruins of the walls, gatehouse and Athelstan's tower now form part of Rougemont ('red hill') Gardens. The city was unique in medieval England in having a man-made pure water supply. The underground passages built as conduits can be seen in Princesshay.

Exeter prospered with the proceeds of the wool trade and from Continental trade through its port, until 1290, when the Countess of Devon built a weir across the river, to spite the locals. However, trade was restored in 1563, when Exeter's early ship canal was opened. The Customs House on the Quay dates from 1681. Nowadays the docks are largely disused, although they were used in a television series 'The Onedin Line', as Liverpool's 19th-century docks.

Exeter Cathedral dates from the early medieval period, although the two towers are Norman. Its magnificent west front has tiers of angels and saints. Around the cathedral precinct some of Exeter's old buildings survived both the air raids and modern development. The best known is the former Mol's Coffee House, where Drake and Hawkins used to meet. They also drank in The Ship Inn in St Martin's Lane. St Martin's Church, consecrated in 1065, has a fine wagon roof and 17th-century gallery. Other interesting churches are the Norman St Mary Arches and St Mary Steps which has a 17th-century clock with moving figures which strike the hour and the quarters. Opposite is an Elizabethan half-timbered building, which was moved from its original site and is consequently known as 'The House that Moved'. Exeter's medieval Guildhall is the oldest municipal building still in use in England; its most distinctive feature is its ornate upper storey which dates from 1593. Next to the Guildhall is the Turk's Head, a 15th-century inn in which Dickens found his original 'Fat Boy' for *Pickwick Papers*. Daniel Boone's grandfather came from Exeter; his father, 'Squire Boone', settled in North

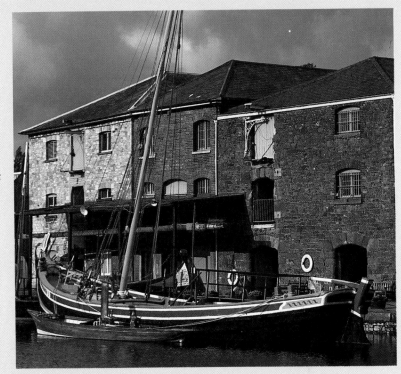

Tagus River barge, Exeter Maritime Museum

Carolina around 1750. Exeter University occupies an attractive campus, and contains the American Arts Documentation Centre.

The parish church at Heavitree has a memorial to Thomas Gorges, Deputy Governor of Maine, and nephew of Sir Ferdinando Gorges.

PLACES TO SEE
Exeter Cathedral The 300ft long nave is the longest span of unbroken Gothic rib-vaulting in the world, and is also noted for the beautifully carved roof bosses. There is much fine wood-carving, including the earliest set of misericords in England, an elaborate Bishop's throne and an exquisite minstrel's gallery. Sir Walter Raleigh's parents are buried in the cathedral, and a memorial to Lt John Graves Simcoe depicts American Indians. Simcoe died in Cathedral Close and is buried in Wolford Chapel, near **Honiton**. Lethbridge in Alberta is named after the Exeter family and there are Lethbridge memorials in the cathedral as well as one to Rachel O'Brien, whose father was the Montreal fur-trader Joseph Frobisher. John Horden, the 19th-century missionary to the Canadian Indians is buried in the cathedral.

The cathedral library has priceless manuscripts including *The Exeter Book*, from the collection of Leofric, Exeter's first bishop; the book is the largest known collection of Anglo Saxon poems. Other items of interest include the city's Domesday Book, and a copy of John Eliot's American Indian Bible, the first translation of the Bible into an Indian language.

Maritime Museum More than 100 craft from all over the world are housed in the docks and canal basin. Some are afloat and can be boarded. A river ferry crosses the river here. Overlooking the river, Colleton Crescent is a splendid Georgian terrace.

Rougemont House Museum contains local archaeological discoveries.

Royal Albert Memorial Museum houses collections of local interest, including natural history, Honiton lace, china and glass, but also has some good paintings and items relating to America.

St Nicholas Priory The restored remains of a Benedictine Priory with Norman undercroft.

F

FAIRFORD
Gloucestershire *4 SP10*
Fairford is one of the most attractive
and least spoiled of the Cotswold
towns. Lying on the gentle River Coln,
its chief glory is its late 15th-century
church built, unusually for England, to
one uniform design by John Tame, a
wealthy cloth merchant. The Christian
faith from Creation to the Last
Judgement is depicted in 28 very fine
stained glass windows, which date
from the 15th and 16th centuries.

   John Keble, poet and cleric, author
of the classic work *The Christian
Year*, was born here in 1792. Keble
College, Oxford was founded in his
memory. Edwin Austin Abbey, the
19th-century American illustrator and
painter, lived with his family in
Morgan Hall, Fairford. Abbey was
highly regarded in his day, and was
chosen by Edward VII to paint his
coronation.

FAIR ISLE
Orkney & Shetland
The most remote inhabited island in
Britain, 3 miles long and under 2 miles
wide, Fair Isle lies midway between the
Orkney and Shetland Isles. The island
is most famous for its intricate knitted
designs. Its bird observatory, (which
offers limited accommodation to
ornithologists) has recorded over 300
species of wild birds ranging from the
alpine swift to the osprey and is noted
for its contribution towards research
into bird migration.

FALKIRK
Central *22 NS88*
Falkirk, situated on the Firth of Forth,
was a centre for coal-mining and for
the great Carron Ironworks, which
began making 'carronades', as the
cannon were known, for Nelson's
navy in 1760. Falkirk Museum has
some interesting local exhibits and just
west of the town is Rough Castle
(AM), one of the 19 Roman forts
which guarded the Antonine Wall. On
the east of the town, in the grounds of
Callendar House, is one of the best-
preserved sections of the wall (AM).

FALKLAND
Fife *23 NO20*
On the fringe of the fertile Howe of
Fife, Falkland is a small and ancient
royal burgh, its cobbled streets
bordered by picturesque old houses
and weavers' cottages. The town is
sited below the Lomond Hills.
Falkland Palace and Gardens (NTS),
the old hunting palace of the Stuarts
until 1625, was built in the mid 16th
century in Renaissance style. Its tennis
court is the oldest in Britain – 1539. Sir
Walter Scott used the Palace in *The
Fair Maid of Perth*.

FALMOUTH
Cornwall *1 SW83*
Sir Walter Raleigh can claim some of
the credit for putting Falmouth on the
map: it was he who saw the
commercial possibilities of this large
natural harbour. It became the first
station for the Royal Mail Packet
Service in 1688, reaching its heyday in
1827 when 39 packet steamers
operated from the port. Nowadays its
dry dock is home to huge modern oil
tankers. The town with its lovely
setting on the Cornish Riviera
developed as a holiday resort in the
19th century following the arrival of
the Great Western Railway. Pendennis
Castle (AM) was one of Henry VIII's
coastal forts and was the last Royalist
stronghold in England to surrender to
Cromwell. Together with St Mawes
Castle (AM) on the opposite side of
Carrick Roads, it guards the harbour.
The church of St Charles the Martyr
was built in the 17th century and
dedicated to Charles I. Among the
18th- and 19th-century buildings near
the harbour is 'King's Pipe' – a
chimney where tobacco smugglers'
dreams literally went up in smoke –
burnt by Excise men.

   Thomas Peter, a founder of New
London, Connecticut, came from
Mylor further up the estuary. The
notorious 17th-century pirate, Peter
Easton, who operated on the channel
coast of England and also from
Newfoundland, was actively
supported by the Killigrews, a Cornish
family whose ancestral home was
Pendennis Castle.

FARNBOROUGH
Hampshire *4 SU85*
To most people, Farnborough means
the Royal Aircraft Establishment and
the biennial International Airshow.
The town itself is unexceptional but
nearby is St Michael's Abbey, built in
1881 in flamboyant French Gothic style
by the Empress Eugénie, wife of
Napoleon III, who lived in exile in
nearby Farnborough Hall, now a
convent. St Peter's Church has a
Norman nave and a 17th-century
tower.

FARNHAM
Surrey *4 SU84*
A small country town of red brick,
whose predominantly Georgian

Falkland town square

Finchingfield

character has been preserved from the encroaching commuter country. A wide street of attractive shops and houses leads to Farnham Castle (AM). The Norman keep is attached to a 15th- to 17th-century building, formerly residence of the Bishops of Guildford.

What is now the 'William Cobbett Inn' was the birthplace in 1763 of William Cobbett, the radical politician, supporter of American independence and author of *Rural Rides*. In 1784 Cobbett enlisted in the British Army and served in Nova Scotia and Frederickstown, New Brunswick. There he attained the rank of sergeant-major and met the woman (or rather girl, she was 13) who was to become his wife. He returned to England in 1791, but had to leave soon after, having made an accusation against his officers. He went to the United States, first teaching in Wilmington, Delaware and later becoming a bookseller in Philadelphia. Continuing his dissidence, Cobbett lived successively in England and America, finally returning to England in 1820 bringing with him the body of Tom Paine. The graves of Cobbett and his parents are in Farnham parish church, where there is also a memorial to him. Willmer House in West Street has much Cobbett material.

Near the station are the ruins of England's first Cistercian house, Waverley Abbey. It is thought that the title of Sir Walter Scott's series of novels derives from here. J M Barrie wrote *Peter Pan* while living in Farnham.

Seven miles north west of Farnham, across the county border in Hampshire, is Elvetham Hall near Hartley Wintney. The Canadian painter and official war artist in World War I, Inglis Sheldon-Williams, lived here as a child. He is particularly associated with Saskatchewan and he set up an art school at Regina.

Charles Poulett Thomson, Lord Sydenham, was Governor-General of the United Province of Upper and Lower Canada from 1839–41. Waverley Abbey House, east of Farnham, was the Thomson house.

FAVERSHAM
Kent   *6 TR06*
There is evidence of a Saxon village here in King's Field and the Romans were later settlers. Once a flourishing port, its main claim to fame is the wealth of Tudor, Stuart and Georgian buildings, of which over 50 are listed for preservation. In the former

Queen's Arms James II was held prisoner after his capture when he tried to flee the country in 1688. The Church of St Mary of Charity is partly Norman, partly Early English in style with particularly fine misericords. The Chart Gunpowder Mills (OACT) date from the late 18th century and are a reminder of the town's importance as a centre of the gunpowder industry.

Three miles south, Hernhill was the birthplace of Edward Johnson, who sailed with John Winthrop. Johnson founded Woburn, Massachusetts and was an early historian of the New England colony.

Four miles south of Faversham is Throwley, associated with military engineer Colonel John Montrésor, active in Canada after Quebec fell. He came back to England in 1778. Montrésor died in prison following seizure of his lands to repay disallowed expenses from his Canadian engineering programmes. His house is Belmont, just north west of Throwley. He gave money for bells in the parish church, acknowledged in an inscription. There are memorials to the Montrésors at Norton parish church, 4 miles west of Faversham.

FILEY
N Yorkshire   *16 TA18*
Charlotte Brontë was a frequent visitor to this clifftop holiday resort, with its sandy beach and elegant hotels. The Romans established a signal station on Carr Naze headland, below which lies Filey Brigg, a mile-long jagged reef forming a natural breakwater, and now part of a nature trail. A few surviving fishing cobles (a type of boat) on the beach are a reminder of more prosperous fishing days for the town. St Oswald's Church, mainly Early English in style, has a fine south doorway and massive tower adorned by a fish-shaped weather vane. The

town lies on the Cleveland Way, a 90-mile, long-distance footpath which runs from Saltburn-on-Sea to **Helmsley**, inland on the North Yorkshire Moors.

FINCHINGFIELD
Essex   *12 TL63*
Duck pond, stream, green, church on the hill and a pleasant jumble of variously shaped and sized houses all combine to make this one of the most photogenic and photographed villages in Britain. The church of St John the Baptist has a Norman tower with an 18th-century bell turret and there is a handsome 15th-century timber-framed Guildhall which houses the museum.

Two miles to the east, Wethersfield was an RAF base in World War II; American airmen were based here. Finchingfield church was renovated with American assistance.

Spains Hall, 1 mile north west, is a red brick Elizabethan mansion (gardens open, OACT, house open by appointment). Its lake was an amalgamation of several ponds, supposedly dug by one resident who maintained a vow of seven years silence, for wrongly accusing his wife.

FIRLE PLACE
E Sussex   *5 TQ40*
Firle Place (OACT) owned by the Gage family since the late 15th century, contains collections of Old Masters, porcelain and furniture, as well as items brought back from America by General Thomas Gage, military governor of Montreal after its capture in 1760, last 'imperial' Governor of Massachusetts, and Commander of the British Forces at the start of the War of Independence. The house itself is predominantly Georgian, built around a Tudor core. In World War II Firle Place played host to Canadian troops.

BONNIE PRINCE CHARLIE

AND FLORA MACDONALD

In 1745 a final Stuart attempt was made to regain the throne from the Hanoverian crown. Charles Edward Stuart, aged twenty-three, son of the unsuccessful 'Old Pretender', handsome and headstrong, landed from a French ship on the Isle of Eriskay, off South Uist in the Western Isles, with only seven supporters – and three of them were Irishmen, and only one Macdonald and he from Ulster. He had pawned all he had, and all his mother's rubies, to finance the adventure. When the local clan-chief Macdonald of Boisdale told him to go home, he replied 'I am come home, sir.'

At Glenfinnan, his HQ on the mainland, he was joined, after some hesitation, by Cameron of Lochiel – whose father lost his estates after the 1715 unrest – and perhaps by half the Highland clans,

many of them Macleods and Macdonalds; he got support as much from poverty as from political or religious conviction. He moved through the Pass of Killiecrankie to Perth and Edinburgh, meeting with little resistance, and he held court in Holyroodhouse. Had he stayed there until French forces came, it might have been a different tale. His staff were split on the strategy. With 6000 men, however, he decided to march on London by way of Carlisle, Penrith, Preston, and by 4 December he had reached Derby. London was in panic, there was a run on the Bank of England, a quick dash might have won him his prize; George II prepared to go back to Hanover. But few Jacobites had joined him; his Highlanders were deserting, and his chief of staff, Lord George Murray, prevailed on

Bonnie Prince Charles by Antonio David, 1732

him to retreat. He did so; to Carlisle and Glasgow, to win a victory at Falkirk in January 1746, and finally he

took a stand on Culloden Moor.

He was outnumbered by two to one, his men tired and hungry; less than half of them were professional troops, who were mainly Scottish and Irish units from France. The Duke of Cumberland, the King's son, had fifteen regular battalions and heavy guns. On 16 April 1746 Cumberland was victorious in the last battle on British soil, and savage in his treatment of the enemy, earning the name 'Butcher' Cumberland. Seven hundred and fifty Highlanders were killed on the field, probably the same number again in the pursuit that followed. The glens were 'harried': Glen Moriston and Lochaber, Keppoch and Glen Nevis, Appin, and west to Moidart. Though seen by the English as a Highland and Scottish revolt, it was in fact a Scottish civil war. Three

The Battle of Culloden, 16 April 1746, from a contemporary print by Laurie and Whittle

Scottish regiments – the Royal Scots, the Royal Scots Fusiliers and the King's Own Scottish Borderers – fought on the Hanoverian side. More Scots fought against the Prince than for him; those for him were the Mackays, the Munros, the Macphersons, the Grants, the MacLeods, the MacNeils, the Macdonalds of the Isles but not of course the Campbells of Invarary (Dukes of Argyll). It was the end of the ill-fated Stuart cause, the end of an 'auld sang'.

Eilean Donan Castle

Flora Macdonald by Richard Wilson

The Young Pretender, with a price of £30,000 on his head, hid for five months; he was passed on by friend to friend and his wanderings – from the braes of Glen Moriston to the islands – have become legends. One who protected him was twenty-four-year-old Flora Macdonald who hid him for ten days on South Uist. Disguised as her maid 'Betty Burke' he sailed from Benbecula to Portree on Skye. On 1 July 1746, he returned to the mainland – promising to reward her – and from Moidart, on 20 September, under the cover of a thick mist and fourteen months after his landing, he sailed back to France on the French rescue ship *L'Heureux*. He probably visited London *incognito* in 1750, and perhaps in 1753, but got no support; after his father's death in 1766, even the Pope ceased to recognize him as King, though he gave him sanctuary. He died in Rome in 1788.

Many Scots emigrated to North America after the '45, particularly to North Carolina. They were encouraged by a skilful Governor, Gabriel Johnston (born a Lowland Scot, who knew some of them from his schooldays), and by a ten-year spell of grace on their tax-bills. Flora Macdonald had been arrested and sent to London in 1746; she was in fact well treated there, released, and returned to Skye. She married in 1750. With her husband Allan and two of their sons in 1774, after twenty-five years' struggle, she too emigrated. American Highlanders opposed the Tidewater and rebellious ('patriot', after July 1776) forces at Moore's Creek Bridge, among them Allan Macdonald. He was thus indirectly fighting for George III. Flora Macdonald, mounted on a white horse, addressed them in Gaelic before the battle. But the patriot forces had obligingly re-moved a number of planks from the bridge and greased the rest, and this 'battle' was over in three minutes. Allan Macdonald and one of his sons were captured. A year later his wife lost her land because she refused to take an oath to the rebellious North Carolina government. She and four children in 1779 returned to Skye. She died there 4 March 1790, aged sixty-eight. She was thus a heroine of two lost causes, in 1745 and 1776.

For whatever reason, much of North America beats to exiles' drums. They look back to the lone shieling and misty island, and all respond with loyalty and affection to the music and the magic of the Hebrides. *Tout finit par des chansons.*

Places to Visit

Eilean Donan Castle, Isle of Eriskay, Isle of Skye, and **Dunvegan Castle,** ancestral home of the Clan Macleod. **Culloden Moor, Arisaig**

Further Reading

J L Campbell, *Canna, the story of a Hebridean Island,* a story by a Catholic Gaelic-speaking naturalist author, living at Canna House and married to American writer, Margaret Fay Shaw. Until 1560 Canna was attached to the Benedictine Abbey of Iona.

Chevalier de Johnstone, *Memoir of the Forty-Five* (London, 1820)

Hugh McDiarmid, *Collected Poems* ('The Rose of all the world is not for me. I want for my part Only the little white rose of Scotland That smells sharp and sweet – and breaks the heart')

John Prebble, *Culloden* (Secker & Warburg, 1961)

Sir Walter Scott, *Waverley*

Robert Louis Stevenson, *The Master of Ballantrae; Kidnapped;* and *Catriona*

FISHBOURNE
W Sussex *4 SU80*
Fishbourne's Roman Palace (OACT)
was a splendid and skilful example of
Roman architecture and, extending
over 6 acres, the biggest site discovered
in Britain. Just west of the important
settlement at Chichester, it was
inhabited during the 2nd and 3rd
centuries AD, the height of Roman
occupation. Archaeologists did not
discover the Palace until 1960 although
in medieval times a ploughman is
known to have cut a furrow across one
of its mosaic pavements. For these
pavements Fishbourne is famous,
especially the centre-piece of the boy
on the dolphin. The museum gives a
good idea of life in the Palace, and a
formal garden has been recreated
along Roman lines in the courtyard
formed by the four wings.

FISHGUARD
Dyfed *7 SM93*
The attractive harbour town was the
setting for the 1971 film version of
Dylan Thomas's *Under Milk Wood*.
Nearby Carregwastad Point was the
scene of the last invasion of Britain
when, in 1797, 120 French troops led
by the Irish-American William Tate,
landed here to raise a rebellion against
George III. The force had intended to
raid Bristol, but was diverted by winds
and landed without opposition.
However, legend has it they mistook
the red cloaks of the local women for
British military uniforms and
surrendered at Goodwick. The oak
table used for the surrender is now in
the Royal Oak in Fishguard.

FISHTOFT
Lincolnshire *11 TF34*
A granite obelisk at Scotia Creek
marks the point from which John
Winthrop's Pilgrims made their first
attempt to sail to religious freedom in
Holland. They were caught, then tried
and imprisoned in Boston. Fishtoft
was also the birthplace of Edmund
Quincy in 1623.

FLAMBOROUGH
Yorkshire *16 TA27*
Among the whitewashed stone
cottages of this seafaring village stands
St Oswald's Church which contains a
rare 18th-century Yorkshire rood
screen and loft. The village, high on
the chalk cliffs, is exposed on three
sides to the North Sea, and has several
dramatic episodes in its history. The
Vikings landed here as part of the
invasion of Britain in the 9th–10th

Flamborough Head

century. Later, in 1779, Flamborough
Head was the scene of the naval battle
in which Scots-born John Paul Jones
defeated the British. Jones, founder of
the American Navy, fought from the
Bonhomme Richard named in honour
of Franklin, after *Poor Richard's
Almanack*. The *Richard* sank but
Jones managed to capture HMS
Serapis and sail her to France. A
toposcope near the lighthouse
commemorates the battle.

FLINT
Clwyd *14 SJ27*
Edward I built the first of his Welsh
castles (AM) here on the banks of the
Dee in 1277. Largely destroyed by the
Puritans in the 17th century, the ruins
still look out over 3 empty miles across
the sands of the Dee to the Wirral
Peninsula. The plan of the castle is
unique in Britain: square, with three
corner towers and a detached keep.
Richard II was held here after his capture by Bolingbroke, later Henry IV.

FOLKESTONE
Kent *6 TR23*
A holiday resort since the coming of
the railways, Folkestone is now a ferry
terminal, but has preserved its
attractive old town with its
picturesque harbour and cobbled
streets, and has a beautiful clifftop
promenade known as the Leas. The
medieval church of St Mary and
Eanswith, named after the
granddaughter of Ethelbert, first
Christian King of Kent, who
established England's first nunnery in
AD 630, has a memorial window to
William Harvey the Folkestone-born

physician to James I, who discovered
the circulation of blood. The Warren,
a landslip basin containing rare plants,
fossils and the remains of two Roman
villas, lies to the east of the town
towards Dover. Dickens took a family
holiday in what is now Copperfield
House, and was visited here by Wilkie
Collins. H G Wells wrote many of his
most famous works when living at
Spade House, Sandgate. Many of his
contemporaries, including Henry
James and George Bernard Shaw,
visited him here. Conrad was part of
this circle; he lived at Pen Farm,
Postling, a few miles north west, where
he wrote *Lord Jim, Typhoon* and
Nostromo. Between Postling and
Hythe is Saltwood Castle, where
Thomas à Becket's murder was
planned.

FORRES
Grampian *27 NJ05*
Forres is mentioned in Shakespeare's
Macbeth as the home of Duncan's
court. $3\frac{1}{2}$ miles south west is
Darnaway Castle where Mary Queen
of Scots stayed in 1562. The scenery of
the area is outstanding. Forres was the
birthplace of Donald Smith
(1820–1914) who was later to become
Lord Strathcona. Apprenticed to the
Hudson's Bay Company in 1838, Smith
worked his way from fur trader to
financier and railway promoter.
Eventually he entered Canadian
politics as a Conservative member for
Winnipeg. In 1897 he became High
Commissioner for Canada in London,
where he lived until his death. Smith
was knighted and then raised to the
peerage.

FORT AUGUSTUS
Highland *26 NH30*
One link in the Hanoverian chain of
defences in the Great Glen (**Glen
More**), Fort Augustus was built after
the 1715 Jacobite Rising and named
after the Duke of Cumberland. Its
remains now share the site with a 19th-
century Benedictine abbey and a
Roman Catholic school. General
Wade extended Fort Augustus in 1730
and built his famous network of roads
to open up the Highlands and control
the clans: the present main road partly
follows the line of the one he built
through the Great Glen connecting
Fort William and **Inverness**. The
village of Fort Augustus, in wooded
hill country at the south-west end of
Loch Ness, near the entry of the
Caledonian Canal, is an angling and
tourist centre. The Great Glen
Exhibition (OACT), in addition to its
historical displays, gives the latest
information on the search for the Loch
Ness Monster.

FORTINGALL
Tayside *26 NN74*
This pretty village of thatched
cottages, lying in a narrow valley at the
entrance of Glen Lyon, was renovated
in the late 19th century by Sir Donald
Currie, a wealthy shipowner and
resident of Glen Lyon House. The way
into the beautiful glen lies over the
Pass of Lyon. In the churchyard is a
huge yew tree, which is said to be 3000
years old and is probably the most
ancient tree in Britain. The
surrounding countryside is full of
prehistoric remains: ring forts, stone
circles, disc barrows and standing
stones. However, the local tradition
that Pontius Pilate was born here while
his father was on an embassy from the
Emperor Augustus, has been dismissed
by archaeologists.

FORT WILLIAM
Highland *26 NN17*
The stone fort built in William III's
reign to help control the clans
withstood Jacobite assaults during the
1715 and 1745 Risings, but met its
match when, save for a gateway, it was
demolished to make way for the
railway. Inverlochy Castle (AM) is
currently (1985) under repair and not
accessible. The town, known variously
in the past as Gordonsburgh,
Duncansburgh, and Maryburgh, and
squeezed between loch and mountain,
is now a well-known tourist centre for
the West Highlands. The West
Highland Museum dates from the 18th

century and is famous for its secret
portrait of Bonnie Prince Charlie,
reflected on a cylinder. 2¼ miles south
east of the Caledonian Canal, begun in
1803 by Thomas Telford, near Spean
Bridge stands the Commando
Memorial marking a World War II
commando training area. An avenue of
beeches known as the Dark Mile, was
planted at Clunes, about 11 miles
north east of Fort William, in 1745 for
Bonnie Prince Charlie who is said to
have buried a fortune in gold at **Loch
Arkaig**, which spreads west from
Clunes.

FOTHERINGHAY
Northamptonshire *11 TL09*
Wild Scotch thistles, reputedly planted
by Mary Queen of Scots, grow on the
earthworks which are the only remains
of the 14th-century castle where Mary
was executed in 1587. Earlier, the
castle was the birthplace of Richard
III. The village itself, with its solid
limestone cottages and 18th-century
bridge over the River Nene, lies on the
edge of what remains of Rockingham
Forest. Its chief glory is the church of
St Mary and All Saints, an imposing
building of cathedral-like proportions.
Its unusual octagonal lantern tower,
rising in stages and topped by a gilt
falcon badge of the House of York, is a
landmark all over the Nene Valley.

FOUNTAINS ABBEY
N Yorkshire *15 SE26*
The ruins of Fountains Abbey (AM)
are some of the best preserved and
most beautiful of England's medieval
relics. The abbey was founded in 1132
by monks from York who came to this
remote location and adopted the
Cistercian Rule. They flourished with
the wool trade, but this prosperity
meant that Fountains Abbey was one
of the first to be sold by Henry VIII at
the Dissolution in 1540. The abbey lies
within the Country Park of Studley
Royal. Nearby is 17th-century
Fountains Hall, built with stone from
the abbey.

FOWEY
Cornwall *1 SX15*
Ruined forts at either side of the
Fowey estuary still appear to guard
this charming Cornish coastal town.
The harbour, and the quaint narrow
streets climbing steeply from it, attract
holidaymakers but the town is also an
important commercial port exporting
large cargoes of china clay. The wide
variety of old buildings include the
ruins of St Catherine's Castle (AM) the

Fountains Abbey

church of St Finbarres, 14th-century in
origin and with a fine 16th-century
tower, and the impressive town hall
built in 1792 but incorporating several
14th-century windows. Noah's Ark, a
14th-century house, houses a museum
of Cornish domestic life. Nearby, there
is safe bathing at sandy Readymoney
Cove. Between Polridmouth and
Polkerris Coves lies '**Menabilly**'. The
house, built in 1600 and added to in the
18th and 19th centuries, was formerly
the home of the Rashleigh family and,
more recently, of Daphne du Maurier.

FRAMLINGHAM
Suffolk *12 TM26*
A handsome market town amid the
open Suffolk farmland, Framlingham
has an impressive ruined castle (AM),
built in 1190 by Roger Bigod, 2nd Earl
of Norfolk, and extensively rebuilt in
the 16th century. The almshouses
within the walls were built from
materials from the Great Hall. As a
result of Bigod's treachery, the castle
was sequestrated and became the seat
of some of the great East Anglian
families: primarily the Howards,
created Dukes of Norfolk after the
Battle of Flodden. St Michael's
Church, a fine example of late
Perpendicular, houses the splendid
Howard family tombs. Several
important Americans had links with
Framlingham. It was the ancestral
home of Josiah Quincy, President
James A Garfield, and Richard Henry
Dana. Thomas Danforth, President of
Maine from 1679–86, and benefactor
and treasurer of Harvard College, left
Framlingham with his father at the age
of 12. His father was to found

Pontcysyllte Aqueduct, Froncysyllte

Framlingham, Massachusetts. The town is surrounded by beautiful Suffolk villages such as Parham, 2 miles to the south, with its moated hall, and Dennington, 2 miles to the north, which has a beautiful 14th-century church. Saxtead Green, 1 mile to the west, has one of the finest Suffolk windmills.

FRASERBURGH
Grampian *28 NJ96*
A trim, embayed town built in the mid-16th century by Alexander Fraser, Laird of Philorth, Fraserburgh is both a port, landing mostly white fish since the decline of the herring, and a resort on the sandy Buchan coast. Town and harbour lie in the protection of Kinnaird Head, a promontory known to Ptolemy, and of Fraserburgh Castle which was built on the headland in 1569; only its central tower survives, adapted as a lighthouse in 1787. At the rocky foot of the castle, the Wine Tower – in fact probably a watchtower – stands unchanged since its construction, probably during the 15th century.

FRENSHAM
Surrey *4 SU84*
Frensham has an extensive common (NT), famous for its wild life, and ancient prehistoric barrows line its crest; over 200 species of birds can be seen here. Frensham Ponds are ideal for fishing and sailing: Great Pond – at over 100 acres one of the biggest in southern England – and Little Pond – where water lilies flourish. The River Wey runs nearby and the three curious-looking hills are called the Devil's Jumps: the largest is Stony Jump (NT), which gives a fine view over Surrey. Frensham's church, although restored, still retains 14th- and 15th-century characteristics. It has a Norman font and a medieval witch's

cauldron, said to belong to Mother Ludlam, denizen of the local caves.

FROME
Somerset *3 ST74*
The heart of this busy market town is well preserved, its steep and narrow streets rich in medieval, Tudor and 18th-century houses. Cheap Street has a watercourse running down its centre. The Bluecoats School near the bridge dates from 1720. Frome was the home town of William Cabell, founder of the Virginian family, and the English poet George Crabbe was a regular visitor. The nearby village of Nunney is delightful. The castle (AM), built as a fortified house in 1373, is said to have been modelled on the Bastille in Paris. It suffered at the hands of the Round-heads in the Civil War. Its moat is said to be the deepest in England.

FRONCYSYLLTE
Clwyd *14 SJ24*
Here, in the Vale of Llangollen, is Telford's 'Stream in the Sky' – the Pontcysyllte Aqueduct. Built between 1795 and 1805, its 18 piers carry the Shropshire Union Canal 120ft high above the River Dee. A pioneering piece of iron-engineering, it connected the Llangollen Canal with the English canal system.

FYLINGDALES
N Yorkshire *20 SE99*
'The geometry of the Space Age at its most alluring and frightening' wrote Pevsner of the three giant pearly-white balls which form part of the Ministry of Defence's Ballistic Missile Early Warning Station and which dominate this high moor inland from **Robin Hood's Bay**. The heather-covered moor is part of the North York Moors National Park and is traversed by the famous Lyke Wake Walk.

GAINSBOROUGH
Lincolnshire *16 SK88*
A three-arched 18th-century bridge links Nottinghamshire to Lincolnshire at Gainsborough, the St Ogg's of George Eliot's *Mill on the Floss*. The River Trent is still the lifeline for the town's many industries; its quayside is lined with fine 18th-century warehouses. The Old Hall, Gainsborough's oldest building, rebuilt in 1480, it is one of the largest medieval buildings in Britain open to the public. Richard III stayed here in 1484, Henry VIII and his sixth wife Catherine Parr also visited. It was closely associated with the early Pilgrims too, many of whom came from the surrounding area. 'Separatist' meetings were first held here. Gainsborough's John Robinson Memorial Church, built by English and American Congregationalists, commemorates 'the Pastor of the Pilgrim Fathers'. Robinson is thought to have written the address given at the departure of the *Mayflower*. He intended to sail with William Brewster's Pilgrims, but died before they left. The church was opened in 1902, the tricentennial of the Gainsborough congregation. Robinson was born in Sturton le Steeple, a small village 4 miles south west of Gainsborough. This was probably the birthplace of the Reverend John Smythe – another Pilgrim. Both men were educated at Cambridge. Smythe organized the congregation at Gainsborough, where Robinson was to come after holding pastorates at **Norwich** and **Scrooby**. Smythe led an early group to religious freedom in Holland in 1607, where he baptized himself, thereby becoming the first of the Se-Baptist sect. Later John Wesley, born 9 miles north west in **Epworth**, preached at the Old Hall.

GAWSWORTH
Cheshire *14 SJ86*
Mary Fitton, one of the Fitton family who owned Gawsworth Hall for four centuries, may have been the 'Dark Lady' of Shakespeare's sonnets. The fine black-and-white Tudor manor house (OACT) has a beamed interior

and outside can be seen a rare tilting ground. The carriage museum is also worth visiting. The mainly 15th-century village church contains a notable range of monuments to the Fittons, including Mary. Many local people, past vicars of the church among them, claim that her ghost haunts the church. Surrounded by woodland, pools, and parkland, the village itself is a delight. In addition to the Fitton manor house, there are two old vicarages and another Elizabethan hall, used as a Cheshire Home. Maggoty Johnson's Wood (NT) is named after England's last professional jester who lived in the village in the 18th century and is buried in the wood.

GEDDINGTON
Northamptonshire   *10 SP88*
In 1290 Eleanor of Castile, wife of Edward I, died near Lincoln and her coffin was taken south for burial at Westminster Abbey. At each of the 12 resting places on the journey memorials were built. Only three now remain, and the best preserved of the Eleanor Crosses is the one erected in this attractive stone-built village.

GIFFORD
Lothian   *24 NT56*
This delightful village on Gifford Water dates from the 18th century. It replaced an earlier village demolished by the 2nd Marquis of Tweeddale to make way for the parkland surrounding Yester House. John Witherspoon, signatory of the Declaration of Independence for New Jersey and President of Princeton, was born here. To the south of the village are the sheep-grazed Lammermuir Hills, ideal for walking and pony-trekking.

GILLINGHAM
Kent   *6 TQ76*
An industrial town on the Medway estuary, Gillingham is the largest of the Medway towns, sharing with its neighbour, Chatham, the former Royal Naval Dockyard, founded by Henry VIII. Exhibits in the Royal Engineers Museum in the suburb of Brompton include relics of General Gordon, killed in Khartoum in 1885.

GIRVAN
Strathclyde   *22 NX19*
Now a seaside resort with sandy beaches, this town at the mouth of the River Girvan, looking out across the Firth of Clyde, grew up round a small

fishing port. There is a well-known whisky distillery in the town, and boat trips can be arranged to see the lonely 1114ft-high rock of Ailsa Craig. Lying to the west, 10 miles out to sea, it is home only to lighthouse keepers and thousands of seabirds. South of the town a beautiful coastal road to Ballantrae negotiates the dramatic Kennedy's Pass.

GLAMIS
Tayside   *28 NO34*
Birthplace of Princess Margaret in 1930, baronial, much-haunted Glamis Castle (OACT) was also the childhood home of the Queen Mother. The tower has 15ft-thick walls and dates from the 14th century, but most of the turreted castle was rebuilt during the late 17th century in the style of a French château. Items of interest include tapestries, furniture, paintings and weapons, and the fine grounds were laid out by 18th-century landscape gardener Capability Brown. From the battlements there are fine views of the Vale of Strathmore, the eastern Grampians and the Sidlaw Hills. The Angus Folk Museum (NTS) is housed in a row of 19th-century cottages.

GLASGOW
Strathclyde   *22 NS56*
Scotland's largest city, and the third most populous city in Britain, Glasgow owes its rapid development during the Industrial Revolution to its situation on the Clyde, only 20 miles from the sea, and surrounded by coalfields. Its

prosperity had begun earlier, in the 17th century, when Port Glasgow, on the Clyde estuary, began to handle a flood of goods from the New World. Heavy industry and ship-building developed in the 19th century, requiring the massive workforce whose cheap housing became the notorious slums of this century.

In recent years there has been a switch to lighter engineering, and an extensive programme of slum-clearance has replaced much of the old city by new flats and road networks. The city's underground, reopened by the Queen in 1979, is now one of the most modern in the world, and its airport lies 7 miles to the west. Smoke begrimed Glasgow is fortunate in its large number of parks and other open spaces, covering in all 6000 acres. Lovely countryside surrounds the city: Campsie Fells and Kilpatrick Hills, almost at its door; the **Trossachs, Loch Lomond** and the Kyles of Bute within easy reach.

Glasgow Cathedral (AM), begun in the 12th century and completed at the end of the 15th, is considered the finest example of pre-Reformation Gothic in Europe. The city's university was established as early as 1451 and treasures in its Hunterian Art Gallery include paintings by Rembrandt, Rubens and Whistler. The Hunterian Museum is based on the wide-ranging collections of an 18th-century surgeon. Glasgow has several other outstanding museums and art galleries, including: the Glasgow Art Gallery and Museum;

Glasgow Cathedral from necropolis

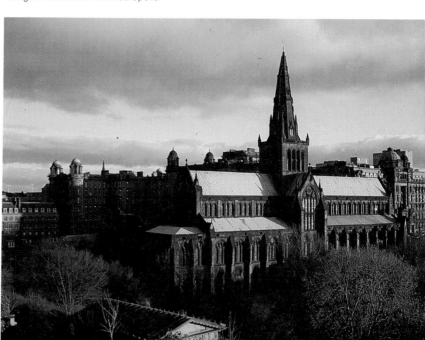

Glencoe, looking east

Haggs Castle, a museum for children; People's Palace, containing a visual record of the history and life of the city; and the Transport Museum. Some 15 miles south west lies Beith, a small town manufacturing gloves and furniture, which has an 18th-century mill. John Witherspoon was a church minister at Beith.

GLASTONBURY
Somerset   *3 ST53*
The ruined abbey is the central attraction of this market town, the so-called 'cradle of English Christianity'. The abbey is on the site of a 7th-century chapel said to have been built by Joseph of Arimathea who had come from the Holy Land to convert the British. According to legend the saint, on arrival in Glastonbury, leant on his staff in prayer, whereupon the staff took root indicating that he should found his religious house here. The original thorn bush was destroyed in the Civil War, but a thorn in the Abbot's kitchen in the abbey is said to be of the same plant. St Mary's Chapel has an underground chapel dedicated to St Joseph. There is no sure evidence of the story of Joseph of Arimathea, but Glastonbury probably had a religious foundation as early as the 5th century. The first abbey was founded in AD 668 and the last was begun in the 13th century, but only completed just before the Dissolution of the Monasteries. Glastonbury is also steeped in Arthurian legend; through the ages writers have speculated that this is the site of Avalon, Arthur's final resting place. The chalice used by Christ at the Last Supper, sought by Arthur's knights as the Holy Grail, is said to lie beneath the Chalice Spring on Glastonbury Tor, brought here by Joseph of Arimathea. As well as the abbey, the town itself had various interesting churches; the George and Pilgrims Inn is one of few surviving pre-Reformation inns. Glastonbury's key industries are sheepskin and leather. The Abbey Tribunal contains finds from prehistoric lake dwellings nearby.

Henry Adams, founder of the New England family, emigrated from the nearby village Barton St David in 1635, while Hector Hugh Monro – 'Saki' – was brought up here.

GLENCOE
Highland   *26 NN15*
Savage peaks and ridges overlook the little whitewashed houses along the straight main street of Glencoe village.

It is not the present village which Scotsmen think of when they hear the name however, but the starkly beautiful glen, a mountain wilderness ascending 1100ft in 10 miles to the vast expanse of Rannoch Moor. Known as 'the Glen of Weeping', it was the scene of the infamous massacre of 38 MacDonalds in 1692, when Campbell troops billeted in the glen turned on their hosts because of their failure to forswear the Jacobite cause. The heather-thatched Glencoe and North Lorn Folk Museum (OACT) in the village houses among other items MacDonald and Jacobite relics, and the Glen Coe Visitor Centre (OACT) at the north end of the glen is close to the site of the massacre. Red deer, ptarmigan, golden eagles and wildcats inhabit the glen, which offers the hill-walker a splendid choice of routes.

GLENEAGLES HOTEL
Tayside   *22 NN91*
On moorland near Auchterarder, palatial Gleneagles Hotel has a 700-acre estate containing a number of golf courses, making it one of Scotland's best known golf resorts. The £1,500,000 Indoor and Country Club complex recently opened has made Gleneagles even more popular.

GLENELG
Highland   *25 NG81*
In summer a car ferry crosses the Sound of Sleat from this scattered village, reached by the steep and winding Mam Rattachan Pass, to the Isle of Skye. To the north are the gaunt ruins of Bernera Barracks, where soldiers were quartered for 70 years following the Jacobite rebellion of 1715. 2 miles south east, in narrow

Glen Beag, are the well-preserved Glenelg Brochs, Dun Telve and Dun Trodden. These 30ft-high defensive towers were probably built by the Picts 2000 years ago.

GLENFINNAN
Highland   *25 NM88*
This hamlet was the rallying point for Bonnie Prince Charlie's clans after he landed from France. A statue of a kilted highlander tops a monument (NTS) at the head of **Loch Shiel**, marking the spot where the prince unfurled his father's standard in 1745 at the beginning of his doomed campaign to regain the throne for his father, the Old Pretender. There is also a Visitor's Centre near the Monument.

GLENGOULANDIE DEER PARK
Tayside   *25 NN75*
Pets must be kept in cars when visiting this park (OACT) where red deer, Highland cattle and other animals and birds are kept in surroundings as much like their natural environment as possible.

GLEN MORE
Highland   *26 NH90*
Overlooked by lofty hills, culminating in 4406ft Ben Nevis, the highest mountain in the British Isles, this remarkable natural feature is better known as the Great Glen, short for the Great Glen of Albin. It divides the mainland of Scotland in two and stretches from **Inverness** down to **Fort William**. The chain of lochs along the glen, including **Loch Ness**, and Telford's Caledonian Canal, enable boats to pass between the North Sea and Atlantic Ocean.

GLOUCESTER

Gloucestershire   9 SO81

Cathedral City of the Cotswolds
'Gloucester town lyes all along on the
bancks of the Severn . . . here are the
fine Lamprys taken in great quantitys
in their season . . . here are very good
Cloysters finely adorn'd with
fretwork . . .'
The Journeys of Celia Fiennes

County capital and an important
inland port on the River Severn,
Gloucester is linked by a canal,
completed in 1827, to docks at
Sharpness on the Bristol Channel 16
miles away. The canal can
accommodate ships of nearly 1000
tons, making the city a commercial
centre with a port that handles the
output of local engineering industries.
A fortified harbour existed here as long
ago as Roman times. Built for the
invasion of Wales during the 1st
century AD, the fort of *Glevum*
guarded the lowest Severn crossing
and the legions' routes into Wales. The
city's main thoroughfares, Northgate,
Southgate, Westgate and Eastgate, still
follow the pattern of the original
Roman roads.

Gloucester is known for the Three
Choirs music festival which takes place
every 3rd year: in the two intervening
years it is held in turn in Hereford and
Worcester. Gloucester's main
attraction is the beautiful cathedral
containing the tomb of Edward II.

A splendid example of Norman
architecture, the main part of the
cathedral, built between 1089 and 1260
contains a massive 174ft-long nave
lined with piers, and a Norman crypt.
The building was partly transformed
by Edward III, and the transepts and
choir, remodelled in the mid 14th
century, mark the birth of the
Perpendicular style in England. These
were redesigned to hold the splendid
tomb of Edward II, murdered at
Berkeley Castle in 1327. The apse was
replaced by Britain's second largest
stained glass window, measuring 72ft
by 38ft. Made in about 1350, it is a
glorious memorial to those who died
at the Battle of Crécy in 1346, and
depicts the Coronation of the Virgin.
There is a memorial to Edward Jenner,
who discovered smallpox vaccine, and
one to John Stafford Smith, son of the
cathedral organist. He composed the
tune that was to become the 'Star
Spangled Banner'. Button Gwinnett, a
signer of the Declaration of
Independence for Georgia, was born at
the Old Rectory, Down Hatherley, 3
miles north, and brought up in
Gloucester.

Originally an abbey, the building
did not become a cathedral until the
reign of Henry VIII. The lovely 14th-
century cloisters, enclosing a delightful
monastic garden with a well, have
exquisite fan vaulting, the earliest in
an English cathedral. The fine, 225ft
pinnacled central tower contains a 3-
ton medieval bell, Great Peter.

In the close, entered by two old
gateways, is a cross to the memory of
Bishop Hooper, a protestant who was
martyred in 1555 during the reign of
Mary I. In one of the alleys leading
into the close is the quaint old shop
immortalized by Beatrix Potter in *The
Tailor of Gloucester*; it is a bookshop
and contains a small museum to this
ever-popular children's writer.

PLACES TO SEE

Bishop Hooper's Lodging In 1555
Bishop Hooper spent the night
before his martyrdom in this
15th–16th-century timber-framed
building. It is now a fascinating
folk-museum, illustrating ancient
crafts.

Blackfriars Abbey The remains of
church and cloister date from the
13th century.

City Museum and Art Gallery The
museum contains many finds
relating to the Roman origins of the
town, including mosaics, and

Edward II's tomb, Gloucester Cathedral

Roman tombstone, Gloucester City
Museum

sculptures. Recent excavation has
revealed the site of a 2-acre Roman
forum, and this would appear to
confirm the theory that the city was
occupied twice by the Romans.
Apart from archaeological finds,
the museum has many other items
of interest.

City East Gate Here, on Eastgate
Street, the Roman and medieval
city defences can be seen in an
underground chamber.

Church of St Mary de Crypt The
grave of Robert Raikes, founder of
the Sunday School Movement and
for many years editor of a local
newspaper, can be found in this
Norman church which stands near
to his house (now the Golden
Fleece Inn) in Southgate Street.
George Whitefield the Evangelical
orator, and leader of the Calvinistic
Methodists attended school here
before going to Pembroke College,
Oxford, where he came under
Wesley's influence. Whitefield was
a highly acclaimed preacher, and
drew vast crowds on his travels.
According to popular legend,
Whitefield's first sermon in St
Mary's de Crypt caused 15 people
to go mad. He was born in 1714 at
the Bell Inn, where his father was
landlord. Whitefield made 7 visits
to America and was in effect the
first great missionary to the
colonies.

New Inn Northgate Street. A half-
timbered 15th-century pilgrim's
hostel whose courtyard has well-
preserved surrounding balconies.

The Old Custom House Built in the
19th century on the quayside, the
building houses the Museum of the
Gloucestershire Regiment.

GLYNDEBOURNE
E Sussex *5 TQ40*
One mile north of Glynde where John Ellman bred the famous Southdown sheep in the 18th century, and where the Elizabethan Glynde Place (OACT) contains fine collections of bronze, pictures and needlework, is Glyndebourne. Here in the 1930s opera-lover John Christie built an opera-house in the grounds of his Tudor manor. Ever since the summer season at Glyndebourne has been synonymous with elegant picnics enjoyed by opera-lovers in evening dress, and is now firmly established in the social calendar.

GOATHLAND
N Yorkshire *20 NZ80*
Sturdy grey stone houses surround the large sheep-grazed greens of this scattered and attractive moorland village, a popular starting point for walks on the North York Moors. Moorland streams cascade over rocks in several spectacular waterfalls, the best known being 70ft-high Mallyan Spout.

GODALMING
Surrey *5 SU94*
An old wool town on the River Wey, with narrow streets, half-timbered buildings and coaching inns, Godalming was an important staging-point on the London to Portsmouth road. Peter the Great was a guest at the King's Arms in 1698; in 1816 Tsar Alexander I and King William Frederick of Prussia dined there. Westbrook Place, now the Meath Home for Epileptics, was the home of the Oglethorpe family. This strongly Royalist family was involved in several conspiracies and attempts to restore the Jacobites to the throne. In 1718 the property passed to James Edward Oglethorpe, who then became MP for Haslemere, and Westbrook became the meeting place for a group of intellectuals who formed the 'Great Philanthropic Movement', working among other things for the reform of London's prisons. Oglethorpe's personal venture for which he was later to foresake Westbrook, was a new settlement in Georgia. He used Westbrook's park as a training ground for prospective pioneers, teaching them relevant skills. The first 120 emigrants reached Georgia in November 1732. Oglethorpe stayed in Georgia and was associated with the Wesleys on their travels. Later James Edward returned to England bringing with him a group of American Indians, whom he held very dear. Later in his life, after various trials and tribulations, Oglethorpe was to become a patron of the arts, and it was largely through his actions that the Government purchased the Sloane Collection, the basis of the British Museum.

GODOLPHIN CROSS
Cornwall *1 SW63*
Near this quiet hamlet, in a secluded woodland setting, is one of Cornwall's most interesting historic houses, Godolphin House (OACT). Former home of the enterprising Earls of Godolphin, it dates mainly from the 16th century. Of particular interest to horse-lovers is the painting by John Wooton of 'Godolphin Arabian'. This stallion owned by the 2nd Earl was one of the three imported Arab stallions from which all British thoroughbred horses descend.

GOODWOOD
W Sussex *4 SU81*
Formerly part of the Goodwood estate, the racecourse here is famous for the 'Glorious Goodwood' meeting in July. Goodwood House (OACT) built by James Wyatt, is a treasure-house of fine pictures, furniture, tapestries and Sèvres porcelain. It was the home of the 4th Duke of Richmond and Lennox, appointed Governor-General of Canada in 1818. He died of rabies the following year, having been bitten by a fox.

GOSFIELD
Essex *12 TL73*
Some of the houses in this tidy village were built by the Courtauld family, who established a silk factory in nearby Halstead in 1826. For a while they also owned Gosfield Hall (OACT), a Tudor and later mansion with a fine gallery. A large lake built on part of the estate in the 18th century is now a recreation centre with paddling and water-skiing areas, and rowing boats available for hire.

GOTHAM
Nottinghamshire *10 SK53*
The medieval population of Gotham took pride in their reputation as fools, which deterred many from the town, including King John, who had intended taking up residence nearby. The village was immortalized by Dr Andrew Borde, 'Merry Andrew', in *Merry Tales of the Mad Men of Gotham*, a collection of rhymes relating among others the tale of the men who sailed to sea in a tub. Several hundred years later Washington Irving was to rename New York 'Gotham'.

GRAMPIANS, THE
Grampians/Highland *26/7*
Britain's largest and highest land mass, the Grampians incorporate the Cairngorm range. Many of the summits exceed 3000ft, and some, in the Cairngorms, top 4000ft. The mountain range stretches from the old county of Argyll in the west to old Aberdeenshire in the north east. Skiing is possible in some parts in winter, particularly around Glenshee.

GRANTCHESTER
Cambridgeshire *11 TL45*
Famous through Rupert Brooke's evocative poem 'The Old Vicarage, Grantchester', this serene village on the River Cam has been loved by generations of students from Cambridge. Brooke lived here before World War I, before him Milton, Spenser, Dryden and Byron were all visitors. Outside the village off the Trumpington road is Byron's Pool. Trumpington Church contains a brass of Sir Roger de Trumpington, the second oldest in Britain, dated 1289. Chaucer used Trumpington Mill as the setting for his *Reeve's Tale*.

GRANTHAM
Lincolnshire *11 SK93*
The beautiful 14th-century spire of St Wulfram's Church is a landmark for miles around this ancient farming and hunting town. The church has a chained library, left to it in 1598. Sir Isaac Newton, formulator of the law of gravity in 1685, was educated at the 15th-century grammar school; he was born in the village of Woolsthorpe 7 miles south. Latterly, Grantham has become famous as the birthplace of Margaret Thatcher, Britain's first woman Prime Minister, whose father owned a grocer's shop in the town. South west of the town Grantham Castle, or Harlaxton Manor, is a fine example of 19th-century architecture. It was used as an English study centre for Stanford University. Several surrounding villages have American connections. At Honington, 5 miles north east, there is a memorial to William and John Smith, founders of Virginia. East of Grantham, Simon and Anne Bradstreet left Horbling to join the pilgrims who sailed in 1630 from Boston, Lincolnshire, in the *Arbella*, Anne being modern America's

St Wulfram's Church, Grantham

first poetess. Just south of Billingborough is Sempringham, home of the Earl of Lincoln, at whose house the Emmanuel College men met to discuss plans for the migration to Massachusetts.

GRASMERE
Cumbria   *18 NY30*

The poet William Wordsworth lived for 14 years in this small village at the northern end of Grasmere lake which he described as 'the loveliest spot that man hath ever found'. From 1799–1808 he lived at Dove Cottage (OACT), a simple lime-washed, slate-roofed stone cottage, originally The Dove and Olive Inn. The Wordsworth Museum is

Grasmere

opposite the house. Many of his contemporaries visited him here, including Coleridge, Sir Walter Scott and Thomas de Quincy who lived in Dove Cottage after the Wordsworths. Wordsworth stayed in Grasmere, living at Allan Bank (NT), and the rectory, later he moved to **Rydal** Mount. Wordsworth is buried in the churchyard of St Oswald's, Grasmere; his simple grave is near those of his wife Mary, three of their children and his sister, Dorothy. Inside the church is a memorial to Sir John Richardson, the arctic explorer and companion of Sir John Franklin; he is buried near the lychgate (d 1865). Grasmere Sports – Cumbria's equivalent of Scotland's Highland Games – features events such as lakeland wrestling, hound-trailing and fell-racing to the summit of Butter Crag and back.

GRAVESEND
Kent   *6 TQ67*

Gravesend's status as a busy port linking coastal and river traffic at the mouth of the Thames has made it a key port of emigration to America. The Serchright Expedition left here in 1556 to seek the North-East Passage. Henry Hudson in the *Hopeful* left Gravesend in 1607 to discover the North-West Passage. In 1629 the Reverend Francis Higginson left for Salem, Massachusetts, where he was to make an early impact on New England's ecclesiastical history. Leonard Calvert and his Catholic founders of Maryland sailed from Gravesend in *The Ark of Avalon* and

The Dove in 1634. George Fox sailed to America in the *Industry* in 1672 and John and Charles Wesley left for Georgia in 1735 from here. Benjamin Franklin landed at Gravesend on his first visit. However, the most lasting link with America can be seen in the Chapel of Unity – an 18th-century building reconsecrated in 1952 and restored by Lady Nancy Astor as a memorial to the Indian princess Pocahontas, daughter of Powhatan. It was she who allegedly saved Captain John Smith from death at the hands of her father. She was later baptized and married Smith's lieutenant John Rolfe. Outside the church is a statue of Pocahontas, inside are two memorial windows and other records relating to her, including a copy of a marriage petition to James I from Rolfe. The King gave consent, overcoming his objections to a commoner marrying a lady of Royal blood. During her time in England Pocahontas was received at the court of Queen Anne, wife of James I. She died just before she and her husband were to revisit her homeland and is buried in Gravesend. The original church of St Mary's was destroyed, but the present building is on the same site.

GREASLY
Nottinghamshire   *15 SK44*

Reverend John Robinson lived in Greasly, 1 mile to the east of Eastwood before he began ministering to the early Separatists (Puritans). 3 miles north east of Greasly is the small mining town of Hucknall; the 12th-century church contains the family vault in which Byron was buried, following his death in Greece. The church and the town contain several memorials and a statue of the poet.

GREAT AYTON
N Yorkshire   *20 NZ51*

Lying beneath the ridges of the Cleveland Hills is the beautiful village of Great Ayton. Here lived Captain James Cook, whose expeditions in the South Seas led to the colonization of Australia and New Zealand. His school is now a museum (OACT); the family house has been reconstructed in Australia and replaced by an obelisk hewn from rocks near Point Hicks, the first Australian land sighted on Cook's voyage of discovery (1768–71). The skyline of Easby Moor is dominated by another Cook monument. 2 miles north east at Newton under Roseberry a path leads to Roseberry Topping, 1057ft, with views to the North Sea.

GREAT BADMINTON
Avon *3 ST88*

Badminton House (open only occasionally), a magnificent Palladian mansion in a 52,000-acre estate, was originally built in 1682 and remodelled by William Kent in the 18th century. The house, home of the Dukes of Beaufort, contains priceless paintings, works of art and Grinling Gibbons carving. The famous Badminton Three Day Event Horse Trials are held in the park each April. On the edge of the estate lies the neat stone built village.

GREAT BOOKHAM
Surrey *5 TQ15*

Great Bookham church is a building of particular interest. The nave walls are 11th century; the north wall shows the remains of contemporary frescoes. Monuments within the church are exceptional, among them is one known as the Geary monument – a memorial to Cornet Geary, killed in action during the Revolutionary War in 1776. It shows British troops marching, with American fighters concealed in the nearby woods. Jane Austen was a frequent visitor to the village where her godfather was rector. A scene in *Emma* is set nearby at **Box Hill**. Fanny Burney wrote *Camilla* while at Fairfield House in the High Street. 2 miles south is Polesden Lacey (NT) where George VI and Queen Elizabeth (now the Queen Mother) spent part of their honeymoon. This 19th century house, containing the Greville collection of pictures, tapestries and furnishings, is set in 140 acres of beautiful grounds which include a superb rose garden.

Viscount Bennett, previously R B Bennett, Canadian Prime Minister 1930–35 and friend of Lord Beaverbrook, came to England disillusioned with politics and his country after the failure of his economic policies and his rejection by the Canadian electorate. From 1938 to his death in 1947 he lived at Mickleham, 2 miles east of Great Bookham. He is buried in St Michael's Church.

GREAT COXWELL
Oxfordshire *4 SU29*

William Morris described the well-preserved stone 13th-century barn (NT) here as being as 'noble as a cathedral'. Built by the Cistercian monks of Beaulieu Abbey, it is 152ft long, 44ft wide and 50ft high. From the limestone village there are wide views extending to the White Horse Hills and the Iron Age fort of Uffington.

GREAT DUNMOW
Essex *11 TL62*

One of the first lifeboats was tested here in 1785 on Doctor's Pond, by the local inventor Lionel Lukin. A unique medieval custom, imported from Brittany in the 13th century and mentioned by Chaucer, takes place here every 4 years. A flitch of bacon is presented to any married couple who have not quarrelled or regretted their marriage for at least a year and a day – recipients being tried by a bewigged amateur judge and counsel. Henry Ainsworth, the historical novelist, revived the ceremony in the mid 19th century. The Town itself is a bustling little place, with many attractive buildings. The Blue Gates of Easton Lodge 2½ miles north west bear a memorial to American airmen.

GREAT TORRINGTON
Devon *2 SX41*

The town affords exquisite views and its site, high above the River Torridge, is one of the finest in Devon. In 1645, Torrington church and 200 imprisoned Royalists were blown up with gunpowder; it was rebuilt in 1651 and has a fine 17th-century pulpit. The little market square has considerable charm. William Cory, the Victorian poet, was born here and lived at Palmer House. Increase Mather, who was born in **Dorchester**, lived and minstered in Great Torrington as well as to a number of other English congregations. He became president of Harvard in 1685, and was probably the most powerful man in the Puritan colonies in America. He died in 1723.

On the south side of the town there is a roadside conical Waterloo monument, and 3 miles south east lies Great Potheridge, 17th-century home of the Monk family. A tablet records General Monk's help in the restoration of Charles II.

GREAT YARMOUTH
Norfolk *12 TG50*

Now one of Britain's most popular seaside resorts, the town was for centuries a centre for the herring fishing industry. These days the harbour is used mainly by cargo ships and vessels servicing North Sea gas and oil rigs. 5 miles of sandy beach provide safe bathing, and the numerous entertainments include two piers with theatres, a leisure centre and a pleasure beach. The town became a resort in the 19th century, but it suffered badly from air raids in World War II, so much so that a 1969 film version of Charles Dickens's *David Copperfield*, which has many scenes in the town, had to be filmed in Southwold. Nevertheless, several fine old buildings survive in Great Yarmouth including the birthplace of Anna Sewell, author of *Black Beauty*. Her half-timbered house opposite St Nicholas's Church (said to be England's largest parish church) is now a museum. George Borrow spent several years here for his wife's health. The Elizabethan House, the Tollhouse and the Old Merchant's House are also interesting historical museums. Other attractions include the House of Wax; the Maritime Museum for East Anglia; and the Merrivale Model Village.

GREENOCK
Strathclyde *22 NS27*

Situated on the Clyde estuary, Greenock was an important industrial and shipbuilding town, suffering severe bomb damage in World War II. Among other exhibits in the McLean Museum and Art Gallery are those connected with shipping, and relics of James Watt, inventor of steam power, who was born here in 1736.

GRETNA GREEN
Dumfries & Galloway *18 NY36*

For over a century this border village was a favourite destination for runaway English lovers wishing to marry without their parents' consent. After a law of 1754, clandestine marriages were banned in England, but in Scotland all that was required was for a couple to declare that they wished to become man and wife in front of witnesses. In Gretna Green it took place over the anvil, which can still be seen. In 1856 a new law required one of the couple to live in Scotland for three weeks, but it was not until another law was passed in 1940 that the village smith was banned from performing the ceremony altogether.

GRIMES GRAVES
Norfolk *12 TL88*

Not graves at all, the 350 holes in the ground and the labyrinth of tunnels that bear this name are in fact the largest prehistoric flint mines (AM) in Europe. Using tools made from deer antlers, Neolithic man extracted flints and exported them throughout the south of England to be used for arrowheads and axes. One of the shafts can be explored; although it is lit, a torch may still be useful.

Grimsby Docks

GRIMSBY
Humberside *16 TA20*
Formerly one of the world's great
fishing ports, Grimsby, which was
named after a legendary Danish
fisherman, Grim, has declined
substantially since, among other
things, the cod war with Iceland in the
1970s. Exhibits in the Welholme
Galleries include Napoleonic and 19th-
century ship models, and marine
paintings. Many emigrants went to
Massachusetts Bay from Grimsby in
the early pilgrim days. South of
Cleethorpes, the adjacent northern
resort town, is Humberston. The
Reverend Hansard Knollys left here
for America in 1638. The area affords
fine views across the Humber estuary
to Spurn Head.

GUILDFORD
Surrey *5 TQ04*
Guildford's impressive modern
Anglican cathedral, consecrated in
1961, looks down on the county town
of Surrey from its hilltop setting on the
outskirts. Close to the cathedral are
the modern buildings of the University
of Surrey, and the Yvonne Arnaud
Theatre was opened in 1965 on the
banks of the River Wey. Despite being
a busy modern shopping centre the
town retains many old buildings, and
its steep High Street has an unchanging
Georgian character, with a very ornate
17th-century Guildhall. All that
remains of the castle is the 12th-
century keep (OACT); nearby is the
house in which Lewis Carroll died in
1898. William Cobbett also died just
outside Guildford at Normandy Farm.
Other places of interest in the town are
the 17th-century Guildford House
Gallery, Guildford Museum and the
Tudor Hospital of the Blessed Trinity
(OACT). Loseley House (OACT) is an
Elizabethan manor built with stone
from Waverley Abbey, lying 2½ miles
south west of Guildford, and contains
fine period furnishings. Other
interesting houses are Elizabethan
Sutton Place, 2½ miles north east, one
of the first non-fortified mansions in
Britain; Clandon Park (NT) with its
Palladian house, and Hatchlands (NT)
which has a Robert Adam interior.

A memorial in the cathedral
commemorates Viscount Bennett, a
former Canadian Prime Minister,
1930–5, who gave a large donation for
the purchase of the cathedral hill to
recall strong connections between
Canadian forces and the area in which
they trained in World War II.

GUISBOROUGH
Cleveland *20 NZ61*
This busy market town, a touring
centre for the nearby Cleveland Hills,
and North Yorkshire Moors, contains
an architectural gem in the remains of
a 12th-century priory (AM). They
include a gatehouse and dovecot, and
the magnificent 14th-century east end
of the building. The work of artists
and craftsmen can be seen at the
Chapel Beck gallery.

GUITING POWER
Gloucestershire *10 SP02*
Through the far-sighted action of a
local landowner, the rural character of
this village of Cotswold stone
buildings clustered round a triangular
green should be preserved. Rare breeds
of farm animals can be seen at the
Cotswold Farm Park (OACT), 1¾
miles north east of the village.

GWEEK
Cornwall *1 SW72*
At the head of the Helford River, this
quiet village has become a popular
destination for tourists, who come to
visit the fascinating Seal Sanctuary.
Here sick and injured seals rescued
from Cornish beaches are cared for in
the well-run hospital and five pools.

H

HADDINGTON
Lothian *24 NT57*
In the 12th century the town was laid
out in a narrow triangle, whose
boundaries can be traced following
High Street, Market Street and
Hardgate. Today this gracious town of
wide streets is one of Scotland's best
preserved, with 129 buildings
scheduled as of special architectural or
historic interest. The splendid Town
House, with its slender spire, was built
by William Adam, father of Robert
Adam, in 1748. The medieval red
sandstone of St Mary's Church, where
John Knox worshipped as a boy, has
been extensively restored.

HADDON HALL
Derbyshire *15 SK26*
A splendid example of a well-
preserved 12th- to 15th-century
medieval and manorial house, Haddon
Hall (OACT) has belonged to the
Manners family since 1567 and
probably looks much the same as it did
300 years ago. Beautifully situated on
the River Wye, its battlemented towers
and turrets of warm-coloured
Derbyshire stone, never used in self-
defence, blend serenely with their
peaceful surroundings. Of particular
interest are the chapel, the long
gallery, panelled in oak and walnut,
and the Mortlake Tapestries.

HADLEIGH
Essex *6 TQ88*
Impressive ruins remain of a 13th-
century castle (AM), rebuilt by
Edward III in the 14th century, but
destroyed during a landslide. A
painting of the ruins by John
Constable can be seen in the Tate
Gallery. From the castle there are
views of the Thames estuary and the
Kent coast.

HADLEIGH
Suffolk *12 TM04*
Fine houses in the long High Street of
this former wool town on a tributary
of the River Stour represent an
unusually wide variety of architectural
styles; timber-framed, brick, plasterwork with and without the decoration
known as pargeting. The 14th- to 15th-

century church contains an unusual 14th-century bench-end depicting a wolf holding the decapitated head of St Edmund, illustrating an old legend. The nearby 15th-century Deanery Tower is all that remains of the palace of Archdeacon Pykenham, while the fine 15th-century timbered Guildhall (open daily) has two overhanging storeys.

HADRIAN'S WALL
see Housesteads
Building of this great wall began in AD 122 after the Emperor's visit to Britain. The 15ft wall was 7½ft thick and ran from Wallsend to the Solway Firth.

HAILSHAM
E Sussex   *6 TQ50*
Two miles west of this pleasant market town situated below the Sussex Downs is Michelham Priory (OACT). The nucleus of this Tudor manor was an Augustinian priory, founded in 1229 and partially destroyed during the Dissolution of the Monasteries in 1536. Approached by an ancient bridge over the wide moat, the priory is entered through a splendid 14th-century gatehouse. The interior contains 17th-century furniture, and other items of interest include Sussex ironwork. The 7-acre grounds contain a Tudor great barn, old wagons and ploughs, and a Sussex craft shop.

Michelham Priory and the River Cuckmere near Hailsham

HALIFAX
W Yorkshire   *15 SE02*
Nineteenth-century industrialization brought great changes to the town. Today it is known, amongst other things, for having the headquarters of the world's largest building society. Architecturally, the Victorian era gave

Halifax its town hall – the work of Sir Giles Barry, designer of the Houses of Parliament – and the folly, Wainhouse Tower, originally a 253ft dye-works chimney, now crowned with a Renaissance-style pinnacle. The ancestors of the famous New England family, Saltonstall, came from the villages of Over and Nether Saltonstall, now part of Halifax. Sir Richard Saltonstall, nephew of a Governor of the Merchant Adventurers Company and Lord Mayor of London, sailed in the *Arbella* in 1630, founding Watertown, Massachusetts. North east of Halifax, Shibden Hall (OACT) contains the Folk Museum of West Yorkshire. The Hall was the birthplace in 1752 of Jeremy Lister, an officer in the 10th Regiment of Foot, who fought at the Battle of Concord, early in the Revolutionary War. His account of the battle is held in Halifax library along with papers and letters relating to the family estate.

HARDWICK HALL
Derbyshire   *15 SK46*
A striking feature of this Elizabethan mansion (OACT), built in 1597 for the Dowager Countess of Shrewsbury ('Bess of Hardwick'), is the large number and size of windows. A symmetrical, stone building, it has a huge tower at each corner topped with decorative open stonework incorporating the letters ES for Elizabeth Shrewsbury. Of particular interest inside are fine tapestries and needlework.
   At Ault Hucknall, 1 mile north, the philosopher Thomas Hobbes is buried in the church. He was tutor to two Earls of Devonshire, and spent the last years of his life at Hardwick Hall.

HAREWOOD
W Yorkshire   *15 SE34*
Rebuilt in the 18th century at the same time as Harewood House (OACT), the long terraces of the village extend from the main gates of this opulent yellowstone mansion, probably the most exquisite in the region. Planned by John Carr of York, the beautiful interior of the house, home of the Earl and Countess of Harewood, was largely decorated by Robert Adam and furnished by Chippendale. The picture collection contains works by John Singer Sargent; Epstein's 'Adam' is also housed here. The park, created by Capability Brown, has a 4-acre fascinating bird garden.

HARLECH
Gwynedd   *13 SH53*
This town of steep narrow streets and granite-built houses above Tremadog Bay is popular with tourists. Built by Edward I on the site of a Celtic fortress, the castle has survived repeated attacks. The beloved Welsh chieftain Owen Glendower, or Owain Glyndwr, was beseiged here by Henry V. The song 'Men of Harlech' commemorates Dafydd ap Einion who held the castle in 1468 during the Wars of the Roses; Harlech was the last British fortress to hold out against the Yorkists, and also the last to stave off the Parliamentarians during the Civil War. However, the song dates only from the 18th century.
   To the north is a National Nature Reserve, Morfa Harlech.

HARLOW
Essex   *6 TL41*
Harlow New Town was conceived in 1947 and was planned to develop alongside the old market town. It was the first town to have a pedestrian precinct and now has a population of 80,000. Passmores House is an early Georgian building converted to a museum, and the Mark Hall Cycle Museum displays more than 50 machines, the earliest dating back to 1819.
   East of Harlow is the hamlet of High Laver. Three men associated with early American history lived here. Oates Manor House (now destroyed) was the home of Sir Francis Masham, to whom Roger Williams, a pioneer of religious freedom, was chaplain. Williams, educated at Charterhouse and Pembroke College, Cambridge, sailed to Boston, Massachusetts, with his wife, Mary. He lived in Salem and Plymouth until, banished from Massachusetts he founded Providence, then returned to England where he met Oliver Cromwell and the Mathers. Williams obtained self-government for Rhode Island and became their first President. John Lake, the philosopher and writer, whose beliefs in life, liberty and property were adopted by Thomas Jefferson in the Declaration of Independence, lived here for the last 14 years of his life. As Secretary to the Lords' proprietors of Carolina he had American interests. His tomb in High Laver church bears a memorial. High Laver's third resident was John Norton, who has the ignominious claim of being the chief persecutor of Quakers in Massachusetts.

Harlech Castle

HARROGATE
N Yorkshire *15 SE35*
An attractive, spacious town of
dignified Victorian stone buildings,
lightened by flowerbeds and open
spaces, Harrogate stands 400–600ft
above sea-level, within easy reach of
the dales. The town's importance as a
spa resort was increased in 1804 when
the Royal Pump Room was erected on
a sulphur well. The Royal Baths,
opened in 1897, became one of the
largest hydrotherapy establishments in
the world. Agatha Christie stayed,
incognito, at the Old Swan, in 1926,
having mysteriously disappeared from
London. On the south side of the town
is a 200-acre common known as the
Stray. A path joins Valley Gardens
where there is an attractive sun
pavilion, and the 60-acre Harlow Car
Gardens, with its comprehensive
collection of plants, shrubs and trees,
and trial grounds for experimental
agriculture. The location and
attractions of the town are capitalized
on by the international conference
centre. Rudding Park, a Regency
mansion, lies 3 miles south east; its
picture collection contains J S Copley's
copy of West's 'Death of Wolfe'.

HARTLEBURY
Hereford & Worcester *9 SO87*
Hartlebury Castle, built originally in
1268, has a 15th-century hall and
includes many 18th-century
alterations. It is the former home of
the Bishops of Worcester. Sir Edwin
Sandys, who helped found Virginia,
was probably born here, the second
son of Archbishop Sandys. Izaak
Walton, the *Compleat Angler*, lived

here as Bishop's steward for 2 years.
Hartlebury Castle now contains a
fascinating folk museum, the Hereford
and Worcester County Museum, with
a varied collection of exhibits.

HARWICH,
Essex *12 TM23*
The ancient walled town and port of
Harwich grew up on a small peninsula
at the mouths of the Stour and Orwell
rivers. It has been a port since
medieval times. Edward III's fleet
gathered here in 1340 before sailing to
victory in the first sea battle of the
Hundred Years War. In 1808 work
began on the 180ft diameter redoubt, a
granite fort with moat and earthworks
built to defend the port against
Napoleon's armies. A unique naval
treadmill crane is preserved on the
green. The narrow, cobbled streets
retain their medieval character.

Harwich was the birthplace of
Christopher Jones who captained the
Mayflower on its voyage in 1620. He
lived at No 21 King's Head Street and
was twice married in nearby St
Nicholas's Church. His house is
marked by a plaque. Two other
Pilgrims, Richard Gardner and John
Alden, were also Harwich men. Round
the bay is Parkestone Quay, departure
point for Continental ferries.
Dovercourt on the south side, is a quiet
resort suburb, Edwardian in flavour.

HASCOMBE
Surrey *5 TQ03*
From 100-acre Winkworth Arboretum,
1 mile north of Hascombe, there are
fine views of the **North Downs**. This
hillside arboretum with two lakes is

especially worth visiting in May and
October for seasonal colours.

HASLEMERE
Surrey *5 SU93*
Situated in hilly, wooded country,
much of it designated an area of
outstanding natural beauty and ideal
for walking, this small town is well
known for its Dolmetsch Musical
Instrument Workshops where there is
a museum of musical instruments. An
annual festival held in July is devoted
to early music. The town also boasts a
unique Educational Museum, founded
in 1888 by a Victorian surgeon, Sir
Jonathan Hutchinson.

HASTINGS
E Sussex *6 TQ80*
In many ways Hastings is a typical
19th-century resort town with its pier,
parade and hotels. However,
reminders of its earlier history can be
seen in the remains of the Norman
castle, built 1067. William the
Conqueror prepared for his decisive
battle with Harold here in 1066, which
took place 6 miles inland at Battle. The
town hall contains a modern Bayeux
Tapestry representing events from the
Battle of Hastings to the 900th
anniversary in 1966, known as the
Hastings Embroidery. Hastings was
one of the Cinque Ports, with a strong
tradition of associated activities,
notably fishing and smuggling. The
fisherman's museum and fishmarket in
Old Hastings are worth a visit. The
market is set on the beach and is
among a series of tall net huts
following a design dating from
Elizabethan times.

During the 19th century, in its
heyday as a seaside town, Hastings
was visited by many writers and poets,
including Byron, Keats, Mary and
Charles Lamb and Christina Rossetti.
36 St Mary's Terrace, Hastings was the
home of Grey Owl, born Archie
Belaney in 1888. At the age of 18
Belaney emigrated to Canada. In 1930
he took up the cause of beavers. As
Grey Owl he claimed to be half
Scottish and half Apache. His pose was
so convincing that on the second of his
visits to England in 1937, Grey Owl
received an audience with the king and
Royal Family.

Four miles north west of Hastings is
Beauport Park, a Georgian mansion
set in 900 acres of wooded estate. This
was the home of General James
Murray, an 18th-century Governor of
Quebec and the name is taken from a
village near Quebec. Murray fought in

the Battle of the Plains of Abraham. A replica of a shield from the gates of Quebec is in the mayor's office in Hastings. Beauport is now a hotel lying in 33 acres of beautiful gardens. 6 miles further north of Hastings is Brede. Stephen Crane, author of *The Red Badge of Courage*, lived here with Lady Cora Stewart. However, he soon became ill, and died in Germany a year later, aged 28. Later, Clare Sheridan, the British sculptress, niece of Jennie Jerome and cousin of Winston Churchill, lived at Brede Place. J M Barrie heard the story which inspired Captain Hook in *Peter Pan* when visiting Brede. The character was based on J M Mahler, a pirate who became a rector, but was blackmailed by a man named Smith.

HATFIELD
Hertfordshire   *5 TL20*
Despite rapid development of the adjacent New Town since 1946, Hatfield old town survives; Fore Street has a row of lovely Georgian houses stepped up the hillside to the 13th-century church of St Ethelreda and the 15th-century Old Palace: Elizabeth I lived here as a child; Elizabeth's Oak is said to be the spot where she heard of her sister Mary's death and her own accession to the throne. The house was built entirely of brick – a startling new fashion for the period. The Old Palace stands at the threshold to Hatfield House, one of Britain's best Jacobean houses (OACT). Hatfield House was built from 1608–12, in the shape of an

E, by Robert Cecil, 1st Earl of Salisbury and Secretary of State to Elizabeth I. Cecil was particularly interested in the Virginia Colony, with a share in any minerals discovered there; the family had many links with America. The house contains items relating to Elizabeth and to the Cecil family, including a letter written by the fatally wounded William Brewster to Cecil. The house, now the home of the Marquess of Salisbury, is surrounded by 1500 acres of parkland, with woods and some farmland. The local church contains the Cecil family chapel and Sir Robert Cecil's tomb, which was ordered before his death to ensure a good likeness.

HATHERSAGE
Derbyshire   *15 SK28*
Beautifully situated above the River Derwent, this sturdy Peak District village was the inspiration for 'Morton' in Charlotte Brontë's *Jane Eyre*. She stayed at the 18th-century vicarage and must have taken her heroine's name from the Eyre family monuments in the church. Robin Hood's friend 'Little John' is said to be buried in a 14ft grave in the churchyard.

HAVERFORDWEST
Dyfed   *7 SM91*
Dominated by the hilltop ruins of a Norman castle 'slighted' by Cromwell during the Civil War, the houses of this important market town crowd the slopes of two hills. There are splendid

views from the castle (OACT), which now houses the town's museum, art gallery and record office. St Mary's Church dates from the 13th to 15th centuries.

HAWARDEN HOUSE
Clwyd   *14 SJ36*
Hawarden is only 6 miles from Chester; its most famous resident was William Ewart Gladstone, four times Prime Minister during Victoria's reign. He came to Hawarden House after 1839 when he married Welsh heiress, Catherine Glynne, and lived here until his death in 1898. One of the elder statesman's hobbies was felling trees in the park, which were then carved into chairs – many of which survive. The village contains many memorials to Gladstone, including St Deiniol's Library and Hall, which contain his library of 32,000 volumes. The parish church also has memorials, including a Burne-Jones window. The grounds of the ruined Hawarden Castle are open to the public.

HAWES
N Yorkshire   *19 SD88*
Situated in the heart of the **Yorkshire Dales** National Park, this village of grey stone cottages on the River Ure is an ideal starting point for exploring the high moors of Wensleydale. There is a National Park Centre and a Folk Museum of the Upper Dales (OACT). A 100ft-high waterfall, Hardraw Force, can be reached by a footpath behind the Green Dragon Inn at Hardraw 1 mile to the north.

HAWICK
Borders   *24 NT51*
Some of the fascinating exhibits in the local museum and art gallery reflect the importance of the wool trade in the history of this large Border town, world-famous for knitwear, and situated in Teviotdale. The Horse Monument in the High Street commemorates the defeat of the English by local youths in 1514, evoked annually in an event known as the Common Riding.

HAWKSHEAD
Cumbria   *18 SD39*
Near the head of Esthwaite Water, halfway between Coniston and Windermere, the stone cottages of this delightful Lake District village are clustered round little courtyards and narrow alleys. The Norman church of St Michael contains the Sandys Chapel, dedicated by Edwin Sandys,

Hatfield House

Hawkshead

Archbishop of York, to his parents. Sandys was born at Esthwaite Hall in 1516. The family bible records the births of his children, including Sir Edwin Sandys, one of the founders of Virginia; the bible is kept in the grammar school, founded in 1585 by the Archbishop. William Wordsworth, who was born at **Cockermouth**, was educated, from 1778–87, at the school, which is now a museum and contains one of the finest medieval school libraries in existence. Nearby is Anne Tyson's cottage where Wordsworth lodged.

The pre-Reformation courthouse (NT), dating from the 15th century is of great interest. Several buildings in Hawkshead, together with land overlooking Esthwaite Water, were given to the National Trust by Beatrix Potter, who lived nearby at **Sawrey**.

HAWORTH
W Yorkshire   *15 SE03*
Situated on the edge of rugged moors, this bleak village is famous for its Brontë associations. The Brontë's parsonage lies at the top of the steep main street, away from the local industries which nestle in the valley. The Parsonage where Anne, Emily and Charlotte lived from 1820–61, is now a Brontë museum, incorporating the Bonnell Collection – material collected over the 30 years devoted by Henry Houston Bonnell of Philadelphia to finding information about the famous literary family. Personal items including clothes and furniture are also preserved. Charlotte was married in the parish church, she died soon after and both she and Emily are buried there. The Brontë Chapel, dedicated in 1964, has a memorial window donated by an American admirer. The Brontës' brother, Branwell, was a frequent visitor to the Black Bull Inn, and he

eventually drank himself to death. The bleak ruin of High Withins on the moor was the setting for *Wuthering Heights*, Emily's most well-known work. A favourite walk of the sisters ran 2 miles west from the cemetery along Enfield Side to the Brontë Waterfall. Nearby, the Keighly and Worth Valley Railway is a revived steam line, with a museum at Haworth station exhibiting one of the largest private collections of standard-gauge and diesel locomotives (and an American steam locomotive) in the country.

HAXEY
Humberside   *16 SK79*
Remnants of the ancient strip system of field division can still be found in this old farming centre. A custom known as Throwing the Hood takes place here every 6 January, Twelfth Night. The game, which resembles a boisterous Rugby match, consists of a competition to get several 'hoods' to various village inns, while costumed 'boggins' try to intercept them. The custom is said to have originated in medieval times when the lady of the manor lost her hood while out riding, and a group of peasants competed to return it.

HAY-ON-WYE
Powys   *8 SO24*
Booklovers come to this small market town set high above one of Britain's most enchanting rivers, the Wye, to visit the largest secondhand bookshop in the world. The town, at the edge of the **Brecon Beacons** National Park, is also the ancestral home of the American writer William Dean Howells. At one time Hay-on-Wye was a centre of the flannel industry, and the oldest part of the town with its narrow, winding streets and little shops is particularly attractive. The

19th-century church of St Mary includes sections dating from the 13th century; the ruins of the Norman castle can also be seen. Outside the town there are beautiful walks and passes through the Black Mountains, including the 1778ft Gospel Pass which leads to the ruins of **Llanthony** Priory.

HEACHAM
Norfolk   *12 TF63*
Heacham was the birthplace of John Rolfe, famous for tobacco cultivation in Virginia and for his marriage to the Algonquin Princess Pocahontas (Rolfe's first wife and daughter died in a series of tragedies in the colonies). The young Pocahontas returned with her husband to Norfolk, where she gave birth to their son Thomas. Pocahontas died soon afterwards before returning to her native land. Her son however was brought up in Virginia and the family flourished. Heacham Hall, a Georgian mansion incorporating the old family house, was built in the 18th century, but was destroyed by fire during World War II; but the parish church and the village have many reminders of Pocahontas. The wife of President Woodrow Wilson traced her ancestry back to Pocahontas whose great-granddaughter married Robert Bolling of Virginia. Norfolk Lavender, the largest growers and distillers of lavender, with fields covering over 100 acres, are based at Caley Mill, on the main coast road A149.

HELMINGHAM
Suffolk   *12 TM15*
The magnificent parkland (OACT) of Helmingham Hall, a moated half-timbered house where the two drawbridges are still raised at night, contains red and fallow deer and Highland cattle.

HELMSLEY
N Yorkshire   *15 SE68*
Situated on the edge of the moors beside the River Rye, this attractive market town of red-roofed, stone-built houses is the start of the Cleveland Way. In Duncombe Park are the ruins of a 12th-century castle (AM), thought to have been built by Walter L'Espec who founded the beautiful Rievaulx Abbey 2 miles north west. Nunnington Hall (NT) 4½ miles south east is a 16th- and 17th-century house with a fine panelled hall and an impressive staircase. The Carlisle Collection of Miniature Rooms should be seen.

ON THE BANKS OF THE CLYDE

Glasgow is a cathedral town, though St Mungo's is now a Presbyterian kirk; the only undamaged survivor among the Gothic churches of southern Scotland. Its municipal coat of arms has the motto, 'Let Glasgow flourish by the preaching of the Word', though in recent years it has omitted all but the first three words. Its population at the time of the Act of Union was approximately 20,000. Today, with a population of over one million, it is the third largest city in Britain, after London and Birmingham, the latter only recently surpassing it in population. Its development is a microcosm of Scotland's industrial history.

Glasgow began to develop after the Act of Union. In the eighteenth century Edinburgh became a centre of the Enlightenment, in its University and in the New Town.

Glasgow, in whose University James Watt was employed, and with Joseph Black and William Cullen on its faculty, looked west, to the trade the Clyde brought and to the products it could export. After 1707 it could trade with English territories overseas as well as the Scottish, and notably with the West Indies for sugar, and the Chesapeake. The main bridge in the city is, locally, still called Jamaica Bridge. The American tobacco fleets came to Glasgow (downriver Port Glasgow was built for them) to Whitehaven and to Bristol, and there were many Scottish factors (agents) working at the tobacco-collecting points on the James, the Rappahannock and the Potomac. The eighteenth-century commercial barons who paraded Virginia Street and the Salt Market in their red gowns were known as the

Tobacco Lords: Glassfords, Cuninghames, Buchanans and Boyles, Dunlops, Spiers and Ritchies, Murdochs and Oswalds. One of Glasgow's suburbs, like a house on the Potomac, is called Mount Vernon – the Victor of Portobello in 1739 had other admirers as well as Lawrence Washington. Sir Walter Scott caught the picture of the enterprising Glasgow trader in his immortal Glasgow Bailie, Nicol Jarvie, in *Rob Roy* – modelled, perhaps, on cherubic David Dale, Robert Owen's father-in-law, and a man of great enterprise.

The War of American Independence in 1776 was a far more worrying blow to Glasgow than the visit of the Young Pretender and his wild clansmen, whom Glasgow opposed, had been thirty years before. Trade dried up, banks went broke – as they would again, with the Amer-

ican Civil War. But, resiliently, they turned to cotton, and built the mills to use it. By 1808 there were 250 linen factories in Scotland. Since the river silted up easily, it was dredged and deepened, and equipped with docks. 'Glasgow', they say, 'made the Clyde, and the Clyde made Glasgow.' In a wider part of the river, twenty miles upstream from the sea, they began the building of ships, culminating in the 1930s in the two *Queens* built at John Brown's yard, Clydebank. Ships and ships' engines, coal and steel, chemicals and dyes, railway engines and track became Glasgow's major products, and it had a world-wide reputation for engineering craftsmanship, for quality, and industry; Clyde-built became a synonym for excellence. It was also a two-way traffic. Then, as today, Americans moved in – in the

New Lanark, Strathclyde

1860s Singer's set themselves up in Bridgeton and then Clydebank; Babcock and Willcox moved to Renfrew and Dumbarton, and, later, companies as various as Hewlett-Packard, and Caterpillar Tractor, Burroughs, Seagrams and a legion more. The Kirk had said that Glasgow flourished by the preaching of the Word; it flourished too by those other Calvinist qualities, effort, industry, sweat, for – as the Pilgrim Fathers and Franklin knew – God helps those who help themselves. Its numbers grew, to feed its shipyards and its factories, Highlanders and Irishmen among them, so that parts of the city have now a forty per cent Catholic population. In the 1840s the Irish came in at the rate of 50,000 a year.

Glasgow is, in style, a total contrast with Edinburgh, and in appearance and character closer to Belfast or Sheffield – or to Pittsburgh (and each of them has had a facelift) – than to any other city in Britain. And now, in the newly constituted Strathclyde region set up after the local government reorganization of 1974, it is still at the centre of, but in territorial area swamped by, a varied countryside stretching downriver and across to the sea, north and south of the Clyde; and only an hour away, in the Trossachs and Loch Lomond, it has a nature reserve all its own.

Glasgow has sent legions of its people to Canada and the United States. Some of them exotic, since two became Indian chiefs: President George Washington in making a settlement with Indians entertained Chief Alexander McGillivray and Chief William McIntosh of the Creek Indians. The Valley of Virginia, the route south and the interiors of the Carolinas were a trail of Scottish names, as their place names (Glasgow and Edinburgh among them) recall. They founded colleges, traded in tobacco and cotton and furs – and went into politics. And, if many Glasgow factors in Dumfries, Virginia or on the Potomac were Loyalists in 1776, the roll-call of the Scots and Scotch-Irish who fought for American Independence is impressive, including John Witherspoon of Paisley and Princeton, who was a signer of the Declaration of Independence.

Moreover, in the nineteenth and early twentieth centuries, many of Glasgow's activities were seen as models for the United States. It was not merely that Glasgow was the workshop of the world; there was a common democratic and Presbyterian culture, sober and church-going, a respect for the Book and for learning, and a faith in God and industry. 'The gospel of wealth', said Andrew Carnegie, 'but echoes Christ's words'. To Glaswegians America was less a foreign country than an idealized Scotland. Indeed Glasgow's industries were the models for much of the New World, as the story of the Donahue brothers indicates – they made a fortune in San Francisco with the first iron works, the first railway engines, the first ironclad ships. Temperance reform and prohibition of the use of the demon rum were common crusades – like anti-slavery itself. Civil reform as carried out in Glasgow interested Jane Addams, F C Howe and Henry Demarest Lloyd; not least its settlement houses for the poor, and even its tramcars. Horace Greeley, the editor of the *New York Tribune* in the 1840s and 1850s, once described Glasgow as 'more American than any city I have seen in Europe. Half of Pittsburgh spliced on to half of Philadelphia would make a city like Glasgow.'

Places to Visit

The Cathedral and the Provand's Lordship House (once a manse of cathedral canons), the only remaining pre-Reformation house in the city (late fifteenth century).
Crookston Castle, home of the Darnley Stuarts.
The Gorbals, no longer the fabled centre of violence it was once said to be.

Glasgow; the cathedral and statue of David Livingstone

New Lanark for David Dale and Robert Owen of New Harmony, Indiana.
People's Museum, Glasgow Green.
Pollok House, for the collection of paintings and exotica made by Glasgow industrialist Sir William Burrell.
Strathclyde University on George Square, and the massive *City Chambers*.
Trades House, Glassford Street (Robert Adam).
The University on Gilmorehill, designed in 1870 by Gilbert Scott, has obvious 'Gothic' similarities with St Pancras Station, London; and the terraces facing it across Kelvingrove Park; its Hunterian Museum is important; see also Charles Rennie Mackintosh's Art School. The University has a remarkable collection of over seventy oil paintings by Whistler.

Further Reading

Bernard Aspinwall, *Portable Utopia*, Glasgow and the US 1820–1920 (Aberdeen University Press, 1984)
Jack House, *Square Mile of Murder* (Chambers, 1955)
Tom Johnston, *Memoirs*. Labour MP, Secretary of State for Scotland in Churchill's war-time government (Collins, 1952)
Charles Oakley, *The Second City* (Blackie, 1945)
Sir Walter Scott, *Rob Roy* (for the portrait of Bailie Nicol Jarvie)

Sail from the Broomielaw 'doon the watter' via Clydebank and Dunoon and the Holy Loch, where the American Polaris submarines come in to refit, and – time permitting – sail through the narrow but beautiful Kyles of Bute to Mull or Oban or Inveraray.

HELSTON
Cornwall   *1 SW62*
A busy market town, Helston is
particularly worth visiting on Floral
Day, on or near 8 May. This is the day
of the ancient Furry Dance, with
dancing up and down the hilly streets,
just as described in the popular song.
Nearby is the fascinating Cornwall
Aero Park with collections of historic
aircraft and motor vehicles. An added
attraction are the reproduction old-
world cobbled streets of Flambards
Village. The story of Cornish tin-
mining is recreated at Poldark Mine,
Wendron, 3 miles north east of
Helston.

HEMEL HEMPSTEAD
Hertfordshire   *5 TL00*
Hemel Hempstead lies to the north of
the Grand Union Canal on the River
Gade. Despite the addition of a
sprawling new town, this Chilterns
market town retains several examples
of its architectural heritage. The
remains of a Roman villa were
discovered in Gadebridge Park; and
Piccott's End 1 mile north, may have
been a pilgrim's hostel, and contains
impressive medieval wall paintings.
Zacchaeus Gould, who emigrated to

America in 1638 and was founder of
the New England Gould family, was
born in Bovingdon 3½ miles south
west.

HENLEY-ON-THAMES
Oxfordshire   *4 SU78*
The Royal Regatta, held on the
Thames each year in early July, has
made Henley internationally famous.
The regatta, which was the first event
of its kind, growing out of the first
Oxford-Cambridge boat race here in
1829, is now firmly established in the
calendar of the affluent. The town is
enhanced by its old coaching inns, its
Regency houses, and of particular note
are the 18th-century 5-arch bridge, the
Norman-towered Perpendicular
church and 15th-century Chantry
House (OACT). Fawley Court,
(OACT July and August), was
designed by Sir Christopher Wren and
is now the Divine Mercy College, and
contains a museum devoted to the
Polish Army. The furnishings are by
Grinling Gibbons. 2 miles west the
Elizabethan Grey's Court retains 14th-
century fortifications and has a donkey
wheel used in Tudor times for raising
water. 4 miles north west is **Stonor
House** and **Park** showing some of
Britain's earliest domestic architecture.

Henley-on-Thames

HEREFORD
Hereford & Worcester   *9 SO54*

Situated on the banks of the River
Wye, Hereford was the Saxon capital
of West Mercia, and a bishopric since
AD 672. The cathedral is mainly
Norman and Decorated in style,
notable for its red sandstone tower.
However, much of the early building
was lost when the West Tower
collapsed in the 18th century. Of
special interest are the fine brasses, the
carved stalls and King Stephen's 800-
year-old chair. The chained library
contains over 1600 books and the
cathedral also houses a unique late
13th-century *Mappa Mundi*, which
depicts the world, flat and centred in
Jerusalem. Vestiges of the old town
can be seen in the town walls and
earthworks from the former castle – a
stronghold against the Welsh. The
museum contains a Bronze Age tomb
and finds from Iron Age forts and from
Magnis, a Roman town at Kenchester
5 miles north west. Modern Hereford's
importance comes from its administrative role in the surrounding
farmland, famed for its cider and red
and white Hereford cattle. To the west
is the beautiful Golden Valley, and to
the south spectacular stretches of the
Wye Valley. The Saxon market centre
of High Town and the Butter Market
is now a shopping precinct and the
town preserves many attractive 17th-
and 18th-century buildings, including
the Green Draper house. David
Garrick the actor and playwright was
born here at the Raven Inn, and Nell
Gwynne, the orange-seller who
became Charles II's favourite mistress,
was born in the town; a plaque in
Gwynne Street commemorates her.
Every third year Hereford is host to the

The Old House

Three Choirs Festival, an event shared with the neighbouring cities of Worcester and Gloucester.

PLACES TO SEE

Churchill Gardens Museum and Brian Hatton Art Gallery A Regency house in fine grounds contains a Victorian nursery, butler's pantry and parlour. The art gallery mainly has works by local artist Brian Hatton. 'Roaring Meg', a locally made mortar, was used by Parliamentary troops in the siege of Goodrich Castle in the Civil War and can be seen in the Gardens.

Museum of Cider A fascinating museum illustrating the history of British and European cidermaking from the 16th century onwards.

Hereford Museum and Art Gallery Exhibitions in the art gallery are changed every month and exhibits in the museum include Roman tessellated pavements.

The Old House (OACT) Jacobean furniture is displayed in the rooms of this beautifully restored 17th-century house in High Town.

St John's and Coningsby Museum Armour and other items connected with the Order and Chapel of Knights of St John are displayed in an early 13th-century hall. Adjoining almshouses were added in 1614.

All Saints Church Like the cathedral, this church too has a chained library, including a 15th-century book on the Seven Deadly Sins.

Hereford Cathedral

HERMITAGE CASTLE
Borders   *24 NY59*
In 1566 Mary Queen of Scots came to this sturdy 14th-century castle (AM) to visit the wounded Earl of Bothwell. A year later she married the earl, after the murder of her husband Lord Darnley.

HERSTMONCEUX
E Sussex   *6 TQ61*
This small village is the setting for an attractive mid 15th-century moated castle. Restored in the 1930s, the fine fortified brick manor house contains the Royal Greenwich Observatory which moved here when Greenwich became too polluted.

HERTFORD
Hertfordshire   *5 TL31*
Four rivers, the Lea, Beane, Mimram and Rib meet at this ancient and picturesque country town. A settlement existed here long before Roman times, and the town has the ruin of a Norman castle on the earlier site of a Saxon stronghold, built to defend London from the Danes. Only a modernized gatehouse remains of the castle where Elizabeth I spent much of her childhood. The town has a Victorian corn exchange, Shire Hall built by James Adam (the brother of Robert), which dates from 1768, and Lombard House, once the home of Chauncy, the county historian. The Friends Meeting House dates from 1670.

Hertford has several American links; All Saints Church has records of the baptism in 1602 of Samuel Stone, who became one of the founders of Connecticut. Stone accompanied the Reverend Thomas Hooker who emigrated to Massachusetts in 1633, as pastor of Newtowne (now Cambridge); later Hooker was to found Hartford, Connecticut named after this English town. During the 18th century a group of 25 Hertfordshire MPs were noted for their united stand against Lord North's Government and their demands for peace with America. 1 mile west, Hertingfordbury church has a monument to Anne Mynne, wife of George Calvert, 1st Lord Baltimore and founder of Maryland, who came from here.

Seven miles west of Hertford, Brocket Hall was the home of Lord Melbourne, Lord Palmerston and Lord Mount Stephen – who helped build the Canadian railways.

◆ HEVER
Kent   *5 TQ44*
From the reign of Henry II (1154–89) a castle could be built only with the King's licence. In 1272 Sir Stephen de Penchester obtained permission from Edward I to convert his house to a castle. Further alterations were made by William de Hever in 1340. A century later Hever Castle, reinforced with portcullises and a drawbridge, became the home of the Boleyn family (family tombs can be seen in the church). It was here that Henry VIII courted his second wife Anne Boleyn, the mother of Elizabeth I. Early this century the American William Waldorf Astor bought and restored the castle (OACT) adding a mock-Tudor village, a 35-acre lake, an Italian garden with maze and Tudor-style flowerbeds. Astor later became a British citizen and received the title 1st Viscount Astor of Hever.

HEXHAM
Northumberland   *19 NY96*
A busy shopping and market centre, beautifully situated on the River Tyne, Hexham is a convenient base for visiting the Northumberland Dales and Hadrian's Wall. From the Seal, a public park originally a monastic enclosure, there are views of the town below. Of particular interest is the abbey dating from the 12th century, with a fine Anglo Saxon crypt remaining from the original church completed in 678. The many treasures in the church include an Anglo Saxon frith stool, font bowl and cross, a Roman monument and altars, and medieval misericords.

HIGH FORCE WATERFALL
Co Durham   *19 NY82*
High Force is reached by a short wooded path opposite the High Force Hotel on the B6277. One of England's most spectacular waterfalls, it is particularly impressive when, swollen by rain, the Tees cascades over the cliff of the Great Whin Sill to plunge to a deep glen-enclosed pool 70ft below.

HINGHAM
Norfolk   *12 TG00*
Elegant Georgian houses cluster round Hingham's two squares – evidence of former prosperity as a market town. Many people emigrated from this area in the early days of the Massachusetts colony. One, the Reverend Robert Peck founded Hingham's namesake in Massachusetts. In the market place a granite boulder from America

commemorates the link between the two towns. Hingham's most lasting connection, however, is its ancestral links with Abraham Lincoln. His direct ancestor Samuel, whose original home was 10 miles north at Swanton Morley, was apprenticed to Francis Lawes, a Norwich weaver; together they sailed from Great Yarmouth to Salem in 1638. Soon after Lincoln joined two of his brothers in Reverend Peck's settlement – a local ledger records 206 emigrants from Hingham. Hingham church contains a bronze bust of the President given by the Lincoln Ancestors Members Association. $4\frac{1}{2}$ miles south, Attleborough was the home of the Reverend William Blackstone, a recluse, who emigrated to America in 1623 and later became the first white resident of Rhode Island.

Banham 5 miles south of Attleborough has a Zoo and Monkey Sanctuary with a colony of woolly monkeys, one of only six in Europe. Here too is the Banham Classic Collection (OACT), a motor museum with over 40 vehicles.

HODNET
Shropshire   9 SJ62
A rare chained 15th-century Nuremberg Bible can be found in the 14th-century church of this small hill town, which has black and white timbered houses typical of north-west England. The beautiful 60-acre landscaped gardens (OACT) of Victorian Hodnet Hall are well worth a visit.

HOGHTON
Lancashire   14 SD62
Hoghton Tower (OACT) contains a magnificent banqueting hall and several state rooms. There is also a collection of antique dolls and dolls' houses. Hoghton lays claim, as do several other mansions, to be the place where James I knighted the loin of beef, hence 'sirloin'.

HOLKER
Cumbria   18 SD37
Magnificent red sandstone 16th-century Holker Hall (OACT) lies in a 122-acre park containing a large herd of deer as well as formal and woodland gardens and children's adventure playground. Additional attractions include the large motor museum, aquarium, and large-gauge model railway.

HOLKHAM
Norfolk   12 TF84
Built by William Kent in 1734 for the 1st Earl of Leicester, this vast Palladian mansion (OACT) is set in magnificent landscaped parkland. The house has a marble hall and the magnificent state rooms with their fine furnishings contain works by Rubens and Van Dyck. The 1st Earl's nephew, Thomas Coke, carried out his pioneering agricultural experiments on the estate and his reforms played a significant part in the Agricultural Revolution.

HONITON
Devon   2 ST10
An attractive small town, Honiton is known principally for its tradition of lacemaking. The industry flourished from Elizabethan times until the 19th century; Queen Victoria's wedding veil was made locally. The Allhallows Museum has a fine collection of lace and lacemaking demonstrations also take place here. Today the town is characterized by its pottery industry and its many antique shops.

Wolford Lodge is a 19th-century house $3\frac{1}{2}$ miles north west of Honiton on the Dunkeswell road. The chapel close to the Lodge was built in 1800 on the site of a former church. It contains many memorial tablets to the Simcoe family. Lieutenant-General John Graves Simcoe is buried in the chapel. He was appointed first Lieutenant-Governor of Upper Canada (now Ontario) in 1791. Previously he had served in the American War of Independence. He left Canada in 1796 and was due to become Commander-in-Chief for India when he died at Exeter in 1806. The chapel is maintained by the John Graves Simcoe Memorial Foundation, Ontario. There is a memorial with the figure of an American Indian on it in Exeter Cathedral. Dunkeswell was the site of a US Naval Air Force base during World War II. 7000 men of Fleet Air Wing 7 were based here, and the parish church contains a memorial to them. The organ was donated by American servicemen in 1945. Lt Joseph Kennedy, eldest brother of the late president, is named in the memorial.

HORNCASTLE
Lincolnshire   16 TF26
One of the principal market towns serving this important agricultural area, Horncastle occupies the site of the Roman town *Banovallum*. It was from here in 1623, that the Reverend William Blackstone left, eventually to

become Rhode Island's first white settler. 6 miles north east, Somersby was the birthplace of Alfred Lord Tennyson in 1809. The poet grew up in the former rectory, where his father was rector. He attended Louth Grammar School for a while, but received most of his early education at home – it was here that he started to write, and together with his brother published his first book of poems the year he went up to Cambridge. He was made Poet Laureate in 1850. The church contains Tennyson memorials.

HORNSEA
Humberside   16 TA24
Lying between the 487-acre freshwater lake of Hornsea Mere and the sea and sandy beach, this Holderness town has become a popular holiday resort. An additional attraction is Hornsea Pottery (OACT), where there are factory tours, a country crafts centre, a mini-zoo and a model village. Further south along the coast a memorial at Mappleton recalls the exploits of John Paul Jones along this coast.

HORRINGER
Suffolk   12 TL86
The 18th-century mansion of Ickworth (NT, OACT) is a vast elliptical rotunda, set in parkland designed by Capability Brown, housing collections of Regency furnishings, silver and pictures – including Benjamin West's 'The Death of General Wolfe'. The house is considered remarkable. The former owners, the Earls of Bristol, are commemorated in the 13th-century church at Horringer.

HOUGHTON
Norfolk   12 TF72
Eighteenth-century Houghton Hall (OACT), approached from the village by a long avenue through beautiful parkland where a herd of white deer roam, was designed for Sir Robert Walpole, England's first prime minister by Colin Campbell and Thomas Ripley, and is one of the finest examples of Palladian architecture in England. State rooms contain interior decorations and furniture by William Kent and there are many family portraits and exquisite porcelain. Traditional heavy horses and Shetland ponies can be seen in the stables.

HOUSESTEADS
Northumberland   19 NY76
Perhaps the finest of the Roman forts on Hadrian's Wall, *Vircovicium* (AM, NT), would have accommodated 1000

Hadrian's Wall from Housesteads

Hull Chamber of Commerce and Shipping

infantrymen in its 5 acres: ramparts, gateways, granaries, latrines, headquarters and barracks are still clearly visible. There is a museum, and from the fort, with its clifftop setting, there are fine views of the wall snaking over the bleak hills of the Border country. To the west is the substantial ruin of a Roman mile-castle.

HUGHENDEN
Buckinghamshire   *4 SU89*
Prime Minister Benjamin Disraeli lived at Hughenden Manor (NT), a large mansion he had remodelled in 1862. It stands in a 169-acre estate which includes the church where he is buried. The statesman's study contains letters from Queen Victoria and remains as it was at the time of his death.

HULL
Humberside   *15 TA02*
The Humber Bridge, opened in 1981, spans the River Humber and is (or was when it was completed) the largest single-span suspension bridge in the world. Previously, the easiest way to reach the city from the south was by ferry from New Holland. Officially named Kingston-upon-Hull, the city was badly damaged in World War II. It contains much modern development, some very striking. Among the parts of the old city that survive is the curiously named 'Land of Green Ginger', a narrow street that recalls Hull's former importance as a trading centre. It was from here that Alexander Selkirk sailed on the voyage that was to make him the model for Daniel Defoe's *Robinson Crusoe*. There is a plaque in the Queen's Gardens. Hull's dockland stretches for 7 miles, handling a wide variety of cargoes and also serving Continental ferries, although in recent years the fishing industry has drastically declined.
In 1921 Hull was the scene of the tragic flight of the airship R38, which

collapsed over the city, killing the 44 Americans and Britons aboard. The western cemetery has a memorial to them.
Displays in the Town Docks Museum illustrate the past importance of fishing, whaling and shipping to the town. Other places to visit include the Transport and Archaeological Museum; Ferens Art Gallery; and 17th-century Wilberforce House where the anti-slavery campaigner William Wilberforce was born.
Ten miles west the Reverend Ezekial Rogers was rector of Rowley. Several of Rogers' relatives were among the early pilgrims and Ezekiel himself left in 1638 in the *St John*, to become the Pastor of Rowley, Massachusetts, named after his birthplace in his honour.
William Wilberforce later became MP for Hull and was the most strident opponent of the slave trade in the British colonies of America. The museum in Wilberforce House contains many items relating to the slave trade in both Britain and America.
David Hartley, MP for Hull, drew up the peace treaty with Benjamin Franklin which ended the war between Britain and America. In the northern suburb of Cottingham, Major General Ralph Burton who fought at the Plains of Abraham, is commemorated.

HUNGERFORD
Berkshire   *4 SU36*
Situated on the Kennet and Avon Canal and also the River Kennet, this pleasant town with a wide High Street and many antique shops, was granted fishing rights by John of Gaunt in the 14th century. This is celebrated at Hocktide (after Easter) by a picturesque ceremony that involves 'tutti-men' (tithe men) who carry decorated poles. The revelry lasts all day, and there is much kissing of pretty girls and distributing of oranges. East Shefford, 5 miles north east in the Lambourn Valley, was owned by David Hartley, MP for **Hull** and chief British peace negotiator with America in 1783.

HUNTINGDON
Cambridgeshire   *11 TL27*
Huntingdon, formerly a county town, now forms a borough with Godmanchester which began its days as a crossroads of the *via Devana*, the Roman road which ran from Colchester to Chester, and Ermine Street, the York to London road. Both towns contain some fine buildings and

the area is rich in history. The coffin bearing Mary Queen of Scots was rested in St George's Church on its journey to Westminster Abbey. Oliver Cromwell was born in Huntingdon and was baptized in 1610 in All Saints Church. He attended the local grammar school, now the Cromwell Museum. The George Inn was owned by Cromwell's grandfather. Hinchingbrooke House, a Tudor manor just outside the town, was built by Sir Richard Cromwell, Oliver's prosperous great-grandfather. The sculpted gatehouse is believed to have come from Ramsey Abbey. After the Restoration the house passed to the Earls of Sandwich; it is now a school and can be visited during the summer. Samuel Pepys the diarist was born just outside the town in Brampton, where the exterior of his family's 15th-century farmhouse can be seen. It was here that Samuel is alleged to have buried his money, away from the expected Dutch invaders. He attended Cromwell's school in Huntingdon.
Ten miles north west is Little Gidding where a fervent religious community was established by Nicholas Ferrar, a member of the Virginia Company in 1625. Ferrar came from a wealthy family but, disillusioned with life, came here with his mother and other friends and relatives to devote his life to prayer and good works. In their prayers the community always remembered the Virginia colony. They rebuilt the church of St John the Evangelist and gained respect; Charles I visited the community several times, finally, in 1646, to seek shelter from Cromwell's forces. The church and house were later sacked by the Parliamentarians as a reprisal. Little Gidding's Society of Friends makes an annual pilgrimage to the church, commemorated in 'Little Gidding' the last of T S Eliot's *Four Quartets*.

Hutton-le-Hole

HUTTON-LE-HOLE
N Yorkshire 20 SE79

One of the prettiest villages in the North York Moors; 2 becks meet here and the red-roofed, stone cottages cluster around a green. In spring the surrounding dales are enlivened with daffodils. The oldest building is Quaker Cottage which dates from 1695 and is associated with John Richardson the missionary to America. Richardson was a close friend of William Penn, founder of Pennsylvania. Ryedale Folk Museum (OACT) has reconstructed buildings such as cruck-framed houses and an Elizabethan glass furnace. A few miles east Cropton was the home of Reverend William Scoresby (1789–1857) and his father the Arctic explorer. Lastingham, 1½ miles east, has a beautiful church with an outstanding 11th-century crypt, built as a shrine to St Cedd.

HYTHE
Kent 6 TR13

A mellow seaside town, Hythe is one of the Cinque Ports and stands on the Royal Military Canal, built for defence in Napoleonic times. The Romney, Hythe and Dymchurch Light Railway has its terminus here and a ½ mile north is Saltwood Castle. This was the stronghold from which Henry II's knights set out to murder Thomas Becket.

I

ICKNIELD WAY

One of the great pre-Roman routes, the Icknield Way is now largely only negotiable by walkers. It starts near **Marlborough** in Wiltshire, crosses the Thames at Goring, intersects with the old Roman road known as Watling Street at Dunstable, then passes by Letchworth and on to the Wash.

IGHTHAM
Kent 6 TQ55

Brick-and-tile cottages are interspersed with half-timbered houses in and around the village square. Ightham is a corruption of Etheham (or Etha's Ham) which was its original name until Norman times. The church of St Peter, which was largely rebuilt during the 14th and 15th centuries, boasts several brasses and sculptures. Also inside is a plaque commemorating one Benjamin Harrison, a local grocer who earned himself national recognition as an archaeologist. His nearby excavations included those of the Iron Age settlement at Oldbury Hill, an ancient camp located across the busy bypass at the end of Sevenoaks Road. The 120-acre site is roughly in the shape of a diamond. Some 2½ miles to the south is Ightham Mote (OACT), a delightfully preserved medieval country house built partly of stone, partly of timber.

Igtham Mote

ILAM
Staffordshire 15 SK15

The River Manifold meanders past this ancient village, which was given a substantial face-lift by Jesse Watts-Russell in the last century, transforming it into a 'model' village. The Hall (NT but not open), also part of Russell's programme, has some 50 wooded acres (OACT) and houses, in part, a youth hostel. Parts of the local church date back to the 13th century. Among several items of interest is a shrine to St Bertram, supposedly the bringer of Christianity to this region. Still earlier are the two Anglo Saxon crosses in the churchyard.

ILCHESTER
Somerset 3 ST52

Although now a quiet little town, Ilchester was an important military station on the Fosse Way in Roman times. Roger Bacon, the remarkable scholar-churchman of the 13th century, was born here. A 700-year-old octagonal mace (the oldest of its kind in England) is housed in the town hall. Some 3 miles north east of the town is Lytes Cary (NT), a medieval manor which preserves its 14th-century chapel and original Great Hall.

ILFRACOMBE
Devon 2 SS54

A popular holiday resort situated on Devon's lovely north coast, Ilfracombe was originally just a quiet fishing harbour, but has since evolved, thanks to a 19th-century enterprise, as a thriving seaside centre. The many large Victorian houses and hotels are necessarily built in terraces, because of the steeply shelving hills that meet the shoreline. Public gardens in this area are particularly well kept. Chambercombe Manor (OACT), situated 1½ miles south east of Ilfracombe, is a mansion which, although largely Elizabethan, has parts which are much more ancient. It is one of the oldest inhabited houses in England. A haunted room and a 12th-century cider-press are among its interesting relics and furnishings. 1 mile to the east, Hele Mill (OACT) has been restored to working condition and produces wholemeal flour. Watermouth Castle, 2½ miles east of the town, offers varied amusements.

ILKLEY
W Yorkshire 15 SE14

Although situated in the River Wharfe valley, this inland health resort is 400ft above sea-level. There are some interesting buildings including Box Tree Cottage and Manor House Museum (OACT), which is built on the site of a Roman fort. All Saints is a 13th-century church with a fine old tower and some rare wood carvings. Three Saxon crosses stand in the churchyard. Several Bronze Age carvings have been found in this area and examples are on display in the garden opposite the church. Nearby Heber's Ghyll is the site of the Swastika Stone, a unique carved relic believed to have been instrumental in ritual fire worship. The surrounding Ilkley Moor remains the bleak but beautiful setting immortalized in the Yorkshire anthem 'On Ilkla Moor baht'at'.

At nearby Denton, Denton Park was the ancestral home of the Fairfax family which included Cromwell's famous general. The family has strong connections with colonial Virginia. The 6th Lord Fairfax (1692–1782) was a grandson of Lord Culpeper, from whom he inherited vast estates in Virginia. Fairfax lived there, selling Denton Park in 1746. A cousin of the family, William Fairfax, was the father-in-law of Lawrence Washington, half-brother and guardian of George Washington. Washington's early years as a surveyor were spent on Fairfax's estates. Lord Fairfax died a bachelor; the title went out of use until 1908 when Albert Kirby Fairfax successfully claimed it, taking the title of 12th peer and a seat in the House of Lords.

ILMINGTON
Warwickshire *10 SP24*
A pleasant Cotswold village, this has all the 'olde-worlde' features such as mossy stone roofs and mullioned windows. Some half-a-dozen buildings in the parish are over 200 years old and include the Rectory, Crab Mill, the Manor House and Foxcote, an impressive Georgian House. The Ilmington Morris Dancers keep alive one of several annual rural events that take place in and around the region. The highest point of the hills (854ft) has fine views of Warwickshire.

ILMINSTER
Somerset *3 ST31*
A bustling market town on the A303 at the foot of the Blackdown Hills. The rows of thatched cottages just off the main road are reminiscent of those in Devon and the focal pillared market house is pleasantly surrounded by a Ham stone square. The local high school dates back to 1586, while the

church is over a century earlier still. Sir William Wadham, founder of the Oxford college named after him, was the church's main benefactor. Jordans, a house on the Taunton road, was the residence of John Speke, discoverer of the source of the Nile. Some 3½ miles north east of Ilminster is **Barrington Court** (NT).

IMMINGHAM
Humberside *15 TA11*
This modern, deep-water port acts as a sister to Grimsby 5 miles further down towards the open sea. In recent years new oil, coal and iron-ore terminals have been established here, and a large refinery is at nearby Killingholme. Near Immingham parish church there is a monument incorporating a piece of rock from Plymouth, Massachusetts and commemorating the Pilgrim Fathers' point of departure for Holland in 1609 prior to their departure for the New World.

INGLETON
N Yorkshire *18 SD67*
A busy little town, Ingleton acts as a useful base from which to visit the abundant caves and waterfalls in the region. Some 3½ miles north east is Ingleborough Hill, an impressive 2373 ft peak with the remains of an Iron Age settlement at its summit. This, with Whernside and Pen-y-Ghent, forms the gruelling course of the Three Peaks race. Beneath Ingleborough is a maze of limestone caves, within which is Gaping Gill, the largest limestone chamber in Britain.

INKPEN
Berkshire *4 SU36*
Le Nôtre, the man who masterminded the gardens at Versailles, stayed for a spell at the village's 17th-century rectory, while the 13th-century church has connections with the Knights Templar. The summits of Inkpen Beacon and Walbury Hill, at 954ft and 974ft respectively, are the highest chalk downs in England. On Inkpen Beacon stands Combe Gibbet, a macabre reminder of the fate of pre-Victorian highwaymen.

INNER HEBRIDES
Highland
The Inner Hebrides comprise Skye, Mull, Jura and Islay, plus a host of smaller islands, some well known, such as Iona, Eigg, Rhum, Tyree and Colonsay, some little visited, such as Canna, Raasay and Coll. Easily the most visited isle is Skye.

The Gaelic name for Skye means 'the Isle of Mist under the Shadow of great mountains'. The island is 50 miles long, and no place is more than 5 miles from the sea, yet Skye has over 1000 miles of craggy coastline, as well as some of Scotland's wildest mountain scenery in the Cuillins. Nowhere in Britain are there better climbing peaks. The range is partly composed of black gabbro rock, one of the safest climbing rocks in the world owing to its rough surface; however, the peaks should only be attempted by experienced walkers and climbers. The island is bound up in myth and legend, and almost every place has tales of fairy bridges, fairy castles and fairy kidnapping associated with it. The richest store of local colour comes from the brief but well-known visit of Bonnie Prince Charlie. After their journey 'over the sea to Skye' from the island of Benbecula, Flora Macdonald brought the Prince, disguised as her Irish maid, to Monkstadt House 2½ miles north of Uig on the northern coast of Skye. There is a Flora Macdonald window in St Columba's Church, Portree. Flora Macdonald's grave is marked by a Celtic cross in Kilmuir churchyard. Close by is the ruined Duntulm Castle, former stronghold of the Macdonalds.

From the ramparts of Dunvegan Castle (OACT), the seat of Clan MacLeod, the Hills of Harris in the Outer Hebrides can be seen. The castle was attacked by John Paul Jones in his raids on the Scottish coast. Among the treasures inside are a lock of Bonnie Prince Charlie's hair, MacLeod family portraits by Ramsay and Raeburn, the 4-pint drinking horn which the 13th chief, Rory More, could empty at a draught, and the Bratach Sith, or Fairy Flag. According to legend, the Fairy Flag was given to the clan in the 14th century, to be used only in the face of imminent defeat of the clan. Its three magical properties gave victory on the battlefield, ensured children in marriage and charmed herring into the loch. The silk flag was twice used in battle with encouraging results. At the Battle of Trumpan in 1597, only two Macdonald raiders escaped the wrath of the MacLeods who attacked after an entire congregation of MacLeods were burned to death at worship.

Other places of interest on Skye include the Clan Donald Centre (OACT) at Armadale Castle, the Skye Black House Folk Museum, a restored crofter's house at Colbost and the Skye Cottage Museum at Kilmuir.

Isle of Skye from Rhum

Eigg and Rhum are bleak but beautiful. Many weirdly formed caverns punctuate Eigg's coastline. In the cave of St Francis a group of 16th-century MacLeods is supposed to have killed 200 people by blocking the cave entrance with fire trapping them inside.

On Mull, much further south, the biggest burgh is Tobermory. Duart Castle (OACT) is the home of the Macleans. The Victorian Torosay Castle (OACT) is set in magnificent gardens.

Iona lies across the water from Mull's most westerly community, Fionnphort. St Columba came here from Ireland in the 6th century to found a monastery. He is thought to have landed at Portna Curaich. Following Columba's death in AD 597, Iona became a place of pilgrimage, and many early Scottish kings and chiefs were buried here. St Oran's Cemetery is considered to be the oldest Christian burial ground in Scotland. King Duncan, said to have been murdered by Macbeth in 1040, was one of the 48 Scottish kings to be buried here. The cathedral was founded in the 13th century – though the present building is more recent. Many interesting tombs survive, and the so-called Columba's Pillow is preserved beneath the East Window. Dr Johnson described Iona as 'that luminary of the Caledonian regions' when he visited in 1773. The island's beauty and peacefulness enhance its continued importance as a place of Christian pilgrimage. The oldest building on Iona is St Oran's Chapel, said to have been founded by

Queen Margaret in 1080. Although largely restored the church has a carved Norman doorway among its 11th-century remains.

Islay at the south of the Inner Hebrides group was the birthplace of Alexander McDougall, who founded the first modern shipyard on the Pacific north-west coast of America. In the south west of the island a memorial on cliffs at the Mull of Oa commemorates the American sailors killed here in World War I when the *Tuscania* and the *Otranto* were hit by torpedoes.

George Orwell lived on Jura after World War II. It was here he wrote *Nineteen Eighty Four*. He left the island in 1950.

INNERLEITHEN
Borders   *23 NT33*
The town is situated on Leithen Water near its junction with the River Tweed. Innerleithen is known for its woollens – the first tweed mill was opened here in 1790. To the south of the town is **Traquair House** (OACT) which is thought to be the model for 'Tullyveolan', the house in Scott's *Waverley*. The town became an attraction when, in 1830, Sir Walter Scott published *St Ronan's Well*, in which he linked Doo's Well with the saint. Each summer the expulsion of the Devil by St Ronan is re-enacted in the St Ronan games.

◗INVERARAY
Strathclyde   *2 NN00*
Near the northern end of Loch Fyne surrounded by beautiful woods is this

picturesque white-walled burgh, the hereditary seat of the Dukes of Argyll heads of the Clan Campbell. It was destroyed by the Royalist Marquis of Montrose in 1644. The new town was built between 1746 and 1780 by the 3rd Duke of Argyll and the castle (OACT) was built by Roger Morris and William Adam, with at least one of his two famous sons. The magnificent interior decoration was carried out by Robert Mylne at a later date. The castle contains many historic relics and a good picture collection. In the grounds is a cannon from the Spanish Armada ship *Florida*. A 5 mile walk up Glen Shira leads to the ruined home of Rob Roy. The town is mentioned by Scott in *Legend of Montrose*, and *Heart of Midlothian*, and by Stevenson in the closing scenes of *Catriona*. A Celtic cross from Iona stands at one end of the main street. The parish church is divided by a wall separating services in Gaelic and English.

• INVERNESS
Highland   *26 NH64*
Known as the 'capital of the Highlands', Inverness is a historic burgh on the River Ness just inland from the Moray Firth. Scotland's King David built the first castle here in the 12th century but of this and subsequent castles built on this site, little evidence remains today and the present castle dates from 1834. At Craig Phaorig are the remains of a fort where the Pictish King Brude was probably visited by St Columba in 565. Two other interesting fortresses are Castle Stewart, 6 miles east, and Aldourie Castle, seat of the Frasers for over 200 years, 7 miles south west on the northernmost tip of Loch Ness. The town's clock tower is the only remnant of a fort built by Cromwell's army during the Civil War.

Inverness was the terminal point for the system of metalled military roads built by the engineer and soldier George Wade during the period 1726–37, following the Rebellion of 1715. Fort George, the town barracks named after Wade, was blown up by Prince Charles Edward's forces in 1746 but a new fort was subsequently built to the north east of the town. Abertarff House on Church Street dates from the mid-16th century; inside is a rare, early spiral staircase. The Town House in Castle Street was the scene of the first Cabinet meeting to be held outside London: Lloyd George, holidaying in Scotland in 1921, called an emergency meeting here to discuss a letter on the question of Irish independence from Eamon de Valera, the Irish politician who became the first President of the Irish Republic. Across the river is St Andrew's Cathedral, a mid-Victorian edifice with notable carved pillars. Other interesting buildings include the library, museum and art gallery. General Ulysses S Grant was an honorary burgess here. Balblain, home of the Rosses, who included Colonel George Ross, lies 15 miles north of Inverness, on the Black Isle peninsula.

Abertarff House, Inverness

INVERURIE
Grampian *27 NJ72*
A royal burgh, located near the confluence of the Don and the Urie, Inverurie has many features and connections of historical interest, including the visit of Mary Queen of Scots in 1562. Brandsbutt Stone (AM) is ½ mile north west of Inverurie and bears ancient inscriptions, while the Easter Aquahorthies Stone Circle is some 2½ miles to the west. Another early Christian monument in the area is the Maiden Stone (AM), 4½ miles north west of Inverurie.

IPSWICH
Suffolk *12 TM14*
The county town of Suffolk acquired its name from an Anglo Saxon settlement called Gippeswic. The town was granted a charter by King John in 1200 and steadily grew in importance, reaching a peak as a flourishing cloth port in the 16th century. Its development then tailed off until the mid 19th century when a second upturn in fortune resulted in its present significance as a port, market town and East Anglian seat of administration. The docks now handle over 2,500,000 tons of cargo a year, ideally placed for European trading.

Architecturally, Ipswich has many places of interest including the Ancient House in Butter Market, built in 1567 (also known as Sparrowe's House after a one-time occupant). The front of the house features the intricate decorative plasterwork known as pargeting, an art characteristic of East Anglia. Beneath the front windows are thematic panels depicting the then known continents of the world. Cardinal Wolsey was born in Ipswich and later founded the Cardinal College of St Mary. All that is left of the building today, though, is the red brick gateway in College Street. Old Ipswich had medieval walls and Northgate Street, Westgate Street and Tower Rampart are all reminders, along with Priory Street which once had houses built by Augustinians, Franciscans, Dominicans and Carmelites.

At the junction of Tavern and Northgate Streets is the Great White Horse Hotel. Murals on the dining-room walls record the activities here of Charles Dickens' Samuel Pickwick, hero of *Pickwick Papers*. Dickens worked here as a reporter and used the town in the book. Rider Haggard, author of *King Solomon's Mines*, attended Ipswich School. Christchurch Mansion, in Christchurch Park, has a fine art gallery which includes works by both Gainsborough, who lived in the town, and Constable, who was born nearby.

Just outside Ipswich, Playford was the house of the anti-slave trade leader Thomas Clarkson, who died at the moated Elizabethan hall; an obelisk commemorates him.

IRONBRIDGE
Shropshire *9 SJ60*
The town is situated in the deep, wooded gorge of the River Severn and developed, like many others in this region, during the Industrial Revolution. The community takes its name from the world's first iron bridge, built here in 1778–81. It was designed by the ironmaster Abraham Darby III as an example of the quality of his cast iron and was cast at his foundry in Coalbrookdale. The bridge is 196ft long, weighs 380 tons and, seen from a distance as it spans the wooded Severn Gorge, presents a romantic and inspiring picture. Abraham Darby I had been the first man to smelt iron using coke, 70 years earlier. His grandson's iron bridge is built using woodworking joints. Nowadays access is restricted to pedestrians. Scattered along the Gorge is a unique series of

museums of industrial history, under the general title of the Ironbridge Gorge Museum. These include: Blists Hill Open Air Museum, which covers 42 acres, recreating the iron, coal and clay industries; Coalbrookdale Museum and Furnace Site, Abraham Darby's original blast furnace; the Coalport China Works Museum; and the Severn Warehouse. 2 miles to the north west of the town are Buildwas Abbey ruins (AM), and 1 mile south west is Benthall Hall (NT), an interesting 16th-century house.

IRVINE
Strathclyde *22 NS33*
A royal burgh located where the River Irvine joins the sea, Irvine and nearby Kilwinning have been paired to form a 'seaside new town', the first in Great Britain. In the centre of Irvine are the ruins of Seagate Castle which Mary Queen of Scots visited in 1563. Robert Burns lived here between 1781 and 1783, working briefly as a flax-dresser in the Glasgow Vennel area. Several misfortunes attended Burns' time in Irvine. He suffered from pleurisy and fire destroyed all his possessions. The Burns Club was inaugurated in 1826 and has since been converted into a museum. Across the Garnock and Irvine estuaries is the Ardeer explosives factory, one of Britain's major production centres for high explosives. The site was chosen in 1873 by the Swedish chemist and inventor of dynamite, Sir Alfred Nobel, who initiated the Nobel Prize.

The world's first iron bridge – after which the town was named

ISLE OF MAN   17 SC38

On a clear day England, Wales, Scotland and Ireland can all be seen from the Isle of Man, one of the smallest independent sovereign countries of the Crown. Annexed by England in the 13th century, it still has its own Parliament, and systems of law and taxation. The native language is a form of Celtic. The sight of the island from the sea inspired three of the many sonnets Wordsworth wrote on a short tour in 1833. Douglas is the island's capital and most popular holiday resort. The 2 miles of seafront promenade is level with the sea, traffic is directed by white-helmeted policemen, and horse-drawn trams still operate. The island's Parliament, the House of Keys at Tynwald, is on Prospect Hill: its Scandinavian origins are older than those of Westminster. The Manx National Museum is also worth a visit. In Noble's Park, the famous tailless Manx cats are bred. Offshore, Conister Rock bears a tower of refuge for shipwrecked mariners. This was erected in 1832 by Sir William Hillary, founder of the National Lifeboat Institution. Sir William once lived on Douglas Head, in what is now the Fort Anne Hotel. A few miles north the small town of Laxey is dominated by the 'Lady Isabella', the world's largest water-wheel, formerly used to pump water from nearby lead mines. South west of Douglas is Castletown, the island's former capital. The town is built around Castle Rushen, one of the finest medieval fortresses in Britain. On the west coast, Peel has links with Ireland, most notably Peel Castle, a 10th-century 50ft structure on St Patrick's Isle. At Ballaugh the church contains a tablet to the Veale family in America. Ramsey, the island's second largest town, was claimed briefly for Scotland in 1313, by Robert the Bruce.

ISLE OF WIGHT
Hampshire   4 SZ37

The Garden Isle was once described as a miniature England cast adrift in the English Channel. Its coastal perimeter extends some 60 miles, varying from pleasant sands, to chines (as the deep coastal ravines are called), grottoes and eye-catching rock formations. Inland, the picturesque landscape is punctuated with stone cottages, thatched farmhouses and secluded villages. The seaboard townships provide excellent facilities for holidaymakers, especially those keen on yachting and fishing. Visitors arrive at Ryde, whose attractions include a pavilion, canoe lake, Appley Gardens and Puckpool Park; it is the home of the Royal Victoria Yacht Club.

Leaving Ryde and moving clockwise round the island, Bembridge is the home of yet another yacht club. The nearby small public school has a library of John Ruskin's works. The last windmill on the island (NT) stands near the B3390. The Maritime Museum has an interesting collection of model ships. Sandown on the south east coast is a popular resort. Battery Gardens are in the grounds of an old fort, while the Museum of Isle of Wight Geology houses, among other exhibits, over 5000 fossils found on the island. A 6-mile cliff walk leads around the bay to Shanklin, where the hurly-burly pier end contrasts with secluded Hope Beach. The old village has thatched cottages festooned by roses, and gardens with exotic trees. 3 miles south west of Shanklin is Ventnor. Predominantly Victorian, the town has imposing hotels with verandahs, an abundance of parks and gardens and, because of its sheltered beach, is known as the Madeira of England. The Russian writer Turgenev holidayed here in 1860. Places of interest include ruined Appuldurcombe House (AM) at Wroxall, and the Museum of the History of Smuggling which traces this profession back over 700 years.

North west of the isle's southernmost tip, St Catherine's Point, lies Blackgang Chine, one of the best known of these deep rocky clefts, which has a large amusement complex to add to its natural attractions. Newport lies some 8 miles inland from Blackgang. This centrally positioned community serves as capital of the island. South west of Newport is Carisbrooke Castle (OACT) where Charles I was imprisoned for a year (1647–8) before his eventual execution in London. He was visited here by his son Henry and daughter Elizabeth. Other places of interest include the Roman Villa (OACT). Freshwater is 10 miles west of Newport where Farringford House, now a hotel, was once the home of Alfred, Lord Tennyson. The Museum of Clocks, with more than 200 exhibits, stands in beautiful countryside. Beyond Freshwater, at the most westerly point of the island, lies Alum Bay, surrounded by cliffs whose strata are many-coloured, and offshore are the Needles, three huge chalk pillars jutting from the sea. At their end is Needles Lighthouse, built in 1858.

Yarmouth stands at the mouth of the Yar opposite mainland Lymington. The harbour is a delight. Yarmouth Castle (AM) was built by Henry VIII, and Fort Victoria, to protect the western approaches to Portsmouth, in 1853; it is now a country park (OACT).

Cowes is Britain's yachting capital; Cowes Castle built by Henry VIII houses the Royal Yacht Squadron. 22 brass guns line Victoria Parade ready to start races and fire Royal Salutes. Cowes was the point of departure for several expeditions to America. Notably, Leonard Calvert, brother of the second Lord Baltimore, led an

The Needles, Isle of Wight

St Mary's, Isles of Scilly

expedition of 200 Roman Catholics to form a colony. They left for Maryland in the *Ark of Avalon* and the *Dove* in 1633. A plaque in the Cowes parade commemorates this. Another Royalist, William D'Avennant, was imprisoned here, after his ship was intercepted on its way to Virginia. He is remembered for his chivalrous poem *Gondibert* (1651). East Cowes across the River Medina, is the centre of the UK hovercraft industry.

One mile south east is Osborne House, Queen Victoria's home at the time of her death in 1901. The house was designed in the style of an Italian villa by Prince Albert and Thomas Cubitt. The apartments are furnished as they were in Queen Victoria's day. The Swiss Cottage, built as a playhouse for the Royal children, now contains the Queen's writing-table and her collection of porcelain. Nearby is Norris Castle, where the young Princess Victoria frequently stayed with her mother.

Among the many other places of interest on the island are Arreton Manor on the Newport–Sandown road; the Isle of Wight Steam Railway at Haven Street, south west of Ryde, and the Flamingo Park at Seaview, a village just along the coast from Ryde. Brading, inland from Sandown, has a Lilliput Doll and Toy Museum, Osborn-Smith's Wax Museum and Animal World, and not far from the town are the remains of a Roman villa and 17th-century Morton Manor.

ISLES OF SCILLY
Cornwall
Twenty-eight perilous miles south west of Land's End lie the Scillies, separated from Cornwall by some of the most dangerous waters around the British coast. Only five islands are inhabited – St Mary's, Tresco, St Martin's, Bryher and St Agnes – many of the others being little more than stumps of rock: in total, the archipelago covers about 3000 acres. Once privately owned, they are now part of the Duchy of Cornwall. St Mary's is the largest island in the group and can be reached from Penzance by helicopter or boat. In the 'capital', Hugh Town, sits the council of the isles, supervisors of the islands' administration. The main square of Hugh Town has a little park where the rites of May are celebrated every year. High above the town on the Hugh Peninsula is Star Castle, an Elizabethan fort-turned-hotel encompassed by 18th-century granite walls. The whole area around here has consequently become known as The Garrison.

St Martin's Island has excellent white sandy beaches; the three small communities here are prosaically named Higher Town, Middle Town and Lower Town. Tresco is an island of contrasts and is the home of the former Lords Proprietors of the island, the Dorrien-Smith family. The house built by their ancestor Augustus Smith in 1841, Tresco Abbey, is world famous for the sub-tropical gardens he planted.

Because the Isles of Scilly enjoy a very mild, virtually frost-free winter a flourishing flower-growing economy has been developed. The season starts in November and reaches its peak in mid March when large quantities of daffodils are exported to mainland Cornwall. These are followed by irises and tulips in April.

IXWORTH
Suffolk *12 TL97*
Ixworth has several Roman connections and in nearby Stow Lane are the remnants of a building believed to have been part of an Iceni camp. Ixworth Abbey (OACT) dates, in part, from 1170 when an Augustinian priory was built here; the remains are incorporated into a 17th-century house. The church of St Mary contains a decorative tomb in memory of Richard Coddington and his wife, and portrait brasses of other members of the Coddington family. Close by is the village of Ixworth Thorpe, where All Saints Church has a thatched roof. The church door is only 5ft high and the pews have carved ends depicting animals, birds and humans.

J

JARROW
Tyne & Wear *20 NZ36*
The town became the centre of attention in the 1930s when unemployed shipyard workers marched to the Houses of Parliament and demanded work. Their plight illustrated the danger of a community depending totally on a single industry. Today the town supports a greater diversification of industry with factories producing furniture, metal goods and chemical products.

Deeper historical roots can be traced through St Paul's Church (OACT), an important Christian shrine that was once part of the monastery where the Venerable Bede wrote many of his 79 books, including the *Ecclesiastical History of the English People*. The Saxon church has seen many architectural changes since its original foundation in 682 by Benedict Biscop. After being sacked by the Danes and then by William the Conqueror, the church was rebuilt in 1074. The Bede Monastery Museum in Jarrow Hall contains archaeological finds from St Paul's Monastery.

JEDBURGH
Borders *24 NT62*
During the Middle Ages Jedburgh was at the centre of the Border Wars between the Scots and the English, changing hands many times. Today it is a quiet town producing tweeds and woollens and set amongst the Border hills. The former county prison, known as 'the Castle', was built in 1823 on the former site of Jedburgh Castle destroyed by order of the Scottish Parliament in 1409. Jedburgh Abbey (AM) was founded in 1118 by Prince David and constantly suffered at the hands of English invaders until 1523 when the Earl of Surrey finally ordered it to be burnt down. The fine Norman tower has been reconstructed and the tracery of the rose window makes this one of Scotland's finest medieval buildings. Mary Queen of Scots House (OACT) is a museum displaying artefacts associated with the Queen's stay in the town in 1566.

JERVAULX ABBEY
N Yorkshire *15 SE18*
Jervaulx Abbey ruins are located 4 miles north west of Masham. Founded in 1156, the great monastery housed Cistercian monks until 1537, when the last abbot was hanged for having taken part (although reluctantly) in the ill-fated 'Pilgrimage of Grace'. The remains are less spectacular than those of Fountains and Rievaulx, but the ground plan can be easily identified and the site, partly overgrown by trees, is in lovely countryside.

JODRELL BANK
Cheshire *14 SJ77*
The Mark 1A radio telescope at Jodrell Bank (OACT), where the Nuffield Radio Astronomy Laboratories are situated, measures 250ft and is one of the largest steerable radio telescopes in the world. Display material, working models, a planetarium and an arboretum can be seen.

JOHN O'GROATS
Highland *30 ND37*
The village of John O'Groats takes its name from a Dutchman, Jan de Groot who arrived in Scotland in the early 16th century, with his 2 brothers. Eventually there were 8 families and Jan built an octagonal house with a door in each side so that they could all live peaceably. Although the house no longer exists, the site is marked by a mound and a flagstaff. John O'Groats looks out to the waters of Pentland Firth and the fine views include those of the Orkney Islands, Stroma and South Ronaldsay. To the east is Duncansby Head with the three Stacks of Duncansby jutting out of the sea. John O'Groats is the most northerly settlement on the British mainland. Land's End, at the tip of the Cornish peninsula, is 877 miles away by road. Dunnet Head, to the west of John O'Groats is the most northerly point.

Duncansby Stacks, John O'Groats

K

KEDLESTON HALL
Derbyshire *10 SK34*
Kedleston Hall (OACT) is an 18th-century mansion in a 500-acre park. The Curzon family has lived in houses on this site since 1100. The mansion is considered one of the greatest achievements of Robert Adam. It has a magnificent marble hall, state rooms and a fine collection of pictures; added attractions are an Indian Museum and a colony of Canada geese in the park.

KEELE
Staffordshire *14 SJ84*
Keele, 3 miles west of Newcastle-under-Lyme, was once an administrative centre of the Knights Templar. The University of Keele, founded in 1962, is well known for its broadly based courses which combine Arts and Social Sciences; the modern buildings grouped around old Keele Hall form an American-style campus.

KEITH
Grampian *27 NJ45*
Keith, an agricultural centre of Strath Isle, was once famous for its Fair. Auld Brig o' Keith over the River Isla dates from 1609. Ruined Milton Tower was once the home of the Oliphant family. The Milton Distillery founded in 1785 and now called Strath Isla, is Scotland's oldest working malt whisky distillery. Just north of the town Newmill was the birthplace of James Gordon Bennett, who established the pioneering *New York Herald*.

KELMSCOT
Oxfordshire *3 SU29*
William Morris, the poet, designer and printer, lived here from 1871 until his death in 1896. His home was the gabled Elizabethan Kelmscott Manor, and a woodcut depicting it formed the frontispiece of his book, *News from Nowhere*. The house was restored in 1968 as a Morris Museum; it can be seen by written arrangement with the owners, the Society of Antiquaries.

KELSO
Borders *24 NT73*
Kelso, a little market town on the Tweed built round a cobbled square,

was described by Scott as 'the most beautiful, if not the most romantic village in Scotland'. The 12th-century abbey (AM) was the greatest of the Border abbeys until its destruction in the 16th century, and the little that remains gives evidence of fine Norman and early Gothic workmanship. Floors Castle (OACT) is an imposing 18th-century building, the home of the Duke and Duchess of Roxburghe; it contains superb English and French furniture, tapestries and paintings. It was also the ancestral home of William Hooper.

KEMNAY
Grampian   *NJ 7316*
Granite from the quarries at Kemnay was used in the building of the Forth Bridge and of the Thames embankment. Castle Fraser (NTS), 2½ miles to the south west, is an impressive example of the Scottish Baronial style built between 1575 and 1636 and incorporating an earlier stronghold; an exhibition tells the story of 'The Castles of Mar'.

KENDAL
Cumbria   *18 SD59*
The 'auld grey town' of Kendal was made a barony by Richard Coeur de Lion in 1189. It has since become the administrative capital and the largest town of the Lake District. The town's motto *Pannus mihi panis* – wool is my bread – comes from the wool industry established here by the Flemish in 1331. Kendal is now most famous for its snuff and mint cake. The River Kent meanders through the Fell country on the edge of the Lake District National Park, overlooked by the remains of Kendal Castle (AM), the birthplace of Catherine Parr. The Abbot Hall Art Gallery is a fine 18th-century house with period furnishings – its collection includes American works; a museum of Lakeland life and industry is housed in the old stables. Kendal museum specializes in natural history and archaeology. The Mayor's Parlour has a collection of pictures by George Romney, the portrait painter who was born here in 1734.

One mile south is the site of *Alauna*, a Roman fort. 3 miles south lies Sizergh Castle (NT), home of the Strickland family for 700 years. Its pele tower was built in 1370 as a defence against border raiders. It contains much fine panelling and early Elizabethan carving. The family has a Washington connection.

KENILWORTH
Warwickshire   *10 SP27*
The town's most important feature is its 12th-century castle (AM) perhaps the finest fortress ruin in the country, and the setting for much of Scott's novel *Kenilworth*. The castle, a stronghold throughout the Dark Ages, was remodelled as a palace by John of Gaunt, the fourth son of Edward III, who added the Great Hall in the 14th century. 200 years later Robert Dudley, Earl of Leicester, built the gatehouse and laid out the pleasure gardens. The Earl entertained Queen Elizabeth I at the castle. The remains of the keep are also of interest. The main street of the original town winds away from the castle's main gateway, the town itself being attractive with several 15th-century half-timbered houses, a fine parish church, with a Norman doorway; nearby are the remains of an Augustinian abbey.

KENMORE
Tayside   *22 NN74*
Today Kenmore is a popular salmon fishing resort, but at the beginning of the 16th century only a ferryman's cottage stood here beside the River Tay; the introduction of market fairs stimulated the development of the village, and it was furthered by the building of the bridge across the Tay in 1744. In the mid 19th century Kenmore was 'restored' in a Victorian mock-rustic style by the 2nd Marquis of Breadalbane, and since this is a conservation area the village looks much the same today. The home of the Breadalbanes was 16th-century Balloch Castle (now ruined); Taymouth Castle was built as a replacement for Balloch, but since the death of the 3rd marquis in 1922 it has been used as hotel, military hospital and school. 1 mile north east of Taymouth Castle is Croft Moraig, the site of a prehistoric double circle of standing stones, 185ft in diameter.

KERSEY
Suffolk   *12 TL94*
At one time most of the working men of England were clad in tough Kersey cloth, while their womenfolk wore the softer fabric made in neighbouring Lindsey. The fine Perpendicular church of this charming village reflects the early prosperity that the wool trade brought; the roof of its south porch is particularly notable, being made up of 16 magnificently carved 15th-century panels. The colour-washed houses lining the main street as it runs steeply

down to a watersplash are dark-timbered with age and include a group of pre-Reformation weavers' cottages.

KESWICK
Cumbria   *18 NY22*
Keswick, an old market town with narrow streets and grey stone buildings, stands on the River Greta between Skiddaw and Derwent Water. Set in magnificent scenery, it is a popular centre for exploring the Lake District. Derwent Water, at 1¼ miles across, is the widest of the lakes. St Herbert, a disciple of St Cuthbert, had a hermitage on the island in the lake in AD 685. John Ruskin declared Friar's Crag headland to be one of Europe's most scenic viewpoints. Hugh Walpole had connections with the area and set some of his works here. Coleridge and later poet Robert Southey lived at Greta House north of the town square; they were visited here by many friends including the Wordsworths and Sir Walter Scott. The Fitz Park Museum has items relating to all the Lake District artists and an Epstein bust of Walpole. Walpole and Southey are buried at Great Crosthwaite, where the church contains a marble bust of Southey.

Lingholm (OACT), on the west shore of Derwent Water, has both formal and woodland gardens, with a large collection of rhododendrons, azaleas and other shrubs. Castlerigg Stone Circle (AM, NT) just outside the town is a most impressive prehistoric circle of 38 stones, 4 of which form a rectangle within the ring. It is also known as the Druids' Circle.

Kersey

SCOTT AND THE BORDERS

The Borders are distinctive. The lower Tweed River and many of its tributaries, and Berwick at its mouth, though they seem to be Scottish, are in England. Berwick, for long one of the original four royal burghs of Scotland, was lost to the English in 1482. Originally Scotland's greatest seaport, and until recently the HQ of the King's Own Scottish Borderers, with Scots (not English) law applying to the Tweed salmon fisheries, its people have Scottish names and (not least) its football team plays soccer in the Scottish League. Yet its walled defences face north – the best preserved Tudor fortification in Britain – and it is governed, not by a provost

Sir Walter Scott

and bailies as a good Scottish burgh would be, but by a mayor and aldermen. The official border runs three miles north. And as a result of this confusion Berwick is still, they say, at war with Russia. When the Crimean War began in 1854, it was still seen, in legal documents, as a separate entity, and so it was Scotland, England and Berwick-on-Tweed that declared war. By 1856 when the peace was signed, Berwick had been legally incorporated into England, and so it was Scotland and England that made peace.

Sir Walter Scott (1771–1832) was born in Edinburgh and raised on his

grandfather's farm near Kelso in Tweeddale, because of his infantile paralysis. He came to his writing late. He collected minstrels' songs, legends and tales, and continued writing because it allowed him to live as a country gentleman while practising as a lawyer in Edinburgh; he served also as sheriff-depute in Selkirkshire, living in his own countryside, which he loved and left rarely – though one of his trips led him to meet and marry his French wife – and built his great baronial-style home at Abbotsford near Melrose, which cost him £76,000. Later, as its splendour and its costs grew, he called it, in private, Conundrum Castle. The sum was a fortune for those days, and it took him the rest of his life to pay off. The failure of his publishers, Constable and Ballantyne, led him to take on the burden of their debts too. His first verse, *The Lay of the Last Minstrel* (1805), ushered in a wave of romantic interest in knights and their ladies, abbeys, castles and kings. His first novel, *Waverley* (1814), was published with no author's name on it, but had phenomenal success, and led to eight more historical novels – the most notable *Old Mortality* and *The Antiquary*. All were products of dedicated labour, writing from 6 am to noon each day, before his other life began – as sheriff, lawyer and farmer and – gradually – as social celebrity in Edinburgh. He could see the clash in contemporary Scotland between its heroic and stormy past, landed, clan-linked and poor, and its vigorous commercial-orientated present, the legacy of the Union with England. By 1820 he was known throughout Europe; he organized, and was host for, George IV's visit to Scotland in 1822, the first visit of a member of the royal house since his great-great-uncle 'Butcher' Cumberland's visit in chase of the Young Pretender

at Culloden; he all but invented the tartan – he himself wore the Campbell tartan for the occasion in 1822; and clan history owes much to his research and popularizing; his literary and romantic impact on the American South in the years before the Civil War was immense. When he died he could say, justly, that he had 'many friends, few unfriends and, I think, no enemies.'

The Borders, on both the Scottish and the English sides, and at each end, from Wallsend to the Solway Firth, have been rich in poets and authors, from Thomas the Rhymer to James Hogg 'The

Ettrick Shepherd', Robert Louis Stevenson and Rabbie Burns (though he was primarily an Ayrshire Scot), Carlyle at Ecclefechan in Dumfriesshire and – in legend at least – Merlin himself, who is said to be buried in the Eildon Hills. Its more recent authors include S R Crockett, Hugh McDiarmid in Langholm (Marxist, Scottish Nationalist and passionate Celt), Gavin Maxwell of the *Ring of Bright Water* and, not least, John Buchan, first Lord Tweedsmuir, a name taken from the lonely hamlet near St Mary's Loch in the deep heart of the Borders, a twentieth-century Walter

The Library, Mellerstain

Abbotsford, Scott's house near Galashiels

Scott. Born in Perth, a son of the Free Kirk manse, largely raised in Glasgow and in his grandmother's and his uncle's home at Broughton in Tweeddale five miles east of Biggar – the country he knew as a boy and round which he built many of his tales, his 'holy land' – Buchan went by way of Glasgow University to Brasenose College, Oxford. At Oxford he knew Aubrey Herbert, whose wartime adventures were incorporated in Buchan's creation of Sandy Arbuthnot (*Greenmantle*). And at Oxford he won the Newdigate Prize for a poem on 'The Pilgrim Fathers'. He identified, thereafter, with the British Establishment, became a publisher with Nelson & Co, and an author. He published at least sixty-eight books, sometimes four a year. He appears, disguised, in his own fiction as 'Edward Leithen'; he became an MP and in the end Governor-General of Canada (hoping privately in fact to be Viceroy of India). Many Scots have since 1603 thus identified with England, many in so doing remaining self-consciously and proudly Scots; many, especially for the first century-and-a-half,

very unpopular in London; some having their sons educated south of the Border (Buchan's own sons went to Eton). The Anglo-Scottish relationship is politically a sensitive area, touched by Calvinism and by snobbery, by pride and strong national feeling, and rich in creative tensions – to which perhaps the only parallels in the US are to be found in Texas or among old-fashioned Dixiecrats?

The Borders, particularly Selkirk, Roxburgh and Peeblesshire, are rich in history, as the annual 'Ridings' testify. On various dates through the summer, each locality confirms its boundaries by riding round them, or by commemorating some historic event. These are colourful equestrian occasions, in appearance suggesting a noisy and jovial clan uprising or even a somewhat hilarious Red Indian revolt. Some of these celebrations recall pagan days, like the Beltane Festival each mid-June in Peebles, a reminder of the days of sun and fire worship.

The Borders too are rich in Lowland earls and lairds – the Dukes of Roxburghe (Ker family) whose seat is Floors

Castle; of Buccleuch: the Scotts, whose seat is Bowhill, near Selkirk; the Earls of Home, whose seat is the Hirsel near Coldstream – Earl Home of the Hirsel, Prime Minister 1963–4 is the 14th Earl of Home, and the 34th in an unbroken descent from the thirteenth century; the Marquess of Lothian, of the Ker family of Ancrum, near Jedburgh; the McEwens of Marchmont; the Stuarts of Traquair; to name only a few of the Scots nobility. Traquair is one of the oldest continually inhabited houses in Scotland. The family, as Catholics, were loyal to the Jacobites and refused to open the gates until a Stuart was on the throne; the gates have stayed closed since 1746.

Just over the border, from Eskdale, came the family of Lord Thomson of Fleet, Canadian newspaper owner and TV pioneer; and of Thomas Telford too, the bridge and canal builder.

Places to Visit

Abbotsford, near Galashiels.
Broughton, The Green, for evidence of John Buchan.

Carlisle
Drybrugh, near Melrose. The White Canons.
Edinburgh, where Sir Walter Scott lived at 39, Castle Street, and Stevenson at 17, Heriot Row.
The Eildon Hills
Flodden Field, where in 1513 English forces defeated the Scots and James IV of Scotland, and many Scots nobles were killed.
Hermitage Castle, fourteenth-century stronghold of the Douglasses.
Jedburgh, The Black Canons.
Kirk Yetholm, capital of the Scots Gypsies and the Romany family of Faa.
Lamberton Bar and **Gretna Green**, the two ends of the Borders, and both sites for Scottish marriages for runaway couples from England.
Mellerstain, near Kelso, home of the Earl of Haddington.
Melrose, a Cistercian foundation.
Winton House, Pencaitland, East Lothian.

Further Reading

George Borrow, *Lavengro*
John Buchan, *The Thirty-Nine Steps, John Burnet of Barns, John McNab, Scholar Gypsies, Memory Hold-the-door* (Hodder & Stoughton 1941) and Janet Adam-Smith, *John Buchan* (Rupert Hart Davies 1965)
James Fergusson, *Lowland Lairds* (Collins 1949)
Michael Joyce, *Edinburgh the Golden Age* (Longman, Green 1951)
Gavin Maxwell, *The House of Elrig, Ring of Bright Water* (Longman, Green 1960)
Sir Walter Scott, *Old Mortality* (for Edinburgh), *Marmion* (for Tantallon Castle, Norham Castle and Flodden Field), *Guy Mannering* (for the Stewartry of Kirkcudbright and Galloway).
Shakespeare, *Henry IV*
Robert Louis Stevenson, *Kidnapped* and *The Master of Ballantrae*

KIDDERMINSTER
Hereford & Worcester   *9 SO87*
Flemish weavers brought prosperity to
Kidderminster in the 13th and 14th
centuries, and the carpet manufacture
for which the town is famous began
during the 18th; a working model of
an old carpet loom can be seen in the
Museum in Exchange Street. The
success of the industry was reinforced
during the 2nd half of the century by
the building of the Staffordshire and
Worcestershire Canal, designed by
James Brindley. 19th-century mills
dominate the town, and little remains
of medieval Kidderminster except the
church of St Mary and All Saints,
which has a 13th-century chancel, a
15th-century Lady Chapel, and
interesting brasses and monuments. Sir
Roland Hill, who introduced the
penny post, was born here in 1795.
Harvington Hall (OACT) stands 3
miles south east; the 16th-century
brick house is built around a late medieval original and contains a warren of
secret passages and priests' holes.

KIDWELLY
Dyfed   *7 SN40*
Kidwelly Castle (AM) was built in a
good strategic position above the River
Gwendraeth by a 12th-century Bishop
of Salisbury and was subsequently
much involved in the struggles of the
Welsh rebels against the English
crown. Additions were made to the
castle in the 13th and 14th centuries –
notably a three-storeyed gatehouse
and an outer ward; the vast ovens also
built at that time can still be seen in the
extensive ruins.

KILBARCHAN
Strathclyde   *22 NS46*
The Weaver's Cottage (NTS) is an
early 18th-century house of cruck
construction; it dates from the days
when cloth-making was a cottage
industry and contains looms and other
weaving equipment. A local weaver-
poet, Robert Allan, is commemorated
by a fountain nearby.

KILDRUMMY CASTLE
Grampian   *27 NJ41*
The ruins of 13th-century Kildrummy
Castle (AM) overlook the valley of the
Don from a height of 800ft, the
original choice of site obviously
influenced by the ravine that guards it
on two sides. Bravely defended by Sir
Nigel Bruce in 1306, it survived until
the Jacobite Rising of 1715, after
which it was dismantled. The grounds
include an attractive water garden, and

the quarry which provided the stone
for the castle has been planted with
alpines and shrubs.

KILLERTON
Devon   *2 SS90*
Eighteenth-century Killerton House
(NT) is the home of the Acland family,
a member of which was a major
fighting with Burgoyne at the Battle of
Saratoga; Major Acland was noted for
his extreme anti-American views. The
house, which contains the Paulise de
Bush collection, is set in 15 acres of
beautiful gardens. 3 miles north east is
Bradninch, where King Charles I
stayed at the old manor house in 1614;
the bed in which he slept is still in
existence. George Boone, grandfather
of the frontiersman Daniel Boone
(1734–1820) was a blacksmith and
weaver here. Squire Boone, Daniel's
father,.was baptized in the parish
church, which contains a fine painted
screen, typical of Devon.

KILLIECRANKIE
Tayside   *26 NN96*
Killiecrankie is best known for the
battle which took place at the head of
the Pass in 1689, when Viscount
Dundee – the 'Bonnie Dundee' of
Scott's ballad – won a decisive victory
for the Jacobite cause, though he was
killed in his moment of triumph. The
National Trust for Scotland owns
much of the Pass, and its Visitor
Centre stands close to the site of the
battle. A steep path runs down to the
narrow opening of the gorge known as
'Soldier's Leap', because a trooper
fleeing from the Highlanders jumped
across the River Garry here.

KILMARNOCK
Strathclyde   *22 NS43*
It was in Kilmarnock that Scotland's
national poet, Robert Burns, published
his first collection, *Poems Chiefly in
the Scottish Dialect*; his intention was
to raise enough money to emigrate to
Jamaica, but the success of the book
persuaded him to remain. A copy of
this first edition and an extensive
collection of original manuscripts are
contained in the Burns Museum, a
Victorian tower built to commemorate
the poet. The Dick Institute includes
displays of archaeological and
geological interest, a collection of
small arms, a children's museum and
an art gallery. Dean Castle (OACT)
contains exhibitions of European arms
and early musical instruments, and
there is a nature trail in the extensive
park. A famous name connected with

Kilmarnock is that of Johnnie Walker,
a grocer in King Street until he began
to blend whisky in 1820.

KILMARTIN
Strathclyde   *21 NR89*
Dunadd Fort (AM), 3 miles south of
Kilmartin, is a prehistoric hill-fort
which was once the capital of the
ancient Scots kingdom of Dalriada.
Other prehistoric remains include the
Temple Wood circle and cist and
several cairns and groups of cup-and-
ring marked rocks. Carnasserie Castle
(AM) overlooks the valley from a high
point about a mile north of Kilmartin,
and the ruins of another castle stand
on the outskirts of the village.

KILVERSTONE
Norfolk   *12 TL88*
Kilverstone 'Latin American' Wildlife
Park is set in the grounds of 17th-
century Kilverstone Hall, the home of
Lord and Lady Fisher; they have
brought together a varied collection of
South American mammals and birds,
and hope to breed from some of the
rarer species. The miniature horse stud
and the English walled garden are also
of interest.

KIMMERIDGE
Dorset   *3 SY97*
Low cliffs of black shale overlook the
small bay where thatched cottages
stand beside the derelict quay of
Kimmeridge. Smedmore House
(OACT) to the south east is originally
Jacobean, with Queen Anne and
Georgian additions, and contains an
exhibition of antique dolls and
marquetry furniture. Ruined Clavel
coastguard tower on the cliffs was
once a summer house belonging to
Smedmore. 1 mile inland, the church in
the tiny village of Steeple very
surprisingly contains representations
of the stars and stripes – the
Washington coat of arms. One is cut
into the stone porch, while the other is
painted in scarlet on the barrel roof. A
branch of the Washingtons were once
squires of Steeple.

KINCARDINE-ON-FORTH
Fife   *23 NS98*
This former port lies on the east bank
of the Forth, its bridge the last to span
the estuary before it widens. A 17th-
century mercat cross stands in the
market place and many old houses
survive. Ruined Tulliallan Castle, a
15th-century building with ground-
floor vaulting, is of great architectural
interest.

Kimmeridge Bay

KINCRAIG
Highland   *26 NH80*

Kincraig stands on the north side of Loch Insh, through which the River Spey flows to be joined by the Freshie. Nearby is the Highland Wildlife Park, which displays native animals of Scotland including species no longer found in the wild.

KINGSBRIDGE
Devon   *2 SX74*

This market town is situated in the South Hams, at the head of the Kingsbridge estuary. It was the birthplace in 1705 of William Cookworthy, who discovered china clay in Cornwall and made the first porcelain in England. An exhibition commemorating his achievement is contained in one of the galleries of the Cookworthy Museum. Kingsbridge has a late 16th-century arcade, The Shambles, and two interesting churches – St Edmund's, with its 13th-century tower, and 16th-century Dodbrooke.

KING'S LYNN
Norfolk   *11 TF62*

To the locals the town is known simply as Lynn. Until the 16th century it was Bishop's Lynn, the area belonging to the See of Norwich, but it was appropriated by Henry VIII at the Dissolution of the Monasteries. By that time it was a flourishing market town. The Tuesday and Saturday markets have gathered round the

churches of St Margaret and St Nicholas since the 12th century. It was also fast becoming one of the busiest ports in England. The elegant 17th-century Customs House, built by Henry Bell, architect and mayor of the town, indicates the status that the town had achieved by then. Prosperity really came, however, with the corn-shipping trade of the 18th century, and the substantial Corn Exchange and elaborate merchants' houses date from this period. The town's historic buildings include St George's Guildhall (NT), faced with chequered flintwork, the largest surviving medieval guildhall in the country and now a theatre. Shakespeare is said to have played here. The Hanseatic Warehouses date from 1428. Thoresby College was founded in 1500 as a college for priests. The timber-framed Hampton Court is also interesting. Lynn Museum has interesting exhibits of local and natural history and the Museum of Social History concentrates on domestic bygones. King's Lynn was the birthplace of Fanny Burney.

The maritime history of King's Lynn has given it several lasting connections with the New World. John Mason, the founder of New Hampshire, was associated with Sir Ferdinando Gorges in his explorations, becoming Vice-Admiral of New England, of which he made the earliest map. Mason was also Governor of Newfoundland; he is buried in Westminster Abbey. Sir Andrew Hammond was Lieutenant-

Governor of Nova Scotia 1780–82. Another emigrant was Daniel Whiting, rector of St Margaret's Church, who left for New England in 1636. Lynn, Massachusetts was so named because of his connections with King's Lynn. 23 New Conduit Street was the birthplace in 1761 of George Vancouver, the explorer. Vancouver spent his early years serving under Captain Cook, then led his own expedition around the Cape of Good Hope, surveying south-west Australia and New Zealand. Vancouver then visited the Hawaiian Islands and sailed up the Pacific Coast of America from California to Vancouver. Rear-Admiral James Burney, also from King's Lynn, sailed with Cook in North American waters. Captain John Smith of the Virginia Colony was apprenticed to a New Lynn merchant, but soon ran away to become a soldier.

Captain Samuel Cresswell, who was with Sir James Clark Ross exploring the Arctic, is buried at North Runcton, 3 miles south east of King's Lynn. The museum at King's Lynn holds sketches by him.

KINGSWINFORD
W Midlands   *9 SO88*

Kingswinford, on the western edge of the Black Country, lies just north of Stourbridge, whose early importance was due to its glass-making industry. Many fine examples of its craftsmanship are included among the exhibits on show at Broadfield House Glass Museum, which covers both English and Continental glass from the late 17th century until the present day. Visitors can also see glass-making tools and an engraving studio.

KINGTON
Hereford & Worcester   *8 SO35*

Kington is a small market town on the River Arrow, famous for its autumn sales of Clun Forest and Kerry sheep. It lies in pleasant hill country, sheltered by Hergest Ridge and Rushock Hill – the latter being crossed by **Offa's Dyke**, the old Mercian defence against the Welsh. Hergest Croft Gardens (OACT) display a variety of trees, shrubs and flowers, together with an old-fashioned kitchen garden and a woodland valley filled with rhododendrons, some 30ft high.

KINGUSSIE
Highland   *26 NH70*

Kingussie, the so-called 'Capital of Badenoch', stands on the wooded slopes of Strath Spey with clear views across to the Cairngorms. The district of Badenoch is sometimes called 'the drowned land' because the Spey floods so often, in spite of its banks having been heightened and reinforced. The Highland Folk Museum, which was originally founded in Iona and maintained by four Scottish universities, covers 200 years of farming and local craftsmanship and includes an old cottage, a reconstructed Hebridean mill and a primitive 'black house'.

KINLOCHEWE
Highland *29 NH06*
The small village of Kinlochewe lies 2 miles beyond the southern end of **Loch Maree**, amid magnificent scenery dominated by the 3217ft 'spear', Slioch. It is a base for climbing and hillwalking and offers excellent fishing for sea trout, brown trout and salmon. To the west stretches the Beinn Eighe National Nature Reserve, the first of its kind in Britain; it covers over 10,000 acres, preserving the remains of ancient Scottish pine forests and protecting such species as deer, wild cats, pine martens and golden eagles. Beinn Eighe itself is of interest geologically, being formed of 750-million-year-old red sandstone topped with 600-million-year-old white quartzite.

KIRKBY LONSDALE
Cumbria *18 SD67*
Kirkby Lonsdale is a little market town attractively set on a hill above the River Lune. John Ruskin, the 19th-century writer, considered his favourite view from the town to be 'one of the loveliest scenes in England and therefore in the world'; Ruskin Walks are signposted near the churchyard. The ancient, three-arched Devil's Bridge (AM) which spans the Lune just outside Kirkby is now closed to traffic. The great pool beneath it is popular with salmon fishermen and aqualung divers. The town has an old market cross and the church, St Mary's, is Norman. The Brontë sisters attended the Clergy Daughters' School at Cowan Bridge, near here, and Kirkby is the model for Lowton in *Jane Eyre*.

KIRKCALDY
Fife *23 NT29*
Economist Adam Smith was born here in 1723 and educated at the Burgh School where Thomas Carlyle later taught. Smith returned to Kirkcaldy, where in 1776 he wrote *The Wealth of Nations*, one of the earliest theoretical justifications of free trade. In 1728 Robert Adam, the illustrious architect, was born here. Kirkcaldy was also the birthplace of Anna, John Buchan's writer sister. Kirkcaldy has three interesting museums; the John McDouall Stuart Museum, which is a memorial to the 19th-century Scottish explorer of Australia; the town Museum and Art Gallery, which has a fine picture collection of works by most of the major Scottish artists – there is also a section on local pottery, including the famous Wemyss Ware; and the Industrial Museum. Ravenscraig (AM) is an impressive ruin on a rocky headland at the eastern end of the town. A few miles north east is Wemyss Castle which belonged to Shakespeare's Macduff; it was also the first meeting place of Mary Queen of Scots and Darnley; the couple married 5 months later.

KIRKCUDBRIGHT
Dumfries & Galloway *17 NX65*
Kirkcudbright, (pronounced Kircoobri) an ancient Royal Burgh on the Dee estuary, is the most important town in the area, with a small harbour at the head of Kirkcudbright Bay. Its name means 'Church of Cuthbert', and part of the old gateway to the town is incorporated in the entrance to the churchyard. Buried here is Billy Marshall, the 18th-century tinker 'king' who lived to be 120 – having reputedly fathered four children after the age of 100. At the Selkirk Arms Hotel in the High Street, Burns wrote the famous Selkirk Grace:

> Some hae meat and canna eat
> And some wad eat that want it,
> But we hae meat and we can eat
> And sae the Lord be thankit.'

The tolbooth is now a memorial to John Paul Jones, imprisoned here in 1773.

The Stewartry (or 'county') Museum includes firearms, domestic and agricultural equipment and a natural history section, while 18th-century Broughton House (OACT) has an interesting library and an attractive garden. McLellan's Castle (AM) is an impressive castellated mansion overlooking the harbour, built in 1582 by Sir Thomas McLellan who was Provost at that time. 4½ miles south east of the town is **Dundrennan** where Mary Queen of Scots spent her last night in Scotland.

KIRKOSWALD
Strathclyde *22 NS20*
Souter Johnnie's Cottage (NTS), a thatched 18th-century house, was once the home of John Davidson, the village cobbler (or 'souter') of Burns' poem 'Tam O'Shanter'; Tam O'Shanter himself lived here. He was Douglas Graham of Shanter who supplied malted grain to a brewhouse in Ayr. Life-size stone figures of the two and their friends stand in the garden of the cottage, now a Burns' Museum.

Kirkcudbright

Barrie Museum, Kirriemuir

KIRKSTALL ABBEY
W Yorkshire *15 SE23*
The ruins of Kirkstall Abbey (AM), lying beside the River Aire, are mainly late Norman. It was founded in 1152 by Cistercian monks from **Fountains Abbey**, who pioneered the exploitation of the iron ore in the area as well as being involved in the more traditional pursuits of farming, spinning, weaving and pottery-making. The original gatehouse now contains an interesting museum in which three Victorian streets have been recreated.

KIRRIEMUIR
Tayside *27 NO35*
Known as 'Thrums' in the writings of J M Barrie (1860–1937), who was born at 9 Brechin Road, now the Barrie Museum (NTS). Barrie was the author of *Peter Pan*. He is buried in the local cemetery. Logie, a 17th-century mansion with lovely gardens, stands 1 mile south. 3 miles north east is Inverquharity Castle.

KNARESBOROUGH
N Yorkshire *15 SE35*
Knaresborough is an attractive town with narrow streets of Georgian houses, steep steps and alleyways. The area is full of caves, the most famous being that named after Mother Shipton, the 15th-century seer; she is said to have predicted trains and aircraft, but most of the prophecies attributed to her were in fact written in the 19th century. The most interesting phenomenon is the Dropping Well, where drips of water containing a lime deposit are gradually petrifying a curious assortment of objects placed beneath them by the owners of the cave and others. On a clifftop high above the river stand the remains of the 14th-century castle (OACT), including the keep, two baileys and gatehouse; the Court House Museum is situated in the castle grounds. The Zoological Gardens at Conyngham Hall contain sea-lions and llamas as well as big cats.

KNEBWORTH
Hertfordshire *11 TL22*
Knebworth House (OACT) has been the home of the Lyttons since it was first built in 1492 and contains many portraits and personal mementoes of the family. It was largely rebuilt in 1843 by the Lord Lytton who wrote *The Last Days of Pompeii*, and some of his manuscripts are on display. The magnificent Tudor banqueting hall, with fine 17th-century plasterwork and panelling, was preserved in the reconstruction. The vast park has now been turned into a Country Park, offering such attractions as a crazy-golf course, skate park, Astroglide, narrow-gauge railway and adventure playground in addition to the more traditional deer park.

KNIGHTON
Powys *8 SO27*
This grey stone market town in the sheep-rearing countryside of the Teme valley has clung tenaciously to its hillside for at least 1000 years. The first settlers were Saxons, followed in the 11th century by the Welsh and then the Normans. A wooden Norman castle stood on the mound which is still called Bryn y Castell, and a hilltop on the other side of the town retains traces of a 12th-century stone stronghold. The old Welsh name for Knighton was Trefyclawdd, 'the town of the dyke', for **Offa's Dyke** (built by an 8th-century King of Mercia to keep Welsh predators out of his domain) runs through it. The Central Wales Railway line still operates, and the station is a charming example of Victorian Gothic, for Sir Richard Green-Price, who first released the land to the railway company, insisted on personally approving all their structures.

KNIGHTSHAYES COURT
Devon *2 SS91*
Nineteenth-century Knightshayes Court (NT) was the home of the Heathcote Amory family and contains Sir Julian Amory's collection of Old Masters. Both outside and inside the house retains a typically Victorian atmosphere of elaborate opulence. The gardens, overlooking the Exe Valley, are large and wooded, with fine shrubs; the topiary is unique.

KNOCKANDO
Grampian *27 NJ22*
At the Tamdhu Distillery (OACT) visitors to Knockando can see the whole process of whisky making. The Cheeryble brothers in Charles Dickens' *Nicholas Nickleby* are said to be based on the Grant brothers, who lived here. There are some ancient carved stones in the churchyard, and the church has an internal gallery.

KNOLE
Kent *5 TQ55*
Knole (NT), one of the largest private houses in England, was the birthplace of Vita Sackville-West in 1892 and is still the home of the Sackville family. Built of Kentish stone, it stands on a rounded hill or 'knoll' (whence the name) just outside **Sevenoaks**, spreading over some 4 acres. The building was begun by Thomas Bourchier, the Archbishop of Canterbury, in the 15th century and was extended in the 17th; the 365 rooms, 52 staircases and 7 courtyards represent the number of days in a year, weeks in a year and days in a week. The state apartments, with their fine plastered ceilings, retain much of the original Jacobean and Caroline furniture, and the house contains priceless collections of pictures, silver, carpets and tapestries. The house, which is set at Knole, and family are rich in literary associations. The manuscript of Virginia Woolf's *Orlando* can be seen in the Great Hall. The 26-acre garden, enclosed by an Elizabethan wall, has changed little since the 17th century, and herds of fallow and Japanese deer roam in the 1000-acre park.

KNOWSLEY
Merseyside *14 SJ49*
Knowsley Hall, the former home of the Earls of Derby, is an impressive 17th–19th-century mansion surrounded by 2500 acres of parkland – part of which has been given over to a Safari Park. The drive-through reserves contain elephants, giraffes, rhinos, monkeys, lions, tigers and many other animals. There are a children's amusement park and pets' corner, and, during the summer months, a dolphinarium.

KNUTSFORD
Cheshire *14 SJ77*
The name derives from the reputed fording of a local stream by King Canute. Knutsford is the 'Cranford' of Mrs Gaskell's novel. Mrs Gaskell, born Elizabeth Stevenson, was brought up by an aunt at Heathwaite House. In 1832 Elizabeth married Reverend William Gaskell in the parish church.

She herself attended the Brook St Unitarian Chapel where she is now buried. Knutsford, an attractive and traditional town, contains many reminders of Mrs Gaskell. These include the memorial tower in King Street and the King's Coffee House built in 1907. The Coffee House was frequented by John Galsworthy and other writers and painters of the day. The interior maintains its original decoration combining Art Nouveau and the Arts and Crafts Movement of the early 20th century. **Tatton Hall** (NT) is to the north of the town.

South of Knutsford, the church of Peover contains an American flag commemorating General George Patton and the American 3rd Army, who were based at Peover Hall during the war.

· KYLE OF LOCHALSH
Highland   *25 NG72*
Kyle of Lochalsh, the end of the romantic 'Road to the Isles', is a busy fishing and shipping village at the western end of Loch Alsh. It is the traditional 'Gateway to Skye', which lies only a short distance away across the waters of Kyle Akin. The railway line from Inverness terminates here, and steamers ply to Mallaig (passenger) and Skye (vehicle).

KYLESKU
Highland   *29 NC23*
Kylesku is one of the most remote places in Britain – and also one of the most beautiful. It stands on an inlet of Eddrachillis Bay in an area of coastline often compared with the Norwegian fjords. 5 miles south east and reached only by boat, Eas-coul-Aulin is the highest waterfall in Britain, with a sheer drop of 658ft.

KYNANCE COVE
Cornwall   *1 SW61*
This cove, in an area of coast owned by the National Trust, is possibly the most spectacular on the Lizard Peninsula. The remarkable cliffs of serpentine rock are streaked with red, purple, and green, and round the beach there are numerous caves with names like 'Devils Letter Box' and 'Ladies' Bathing Pool'. To the north west stand the magnificent cliffs known as Pigeon Hugo and The Horse. Just offshore is Asparagus Island (so called because the plant grows there in abundance), where the sea spouts dramatically through a rock known as the Devil's Bellows.

L

LACOCK
Wiltshire   *3 ST96*
Lacock is owned almost entirely by the National Trust; the oldest buildings in its twisting streets date back to medieval times and none is later than the 18th century, the village as a whole presenting an attractive blend of grey stone, red brick, whitewashed and half-timbered constructions. There are a 14th-century church and tithe barn, ancient inns and weavers' houses, a King John hunting lodge, an old lockup, a stepped cross and a packhorse bridge. The most impressive building, however, is the riverside abbey founded by the Countess of Salisbury in the 13th century and converted into a house by Sir William Sharington shortly after suppression of the monastery in 1539. The original sacristy, chapter house and cloisters were preserved and a large courtyard, octagonal tower and twisted chimney stacks were added. A Gothic-style entrance hall and great hall were built on in the 18th century by the Talbot family, into whose hands the abbey had then passed; a museum housed at the entrance to the abbey traces the work of W H Fox-Talbot, the pioneer of photography who produced the first photographic prints in 1838 and was awarded the Royal Society Medal for his achievement.

LAIRG
Highland   *30 NC50*
Lairg is a market village where important lamb sales are held, but its beautiful setting in wild countryside at the end of Loch Shin makes it popular with anglers and holidaymakers, whilst archaeologists are drawn to the area by the presence of prehistoric circles and tumuli. In woodland about 3 miles south of the village are the spectacular waterfalls of the River Shin, where salmon can be seen leaping at certain times of the year.

LAKENHEATH
Suffolk   *12 TL78*
There has been a United States Air Force station at Lakenheath since 1941, and it is still one of the largest of such bases in the country. St Mary's Church is particularly fine, with a Norman chancel arch and a 16th-century wooden roof embellished with angels; the bench ends in the nave and the 15th-century pulpit also have beautifully carved motifs.

LAMBERHURST
Kent   *6 TQ63*
Lamberhurst, its long main street crossing the River Teise, looks substantially as it has for hundreds of years. It is known for its flourishing vineyard. The ruins of Bayham Abbey (OACT), founded in the 13th century, are situated in the grounds of a modern house 2 miles to the west, and those of moated Scotney Castle (NT), set in beautiful landscaped grounds lie to the south east. Owl House, the one-time haunt of smugglers, is a small half-timbered house set in large gardens (OACT).

Scotney Castle, Lamberhurst

LANCASTER
Lancashire 18 SD46

The name of the city indicates its origin: the Roman *castrum*, or camp, beside the River Lune. Flint tools found around the rock of Castle Hill indicate that prehistoric man had also settled here. After the Romans left, the Saxons took over the site, and after the Conquest, the town passed to Roger de Poitou, who built the first Norman castle. The keep dates from about 1100 and both King John and John of Gaunt, first Duke of Lancaster, and ancestor of the Royal House of Lancaster (the Duchy of Lancaster still belongs to the Crown) added to the fortifications. Further additions were made by Elizabeth I.

For many hundreds of years Lancaster was an important port and in the 18th century was England's chief port for trade with America.

At Sunderland Point, south west on the Lune estuary, Britain's first bale of American cotton was unloaded, starting the close links between the north-western textile regions and the American South. The Customs House on St George's Quay, designed by Richard Gillow, one of the family of furniture-makers whose workshops were in Lancaster, dates from this period, as do the many Georgian houses in the principal streets. As the River Lune silted up and Liverpool expanded, Lancaster's maritime trade declined, but in the 19th century many cotton mills were built in the southern part of the town. Most of these have now closed or been converted to other uses, but several still stand near the canal.

As the county town of Lancashire, Lancaster is an important administrative centre and in the 1960s was selected as the site for a new university.

PLACES TO SEE

Castle and Shire Hall Dominating the city from the heights of Castle Hill, Lancaster Castle still looks medieval, though, of course, much restored. It was and is still used as a gaol, and among its famous prisoners were the so-called 'Lancashire Witches' in 1612, and George Fox, founder of the Society of Friends. George Whitfield, the evangelical orator, preached here in the Friends Meeting House, which dates from 1690. The law courts are also housed here but – subject to court requirements – parts of the castle and Shire Hall, with its collection of more than 600 coats of arms, including those of all the sovereigns since Richard I, can be visited.

Shire Hall's 18th-century ceiling

The Priory Church of St Mary stands near the castle and occupies the site of a 2nd-century Roman church. Most of the present building dates from the 15th century when the church belonged to the convent of Syon, but there are traces of older Saxon and Norman buildings. The choir stalls, with their exquisitely carved canopies, date from the 14th century and came originally from Cockersand or Furness Abbey.

Judge's Lodgings Visiting judges were lodged in this elegant Georgian house, now a fascinating museum decorated in period, with furniture made by Gillow. The Barry Elder Doll Collection is here, with an interesting collection of other toys and children's games displayed in the old nurseries.

Hornsea Pottery Guided factory tours and 42 acres of landscaped parkland are available to visitors to the pottery.

The Music Room In fact this is a tall, narrow house, which takes its name from the first-floor music room, famous for its elaborate plaster ceiling cast in about 1730 by Italian craftsmen. The Landmark Trust owns the house, and the room can be seen sometimes.

The City Museum Housed in the dignified Old Town Hall, the museum contains archaeological finds and displays of local crafts. The museum of the King's Own Royal (Lancaster) Regiment which served in America in the Revolutionary War and also in 1812 is housed here. The collection includes several George Washington medals.

St Peter's Cathedral, Roman Catholic, dates from 1859. Ornate and highly gilded, its style is of the 1300s.

LAMPETER
Dyfed 7 SN54

Lampeter, once famous for its horse fair, has had a market since 1284 and is still an important centre for the sale of the disease-resistant cattle bred in the area. It has a Victorian town hall and a parish church which was completely rebuilt in the 19th century, though some 17th-century memorials are preserved in the porch. St David's College (now part of the University of Wales) is noted for its library containing some 80,000 books, ancient manuscripts and first editions. The 19th-century building is an unspoiled example of early Gothic revival, and a nearby mound marks the site of a medieval castle.

LANARK
Strathclyde 22 NS84

The market town of Lanark, set high above the River Clyde, is an ancient Royal Burgh. David I built a castle here in the 12th century. It looks over Cora Linn, which has the most spectacular of the Clyde Falls, a magnificent 90ft plunge. To the west of the town, Cartland Crags rise to 400ft over a chasm nearly a mile long, by Mouse Water. Two time-honoured rituals are still observed in the town – Whippity Scoorie at the beginning of March (believed to originate in a pagan festival to drive away winter) and pageants to celebrate the Beating of the Bounds in June.

One mile south, New Lanark was the creation of Glasgow merchant David Dale, who acquired an area of marshland and, in 1784, built a textile village in conjunction with Richard Arkwright. He built cottages for his workforce, mostly dispossessed crofters. New Lanark is the best Scottish example of an industrial village. The socialist tradition continued when Robert Owen married Dale's daughter. He abolished child labour and built schools and shops, making New Lanark a 'model' community. Owen was forced to abandon his projects in 1825. Owen's son, Robert Dale Owen, founded the settlement of New Harmony, Indiana, carrying on his father's utopian socialist principles.

LAND'S END
Cornwall 1 SW32

England's most westerly point, Land's End is a particularly dramatic piece of coastline with brownish granite cliffs plunging into the Atlantic. On a clear day there are impressive views of the

Longships and Wolf Rock lighthouses. Inland is Sennen, England's westernmost village. According to legend, King Arthur, leading the forces of seven Cornish chieftains, routed the Danes here. A banquet to celebrate the victory was held on a large rock known as the Table Men, which lies about $\frac{1}{4}$ mile north of Sennen's church. Sennen has its own small harbour and beautiful bathing beaches.

LANHYDROCK HOUSE
Cornwall   *1 SX06*
Lanhydrock House (NT) 2½ miles south east of **Bodmin** is approached by an avenue of ancient beeches and sycamores, running through flowering trees and shrubs to the formal gardens of lawns, rose beds and clipped cypresses around the house. The brown stone building is simple in design and dates back to the 17th century, though much of it was rebuilt after a fire in 1881. Inside, the atmosphere is informal and the house is still lived in. The daily routines of earlier days are illustrated by the collection of curios in the kitchen and buttery. Lanhydrock's showpiece, however, is the original 17th-century plaster ceiling of the long gallery in the north wing, which local craftsmen decorated with early Old Testament scenes. The house is now used as an American training centre.

Lanhydrock House

LAUDER
Borders   *24 NT54*
Lauder, the only Royal Burgh in old Berwickshire, claims to have been granted this distinction during the reign of William the Lion, and it has certainly held its charter since 1502. The church is 16th century, with an octagonal spire, and magnificent Thirlestane Castle (OACT), just outside the town, also dates back to this period though with later additions; it now houses the Border Country Life Museum. Old Lauder Bridge set the scene for the hanging of several favourites of James III by the Earl of Angus in 1482, and the days of the old street fairs are recalled by the curious little stepped tolbooth where stallholders used to pay their dues. Lauder Common Riding, a horse-riding festival held here each June, is one of the oldest in the country, and the Leader Water has excellent fishing.

LAUGHARNE
Dyfed   *7 SN31*
Laugharne (pronounced 'Larn') was a town on the border known as the 'Landsker', which separated 'Little England' beyond Wales, with its strong Norman and Flemish influences, from 'Welsh Wales'. The town is charming, with Georgian terraced streets, an old harbour and the castle, converted by Sir John

Perrot, illegitimate son of Henry VIII.
    Richard Hughes, author of *In Hazard* and *High Wind in Jamaica*, lived here for 11 years. It was Hughes who first brought Dylan Thomas to the town, which eventually became his home from 1949 until his untimely death in New York in 1953. Thomas lived in the Georgian boathouse on the steep banks of the River Taf, overlooking the estuary and he is buried in St Martin's churchyard. The local area features in several of Thomas's poems, and although the poet denied it, the locals believe that *Under Milk Wood* was based on Laugharne and Thomas's most famous work is re-enacted there regularly.
    Along the coast at Pendine Sands Malcolm Campbell broke the land speed record in 1927 in *Bluebird*.

LAUNCESTON
Cornwall   *1 SX38*
Launceston once guarded the main route into Cornwall from Devon, and it was the county capital until 1838. A primitive motte-and-bailey stronghold was built here in the 11th century, but the present castle (AM) dates from the 13th. When it fell into disrepair after the Civil War, one tower continued to be used as a prison, and public executions were carried out below its walls until 1821. Lawrence House (NT) is one of the many interesting Georgian buildings in the old streets around the Square; it now houses a local history museum, but during the Napoleonic Wars it was a favourite rendezvous with French prisoners on parole. St Thomas's Church is notable for its large Norman font, and St Mary Magdelene's has fine woodwork inside and remarkable 16th-century carving on the granite exterior.

LAVENHAM
Suffolk   *12 TL94*
The finest of the Suffolk wool towns, with beautiful medieval timber houses. The market square is dominated by a 16th-century cross. In the past the Guildhall (NT) has been used as a prison, a workhouse and an almshouse. The Swan Hotel incorporates the old Wool'Hall. Inside a section of the bar-counter is scored with the signatures of American airmen who were based in the district during World War II. Lavenham church has a massive tower which was built largely by John de Vere, 13th Earl of Oxford, and by Thomas Spring a local clothier. John Constable went to school in the town and was a regular

visitor to the Taylors of Shilling Old Grange. Jane Taylor was the author of 'Twinkle, Twinkle Little Star'; she and her sister wrote many children's rhymes.

A plaque at Boxted airfield, west of Lavenham, commemorates US airmen operating from here during the war.

LAXTON
Nottinghamshire   *16 SK76*
The village of Laxton somehow evaded the Enclosures Acts of the 18th century, and its arable land is still divided into three enormous tracts (West, South and Mill Fields) which are farmed on the 3-year rotation basis, one being left fallow each year. The fields are overseen by the Court of the Manor, acting for the Lord of the Manor (now the Ministry of Agriculture). A foreman and jurors apportion strips of land to local farmers on a yearly basis and see that boundaries are respected and ditches cleared – a system of administration practised since medieval times and an almost unique survival of strip-farming.

LEAMINGTON SPA
Warwickshire   *10 SP36*
Situated on the River Leam, the town gained the prefix 'Royal' when Queen Victoria visited in 1838. Leamington's heyday was in Regency and early Victorian times; its character and most impressive buildings date from this period. John Ruskin was brought here as a young boy suffering from a tubercular complaint. Today over 50,000 people every year are treated for rheumatic complaints in the natural spring waters of the Pump Rooms.

Benedict Arnold, great-grandfather of General Benedict Arnold and three times Governor of Rhode Island, left Leamington for America in 1635 as a boy. There may be a connection between Chesterton Mill, and one at Newport, Rhode Island, referred to both in Arnold's will and in Longfellow's 'Skeleton in Armour'. Chesterton Mill, 3 miles south east of Leamington, was built in 1632 by Inigo Jones. Nathaniel Hawthorne lived here for a while, at 10 Landsdowne Circus, now Hawthorne House. Hawthorne described Leamington then as the 'prettiest, cheerfulest and cleanest of English towns'. Ambrose Bierce also stayed here.

The architect of Landsdowne Crescent was William Thomas, who went to Canada in 1843 and built a distinguished career there. His decorated neo-Gothic style features in many major Canadian buildings. A plaque to him is in the Crescent.

LECHLADE
Gloucestershire   *3 SU29*
Today only pleasure craft cluster round Lechlade's old wharves, but in the 17th century they were used by barges carrying stone for the building of St Paul's Cathedral. Halfpenny Bridge spans the Thames here, its name a reminder of the toll once payable. St John's Bridge stands ½ mile to the east, where the Leach meets the Thames and the borders of Gloucestershire, Wiltshire and Oxfordshire come together. Outside the town the Thames, flowing through a pleasant park, is referred to locally as the Isis, just as at Oxford. The poet Shelley stayed at a local inn and was inspired by the serenity of the riverside scene to write *Stanzas in a Summer Evening Churchyard*.

LEDBURY
Hereford & Worcester   *9 SO73*
Ledbury stands not far from the Malvern Hills, in rich pastureland intersected by slow-moving streams, a small and pleasant town in England's second most important hop-growing region after Kent. The 17th-century Market House (AM) is particularly striking, raised on pillars of oak and timbered in a herringbone pattern, whilst there is an excellent example of 16th-century building in the Feathers Hotel. The illusion of being transported back in time is strongest, however, in a nearby lane – narrow, cobbled, and overhung by the projecting upper storeys of ancient houses. At the end of the lane stands the impressive church of St Michael and All Angels, basically Norman, but containing memorials dating back to the Middle Ages. Eastnor Castle (OACT), 2 miles to the east is a 19th-century Baronial style house set in a deer park and containing fine furnishings, pictures and an extensive collection of weaponry and suits of armour.

John Masefield, the late Poet Laureate, was born here in 1878, He ran away to sea at an early age and travelled extensively in the United States. The Brownings and Wordsworth used to visit Ledbury.

LEEDS
Kent   *6 TQ85*
Leeds Castle (OACT) was named after Led, chief minister of a 9th-century King of Kent, Ethelbert IV. It stands on two islands in a lake formed by the River Len and was described by Lord Conway as 'the loveliest castle in the world' – though the 12th-century architects of the present structure were more concerned with its effectiveness as an impregnable stronghold. It became known as 'Lady's Castle' because of the number of Queens of England who occupied it: Eleanor and Margaret (the two wives of Edward I), Philippa of Hainhault (wife of Edward III), Catherine de Valois (Henry V's queen) and Katherine of Aragon all lived here at various times, and Elizabeth I was held prisoner here before she was crowned. King Henry VIII made it an official Royal Residence. In the 17th century the castle was owned by Lord Culpeper, Governor of Virginia 1680–3. His grandson, 6th Baron Fairfax, left Leeds in 1746 and emigrated to a 5 million acre estate in Virginia. Later he employed the young George Washington as a surveyor and became his lifelong friend. In 1908 a member of the Virginia branch of the family successfully claimed his title and became the first American to take a seat in the House of Lords. Leeds Castle is now a conference centre, open to the public at weekends in winter and most afternoons in summer.

LEEDS
W Yorkshire   *15 SE33*
Originally a wool town, Leeds has developed into a world centre for ready-made clothing; it is also involved in the manufacture of a large

The Ivanhoe Clock in Leeds

variety of commodities ranging from footwear to ferro-concrete constructions. Despite progress, the old town is still evident. The Grammar School was founded in 1552 and both the Corn Exchange and Town Hall are 19th century. St John's Church has interesting 17th-century woodwork, while St Peter's preserves a restored pre-Conquest cross. 3 miles north west of the town stand the extensive remains of **Kirkstall Abbey** now a museum of folk studies. To the south east lies Temple Newsam (OACT), a splendid house which was the birthplace of Lord Darnley. Middleton Colliery Railway (OACT), dating from 1758 and the oldest in existence, is still in operation, manned by a group of enthusiasts. As a young man one of America's most famous preachers, the Reverend Robert Collyer, worked as a 'bell ringer' at the Washburn Valley mills, north of Leeds. These mills were demolished to make way for reservoirs. The Collyer's bell which now rings in Cornell University was presented by the preacher himself.

LEICESTER
Leicestershire   *10 SK 50*
Leicester's development from a small county town to the sprawling industrial city of today was prompted by the coming of the railway in the 19th century, for this provided easy access to the coalfields. The stocking frame was invented in Leicester, where hosiery and footwear are still strong trades. At the height of the Industrial Revolution in 1841, Thomas Cook's first organized expedition took place from here to **Loughborough**.

There was a settlement here in Roman times: the Jewry Wall is believed to date from AD 130, and excavations have also revealed a public bath and shops. Of the Norman castle only motte and great hall remain, the latter used as a law court. St Mary de Castro, the church of the castle, is also basically Norman, and St Martin's Cathedral has its origin in a 13th-century church. The richness of the city's history is reflected in its many museums: Newarke House Museum concentrates on the period from 1500 to the present day, while the Leicestershire Museum and Art Gallery includes exhibitions on ceramics, natural history and Egyptology, together with a notable collection of German Expressionist paintings and a collection of Americana, including letters written by John Paul Jones to George

Washington. The Museum of the Royal Leicestershire Regiment is housed in the 15th-century Magazine Gateway, and the Wygston's House Museum of English Costume in a building which is basically late medieval. Giant beam engines are displayed in the Leicester Museum of Technology, and the results of various digs in the Jewry Wall Museum. The medieval Guildhall (OACT) survives, as does the 18th-century mansion of Belgrave Hall (OACT). Leicester University founded the country's only School of English Local History.

Leicester was the birthplace of William Bradford, the printer of Pennsylvania's first newspaper. West of the city, the village of Markfield was the birthplace of Thomas Hooker, founder of Hartford, Connecticut. Peckleton is the ancestral home of the William Howard Taft family.

LEIGHTON HALL
Lancashire   *18 SD 47*
Standing in extensive grounds, Leighton Hall (OACT) is a fine stone mansion to which an attractive neo-Gothic facade was added in the early 19th century; sheltered by Warton Crag, it looks north towards the Lake District. In 1822 it was bought by Richard Gillow, a member of the famous furniture-making family, and a superb collection of their early work is on display. Many birds of prey are kept in the grounds, where they are flown, weather permitting.

LEITH
Lothian   *23 NT 27*
Leith, which has officially been part of Edinburgh since 1920, stands where the Water of Leith enters the Firth of Forth. It is a seaport with a busy modern dock and container quay; shipyards, sawmills and chemical works are the other major employers of labour in the area. The town was twice sacked by the English, in 1544 and 1547. When Mary Queen of Scots returned from France (where she had spent her childhood) in 1561, she landed here and stayed at the home of a local merchant – Lamb's House (NT), which still stands, used now as an old people's home. St Mary's Church is restored 15th century and Trinity House has an interesting collection of paintings. Charles I played golf on Leith links, now a park, in 1641. The shore was the old landing place and a stone on the quay commemorates the visit of George IV in 1822.

LELANT
Cornwall   *1 SW 53*
Lelant is a delightful village and golfing resort set on the estuary of the River Hayle; its church, Norman and Perpendicular, has an interesting 18th-century sundial. The greatest attraction to visitors, however, is Lelant Model Village (OACT), where scale models of many of the country's notable buildings are displayed in landscaped grounds. A museum illustrates Cornish crafts and history (with particular emphasis on shipwrecks, smugglers and tin-mining), and the work of local artists is on sale. The grounds also include water gardens, a junior assault course and children's playground and a model railway exhibition.

LEOMINSTER
Hereford & Worcester   *9 SO 45*
Leominster stands at the junction of the Rivers Pinsley and Lugg, in countryside chequered with cider-apple orchards and hop-fields. Today the famous Herefordshire cattle are exported all over the world from here, but the town's traditional involvement is with sheep, for 13th-century monks bred the sturdy Ryelands whose wool – the fine-textured 'Lemster Ore' – was in great demand until the 18th century. Ryelands were exported to Australia, New Zealand and South America. The grey stone, three-naved priory (founded, according to tradition, by Earl Leofric, husband of Lady Godiva, in the 11th century) has some fine windows and contains an old ducking stool once used for the punishment of nagging wives. Grange Court, a 17th-century brick and timber house, originally served as the Town Hall and stood at the central crossroads, but it was moved to its present site in 1855. Leominster's architecture spans many centuries – there are medieval buildings in the High Street, Tudor in Draper's Row, Jacobean in Pinsley Road and Georgian in Broad Street and Etnam Street. The Leominster and District Folk Museum has displays of smocks, corn dollies and many agricultural implements. Berrington Hall (NT), built by Henry Holland in 1778, lies 4 miles to the north east of the town. 1 mile west of Berrington Hall is Eye Manor, the country house of Ferdinando Gorges.

Richard Hakluyt, the geographer and adventurer of the South Virginia Company, was born into a Welsh family which had settled in Eaton, a suburb of Leominster, in the 13th century. Hakluyt was educated at Westminster School and Christ Church, Oxford. His maps were the first to bear the name 'Virginia' – this appeared in a work on English and French voyages to the American coast, commissioned by Sir Walter 'Rahly' (Raleigh). He was offered the living of the Jamestown settlement, Virginia, but never took this up. Hakluyt, to whom Britain owed many of its early American possessions, is buried in Westminster Abbey.

LEUCHARS
Fife *24 NO42*
The Norman church at Leuchars, built by the de Quincy family, is one of the finest in Scotland. The bell turret was added in the 17th century, but the original chancel and apse have survived and the building is elaborately carved, both inside and out; the Earlshall stones date from 1584 and 1635. On the edge of Tentsmuir, an area of great beauty encompassing forestry plantations and a nature reserve, stands the late 16th-century Earlshall Castle (OACT).

LEVENS
Cumbria *18 SD48*
Levens Hall (OACT) stands in 100 acres of parkland through which flows the River Kent; its topiary gardens are probably the best of their kind in the country and were designed in about 1700 by a Frenchman called Beaumont, who also remodelled the gardens of Hampton Court for James II. The house itself is a fine Elizabethan mansion incorporating part of a 14th-century pele tower (built to protect the border against the Scots). The richly carved panels and moulded ceilings were added by James Bellingham, who bought the house in 1580. The former brewhouse has a unique collection of steam-driven traction engines.

LEWES
E Sussex *5 TQ41*
The site of Lewes, on the River Ouse and in a hollow of the downs, was chosen by the Normans as the ideal place for a defensive stronghold, and a castle stood here until the 17th century, when much of the fabric was sold as building material. The only parts to survive were a stone keep (AM) and a gatehouse, now known as Barbican House and containing a museum of Sussex archaeology. Most of the old buildings in Lewes, including the market tower which holds the town bell, are 18th-century,

Lewes Castle

and many are attractively tile-hung. One house in Southover, however, dates from 1559; it was given to Anne of Cleves by Henry VIII and it now holds a museum of local history.

One of Lewes' most famous residents, Tom Paine, whose ideas and works, such as *The Age of Reason* and *The Rights of Man*, greatly influenced the revolution in the colonies, described the town as 'the cradle of American Independence'. Paine married the daughter of a local tobacconist and lived at Bull House from 1768 to 1774, when the marriage broke up and Paine left for America. The half-timbered Bull House is now a restaurant and bears a plaque to Paine. Also in the High Street, The White Hart Hotel was the meeting place of Paine and his political associates, known as the 'Headstrong Club'. Lewes has strong Protestant associations, and the torchlit Guy Fawkes procession each November is particularly impressive.

The history of the British army is traced in the Military Heritage Museum at Regency House. St Michael's Church has a curious round tower, and St Anne's and St John's are both partly Norman – the former having a Norman font and the latter a carved stone covering the grave of one of William the Conqueror's daughters.

The 17th-century diarist John Evelyn went to school in Lewes and spent periods of his life with his grandparents at Southore Grange, near

South Malling. South Malling church contains records of John Harvard's marriage in 1636 to Ann Sadler, the sister of a university friend, and daughter of the Reverend John Sadler, rector of the adjacent parish of Ringmer. The Lady Chapel of Ringmer church is a memorial to Reverend Sadler; there is also a monument to Sir William Springett, the father of William Penn's first wife, Gulielma.

Malcom Lowry (1909–57), author of *Under the Volcano*, is buried in the churchyard at Ripe, near Lewes. Between 1940 and 1954 he lived near Dollarton, Burrard Inlet, British Columbia. At Ripe in the last years of his life he lived at the White Cottage.

LILFORD PARK
Northamptonshire *11 TL08*
Herds of deer roam freely in the 240 acres of Lilford Park (OACT), once the home of the 4th Baron of Lilford, who first created its impressive aviaries and gardens. 17th-century Lilford Hall is opened to the public only for certain events, but the aviaries have been rebuilt and stocked with hundreds of birds – including the Lilford Crane and the Little Owl, the latter first established in Britain through birds released from here. The Park offers pleasant riverside walks and picnic spots, a children's farm with pony rides, craft and antique centres and a museum. It is the venue of the East of England Motor Show.

LICHFIELD
Staffordshire *10 SK10*

A rapidly modernizing city, dominated by the famous cathedral. It is the only English cathedral with 3 spires, known as 'The Ladies of the Vale'. The central spire was destroyed by Cromwellian troops and then rebuilt. Originally consecrated in AD 700 by St Chad, Bishop of Mercia, Lichfield Cathedral became a place of pilgrimage. The present building was largely completed between 1195 and 1325 with money donated by pilgrims. The Cathedral Library contains the St Chad's Gospels, one of the finest illuminated manuscripts in Europe.

Lichfield was the birthplace of Samuel Johnson. His house is now a Johnsonian Museum, and there is a statue of him in the cobbled square, while opposite is a monument to James Boswell, his biographer. David Garrick (1717–79), the famous Shakespearian actor, was taught at the old grammar school by Samuel Johnson. Another famous son of Lichfield was Elias Ashmole, the antiquarian who left his priceless collection to Oxford University. This now forms part of the Ashmolean Museum.

Major André, the British soldier

Samuel Johnson plaque

IIS PENANCE IN UTTOXETER MARKET

hanged as a spy by George Washington, has connections with Lichfield. It was here, in the house of the Reverend Thomas Seward, that he met his lifelong love, Miss Honora Sneyd. Although her parents would not consent to marriage between them, André remained devoted. In the museum are paintings of André and early editions of the Monody on his deathy by Anna Seward, a poet known as the 'Swan of Lichfield'.

The Staffordshire Regimental Museum at Whittington Barracks has, among its collections, relics of the American War of Independence. During World War II the Barracks were the headquarters of the 10th Replacement Depot of the American Army. The west window of the garrison church was given by them and an American flag always hangs here. At Wall, 2 miles south west, is *Letocetum* a Roman posting station on Watling Street. Its excavated bathhouse is the most complete example in Britain.

PLACES TO SEE
Cathedral of St Mary and St Chad The present building, begun in 1195, was completed in 1338, but the intricate carvings of the west front are mostly 19th-century work. Inside, the windows of the Lady Chapel, all except 2, are of 16th-century Flemish glass, and there is an exquisite sculpture by Sir Francis Chantrey of two sleeping children. In complete contrast is the bronze head of Bishop Woods by Epstein.

Vicar's Close Entered through an archway off the gracious 18th-century Close, the lodgings of the vicar's choir, who used to be attached to the cathedral, are delightful half-timbered houses.

Samuel Johnson Birthplace Museum The 8 rooms of this attractive 18th-century house built by his father, Michael Johnson, are devoted to relics of Samuel Johnson and his work.

St Chad's Church Memorials to Dr Johnson's step-daughter, Lucy Porter, and an old family servant, Catherine Chambers, can be seen in this restored medieval church, said to be built on the site of the monastery founded by St Chad, Lichfield's first bishop and the 'apostle of the Midlands' in 669.

Hanch Hall 3 miles north west of the city, the mansion (OACT) is a blend of Tudor and later architecture.

LINDISFARNE
Northumberland *24 NU14*

Lindisfarne, or Holy Island, is accessible from the mainland by a causeway which is covered at high tide. Missionaries from Iona who settled here in the 7th century, led by St Aidan, who founded the first monastery on the island, and later St Cuthbert, brought Christianity to Northumbria. The island was probably visited by Viking raiders in 793. The monks were driven out by the Danes in 875, but a Benedictine Priory was established in the 11th century, and its remains (OACT) incorporate a museum. A small, 16th-century castle (NT), restored by Sir Edwin Lutyens, stands on a rocky point. The island has been designated an area of outstanding natural beauty and part of it is a National Nature Reserve; the limestone cliffs and sand dunes of the north shore teem with birdlife, and seals are often seen offshore.

LINLITHGOW
Lothian *23 NS97*

The ancient Royal Palace of Linlithgow overlooks the town loch. The palace is probably Scotland's finest and dates from 1424 when James I built it on the site of another, destroyed by fire. James V and his daughter, Mary Queen of Scots, were born here. Their palace, too, was destroyed by a fire in 1746 started, probably inadvertently, by the Duke of Cumberland's troops. In the town is the church of St Michael, also rebuilt in 1424; it is one of the finest in Scotland. The original crown steeple of the tower was renewed for safety in the 1820s – a symbolic 20th-century crown of thorns replaces it. The oldest bell dates from 1490 and was tolled in 1513 after the Scots' defeat at Flodden. There are several late 16th-century houses in the High Street. The ruins of Blackness Castle (AM) are 4 miles north east; to the east is the House of Binns (NTS), a magnificent 17th-century house, with beautifully moulded plaster ceilings inside.

LINTON
Cambridgeshire *11 TL54*

Linton, an attractive village with timber-and-plaster houses and a half-timbered Guildhall, stands on the River Granta. The church, which dates back to the 13th century, has some interesting brasses and monuments. Linton Zoological Gardens stress the importance of conservation of threatened species, and snakes, insects

Lindisfarne

and spiders are on display as well as
the more usual animals and birds. The
zoo's 10 acres are laid out with
flowerbeds, shrubberies and exotic
trees, and its enclosures are
attractively landscaped – each being
made as similar as possible to the
natural environment of the native
country of its occupants.

LIPHOOK
Hampshire   *4 SU83*
Liphook's Royal Anchor Hotel is a
well-known 17th-century coaching inn
whose famous patrons have included
Queen Victoria and General Blüchner.
Bohunt Manor Gardens (OACT), the
property of the World Wildlife Fund,
offer woodland and lakeside walks,
fine roses and herbaceous borders and
a water garden; there is also a
collection of over a hundred
ornamental ducks, geese and crane. At
Hollycombe House Gardens (OACT)
a remarkable array of steam-driven
fair machinery and a 2ft gauge railway
are displayed against a woodland
setting, and there are occasional
demonstrations of ploughing,
threshing or steam-rolling. Nearby lie
the beauty spot known as Waggoners
Wells (a string of ponds first
constructed for the iron industry), and
40 acres of Bramshott Chase belonging
to the National Trust.

LIPPITT'S HILL
Essex   *5 TQ39*
Near to High Beach at Lippitt's Hill the
first American anti-aircraft gun was
installed to defend London. Chigwell
has further American associations,
William Penn went to school here
(his family lived in Walthamstow
5 miles further south west, into
London). Charles Dickens wrote part
of Barnaby Rudge at Chigwell. The
William Morris Gallery at Walthamstow
contains work of the artist and
craftsman, and of his American
furniture designer, George Jack.

LITTLE GADDESDEN
Hertfordshire   *5 SP91*
Little Gaddesden is a beautiful old
village set against a magnificent
backcloth of beechwoods and
bracken-covered commons. Its
Perpendicular church has several
interesting monuments. The manor
house is Elizabethan, and John
o'Gaddesden's House – timber-framed
with an overhanging upper floor and a
timber roof – was built in the 15th
century. Ashridge Management
College occupies Ashridge House
(OACT), a large neo-Gothic mansion
rebuilt by James Wyatt in 1808 on the
site of a 13th-century original. It stands
amid wooded parkland laid out by
Capability Brown and gardens
designed by Humphry Repton, the
National Trust owning the majority of
the estate.

LIVERPOOL
Merseyside   *14 SJ49*
The north bank of the famous River
Mersey was first settled in the 1st
century AD, and had grown into a
sizeable fishing village by 1207 when
King John granted a charter. It was
Liverpool's coastal location which
influenced its greatest development,
first as one point in the triangular slave
trade with Africa and the West Indies;
then with the American colonies and
the young Republic whose cotton
fuelled the textile industry of north-
west England. By the mid 19th century
and the introduction of steamships,
modern Liverpool had finally emerged,
serving as a principal port of trade and
emigration. Today the 7-mile dock is
one of the finest in the world, with the
famous Liver Building its crowning
glory, although trade has declined
leaving parts redundant. Liverpool's
connections with America are
profound, and a statue of Columbus in
the city's Sudley Park bears the
inscription 'The discoverer of America
was the maker of Liverpool'.

Richard Mather, the father of
Increase, Nathaniel and Samuel, early
graduates of Harvard, was a minister
at Toxteth chapel from 1618–35. (He
was born at Lowton, near Warrington,
Lancashire). During his time in
Liverpool, Mather was twice
suspended for Nonconformity. Finally
in 1635 he emigrated to Dorchester,
Massachusetts where he remained as
minister until his death in 1669.
Toxteth's Nonconformist chapel
contains a portrait of Mather and a
room kept in his memory. A relief on
the bronze doors depicts his journey to

America. Robert Morris, one of the
signers of the Declaration of
Independence, was from Liverpool.
James Gore King was a Liverpool
banker who acted as Assistant
Adjutant General in the war of 1812;
25 years later he secured a huge loan of
$5 million from the Bank of England
for the American banks.

The poet Arthur Hugh Clough was
born here in 1819. The son of a cotton
merchant in Liverpool, Clough was
brought up in Carolina but educated in
England. He lectured at Harvard and
his words were used by Winston
Churchill in his famous broadcast to
America in 1940 following the fall of
France. It was through Liverpool that
William Cobbett returned Tom Paine's
remains to his native country in 1819.

Nathaniel Hawthorne was US
consul here in 1853. Washington Irving
was involved with a business
partnership with his brother here in
1818; it is said that the failure of this
venture was the start of Irving's
literary career. Ralph Waldo Emerson
came to Liverpool in 1848. Dickens
also made frequent visits to the city.
Matthew Arnold died in Liverpool,
meeting his daughter as she returned
from America. Both Herman Melville
and John Masefield experienced
Liverpool as sailors.

Liverpool was the scene of massive
emigration, especially by the Irish
escaping the famine of the 1840s. The
old Cunard Building, now the
Customs House, recalls the Quaker
family who built up the shipping line,
operating first on the North American
coast, and then Transatlantic from the
United States and Canada to Britain.
In the County Museum there are
exhibits dealing with these routes and
materials dealing with the King's
Regiments' exploits in Canada.

Liverpool's strategic importance as
the port of a major industrial region
led to severe destruction during World
War II. Along with industrial decline,
this has left modern Liverpool with
many problems. However, the city is
renowned for its character and
resourcefulness. The 1960s produced
The Beatles and the sound of
Merseybeat.

There are also two cathedrals, both
built this century – the Anglican,
Gothic-style church begun in 1904 by
Sir Giles Gilbert Scott, and the striking
Roman Catholic Metropolitan
cathedral, consecrated in 1967. A
contemporary design by Sir Frederick
Gibberd, it is capped with a stained
glass lantern tower. In the cemetery of

139

The Liver Building from Liverpool's dockland

the Anglican cathedral is the grave of Arthur Richardson VC, a Canadian mountie originally from Liverpool.

The Walker Art Gallery has an outstanding collection of European paintings and includes several American works. The Sudley Art Gallery concentrates on British paintings. Housed in restored 19th-century quays on the waterfront, is the Merseyside Maritime Museum.

The City Library is one of the country's largest, with over 2,000,000 reference books, and the largest American collection in a British public library. Liverpool Museum too has many splendid items relating to the trade with the colonies.

Liverpool University is of high repute and the Royal Philharmonic Orchestra is renowned. Britain's Grand National is held each spring at Aintree, and Liverpool is famous for its two football clubs – Everton, and Liverpool with their well-known 'kop'.

Two tunnels beneath the Mersey join Liverpool with **Birkenhead**, which has American links.

LIZARD
Cornwall   *1 SW71*
Lizard Point, the tip of the Lizard Peninsula, is the southernmost point in England. The name comes from the Cornish words 'lis' (place) and 'ard' (high). The famous veined serpentine rock is found only here. The scenery is dramatic, as towering walls of cliff and magnificent rock pinnacles stretch down to turbulent seas on a stretch of coast notorious for shipwrecks. There are sandy beaches to the east at Housel Bay, and **Kynance Cove** lies west of the Point. A few miles inland, on Goonhilly Downs, stands the Post Office's satellite tracking station.

LINCOLN
Lincolnshire   *16 SK97*

When the Romans invaded Britain they found at Lincoln a Celtic hill-fort named *Lindon*, the 'fort by the pool'. They took over the name, changing it to the Latin form, *Lindum Colonia*, from which we get Lincoln. A relic of the Roman town can be seen in Bailgate, where the Roman north gate is partly preserved in Newport Arch; fragments of the east gate can be seen in the courtyard of the hotel of that name. The historic centre of this ancient city is remarkably untouched; narrow medieval streets such as the Strait, Steep Hill and Bailgate contain many interesting and historic buildings. Some are half-timbered, like the quaintly named Cardinal's Hat, which is thought to be named after Cardinal Wolsey who was Bishop of Lincoln for one year (1514–5); and some are of stone, like the two remarkable Norman houses of Aaron the Jew, probably England's oldest inhabited house. These buildings both date from the 12th century, when the Normans were encouraging Jews to settle in prosperous towns so that they could help to finance trade.

Lincoln Cathedral

Before it turned to engineering, Lincoln was an important centre of the cloth industry, and was particularly famous for a type of cloth devotees of the Robin Hood story will remember as Lincoln Green. Lincoln is dominated by its majestic three-towered cathedral, crowning the steep hill that rises so dramatically from the Lincolnshire plain. Complementing the cathedral in size if not in grandeur is the great limestone castle, built in 1080 to control this eastern corner of the kingdom.

Lincoln's hinterland is rich in Pilgrim connections. Thomas Pownall, a Governor of Massachusetts and South Carolina, was born in Minster Yard, and Francis Bernard, Pownall's successor as Governor of New Jersey and Massachusetts, was once a steward to the city of Lincoln and lived at College House on the Minster Green. The surrounding fenland was drained during the American War of Independence and many pieces of land were given American names such as New York, Maryland and Bunker Hill.

PLACES TO SEE

Lincoln Cathedral The impressive west front, decorated with many statues, is all that remains of the first cathedral the Normans built. Most of the rest of this majestic building dates from the 13th century when St Hugh of Avalon was bishop. St Hugh's Choir, with its lovely choir stalls, and the Angel Choir, so-called from the 28 carved angels supporting the roof, are particularly fine. Among the carvings in the Angel Choir is the figure of the legendary Lincoln Imp, turned to stone for his misdeeds. Ancient stained glass has survived in some windows, particularly the two rose windows of the transepts, known as the Dean's Eye and the Bishop's Eye. Among the cathedral treasures is one of the four extant original copies of Magna Carta. The Seamen's Chapel has memorial windows to Lincolnshire people who helped shape the early history of America. Captain John Smith of the Virginia Colony is depicted, along with the Pilgrim Fathers of the *Arbella*.

Lincoln Castle Although alterations have been made over the years, the basic plan of this great walled fortress with its 2 massive towers is unchanged. In Cobb Hall prisoners were kept chained to iron rings, and until 1859 the town gallows stood on its roof. The prison chapel has narrow enclosed cubicles, partitioned so as to allow prisoners to see only the preacher and not each other.

Greyfriars City and County Museum Housed in part of an old Franciscan friary, the museum contains archaeological finds, arms and armour, items relating to Sir John Franklin, the explorer of the American north west, and early American paintings.

Usher Gallery Founded in 1927, the gallery contains many paintings by Peter de Wint, who drew his inspiration mostly from the Lincolnshire countryside, and a room devoted to Alfred, Lord Tennyson.

The Museum of Lincolnshire Life Exhibits range from Elizabethan to modern times.

Museum of the 10th Foot Royal Lincolnshire Regiment Housed in Sobraon Barracks, exhibits cover regimental history from the 18th century on. The regiment fought in America; the first British soldiers to fall at Concord Bridge were from the Lincoln Regiment.

LLANBERIS
Gwynedd *13 SH56*
This little town is the starting point for the easiest walk to Snowdon's summit and also the terminus of the Snowdon Mountain Railway (OACT) – established in 1896 to carry tourists to the top of the mountain, and the only rack and pinion steam railway in Britain. Llanberis Lake Railway (OACT), by contrast, uses the old line from Dinorwic Quarries to Port Dinorwic, following the valley along Llyn Padarn. The huge Dinorwic slate quarries were once the world's greatest, but they were closed in 1969 because of the decline in demand for the material. The Welsh Slate Museum (OACT) contains much of the original machinery used in the workshops, together with the 54ft waterwheel that provided the power to operate it. Llanberis was the birthplace of Thomas Jefferson's mother. Jefferson himself was brought up to speak his mother's native tongue. Just outside the town are the ruins of Dolbadarn Castle (AM), a native Welsh fortress with a three-storeyed, 13th-century round tower, overlook the valley.

LLANDAFF
S Glamorgan *8 ST17*
The little city of Llandaff officially became part of Cardiff in 1922, but it still retains a sense of identity, clustered closely round its ancient cathedral. The present building, begun in the 12th century, stands on the site of a church founded by St Teilo in the 6th; it has survived several periods of ill-treatment and neglect – and even a German landmine. The interior is dominated by Epstein's soaring aluminium figure of Christ in Majesty. Many of the windows were decorated by the Pre-Raphaelites; Burne-Jones, Swinburne and William and Jane Morris were models in Llandaff's Rossetti Triptych. Outside, by contrast, is a 10th-century Celtic cross. Geoffrey of Monmouth, whose *Historia Regum Britanniae* was a major contribution to Arthurian legend, was archdeacon of Llandaff c1140. The first man to translate the Bible into Welsh, William Morgan, was consecrated here in 1595. The cathedral grounds contain the remains of a 13th-century bell tower, and a public garden lies inside the ruins of a former bishop's palace, sacked by Owain Glyndwr in 1402.

Francis Lewis, a signatory of the Declaration of Independence, was born in Llandaff in 1713.

LLANDDEWI BREFI
Dyfed *8 SN65*
The village, its huddle of colour-washed cottages a reassuring sight against the wild beauty of the hills that surround it on three sides, is set well off the main road in the Teifi valley. The mound on which the 13th-century church stands is said to have risen miraculously beneath the feet of St David as he spoke against the Heresy of Pelagius in the 6th century. A modern sculpture by Mancini shows the saint as a barefooted traveller with a stout staff and the dove of peace on his shoulder; St David's Staff is one of five carved Celtic stone crosses which survive. The 'dewi' of the village's name is the Welsh form of 'David' and 'Brefi' refers to a little stream which flows through it to join the Teifi.

LLANDOVERY
Dyfed *8 SN73*
Llandovery, its name meaning 'the church amidst the waters', stands where the Rivers Bran and Gwydderig run into the Tywi. The church is St Mary's on the Hill, with fine tie-beam roof and barrel-vaulted chancel; it is built within the walls of the Roman fort that once stood here, and its fabric includes some Roman tiles. The town is the traditional market centre of the upper Tywi valley, and the Victorian and Georgian houses in the streets round the cobbled square are interspersed with a surprising number of old inns, for at one time Llandovery was the only town in the area permitted to keep taverns. George Borrow stayed in Llandovery on his travels.

Three miles east of Llandovery, Pentre ty gwyn was the birthplace in 1717 of William Williams, or *Pantycelyn*, the writer and prominent leader of the Welsh Methodist movement. Williams wrote many hymns and poems in Welsh. He is buried at Llanfair ar y Bryn just outside Llandovery, where there is also a memorial chapel to him. South west at Llangadog *Hwyrnos*, traditional Welsh evenings of song, folktales and food, are created at the country mansion, Plas Glanserin.

LLANDRINDOD WELLS
Powys *8 SO06*
The waters of Llandrindod Wells first became famous in the reign of Charles II, and by the 1850s it was the largest and most popular of the Welsh spas, with some 80,000 visitors a year. The original hamlet quickly expanded to provide all the attractions of a

fashionable watering place; parks and gardens were laid out, surrounded by wide streets lined with extravagant hotels, ballrooms, eating-houses and gaming rooms. Today the town, its broad streets and 19th-century architecture substantially unchanged, is the administrative capital of the newly formed county of Powys and is developing as a conference centre; it is also popular as an inland resort, offering an excellent base for touring as well as facilities for golf, bowls, angling and boating. Visitors can glimpse the glories of Llandrindod's fashionable era in the Victorian Spa Gallery of the War Memorial Gardens Museum, which also contains the Paterson Doll Collection and an exhibition of finds from *Castell Collen*, a Roman camp to the north.

LLANDUDNO
Gwynedd   13 SH78
The resort of Llandudno, the largest in Wales, lies on a crescent of sandy bay dominated by the huge limestone headland of Great Orme. There are panoramic views from the 678ft-high clifftop, which can be reached by Edwardian tramway, funicular railway or modern cabin-lift, and a 5-mile Marine Drive has been cut into the side of the cliff. St Tudno's Church, on the north slope of the Orme, dates back to the 12th century (though St Tudno's mission here probably began some 600 years earlier); the font is medieval, and the roof above the altar bears the stigmata – the marks of Christ's wounds. On the lower slopes, overlooking town and bay, are the Happy Valley Rock Gardens and the terraced Haufe Gardens. Llandudno has two museums: the Rapallo House Museum and Art Gallery displays a traditional Welsh kitchen, weaponry and Roman relics, as well as collections of porcelain, sculpture and pictures; the Dolls Museum has over a thousand dolls, representing various eras of fashion, and the same building houses a large model railway. A stone on the promenade depicts the White Rabbit consulting his watch – for Lewis Carroll was here, staying with the Liddells and their daughter Alice, when he decided to write his book.

LLANFIHANGEL CRUCORNEY
Gwent   8 SO32
Set beside the River Monnow, this village has old stone houses and an ancient inn. The church porch contains a carved stone commemorating an 18th-century

blacksmith. Llanfihangel Court (OACT) is a Tudor house standing in attractive gardens; it has a fine yew staircase and a number of interesting portraits and furnishings.

LLANGOLLEN
Clwyd   14 SJ24
Llangollen, a small town on the River Dee, was once a slate-quarrying centre, but the beautiful vale has been scarcely touched by industrial development and is famous as the setting of the International Music Eisteddfod, held here each summer since 1947, when music of every kind is performed. **Valle Crucis Abbey** (AM) was founded in 1201 by Madog ap Gruffydd, Prince of Powys, and most of the remains date from that period. The 14th-century stone bridge that spans the river is acclaimed as one of the Seven Wonders of Wales. Llangollen attracted considerable attention in the 18th century, when two aristocratic Irishwomen, Lady Eleanor Butler and the Honourable Sarah Ponsonby, set up a curious but lively home at Plas Newydd, Llangollen. Among the many society guests of the 'Ladies of Llangollen' were Wordsworth, Sir Walter Scott, Robert Southey and the Duke of Wellington. Llangollen Station (OACT), in the town centre, is a restored Great Western station complete with locomotives and rolling stock; trains run to Fford Junction during the summer months. The Canal Exhibition Centre uses models, murals and films to tell the story of Britain's great canal era; it is possible to take a trip on a horse-drawn passenger boat.

LLANIDLOES
Powys   8 SN98
At the heart of the little town of Llanidloes is its unique Market House, a half-timbered building standing on pillars, the open space beneath once having been used for traders' stalls. The upper storey now houses a museum (OACT), but over the centuries it has been a meeting house for Quakers, a chapel for Wesleyan Baptists, a public library, a working men's institute and a court house.

LLANRWST
Gwynedd   13 SH86
Llanrwst is a pleasant old market town in the Conwy valley. Gwydyr Castle (OACT), a magnificently furnished Tudor palace, stands in beautiful grounds where peacocks and tropical birds are kept. Gwydyr Uchaf Chapel (AM), once the private chapel of the

castle but now used as an exhibition centre, has a rare Welsh painted roof dating from 1673.

LLANTHONY
Gwent   8 SO22
The ruins of 13th-century Llanthony Priory (AM) stand in the beautiful unspoiled valley of the River Honddu, with the Black Mountains on the west and 1748ft Hatteral Hill rising to the east. This is border country (the English boundary a mile away also defining the limit of the **Brecon Beacons** National Park and following the path of **Offa's Dyke**), and the Priory was founded by a Marcher Lord of Hereford, Hugh de Lacy. The original 12th-century community numbered 40, but the remoteness of the spot made for a primitive existence which many monks shunned, and by the time of the Dissolution only 5 remained. What was the Prior's house is now an hotel, and a church contemporary with the priory still stands, retaining some Norman features, though restored.

LLANTRISANT
Mid Glamorgan   8 ST08
The remains of an Iron Age fort to the east of Llantrisant indicate that the potential of this site – an easily defended ridge overlooking the Ely valley and the Vale of Glamorgan – was recognized many centuries ago. There were native Welsh rulers here long before they were ousted by the Normans whose ruined castle keep can be seen today, overlooking an attractive little town with steep streets running down the hillside. The church, though much restored in the 19th century, is Norman; it has a 13th-century font, and an ancient slab of stone bearing three crosses is set into the outside of the north wall. The coming of the Royal Mint in 1967 led to the development of a virtually separate new town to the south of the old. The legality of cremation was established in a trial involving an inhabitant of Llantrisant: Dr William Price, a famous 19th-century eccentric who tried to live according to what he imagined would have been the teaching of the Druids, defended successfully his right to burn the body of his dead child, instead of having it buried as was customary at the time. When he himself died 10 years later, he too was cremated. A plaque commemorates this extraordinary figure.

LLANYSTUMDWY
Gwynedd *13 SH43*

Llanystumdwy is the burial place of David Lloyd George, one of Britain's most remarkable statesmen and a social reformer who took the first steps towards the Welfare State. He was brought at the age of 1 to live with his uncle, the village cobbler, after his father died. The cottage where he was brought up (OACT) stands, marked by a plaque, on the Criccieth to Pwllheli road. In later life he returned to live at Ty Newydd, a Jacobean mansion near the village, and it was his wish that he should be buried on a wooded bank above the River Dwyfor, his monument a boulder carved only with the initials DLG and the dates of his life. The Lloyd George museum includes a copy of the Treaty of Versailles.

LOCH ARKAIG
Highland *26 NN09*

Bonnie Prince Charlie's treasure is said to have been buried by the Jacobites here. The surrounding countryside is the traditional home of the Clan Cameron, strong supporters of Charles Edward. Achnacarry House at the head of the Loch replaces the original castle burned in 1746, as a punishment of the chief's support of the '45 Rising. Among the tree-lined avenues on the estate is the Dark Mile, planted for the Prince, who wandered the rugged hill country after the Rising.

LOCH AWE
Strathclyde *21 NN01*

Loch Awe is long and narrow, 22 miles long and only about a mile wide in most places. A ruined castle stands at each end – Fincharn in the south and Kilchurn to the north – and there is another on the island of Fraoch Eilean, whilst the Isle of Inishail has an ancient chapel and burial ground. To the north towers 3689ft Ben Cruachan, where the world's second-largest hydro-electric power station pumps water from the loch to a reservoir 1315ft up the mountain.

LOCH FYNE
Strathclyde *21 NR99*

Loch Fyne, one of the longest sea lochs in Scotland, stretches 40 miles from the Sound of Bute. It is famed for the spectacular scenery at its mountainous head, and – more mundanely – for its herring catch, a large proportion of which is smoked to make kippers.

LOCHGILPHEAD
Strathclyde *21 NR88*

Four miles north west of Lochgilphead, a town at the head of Lock Gilp, an inlet of **Loch Fyne**, is Dunadd Fort (AM). This ancient hill-fort was the site of the ancient kingdom of Dalriada (c500–800), out of which came the Celtic kingdom of Scotland. The highest rock on the site is carved with the figure of a bow and the sign of a footprint – this is thought to be where the early Scottish kings were invested.

LOCH KATRINE
Central *22 NN40*

Loch Katrine, which inspired Scott's *The Lady of the Lake*, is considered one of the loveliest in Scotland. Lying beneath the Achray Forest, the loch is not accessible by car. However, walks or a steamer trip give some idea of the rugged beauty of the surrounding **Trossachs**. Ellen's Isle is named after Ellen Douglas, the original 'Lady of the Lake'. This is MacGregor country, and until the 18th century they used the island to hide cattle stolen in raids on the lowlands. Glengyle, on the north shore, was the birthplace of the famous MacGregor brigand, Rob Roy.

LOCH LEVEN
Tayside *24 NO10*

Well known for its salmon trout, Loch Leven is the site of international trout angling competitions each year; in winter it is also a centre for the sport of curling. The ruins of 15th-century Loch Leven Castle (AM) from which Mary Queen of Scots escaped in 1568 with the help of a gaoler, stand on an island which can be visited by boat in the summer months. 17th-century Kinross House built by Sir William Bruce, the architect of the Palace of Holyroodhouse in **Edinburgh**, is set in beautiful grounds (gardens OACT) on the west shore between the town of Kinross and the waterside. The Tolbooth at Kinross has fine decoration by Robert Adam.

LOCH LOCHY
Highland *26 NN29*

Loch Lochy is the second largest of the chain of inland lakes that runs along the Great Glen, forming part of the Caledonian Canal. The hilly shores, wooded in many places, reach their greatest height in Glengarry Forest to the north east. The Laggan Locks, at the north end, allow vessels using the Canal to be raised from the level of Loch Lochy to that of its highest

section, Loch Oich. The Letterfinlay Inn on the eastern shore of Loch Lochy was used as a hostel by General Wade's soldiers while they built the Inverness to Fort William road in the 18th century. Later Wordsworth and his sisters were visitors.

LOCH LOMOND
Strathclyde & Central *22 NS39*

A prisoner of Prince Charles Edward is said to have composed the song 'Loch Lomond' on the eve of his execution in Carlisle, the 'low road' being the path that his spirit would take back to its native land when released by death. Loch Lomond, the 'Queen of Scottish Lakes' and the largest in Great Britain, runs from Ardlui in the north to Balloch in the south – a distance of some 23 miles – and varies in width between 5 miles and ¾ of a mile. There are 30 islands in its length, the most significant being Inchmurrin (with the ruins of Lennox Castle) and Inchcailloch (where the remains of a former nunnery lie near the burial ground of the MacGregor clan). There is good fishing for trout, pike and powan (a white freshwater herring). A National Nature Reserve covers the south-west corner of the loch and five of its islands.

LOCHMABEN
Dumfries & Galloway *18 NY08*

The small Annandale town of Lochmaben has Castle Loch to the south east, Kirk and Mill Lochs to the south west and north west. The vendace, a rare fish with a heart-shaped mark on its head, is found in Castle and Mill Lochs. Castle Loch is also a nature reserve, and at its south end stand the ruins of Lochmaben Castle. Robert the Bruce may have been born here on what is now the site of Lochmaben Castle. The castle was built in the 14th century. Mary Queen of Scots visited in 1565.

Three miles south west, Skipmyre was the birthplace in 1858 of William Paterson, a founder of the Bank of England, who tried unsuccessfully to establish a settlement on the Isthmus of Panama.

Rammerscales (OACT) is a house with many Jacobite relics; it has associations with Flora Macdonald.

LOCH MAREE
Highland *29 NG97*

Loch Maree is probably Scotland's most beautiful inland loch, its south-east shore dominated by the huge mass of Slioch and the south-west lying within the Ben Eighe National Nature Reserve. Tiny Isle Maree still bears oaks – the sacred trees of the Druids who once worshipped here; there are traces of a very early chapel, superseded by the 7th-century hermitage of St Maelrubha. All the islets on the loch are controlled by the Nature Conservancy authorities, from whom permission must be obtained before landing, for the area affords a valuable refuge for threatened wildlife.

LOCH NESS
Highland *26 NH52*

Loch Ness is the largest of the Great Glen lochs (see Loch Lochy). Its waters, dark with peaty soil washed down by the rivers and streams that feed it, are over 900ft deep in places and have never been known to freeze. The view to the west is particularly beautiful, with the ruins of Urquhart Castle (AM) guarding the entrance to Glen Urquhart. The loch's legendary monster is world famous, and tales of sightings go back to the 7th century. Many modern sightings seem well authenticated, and it is now being suggested that unknown fish, giant slug-like creatures, or even fish-eating dinosaurs could exist in the depths. Similar claims have been made for other lochs, and for deepwater lakes in Ireland, Norway and Canada.

LOCH SHIEL
Highland *25 NM87*

Loch Shiel is one of the finest freshwater lochs in the Highlands, with wonderful mountain scenery at its north end and 2895ft Bheinn Odhar Bheag rising from its west shore. No more than a mile wide at any point, it stretches from Acharacle to **Glenfinnan Monument** (NTS), the tribute raised to the Highlanders who died for Bonnie Prince Charlie in the '45 Rising. The loch is touched by public roads only at its head and its foot; none runs along its shores.

LOCKERBIE
Dumfries & Galloway *18 NY18*

The market town of Lockerbie is famous for its August Lamb Fair, which has taken place ever since the 17th century. In 1593 one of the last of the Border family feuds ended here, when the Johnstones slaughtered 700 Maxwells and chopped off the ears of many of their victims – a method of mutilation subsequently known as the 'Lockerbie Nick'. South east is **Ecclefechan**, birthplace of Thomas Carlyle.

LONG CRENDON
Buckinghamshire *39 SP60*

Long Crendon is an attractive village with straggling thatched cottages, set where a four-arched bridge spans the River Thames. Needle-making was introduced here in the 16th century and continued until the work was taken over by factories in the 1830s. Long Crendon Manor, part stone and part timber-framed, dates from the 13th century and has a courtyard guarded by a stone gatehouse. The Court House (NT) is a late 14th-century building which was probably first used as a wool staple hall or store, but manorial courts were held here in the 15th century by the stewards of Catherine, wife of Henry V, who owned the manor at that time. The tall-towered grey stone church was begun in the 13th century.

LONGLEAT
Wiltshire *3 ST84*

Longleat House (OACT), one of the most visited stately homes in the country, was built in 1568 for Sir John Thynne, an ancestor of the Marquess of Bath, who owns it today. The 1st Marquess of Bath, Thomas Thynne (1734–96), resigned from Lord North's Government in 1779 in opposition to its policies on America and Ireland.

As a result of 19th-century renovations, the house has exquisite Venetian ceilings and Italian decor, and it contains fine paintings, tapestries and leatherwork. The family's state robes are on show, together with their state coach and a waistcoat said to have been worn by King Charles I at his execution. There are fully equipped Victorian kitchens. A shop sells culinary goods and gifts. The grounds were landscaped by Capability Brown.

The great attraction at Longleat now, however, is the Safari Park, famous for its lions but also including elephants, tigers, buffaloes and antelope. It is open in summer and visitors can also take a Safari Boat, cruising through groups of sea lions and hippos and passing the ape islands. Additional attractions for children are Leisureland (an exciting adventure playground), donkey and camel rides, and Pets' Corner with its chimps' tea-party.

The village of Horningsham 1 mile south has one of Britain's oldest Non-conformist chapels. The thatched church was built in 1568 by Scottish workers from the Longleat estate.

LONG MELFORD
Suffolk *12 TL84*

Long Melford, with its attractive main street, almost 2 miles long, of fine old shops and houses, is one of the most impressive villages in Suffolk. At the upper end of its triangular green stands Melford Hall (NT), a turreted, red brick Tudor house containing collections of fine paintings, furniture and porcelain. It was built in the 16th century by Sir William Cordell, Speaker of the House of Commons and Master of the Rolls during the reign of Queen Elizabeth I. He died in 1580 and is commemorated by a fine monument in the church. Kentwell Hall (OACT) lies to the north of the village, surrounded by a moat and beautiful gardens and approached by a 300-year-old avenue of lime trees. Holy Trinity Church is a huge 15th-century building occupying the site of a Roman temple; its exterior is decorated with flushwork and the interior has notable stained glass and beautiful worked pillars. The Lady Chapel still has a child's multiplication table on the wall, dating from its days as a schoolroom, between 1669 and 1880. The poet Edmund Blunden ended his days at Hallmill in 1974. He is buried in the churchyard. The Bull Inn is also 15th century.

LOOE
Cornwall *1 SX25*

Although a 15th-century bridge had spanned the river here, East and West Looe were separate entities until the building of the Victorian bridge in 1883. After this date the two towns merged, still much involved in fishing but also developing as a holiday resort. Today Looe is England's foremost shark-fishing centre and the venue each autumn of the British Sea Angling Festival, but it is also an ideal place for a family holiday, offering fine surfing conditions and excellent bathing from large sandy beaches. West Looe is centred round its picturesque quay and the church of St Nicholas – built mainly from the timbers of wrecked ships, and containing in its tower a Scold's Cage for the incarceration of nagging wives. In East Looe stands the 16th-century Guildhall, its upper floor now housing a museum; the building was once used as a gaol, and the old stocks and pillory can be seen downstairs. Looe Aquarium displays examples of fish caught locally and includes a shark museum, whilst at Murrayton there is a woolly monkey sanctuary.

LONDON

London History and London Landmarks

LONDON'S HISTORY begins in the middle of the 1st century AD when the invading troops of the Roman Emperor Claudius swept across south-east Britain to the Thames. The area was uninhabited marshland, and the Romans had to bridge the river to get to Colchester, then the most important town in the south east. In time, they built roads converging on the bridge, river traffic increased, and a settlement grew up which they named Londinium. Its position ensured its prosperity and by the 3rd century it had become the centre of Roman administration and a prosperous walled city with a fort, a large temple, a basilica and a governor's palace. Recent excavations have shown that the present London Bridge is sited only a few hundred yards from the Roman one. Until the 17th century, London Bridge, lined on both sides with shops and houses, was the only access to the city from the south, and until the 16th century London stayed more or less confined within the limits of the Roman walls. Southwark, on the south side of the bridge, was outside the jurisduction of the city authorities, and by medieval times had become a refuge for criminals and the quarter where playhouses such as the Globe, forbidden within the City, could flourish.

Until after the reign of Edward the Confessor, English kings were not crowned at London. However, Edward had completed the rebuilding of Westminster Abbey just before his death, and Harold, his successor, was crowned there, as was William the Conquerer, who made Westminster his capital, at the same time conferring on London the status and privileges of a city, but also building the Tower as a symbol of his authority. London thus became truly the capital of England – but for centuries there were two centres of authority – Westminster where the monarch had his palace and where eventually parliament met, and the City where the powerful merchants guilds were supreme. Gradually wealthy landowners built themselves residences along the Strand, which linked the two centres, and the legal profession set themselves up on the site of the Temple of the Knights of St John.

From the 17th century onwards, London grew at an amazing rate, spreading far beyond the Roman and medieval walls. Even the Great Fire of 1666, to which we owe the creation of St Paul's Cathedral and many other churches designed by Wren, did not halt expansion, and surrounding villages like Chelsea, Marylebone, Islington, Kensington, Hampstead and Highgate were gradually swallowed up. The Victorian era, especially after the building of the railways, saw a phenomenal growth in size and population as trade with the Empire boomed and by 1901 the population of the capital stood at 4½ million, more than four times the number there had been in 1801.

The devastation of World War II has resulted in massive new office blocks, and whole areas of houses have been demolished to make way for high-rise or high-density flats, which have, say many, brought more problems than they have solved. Other post-war developments, such as the Barbican and the South Bank Arts Centre, have been widely acclaimed. Despite the drift of people from the centre, where housing is scarce and expensive, to the suburbs, London continues to grow and efforts are being made to attract industry back to the centre.

Kensington is notable for its complex of museums (see 'A London Directory') and has a number of embassies. Princes Gate in Kensington Road was formerly the official residence of American ambassadors. The poet Ezra Pound once lived in Kensington Church Street. William Penn was a guest at Holland House in 1684. The Commonwealth Institute includes good Canadian displays and is one of the most attractive museums in London. The area around the world-famous store, Harrods, was once the residence of many Loyalist refugees escaping from the Revolutionary War in America. Thomas Hutchinson, Governor of Massachusetts, died here in 1781. The writer, William Dean Howells, lived in Pelham Crescent.

Leicester Square Devoted almost entirely to the cinema and other entertainments, the square was laid out in the 17th century on land belonging to the Earls of Leicester. Among Americans who once lived in the square were Benjamin West, and the artists J S Copley and John Trumbull. Nearby Gerrard Street was once the home of James Boswell and of Edmund Burke. The streets between the square and Shaftesbury Avenue form the nucleus of London's Chinatown. Sir Edmund Andros, founder of William and Mary College, is buried at St Anne's Church in Dean Street, Soho.

Pall Mall Pall Mall has many exclusive clubs, including the Athenaeum and the Reform. British Columbia House, Nova Scotia House, Ontario House, Quebec House and Saskatchewan House are all in this area. The Institute of Contemporary Arts, a centre of major importance to the visual arts in Britain, is in the Mall, which runs parallel to Pall Mall.

Trafalgar Square Famous for its flocks of pigeons and as a rallying point for demonstrations of all kinds, Trafalgar Square, on the site of the old Royal Mews, commemorates Lord Nelson's victory over the French in 1805. It was laid out between 1829 and 1841, but Landseer's lions, flanking Nelson's Column, were added in 1867 and the fountains, in 1948. Canada House on the west side of Trafalgar Square was built in the early 19th century as the Union Club, bought for Canada in 1921 and opened in 1925.

Whitehall The old palace of Whitehall, burned down in 1698, was made the official residence of the sovereign by Henry VIII. The site is now occupied by government departments such as the Foreign Office, the old Admiralty buildings, the Ministry of Defence and Great Scotland Yard. Visits can be made by arrangement to the War Rooms where Sir Winston Churchill lived and worked during World War II. The Banqueting Hall, a Palladian masterpiece by Inigo Jones, was planned as the start of a new royal palace. The ceiling of the main hall was painted for Charles I by Rubens. In the centre of the road is the Cenotaph, designed by Sir Edwin Lutyens and unveiled in 1920. Memorial services are held here every year in November. Leading off Whitehall is Downing Street, home of the Prime Minister and the Chancellor of the Exchequer. Downing Street was named after Sir George Downing, Harvard's second graduate, who once owned the street.

Mayfair extends from Oxford Street in the north to Piccadilly in the south, and is bounded by Regent Street in the east and Park Lane in the west. It is a very fashionable area, dominated by major hotels and businesses. General John Burgoyne, Edwin Arlington Robinson, James Russell Lowell and Ralph Waldo Emerson all lived in Curzon Street, and Joseph Priestley, who discovered oxygen and emigrated to America in 1794, lived in Berkeley Square. Grosvenor Square is home to the American Embassy. The first United States Minister to Britain, John Adams, lived in this square. MacDonald House was the American Embasssy from 1938 to 1960 then it was bought by Canada and is used by the High Commission. 12 Upper Brook Street served as the

Canadian High Commissioner's residence from the late 1940s to the 1980s. Washington Irving, Winston Churchill and Somerset Maugham all lived in Mount Street. Alberta House is also in Mount Street.

Royal Albert Hall and Albert Memorial Much loved as the home of the Proms, the Royal Albert Hall, an immense, domed, circular structure opened in 1871, commemorates the Prince Consort, as does the elaborate Gothic memorial opposite, showing the Prince seated under a canopy and reading a catalogue of the Great Exhibition.

Marble Arch Made redundant as a gateway almost as soon as it was built, Nash's imposing archway had to be moved from Buckingham Palace because it was too narrow to admit Victoria's State Coach, and was re-erected as the entrance to Hyde Park. By 1908, however, the traffice was too much for it, and it was removed to its present site, islanded by traffic on all sides, at the west end of Oxford Street, on the spot where the notorious Tyburn gallows used to stand.

Portland Place Portland Place is a fine 18th-century street and site of the British Broadcasting Corporation. The American Embassy was at No 98 from 1863 to 1866. Here, and in Langham Place, many Americans have lived including Henry Brooks Adams, Longfellow and Mark Twain.

Piccadilly Circus The centre of London's West End and theatreland, Piccadilly Circus was once known as the hub of the Empire. Piccadilly is renowned for its exclusive shops. The area to the south is known as St James (**see** London's Shops; Piccadilly; and Gardens; and Palaces; St James' Palace).

The Royal Albert Hall

The church of St James's, Piccadilly, is a Wren church and contains work by Grinling Gibbons. Many famous people were buried here. The best known street in St James is Jermyn Street with shops for hand-made men's shirts and its famous speciality cheese shop. Benjamin Franklin lived in Craven St, while novelist Sinclair Lewis lived in Bury Street. The Fine Art Auctioneers, Christie's, are based in King Street. St James's Place was once the home of several literary figures, including

James Fenimore Cooper and Nathaniel Hawthorne. Opposite Fortnum and Mason, Piccadilly's most famous store, is the Regency Burlington Arcade and Burlington House, home of the Royal Academy of Arts, founded by George III in 1768. Sir Joshua Reynolds was the first President of the Academy and Benjamin West, the second. The Royal Academy moved to its present site in 1868; its regular exhibitions are among the most important in the country. On the north

Piccadilly Circus

side of Piccadilly are the more exclusive shopping streets such as Savile Row, famous for its tailors, and Cork Street with its art galleries, also the home of philanthropist George Peabody. Bond Street has many jewellers and couturiers as well as Sotheby's, the Fine Art Auctioneers. Lord Cornwallis and Charles Fox both lived in Grafton Street. Further west along the Piccadilly thoroughfare is the celebrated hotel, The Ritz, which opened in 1906. Brown's Hotel in Dover Street has entertained many Americans including Mark Twain, Theodore, Franklin and Eleanor Roosevelt.

Westminster Abbey Since the consecration of the abbey on 28 December 1065, the coronation of every English monarch has been held here, with the exception of the two uncrowned kings, Edward V and Edward VIII. It is also the burial place of all English monarchs from the time of Henry III (to whom we owe the rebuilding in Early English style of most of the abbey) to the reign of George III. Their tombs, particularly that of Edward the Confessor and that of Henry VII, housed in the beautiful, fan-vaulted chapel he had built in the early 16th century, are magnificent, but outnumbered by the thousand or so monuments to the great and famous. Poets' Corner is the best-known section, where many distinguished writers are remembered such as Shakespeare, Milton and Wordsworth. There is an Epstein bust of William Blake and tributes to the Americans, Longfellow and T S Eliot. Statesmen honoured include Disraeli and Gladstone, Churchill and Attlee. Many tombs and memorials commemorate eminent people connected with America such as the Wesleys, General Howe, Captain John Mason

(founder of New Hampshire), Richard Hakluyt (responsible for early maps of the American coast), General Burgoyne and Major John André. There is also a monument to Franklin D Roosevelt. Many of the tributes were given by Americans and the memorial to Britain's Unknown Warrior was granted a United States Congressional Medal of Honour. Of particular interest to Canadians are monuments to Wolfe, Sir Charles Saunders (who transported Wolfe's army to the Heights of Abraham), to the explorer Sir John Franklin, George Montagu, Earl of Halifax whose name was given to Halifax, Nova Scotia in 1749, and to Bonar Law, the only Candian-born British Prime Minister. Next to the abbey in Parliament Square is St Margaret's, Westminister, the parish church of the House of Commons. The headless body of Sir Walter Raleigh may have been buried here, although he may actually have been laid to rest in Beddington Park churchyard, Surrey. A plaque in St Margaret's commemorates the early American adventurer. A Raleigh memorial window donated by Americans, bears an inscription written by James Russell Lowell. Other windows commemorate people associated with colonial America and there is a memorial to James Rumsey, who invented the American steam boat and was buried here in 1792. Behind the abbey is Westminster School, whose alumni include Charles Wesley, Jeremy Bentham, Richard Hakluyt and Arthur Middleton, a signatory to the Declaration of Independence. Edmund Burke lived in Dean's Yard.

Bloomsbury Bloomsbury is the area around the British Museum, centred on

Bloomsbury Square. It gave its name, early this century, to the Bloomsbury Group, a number of writers and artists including E M Forster, Duncan Grant and Virginia Woolf. Gertrude Stein lived at 20 Bloomsbury Square. T S Eliot worked for many years at the publishers, Faber and Faber, then in Russell Square. Ralph Waldo Emerson stayed at 63 Southampton Row. The Poetry Bookshop, an important literary landmark from 1913 to 1926 was in Boswell Street. Robert Frost lived there. The Institute of United States Studies is in Tavistock Square. At the Thomas Coram Foundation for Children in Brunswick Square there are pictures by Benjamin West and John Singleton Copley. The Trades Union Congress, hub of British labour unions, is in Great Russell Street and has a memorial by Epstein. The administrative centre of the University of London is in Malet Street.

Fleet Street and the Strand Although many newspapers, including *The Times*, now have their offices elsewhere in London, Fleet Street is still synonymous with the power of the Press. The Daily Express Building will always be associated with the millionaire and newspaper magnate, Lord Beaverbrook, who was born in Maple, Ontario. Many of its pubs are the haunt of journalists and some, such as the Cheshire Cheese, have a long and distinguished history. The great Dr Johnson had his house in Gough Square, one of the many courts leading off the street. Fleet Street, which takes its name from the old Fleet River, runs from Ludgate to Temple Bar, the old boundary of the City with Westminster. The archway was removed in 1878, but a memorial plinth remains. St Bride's Church, designed by Wren, is known as the parish church of the Press, and its

spire is said to have been the inspiration for the traditional three-tier wedding cake. The parents of Pilgrim Edward Winslow, third Governor of Plymouth, Massachusetts, were married here and there is a bust of Virginia Dare, the first child to be born in America of English parents. The Strand is the continuation of Fleet Street towards Trafalgar Square. As the name suggests, this was the river bank until the building of the Embankment. Between the Strand and the river lie two of London's four Inns of Court, the Inner and Middle Temple, a peaceful enclave of mostly 17th-century courts, linked by steps and alleys. The Middle Temple has the closest links with America. John Dickinson who helped draft the Declaration of Independence and was later Governor of Pennsylvania was a member, and five others also signed the Declaration. The largest American legal library outside the States is here and much of the restoration of the Middle Temple hall after World War II was financed by the American Bar Association. William Penn was a member of Lincoln's Inn. The northern side of Lincoln's Inn Fields is called Canada Walk and recalls its association with the Royal Canadian Air Force during World War II. The Temple Round Church, one of only five in England, dates back to the time of the Knights Templar who originally occupied this site in the 12th century. Two other famous churches, both on islands in the Strand, are St Mary-le-Strand, designed by James Gibbs in 1714–19 and St Clement Danes of nursery rhyme fame and, since its rebuilding after World War II, the RAF church with plaques to American and Canadian airmen and books of remembrance. Three Canadian VCs are recorded: Billy Bishop, William Barker and Alan McLeod.

Old Bailey Properly called the Central Criminal Court, the Old Bailey, crowned by the traditional figure of Justice, takes its popular name from the street where it is sited, near St Paul's. It was built where the old Newgate Prison, scene of public executions until 1868, used to stand.

The Monument Despite the towering office blocks, the Monument is still one of the City's most visible landmarks. Erected in 1677, it commemorates the Great Fire of 1666. From the top there are splendid views of the City (202ft is the distance from its base to the place in Pudding Lane where the fire started).

The Monument offers a magnificent city panorama

The Bank of England This massive, windowless stone fortress stands rock-solid (whatever the state of the pound) in Threadneedle Street. Sir John Soane's original designs for the building can be seen in the Soane Museum (p156), but much of his structure was rebuilt by Sir Herbert Baker in the 1920s. Nearby are the Stock Exchange in Throgmorton Street, and Lloyds of London in Lime Street.

London owes its existence to the Thames and to the bridge the Romans built in the 1st century AD. Until less than a hundred years ago the river was busy with shipping of all kinds but nowadays even the distinctive flat-bottomed lighters have all but disappeared and the sailing barges are museum pieces. To travel down the Thames from Westminster Pier to Greenwich in one of the many pleasure launches is to voyage past a fascinating panorama. After the splendours of Westminster, the City and the Tower of London, the scene changes to the warehouses and docks of the Pool of London and Limehouse, ending in the open spaces of Greenwich, and the Royal Naval College.

Chelsea Cheyne Walk, Chelsea, and its immediate surroundings has more literary associations than any other street in London. Thomas Carlyle, George Eliot, Elizabeth Gaskell, Charles Swinburne, George Meredith, Henry James and T S Eliot all lived here at various times as well as the artists J M W Turner, Whistler and John Singer Sargent. Oscar Wilde lived in Tite Street, as did the American painter Edwin Austin Abbey.

Westminster Pier and Bridge Westminster Pier, just north of the bridge, is the embarkation point for many of the trips up and down the river. The bridge itself, built in the 19th century, seems to blend in with the Houses of Parliament.

The Houses of Parliament Kings from Edward the Confessor to Henry VIII lived here, but the Court had to move to St James in 1515, after a fire, and Henry VIII then built himself a new palace at Whitehall. Westminster Palace became the Houses of Parliament. In 1834 most of the old palace burnt down. Charles Barry designed the present Gothic building, and much of its intricate decoration was entrusted to Augustus Pugin. The buildings are 940ft long and include 1100 apartments and two miles of corridors. The clock tower at the north end, although smaller than the imposing Victoria Tower at the south end, is affectionately known the world over as Big Ben, although properly speaking this is the name of the 13½ ton bell that strikes the hours.

Westminster Hall, 240ft long, may well be the largest Norman hall in Europe. Its magnificent hammerbeam roof dates from the reign of Richard II. In the Houses of Parliament are a number of paintings including ones depicting the Pilgrim Fathers embarking for the New World, Henry VII granting a charter for exploration to the Cabots and a John Singleton Copley showing the death of William Pitt. The table of the House of Commons is made of Canadian oak.

County Hall A modern building with 750ft of river frontage; recently the administrative headquarters of the Greater London Council.

Lambeth Palace Lambeth Palace is the Archbishop of Canterbury's official residence. Just beside it, in Lambeth Road, is the church of St-Mary-at-Lambeth. Captain William Bligh of the *Bounty* is buried here. He served with Cook on his third voyage. The church is now a Museum of Garden History. The Tradescants,

famous 17th-century gardeners, are buried here. Their garden, incorporating specimens from North America, was in Lambeth.

Cleopatra's Needle This 69½ft-tall obelisk was given to this country in 1819 by the Viceroy of Egypt. It had been erected at Heliopolis in about 1500 BC – but it has no real connection with Cleopatra.

The South Bank Complex This complex includes the Royal Festival Hall, National Theare and National Film Theatre, the Purcell Room, the Hayward Gallery and the Queen Elizabeth Hall.

Southwark Cathedral, London Bridge, has a Harvard chapel. John Harvard was baptized in the cathedral in 1607 and went to Massachusetts in 1623. The chapel contains a window by the American artist John La Farge. From the cathedral there is a Pilgrim Trail leading to the Pilgrim Fathers' Memorial Church, opened in 1956.

Westminster

The Tower of London

The Barbican London's most ambitious scheme for making the City a place to live as well as to work, the Barbican is a massive, self-contained complex west of Moorgate. Flats and tower blocks look out onto a series of courtyards, gardens and a lake. At one end is the Museum of London (p156), at the other, an arts centre incorporating exhibition halls, a concert hall and a theatre, now the home of the Royal Shakespeare Company.

Other points of interest in the City include the church of St Mary Woolnoth, Lombard Street, which is mentioned by T S Eliot in *The Waste Land* and has strong associations with British Columbia. St Giles, Cripplegate was Martin Frobisher's parish church and contains a memorial. He led three expeditions in search of the North-West Passage and was buried here in 1594. Milton's grave is here. Henry Hudson and his crew received communion in the church of St Ethelburga-the-Virgin, Bishopsgate, before their 1607 voyage seeking the North-West Passage. He is commemorated in stained glass windows in the church. Just off Tower Hill is All-Hallows-by-the-Tower where William Penn was baptised in 1644. It was extensively damaged in World War II and restored with American and Canadian gifts. Outside the Royal Exchange is a statue of American philanthropist, George Peabody. Beaver House, Great Trinity Square, was formerly headquarters of the Hudson's Bay Company. It is no longer owned by the company and is not open to the public.

Bunhill Fields Bunhill Fields in City Road just north of the City of London contains the graves of William Blake, John Bunyan, Daniel Defoe, Susannah, mother of John and Charles Wesley, Nathaniel Mather, son of Richard Mather, and Edmund Quincy. John Wesley's house is opposite Bunhill Fields at 47 City Road. His grave is behind the chapel. George Fox is buried in the Quaker graveyard.

Waterloo Bridge By the 1920s John Rennie's 19th-century Waterloo Bridge was showing signs of structural weakness, and work began on this elegant replacement, designed by Sir Giles Gilbert Scott, in 1939.

Somerset House Elizabeth I lived in the palace that once stood on this site, and Oliver Cromwell lay in state here before his funeral. The present building dates from 1776 and a large part of it is occupied by the Registrar General's staff.

St Paul's Cathedral Sir Christopher Wren's magnificent Baroque cathedral replaced Old St Paul's, destroyed in the Great Fire of London in 1666. Seen from the river, it retains its majesty despite surrounding office blocks. The height to the top of its cross is 365ft, and the dome is 112ft in diameter, with three galleries – the famous Whispering Gallery, the Stone Gallery and the Golden Gallery, the two latter giving fine views over London and the Thames. In the crypt are the tombs of Lord Nelson and the Duke of Wellington. Benjamin West and Edwin Austin Abbey are buried in St Paul's and among other memorials of North American interest are busts of George Washington and Sir John A MacDonald, Canada's first Prime Minister, as well as a memorial to Lord Thomson of Fleet, Canadian newspaper proprietor.

London Bridge The medieval London Bridge was a remarkable structure, its 950ft length supported on 19 piers and bearing shops, houses and a chapel. The buildings were demolished in 1760 because of the danger of fire, and in 1832 the bridge itself was replaced by a five-arched granite bridge designed by John Rennie. This was dismantled stone by stone and reassembled in the USA when the new bridge was built in 1968.

HMS Belfast Almost opposite the Custom House is moored HMS *Belfast*, a World War II cruiser – one of the largest and most powerful ever built for the Royal Navy – now a museum.

The Tower of London The Tower, easternmost point of the City of London, has served as fortress and prison and now houses the beautiful Crown Jewels and a fine collection of weapons and armour. The White Tower was the original building begun by William the Conqueror in the 11th century and additions have been made ever since. The Bloody Tower is the best known and over the centuries many important figures were held here. The most notorious incident in its history was the mysterious death of the young Edward V and his brother during the reign of Richard III. Sir Walter Raleigh was imprisoned in the Tower three times. It was here he wrote his *History of the World* – first edition can be seen in a reconstruction of his room. William Penn was another prisoner, and wrote *No Cross, No Crown* here. Sir Isaac Pennington and Sir Henry Vane, a Puritan and Governor of Massachusetts, were also prisoners. Henry Laurens, a South Carolina merchant, was the only born American to be held in the Tower. He was captured at sea in 1780 and imprisoned here for eighteen months before he was freed in exchange for Cornwallis. Prisoners were held here for treason and many were executed on Tower Green or on Tower Hill. Anne Boleyn, Lady Jane Grey, the Earl of Essex, The Duke of Monmouth and Sir Henry Vane were all executed here. In World War I Sir Roger Casement, the Irish patriot, was imprisoned here before his execution. Traitor's Gate which leads to the river is also a reminder of the prison's status.

Tower Bridge This, the most spectacular of London's bridges, was designed in the late 19th century by Sir John Wolfe-Barry. The roadway between the Gothic towers is carried on twin bascules which are raised to allow ships to enter the Pool of London; the original machinery is still in working order, though the steam engines have been replaced by electric motors for reasons of economy. A pedestrian high-level walkway has now been opened between the towers, and the original machinery can be inspected.

St Katharine's Dock The buildings have now been adapted to a variety of uses and the docks themselves converted to marinas. The Maritime Trust's History Ship Collection illustrates the evolution from sail to steam and also includes the RRS *Discovery*, Captain Scott's Vessel.

Execution Dock Pirates and sailors found guilty of serious crime on the high seas were hanged in chains here until three tides had washed over them. Nearby is the famous Prospect of Whitby public house.

The Grapes This picturesque old limestone pub stands near Regent's Canal Dock. Regent's Canal and the Grand Union Canal enabled goods to be shipped by barge from the Midlands to the Thames.

The Isle of Dogs Charles II had his royal kennels here and this gave the island its name. Brunel's steamship *Great Eastern* was launched from a site near Millwall Docks.

Greenwich The river gives the best view of Wren's superb Royal Naval College (p156 originally a naval hospital). Behind this and behind the Queen's House (now part of the National Maritime Museum, p155) rise the landscaped acres of Greenwich Park and at the top of the rise stands the Old Royal Observatory (p156). Moored near the pier are two historic ships, *Cutty Sark* and *Gypsy Moth IV* (p155). There is a statue of General James Wolfe next to the Greenwich Observatory. His family lived in Macartney House, East Street, and he is buried in the family vault at St Alfege Church.

Royal Military Academy at Woolwich Many graduates of the Royal Military Academy at Woolwich played a part in the history of North America, including John By, who built the Ridean Canal and the Duke of Connaught, Governor General of Canada 1911–16. Although the Academy is now merged with Sandhurst Military Academy, the building of 1805 is still intact and contains a museum.

Parks and Palaces

London is well blessed with open spaces; they range from the compact green squares of residential districts to great open spaces like Hampstead Heath. Best known, however, are the royal parks, tracts of land still owned by the Crown though the public is privileged to use them. London is also rich in royal palaces, as some past monarchs, such as Henry VIII, were keen builders. Today 'the Palace' denotes Buckingham Palace – but this has only been so for a comparatively short time, Queen Victoria being the first monarch to make her home there. The English Court remains 'the Court of St James', and it is to this that foreign ambassadors are still appointed.

Green Park Charles II purchased this extension to St James's Park, from which it is divided only by The Mall, in 1667. He was fond of walking, and Constitution Hill, which runs alongside, is thought to have been the route of his favourite 'constitutional'. Green Park differs from the other royal parks in having no flowerbeds and no water.

Greenwich Park Greenwich Park was enclosed in 1433 to form a setting for Bella Court Palace, built there a few years earlier by the Duke of Gloucester. In Tudor times it was popular as a hunting chase, and it was not until the reign of Charles II (who had a palace there) that the present, semi-formal layout was achieved. Wide expanses of lawn, broken by avenues of trees and an ornamental pond, sweep up towards Blackheath from the Maritime Museum and the Queen's House on the riverside. Fallow deer roam in a 13-acre tract of bracken and wild flowers known as The Wilderness, and there are three bird sanctuaries. The Old Royal Observatory (now a museum) stands in the park, as does a stone bearing a strip of brass marking the Meridian – zero degrees Longitude – to which measurements made all round the world are referred.

Regent's Park Marylebone Park was renamed after the Prince Regent, later to become George IV, who was responsible for the elegant Nash residences built round its fringe; these were part of a huge neo-Classical development that would have covered the park itself had it been completed. Fortunately this was not feasible, and Nash laid out the area more or less as we know it today, with Inner and Outer Circles, artificial lake and Regent's Canal. Today there is boating on the lake, and pleasure cruises on the canal pass through London Zoo at the north end of the park. The Inner Circle encloses the rose beds of Queen Mary's Garden, together with the Open Air Theatre where performances of Shakespearian plays are given during the summer months.

Richmond Park This, the largest of the royal parks, was originally an area of wild countryside enclosed by Charles I and used for hunting by his successors; King Henry VIII's Mound was constructed as a vantage point from which the monarch might survey the killing of his deer. The park is still fairly wild, the deer roaming freely through its coppices, but exotic shrubs have been introduced and the 18-acre Pen Ponds have been developed for fishing.

Londoners owe their continued right to use the park to an 18th-century brewer called John Lewis, who opposed the Crown's attempts to bar the public.

St James's Park Until the reign of Henry VIII a 12th-century hospice for lepers, dedicated to St James the Less, stood here; Henry replaced it with St James's Palace, stocking the grounds with deer for the royal hunt. James I used the park to house a menagerie of animals from all over the world, many of them the gift of foreign royalty. The park remained swampy grassland, however, till the reign of Charles II, when it was redesigned in the formal French style. One of its attractions was an aviary (along the road still known as Birdcage Walk), and the islands of the ornamental lake were stocked with a collection of wildfowl.

Buckingham Palace, showing its central courtyard

Buckingham Palace, *The Mall, SW1* Buckingham Palace – formerly Buckingham House, built in 1703 for the Duke of Buckingham and Chandos – has been the principal home of the sovereign since Queen Victoria came to the throne in 1837. The original brick building was bought by George III in 1761 as a dower house for Queen Charlotte, and in the reign of George IV it was remodelled and clad in Bath Stone by John Nash. Victoria put on a new frontage, however, having Marble Arch (Nash's grand entrance) moved to Hyde Park because it was too narrow for the state coach. In 1912 the east front of the building was refaced again, being given a Classical façade of Portland stone to blend with the Victoria Memorial which stands opposite the top of the Mall. Buckingham Palace is open to the public only on such occasions as investitures, though it is possible to visit the Royal Mews and the Queen's Gallery (see p156).

Hampton Court Palace, *Hampton Court Road, Kingston-upon-Thames* When Cardinal Wolsey began work on Hampton Court in 1514 he intended to become the owner of one of the most magnificent palaces in Europe; later, however, he gave it to Henry VIII in a vain attempt to curry favour. Hampton Court, in its fine riverside park, was one of the king's favourite residences. He was often there, playing Royal Tennis (today's 'real' tennis) in the enclosed court and jousting in the area where the Tiltyard Gardens are now. Five of his wives lived there, and the ghosts of two (Jane Seymour and Catherine Howard) apparently haunt it. Anne Boleyn's Gateway, a fine example of Tudor brickwork, dates from this time, surmounted by Henry's

Hampton Court

fine astronomical clock. The intricate gardens, with their famous maze, were added by Charles II and are reminiscent of Versailles. The last monarch to live there was George II, and afterwards the palace, after extensive restoration, was opened to the public. There are priceless paintings to be seen, and fine tapestries and furniture – but perhaps most impressive of all is the magnificent hammerbeam roof in the Great Hall.

Hyde Park Henry VIII designed Hyde Park specifically for the purpose of hunting when the land, previously the property of the Abbey of Westminster, came into his possession at the Dissolution. In Stuart times the park was used for horse-racing, and the $1\frac{1}{2}$ miles of Rotten Row (a corruption of 'Route du Roi') is still popular with riders. The Serpentine Lake was formed at the instigation of Queen Caroline by damming the underground River Westbourne; it provides facilities for rowing and sailing – or even year-round bathing for the intrepid few! At the north-

east corner of the park, nearest to Marble Arch, is Speakers' Corner, where anyone prepared to face the heckling of bystanders can have his say.

Wellington Court At the southern end of the park, this was the home of Mark Twain at the beginning of the century. To the north, Radnor Place along the Bayswater Road was home to James Russell Lowell while Bret Harte lived at Lancaster Gate.

Kensington Gardens Kensington Gardens were once part of Hyde Park, but when William III came to the throne in 1689 he feared the effect of Whitehall Palace's damp atmosphere on his asthma and so acquired Nottingham House, at the west end of the park. This became Kensington Palace, its grounds Kensington Gardens – more formal than Hyde Park, though now divided from it only by a road and sharing the same stretch of water. Generations of children have flocked here to see the statue of Sir James Barrie's Peter Pan, the fantastically carved Elphin Oak and the craft of model boat enthusiasts on the Round Pond.

Kensington Palace, *Kensington Gardens, W8* Nottingham House, the London home of the Earl of Nottingham, was purchased by William III in 1683 and was remodelled as Kensington Palace by Sir Christopher Wren. It remained the home of the reigning monarch until George II died here in 1760; it was also the birthplace of Queen Victoria, who lived here until her accession to the throne. It is now the home of Princess Margaret, but the State Apartments, where there is fine work by Wren, Grinling Gibbons and William Kent, are open.

St James's Palace, *St James's St, SW1* This rambling, rectangular brick mansion was built for Henry VIII. It remained the official residence of the sovereign until the time of Victoria and was the birthplace of Charles II, James II, Mary II, Queen Anne and George IV. Charles I spent his last night in its guardroom before going to the scaffold in Whitehall. All that remains of the original structure is a fine Tudor gatehouse, in front of which the Brigade of Guards parades each day.

The Chapel Royal has been much altered over the centuries, but it has the original Holbein ceiling; William III, Mary II, Queen Anne, George IV, Victoria and George V were married there, and it is the setting for the annual Royal Epiphany Gifts Service (see below). The chapel is open to the public for services from October to Palm Sunday, though the palace itself is not, being occupied by various Court officials.

London's Pageantry

Pageantry and ceremonial are colourful parts of London life, observed not only in the panoply of state and civic occasions but also in the meticulous observance of minor rituals so old that their origins have in some cases become obscured by time.

ROYAL CEREMONIES

The State Opening of Parliament (*Late October or early November*) After the summer recess, the new session of Parliament is opened by a speech from the Monarch. The Monarch, accompanied by other members of the royal family, rides from Buckingham Palace in the Irish State Coach, a gun salute heralding their arrival at Westminster. After changing into royal robes and crown in the Robing Room, the Monarch is escorted to the Upper Chamber, where the Lords in their ceremonial robes are already assembled. The official known as Black Rod summons the Speaker and Members of the House of Commons, having first knocked three times on the door with his staff, and the Monarch then outlines the proposed government legislation for the coming session.

Trooping the Colour (*Second Saturday in June*) This ceremony takes place on Horse Guards Parade on the occasion of the sovereign's official birthday. Wearing the uniform of one of the regiments of which he or she is Colonel-in-Chief, the sovereign rides out from Buckingham Palace and takes the salute of the Brigade of Guards and the Household Cavalry. This is followed by a display of marching and the 'trooping' (display) of the 'colour' (or flag) of one of the five regiments of foot guards.

The Distribution of the Royal Maundy Money (*March*) Each Maundy Thursday the sovereign personally distributes alms (now purses of money, representing the original gifts of food and clothing) and, since the reign of Charles II, a purse of specially minted Maundy money, to old folk chosen from various parts of London.

DAILY CEREMONIES

The Ceremony of the Keys (*10 pm*) Each evening the gates of the Tower of London are locked by the chief Warder of the Yeoman Warders who is ceremonially challenged by a sentry as he nears the Bloody Tower. At 10 pm the Last Post is sounded and the Chief Warder hands over his keys to the Resident Governor and Major in the Queen's House. Applications to attend the ceremony can be made at the constable's office in the Tower.

The Changing of the Guard at Buckingham Palace (*11.30 am daily – winter alternate days*) The guard, usually formed from one of the regiments of Foot Guards (the Scots, Irish, Welsh, Coldstream and Grenadier) is changed each morning. A band leads the new guard to the palace and the old one back to its barracks.

The Mounting of the Guard (*11 am weekdays, 10 am Sundays*) The Mounting of the Guard takes place at the Horse Guards, opposite Whitehall. The guard is formed from two units of the Household Cavalry – the Blues (identified by the red plumes on their helmets) and the Life Guards (white plumed).

CIVIC CEREMONIES

Election of the Lord Mayor and Lord Mayor's Show A new Lord Mayor of London is elected every year on 29 September, Michaelmas Day. The retiring holder of the office and his aldermen attend a service at St Lawrence Jewry and then process to the Guildhall, where they make the final choice from the candidates put forward by the livery companies; the City bells ring as the old and new Lord Mayors ride to the Mansion House together in the state coach. On 8 November, after attending a luncheon at the Mansion House, together with liverymen of their companies, they go in procession to the Guildhall, where the insignia of office are finally transferred; bells ring in all the City churches as they return to the Mansion House. The new Lord Mayor publicly assumes office on the second Saturday in November, in the 600-year-old ritual of the Lord Mayor's Show. He is flanked by a bodyguard of pikemen and musketeers as he rides to the Royal Courts of Justice in the ceremonial coach, behind a procession of colourful floats depicting some aspect of London's history. The Lord Mayor's Banquet takes place at the Guildhall on the following Monday.

Processions In early January the Lord Mayor and his officers lead processions to the opening session of the Central Criminal Court (Old Bailey); to the first sitting of the newly elected Court of Common Council (January) and the church of St Lawrence Jewry for the Spital Sermon, preached by a bishop on an Easter theme (second Wednesday after Easter).

OTHER CEREMONIES

John Stow's Quill Ceremony (*Around 5 April*) During the memorial service for John Stow, 16th-century author of *The Survey of London*, at the church of St Andrew Undershaft, the Lord Mayor places a new quill in the hand of Stow's statue.

Royal Epiphany Gifts Service (*6 January*) Officers of the Household offer up gold, frankincense and myrrh – the currency equivalent of the gold then being distributed to old people – at a service in St James's Chapel.

Charles I Commemoration Ceremony (*30 January*) Each year, members of the Society of King Charles the Martyr and the Royal Stuart Society process from St Martin-in-the-Fields to the king's statue in Trafalgar Square to commemorate his execution on that day in 1649.

The Blessing of the Throats (*3 February, St Blaise's Day*) Throat sufferers commemorate St Blaise, who, on his way to a martyr's death, saved a child who was choking on a fishbone, in a service at St Ethelreda's Church in Holborn.

Cakes and Ale Sermon (*Ash Wednesday*) Members of the Stationers' Company walk to St Paul's Cathedral to hear a sermon preached in accordance with the wishes of John Norton, a member of their Company who died during the reign of James I. Cakes and ale are distributed.

Oranges and Lemons Children's Service (*End March*) The children from the local primary school attend a service to commemorate the restoration of the famous bells at St Clement Danes Church in the Strand, and each receives an orange and a lemon.

Hot Cross Buns Service (*Good Friday*) Morning service at St Bartholomew-the-Great, Smithfield, ends with the distribution of hot-cross buns and money (provided by an ancient charity) to 21 local widows.

Oak Apple Day (*29 May*) Chelsea Pensioners celebrate the escape of the founder of the Royal Hospital, Charles II, after the Battle of Worcester, decorating his statue with oak leaves in memory of the oak tree in which he hid.

Swan Upping (*Around the last Monday in July*) The swans on the Thames between London Bridge and Henley belong to the Monarch and the Companies of Vintners and Dyers. The Monarch's Swan Keeper and the Swan Wardens and Swan Markers of the two Companies inspect the swans and mark the cygnets.

Doggett's Coat and Badge Race (*Late July/early August*) Six Thames watermen row against the tide from London Bridge to Chelsea Bridge, and the winner is presented with a scarlet coat with silver buttons and badge. This is the oldest rowing event in the world, instituted in 1715.

Quit Rents Ceremony (*Late October*) In this, one of the oldest public ceremonies carried out in London, the City Solicitor makes token payment for two properties. The rents, accepted by the Queen's Remembrancer at the Royal Courts of Justice, comprise two faggots of wood, a billhook and a hatchet (for land in Shropshire) and six horseshoes and sixty-one nails (for a forge which once stood in the Strand).

Pearly King at Battersea

Calendar of Events

For Royal and Civic Occasions, see 'London's Pageantry'. Precise dates for most events may vary from year to year.

JANUARY
International Boat Show
(*Earl's Court*)

FEBRUARY
Cruft's Dog Show
(*Earl's Court*)

MARCH
Daily Mail Ideal Home Exhibition
(*Earl's Court*)
Druid Observance of Spring Equinox
(*Tower Hill*) around 21 Mar
Harness Horse Parade
(*Regent's Park*) Easter Monday
Easter Parade
(*Battersea*) Easter Sunday
Oxford and Cambridge Boat Race
(*Putney to Mortlake*) end Mar/Apr

APRIL
London Marathon
Milk Cup Football Final
(*Wembley Stadium*)

MAY
May Day Procession
(*Hyde Park*) 1 May
Rugby League Cup Final*
(*Wembley Stadium*)
Summer Exhibition Opens
(*Royal Academy*)
London to Brighton Walk
(*From Westminster Bridge*)
FA Cup Final
(*Wembley Stadium*)
Chelsea Flower Show
(*Royal Chelsea Hospital*) end May/Jun

JUNE
Cricket Test Matches
(*Lord's*)
Lawn Tennis Championships
(*Wimbledon*) end Jun/Jul

JULY
Royal Tournament
(*Earl's Court*)
AAA Championships
(*Crystal Palace*)
Royal International Horse Show
(*Wembley Arena*)
Cricket – Benson & Hedges Cup Final
(*Lord's*)
First Night of the Proms
(*Royal Albert Hall*)
Open Air Theatre Season Starts
(*Regent's Park*)

AUGUST
Greater London Horse Show
(*Clapham Common*) Bank Holiday
Cricket – Test Matches**
(*The Oval*)
Outdoor Theatre Season Starts
(*Holland Park*)
Cricket – NatWest Bank Trophy Final
(*Lord's*)

SEPTEMBER
Battle of Britain Thanksgiving Service
(*Westminster Abbey*) around 15 Sep
Druid Observance of Autumn Equinox
(*Primrose Hill*) around 23 Sep
Last Night of the Proms
(*Royal Albert Hall*)

OCTOBER
Costermongers' Harvest Festival
(*St Martin-in-the-Fields*) 1st Sunday
Horse of the Year Show
(*Wembley Arena*)
Trafalgar Day Service and Parade
(*Trafalgar Square*)

NOVEMBER
RAC London to Brighton Veteran Car Run
(*From Hyde Park*)
Remembrance Day Service
(*Whitehall – the Cenotaph*)
Sunday nearest 11 Nov

DECEMBER
Smithfield Show
(*Earl's Court*)
International Show Jumping
(*Olympia*)
Carol Singing and Lighting of the Christmas Tree
(*Trafalgar Square*) from 16 Dec
Switching on the Decorations
(*Regent Street*)
New Year's Eve Celebrations
(*Trafalgar Square*)

* Rugby Union: Of matches involving England versus Scotland, Wales, Ireland and France, two take place at Twickenham between January and March in any given year. Matches against other foreign touring teams may also be held.
** Subject to fixtures.

Shops and Markets

Oxford Street, Bond Street, Regent Street and Knightsbridge are the traditional heart of London's shopping area, and many of the long-established department stores are found here. Charing Cross Road has its bookshops; Savile Row its high-class tailors; Soho its delicatessens; Tottenham Court Road its furniture. Street traders flourished before the days of shops and their 'cries' are an evocative echo of Old London. Cheapside was once the centre of the City's trading ('ceap' being the Saxon word for barter or sale) but today there are markets all over the capital – large central wholesale markets and local 'village' and specialist markets.

Bond Street Where Oxford Street is famous for department stores Bond Street is traditionally known for jewellers, art dealers and expensive boutiques. Many of the best of the latter have now colonized South Molton Street, an attractive pedestrian way which leads off Brook Street.

Knightsbridge Harrods, the largest department store in Europe, lords it over the many expensive shops in Knightsbridge. Its magnificent foodhalls are a study in themselves, but every department is worth a visit, for the legend is that Harrods sells everything. For those who are daunted by the sheer size of the place, the streets round about, such as Beauchamp Place and Sloane Street, are full of interesting smaller shops and boutiques.

Harrods at night

Oxford Street Selfridges is the doyen of Oxford Street, with John Lewis, C & A, Marks and Spencer and a number of others also competing to attract the millions of shoppers who descend on the West End at weekends and, above all, at sales time.

Piccadilly Not many shops have held their own against the tourist and airline offices that now dominate Piccadilly, but Fortnum and Mason stands firm, still supplying the finest in food and drink and a select range of fashion from its original elegant premises. Swaine, Ardeney, Brigg & Sons specialize in riding equipment, leather goods and umbrellas. Richoux sells tempting pastries and confectionery and Hatchards, books. Facing these establishments, Burlington Arcade has many luxuries for sale, as has Jermyn Street, with its famous cheese shop, Paxton and Whitfield. Well-dressed gentlemen might order hand-made shirts in Jermyn Street, or perfume as a gift from J Floris, established here in 1739, on their way into the Haymarket to buy snuff, tobacco or cigars from Fribourg and Treyer, whose bow-windowed premises have been here since 1720. At the other end of Jermyn Street, in St James's Street, it is still possible to have a bowler hat made to measure at James Lock, or fine leather shoes made at John Lobb, a few doors away.

Regent Street Most of the shops are to be found near Oxford Circus, where easily the most famous are Liberty

and Jaeger. Liberty, housed in a distinctive, Tudor-style building, has always been a by-word for its beautiful fabrics. Nearby is Hamley's toyshop, a three-storey wonderland for children.

Tottenham Court and Charing Cross Roads High fashion in clothes is not to be found in either of these streets, but the best of modern furniture is displayed at Heal & Son and Habitat in Tottenham Court Road, and the whole range of bookshops, from paperback to antiquarian can be found in Charing Cross Road, where Foyles, occupying two buildings, sells not only these but very nearly all other categories of books.

TRADE MARKETS
New Covent Garden This famous flower, fruit and vegetable market is now sited at Nine Elms, Battersea, but for hundreds of years it was held in the square in front of St Paul's Church, north of the Strand. It was originally the *Convent Garden* – a walled enclosure used by the monks of Westminster Abbey. After the Dissolution the land was eventually granted to the Earls of Bedford; the 4th Earl obtained permission from Charles I to build on the site, and an Italian-style piazza surrounded by gentlemen's residences was designed by Inigo Jones. Traders were soon attracted by the central square and its covered walks, and the market was well known by the end of the 17th century. The 19th century saw the erection of special market buildings, and the second

half of the 20th century the traffic problems that brought about its removal to the Nine Elms site. The old market has become the lively centre of a revitalized area; craft goods of high quality are sold at many of the stalls in the central market area, and a host of shops and restaurants have opened in the surrounding streets.

Billingsgate Billingsgate Fish Market has also been moved from its original site because of traffic congestion in the City streets. It grew up round a medieval quay just below London Bridge, probably as early as the 9th century, although it did not receive its charter until 400 years later. In 1875 an arcaded building (which still stands) was erected to bring together the sale of all kinds of fish, 'wet, dry and shell', but in 1981 the market was transferred to a new site at the less busy West India Docks. The name of Billingsgate has long been synonymous with bad language – its tradition of colourful expletive dating back to the original fishwives who squabbled round the quay, but ably maintained by today's hard-pressed porter, carrying anything up to a hundredweight of fish balanced on his flat-topped 'bobbing' hat.

Borough Market This Southwark market, a direct decendant of one held on old London Bridge, occupies buildings beneath the arches on a viaduct serving London Bridge station.

Smithfield Smithfield, now one of the world's largest meat markets and famous for the quality of its beef, pork and lamb, dealt originally in hay, horses, cattle and sheep; its name recalls the 'smooth field' just outside the city walls to which the animals were driven through the streets of London until the practice was restricted by statute in

Smithfield Market

the middle of the 19th century. At about the same time the market was modernized, when Sir Horace Jones built the Renaissance-style Central Meat Market Arcade, capable of holding up to 400 truckloads of meat at a time.

Spitalfields The name of Spitalfields Market, in the East End, like that of Covent Garden recalls earlier Church ownership of the site: in the 12th century a priory dedicated to St Mary Spital was founded here. The surrounding land was fertile, and by the time of Charles II the volume of local produce for sale was such that he granted a market charter. During the 18th and 19th centuries the area was built up with close-packed houses that subsequently deteriorated into slums, but the market continued to deal in flowers, fruit and vegetables, though no longer locally produced.

STREET MARKETS

Berwick Street Market, *Berwick St, W1* One of the few survivors of the old Soho, Berwick Street Market (Monday to Saturday) offers excellent value in fruit and vegetables, and there are also shellfish, clothing and household goods stalls.

Brixton Market, *Electric Avenue, SW9* Brixton (Monday to Saturday) is a general market which reflects colourfully the local community it serves. Because of the largely West Indian population, many stalls are piled with exotic fruit and vegetables, and the compelling rhythms of Caribbean music throb in the background.

Camden Passage Market, *Camden Passage, N1* This market which has grown up near the Angel, Islington, is devoted to antiques, curios and bric-à-brac of all kinds. Some of its shops and stalls open all week, but Saturday is the liveliest day.

Columbia Road Market, *Shoreditch, E2* Well known to keen gardeners, Columbia Road Market (Sunday mornings) offers a wide variety of flowers, plants and shrubs.

Dingwalls Market, *Camden Lock, NW6* Antiques, bric-à-brac, period clothes and crafts are on sale (Saturdays) in this lively market.

Leadenhall Market, *Gracechurch St, EC3* Specializing in meat and poultry, this City market (Monday to Friday) also offers fish, fruit and vegetables and plants. Its origins go back to the 14th century.

New Caledonian Market, *Bermondsey Sq, SE1* The New Caledonian is primarily a dealers' market in antiques, though members of the public are not excluded. Much of the serious trading, however, takes place before the official opening time of 7 am on a Friday.

Petticoat Lane, *Middlesex St, E1* This is probably the most famous of London's street markets, typically Cockney in character and very popular with tourists. It is actually sited in Middlesex Street but was dubbed Petticoat Lane in the 17th century, when it was the place where the local poor could buy cast-off clothing of their richer neighbours. Today's market (Sunday mornings) still sells clothing of all sorts, but it also deals in most household items.

Portobello Road, *Notting Hill, W11* A general market during the week, with a West Indian flavour, Portobello Road assumes its distinctive character on a Saturday, when a multitude of antique stalls, arcades and shops are opened up. The items offered for sale range from expensive antiques through Victoriana to pure junk. The scene is enlivened by buskers and street entertainers.

A London Directory

EXPERIENCE MUSEUMS
London Dungeon, *Tooley St, SE1*: Recreation of scenes of medieval torture in realistic settings.
London Experience, *Coventry St, W1*: London life and times displayed through different media.
Madame Tussaud's, *Marylebone Rd, NW1*: The famous collection of waxworks, including the fearful Chamber of Horrors.
The Planetarium, *Marylebone Rd, NW1*: Representations of planetary motions are projected on to the inside of the building's huge dome.

MARITIME MUSEUMS
HMS Belfast, *Symons Wharf, Vine Lane, SE1*: One of the largest cruisers ever built for the Royal Navy (11,000 tons).
Historic Ships Collection, *St Katharine's Dock, E1*: A collection of 18th- and 19th-century sail and steam vessels owned by the Maritime Trust.
Cutty Sark and Gypsy Moth IV, *Greenwich Pier, SE10*: The last of the clipper ships and Sir Francis Chichester's 'round-the-world' yacht lie side by side at Greenwich.
National Maritime Museum, *Romney Rd, SE10*: The magnificent collection includes exhibitions on Nelson and Captain Cook. (See Old Royal Observatory p156).

HMS Belfast

Royal Naval College, *London SE10:* Wren, Hawksmoor and Vanbrugh were among the architects of these elegant buildings. The chapel and the Painted Hall only are open.

MILITARY MUSEUMS
Imperial War Museum, *Lambeth Rd, SE1:* Exhibits cover both world wars and other British and Commonwealth operations.
National Army Museum, *Royal Hospital Rd, SW3:* History of the British, Indian, Colonial forces since 1485.
Royal Air Force Museum, *Aerodrome Rd, NW9:* 40 historic aircraft.

MUSIC MUSEUMS
Horniman Museum, see 'General Interest'.
National Musical Museum, *368 High St, Brentford:* Far-reaching collection of old instruments, including automatic pianos.
Royal College of Music, Museum of Instruments, *Prince Consort Rd, SW7:* Includes rare instruments, some dating back to the 15th century.
Fenton House, *Hampstead Grove, NW3:* Early keyboard instruments.

'PERSONALITY MUSEUMS'
Carlyle's House, *24 Cheyne Row, SW3:* Manuscripts and personal possessions of the writer known as the 'Sage of Chelsea'.
Dickens' House, *48 Doughty St, WC1:* Many of the author's personal belongings are preserved here.
Dr Johnson's House, *17 Gough Sq, EC4:* Dr Johnson lived here from 1748–58 and compiled his famous dictionary in the attic.
Keats House (Wentworth Place), *Keats Grove, NW3:* The two Regency houses where Keats and Fanny Brawne lived from 1818–20, when Keats wrote some of his best work.
Leighton House, *Holland Park Rd, W14:* Contains

paintings and sculpture by Lord Leighton, also a fabulous Arab Hall.
Sir John Soane's Museum, *13 Lincoln's Inn Fields, WC2:* Antiquities, curiosities and pictures in the setting of the house where he lived from 1812–37.
Wellington Museum, *Apsley House, Hyde Park Corner, Piccadilly W1:* The home of the Duke of Wellington, once known as No 1 London. Wellington Museum has an enormous marble statue of Napoleon, and a good collection of pictures including a John Singleton Copley.

MUSEUMS OF GENERAL INTEREST
(see also 'National Collections'.)
Bear Gardens Museum, *Bear Gardens, SE1:* On the site of the last bear-baiting ring on Bankside, the museum's exhibits relate to Elizabethan theatre, with scale models.
Bethnal Green Museum of Childhood, *Cambridge Heath Rd, E2:* Dolls' houses and model soldiers are among the toys exhibited.
Geffrye Museum, *Kingland Rd, E2:* Furniture and woodwork from the 16th century to 1939.
Horniman Museum, *London Rd, SE23:* Ethnographical and large natural history collections; also musical instruments.
London Transport Museum, *39 Wellington St, WC2:* Tells the story of the development of London transport, with old trams, trolleybuses, etc.
Museum of London, *London Wall, EC2:* Sited in the Barbican, the museum is devoted to the story of London and its people, from prehistoric times to the present.
Museum of Mankind, *Burlington Gdns, W1:* Houses the ethnography department of the British Museum. Special exhibitions of the culture of tribal and village societies outside western Europe. Small permanent display.

Old Royal Observatory, *Greenwich Park, SE10:* Exhibitions of astronomical, horological and navigational interest. It is now a part of the National Maritime Museum (see p155
Pollock's Toy Museum, *1 Scala St, W1:* Old theatres, toys and children's games are on display in two charming old houses.
Public Record Office Museum, *Chancery Lane, WC2:* The national archives on show include the Domesday Book.
Wallace Collection, see 'Art Galleries'.

THE NATIONAL COLLECTIONS
British Museum, *Great Russell St, WC1:* Contains a wealth of archaeological treasures, books, manuscripts, and much more. besides.
Commonwealth Institute, *Kensington High Street, SW7:* Fascinating displays and exhibitions from the British Commonwealth.
Geological Museum, *Exhibition Rd, SW7:* A piece of the moon is among the exhibits relating to geology and mineralogy: the world's largest exhibition on basic earth science is here.
National Gallery, *Trafalgar Sq, WC2:* Contains one of the world's most important collections of European Old Master paintings.
National Portrait Gallery, *St Martin's Pl, WC2:* Paintings, engravings, photos and sculpture representing famous national figures and including many figures who have played a part in North American history as well as works by American and Canadian artists.
Natural History Museum, *Cromwell Rd, SW7:* Five departments relate to botany, zoology, entomology, mineralogy and palaeontology.
Science Museum, *Exhibition Rd, SW7:* Exhibits demonstrate the sciences and the development of technology – often with the

help of working models.
Tate Gallery, *Millbank, SW1:* Contains the national collection of the work of British artists from the 16th to early 20th centuries and collections of modern art generally.
Victoria and Albert Museum, *Cromwell Rd, SW7:* Covers both fine and applied art, exhibiting work from all parts of the world and all periods. Includes sculpture, ceramics, furniture and costume.

ART GALLERIES
Courtauld Institute Gallery, *Woburn Sq, WC1:* Impressionist and post-Impressionist paintings, Old Master drawings and Italian primitives.
Dulwich College Picture Gallery, *College Rd, SE21:* The oldest public picture gallery in England, with works by Gainsborough, Reynolds, Rembrandt and Rubens.
Hayward Gallery, *The South Bank, SE1:* Used by the Arts Council for exhibitions.
Institute of Contemporary Arts, *Nash House, 12 Carlton House Terrace, SW1:* Displays, often controversial, of modern art.
Iveagh Bequest, *Kenwood, Hampstead Lane, NW3:* Old Master paintings.
Queen's Gallery, *Buckingham Palace, SW1:* Constantly changing display of art treasures from the royal collection.
Royal Academy of Arts, *Burlington House, W1:* In summer, exhibition of works of living artists. Important special exhibitions on occasion.
Serpentine Gallery, *Kensington Gdns, W2:* Monthly exhibitions of the work of contemporary artists.
Wallace Collection, *Hertford House, Manchester Sq, W1:* British and European paintings, including some by Rubens, Titian, Holbein and Frans Hals. Also sculpture, ceramics, and furniture.

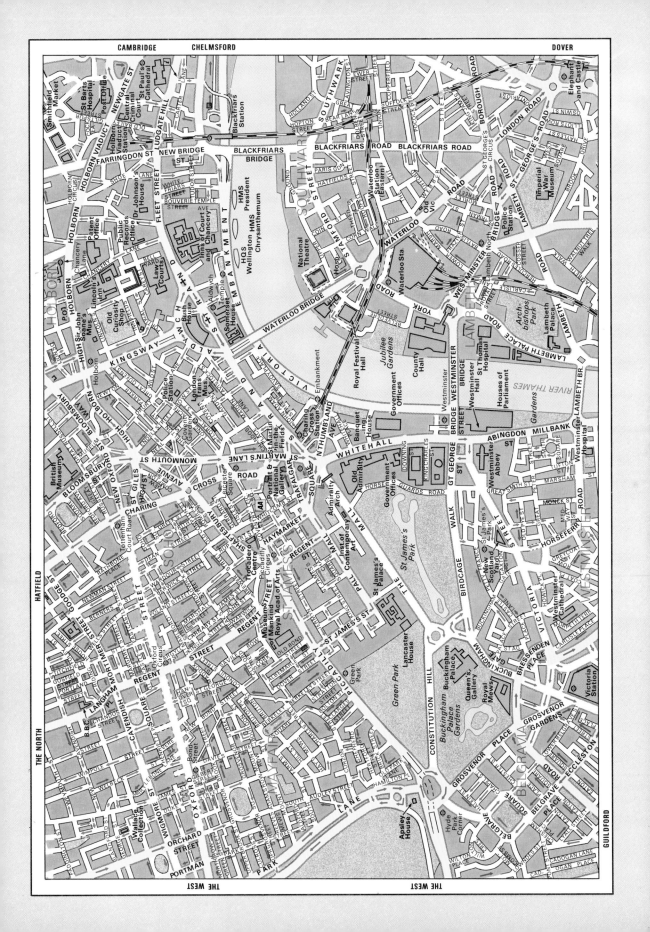

LUDLOW
Shropshire   *9 SJ51*

In Ludlow, wide Georgian streets contrast with narrow medieval alleys, and elegant 18th-century brick and stucco rubs shoulders with half-timbered Tudor buildings with leaning walls and steep-pitched roofs. In the 12th century Ludlow was a 'planned town', its streets designed on a grid-iron pattern that can still be traced today. The most famous of all the timbered buildings, the Feathers Hotel, its exterior ornamented with heads and other carvings, has stood in the Bull Ring, where bulls used to be penned before market, since 1603. Even older is the Bull Inn, and another attractive old tavern is the Angel, its overhanging upper storeys supported on slender columns. More ancient than the inns and overlooking the church is the Reader's House, a medieval stone building with an attractive three-storey timbered porch. Mary Queen of Scots is thought to have been held prisoner here for some time.

Ludlow, built on a steep hill washed on 2 sides by the Rivers Corve and Teme, has, since earliest times been recognized as a strategic site, and the Normans were quick to take advantage of this. The castle, now an impressive ruin, crowns the hilltop, looking out over the Welsh Marches, as it has done since it was built in 1085 by the Earl of Shrewsbury, Roger Montgomery, or his henchman Roger de Lacy. Apart from a period of just under 100 years, from 1461 to 1552, when it was a royal castle, Ludlow retained its connection with the earls, and it was for the children of the Countess of Shrewsbury that Milton

wrote his masque *Comus*, which the children first performed at the castle in 1634. One of Shakespeare's plays is always performed here during the annual Ludlow Festival. If the castle forms one focus of attention in Ludlow, the other is provided by St Laurence's Church, cathedral-like in the nobility of its design, and dating from the 15th century. Its tower stands, at 135ft, higher even than the castle.

PLACES TO SEE
Ludlow Castle (OACT) Although now ruined, the castle is still impressive. As a royal residence, however, its history is sad, for it was from here that Edward IV's young sons, the 'princes in the Tower', set out on their last, ill-omened journey, to meet their deaths either at the hands of Richard III or of Henry VII, according to your point of view. Henry's own eldest son, Prince Arthur, brought his young bride, Katherine of Aragon, to live at Ludlow for a short period, before his untimely death. Their apartments and the terraced gardens he had made for her can still be seen. There is also a rare example of a Norman round chapel.

Ludlow Museum The classical stone Butter Cross, built in 1746, houses the town's museum on its first floor.

St Laurence's Church The interior is lit by a magnificent east window, depicting the life and miracles of the saint, and there is a famous set of misericords in the choir. In the churchyard, the ashes of the poet A E Housman were buried in 1936.

Broad Street

LOSTWITHIEL
Cornwall   *1 SX15*
A medieval bridge (AM) crosses the River Fowey at Lostwithiel, now a popular touring centre but once the capital of Cornwall and a centre for the tin trade. 14th-century Duchy House in Quay Street includes the remains of an old Stannary Court where the regulations of the local tin mines were administered. The remains of Restormel Castle (OACT), dating back to the 12th or 13th centuries overlook the valley about 1 mile away; from here the Duke of Cornwall once ruled the area.

LOTHERTON HALL
N Yorkshire   *15 SE43*
Eighteenth-century Lotherton Hall (OACT) is now a country house museum, containing fine furniture, silver and ceramics from the Gascoigne Collection (the Gascoignes being the former occupants of the house); English works of art are also on display and there are fashion galleries and exhibitions of contemporary crafts. The small chapel nearby has a noteworthy beamed roof and an elaborately carved pulpit. The grounds include Edwardian and Bird Gardens.

LOUGHBOROUGH
Leicestershire   *10 SK51*
Today Loughborough is involved in hosiery manufacture and engineering industries, but it is internationally famous for its bell foundry, brought here from Oxford by John Taylor in 1858 and responsible for casting Great Paul for St Paul's Cathedral. All Saints Church (dating from the 14th century, but restored by Sir Gilbert Scott in the 19th) has memorials to the Taylor family – and, appropriately, a peal of 10 bells. A Victory Peal of 5,041 changes was rung here in 1919, and the War Memorial built in Queen's Park in 1923 took the form of a tower containing a carillon of 47 bells. Loughborough Central contains a museum and locomotive depot.

LOUTH
Lincolnshire   *16 TF38*
A well-preserved Georgian market town. The most imposing feature of Louth is the spire of St James's Church which dates from 1515. Tennyson was educated at the grammar school here for 5 years, and his work was first published in Louth. Captain John Smith, founder of Virginia, was also educated at the school, where there is a bust of him. This was presented by

THE LAND OF STEEL BONNETS

At the western end of the Borders is the land of the reivers, guerrillas in steel bonnets. When there was no stability on one or other side of the border, the local clans exploited the power vacuum, and especially so from the thirteenth century until the union of the Scottish and English Crowns. Chillingham pure-bred cattle were kept deliberately wild, so that they couldn't be stolen! If your name is here, this is your country. If you are not afraid of the consequences of tracking down ancestors, pay it a visit!

Armstrong	Ker(r)
Beattie	Laidlaw
Bell	Little
Burn	Lowther
Charlton	Maxwell
Collingwood	Milburn
Croser	Musgrave
Dacre	Nixon
Dodd	Pringle
Elliot	Ridley
Fenwick	Robson
Forster	Rutherford
Graham	Routledge
Hall	Scott
Hetherington	Storey
Hume	Tait
Irvine	Trotter
Johnstone	Turnbull

The Borders author and historian, George Macdonald Fraser, has written:

'The Grahams live in the Debateable Land, the Scotts in Teviotdale, the Humes on the Merse, the Fenwicks and Forsters on the Middle March. There are fewer Musgraves and Dacres than there once were, but the Charltons play football for England, a Nixon sits in the White House (with Scotts, Cliffords and Percies high in US government), and not very long ago Albert Armstrong had a stall in Carlisle Market.

'But there is very little to remind the visitor to these quiet fields, humdrum little towns and villages, lonely hills and lovely valleys, that this was once a fierce and bloody frontier. Strife and raid and burning and murder seem so out of place and remote, that it is hard to imagine that they were the daily business of the people of the Borders...

'Comparisons have been made between the Border reivers and the Indian North-West frontier – which is not a bad parallel – and the cattle rustlers of the American West. There are certainly strong resemblances there, provided one remembers to separate Western myth from Western reality. One of the canons of the Western code, in its Hollywood translation, is that good triumphs and the villain bites the dust. If anyone believes that, the story of the Border reivers should convince him otherwise. Its moral is clear: there is little justice to be had. The good man survives, if he is lucky, but the villain becomes the first Lord Roxburgh.'

Places to Visit
Carlisle Castle
The Hermitage, Liddesdale

Further Reading
George Macdonald Fraser, *The Steel Bonnets* (Pan Books 1971)

General Lord Baden-Powell, founder of the Boy Scout Movement. 8 miles east of Louth on the North Sea coast is Saltfleetby where Thomas Pownall, Governor of New Jersey and Massachusetts, was born. Pownall was a Fellow of the Royal Society and a very influential man, friend of Benjamin Franklin and Josiah Quincy.

LOWESTOFT
Suffolk   *12 TM59*
The great fishing fleets are now a thing of the past, but Lowestoft is still a busy port, with trawlers docking and unloading. The lifeboat is famous, and the station was founded in 1801, 20 years before the RNLI came into being. The Maritime Museum contains model ships and fishing gear. Joseph Conrad first set foot in England here in 1878. Lowestoft was badly damaged in the war but the 'Scores' are a reminder of the old town: these narrow alleyways descend steeply from the level of the High Street until they reach the shore where the fish

houses for curing herrings used to stand. South town is developing a 'seaside' atmosphere and offers attractions for children – notably a boating lake and a miniature steam railway. Lowestoft Ness is Britain's most easterly point. Nearby Oulton Broad is popular for water sports and is used for yacht, dinghy and motor boat racing. The East Anglia Transport Museum, with all types of old cars and commercial vehicles is an added attraction.

LULWORTH
Dorset   *3 SY87*
Lulworth Cove, deep in Hardy country, is an exquisite small bay backed by magnificent chalk cliffs, its waters almost totally enclosed by two arms of Portland and Purbeck stone. Stair Hole, with its strangely twisted rock strata, is of considerable geological interest. **Durdle Door**, the natural rock arch that juts out into the sea just west of the cove, is a spectacular sight on stormy days,

when huge waves crash through it. Lulworth Castle, gutted by fire in 1929, stands in 600 acres of woodland. The adjoining Rotunda (built in 1786) is the first Roman Catholic church for which Royal permission was given after the Reformation, George III agreed to it on condition that it did not *look* like a church. Archbishop Carroll (1735–1815), the first Roman Catholic bishop of the United States, was consecrated here.

LUNDY
Devon   *1 SS14*
This tiny granite island stands in the Bristol Channel, about 12 miles off Hartland Point and is easily accessible by steamer from Ilfracombe; since 1969 it has been owned by the National Trust, which leases it to the Landmark Trust. The scanty ruins of Marisco Castle, the stronghold of a piratical family who once ruled the island, lie near the quay. The Shutter Rock will be familiar to readers of Kingsley's *Westward Ho!* (see

Bideford). Puffins and other seabirds breed on the rocky coastline, which also offers some of the finest sea cliff climbing in England. The word 'Lundy' is derived from the old Norse word for puffin.

LUTON
Bedfordshire   11 TL02
Light engineering and operation of an international airport have superseded the manufacture of pillow-lace and straw hats as Luton's industries, though these crafts of a bygone era are illustrated in the museum in Wardown Park. Luton Hoo (OACT) is a palatial mansion, originally designed by Robert Adam and set in a 1500-acre park. It houses the magnificent Wernher collection of pictures, tapestries, porcelain and Russian Fabergé jewels.

LUTTERWORTH
Leicestershire   10 SP58
John Wyclif, the reformer who attacked the wrongful use of papal power in politics, was rector at the parish church of Lutterworth from 1374–84 and is commemorated by an obelisk. The church itself was much restored in the 19th century, a massive tower replacing the original spire, but it still contains some 15th-century wall paintings. Wyclif worked on the first English translation of the Bible here. He was buried in the churchyard, but his body was later exhumed, cremated and the ashes cast into the River Swift.

Three miles north west is Claybrooke Magna, where Francis Higginson was born, the son of the vicar, c1588. Higginson emigrated in 1629, becoming famous as pastor of Salem, Massachusetts.

LUXULYAN
Cornwall   1 SX05
Luxulyan is a small, pretty village on the side of an exceptionally beautiful Cornish valley which runs deep between wooded hillsides. The church, a plain building of large granite blocks, is basically 15th-century. Granite was also used for the viaduct which spans the road outside the village; it still carries a water supply for the china clay industry, though the railway that once transported stone from local quarries no longer exists. A Nuclear Power Station (OACT) lies 4 miles south east.

LYBSTER
Highland   30 ND23
The village of Lybster stands on Lybster Bay, on the wild and rugged coastline south west of Clyth Ness, and has a small fishing industry. The church has a west door and chancel entrance of ancient local design and is built of locally dressed flagstones. The Grey Cairns of Camster (AM), two megalithic chambered cairns almost 5000 years old, lie about 5 miles north of the village.

LYDD
Kent   6 TR02
This busy little town, once on the coast but now standing 3 miles inland, is said to have the lowest rainfall in England; it also has the distinction of having given its name to the explosive lyddite, tested near here in the late 19th century. The fine 130ft tower of 'the Cathedral of Romney Marsh' still stands, despite bomb damage during the last war, and inside the church are 16th-century brasses and a 15th-century screen.

LYDFORD
Devon   2 SX58
In the days of tin-mining Lydford was an important centre, and one of Devon's four 'stannary' towns, with the right of assaying metal and minting coins. Although now no more than a moorland village, it remains one of England's largest civil parishes, covering the greater part of Dartmoor. Today's village is dominated by the remains of the 12th-century castle (AM); at one time the upper floor was a Stannary Court, administering the mining laws, and the lower floor was used as a prison. Lydford Gorge (NT) is a deep, wooded ravine about a mile long from which the River Lyd emerges to be joined by a stream at the 90ft-high White Lady waterfall.

LYDIARD
Wiltshire   3 SU18
Lydiard Park (OACT) is a pleasant, mainly Georgian manor house, for generations the home of the St John family but now the property of Thamesdown Borough. It has fine rococo ceilings and there is a small agricultural museum in the stable block. In the park stands St Mary's, the parish church of Lydiard Tregoze, dating back to the 14th century and rich in memorials to the St Johns. Particularly striking are the Golden Cavalier, a gilded life-size figure of Edward St John, killed in the Civil War, and the vast canopied tomb of St John, his two wives and thirteen children. The church also has ancient stained glass and a triptych in a cabinet.

LYME REGIS
Dorset   3 SY39
Lyme Regis became a fashionable south coast resort in the 18th century. Its first importance was as a medieval port, earning its royal title when Edward I sheltered by the Cobb during the wars against the French. Later the Duke of Monmouth landed here in 1685 to lead the ill-fated rebellion against James II. The town was a smuggling stronghold, but regained respectability in the days of Jane Austen. The massive, curving breakwater, the Cobb, was the scene of Louisa Musgrove's fall in *Persuasion*, and more recently was a setting in John Fowles' *The French Lieutenant's Woman*. The town is substantially unchanged today, with Georgian houses lining the steep main street that runs down to the harbour and shingle beach. There are fine views along the bay, much of which is a nature reserve, dominated by Golden Cap – at 617ft, it is the highest cliff on the south coast. The cliff area running round to Charmouth is rich in fossils; many finds can be seen in the town museum. The most famous fossil, discovered in the Undercliff, was the 21ft ichthyosaurus found in 1811 by Mary Anning, the 12-year-old daughter of a local carpenter.

Lyme Regis was the birthplace of Sir George Somers, who discovered Bermuda when his expedition was wrecked there in 1609. Somers lived 6 miles east of Lyme Regis at Berne Manor, Whitchurch Canicorum, where he is buried in the church. Lyme Regis is also the home of Thomas Coram, who became a successful shipbuilder at Taunton, Massachusetts. He was associated with Oglethorpe in Georgia; the Foundling Hospital he endowed has a group portrait which includes the two men.

LYMINGTON
Hampshire   4 SZ39
The ancient town of Lymington has become a sailing centre, its tidal harbour usually packed with yachts, and Pier Station the departure point for car ferries to the Isle of Wight. The church and many of the houses reflect the prosperity of the area in the 18th century. Part of Pressgang Cottage, a former inn, was the headquarters of an 18th-century pressgang, and the old Harbour Master's office was once a bathhouse. Historian Edward Gibbon

represented the town as an MP. 2 miles north is the village of **Boldre**.

LYMPNE
Kent *6 TR13*
Lympne was a coastal village until the sea receded, and the Romans built a fort here as part of their defences. Its ruins, known as Studfall Castle, stand about 300 yds from Lympne Castle (OACT), a fortified manor house which still retains its Norman appearance despite extensive restoration. The grounds offer wide views over Romney Marsh and across the channel to France. Port Lympne Zoo Park and Gardens lie just west of the village; the animals on view include Indian elephants, Siberian and Indian tigers, leopards, monkeys, wolves, rhino and bison. At the centre of the 15 acres of spectacular garden stands the mansion (OACT) in whose library the Treaty of Paris was signed after World War I. The Rex Whistler 'tent' room is very fine.

LYNDHURST
Hampshire *4 SU20*
A typical New Forest village, set in attractive woodland scenery and roamed by untamed ponies, Lyndhurst is popular with tourists. The huge old Knightswood oak, with a girth of more than 21ft is thought to be about 600 years old. The church is 19th century, with work by Leighton, Burne-Jones and Millais; a Mrs Hargreaves buried in the churchyard was formerly Alice Liddell, the original of Lewis Carroll's heroine. Six times a year the ancient Verderers' Court still sits in 17th-century Queen's House to administer the forest laws.

LYNMOUTH
Devon *2 SS74*
Lynmouth is an attractive little resort at the mouth of the East and West Lyn Rivers; it has a small shingle beach, and charming thatched cottages line the narrow street by the harbour. Countisbury Hill, rising over 1000ft to the east, includes some of the steepest cliffs in England (NT) and nearby the East Lyn converges with Hoar Oak Waters in wooded Watersmeet Valley (NT). The lighthouse at Foreland Point (NT) is also surrounded by exceptionally beautiful scenery. Lynmouth will always be remembered, however, for the floods caused by a freak storm over Exmoor in 1952, when 28 bridges were swept away, 100 houses damaged or destroyed and 31 lives lost.

• MACCLESFIELD
Cheshire *14 SJ97*
According to the Domesday Book, Macclesfield used to belong to the Saxon Edwin, Earl of Chester. Edward I and his queen, Eleanor, founded the hilltop church of St Michael and All Angels, which can either be entered from the Market Place or from the valley below by a steep climb up 108 cobbled steps. Macclesfield was, until about the middle of this century, a silk-manufacturing town, as several fine 18th-century mills by the River Bollin testify, but many of them have either been demolished or converted to other trades. The town's museum, including a silk museum, and art gallery stands in West Park, and nearby is an enormous boulder, said to have been brought down by glacial action during the Ice Age.

MACHYNLLETH
Powys *8 SH70*
A modest and quietly elegant Welsh town gracing the Dyfi valley, Machynlleth dates from the Iron Age. It was originally three villages which shared a common market cross, replaced in 1873 by a clock tower to mark the coming of age of Lord Castlereagh. In 1404, having liberated his fellow countrymen from the thrall of Henry IV, Owen Glendower declared Machynlleth the capital of Wales. His Parliament House, to which extensions have been made over the years, is now the Owen Glendower Institute. There is also the pioneering Centre for Alternative Technology, a working demonstration of ways of living by using only a minimum of the Earth's dwindling resources.

MADRON
Cornwall *1 SW43*
The church of St Maddern used to be the parish church of Penzance. Situated on high ground above Mount's Bay, this village – with its granite cottages – overlooks St **Michael's Mount**, the island castle that so closely resembles its namesake, Mont St Michel, in Brittany. A 3 mile walk will take you to the ancient Men-

an-Tol Stone, reputed to have healing powers: sufferers used to crawl through the 'porthole' aperture to be cured of their ailments.

MAIDEN CASTLE
Dorset *3 SY68*
Set on a hilltop to the south west of **Dorchester**, this Iron Age fort (AM) is one of the largest earthworks in Europe, with a perimeter of over 2 miles and terraced ramparts rising to more than 80ft. Finds of pottery and tools indicate that the site was first occupied c2000 BC, but fortified in approximately 300 BC. Earlier this century, excavations revealed an ammunition store containing 20,000 sling-stones and a mass grave. Some of the skeletons had axes embedded in their skulls. Vespasian and the Romans captured the hill-fort in AD 43.

MAIDENHEAD
Berkshire *4 SU88*
At one time an important stage-post on the London-Bath road, Maidenhead's heyday was in Edwardian times, when Boulter's Lock became a popular boating rendezvous, and Skindles, the waterside restaurant, was patronized by 'bright young things'. Maidenhead's image owes much to Evelyn Waugh. The Brunel railway bridge features in Turner's painting 'Rain, Steam and Speed'. Just outside the town at Littlewick Green is the Courage Shire Horse Centre (OACT).

• MAIDSTONE
Kent *6 TQ75*
Maidstone has been an administrative centre since Saxon times; indeed the first trial ever to be recorded in England took place on Penenden Heath. Maidstone's geographical position made it a natural collecting point for the fruit, vegetables and hops grown in the Vale of Kent. Maidstone's Domesday Book records milling, eel-fishing and salt-crystallizing among the town's industries. Wat Tyler, leader of the Peasants' Revolt, was a Maidstone man, and Sir Thomas Wyatt led the men of Kent from Maidstone in their rebellion against Mary I. All Saints' parish church contains a memorial tablet to Lawrence Washington, a collateral ancestor of George Washington. The tablet bears a modified stars and stripes – the oldest known representation of the family arms.
South east of Maidstone in the fine village church of East Sutton, is the

tomb of Richard Argall. After his death his wife Mary married Lawrence Washington of Maidstone. Mary was the mother of Samuel Argall, Deputy Governor of Virginia 1617–19, who was very active in keeping foreigners out of British America. Sutton Valence nearby is an attractive village overlooking the Wealden valleys. It has the remains of a Norman castle. The grave of John Willes 1777–1852 who introduced round-arm bowling into cricket, is in the churchyard.

MALDON
Essex 6 TL80
Maldon, a delightful town on the River Blackwater, is noted for the quality of its salt. All Saints Church is unique in having the only triangular tower in the country. There is an interesting 15th-century Moot Hall. The Reverend Lawrence Washington, father of John who emigrated to Virginia in 1657, and great-great-grandfather of George Washington, was a rector of Purleigh 4 miles south, and a Fellow of Brasenose College, Oxford, and is buried in the churchyard. His father was Lawrence Washington of Sulgrave.

Captain Christopher Jones of the *Mayflower* was probably baptized here, though he was born in Harwich and several Maldon men were early members of the Massachusetts Assembly. General Horatio Gates, born here, emigrated to America and was instrumental in Burgoyne's defeat at Saratoga in 1777. 8 miles south, Archbishop Sandys lived at Woodham Ferrars.

MALHAM
N Yorkshire 15 SD96
Malham, really, is more a landscape than a village, though there is a pleasant cluster of houses, an inn, a humpbacked bridge and Tarn House (NT), now the Field Studies Centre, where Charles Kingsley wrote a part of *The Water Babies*, inspired by the black streaks on the limestone cliffs, which made him think of chimney sweeps. Three of Yorkshire's most celebrated natural features lie within relatively easy walking distance: Malham Cove, the 240ft high limestone cliff created by the Craven Fault, at the top Malham's famous limestone pavement; the dramatically impressive rock bowl of Gordale Scar, where the water hurls itself down a 250ft ravine up which you can climb when the water is not in full spate; and finally, Malham Tarn, a 150-acre

moorland lake. Through Malham passes the 250-mile long-distance pathway, the Pennine Way. The Yorkshire Dales National Park Centre is situated in the village.

MALMESBURY
Wiltshire 3 ST98
An abbey was founded at Malmesbury in the 7th century; King Athelstan, grandfather of King Alfred, was buried in its grounds. The town, which claims to be England's oldest borough, is still overlooked by its abbey, now the parish church. The present, partly ruined building, dates from the 12th century; the south porch has superb Romanesque carvings. A window depicts the local legend of Egelmer, a monk who attempted to fly with artificial wings. Malmesbury Abbey survived the Dissolution due to a local businessman installing looms in the building. The greatest of Malmesbury's beautiful Cotswold stone houses were built during the 17th and 18th centuries by the town's rich weavers. The base of Malmesbury Hill is surrounded by water and 6 bridges lead in to the Market Square. The octagonal Perpendicular market cross is Tudor. Thomas Hobbes the philosopher was born here in 1558, and Joseph Addison the writer and statesman was MP from 1710–19.

The bells in the tower of the 15th-century church at Garsdon 2¾ miles east, were given by Richard Moody, a servant of Henry VIII, who was given Garsdon Manor as a gift. He later sold the house to the Washingtons. The church contains the tombs of Sir Lawrence Washington, a cousin of the direct ancestors of George, that of a son and daughter and of Eleanor Guise, his wife. Sir Lawrence's tomb, restored in 1906 by Bishop Potter of New York, shows a stars and stripes dating from 1640.

South of Minety, to the east of Garsdon, was Penn's Lodge, seat of the Penn family, hereditary stewards of Malmesbury Abbey. Admiral Sir William Penn, father of William, the Quaker and founder of Pennsylvania, was born here.

MALPAS
Cheshire 14 SJ44
The name Malpas is derived from the Norman, meaning 'bad walk'. The badness was created by marauding Welshmen who, despite the building of a castle by the Normans, constantly harassed travellers along the road that marked the border between England

and Wales. A mixture of timbered and Georgian houses makes Malpas wholly delightful. The red sandstone church stands at the top of a flight of steps, beneath which is the village cross. Overton Hall is the ancestral home of the Allports. Various Allports settled in Pennsylvania, Virginia and Massachusetts and there are descendants in Mustoka, Ontario.

MALVERNS, THE
Hereford & Worcester 9 SO74
The Malvern Hills cover an area of 40 sq miles and are designated an area of outstanding natural beauty. The highest point is the Worcestershire Beacon – 1394ft above sea-level – but the flatness of the surrounding land makes them appear higher. Nestling at their foot are no fewer than six places each with the name of Malvern: Great Malvern, Little Malvern, North Malvern, West Malvern, Malvern Wells and Malvern Link. The hills are rich not only in beauty but also in mineral water. More than a million bottles are sold each year, some of them to HM Yacht *Britannia*: the Queen drinks it on her overseas tours as a precaution against ill-health. Great Malvern is also famous for its public school where C S Lewis was a pupil and W H Auden taught. Its drama festivals have associations with George Bernard Shaw, J M Barrie and the music of Elgar. On the road to Malvern Wells is Elgar's modest gravestone. Elgar used to enjoy flying kites on the hills – and during his walks found inspiration for his music. Jenny Lind, the 'Swedish Nightingale', is buried in Malvern cemetery. Her last operatic performance was in 1883 at a charity concert in Malvern.

MANCHESTER
Gtr Manchester 14 SJ89
Manchester was first a Roman camp and by the 14th century a small weaving town, but it was coal and the cotton trade which caused Manchester to grow into the vast industrial centre it became in the 18th and 19th centuries. The construction of the Manchester Ship Canal gave easy access to the flourishing port of Liverpool, and trade with the New World. Manchester and the textile industry underpinned the hopes of the American South that the cotton trade would eventually mean victory for their cause. However the cotton workers' sympathy lay with the Union and a statue of Abraham Lincoln in Plattfields Park commemorates this.

WASHINGTON COUNTRY

George Washington was born at Wakefield on the Potomac River on 11 February 1732 (Old Style), 22 February 1732 (New Style). Though 22 February later became the 'official' birthday, Washington himself often celebrated on the eleventh, or, on occasion, on both. He was the third son of Augustine Washington, the first child by his second wife, Mary Ball. On both sides of his family, Washington could claim 'Cavalier' descent. His great-grandfather, John Washington, had been driven from England because of the sufferings inflicted by the Pur-

George Washington portrait in Sulgrave Manor

itans on his father, the Reverend Lawrence Washington, a 'Scandalous, Malignant Priest', 'a common frequenter of Ale-Houses'. (He is buried in Maldon churchyard in Essex.) John reached the Northern Neck in 1657, as mate on the *Sea Horse of London*. Other members of the family served the Stuarts, and one held Worcester for the King for a few months in 1646. His mother, Mary Ball, much younger than her husband and socially his inferior, was an orphaned daughter of another fortune-seeker whose parents had left England during the Commonwealth. One of his grandmothers is buried in Whitehaven, Cumbria; his favourite half-brother, Lawrence (his

boyhood hero), his father, uncle and grandfather were all educated at Appleby Grammar School in Westmorland.

The Washington story goes back to 1183, when William de Hertburn, a tenant of the Bishop of Durham, became the owner of the manor of Wessyngton, and took its name for his family. One of the Wessyngtons was a notable prior and archivist of Washington Old Hall, in County Durham; it is a twelfth-century building, much restored in the seventeenth century, which was given to the American people in 1975. It stands now at the centre of Washington New Town.

John, the youngest son of Walter de Wessyngton, fought with Henry III at Lewes in 1264. He moved to Kendal in the Lake District and there are many Washington family links with Whitehaven and Northampton; his son in turn settled in Northamptonshire. The family profited from the Dissolution of the Monasteries

in Henry VIII's reign; Lawrence Washington, the most substantial of George Washington's ancestors in the two centuries before the first President's birth, bought the Sulgrave estate in 1539 for the sum of £324 14s 10d. Like George Washington himself, Lawrence's personal fortune owed much to his wife. It was he who built Sulgrave Manor, an unpretentious and comfortable residence of local stone. Before the last Washingtons left it in 1659, it had been a notable centre of the local wool trade. Windows in the manor and in Sulgrave parish church contain the oldest surviving representations of the Washington coat of arms, with its stars and stripes motif, which provided a basis for the American national flag.

The ancestral home was rescued from obscurity in January 1914 when a group of British subscribers purchased the house for the sum of £8400 as a memorial to two hundred years of Anglo-American peace. The King and the Prince of Wales sub-

scribed to the restoration fund, which owed much to Lord Lee of Fareham, who also gave Chequers to the nation for use as the country residence of the Prime Minister. Sulgrave Manor contains a number of Washington relics, and is maintained by an Anglo-American charitable Trust. After leaving Sulgrave Manor, part of the family moved to the picturesque village of Great Brington, in the churchyard of which many of the family are buried.

In the other direction from Banbury is Wroxton Abbey, dating from 1480, the home of Lord North, George III's Prime Minister, and George Washington's political opponent. It has been for some eight generations the home of the Marquess of Northampton. It is now the English campus of the Fairleigh Dickinson University of New Jersey.

Washington Old Hall

163

Harriet Beecher Stowe, the anti-slavery author of *Uncle Tom's Cabin*, was one of the many literary guests at the Manchester home of Mrs Gaskell, herself concerned with social injustice in Britain. With the growth of industry came apalling social conditions which ultimately led to riots, and the notorious Massacre of Peterloo in 1819. Manchester was also, however, a centre for Radical thought and the campaigning *Manchester Guardian* newspaper was founded in 1821 to give expression to new political ideas. Robert Owen, the Utopian Socialist who inspired co-operative communities such as New Harmony in Indiana, was active in Manchester where co-operative societies were strong.

The old city centre was a monument to Victorian pride and prosperity and the majestic Gothic town hall (OACT) stood at the centre of street upon street of solid Victorian commercial buildings, most of which have been swept away in an orgy of redevelopment. The past survives, however, in enclaves such as King's Street, and St Anne's Square, the most elegant part of the shopping centre, and in an old half-timbered pub, which used to stand in the Shambles, and is now marooned incongruously behind the new Piccadilly shopping arcades. Many emigrants left Manchester for America, among them Pilgrim Ralph Smith who came from Denton; the Reverend Samuel Gorton, of Gorton, founded Warwick, Rhode Island which he named after his patron the Earl of Warwick. From Hyde came Edward Hyde, a 17th-century Governor of North Carolina, and George Hide who governed New York a century later. In 1774, a Manchester factory worker Ann Lee left for America and, claiming special powers, founded the sect known as 'the Shakers' – seceders from the Society of Friends.

Manchester has three great libraries, the oldest being the 17th-century Chetham Library (open by arrangement), the first free public library in Europe. The John Rylands (OACT) has a superb collection of jewelled medieval bindings, and the Central Reference Library has one of the most extensive collections of books in the country; there is a lively theatre in the basement. The Free Trade Hall, although suffering bomb damage in 1940, has been restored, and is known as the birthplace of one of Manchester's great prides, the Hallé Orchestra. Among the many museums

Barton Swing Bridge on Manchester Ship Canal

and art galleries are the Whitworth Art Gallery, run by the university, which has a distinguished collection of Pre-Raphaelite and European paintings; the City Art Gallery which contains many treasures, including a collection of the Decorative Arts, furniture and sculpture, and more American works than any other provincial gallery, including Epstein's 'Joseph Conrad'; the Manchester Museum concentrating on archaeology and natural history; the Museum of Transport and the North-Western Museum of Science and Industry.

MANSFIELD
Nottinghamshire *15 SK56*
Mansfield today is an important industrial and mining centre. It used to be a small market town in the middle of **Sherwood Forest**. Indeed a plaque in Westgate marks the site of the so-called 'centre oak', which had to be felled in 1940. Evidence of Mansfield's antiquity can be found in the 'rock houses', or cliff-dwellings cut in the sandstone beside the Southwell road, which were still inhabited at the end of the 19th century. The town is dominated by a vast railway viaduct and in the market place stands the Moot Hall, erected in 1752. While living in Mansfield in 1647, George Fox founded the Society of Friends.

MARGATE
Kent *6 TR37*
In the 18th century the English discovered that sea-bathing was good for the health. The bathing machine was invented by a Margate Quaker

named Benjamin Beale. Tom Paine, Keats and Mary and Charles Lamb were among those who stayed here. 20th-century Margate is often called the Blackpool of the South and has, in Dreamland, a full-scale funfair. Amidst all the modern entertainments, Margate preserves two historic buildings: Salmeston Grange (OACT), a restored medieval grange, and the Tudor House (OACT) which contains the town's museum. A plaque on Droit Building at the pierhead recalls the Dunkirk evacuation in World War II.

MARKET BOSWORTH
Leicestershire *10 SK40*
A tree-lined avenue marks the entrance to this small stone-built town, where markets have been held since 1285.

Market Bosworth Grammar School

The present market is one of only seven in England which are privately owned. The Dixie family came to live in the local manor house in 1567 and are still there, the parish church has many Dixie memorials and the local school was endowed by the family. Thomas Hooker, (born in Markfield, Leicester) founder of Hartford, Connecticut began his education here, later winning a scholarship to Cambridge, where he was a contemporary of John Harvard. Samuel Johnson taught at the school. Market Bosworth lies 1 mile north of Bosworth Field, where in 1485 the Wars of the Roses were brought to a close when Richard III was slain by Henry Tudor. The battlefield has a battle trail and an information centre.

MARKET HARBOROUGH
Leicestershire *10 SP78*
Deep in hunting country – in this case, the Fernie Hunt – Market Harborough was the creation of Henry II. Some say that the church of St Dionysius was founded by John of Gaunt – though the decorations and the Perpendicular style of architecture suggests that this is unlikely. Every November, the bells are rung to celebrate the rescue of a merchant who lost his way on the Welland marshes in 1500. The ringers receive the modest reward of 'one shilling for beer'. At West Langton, 4½ miles north west, Langton Hall (OACT), dating from the 15th century, contains a fine collection of furniture.

MARLBOROUGH
Wiltshire *3 SU16*
Marlborough College, the famous public school attended by Sir John Betjeman and William Morris, to name but two ex-pupils, is said to be the burial place of King Arthur's magician, Merlin. The wide High Street of the town is particularly attractive, with its handsome colonnades and a church at either end. In the 17th century Marlborough suffered a series of disastrous fires which caused the local authorities to ban the use of thatch.

MARLOW
Buckinghamshire *4 SU88*
The most outstanding feature of this busy Thames-side town is its elegant suspension bridge, begun in 1829. Beside the bridge is a monument to Charles Frohman the theatrical manager drowned aboard the *Titanic* in 1912. The riverside view is dominated by the spire of All Saints

parish church, inside which is the Horsepoole monument bearing the Washington coat of arms. Meanwhile, St Peter's Church preserves an object said to be the hand of St James the Apostle, brought here from Reading Abbey. The Shelleys lived at Albion House, West Street and it was here that Mary wrote *Frankenstein* (1818). Dick Turpin is said to have frequented the Crown Hotel and the Compleat Angler Inn is named after Izaak Walton, who fished here. The willow tree in the gardens is said to have been planted by the Duke of Wellington.

MARSTON MOOR
N Yorkshire *15 SE45*
On 2 July 1644, a battle was fought here that marked a turning point in the Civil War. Sir Thomas Fairfax had learned that 20,000 Royalists, under Prince Rupert, were on their way from Lancashire to join the King. His object was to prevent these reinforcements from linking up with the main army. He failed, and the Royalists appeared to have won. Later in the day, however, Cromwell led a cavalry charge, which took the opposition's commanders, who were at supper, by surprise. By 10 pm 4000 Royalist troops lay dead; while only 300 Roundheads lost their lives.

MATLOCK
Derbyshire *15 SK36*
There are several Matlocks – each adjoining the other and following the line of the beautifully wooded Derwent Valley. Matlock Bath became famous as a spa in the 19th century. The Grand Pavilion is the scene of an annual festival, and between the Pavilion and the river, the Derwent Gardens display their finery and contain some splendid grottoes. On the far bank, the 'Lovers' Walks' are suitably romantic. The town is dominated by the Heights of Abraham, which rise to 1000ft. They were so named by an officer who had fought with Wolfe at Quebec, and who likened them to the plateau on which the General fought his last battle. The Victoria Prospect Tower, perched on the highest point, affords impressive views, and Nestus Mine and Great Masson Cavern are exciting to explore, as is the Peak District Mining Museum. Near Matlock, Riber Castle (OACT) has a fauna reserve and a collection of rare breeds of farm animals. Honest John Oliver, premier of British Columbia (1918–27) was born in Hartington, 15 miles west.

MAUCHLINE
Strathclyde *22 NS42*
Robert Burns lived with his family 2½ miles north west at Lochlea until his father's death in 1784. In 1788, he began his married life in the building now named Burns' House in Mauchline. Gavin Hamilton, the friend at whose house the ceremony took place, is buried in the churchyard – and so, too, are some of the poet's children. Mauchline is mentioned in several of Burns' works, and you can still take a drink at the Possie Nansie's Tavern. The Memorial Tower contains a Burns museum. Apart from its associations with the bard, Mauchline is famous for its particularly fine curling stones.

MAYBOLE
Strathclyde *22 NS30*
Maybole used to be the capital of Carrick – the southern division of Ayrshire. It was also the stronghold of the redoubtable Earls of Cassillis, heads of the Kennedys. 28 baronial mansions have existed in the area, but only one survives – the restored 17th-century 'Castle' in the High Street, which was originally the Earl's town house. 2 miles south west of the town are the ruins of 13th-century Crossraguel Abbey. 5 miles north east on the road to the fishing village of Dunure is a phenomenon known as the 'Electric Brae', where the road appears to descend when in fact it ascends.

MEDMENHAM
Buckinghamshire *4 SU88*
Medmenham, with its handsome church and its no less picturesque Dog and Badger Inn stands beside the Thames. The ruined abbey – now part of a private house – was where Sir Francis Dashwood and his fellow members of the notorious Hell Fire Club met in the mid 18th century.

MELBOURNE
Derbyshire *10 SK32*
Lord Melbourne (1779–1848), Queen Victoria's first Prime Minister, was born at the Hall (OACT). Years later, Melbourne in Australia, still no more than a small settlement, was named after him. Melbourne Hall is one of Derbyshire's most delightful stately homes. The formal gardens were laid out by Henry Wise in the style of Versailles. The splendid wrought-iron pergola known as the 'Bird Cage' is the work of Robert Bakewell. Thomas Cook, who created package travel, was Melbourne's other famous son.

MELROSE
Borders *24 NT53*
The best description of Melrose Abbey
(AM) is by Sir Walter Scott in *The Lay
of the Last Minstrel*. Founded in 1136
by David I for Cistercian monks from
Rievaulx in Yorkshire, it is
undoubtedly the finest ruined abbey in
Scotland. The heart of Robert the
Bruce is said to be buried beneath the
east window of the chancel. He was to
have been laid to rest in the Holy
Land, but Sir James Douglas, who was
carrying his heart there, was killed
fighting the Moors in Spain. According
to tradition, Sir James hurled the
casket at the enemy shouting 'Go first,
brave heart.' Bruce's heart was later
returned to Scotland and buried here.
Sir Walter Scott made his home at
Abbotsford House (OACT), 2 miles
west of Melrose. A fine example of the
Scottish Baronial style, the house
contains many mementoes of the man
who wrote so vividly of the Borders
and Scotland's history, including his
9000 volume library. The house is
occupied by a descendant. The writer
himself, is buried 7 miles away at
Dryburgh Abbey.

MELTON MOWBRAY
Leicestershire *10 SK71*
Pork pies, Stilton cheese, and the
Quorn Hunt are Melton Mowbray's
most famous contributions to English
life. On a more spiritual level St
Mary's Church, with its 100ft tower, is
one of the finest parish churches in
Leicestershire. Alongside is a house
given by Henry VIII to Ann of Cleves
'so long as she remained in England'.
However, the 'Flanders mare' bolted
and there is nothing to suggest she ever
lived in the house. At Thorpe End is
the Melton Carnegie Museum of Local
History.

MENABILLY
Cornwall *1 SX05*
Menabilly, near **Fowey**, was the home
for 26 years of the writer Daphne Du
Maurier. It is a very secret place,
concealed by trees from even the most
prying eyes. It appears in *The King's
General* and it can be identified
without much difficulty as Manderley
– the setting of *Rebecca*, though
Victorian Gothic Caerhays, a few
miles along the coast, was recently
used in a television adaptation. The
boathouse in which Rebecca died in
the novel still stands at Polridmouth
beach. It has been restored and
overlooks a lake separated from the
shore by a stone wall.

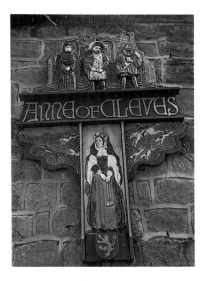

Plaque to Anne of Cleves, Melton Mowbray

MENAI BRIDGE
Gwynedd *13 SH57*
One mile to the west was Stephenson's
tubular railway bridge. Severely
damaged by fire in 1970, it was later
rebuilt with open steel arches and a
new road deck above, carrying the A5
to Holyhead. The first bridge to link
Anglesey with Gwynedd was designed
by Thomas Telford in 1826. Not only
is it 1000ft long, 28ft wide and 100ft
above the highest level of the tide: it
was also the first major suspension
bridge to be built – a triumph of 19th-
century engineering. In Water Street is
a fascinating Museum of Childhood.

MENSTRIE
Central *22 NS89*
Lying in the shadow of 1375ft Dumyat
peak, Menstrie is notable for its large
distillery and its castle (NTS). The
latter, built in the 16th century, was
the birthplace of Sir William
Alexander, who, as James VI's
Lieutenant for the plantation of Nova
Scotia, founded the Canadian
province. One of the rooms contains
107 coats of arms of existing baronets
belonging to an Order created in 1625
to finance the Nova Scotia project.
Other rooms have been furnished as
Nova Scotia commemoration rooms.
In 1734, Sir Ralph Abercromby, victor
of the Battle of Aboukir Bay in 1801
(when he was killed) in the Napoleonic
Wars, was born in the town.

MERIDEN
W Midlands *10 SP28*
In the centre of the village, a medieval
cross marks the centre – of England.
Its exactitude is open to question, but
most Meriden inhabitants support the

theory. Meriden also has one of the
oldest archery societies in the country,
the Woodmen of Arden, which was
formed in 1785. In 1788, it established
its headquarters in Forest Hall – just to
the west of centre.

MERTHYR TYDFIL
Mid Glamorgan *8 SO00*
Originally named after a martyred
Christian princess, modern Merthyr
Tydfil was created and then destroyed
by the vagaries of the iron and coal
industries. In 1804, the first steam
locomotive – the invention of the
Cornish genius Richard Trevethick –
was built here. By 1831, Merthyr was
the largest iron and steel
manufacturing centre in the world –
and the largest town in Wales. Its
population exceeded the sum of
inhabitants of Swansea, Newport and
Cardiff. A century later saw Merthyr
Tydfil sadly reduced. $\frac{1}{5}$ of its people
was unemployed: many had moved on
to seek livelihoods elsewhere and the
gates of the ironworks were closed.
Keir Hardie, the pioneer of British
Socialism, represented Merthyr in the
House of Commons at the turn of the
century. **Cyfarthfa** Castle (OACT),
built by the ironmaster William
Crawshay, is now used as a museum
and art gallery. Train rides into the
Brecon Beacons can be taken from
Pant station (off A465) on the Brecon
Mountain Railway. 10 miles south is
Aberfan, the scene of an industrial
tragedy in 1966, when a slagheap
collapsed burying a school and killing
144 people.

METHLICK
Grampian *27 NJ83*
For over 500 years, Haddo House
(NTS), 2 miles south east of Methlick,
was the seat of the Gordons of Haddo,
Earls of Aberdeen. The present
building is a handsome Georgian
mansion built by William Adam in
1732; operas and concerts are
performed here. Also in the vicinity are
the ruins of Gight Castle. Situated in a
delightfully wooded setting, it has
never recovered from the events of
1639, when it was besieged by the
Duke of Montrose. Catherine Gordon
of Gight, Lord Byron's mother, was
heiress to the estate, but had to sell it
to pay her husband's debts.

MEVAGISSEY
Cornwall *1 SX04*
In summer, Mevagissey is so crowded
with tourists that it is hard to
appreciate the beauties of this

delightful little fishing village. As well as pilchard fishing, smuggling was once an important local industry: Mevagissey-built boats were so fast they could outsail the Revenue cutters. A former boatbuilder's workshop now contains a folk museum (OACT).

MEY
Highland   *30 ND27*
The Castle of Mey is the Queen Mother's personal residence in Scotland, purchased in 1953. Overlooking the Pentland Firth, and not far from John o'Groats, the setting is bleak. Nevertheless, the gardens (OACT) are magnificent and the Queen Mother has carried out a great deal of renovation.

MICKLETON
Gloucestershire   *10 SP14*
Hidcote Manor Gardens, (NT), which are laid out as an American Garden, lie just outside the attractive village and adjoining them is Kiftsgate Court Garden (OACT), famous for its display of old-fashioned roses, among them the R Filipes Kiftsgate, heralded as the largest rose in England.

MIDDLEHAM
N Yorkshire   *20 SE18*
Formerly the capital of Wensleydale, Middleham is a small but pretty village. The castle (AM), now in ruins, was once known as 'the Windsor of the North', when the great Neville family owned it. Richard III acquired it in 1471, and his eldest son was born here. The 13th-century chapel and the 14th-century gatehouse survive.

MIDDLESBROUGH
Cleveland   *20 NZ41*
In 1831 work began on an extension of the Stockton and Darlington Railway – with dramatic effects on Middlesbrough. What had been a village community of about 40 people became transformed during the next four decades into a town with 40,000 inhabitants. Its importance came partly from the docks, from which coal mined in South Durham was exported – and partly from the discovery of iron ore in the Cleveland Hills where the first iron works opened in 1841. The Dorman Museum tells the history of Cleveland, and at nearby Marton is the Captain Cook Birthplace Museum: the great explorer was born here in 1728. Middlesbrough is not only known for industry but also for its parks and in 1982 it was declared Britain's Floral City. Ormesby Hall is on the outskirts.

MIDDLETON-IN-TEESDALE
Co Durham   *19 NY92*
Between the mid 18th and early 20th centuries, Teesdale prospered from its lead mines, which were run by a Quaker-owned organization named the London Lead Company. The firm's preoccupation with the welfare of its employees is evident in the fine stone buildings. The former head office, Middleton House, now provides accommodation for private shooting parties. The village church has a detached bell tower – rare in this part of the country. One of its three bells can be traced back to 1558. Not far away are the famous waterfalls: Cauldron Snout and **High Force**.

MIDDLE WOODFORD
Wiltshire   *3 SU13*
Some time in the 14th century, Heale House at Middle Woodford was built. Charles II took shelter there five days after the Battle of Worcester in 1651. But many years later, in 1835, a fire broke out. Parts of the building survived; others have since been restored. Nowadays, it looks much as Charles II found it. The gardens, covering 5 acres (OACT), are attractive – especially the water garden with its magnolias and acers, which surrounds a Japanese teahouse and is spanned by a nicely designed bridge.

MIDHURST
W Sussex   *4 SU82*
Midhurst has associations with H G Wells, who worked in a chemist's shop and studied and, later, taught at the grammar school. The 17th-century house Cowdray Park (OACT), now in ruins, was originally the home of Sir Anthony Browne, Master of Horse to Henry VIII. Early in the 20th century, it was bought by Viscount Cowdray of Midhurst who restored it. Within the park, there is a famous polo ground; matches are played at weekends during the season, which lasts from April to August. The Angel Hotel was named by a group of Pilgrim Fathers travelling to the port of Southampton – other Angel Inns were often named in a similar way. Midhurst's Curfew Gardens were given by a grateful traveller who found his way by following the sound of Midhurst's church bells. At 8pm each evening the curfew is still rung.

MILDENHALL
Suffolk   *12 TL77*
The setting for the huge American Air Force base is, in fact, a rather lovely village situated beside the River Lark. Of particular interest is the church of St Mary, with its 110ft tower and its elaborately carved roof. Biblical scenes, a host of angels, and fantastic beasts are depicted. The Puritan zealots did their best to destroy it in the 17th century, but only managed to fire off a few shots in its direction. In 1946, the Mildenhall Treasure – which consisted of a rich hoard of 4th-century Roman silver dishes, some of them probably manufactured in Rome itself – was discovered at nearby Thistley Green. It is now in the British Museum.

MILFORD HAVEN
Dyfed   *7 SM80*
Milford Haven (the haven) is an inlet 20 miles long, cutting into the south-west corner of Wales. Nelson described it as one of the world's finest natural harbours. A century or so earlier, Defoe had listed 16 creeks, 5 bays and 13 anchorages for shipping. He suggested that a thousand vessels could moor there 'and not the top mast of one be seen from another'. Henry II used it as a base for his invasion of Ireland in 1171. In 1485, Henry Tudor landed on its shore before proceeding to Bosworth Field and winning the crown of England. Milford Haven (the town) was founded in 1793 on land belonging to Sir William Hamilton, husband of Nelson's mistress. Samuel Starbuck and other religious dissidents from America established the port in order to continue their whale oil business during the Revolutionary War. The community originated in East Anglia, travelled to Nantucket and from there went to Nova Scotia. Milford Haven was patterned on New Amsterdam (New York), with three straight streets parallel to the waterfront crossed at right angles by three others. The port is now a major oil terminal.

MILTON ABBAS
Dorset   *3 ST80*
The abbey founded by Athelstan in 938 was eventually converted into a mansion in the 18th century by Joseph Damer, subsequently Earl of Dorchester. The mansion (OACT) is now a public school, and the magnificent abbey church a school chapel. Milton Abbas was a market town, which Damer had razed because it obscured his view, and created instead a model village of thatched cottages. Robert Worth Bingham, US Ambassador in London, claimed

Bingham's Melcombe just to the west as his ancestral home. The manor has an ancient bowling green and a grand yew hedge.

MILTON KEYNES
Buckinghamshire *10 SP83*
In the late 1960s, the wind of change blew on Milton Keynes, when this formerly rather picturesque little village hard by the M1 was designated a New Town. The overwhelming impression nowadays is of ring-roads, concrete, walls of glass, and the very modern architecture of the vast shopping centre. Among the new enterprises is the Open University, which was established in 1971. North west of Milton Keynes, Stony Stratford was the birthplace of Theophilus Eaton, founder and life Governor of New Haven, Connecticut. Eaton had connections with the Yale family. The tower windmill at Bradwell was restored with donations from American servicemen stationed there during the War.

Milton Abbas

MINCHINHAMPTON
Gloucestershire *3 SO80*
Minchinhampton, crowning a high ridge of the Cotswolds, has ancient links with Normandy: William I's wife, Matilda, persuaded the king to give the Manor of Hampton to the

Abbaye-aux Dames at Caen. The restored cruciform church, with its curious tower, is interesting, as is the 17th-century market hall, raised on a forest of pillars. Anyone concerned with a child's health may care to consult the perforated Long Stone. It displays a legendary (though, perhaps, not infallible) cure for infantile rickets. For golfers, the Minchinhampton course is famous.

MINEHEAD
Somerset *2 SS94*
Until the late 18th century, Minehead used to be quite an important port – for herring fishing and for the shipping of wool, hides, cattle and coal. But then the harbour began to silt up, and the herring shoals vanished. Minehead fell upon hard times until, in 1854, the railway came to the rescue and the town opened its doors to tourists. Traces of its former role can be seen in the 1630 Fishermen's Chapel. Every May Day, a Hobby Horse festival takes place, similar to that at **Padstow**.

MINIONS
Cornwall *1 SX27*
This area of **Bodmin Moor** is rich in ancient monuments, few more impressive than the line of three neighbouring circles of standing stones known as The Hurlers. A centuries-old legend, reported by the 16th-century historian Camden, explains the stones as 'men sometime transformed into stones, for profaning the Lord's Day with hurling the ball.' Camden did not believe the tale, and the stones are, of course, far more ancient than the coming of Christianity to these shores. The nearby Round Barrow, on the summit of the hill, once yielded an early Bronze Age treasure of considerable importance, now in the British Museum.

MINSTEAD
Hampshire *4 SU21*
An enchanting New Forest village where the original main street leads to the church, notable for its 'parlour pews' – each one private, and belonging to the occupants of the big houses in the neighbourhood. Sir Arthur Conan Doyle is buried in the graveyard. The creator of Sherlock Holmes greatly loved the New Forest, spending much of his last years at Bignell Wood in Minstead. Conan Doyle's historical novel *The White Company* was set in the area and was

written 2 miles south of Minstead at Emery Down. Furzey Gardens (OACT) covers 8 acres of woodland glades, in the midst of which is an Art and Craft Gallery.

Six miles south west of Minstead, an altar and wooden cross stand on Mogshade Hill near Bolderwood, where the 3rd Canadian Division prayed on the day before D-Day, 1944.

MINSTER LOVELL
Oxfordshire *10 SP31*
Situated beside the River Windrush, which ambles companionably by, Minster Lovell is the most beautiful village in the area. It is, then, strange to find its ruined 15th-century hall (AM) so haunted by tragedy. Francis Lovell (or 'Lovell the Dog' as his critics called him) was a follower of Richard III. After the disaster at Bosworth, he escaped to the Continent. Two years later, he unwisely returned to England to carry out a plot against Henry VII and to put the pretender Lambert Simnel on the throne. Hounded by the authorities, he found sanctuary in the Hall, where he went to earth in a small room. And there, by all accounts, he starved to death when the only servant who knew his whereabouts died. In 1718, a skeleton sitting at a table, with the skeleton of his faithful dog, was discovered, during alterations. Another tale, that of the Mistletoe Bough, concerns the bride of one of the Lovells who, during a game of hide-and-seek hid in an old chest, the lid of which she could not then raise. She was never found . . . but years later a skeleton was found in that chest.

MOELFRE
Anglesey *13 SH58*
Moelfre on the north coast was the birthplace of Goronwy Owen, the Welsh poet and earlier settler of Brunswick County, Virginia. It was off here that the *Royal Charter* was wrecked in a storm in 1859. 460 lives were lost and bullion and valuables worth over £400,000 from Australia were later recovered. The story was used by Dickens in *The Uncommercial Traveller*.

MOFFAT
Dumfries & Galloway *23 NT10*
Moffat lies at the heart of the Lowlands sheep farming country. In the High Street a large bronze ram tops the column fountain, a reminder of the prosperity of the wool trade brought to the town. Moffat's popularity was boosted in the 17th century with the

discovery of a sulphur spring just to the north. Among the distinguished visitors who came to take the waters were James Boswell, and Robert Burns who wrote the drinking song 'O Willie brew'd a peck o' Malt' here. Moffat's famous sons include John Macadam, the road engineer, and Air Chief Marshall Lord Dowding, whose airmen won the Battle of Britain. St Ninian's preparatory school was founded by Lord Dowding's father. Enriching the town is the magnificent scenery of the Annandale hill country. The river Annan provides excellent fishing and walkers will delight in the 200ft Grey Mare's Tail waterfall described by Scott in *Marmion*, and the sheer-sided Devil's Beef Tub, mentioned in *Red Gauntlet* and thought to have been a cattle raiders' cache.

MOLD
Clwyd *14 SJ26*
Mold is the administrative centre of Clwyd. After the Norman conquest, Lord Robert de Monte Alto built a castle on a mound, north of the town, however nothing remains of it. The 15th-century church contains some remarkable animal frescoes. Mold was the birthplace of the Welsh language writer Daniel Owen. Owen came from a poor family, but became a preacher and studied at the Calvinistic College in **Bala**, returning to Mold to support his family.

MONIAIVE
Dumfries & Galloway *22 NX79*
The village has a monument to James Renwick – the last of the Covenanters to die for the cause – who was executed at Edinburgh, in 1688, aged 26. It also has Maxwelton House (OACT), the family home of Annie Laurie (1682–1764), whose rejected suitor William Douglas immortalized her in a poem, which was put to music in 1755. Annie eventually married and lived at Craigdarroch 2½ miles west of Moniaive in a William Adam house. She is buried in the churchyard at Glencairn near Maxwelton.

MONMOUTH
Gwent *9 SO51*
The Romans established *Blestium*, a military base, at the site between three rivers where Monmouth now stands. Some centuries later the Normans built a castle, later to become the birthplace of Henry V, outside the 18th-century Shire Hall. The castle was destroyed in the Civil War, but the Monnow Bridge,

Monnow Bridge, Monmouth

Britain's only surviving fortified bridge, remains. Its 13th-century tower formed one of the four medieval gates to the town. Nelson visited the town in 1802, and the Monmouth Museum contains his sword and models of his ships, while the Naval Temple (NT) on Kymin Hill has many maritime relics. Monmouth was also the birthplace of C S Rolls – the 'Rolls' of Rolls-Royce, whose father, Lord Llangattock, lived near Monmouth.

MONTACUTE
Somerset *3 ST51*
Montacute (the name comes from the Latin *mons acutus*, meaning 'steep hill') is an ancient and lovely village of golden Ham stone, the showpiece of which is the magnificent Tudor mansion, Montacute House (NT). Its superb Long Gallery contains a collection of Tudor and Stuart portraits from the National Portrait Gallery. Wooded St Michael's Hill, once the site of a Norman castle, is topped by an 18th-century folly. In the 11th century a miracle-working cross was apparently unearthed from the hill and taken to **Waltham Abbey**. Sir Edward Phelips, for whom Montacute was built, led the prosecution speeches at the trial of Guy Fawkes in 1606. A later occupant was Lord Curzon, who lived here between 1915 and 1925.

Five miles west, at South Petherton, the Reverend Thomas Coke was

dismissed as curate in 1776 for holding open air services similar to those of John Wesley. Coke was eventually to found the American Methodist Episcopal Church.

MONTGOMERY
Powys *8 SO29*
Elizabethan, Jacobean and Georgian houses characterize the streets of this handsome small town, formerly the county capital of Montgomeryshire. The town's name comes from its first Norman overlord, Roger de Montgomery. The castle he built was rebuilt in the reign of Henry III but is now a ruin (AM). A curiosity in the churchyard is the grave of John Davies, hanged in 1821 for highway robbery. He died protesting his innocence and swore that no grass would grow on his grave for 100 years: there is reported still to be a bald patch. The church itself has interesting monuments to the Herbert family who owned the castle. The 17th-century cleric and poet George Herbert was a member of this family.

MONTROSE
Tayside *27 NO75*
Montrose, with its 4 sq-mile basin on the River Esk, is one of several Scottish ports that have gained a new lease of life from servicing North Sea oil rigs. The town was the birthplace in 1612 of James Graham, Marquess of

Montrose, one of Scotland's greatest soldiers who was born here in a house in Castle Place, Old Montrose. The High Street is dominated by the 220ft church steeple; many small courtyards lead off the street and no two are alike. A curfew is rung every night at 10pm from St Peter's Church. The Museum and Art Gallery (OACT) tells the long, interesting history of this old royal burgh.

MORETON-IN-MARSH
Gloucestershire   *10 SP23*
The main street of this attractive village on the edge of the Cotswolds was part of the Roman highway known as the Fosse Way. Overlooking it, the Curfew Tower includes a lock-up in its amenities. 2 miles to the north west of Moreton-in-Marsh is the extensive Batsford Arboretum and 3 miles to the south west is Sezincote (OACT), an interesting house, said to have been the inspiration for Brighton Pavilion, with an attractive water garden.

MORPETH
Northumberland   *20 NZ28*
Morpeth is an attractive town, built on a bend of the River Wansbeck and a good starting point from which to explore the Northumberland hills and coast. The gatehouse is all that remains of the castle, though a footpath near the site affords good views of the town. Morpeth's clock tower, designed by Vanbrugh, used to serve also as a prison and still diligently sounds the curfew each evening. St Mary's Church preserves a 14th-century 'Tree of Jesse' window, and in the churchyard stands a 19th-century watchtower, built to protect the graves from body snatchers.

Sir George Downing, an early graduate of Harvard and nephew of John Winthrop, was MP for Morpeth from 1660 until his death in 1684. His name is recalled in Downing Street, London.

MORWELLHAM
Devon   *2 SX46*
Morwellham Quay, near Tavistock, developed as a port for copper mines. In the late 19th century it was the largest exporter of raw arsenic, used for lead bullets and insecticides. Much of this trade was with North America, where insecticides were needed to control the boll weevil on the Southern cotton plantations. At the Morwellham Open Air Musuem quay workers, coachmen, blacksmiths and coopers dressed in period costume re-enact scenes from the past.

MOTTISFONT
Hampshire   *4 SU32*
Mottisfont Abbey (NT), near the River Test, is a lovely sight – with elegant lawns, some enormous old trees, and with water meadows beyond. Founded by the Austin Canons at the beginning of the 13th century, Henry VIII gave the priory to his Lord Chamberlain – William, Lord Sandys – at the Dissolution. Sandys pulled down much of it, converting the nave of the abbey church into a house.

MOUSEHOLE
Cornwall   *1 SW42*
This is a pretty little village that used to thrive off its harvest of pilchards. In 1595, four Spanish galleys eluded the Elizabethan warships, and landed 200 Spaniards – who burned Mousehole to the ground. Only the 15th-century Keigwin Arms (no longer a pub) survived. Dolly Pentreath, the last person known to have spoken Cornish as her native tongue, died here in 1777.

MUCH HADHAM
Hertfordshire   *11 TL41*
There are those who hold that Much Hadham is the prettiest village in Hertfordshire, and they may very well be right. The long main street is rich with Georgian and other period houses – nearly all of them worth a second glance. For nearly 900 years, Much Hadham was a manor of the Bishop of London, who used the Palace as his out-of-town retreat. It was also the birthplace of Edmund Tudor, father of Henry VII. The sculptor Henry Moore has made his home here; two heads sculpted by him are in the church.

MUCH WENLOCK
Shropshire   *9 SO69*
Much Wenlock lies at the northern end of Wenlock Edge, the landscape celebrated in the poetry of A E Housman. The atmosphere of a medieval market town prevails. The stocks still stand outside the Guildhall (OACT), which rests on wooden pillars, and the old Market Hall is now a local history museum (OACT). A lane leads to the ruins of St Mildburga's Priory, founded in the 11th century.

MULLION
Cornwall   *1 SW61*
Mullion church has a magnificent set of 16th-century bench ends and parts of the tower are built of serpentine, a multi-coloured stone peculiar to the Lizard peninsula. The village –

Mousehole

perhaps the most beautiful in Cornwall – looks out onto Mullion Cove.

Two miles north, the tiny church at Cury contains a stained glass memorial window to Robert Bonython, an ancestor of the poet Longfellow. 1 mile north west is Poldhu Point and the cave where Marconi received the first ever transatlantic morse signals in 1901. The site of the radio station is marked by a memorial.

MUMBLES, THE
W Glamorgan   *7 SS68*
The Mumbles is a peninsula with two islands at its head, on the outer of which there is a lighthouse that was established in 1794. The Mumbles, and Oystermouth, are now a popular resort with a pier (1898), Winter Gardens, and vestiges of the Mumbles railway – which ran from Oystermouth to Mumbles Head (but was, alas, axed in 1960). Oystermouth Castle ruins date from the 13th and 14th centuries (OACT). A few miles north west is Ilston, where the ruins of Wales' first Baptist church, founded in 1647 by John Miles, can be seen. Difficulties forced Miles to leave Wales in 1662; he and a group of Baptists emigrated to Massachusetts where they founded Swanzey.

MUNCASTER
Cumbria   *18 SD19*
Muncaster Castle (OACT) stands on land that has been owned by the Pennington family since the 13th century. It was reconstructed in the 19th century but one of the original towers survives. It contains among many other things, a bowl presented by Henry VI, who found sanctuary there after his defeat at the Battle of Towton in 1464. This, known as the 'luck' of Muncaster, is said to ensure the unbroken succession of the Pennington family who have lived here since the 13th century. The grounds contain a bird garden, a Himalayan bear garden, and a flamingo pool. At Muncaster Mill (OACT), 1 mile away you can buy stoneground flour.

BENJAMIN FRANKLIN'S BRITAIN

Like many of the Washingtons, the Franklin roots lie deep in Northamptonshire soil, in Ecton, five miles from the county town, where they were for generations yeomen and blacksmiths – 'leather-apron' men – and dedicated Protestants. Franklin enjoyed tracing his ancestors and visiting his relatives in his London years from 1757 to 1762, and again from 1764 to 1775. Benjamin's father Josiah emigrated in 1685; he was already married, and had three children. In all, from two wives, he had seventeen children; Benjamin was the youngest boy and, 'born on a Sunday' to a very pious and fecund Nantucket girl, was at first dedicated to the church. It would have been a singularly inappropriate vocation, although in the pro-verbs of *Poor Richard*, as in the Biblical cadences in his prose style, he reveals he was very much a product of the strict Calvinist home in Milk Street, Boston.

Throughout his fifteen years on mission in London, Franklin lived in Craven Street off the Strand. It became a second home, a scientific workshop and a strategic centre; he haunted the coffee shops of the Strand, Fleet Street and St James's, especially the Pennsylvania coffee house in Birchin Lane or the London House at 42 Ludgate Hill. His natural cronies were the Scots and Dissenting journalists, and he greatly enjoyed his visits to Scotland, notably to Edinburgh, of which city he became a Freeman in 1768, to St Andrews where he was awarded an LLD (at the time it had more pubs than students, it should be said) and the homes of Scottish friends, notably that of Lord Kames in Blair Drummond in Perthshire, where the trees he planted still flourish. The six weeks of 'densest happiness' he ever had, he said, were spent in Scotland. He was the guest of Lord Despencer (Francis Dashwood) in his exotic estate at West Wycombe, and of Lord Shelburne, and it was to his stay at Twyford near Winchester as the guest of Bishop Shipley that we owe the first part of his *Autobiography*. He returned home on the *Pennsylvania Packet* in March–April 1775; the Declaration of Independence, which, with Jefferson, he helped draft, came a year later.

Places to Visit

36, Craven Street, London (now a Franklin Centre).
Twyford House, near Winchester.
West Wycombe, Buckinghamshire.

Further Reading

Whitfield Bell, '*My Dear Girl*', his delightful letters, especially to the Shipley girls (Philadelphia, American Philosophical Society 1956)
Claude Lopez, *The Private Franklin* (Norton 1975)
Nolan, *Benjamin Franklin in Scotland and Ireland* (University of Pennsylvania Press 1956)
Esmond Wright, *Franklin of Philadelphia* (Harvard University Press 1986)

Franklin's Experiment

N

NAILSWORTH
Gloucestershire *3 ST89*
Nailsworth is an ancient wool town. In the steep narrow streets are several good examples of Georgian architecture. The former cloth mills are fascinating to anyone remotely interested in industrial archaeology, and the 1680 Friends Meeting House deserves to be seen. The 'Supertramp' poet, W H Davies, who wrote 'What is this life if, full of care, We have no time to stand and stare?', died here in 1940. Nailsworth Ladder, a hill with a 1:3 gradient, is used for car-testing.

NAIRN
Highland *26 NH85*
Nairn has sometimes been called the Brighton of the North. As this suggests it is a popular seaside resort – with 3 golf courses, a climate that shows a surprisingly sunny disposition and an annual Highland Games. The harbour was made to a plan by Thomas Telford. About 3 miles to the south, Rait Castle, a 14th-century ruin, was the scene of a massacre of the Comyns by the Mackintoshes.

NASEBY
Northamptonshire *10 SP67*
Naseby is famous for its Civil War battle, fought in 1645. The Royalists might have fared better if Prince Rupert of the Rhine had not ridden off into the town to attack the Roundheads' baggage train – thus exposing a flank. But the Royalist defeat was eclipsed by the capture of letters written by King Charles seeking help from foreign powers. The discovery caused many who had hitherto been indifferent to the outcome of the war to take Parliament's side. A memorial marks the scene of the affray and there is a Battle and Farm Museum nearby (OACT).

NEEDHAM MARKET
Suffolk *12 TM05*
Joseph Priestley, a minister of the Congregational Church at Needham Market, was also a gifted scientist. In 1774, he isolated a gas which he called 'Dephlogisticated air', in other words, he 'discovered' oxygen. Benjamin Franklin encouraged his scientific interests. In 1793 he publicly supported the French Revolution and was forced to leave England. He settled in America where he was a friend of Jefferson and John Adams. He died in 1804 in Northumberland, Pennsylvania. The village church has a fine wooden hammerbeam roof.

NETHER STOWEY
Somerset *2 ST13*
The cottage (NT) in which Samuel Taylor Coleridge wrote 'The Rime of the Ancient Mariner' and 'Kubla Khan' in this attractive village can be visited. Adjoining the church is Stowey Court which dates from the 15th century. The adjacent **Quantock Hills** provide fine country for excursions.

NETHER WINCHENDON
Buckinghamshire *4 SP70*
Nether Winchendon House (OACT) 7 miles south west of **Aylesbury** is a Tudor manor to which additions were made in the 18th century. Originally the home of monks who served in the churches and worked the land, it later became the property of Sir Francis Bernard who, in 1758, was appointed Governor of New Jersey – and then of Massachusetts Bay in 1760. The house contains his maps and several portraits.

NEW ABBEY
Dumfries & Galloway *18 NX96*
New Abbey is not of course *new*, nor is it the name of the abbey. Sweetheart Abbey (AM), called 'New' to avoid confusion with nearby **Dundrennan**, was founded in 1273 by Devorgilla, wife of John Baliol – who created the Oxford college of that name in her husband's memory and, after his death, had his heart embalmed in a silver and ivory casket and buried with her. The red sandstone ruins are remarkably beautiful. Just outside the village is Shambellie House Museum of Costume which is run by the Royal Scottish Museum.

South of New Abbey is Kirkbean where the font in the parish church was presented by the US Navy to commemorate John Paul Jones, the so-called Father of the American Navy. Born John Paul at Arbigland (the cottage still stands), he became a cabin boy at the age of 12. After plying the slave routes, Paul became a captain, and following a series of misadventures involving two deaths, he left for America where he changed his name to Jones. At the outset of the Revolutionary War Jones joined the Continental Navy (fighting for France and earning the title of Rear Admiral in Russia). He was known in Britain for his daring raids on the coast and for sinking several British ships. Arbigland House was also the birthplace of Doctor Craik, Washington's personal medical assistant.

NEWARK-ON-TRENT
Nottinghamshire *16 SK85*
The first recorded owner of Newark is that celebrated lady, Godiva, wife of Mercia's Earl Leofric. Remains of the 12th-century castle, notably the impressive main gateway and chapel and the west wall, overlook this attractive old town. During King John's struggle with the barons, which concluded with the signing of the Magna Carta, the barons captured Newark, held it for a year and then lost it to the King, who later, in 1216, died there from overeating. The centre of Newark is the cobblestoned market place with its many interesting old inns. Lord Byron lodged at the Clinton Arms (formerly the Kingston Arms), while supervising publication of his first book of poems. Gladstone as an ambitious young orator gave his first political speech from one of the windows. Sir Henry Clinton, who captured Charleston in 1780, was MP for Newark. There are two museums – the District Council Museum and the fascinating Millgate Museum of Social and Folk life. An interesting piece of Victorian social history is the flamboyant Ossington Coffee Palace, built to advance the cause of temperance.

Four miles south west Stoke Hall was the home of Lord Pauncefote Britain's first ambassador to America – he is buried at East Stoke. 8 miles south west is Screveton, the home of Edward Whalley, a cousin of Oliver Cromwell, who guarded Charles I when he was confined at Hampton Court, and was one of the judges who signed the King's death warrant. After the Restoration Whalley fled to New England where records show that he lived at Hadley, Massachusetts. The parish church contains the family tomb of his grandfather Richard Whalley, who is buried with his wife and 25 children.

Francis Brooke, who wrote Canada's first novel *The History of Emily Montague*, was christened in the parish church at Claypole, 5 miles south east of Newark.

Newark-on-Trent

NEWBURY
Berkshire *4 SU46*
Newbury was formerly an important
centre of the cloth trade. Its most
famous citizen was Jack of Newbury
who distinguished himself in peace and
war. As a prosperous clothier, he
financed the rebuilding of the church;
as a warrior he led 150 men at Flodden
in 1513. The Jacobean Cloth Hall has
been restored and is now a museum.
The River Kennet, spanned by an 18th-
century bridge, and the Kennet and
Avon Canal add to the attractions, and
Newbury Racecourse is suitably
frequented by characters that appear
to have wandered out of a Dick
Francis novel. The Reverend Thomas
Parker was rector here. In 1634 he was
forced to emigrate for his Puritan
views; Newbury, Massachusetts, was
named in his honour. 1 mile north is
Donnington Castle, successfully
defended during the Civil War by
Royalist Sir John Boys. Just south of
Newbury is Greenham Common, the
scene of the peace camp of women
opposed to the siting of nuclear mis-
siles at the American air base here.

NEWBY HALL
N Yorkshire *15 SE36*
Robert Adam, architect to George III,
MP for Kinross, and designer of
projects that included the streets of
London and country mansions for the
nobility and gentry, achieved one of
his finest works at Newby Hall
(OACT) in the late 17th century for
coal magnate Sir Edward Blackett.
Later that century, the house passed to
William Weddle who, when making
the Grand Tour of Europe, acquired
the collection of sculpture now on
display and a rare complete set of
Gobelin tapestries. Some 25 acres of
gardens contain a miniature railway.

NEWCASTLE EMLYN
Dyfed *7 SN34*
Newcastle Emlyn is a long street of
pleasant houses leading down to the
Teifi. The first printing press in Wales
was installed here in 1718 by Isaac
Carter and the first printed Welsh
book produced in 1719 – an
achievement recalled by a plaque
mounted on the side of a house near
the river. The castle, founded in the
13th century and extensively rebuilt in
the 15th, was ruined in the Civil War.
Felin Geri Mill (OACT), 2 miles away,
is one of the last commercially
operated water-mills in the country
producing stoneground flour regularly.
Visitors can see all stages of
production and there is also a mill
museum.

NEW FOREST, THE
Hampshire *4 SU30*
The New Forest covers approximately
145 sq miles between the River Avon
and Southampton Water. Partly
owned by the Crown, it is a mixture of
wood and heathland. William I
appropriated it in 1079 and designated
it a royal hunting preserve, imposing
fierce penalties on local villagers –
death for killing deer, blinding merely
for disturbing them. Five common
rights survived and in many cases still
survive for the inhabitants of the
Forest: pannage, the right to let pigs
forage; turbage, the right to cut peat or
turves; estover, the right to cut

New Forest ponies grazing alongside
the cows.

firewood; marl, the right to improve
the soil; and pasturage, the right to
graze stock. The most famous event
associated with the Forest is the
shooting of William Rufus (described
as 'loathsome to well nigh all his
people') by Walter Tyrrell. An obelisk
marks the spot where he is thought to
have fallen. Eventually, in the Tudor
period, deer ceased to be protected
because of the importance of New
Forest timber for building warships.
Herds of red, roe and fallow deer roam
freely, as do the famous ponies.
Verderers' Courts, which administer
Forest laws, are held at **Lyndhurst**, one
of the prettiest towns.

NEWLYN
Cornwall *1 SW42*
In the late 19th and early 20th
centuries Newlyn attracted a colony of
artists, among them Dame Laura
Knight, Stanhope-Forbes and Frank
Bramley; the Passmore Edwards
Gallery recalls their work. About 3
miles south west is a Bronze Age stone
group, which according to legend are
maidens turned to stone as a
punishment for dancing on a Sunday.

NEWMARKET
Suffolk *12 TL66*
James I built a palace here as a base for
his hunting and hawking expeditions
and when, in 1619, the first horse race
took place on Newmarket Heath, His
Majesty was a delighted spectator.
Charles II did rather better: he actually
rode in events. In 1752, the Jockey
Club (the ruling body of the Turf) took
note of Newmarket's importance and
moved its headquarters from the Star
and Garter Inn in London. Nowadays,
the statistics that proclaim this town
on the Suffolk/Cambridgeshire border
as the capital of the racing world are
impressive. There are more than 40
training stables, 1500 race horses in
residence, two race courses, more than
4000 race horses sold each year for a
sum adding up to several million
pounds, and 35 stud farms. The
National Stud and the Equine
Research Station are situated here.
Newmarket's most famous races are
the One Thousand and Two
Thousand Guineas (both held in the
spring), the Cesarewich and
Cambridgeshire (in October).
Newmarket's elegant Regency
Assembly Rooms are the home of the
National Racing Museum. Exhibits
include famous racing silks, paintings,
and equine equipment and
memorabilia of all sorts.

NEWCASTLE UPON TYNE
Tyne & Wear   20 NZ26

Northumbria's Capital
'Newcastle is a spacious, extended,
infinitely populous place; 'tis seated
upon the river Tyne, which is here a
noble, large and deep river and ships
... may come safely up to the very
town.'
Daniel Defoe, *A Tour through the*
Whole Island

Newcastle is a true regional capital,
clinging to the north bank of the River
Tyne which is spanned by seven city
bridges. The most famous is the great,
arched suspension bridge that carries
the A1, and the oldest is Robert
Stephenson's high level, combined
road and rail bridge, erected in 1849.
Between the two is the elegant swing
bridge, turning on a central pivot, built
in 1876. The other three bridges are
20th century, one carrying the metro,
an over and underground railway
system which opened in 1980.
  Newcastle began life as a Roman
fort on Hadrian's Wall; later, a
community of monks made a
settlement here called Monkchester,
and finally the Normans came and
built their 'new' castle on the site of an
old Roman fort. The castle keep and
gatehouse remain today as museums,
not far from the riverside. For
centuries, the town lived on the river,
confined within walls for protection
against the Scots. All its finest pre 19th-
century buildings are to be found in
this area, notably the handsome 18th-
century Guildhall; a group of tall,
17th-century merchants' houses on
Sandhill; the beautiful elliptical
church of All Saints, now an urban
studies centre; and St Nicholas'
Cathedral, originally the parish
church, built in the 14th century at a
period when Newcastle was reckoned
to be the third most prosperous town
in England. In Tudor times, the
surrounding coalfields began to be
exploited on a large scale. But the real
boom came in the 19th century, with
the development of heavy engineering
and shipbuilding, and from this
period, between 1825 and 1840, dates
Newcastle's second phase of fine
building, in a style that came to be
known as 'Tyneside Classical'. This
century has brought a third phase of
building, and though some of the high-
rise office blocks seem soulless, the
new Civic Centre is impressive, as is
the architecture of the nearby
university and museum buildings.
South of the Tyne are **Jarrow** and
Washington.

PLACES TO SEE
Black Gate Museum The 13th-century
castle gatehouse houses Britain's only
bagpipe museum – which of course
lays special emphasis on
Northumbrian pipes – though there
are exhibits from all over the world.

Blackfriars This old Dominican priory
used to be the temporary 'palace' of
visiting royalty and Edward I received
the King of Scotland here in 1334. It
now houses a tourist and exhibition
heritage centre.

Castle Keep Begun in the reign of
Henry II, the keep which, with the
gatehouse, is the only part of the castle
to survive, was restored in the 19th
century; Great Hall, Garrison Room
and Chapel can be visited.

Newcastle city centre; the old and new

John George Joicey Museum Housed
in Holy Jesus Hospital, a 17th-century
almshouse, the museum is devoted to
city history and to the work of the
engraver Thomas Bewick, who
worked in Newcastle.

Hancock Museum This superb natural
history museum is named after John
Hancock and houses his famous
collection of birds.

Museum of Antiquities Part of the
university complex, the museum has a
fine collection of Roman relics.

Museum of Science and Engineering
As befits a city of heavy engineering,
the museum has more than 80 full-size
engines on display.

Laing Art Gallery A good regional
gallery containing works by John
Singer Sargent who painted in the city.

NEWMILNS
Strathclyde *22 NS53*
East of Kilmarnock along the River
Irvine are the three lacemaking and
muslin towns of Galston, Newmilns
and Darvel, where Dutch and
Huguenot immigrants settled in the
17th century. Sir Alexander Fleming
who discovered penicillin was born in
Darvel in 1881. During the American
Civil War when most of Britain
favoured the South, a number of
Newmilns weavers formed an anti-
slavery society led by John Donall (the
Manchester textile workers similarly
supported the Union). In return for
their support, Abraham Lincoln sent
the weavers an American flag, which
was subsequently used on all
ceremonial occasions and at the great
Ayrshire Reform Demonstration in
Kilmarnock in 1884. The original flag
has now been replaced.

NEWPORT
Essex *11 TL53*
This attractive Essex village has
several timbered houses that deserve
attention – notably Crown House with
its richly pargeted front and Monks'
Barn. The Links, which is Georgian,
used to be the House of Correction or
workhouse. The 13th-century church
contains an old chest of the same date
with some interesting early paintings.
The delightfully named Mole Hole
Wildlife Park (OACT) occupies the
grounds of an Elizabethan Manor. 3
miles east is Debden where Sir Harry
Vane, the younger, was baptized in
1613. The Vane family had strong
connections with Massachusetts.

NEWPORT
Gwent *8 ST38*
A fast growing modern town,
Newport was originally called
Gwynllyw after the Christian warrior
who governed the town and was
eventually canonized. The Norman
cathedral (a parish church until 1949)
is dedicated to the saint, though they
now refer to him as St Woolos. The
15th-century castle, now ruined,
controls the river crossing. The poet
W H Davies, author of *Autobiography
of a Supertramp*, was born here and is
commemorated by an Epstein bust in
the town's museum. Davies sailed to
America in 1893. Tredegar House
(OACT) is accounted the finest
restoration house in Wales. Parts date
back to the 16th century and it is set in
lovely grounds. At **Caerleon** is a fine
ruined Roman amphitheatre and
barracks. Caerleon is a possible site of

Camelot, linked by both Malory in
Morte D'Arthur and Tennyson in
Idylls of the King.

NEWQUAY
Cornwall *1 SW86*
Good bathing, excellent surfing and a
favourable climate combine to make
Newquay one of the most popular
resorts in Cornwall. Its sandy beach is
backed by tall cliffs, pierced with
enticing caves. Evidence of Newquay's
past as a fishing port when pilchards
were plentiful is provided by the Old
Huer's Hut on the cliffs. The Huer was
the man who kept watch for the
appearance of the shoals and warned
the fishermen to make ready. Trenance
Park, in a valley to the east of the
town, is the setting for Newquay Zoo.
3 miles south east Trerice Manor is a
fine Elizabethan manor house (NT).

• NEW ROMNEY
Kent *6 TR02*
New Romney was one of the original
Cinque Ports; but nature interfered in
1287, changing the coastline and
leaving the town high and dry 1 mile
from the sea. However, the upheaval
indirectly produced Romney Marsh
(important sheep farming country) and
New Romney is the capital. There
were once five churches in the town.
Now there is only one: the parish
church of St Nicholas, in which the
mayor is still elected. The station is an
important feature of that delightful
mini-railway, the Romney, Hythe and
Dymchurch. 2 miles north is St Mary
in the Marsh where E Nesbitt, author
of *The Railway Children*, is buried. In
the same churchyard, Noël Coward sat
while writing some of his plays; later
he bought a 17th-century farmhouse,
Goldenhurst, at nearby Aldington.

NEWSTEAD
Nottinghamshire *15 SK55*
Newstead Abbey (OACT), set in a
wooded park 9 miles north of
Nottingham, was founded in 1170 by
Henry II for Augustinian canons after
the murder of Thomas à Becket. After
the Dissolution, it was given to Sir
John Byron, an ancestor of the famous
poet, who could not afford to live in
the ancestral home until 1808, and
even then, he was heavily in debt.
Some years later, when he left England
for good, Byron sold the property to
an old schoolfriend but the house has
many items relating to the poet,
including the table at which *Childe
Harold* was written and an elaborate
grave in the grounds to his

Newfoundland dog, Boatswain.
Byron, who died in Greece, is buried 3
miles south at Hucknall church. The
famous 19th-century explorer and
missionary David Livingstone wrote
his journals here and Washington
Irving was a guest here. He wrote
Abbotsford and Newstead in 1835.

NEWTON ABBOT
Devon *1 SX87*
When the railway came to Newton
Abbot, the town was transformed
from a sleepy little place into an
important junction and a lively market
town. It also served as a centre for the
clay mines between Kingsteignton and
Bovey Tracey. Forde House, in the
centre, provided Charles I with
overnight accommodation (in 1625)
and, later, William of Orange, who
was on his way to London. The town's
name, incidentally, originated in the
13th century. It was the 'new town' of
the abbot of Torre Abbey. Nowadays,
it is a gathering point for tourists,
either bound for the coast or for
Dartmoor. Bradley Manor (NT), a
15th-century house with an interesting
Great Hall, lies in the valley of the
River Lemon. In the 18th century
Newton Abbot was a major recruiting
centre for hands for the
Newfoundland cod trade. Dried fish
was stored in the town and ships'
goods were made and sold.

NEWTONMORE
Highland *26 NN79*
Newtonmore is the most southerly of
the Speyside resorts: a base for skiing
and pony-trekking. It was, indeed,
here that in 1952, the latter activity
was introduced to Britain. There are
some good rides into the black
Monadhliath Mountains and some fine
views of the Cairngorms. The exhibits
in the Clan Macpherson House and
Museum include a gift from a fairy to
the clan, known as the Black Charter.
A Macpherson who fought in America
is buried nearby.

NEWTON STEWART
Dumfries & Galloway *17 NX46*
At Newton Stewart you can visit a mill
and watch mohair rugs and scarves
being made; you can admire the 57ft
edifice erected in 1875 to honour the
5th Earl of Galloway (Stewart is the
family name: one of his ancestors
persuaded Charles II to grant the town
a charter), and the bridge spanning the
River Cree designed by John Rennie. It
is an attractive little market town and
a good centre from which to walk.

NEWTOWN
Powys *8 SO19*
Newtown is the second largest town in Powys. It used to be an important flannel and tweed manufacturing centre; nowadays, much of its wealth is accounted for by its role as market place to the surrounding sheep farming and agricultural community. Edward I granted it a charter – largely because he saw it as a good point from which to control a ford across the Severn. In those days, it was known as Llanfair until, in the 16th century, it was referred to as Nova Villa. This, perhaps, was harping too much on any Roman origins it may have had, and it soon became translated into Newtown. Robert Owen the reformer and father of the Co-operative Movement was born and died here and is commemorated in the Robert Owen Memorial Museum.

Wool-weaving house, Newtown

NORTHALLERTON
N Yorkshire *20 SE39*
The town is known as the 'capital' of North Yorkshire. The Old Fleece Inn is partly medieval and the church, which has a 15th-century pinnacled tower and a Jacobean font, is surrounded by fine old houses. 6½ miles north west is Kiplin Hall, home of the Calverts, built in 1616. Sir George Calvert, Baron Baltimore, set up a Newfoundland colony, Avalon, in the 1620s. He was later given the land which is now Maryland. This American territory was pioneered by Baltimore's two sons with 300 Yorkshire colonists.

NORTHAMPTON
Northamptonshire *10 SP76*
Northampton's long connection with the now beleaguered boot and shoe trade can be said to have started in the Civil War when the town made footwear for Cromwell's army. The trade flourished, and during the Napoleonic Wars Northampton again made army boots. Fittingly, both the town's museums have large collections: footwear at the Central Museum, with such famous items as Nijinsky's ballet shoes and Queen Victoria's wedding shoes on display; other sorts of leather at the Leathercraft Museum. Northampton is an ancient town with many handsome buildings, most dating from the 17th century and later. It has several imposing churches including All Saints, rebuilt after a devastating fire in 1675, and Holy Sepulchre, one of the few surviving round churches in England, founded in the 12th century on the model of the Holy Sepulchre at Jerusalem. Delapre Abbey (OACT), a mainly 17th-century house, is now the County Records Office. The vast market square is thought to be the largest in the country and dates from the days of the cattle drovers when Northampton was an important market. Abington Park Museum, set in landscaped grounds, is an old manor house with interesting collections of porcelain, lace and toys.

Northampton lies in an area exceptionally rich in Pilgrim associations. To the west, **Daventry** and the **Althorp** area have many American connections. South east is **Sulgrave Manor**, owned by Lawrence Washington, who was mayor of Northampton in 1532 and 1545. Northampton was the home of the Dudley family, who accompanied John Winthrop's Pilgrims to the New World in 1630. Thomas Dudley was Winthrop's second-in-command and he served 4 terms as Governor of Massachusetts. Joseph Dudley, son of Thomas, also held this post. Anne Dudley, as Mrs Bradstreet, was North America's first woman poet. 3 miles east of Northampton is Little Houghton, ancestral home of the Randolph family of Virginia. William Randolph, who emigrated in 1674, was a brother of Thomas Randolph, poet and dramatist, a friend of Ben Jonson, and a member of the Virginia Council. Later, in 1774, Peyton Randolph, friend of George Washington, would become President of the First Continental Congress. Castle Ashby

was the home of the Marquis of Northampton, where Bret Harte was entertained and did much of his work. South, Horton was the birthplace of Sir Ralph Lane, the first Governor of Virginia. 5 miles east of Northampton, Ecton was the ancestral home of the Franklins, the parish records showing entries for the Franklin family as far back as 1558. The family were smiths and yeomen; a portion of the ancestral home survives as the old forge barn. Benjamin was the son of Josiah, a tallow chandler who left Ecton for **Banbury**, Oxfordshire, and thence Boston, Massachusetts where Ben was born. Benjamin's uncle and aunt Thomas Franklin and his wife are buried in the churchyard. Thomas collected money to pay for the church chimes which still play Purcell's 'Britons, Strike Home!', formerly the English national anthem. A memorial in the church commemorates the family. The church in the neighbouring village of Earls Barton has one of the finest Saxon towers in England.

NORTH BERWICK
Lothian *24 NT58*
North Berwick, an ancient royal burgh 23 miles from Edinburgh, is a popular seaside resort and a residential area for commuters to the city. Among its attractions are two particularly good golf courses. 1 mile south, a volcanic hill named North Berwick Law (613ft) has the ruins of a watchtower on its summit (used during the Napoleonic Wars) and an archway constructed from the jawbone of a whale. Bass Rock, 3 miles out to sea, has a famous lighthouse. For a while after 1671, the rock was used as a place of imprisonment for Covenanters. Bass Rock and the other Firth of Forth islands, Fidra and Eyebroughty, are now a nature reserve. Tantallon Castle (AM), ruined by General Monk in 1651, commands a wild headland 3 miles east of the town.

South at East Fortune a monument marks the first Atlantic double crossing by air in 1919 by the Airship R34. The Museum of Flight is situated at East Fortune Airfield, part of the Royal Scottish Museum. Exhibits, some of which can be operated by visitors, include a Spitfire, a de Haviland Sea Venom and Hawker Sea Hawk.

NORTH DOWNS, THE
Kent and Surrey *5, 6*
This range of rolling chalk hills was the northern edge of a great dome that, 140 million years ago, covered all

south-east England and joined it to France. It, and the **South Downs**, are all that remains, the highest point is near Woldingham (900ft) and has a large chalk pit at its base. **Box Hill** (nearly 600ft) is particularly beautiful. The Pilgrims' Way, along which the devout travelled from Winchester to Canterbury, follows the Downs for part of its route. The North Downs reach an abrupt but impressive conclusion in the white cliffs of Dover.

NORTHIAM
E Sussex   *6 TQ82*
A pretty village in the Rother Valley, Northiam's old houses cluster round the traditional village green, shaded by an ancient oak tree under whose branches Elizabeth I is reputed to have breakfasted. Great Dixter (OACT) a 15th-century timbered manor house with a unique great hall, was restored by Sir Edwin Lutyens, who consulted the famous Gertrude Jekyll about the planting of the gardens. Brickwall (OACT), now a school, is a 17th-century Jacobean house with 18th-century gardens.

NORTHLEACH
Gloucestershire   *10 SP11*
Northleach used to be one of the most prosperous Cotswold wool towns: and this wealth is reflected in its attractive old buildings. The great 15th-century church, with its clerestory, its vaulted roof, its brasses remembering bygone woolstaplers, and the humour in its carvings is a near perfect example of a wool church. The Cotswold Countryside Collection, a fascinating series of exhibits, is housed in the former House of Correction. Just north east of the town is the village of Farmington, where the pump house on the green was restored by Americans from Farmington, Connecticut.

NORTHUMBERLAND NATIONAL PARK
19, 24
Covering 398 sq miles, the National Park boundaries are the **Cheviot Hills** in the north and **Hadrian's Wall** in the south. This is magnificent, sparsely populated hill country, where the remains of ancient hill-forts and cup-and-ring marked stones, testify to the presence of early settlers. The long distance footpath, the Pennine Way, passes through the park, and there are Information Centres at Byreness, Ingram and Rothbury.

The Anderton boat-lift, Northwich

NORTHWICH
Cheshire   *14 SJ67*
Northwich's motto is *Sal est Vita*, 'salt is life'. And for this Cheshire town which sits on top of a huge rock-salt bed it is. Salt-mining has been a major industry since Roman times, now much of it is bought by the chemical industry. Not far away is the Anderton boat-lift. This remarkable piece of engineering was assembled in 1875 to raise (and lower) barges and pleasure craft of up to 100 tons 50ft from the River Weaver to the Trent and Mersey Canal above Anderton. Arley Hall (OACT) is an impressive Victorian house, set in lovely gardens 5 miles north, and Vale Royal Abbey (OACT) is a 16th-century house built on the site of a Cistercian abbey.

NORTH YORK MOORS NATIONAL PARK
16, 20
This area, designated a National Park in 1952, covers 550 sq miles extending from the Cleveland and Hambleton Hills, the highest ground, to the coast north of **Scarborough** and to the Vale

of Pickering in the south. The colours on the predominantly high ground range from the purple of heather in August to the bronze of dying bracken in autumn. Attractive, steep-sided valleys break up the mass: moorland villages, early Christian crosses and the ruins of abbeys are scattered sparsely across the landscape. The Cleveland Way circles the northern edges of the Park, and the 40-mile Lyke Wake Walk crosses the moors from **Osmotherley** to Ravenscar. The North York Moors Railway travels from **Pickering** to Grosmont.

NOTTINGHAM
Nottinghamshire   *10 SK54*
Boots, Players and Raleigh are among some of the firms that have made Nottingham into a modern city, proudly proclaiming itself as 'Queen of the Midlands'. A more traditional industry is lace-making, and the old Lace Market still survives in the centre of the town. Nottingham Castle (OACT), which used to feature on Players' cigarette packets, crowns a high sandstone ridge overlooking the

city. King John commanded it while Richard the Lionheart was occupied with the Crusades, and in this period the legends of Robin Hood and the Sheriff of Nottingham gained popularity. The Trip to Jerusalem Inn, built into the sides of the cliff, claims to be England's oldest inn, but there are several other contenders for the title. The great Council House stands on the site of Nottingham's famous Goose Fair, which is still held annually in October. St Mary's Church, in the Lace Market is a noble 15th-century edifice and contains a painting of the Madonna and Child by Fra Bartolomeo. The Brewhouse Yard Museum depicts life in bygone times, with 'period' rooms and cottage gardens; the Canal Museum depicts the history of the River Trent; the Industrial Museum and the Museum of Costume and Textiles portray the history of trade and industry in the city, and the Natural History Museum is housed in 16th-century Wollaton Hall. 4 miles east of Nottingham is the Holme Pierrepont Hall (OACT) a Tudor manor house with a fine collection of English oak furniture.

Langar was the ancestral home of the Howe family, many of whom are buried in the church. One generation

Robin Hood statue

of this family produced three brothers whose involvement in America is still remembered. George Augustus Howe, the 3rd Viscount, was killed in 1758, fighting the French at Ticonderoga; Westminster Abbey has a memorial to him. The 4th Viscount and 1st Earl, Richard Howe, was Admiral in Command of the British Fleet of North America in 1776. Richard sympathized with the colonists; he defended Rhode Island against the French, but later refused to serve under Lord North's ministry. His grave is in Langar Church. The youngest of the three brothers was the 5th Viscount, General William Howe, who captured Louisberg and Quebec in 1759. General Howe was victorious at Bunker Hill, becoming Chief Commander in the American Colonies and his troops also won the battles of White Plains and Brandywine. General Howe, like his brothers, was not unsympathetic to the American cause and as an MP for Nottingham took a particular interest in the subject.

NUNEATON
Warwickshire *10 SP39*
A manufacturing town involved principally in the production of bricks, woollen goods and hats. The town has some interesting buildings. Nuneaton's most famous daughter is George Eliot, who was christened Mary Ann Evans at Chilvers Coton church south of the town. She was born in 1819 at South Farm in the estate of Arbury Hall, and later lived nearby at Griff House. Much of the inspiration for her works came from the surrounding countryside and the characters she knew there. Arbury Hall (OACT), the seat of the Newdegate family since the 16th century, was built on the site of an Augustinian priory. Originally Elizabethan, the hall was transformed in the 18th century into an outstanding Gothic mansion. It has fine interiors and landscaped gardens. A monument in the village of Fenny Drayton 4 miles north marks the birthplace of George Fox, son of a local weaver. In 1647, when living in Mansfield, Nottinghamshire, Fox was to found the Society of Friends.

NORWICH
Norfolk *12 TG20*

One of England's most attractive provincial capitals, Norwich lies on the River Wensum, a compact cathedral city which bears the marks, in many fine and ancient buildings, of 1000 years of history. If a city can be said to have a colour, then that of Norwich is yellow – from the mustard milled by Messrs Colman, whose quaint Old Mustard Shop in Bridewell Alley is a major tourist attraction – and from the Norwich canary, a breed which the locals developed from the cage birds originally imported by the 'strangers', as the Flemish weavers who settled in the city were known: 'Canaries' is now the nickname of the Norwich football team.

The city centre is the wide, sloping market place, overlooked at one end by the stern keep of the Norman castle, raised high on a mound; at the other by the neo-Egyptian City Hall. It has a large produce market, around which is a network of charming old streets, alleys and arcades. Picturesque Elm Hill leads down to Tombland, the old market place, and two imposing medieval gateways give access to the Cathedral Close. The cathedral, crowned by a 315ft spire added in the 15th century, is surrounded by a large Close, whose lawns run down to the Wensum at Pull's Ferry, a 15th-century watergate, often painted by the artists of the Norwich School, whose leading figures were John Sell Cotman and John Crome.

The city has rightly made great efforts to preserve its past and has won several Heritage Awards, but some of

Guildhall, Norwich

the new buildings are adventurous in design – particularly those at the University of East Anglia, by Sir Denys Lasdun, and the gleaming aluminium-clad Sainsbury Centre for the Visual Arts, an art gallery and study centre designed by Norman Foster.

Norwich claims two pilgrim connections. John Jenney was born in the vicinity of the Royal Hotel in 1594, and the Reverend John Robinson was a minister at St Andrew's. Inside the church is a monument to the Lincolns, also commemorated in St Mary's. Edith Cavell, the famous World War I nurse, is buried behind the cathedral. Norwich was the birthplace of the writer Harriet Martineau. East Anglia was an important area of emigration to America; the links were reinforced during World War II, when there were no fewer than 21 air bases in Norfolk.

PLACES TO SEE

Norwich Castle The 12th-century keep contains a museum of local and natural history, and an outstanding collection of paintings by Crome, Cotman and others of the Norwich School.

The Guildhall Built by forced labour in the 15th century, in a distinctive chequered flint pattern.

The Assembly House This gracious 17th- and 18th-century building is used for exhibitions, and the spacious Music Room is a restaurant.

Strangers' Hall This rambling 14th- and 15th-century building named after the immigrant Flemish weavers who settled in the area, houses a folk museum with many period rooms, displays of toys and costumes and old shop signs.

Bridewell Museum A flint-face medieval merchant's house, used as a bridewell from 1583 to 1828, the building now contains a fascinating museum of local crafts and industries.

St Peter Hungate Church Museum A museum of church art is housed in this fine, 15th-century, now redundant, church.

Norwich Cathedral Built of stone specially imported from Caen in Normandy by the first Bishop of Norwich, Herbert de Losinga, the cathedral is a masterpiece of Gothic architecture. Its cloisters, the largest in Europe, and its lofty, vaulted nave and chancel are ornamented with 600 finely carved roof bosses.

OAKHAM
Leicestershire   10 SK80
Oakham is now in Leicestershire, but locals do not forget that they belong to the vanished county of Rutland, and that Oakham is their county town. It is a most attractive old place, preserving its ancient stocks under the buttercross in the cobbled market square. There has been a castle here since before the Conquest, but all that now remains is the 12th-century aisled hall, where there is a unique collection of horseshoes, dating perhaps from the 11th century when William I's farrier lived here, collecting a horseshoe from every noble or royal person who passed through the town. One Oakham resident was the dwarf Jeffery Hudson, who was presented in a pie to Charles II. Rutland County Museum used to be housed in the old 16th-century schoolroom of Oakham Grammar School, but is now in a former indoor riding school. The school was founded by Robert Johnson who also founded the public school 6 miles south at Uppingham. A number of men educated at Uppingham settled in Canada, notably in the 19th century. One was Walter Skrine whose wife, Agnes Higginson, was the poet Moira O'Neill. Rutland Farm Park on Uppingham Road in Oakham is a working farm with many rare breeds of animals. One of Britain's largest manmade lakes, Rutland Water, lies between Oakham and Stamford, a local beauty spot.

OARE
Somerset   2 SS84
Set in the heart of *Lorna Doone* country, Oare's tiny church was, in the novel, the scene of Lorna's marriage to John Ridd. All around is some of the most beautiful countryside in Exmoor, and just west of the village a footpath leads up the valley of Badgworthy Water to Lank and Hoccombe Combes, which were R D Blackmore's models for Doone Valley.

OBAN
Strathclyde   25 NM83
Overlooking the town is MacCaig's Tower, an unfinished replica of the

The church at Oare

Colosseum in Rome. It was built in 1890 by a banker, John Stuart MacCaig, as a memorial to his family and to give work to local craftsmen during the depression of the 1890s. Oban is a popular highland resort, with all the usual amenities, including golf, and is an ideal base for exploring the beautiful countryside of Lorne. Games Day, or the Argyllshire Gathering, takes place here at the end of August. At the Oban glassworks on Lochavullin estate, Caithness glass is made, and MacDonald's Mill (OACT) demonstrates spinning and weaving. Dunstaffnage Castle (AM) is a ruined Campbell stronghold where Flora Macdonald was once imprisoned. There are car ferries from Oban to many of the islands of the **Inner** and **Outer Hebrides**: Mull, Iona, Coll, Tiree, Barra, South Uist, Colonsay and Lismore. There are fine views from Pulpit Hill.

OFFA'S DYKE
8, 13
The dyke was an earthworks, built in the 8th century by Offa, King of Mercia, to mark the western boundary of his kingdom and to provide a defence against Welsh raiders. A long distance footpath follows, as far as possible, the original line of the dyke for about 168 miles, from the River Severn near Chepstow to the sea near Prestatyn in North Wales.

OFFHAM
Kent   6 TQ65
On the Green is what is thought to be the only remaining quintain, or tilting pole, in England. The idea was to ride at the T-shaped pole and attempt to hit a revolving bar with a lance, as practice for jousting, without falling off. The sport is revived on May Day.

OKEHAMPTON
Devon *2 SX59*

The high tors of Dartmoor, High Willhays and Yes Tor, brood over this busy market town on the edges of the National Park. Its castle (AM), overlooking the river, was once the seat of the Courtenay family, Earls of Devon, until they moved to Powderham Castle near Exeter. East of Okehampton is Sticklepath and the Museum of Rural Industry at the old Finch brothers' foundry, which operated from 1814 until 1960, generating power with its waterwheels. 1 mile east of Sticklepath is South Tawton. John Endecott, first official Governor of Plymouth, Massachusetts, took his name from the estate here.

OLD DEER
Grampian *28 NJ94*

Ruined Deer Abbey (AM) lies in a delightful setting in the grounds of Pitfour House. These buildings date from the 13th century, but the first monastery at Deer was a Celtic one, founded by St Columba in the 6th century. The famous *Book of Deer* now in Cambridge University Library, was compiled by Celtic monks: it contains the first known characters of Gaelic script.

OLDHAM
Gtr Manchester *14 SD90*

One of the great cotton towns of the north west, Oldham owes much to the Industrial Revolution and the mechanization of spinning and weaving. Nowadays foreign competition has hit traditional industry hard. Like **Manchester** in the 19th century, Oldham was a centre of radical thought, and elected William Cobbett as its first MP in 1832. In 1900 it returned to Parliament Britain's greatest modern statesman, Sir Winston Churchill. His bust by Epstein is one of the many fine exhibits in the Central Art Gallery, which is also noted for its collection of English watercolours. The imposing 19th-century Town Hall is a copy of the Temple of Ceres, near Athens.

OLD SARUM
Wiltshire *3 SU13*

Remains of the castle, cathedral, and traces of the surrounding wall are now all that remain of Old Sarum, a site that was inhabited in the Iron Age and became in medieval times a flourishing town and an important Episcopal See. However a bitter feud broke out between the clergy and the military at the castle, and there was a serious water shortage, so Bishop Herbert Poore decided to move himself and his cathedral. He died before he could accomplish this plan, but his brother and successor, Richard, began to build the new cathedral in 1220 and by 1258 it was finished. A new town, **Salisbury**, grew up around the cathedral and by the 19th century Sarum had dwindled to a hamlet. It was one of the most notorious of the 'Rotten Boroughs', returning two MPs to parliament, although there were only ten voters, until the Reform Bill of 1832. Among these was William Pitt the Elder – the 18th-century Prime Minister.

OLNEY
Buckinghamshire *10 SP85*

Annually on Shrove Tuesday the ringing of a handbell summons determined Olney housewives wielding frying pans to the famous pancake race. Competitors run from the market place to the handsome 14th-century church, and must toss and catch a pancake three times before completing the course. The custom is said to date back to the 15th century. The annual pancake race at Liberal, Kansas, is similarly famous. The poet William Cowper lived in Olney for many years and worked with his friend, the curate John Newton, to write the famous Olney hymns – among them such old favourites as 'Hark, my soul, it is the Lord', and 'Glorious things of Thee are spoken'. The cottage where he lived with his companion, Mary Unwin, is now a museum. 6 miles north east in Bedfordshire is Odell from where the Reverend Peter Bulkley emigrated to New England, where he became pastor at The Church in the Wilderness at Concord, New Hampshire. Ralph Waldo Emerson was a descendant.

ORKNEY
Highland *28*

Mainland, once more romantically called *Hrossey* ('the horse island') when Orkney was a Viking kingdom, is the largest of the 67 islands in the group which lies off the northernmost tip of the Scottish mainland. There are regular flights from the mainland and a ferry from Scrabster.

Unlike the Western Isles, Orkney is a fertile place with low, rounded hills and a surprisingly mild climate which favours farming. The exception is Hoy – 'the high island' – with its towering 1000ft cliffs and the dramatic, wave-lashed rock stack known as the 'Old Man of Hoy'.

The early settlers of Orkney were Picts and Celts, and from these times the islands are rich in monuments and remains, an archaeologist's paradise. The great chambered tomb of Maes Howe (AM) near Finstown on Mainland, is the finest megalithic tomb in West Europe. Nearby is the slightly later Ring of Brogar (AM), another of the many relics of Orkney's distant past. The Vikings ousted the native Picts in the 9th century, and Orkney remained a part of Norway and Denmark, until 1468 when the islands were given to Scotland as part of the dowry of Margaret of Norway on her marriage to James III of Scotland. Nordic traditions are still evident in the speech and customs of the Orcadians. The peaceful, timeless quality of Orkney is now threatened by the booming North Sea Oil industry: the little island of Flotta, in the World War II harbour of Scapa Flow, is now a terminal for North Sea Oil.

Kirkwall on Mainland is the capital of Orkney, a charming old city of high, gabled houses and narrow streets. The beautiful St Magnus Cathedral, founded in 1137, commemorates an early Norse ruler of Orkney, murdered by his cousin in 1115. Nearby are the ruins of two palaces; the 13th-century Bishop's Palace (AM) and the 17th-century Earl Patrick's Palace (AM) built for the tyrannical 2nd Earl of Orkney. Tankerness House, a 16th-century town house, is now a museum of Orkney life, and at the little settlement of Harray in the island's interior, is a restored Orkney farmstead, the Corrigall Farm Museum. Near Dounby are other historic relics: Skara Brae, a remarkable survival of incredibly well-preserved Stone Age houses; the Brough of Birsay, ruins of a Romanesque church and early Viking dwellings, and Click Mill (AM), a rare Orcadian horizontal water-mill. Stromness is also an attractive township, with distant views of Hoy. It has an interesting maritime museum, and a modern arts centre housed in an 18th-century warehouse. On Mainland is Login's Well, associated with Captain Cook and Sir John Franklin, explorer of the North-West Passage. North of Marwick is the Kitchener Memorial. The cruiser *Hampshire* was sunk off the coast in 1916 while taking Kitchener to Russia.

South of Mainland and connected to

Skara Brae, Orkney

it by the Churchill Barriers, causeways built to guard the approaches to Scapa Flow during World War II, are the islands of Burray, South Ronaldsay, Glimps Holm and Lamb Holm. Italian prisoners of war built the causeways, and also built themselves a chapel on Lamb Holm, elaborately and beautifully painted, which still stands as a memento. On the west side of Scapa Flow is mountainous Hoy, legendary home of many a troll and giant in Orcadian folk tales. The composer Peter Maxwell Davies has made his home here, and the crofters are beginning to return to the long abandoned village of Rackwick.

North of Mainland, Rousay is said to have the loveliest scenery, and Sanday is another popular holiday island. The other major islands are Stronsay, Eday, Westray and Papa Westray, and the most northerly of all, North Ronaldsay, with its unique flocks of sheep, who feed on seaweed.

OSMOTHERLEY
N Yorkshire   *20 SE49*
The Hambleton Hills form the setting for this attractive stone-built village on the edge of the **North York Moors National Park**. It is also the starting point for the Lyke Wake Walk, a 40-mile footpath which ends at Ravenscar, and the Cleveland Way also passes through the village. John Wesley once preached here, using as his pulpit a stone table which can still be seen. 1 mile to the north west are

the ruins (AM, NT) of Mount Grace Priory, founded in the 14th century by the Carthusians.

OSTERLEY
Gtr London   *5 TQ17*
Osterley Park (NT), administered by the Victoria and Albert Museum in London, is an Elizabethan mansion encased in a magnificent 18th-century exterior designed by Robert Adam for the wealthy Child banking family. Almost all of its exquisite interior decorations have remained intact.

OSWESTRY
Shropshire   *13 SJ22*
A town fought over by England and Wales for centuries, Oswestry

Osterley Park

nowadays makes an excellent centre for visiting both the Shropshire and the North Wales countryside. Few of its medieval buildings survived the years of conflict, but the old grammar school dating from 1407, is still there, now divided into cottages. In the parish church are monuments of Hugh Yale and his wife – related to Elihu Yale, benefactor of the American university. The interesting Llwyd Mansion, a black and white 17th-century timbered building bears the insignia of the Holy Roman Empire, a double-headed eagle, on its walls. The arms were granted to an ancestor of the family for service in the Crusades. To the north of the town is the Iron Age hill-fort known as Old Oswestry (AM).

OTLEY
W Yorkshire   *15 SE24*
Otley is a market town on the River Wharfe, near the southern end of the beautiful Washburn Valley. There are some interesting buildings, and a Victorian maypole stands at Cross Green. Thomas Chippendale the furniture designer was born here in 1718. North east of the town Farnley Hall is Elizabethan with Georgian additions. It is associated with the Fairfax family and was visited by J M W Turner. East of Otley is Bramhope where there is a puritan chapel.

South is Guiseley, the ancestral home of the Longfellows. William, an ancestor of Henry Wadsworth Longfellow, emigrated from here in 1676 to Newbury, Massachusetts. The church contains a memorial to the poet; many family tombs are in the churchyard, which contains a Saxon cross. The Reverend Brontë and his wife, parents of the famous sisters, married here in 1812.

OXFORD
Oxfordshire 10 SP50

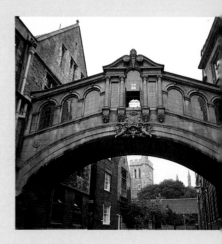

Bridge of Sighs

City of Dreaming Spires

'*Towery city and branchy between
towers;
Cuckoo-echoing, bell-swarmèd, lark-
charmèd, rook-racked, river-rounded;
The dapple-eared lily below thee; . . .*'
Gerard Manley Hopkins,
Duns Scotus's Oxford

Although a flourishing industrial town
has grown up at Cowley where Lord
Nuffield founded his bicycle and later
his Morris car works, alongside
Matthew Arnold's city of 'dreaming
spires', Oxford remains a university
town, *par excellence*, its streets
dominated by the stone-built walls and
quadrangles of its ancient colleges and
in term-time by flocks of black-
gowned undergraduates on foot or on
bicycle. The Broad, where that famous
Oxford institution Blackwell's
Bookshop is to be found, the High,
Cornmarket and the narrow lanes
leading off them are the centre of
university life, and where most of the
old colleges, public houses frequented
by the students, good restaurants and
shops are to be found. In spring and
summer the University Parks and the
Rivers Cherwell and Isis, as the
Thames is known here, from its old
name of 'Tamesis', come into their
own. On May Morning at 5 am the
Cherwell is packed with punts at
Magdalen Bridge to hear the
Choristers of Magdalen sing a Latin
hymn to salute May Day from
Magdalen Tower. Eights Week, on the
Isis, also takes place in May, when the
college crews compete for 'Head of the
River', watched by crowds along the
banks.

Academic life came to Oxford in a
modest way in the 12th century, but
really dates from the 13th century
when foreign students expelled from
the Sorbonne in Paris, came here and
attached themselves to 'halls'
belonging to religious orders. Learning
was at that time in the hands of the
church and all students were 'clerics'
benefiting from the privileges of the
clergy, and this gave rise to frequent
troubles between 'town' and 'gown':
until quite late in the 19th century,
university dons were required to be
celibate. Among the oldest
foundations are Merton College,
founded in 1264, St Edmund's Hall, the
only survivor of the medieval monastic
halls that predated the college system,
and University College. Others
followed thick and fast, throughout
the medieval and Renaissance periods,
and there are now quite a few 20th-
century foundations. The five
'women's' colleges were established,
not without severe opposition, in the
late 19th century. In the last 10 years
however, again not without debate,
the trend has been for all colleges to
admit undergraduates of both sexes,
and only a few are holding fast to the
old ways.

Oxford has at various times played
its part in history. In Mary I's reign,
the Protestant martyrs Latimer,
Cranmer and Ridley were tried at St
Mary's Church for heresy and burned
to death: Martyrs' Memorial in St
Giles commemorates them. During the
Civil War, Oxford declared for the
Royalist cause, and was Charles I's
headquarters for three years. It has
since led a quieter life, but is
remembered in this century for the
famous 1930s' 'King and Country'
debate at the Oxford Union, that early
training ground of many politicians.

Many people of distinction have
been at Oxford, a considerable
number with North American
associations. The poet T S Eliot was at
Merton College, Vincent Massey, the
first Canadian-born Governor-General
of his country, at Balliol and Lester
Pearson, later Prime Minister of
Canada, at St John's. In earlier periods
there were many links between Oxford
and the New World. Sir John Popham
was at Balliol, Richard Mather at
Brasenose. From Christchurch came
Lord Grenville, Richard Hakluyt and
William Penn. The Wesleys were there
too. The Reverend Thomas Coke who
founded the American Episcopal
Church was at Jesus College. John
Mason was at Magdalen and the
Reverend John White at New College.
Oriel College has two very
distinguished associations, Sir Walter
Raleigh and Cecil Rhodes. Rhodes
made his fortune in Africa and formed
a trust to give Oxford scholarships to
students from the British
Commonwealth and the United States.
This has been a means of bringing
many brilliant people to Oxford.
Rhodes House is in Parks Road, and
there is a tablet at 6 King Edward
Street. Another benefactor, James
Smithson, was at Pembroke. His
money set up the Smithsonian Institute
in Washington DC. George Calvert,
1st Lord Baltimore, was at Trinity.
Ruskin College was set up by Walter
Vrooman and American Ruskin
admirers to give working men
opportunities at Oxford. The
Washington arms are in Trinity
Chapel.

PLACES TO SEE

The Colleges Most are open to
visitors, and detailed information
can be obtained from the Official
Information Bureau in Carfax
Tower. The following are among
the best known, but there are many
more worth visiting.

All Souls Founded in 1437 by Henry
Chichele, it admits no undergraduates, only graduate fellows,
elected for academic distinction.

Balliol Founded in the 13th century
by John de Baliol, its most famous
Master was Benjamin Jowett, the
outstanding Greek scholar of the
19th century.

Christchurch Known as 'The
House', has the largest and most
famous quadrangle, Tom Quad, in
Oxford, and a superb hall. It was
founded by Cardinal Wolsey and
its handsome chapel is the city's
cathedral. Bishop Berkeley, the
Irish philosopher, who lived in
America for 3 years from 1728, is
buried in the cathedral. He gave an
organ to Trinity Church, Newport,
RI.

Magdalen Some say this is the most
beautiful of the Oxford colleges. Its
lovely Bell Tower is a noted
landmark, and it is set in extensive
grounds with a deer park.

Merton College Beautiful gardens
and a 14th-century library are its
outstanding features.

Queen's College Named after
Philippa, Queen of Edward III, its
classical buildings are by Wren and
Hawksmoor.

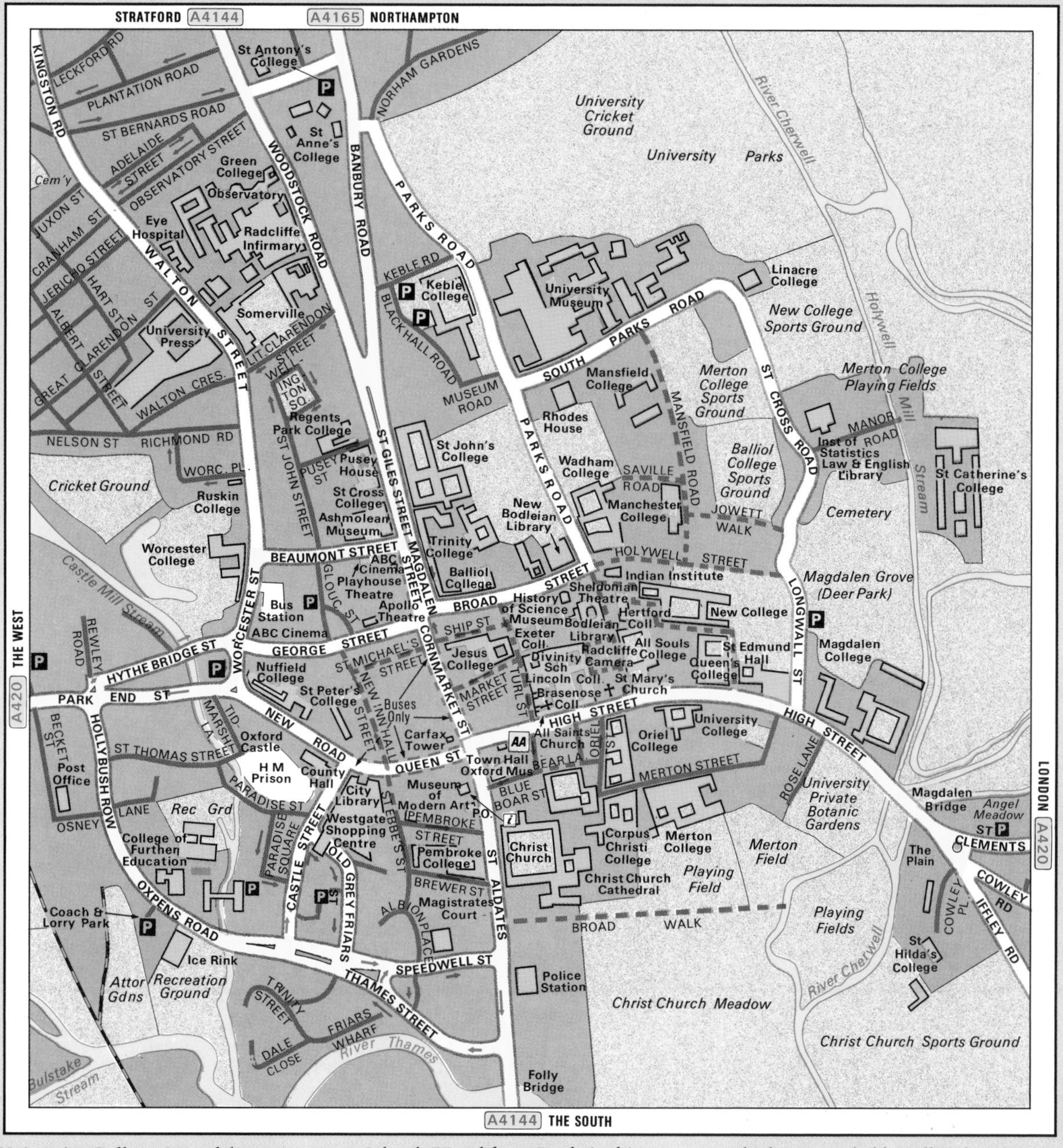
STRATFORD A4144
A4165 NORTHAMPTON
THE WEST A420
LONDON A420
A4144 THE SOUTH
KINGSTON RD
LECKFORD RD
PLANTATION ROAD
ST BERNARDS ROAD
ADELAIDE STREET
OBSERVATORY STREET
Cem'y
JUXON ST
CRANHAM ST
JERICHO STREET
HART ST
ALBERT ST
GREAT CLARENDON ST
WALTON STREET
WALTON CRES.
NELSON ST
RICHMOND RD
WORC. PL
St Antony's College
St Anne's College
NORHAM GARDENS
Green College
Observatory
Eye Hospital
Radcliffe Infirmary
WOODSTOCK ROAD
BANBURY ROAD
University Cricket Ground
University Parks
River Cherwell
PARKS ROAD
KEBLE RD
Keble College
BLACKHALL ROAD
University Museum
SOUTH PARKS ROAD
Linacre College
New College Sports Ground
Holywell Mill Stream
Somerville
LIT CLARENDON ST
WELLINGTON SQ.
University Press
Regents Park College
MUSEUM ROAD
Mansfield College
Rhodes House
Merton College Sports Ground
ST CROSS ROAD
Merton College Playing Fields
MANOR ROAD
MANSFIELD ROAD
Inst of Statistics
Law & English Library
St Catherine's College
Balliol College Sports Ground
Cemetery
St John's College
ST GILES STREET
PUSEY ST
Pusey House
ST JOHN STREET
St Cross College
Ashmolean Museum
Wadham College
SAVILLE ROAD
Manchester College
JOWETT WALK
New Bodleian Library
Cricket Ground
Ruskin College
Worcester College
Castle Mill Stream
BEAUMONT STREET
ABC Cinema
Playhouse Theatre
Apollo Theatre
Trinity College
Balliol College
HOLYWELL STREET
Indian Institute
Magdalen Grove (Deer Park)
Sheldonian Theatre
BROAD STREET
History of Science Museum
Bodleian Library
Hertford Coll
New College
LONGWALL ST
Bus Station
ABC Cinema
GLOUC. ST
MAGDALEN STREET
WORCESTER ST
REWLEY ROAD
HYTHE BRIDGE ST
GEORGE STREET
ST MICHAEL'S STREET
SHIP ST
Exeter Coll.
Jesus College
Divinity Sch
Radcliffe Camera
All Souls College
St Edmund Hall
Queen's College
Magdalen College
Nuffield College
PARK END ST
NEW INN HALL STREET
CORNMARKET ST
MARKET STREET
TURL ST
Lincoln Coll.
St Mary's Church
Brasenose Coll
St Peter's College
Buses Only
HIGH STREET
BECKET ST
HOLLYBUSH ROW
TIDMARSH LA
NEW ROAD
Oxford Castle
Carfax Tower
All Saints Church
ORIEL ST
Oriel College
University College
ROSE LANE
ST THOMAS STREET
Post Office
H M Prison
County Hall
QUEEN ST
Town Hall
Oxford Mus
BEAR LA
MERTON STREET
University Private Botanic Gardens
Magdalen Bridge
Angel Meadow
ST CLEMENTS
PARADISE ST
City Library
Museum of Modern Art
BLUE BOAR ST
P.O.
OSNEY LANE
Rec Grd
Westgate Shopping Centre
PEMBROKE STREET
ST EBBE'S ST
Christ Church
Corpus Christi College
Merton College
Merton Field
The Plain
College of Further Education
PARADISE SQUARE
CASTLE STREET
OLD GREY FRIARS ST
Pembroke College
ST ALDATES
BREWER ST
Christ Church Cathedral
Playing Field
COWLEY PL.
COWLEY RD
IFFLEY RD
Coach & Lorry Park
OXPENS ROAD
Magistrates Court
ALBION PLACE
BROAD WALK
Playing Fields
St Hilda's College
Ice Rink
SPEEDWELL ST
Attor Gdns
Recreation Ground
TRINITY STREET
THAMES STREET
Police Station
Christ Church Meadow
FRIARS WHARF
DALE CLOSE
River Thames
Bulstake Stream
Folly Bridge
Christ Church Sports Ground

University College One of three claimants to the title of Oxford's 'oldest college'.

Ashmolean Museum The basis of the museum was the collection of the 17th-century antiquary Elias Ashmole. It has a notable collection of Oriental treasures.

Bodleian Library One of the oldest and most famous libraries in the world, the Bodleian has an unrivalled collection of rare books and manuscripts. Of interest to the visitor are Duke Humphrey's Library and the Old Divinity School. Wood from Drake's ship the *Golden Hind* has been used to make a chair which is in the Bodleian.

Museum of the History of Science Housed in the original Ashmolean buildings, the museum concentrates on early astronomical, mathematical and optical instruments.

Museum of Modern Art Exhibitions of 20th-century art are held here.

Sheldonian Theatre Degrees are conferred in this Wren building, which is encircled by pillars bearing the busts of Roman emperors. From the cupola there are splendid views over the city.

Radcliffe Camera is a Classical domed building, used as a reading room for the Bodleian.

University Museums Set in the extensive grounds of the University Parks, the museums have geological and scientific collections.

University Private Botanic Garden near Magdalen Bridge is the oldest in the country.

OTTERY ST MARY
Devon *2 SY19*

The magnificent 14th-century collegiate church is out of all proportion to the size of this small town on the River Otter. The church was originally a dependency of the Cathedral of Rouen in France, and was bought in 1335 by the Bishop of Exeter, who made it into a slightly smaller version of his own cathedral. It contains a rare Tudor clock which shows the phases of the moon. Samuel Taylor Coleridge was born in Ottery, the son of the vicar. Among his works is a sonnet 'To the River Otter'. Celebrations in Ottery St Mary on 5 November include a carnival, and the ancient custom of carrying burning tar barrels.

North west of the town is Cadhay (OACT), one of the finest Tudor manor houses in the country.

Memorial plaque to Coleridge, Ottery St Mary church

OULTON BROAD
Suffolk *12 TM59*

The most southerly of the Broads, this popular yachting centre lies to the west of **Lowestoft**. George Borrow lived and worked here. The waters of the Broad were the first testing ground for the hovercraft.

OUNDLE
Northamptonshire *11 TL08*

Set beside a loop of the River Nene, Oundle is a busy sailing centre and a picturesque market town built of the local limestone. The buildings of

Arnol, Isle of Lewis

Oundle Public School were founded by William Laxton, a grocer who became Lord Mayor of London in the 16th century. 1½ miles north is Cotterstock Hall (gardens OACT), where Thomas Dryden wrote his *Fables*. Cotterstock was the birthplace in 1752 of Lieutenant John Graves Simcoe, first Governor of Upper Canada. In the church is a memorial to his father, Captain John Simcoe, who died in 1759 serving with Wolfe before the fall of Quebec. 4 miles south west is Lyveden New Bield, a cruciform building, designed to symbolize the Passion. The house was left unfinished because Sir Thomas Tresham's family became involved in the Gunpowder Plot; his grandson, Francis, was one of the conspirators.

Four miles south of Oundle is Achurch, birthplace of Edmund Quincy, the first known American ancestor of the famous family. He emigrated in 1633, receiving a grant of land at Mount Wollaston, now called Quincy after John Quincy, Edmund's grandson. Other descendants include Josiah Quincy, the patriot and contributor to the *Boston Gazette*; and Edmund Quincy the Younger, a judge, who died on a visit to London. The 'father' of Maryland, Robert Browne, was rector here for 40 years.

OUTER HEBRIDES, THE
Highland *29*

From the windswept headland of the Butt of Lewis in the north to Barra Head Lighthouse on the tiny Island of

Berneray in the south, the 'Long Island' or the 'Western Isles' as they are also known, stretch for 130 miles. The main islands are Lewis and Harris, North Uist, Benbecula, South Uist, Barra and Eriskay. Causeways and bridges now link the Uists and Benbecula. Ferry services run from the mainland from Ullapool to Lewis; from Uig to Harris; and from Oban to South Uist and Barra.

The Western Isles are one of the last outposts of the Gaelic way of life, and the crofters are resistant to change, as two well-intentioned improvers, Sir James Matheson and Lord Leverhulme discovered. Matheson bought the islands in the 19th century and spent a fortune on building roads and bridges. He built himself the Castle of Lews, now a technical college, at Stornoway, importing tons of soil from the mainland to establish the lovely gardens (OACT) where he planted the islands' only extensive woodlands. After World War I Lord Leverhulme bought Lewis and Harris, improved the harbour at Stornoway and tried to set up commercial fisheries, but the crofters did not take kindly to working in factories and his schemes came to nothing. The product for which the islands are mainly known is Harris Tweed. Throughout Harris and Lewis the tweeds, 28½ inches wide and 80ft long, are woven on handlooms from 'virgin wool spun, dyed and finished in the Outer Hebrides, and handwoven by the islanders in their own homes'. The various island tourist offices give details of weavers' workshops which can be visited.

The traditional home of the island crofters was the 'Black House', a low, thatched, windowless building with an open central fire, and one room in which both humans and animals sheltered. Two of these, at Arnol on the north-west coast of Lewis, and at Eochar on South Uist have been restored as crofting museums.

The islands, despite their inhospitable climate and infertile soils, have been inhabited since prehistoric times, as the wealth of prehistoric monuments shows. Most impressive of all is the great stone circle and avenue of Standing Stones (AM) occupying a bleak moorland site at Callanish, overlooking a remote inlet of the western coast. Not far away is another impressive relic, Carloway Broch (AM), a massive Iron Age stone tower, still standing 30ft high.

Harris is the most mountainous of the Western Isles, and has some lovely beaches in the south west, although only the hardy would bathe in the chilly Atlantic waters. The main settlements are Tarbert in the north, and Rodel in the south. The wild, remote promontory of Toe Head is one of the few British breeding grounds of the Golden Eagle.

North Uist and Benbecula are watery islands, the land mass broken up by a confusing maze of lochans, inlets and islets. Army rocket ranges on Benbecula add a touch of the surreal to this almost deserted landscape. The island of Eriskay was the setting for Sir Compton Mackenzie's novel, later filmed, *Whisky Galore*, based on the wreck of the SS *Politician* with its cargo of 20,000 cases of whisky in World War II. Eriskay, where Bonnie Prince Charlie first set foot on Scottish soil when he came from France, and Barra, are noted for their Gaelic folk songs.

OXBOROUGH
Norfolk *12 TF70*
Surrounded by a water-filled moat 15th-century Oxburgh Hall (NT) appears as a romantic evocation of an idyllic past. Even when it was built for Sir Edward Bedingfield, the moat, drawbridge and magnificent brick gatehouse can scarcely have served a defensive purpose. Among the many interesting relics of the Bedingfield family are needlework wall hangings worked by the imprisoned Mary Queen of Scots and her gaoler, the Countess of Shrewsbury.

PADIHAM
Lancashire *14 SD73*
Miss Rachel Kay-Shuttleworth's outstanding collection of textiles, embroideries, lace and the decorative arts is the centre of interest at Gawthorpe Hall (NT), a late Elizabethan mansion redesigned by Sir Charles Barry in the Victorian period. The rooms contain much handsome furniture, and the ceilings of the drawing room and long gallery are elaborately decorated. The house is the ancestral home of the Shuttleworths. Edward Shuttleworth, the Canadian pharmacist, left England for Canada with his father in the 1850s.

PADSTOW
Cornwall *1 SW97*
In the 6th century St Petroc is said to have founded a monastery here on the Camel estuary. The mainly decorated church has a carved font and memorials to the family who have lived at nearby Prideaux Place for nearly 400 years. The Elizabethan mansion has one of England's oldest deer parks. Ancient streets slope down to Padstow harbour. On South Quay is Raleigh Court, where Sir Walter Raleigh presided as Warden of Cornwall. D H Lawrence stayed in Padstow in 1915, intending to emigrate to Florida with a group of friends. Padstow's most celebrated event is the May Day procession when the Hobby Horse, draped in a hooped skirt, frolics through the streets led by the 'Teaser' and a band of attendants. The ancient custom, celebrating the defeat of winter, is believed to be among the oldest dance festivals in Europe. In the prettily named Fentonluna Lane is a Tropical Bird and Butterfly Garden.

PAIGNTON
Devon *2 SX86*
A Torbay resort, Paignton's many attractions include a large and interesting zoo, and several historic homes. The most outstanding is Oldway Mansion (OACT), built in 1871 by the American sewing machine millionaire, Isaac Merritt Singer. The house, completed in 1875, was known to the family as the 'Wigwam'. In 1904

Singer's son, Paris, began making alterations in the style of the Palace of Versailles. During World War II, Oldway was used as an American women's hospital. Kirkham House (OACT), a priest's or chantry house, has been restored to its 16th-century appearance as a museum of domestic life. At Higher Blagdon is the Torbay Aircraft Museum, with exhibits dating from 1924 to 1954. Steam trains run in summer along a stretch of the old Great Western line from Paignton to Kingswear, where there is a ferry to **Dartmouth**. Inland is **Compton Castle** (NT), former home of Sir Humphrey Gilbert.

PAINSWICK
Gloucestershire *9 SO80*
Painswick's lovely old streets slope down a high Cotswold hillside. Although nowadays a quiet place, it was once a wool town of considerable importance, as the many handsomely decorated table tombs in the churchyard show. 99 yew trees stand sentinel around the churchyard, and by tradition the hundredth would never grow. A 'clipping' ceremony takes place here on Painswick Feast Sunday around 19 September when the church is encircled by a ring of children. Afterwards Painswickians eat 'puppy-dog pie'. What the origins of this delicacy may have been can only be imagined: nowadays it is a cake containing a china dog. Painswick House (OACT) has splendid 18th-century reception rooms.

PAISLEY
Strathclyde *22 NS46*
The Museum and Art Gallery houses a priceless collection of the Paisley shawls for which the town has been famous for more than 200 years; their distinctive pattern was introduced from Kashmir in 1770. Paisley's most attractive building is the 17th-century Place of Paisley, a tall building with crow-stepped gables. Alexander Wilson, a Paisley weaver, emigrated to Philadelphia in 1791, where he became famous as a poet and ornithologist.

PANGBOURNE
Berkshire *4 SU67*
A church cottage in this quietly elegant town on the River Pang was the home of Kenneth Grahame, author of *The Wind in the Willows*. H Shephard's famous illustrations were inspired by the river here. Jerome K Jerome's heroes in *Three Men in a Boat* stayed here at the Swan Hotel.

PARC
Gwynedd *13 SH83*
Cyffdy Farm Park (OACT) is the rare-breed centre of northern Wales. There is a museum of old farm implements, but the real attraction is the animals – among them llamas and goats as well as traditional old breeds of sheep, cattle and poultry.

PARSON DROVE
Cambridgeshire *11 TF30*
Woad, a dye extracted from the woad plant, continued in use until quite recent times. Parson Drove, lost in the Cambridgeshire fens, was a centre of this traditional industry until synthetic indigo was introduced at the end of the 19th century.

PASTON
Norfolk *12 TG33*
Much of what we know of everyday life and business in the 15th century comes from the Paston letters, exchanged between members of this remarkable merchant family from 1422 to 1509. The mansion where they lived in the pleasant north Norfolk village is no more, but a great flint barn, 163ft long, stands as a reminder of their history. Memorials to some of the family are in the thatched church.

PEAK DISTRICT, THE
Derbyshire/Staffordshire *15*
Derbyshire and Staffordshire share the superb hill scenery of this lovely area of the Pennines between them. The landscape, too, is divided; between the limestone hills of the 'White Peak' in the south and the harsh moorland of the millstone-grit country to the north. The Peak District National Park covers about 540 sq miles. Good touring centres are **Matlock**, **Buxton**, and **Ashbourne**. Kinderscout at 2088ft and Bleaklow Hill at 2060ft are the highest points, but the Peak District is more famous for its low ground than for its hills: Dovedale, Monsal Dale, Lathkill Dale, Edale and the valleys of the Rivers Manifold, Goyt and Dane are among the most popular beauty spots.

PEAKIRK
Cambridgeshire *11 TF10*
Rare and unusual birds inhabit the waterfowl gardens of the Wildfowl Trust at Peakirk. Trumpeter, Black-necked and Coscoroba Swans are among the 100 or more different species of waterfowl that can be seen here. The village itself is stone built, and set in unspoiled countryside on the

edge of the Fens. At Northborough is the 14th-century Manor House, home of the Claybrooke family in the 16th century. John Claybrooke married Cromwell's daughter, Elizabeth. Three members of this family were early emigrants to America; one was a signatory to the Liberation of Pennsylvania. A Claybrooke was the first recruit to Washington's army, and another descendant printed the Declaration of Independence and Washington's final address to the people of America.

PEDDAR'S WAY
Norfolk *12*
One of Britain's ancient trackways, believed to predate the medieval period, Peddar's Way runs from the Wash near Hunstanton, passing near **Swaffham** and across the Breckland to a point just east of **Thetford** near the Norfolk and Suffolk border.

PEEBLES
Borders *23 NT23*
Three salmon appear on the town's coat of arms, aptly, as the dignified old county town of Peeblesshire on the River Tweed is a noted centre for salmon fishing. Tweeds and knitwear are manufactured here. The Chambers Institute, a museum and library, was

Mercat Cross, Peebles

built by William and Robert Chambers, of Chambers Dictionary and Encyclopaedias, who were born here. Other residents were Mungo Park, the explorer of the Niger, who worked here as a surgeon, and Anna Buchan, sister of John and a writer in her own right. The wooded hills above the river are dominated by 15th-century Neidpath Castle (OACT), where Scott was a frequent visitor; south east of the town are pleasant, wooded Kailzie Gardens (OACT).

PEMBROKE
Dyfed *7 SM90*
Pembroke Castle (AM), on its rocky headland above the town, is protected on three sides by the sea. The massive circular keep, dating from about 1200, stands within a curtain wall fortified by six towers and a forbidding gatehouse. This was the birthplace in 1457 of Henry Tudor, who was to emerge victorious as King of England after the Battle of Bosworth in 1485. Beneath it is a huge limestone cavern called the Wogan, which opens onto the river and was formerly linked to the castle by a winding staircase.

PEMBROKESHIRE COAST
   NATIONAL PARK *7*
A 167-mile footpath follows the wild coastline of Pembrokeshire from Amroth to St Dogmaels. The wild coast and its outlying islands are part of the National Park, which stretches inland to encompass the Preseli Hills and **Milford Haven**.

PENDEEN
Cornwall *1 SW33*
The Penwith peninsula is dotted with the gaunt ruins of engine-houses – the last visible remains of the once prosperous Cornish tin industry. Geevor tin mine near the hamlet of Pendeen is still worked however, and has a museum (OACT) showing the history of tin-mining in Cornwall.

PENDLE HILL
Lancashire *14 SD74*
The 1831ft Hill affords spectacular views westwards across the Forest of Bowland, to the Fylde Plain and the Irish Sea beyond. Pendle is most famous for its associations with witches; 19 of the witches tried at Lancaster Castle in 1612 were from this area, and 10 of them were hanged. Pendle has other connotations, for it was here in 1652 that George Fox had the vision which led him to found the Society of Friends.

STATELY REVELRIES

Wild-Life Parks

Many country houses have wild-life parks, aviaries, small railways etc. One of the most interesting is at Cricket St Thomas, near Chard in Somerset, the house and grounds being those used for the TV series 'To the Manor Born'. It includes a Heavy Horse Centre and a tropical aviary. Longleat, near Salisbury, offers lions, and the Earl of Lonsdale's game park at Lowther near Penrith in the Lake District has deer, wolves and otter – and a miniature railway.

There are many to choose from:

Alfriston, E Sussex: Drusillas Zoo Park
Burford, Oxfordshire: Cotswold Wild Life Park
Chester Zoo
Harewood House, near Leeds
Highland Wild-Life Park, Kincraig, near Kingussie, Inverness-shire
Holker Hall, near Grange Over Sands, South Lakeland
Knebworth House, near Stevenage, Hertfordshire
Penscynor Wild-Life Park, Cilfrew, Neath, W Glamorgan
Scone Palace, Perth (for Highland cattle)
Slimbridge

Tredegar House Country Park, Newport, Gwent
Twycross Zoo, Atherstone, Warwickshire

And note also
The Buckfast Butterfly Centre, Buckfastleigh, Devon
The Cornish Seal Sanctuary, Gweek, near Helston, Cornwall
The Swannery, Abbotsbury

For horses
The Dinosaur Museum, Dorchester
The National Horseracing Museum, Newmarket
The Shire Horse Centre, Maidenhead
The Wernher Collection, Luton Hoo, Bedfordshire

Above:
A medieval banquet

Left:
An open-air concert at Kenwood

Crinolines and Chopin

Country house musical soirées are now fashionable. See – and listen – at (among others):
Charlecote Park, Stratford-upon-Avon
Osterley Park, Middlesex
Sudeley Castle, Cheltenham
and, at a higher level:
Aldeburgh, or more accurately, Snape village, 9 miles away in east Suffolk, a few miles from Sutton Hoo.
Glyndebourne, near Brighton, Sussex

Medieval Banquets

Adamton Courte, Prestwick
Balls Farm, North Petherton, Somerset
Caldicot Castle, Chepstow, South Wales
Coombe Abbey, Coventry
Dalhousie Courte, Edinburgh
Lumley Castle, Durham
Old Vicarage, Bridgnorth (Edwardian)
Pen-y-bont Fawr, Corwen, Clwyd
Ruthin
Seaton Delaval Hall, near Newcastle-upon-Tyne
Worsley Old Hall, Worsley, Manchester

PENMACHNO
Gwynedd *13 SH75*
A former quarrymen's village, Penmachno lies in the little valley east of **Betws-y-Coed**. Its woollen mill (OACT) has an interesting history, having been set up in 1650 as a fulling mill. Cloth is still woven on 19th-century power looms. At Ty Mawr, 2 miles north west, is the cottage (NT) where Bishop William Morgan was born in 1545. He is revered for his translation, the first ever, of the Bible into Welsh.

PENMAENMAWR
Gwynedd *13 SH77*
Penmaenmawr was made popular by Lord Gladstone who made it his summer retreat. Although quarrying has carried off the top of the mountain, leaving only a single rocky crag to mark its original height, Penmaenmawr is nonetheless worth climbing up the steep hillside to the Druid's Circle, one of the best known groups of standing stones in Wales.

PENN
Buckinghamshire *5 SU99*
Following the death of his father in 1670, William Penn, founder of Pennsylvania, came to live in the village. Here he wrote two of his early books. Penn believed himself to be descended from a local family. However, the relationship has never been established. Nevertheless the area's links with William are indisputable and its Quaker connections are not forgotten.

Four miles south east at Jordans is the Quaker Meeting House built in 1687 following James II's Declaration of Indulgence. It is still in use today. Here William Penn is buried along with his two wives Gulielma Springett and Hannah Callowhill. Old Jordans, the farmhouse, is today used as a Quaker hostel, and the Mayflower Barn, reputedly built from timbers of the *Mayflower*, is also part of the centre.

• PENNINES, THE
14, 18, 19
Often called the backbone of England, this range of ancient hills, their weathered summits clothed in open heath and moorland, stretches from Derbyshire in the south to the Cheviot Hills on the Scottish border. The hills are sparsely populated, dotted with scattered sheep farms and stone-built villages; trees, except where the Forestry Commission has been active, are few. The Peak District National Park, the Yorkshire Dales National Park and the Northumberland National Park preserve much of its most unspoiled scenery. A 250-mile long distance footpath, the Pennine Way, the longest in Britain, runs from Edale in Derbyshire to Kirk Yetholm on the Scottish border. It can be walked in 14 days, or even less by the exceptionally fit.

PENRITH
Cumbria *18 NY42*
Literary associations – with Wordsworth, Scott and Coleridge – are strong in Penrith, a historic town, well situated as a touring centre both for the Lake District and for the Eden Valley. The parish church dates from the 12th century, though it was extensively remodelled in the 18th. In the churchyard is the so-called Giant's Grave, reputedly the tomb of Owen Caesarius, King of Cumbria in the 10th century. Nearby is the shaft of a contemporary cross, locally named the 'Giant's Thumb'. The site of Penrith Beacon to the north east of the town is marked by a memorial built in 1719.

Just to the north of Penrith is Edenhall, ancestral home of the Musgrave family; this was the home of the famous Luck of Edenhall goblet, now kept in the Victoria and Albert Museum, London.

In 1888, Eva Hassell was born at the manor house on the Dalemain estate 3 miles south west of Penrith. She began her mission work in Canada in 1920 and continued till 1973 when she was 87. Her mission used vans to tour the country and she organized many charities, working in Canada in the summer and from Dalemain in the winter.

PENSHURST
Kent *5 TQ54*
Old cottages and houses of the 16th, 17th and 18th centuries are much in evidence in this delightful Kentish village, and serve as a foretaste for the glories of Penshurst Place (OACT) ancestral home of the Sidney family and inspiration of Sir Philip Sidney's romance, *Arcadia*. One Algernon Sidney, a close friend of William Penn, helped draw up the Pennsylvania Constitution. The oldest parts of the manor, which is set in beautiful gardens, date from the 14th century, and the superb Baron's Hall, roofed with chestnut beams, is also of this period. The state rooms are splendidly furnished and there is also a fascinating collection of old toys. The Sidney family became Earls of Leicester, and at the entrance to the churchyard is a small open-ended square of old, timbered cottages called Leicester Square. One of the houses has been built around the lychgate of the medieval church, which contains the Sidney family chapel.

PENZANCE
Cornwall *1 SW43*
As a port for the Cornish tin trade and a haven for smugglers, Penzance, the most westerly town in England, flourished long before the arrival of the railway and its development as a seaside resort. Penlee Park contains a natural and local history museum, and the Roland Morris Maritime Museum displays objects recovered from ships wrecked off the Scilly Isles. Exotic plants flourish in Morrab Gardens, and the exotic Egyptian House is a local curiosity, restored by the Landmark Trust and used as a holiday home. At Trengwainton Gardens (NT) 2 miles west, many exotic plants are grown in walled gardens and woodland glades. Sir Humphry Davy, inventor of the miners' safety lamp, was born and educated in Penzance. Richard Trevithick, the early maker of steam locomotives, was an engineer at the nearby Ding Dong Mine. Ferry and helicopter services run between Penzance and the Scilly Isles.

PERTH
Tayside *23 NO12*
Sir Walter Scott's 'Fair Maid of Perth' was Catherine Glover and the 14th-century house (OACT) where she lived is now a crafts centre. Perth was the capital of the Scottish Kingdom until 1437, and as such, the ancient royal burgh at the head of the Tay estuary is rich in historical associations. St John's Kirk, built in the 15th century, is famous for the fiery sermon preached by John Knox in 1559 against church idolatry, which was one of the events which inspired the Reformation. Balhousie Castle, (OACT) near North Inch golf course, houses the Black Watch Regimental Museum. The Black Watch has many American connections and its pipe-band played at the funeral of John F Kennedy. Also of interest are the Perth Museum and Art Gallery, and a Caithness Glass factory, which is open to visitors. Branklyn Garden (NTS) on the road to Dundee, is famous for rhododendrons, shrubs and alpine plants, and has been called the finest garden of its size (2 acres) in Britain.

St John's Kirk, Perth, overlooking the River Tay with Perth's Old Bridge (1772) in the distance

PETERBOROUGH
Cambridgeshire *11 TL10*
Peterborough Cathedral dates from the 12th and early 13th centuries. It is a magnificent structure, built of local Barnack stone. Inside, the ceiling of the nave is decorated with figures of saints, kings, and many grotesques. Two queens were buried in front of the retrochoir: Katherine of Aragon and Mary Queen of Scots, both interred by the same gravedigger, Robert Scarlett, whose epitaph can also be seen: the body of Mary Queen of Scots was later removed to Westminster Abbey. In recent years Peterborough has expanded at an enormous rate, and the modern roads and buildings tend to obscure the legacy of the past. The Longthorpe Tower (AM) is a good example of a medieval fortified house. North of Peterborough are **Peakirk** and Northborough Castle.

PETERLEE
Co Durham *20 NZ44*
Founded in the 1950s in an effort to bring new employment to this part of the north east, Peterlee is a flourishing industrial town and has an attractive shopping centre. The town is named after Peter Lee, who started work down the mines at the age of ten, in 1874, and rose to become President of the Miners' Union. Castle Eden Dene (OACT) is a 3-mile stretch of natural woodland, owned by the corporation and kept as a nature reserve.

PETWORTH
W Sussex *5 SU92*
Though the Petworth estates have belonged to the Earls of Northumberland since 1150, it was the 6th Duke of Somerset, husband of the Percy heiress, who was responsible for the remodelling of this superb house in 1688. Petworth House (NT) stands in a park designed by Capability Brown in 1752. Turner painted it, an artist much admired by the then owner, the 3rd Earl of Egremont, a descendant of the Duke of Somerset. A number of Turner's paintings are among the masterpieces of European art that hang in Petworth's richly decorated and furnished rooms. The magnificence of the stately house should not cause the visitor to overlook the delights of the small town of Petworth with its old, narrow streets and timbered houses. The Angel Inn, like many others in Hampshire, was named by passing Pilgrims.

PEVENSEY
E Sussex *6 TQ60*
To guard the southern coast, the Romans built their fort of *Anderida* on a spit of land then open to the sea. In AD 491 it was besieged by and fell to Aelle, King of the South Saxons, who massacred all the Romano-British defenders. When William the Conqueror landed in Pevensey Bay in 1066, he found the fort abandoned, and promptly had a castle (AM) built on the site. Over the centuries it has been fortified many times: in World War II, camouflaged pill boxes, still difficult to spot, were built into the ancient walls. In the village High Street stands the Old Mint House (OACT) built in 1342 as a mint. In 1542 Henry VIII's physician, Dr Andrew Borde, made alterations to it and used it as a residence.

PICKERING
N Yorkshire *16 SE78*
Pickering is a lively market town with steep narrow streets climbing the hillside. Looking down from a height over the market place stands Pickering's parish church, the walls of its nave decorated with a series of remarkably vivid wall paintings depicting legends of the saints, and believed to date from the 15th century. In the chancel is a monument to Nicholas and Robert King of Pickering, surveyors who helped and then succeeded L'Enfant in planning Washington DC. Below, two brasses commemorate Walter Hines Page, US Ambassador to London during World War I, and the Anglo-American Alliance in 1917. Pickering Castle, also high above the town, is very much a ruin, but the North York Moors Railway, closed by British Rail, has been restored. The Beck Isle Museum of Rural Life contains interesting folk and local history displays.

Wall paintings dating from the 15th century in Pickering's parish church

PILGRIMS' WAY
Hampshire/Kent *4, 5, 6*
This was a medieval route linking the two great cathedral cities of the south, Winchester and Canterbury, and their shrines of St Swithun and St Thomas à Becket. It led across the slope of the **North Downs**, following for part of the way the line of a prehistoric track. Like the **Ridgeway**, it is now a long distance footpath.

PLYMOUTH

Devon 2 *SY55*

'I reach the marble-streeted town, whose "Sound" outbreathes, its air of sharp sea-salts.'

Thomas Hardy, *The Marble-Streeted Town.*

Its site at the head of Plymouth Sound, between the estuaries of the Rivers Plym and Tamar, has made Plymouth a maritime city from its earliest days. The Hawkins family, Drake, Humphrey Gilbert, Sir Ferdinando Gorges (a Plymouth man), Martin Frobisher, Raleigh – all had Plymouth as their base and their exploits helped to bring fame and prosperity to this Devon city. It is said that Gorges, the Governor of Plymouth, was turned to thoughts of the Americas by the sight of 5 American Indians brought from Maine in 1605. Humphrey Gilbert's Newfoundland voyage is remembered in a plaque on Plymouth Hoe. Martin Frobisher made 3 voyages to the Canadian coast, seeking the North-West Passage. Trade and exploration went hand-in-hand and Plymouth's prosperity was, in part, built on the Newfoundland fish trade.

Towards the end of the 17th century William III ordered the Devonport marshes to be drained, and the Royal Naval Dockyard to be built, thus giving the Navy an official presence in Plymouth. In World War II German bombs reduced the centre to rubble, but it has since risen again, its many new buildings dominated by the soaring 2000ft tower of the Civic Centre, from the top of which there are magnificent views. The Hoe (meaning 'High Place') is another excellent vantage point. Here, as every schoolchild knows, Sir Francis Drake, circumnavigator of the world, was enjoying a game of bowls in 1588 when the Armada was sighted, and insisted on finishing his game before setting sail to defeat the Spanish. There is a statue on the Hoe. There are plaques commemorating historic journeys on the Mayflower Steps in Sutton Pool, the ancient harbour which was the nucleus of the modern city. Most famous of all was the voyage of the Pilgrim Fathers, who sailed for New England in the New World in their little ship *Mayflower* on 6 September 1620. Some of the Pilgrims slept the last night at No 9 the Barbican. They landed at Plymouth Rock, Massachusetts on 21 December 1620. The name had first been used earlier than this though. New Plymouth appears first on Captain John Smith's

Sir Francis Drake, Plymouth Hoe

map of 1614. In 1630 Reverend John White set sail from here in the *Mary and John*. Many people in his party were from Dorchester. Just over 150 years after the Pilgrims, in 1772, Captain James Cook set out on his round-the-world voyage of exploration, to be followed nearly 200 years later, in 1967, by Sir Francis Chichester, who landed here on his return from his solo voyage. Around Sutton Pool in the area known as the Barbican is all that remains of Drake's Plymouth. Here, the narrow streets sloping down to the Quay contain several Tudor houses. Although this attractive and historic quarter has been sensitively preserved, Plymouth looks firmly to its future as a modern, commercial city.

There are a number of other interesting New World connections with Plymouth. Millbay Prison housed American prisoners in the War of Independence before they were transferred to Princetown, the prison town on Dartmoor. Millbay held American inmates again in the War of 1812. Two American sailors who died in the war are buried in St Andrew's churchyard. The Door of Unity, Prysten House, which leads into the churchyard, commemorates them. The entrails of Martin Frobisher are also buried at St Andrew's. His body is in London. Brook Watson, who figures in the American artist, John Singleton Copley's first major picture 'Watson and the Shark' (1778) was a Plymouth man. As a boy, Watson lost a leg to a shark while swimming in Havana harbour, and later commissioned the picture. He was with Wolfe at Louisbourg and a Lord Mayor of London. Sir George Arthur, Lieutenant-Governor of Upper Canada 1838–41, was from Plymouth. The son of New York's William

Waldorf Astor was a Mayor of Plymouth and Nancy Langhorne of Virginia, Lady Astor was the first woman to take a seat in the British parliament (in 1919) as member for Sutton, Plymouth. She was a member for 25 years.

As can be expected, North American connections will be found in the villages near this major centre. Fardell, at Cornwood, 10 miles north east of Plymouth, was the family home of the Raleighs from 1303, though Walter Raleigh himself was born at Hayes Barton, near **Budleigh Salterton**. At Noss Mayo, south east of Plymouth along the coast, Edward Baring, later Lord Revelstoke, the financier whose money saved the Canadian Pacific Railway in 1885, is commemorated in stained glass in St Peter's Church. The area around Slapton, 25 miles east of Plymouth, was used as the major training area for the D-Day invasions in World War II and there are memorials at Slapton, Dartmouth and Salcombe to American servicemen who sailed from South Devon for the 1944 Normandy landings.

Customs House, Barbican

PLACES TO SEE
Aquarium of the Marine Biological Association Fish and other kinds of marine life can be viewed in this fascinating aquarium.

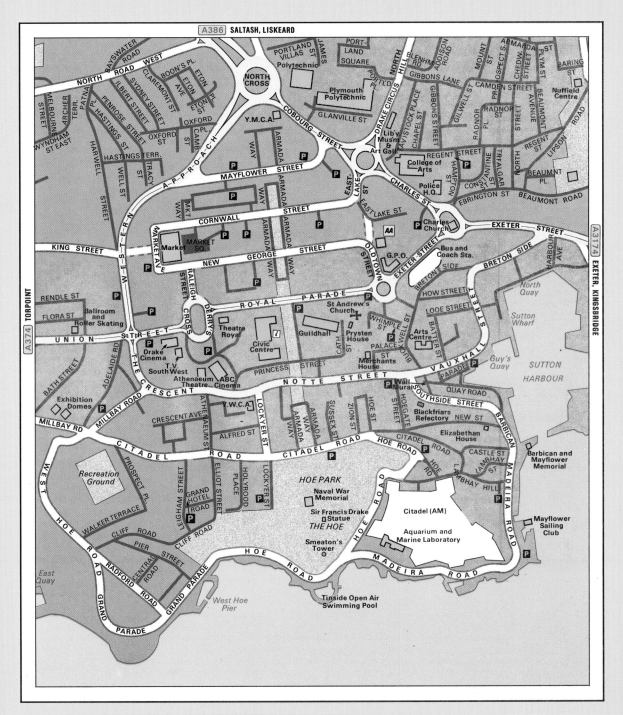

A374 TORPOINT

A3174 EXETER, KINGSBRIDGE

Blackfriars Only the 16th-century refectory of this Dominican priory remains, on land belonging to a distillery where the famous 'Plymouth Gin' is made'.

City Museum and Art Gallery Paintings, including some by Sir Joshua Reynolds, drawings, and finds from Dartmoor are among the collections displayed.

The Merchant's House One of the old houses in the Barbican district has been restored as a museum of Plymouth history.

Prysten House This is Plymouth's oldest house, built by a merchant in 1490 and used as a priests' house by monks of Plympton Priory. It has exhibits relating to the *Mayflower*.

Royal Citadel The barracks beside the Hoe date from the reign of Charles II, and feature a magnificent Baroque gateway designed by Sir Thomas Fitz.

St Andrew's Church Plymouth's parish church, restored after bomb damage during World War II, with fine modern windows designed by John Piper.

PILTDOWN
E Sussex *5 TQ42*
Piltdown is famous as the site of the
discovery of the remains of Piltdown
Man, one of the most notorious of all
archaeological forgeries. The skull was
'discovered' in 1912 by Charles
Dawson, and acclaimed by
archaeologists as the 'missing link'
between man and ape. The hoax lasted
until 1953 when tests proved that an
ape's jaw-bone and a tooth had been
cleverly grafted onto genuine
fragments of a prehistoric skull.

PLOCKTON
Highland *25 NG83*
Now safely in the care of the National
Trust for Scotland, this delightful
village on the shores of Loch Carron,
set in beautiful mountain scenery, has
had a chequered history. In 1801 most
of the existing crofters were evicted to
make way for a sheep-farming
settlement planned by the new
landlord, Hugh Innes. His plans did
not get far, but his descendants tried to
improve the fishing and the harbour.
In 1850 Sir Alexander Matheson
bought the area and built himself a
castle, before moving on to grander
projects on Lewis and Harris in the
Outer Hebrides. Finally the estate was
acquired by Sir Daniel Hamilton, who
gave it to the Scottish National Trust.
The village is sheltered by its
surrounding hills, and the Gulf Stream
causes palm trees to flourish.

PLYMPTON
Devon *2 SX55*
The two villages of Plympton St Mary
and Plympton St Maurice are
nowadays almost part of **Plymouth**.
The painter Sir Joshua Reynolds was
born at Plympton St Maurice in 1723
and was educated at the local grammar
school. Many of his paintings hang in
Saltram House (NT), a Tudor house
refronted in the 18th century,
beautifully furnished, and built for the
Parker family. 2 miles north east of
Plympton Sir John Colbourne, in
command of forces in Canada in the
rebellion of 1837 and later Governor of
British North America, is buried in the
churchyard at Newton Ferrers. He
lived at Beechwood, a house near
Uparkwell. 3 miles north east of
Plympton is the Dartmoor Wild Life
Park, occupying 25 acres.

POLPERRO
Cornwall *1 SX25*
One of Cornwall's most enchanting
fishing villages, Polperro lies at the
foot of a deep wooded combe. One of
the cottages houses a museum of
smuggling and an exhibition. The
Land of Legend portrays Cornwall's
past history and includes a model
Polperro Village.

POLSTEAD
Suffolk *12 TL93*
Notoriety came to this quiet little
village in 1827 when Maria Marten
was murdered at the Red Barn which
stood near the church. The case was
turned into a popular Victorian
melodrama, *Maria Marten or The
Murder at the Red Barn*. West, at
Assington, Nathaniel Rogers, pastor of
Ipswich, Massachusetts had a
ministry.

PONTEFRACT
W Yorkshire *15 SE42*
The round black sweets known as
Pontefract cakes were originally made
of locally grown liquorice, but
nowadays it is imported. Where the
liquorice field once was, stand the
ruins of Pontefract Castle, where
Richard II was imprisoned and
eventually murdered. Many people
were executed here in the Wars of the
Roses and its reputation was so
sinister that the townspeople
petitioned Cromwell to pull it down. A
painting of the castle before its
destruction hangs in Pontefract
Museum. Nostell Priory (NT) was
built as a house in 1733 on the site of
an Augustinian priory, and about 30
years later Robert Adam remodelled a
large part of it. There are many good
paintings and some excellent
Chippendale furniture, and murals by
Angelica Kauffmann.

PONTYPRIDD
Mid Glamorgan *8 ST09*
Anchor chains for Nelson's Fleet, and,
more recently for liners such as *Queen
Elizabeth* and *Queen Mary* were made
in this Rhondda Valley town. It is
claimed that the 18th-century bridge
over the River Taff was designed by a
self-taught engineer, William Edwards.
It is considered a masterpiece. On a
house in Mill Street is a plaque
commemorating Evan and James
James, clothmakers who wrote *Hen
Wlad Fy Nhadau*, 'Land of My
Fathers', the Welsh national anthem.

POOLE
Dorset *3 SZ09*
Yachts and pleasure boats of all kinds
throng Poole's enormous bay, a
natural harbour, said to measure more
than 100 miles round. Encroaching
suburban development has now linked
Poole to its neighbour, **Bournemouth**,
but Poole is much the older town of
the two. The 18th-century atmosphere
of Poole's old town is remarkably well
preserved. Scalpen's Court and the
former Guildhall both contain
museums of local history, while at
Poole Quay a maritime museum is
housed in the 15th-century cellars.
Poole Pottery was founded in 1875 and
its quayside works are open to the
public. Marconi conducted early
wireless experiments here in 1898. The
town's greatest asset, however, is its
natural harbour. Warehouses, harbour
offices and ships' chandlers still line the
harbour. Now a popular yachting
centre, Poole was formerly the
administrative centre of Dorset.

It was the Newfoundland cod trade
that helped build Poole's finest
buildings. Local families, the Lesters,
the Garlands, the Spurriers, seamen
and merchants, ensured close links
between Canada and Poole in the 18th
and 19th centuries. The trade attracted
population and also settlement in
Canada. Pillars of Newfoundland pine
are to be found in the parish church, a
reminder of the Canada timber trade.
Nearby is Brownsea Island.

POOLEWE
Highland *29 NG88*
Despite the fact that it lies on a more
northerly latitude than Moscow,
subtropical plants flourish in the
remarkable gardens of Inverewe
House (NTS), created by Osgood
MacKenzie in 1862. He imported soil
specially, planted extensive woodlands
to shelter his more delicate plants, and
the result is a maze of winding
woodland walks where the flowers are
at their best in spring and early
summer.

PORLOCK
Somerset *2 SS84*
From the west visitors have a choice of
routes into this attractive village, the
steep 1 in 4 Porlock Hill or the gentler
toll roads. It occupies a beautiful site,
caught between Exmoor and the sea,
but to get to the pebbly shore, visitors
must first go to Porlock Weir, a tiny
place clustered around a small
harbour. From here, a footpath leads
to Culbone Church which is 'the
smallest parish church in England',
and occupies a lovely site beside a
stream. Porlock holds a unique place
in literature as the home of the
anonymous 'person from Porlock'

whose inconvenient visit interrupted Coleridge and caused him to abandon his unfinished poem, 'Kubla Khan'.

PORTHCURNO
Cornwall *1 SW32*
Occupying a superb site 200ft up on the cliffs below the village, Minack Theatre, an open air amphitheatre, modelled on the theatres of ancient Greece, was created in 1932 by Miss Rowena Cade. There is a regular summer season of plays which attracts audiences from all over the world. Porthcurno has a fine beach of almost white sand.

PORTHMADOG
Gwynedd *13 SH53*
A mile-long embankment along which a toll road runs, built in the early 1800s by William Madocks, created the safe harbour that made Porthmadog one of the best ports on the Welsh coast and ensured its prosperity. Extensive sandy beaches, such as Black Rock Sands have made it a popular tourist resort. It is also the start of the famous Ffestiniog narrow-gauge railway, which runs from the Harbour Station to the old slate quarry town of **Blaenau Ffestiniog**. There is a Railway Museum at the station. Porthmadog Pottery (OACT) offers visitors guided tours. Borth-y-Gest, 1 mile away, is said to be Prince Madog's point of departure on his voyage of discovery to America in the 12th century. 1 mile inland is **Tremadog**.

PORTLAND, ISLE OF
Dorset *3 SY67*
An isthmus and the pebble spit of Chesil Bank are all that join Portland to the mainland. The inhabitants of the scattered villages long claimed to have distinct ancestry from their neighbours on the mainland, and jealously preserved their own customs and traditions, including smuggling. For many centuries, Portland has been a defensive site; in the 19th-century, a large harbour was built here using convict labour – and Portland is still an important naval base. The southern tip of Portland Bill is graced by an old lighthouse – now a bird-watching station. Portland Museum (OACT) is housed in a cottage associated with Thomas Hardy's *The Well-Beloved*. William Wordsworth's brother was drowned off Portland. The Normans built the now ruined Bow and Arrow Castle, and in the 16th century Henry VIII added Portland Castle (OACT). Pennsylvania Castle was built in 1800

by John Penn, a Governor of Pennsylvania and grandson of its founder. It was designed by James Wyatt. Many architects have made use of the beautiful Portland stone, among them Sir Christopher Wren, who used it for St Paul's Cathedral. The United Nations Buildings in New York are also made of Portland stone.

In Southwell parish church, towards the tip of Portland Bill, there is a Nova Scotian flag and a memorial tablet to people who died on the *Forest*, out of Nova Scotia, which, in 1879, tragically collided with the *Avalanche* with great loss of life.

PORTMEIRION
Gwynedd *13 SH53*
The inspiration for this delightful fantasy, created by the architect Sir Clough Williams Ellis, who died in 1978, was the Italian fishing village of Portofino. On his return to Britain he searched for a suitable site, and finally found the ideal setting on a wooded, rocky promontory between **Porthmadog** and **Harlech**. Graceful, Italianate buildings, dominated by an elegant campanile, surround the main square, and all manner of exotic plants flourish in the picturesque streets. All the cottages are let as holiday homes, and there are also hotels, restaurants and shops. The famous and controversial American architect of the 'Prairie School', Frank Lloyd Wright, was a close friend of Williams Ellis and a frequent visitor to Portmeirion. (Day visitors must pay an entrance fee.)

PORT OF MENTEITH
Central *22 NN50*
The resort lies on the shores of the beautiful Lake of Menteith, sheltered by the Menteith Hills. Ferries run to an island in the lake where the ruins of Inchmaholme Priory (AM) can be seen. It was founded as an Augustinian House in 1238. The 4-year-old Mary Queen of Scots took refuge here in 1543 and the garden where she played, known as Queen Mary's Bower, still remains.

PORT SUNLIGHT
Merseyside *14 SJ38*
The name of this Victorian 'model village' commemorates Sunlight soap, the product that helped to found the vast fortune of William Hesketh Lever, who became the 1st Viscount Leverhulme. The Lady Lever Art Gallery and Museum contains a magnificent collection of English painting and furniture.

Porthmadog

POTTERIES, THE
Staffordshire *14 SJ84*
This is the name given to the towns which were joined to Stoke to make the modern city of **Stoke-on-Trent**: Tunstall, Burslem, Hanley, Fenton and Longton. The district is famous for its china and earthenware.

PRESTON
Lancashire *14 SD52*
Preston was one of the most important centres of the cotton trade, and one of the cradles of the Industrial Revolution. The inventor of the spinning-frame, Richard Arkwright, was born at Preston, but had to take his invention to **Nottingham** to avoid riots. In the Harris Museum exhibits tell the history of the cotton trade, and there are interesting archaeological remains and collections of glass and ceramics. The poet of the Canadian North and the Klondike, Richard Service, was born here.

PRESTONPANS
Lothian *24 NT37*
The famous battle took place in 1745 when Bonnie Prince Charlie's army won an astonishing and decisive victory in a mere ten minutes. The town was once a centre of salt-panning and was also famous for its oysters. Many of its attractive houses date from the 17th century, as does the fine Mercat Cross.

PORTSMOUTH

Hampshire   4 SZ09

The first monarch to appreciate the strategic importance of Portsea Island in the defence of the English Channel was Richard the Lionheart, who ordered the first docks to be built in 1194: 'It pleased the Lord King Richard to build the new town of Portsmouth', reads the entry in the Curia Regis rolls of that year. Over the centuries, succeeding monarchs have improved the defences and extended the docks to ensure that Portsmouth remained an impregnable fortress and secure base for the navy in times of war. The King's Bastion and the Long Curtain Battery are all that remain of the medieval defensive ramparts, but the Round Tower, earliest of the fortifications, and the Square Tower, built by Henry VII, still remain, as do the sea and land forts built in the Victorian era.

The docks have grown steadily since the 12th century: in 1495 the world's first dry dock was constructed, and by the reign of Henry VIII, the docks had extended to cover about 8 acres of land – they now cover about 300 acres. Henry not only built Southsea Castle to improve the defences, he also built ships, including the pride of his fleet, the *Mary Rose*, which tragically sank with all hands just off the coast. In 1982, in one of the most exciting marine salvage operations ever undertaken, she was raised from the seabed and is now on display. During the Napoleonic Wars the town played a key role as a base for the British fleet, and Nelson set out from here to take command at Trafalgar on 21 October 1805. The *Victory*, his flagship, was eventually brought to dry dock in Portsmouth Docks.

Portsmouth suffered much from bombing in World War II, and the centre has been largely rebuilt. The old town, clustered around the harbour mouth, has been restored, and is now an attractive and fashionable area. In these old streets stands the cathedral, raised from the status of parish church in the 1920s.

Portsmouth was the birthplace of the novelist George Meredith and of the engineer Isambard Kingdom Brunel.

John Mason, from **King's Lynn**, lived for some time in Portsmouth, at Buckingham House in High Street. He founded New Hampshire and was one of the early Governors of Newfoundland, making its first English map and writing about it to encourage emigration. Mason died in 1636 and is buried in Westminster Abbey. There is a plaque at the cathedral. General Wolfe left England at Portsmouth bound for Canada in 1758 and the next year his body came back, in state, following his victory and death at Quebec. During the 18th century, Quebec House in Bath Square was a rendezvous for travellers to North America. Robert Moncton who served in the battle for Quebec and was later Lieutenant-Governor of Nova Scotia, was an MP for Portsmouth. Sir John Franklin set out from Portsmouth on his last expedition. And Canadian troops left here, bound for Europe on D-Day, and earlier, in 1942, for the Dieppe Raid.

Southsea, Portsmouth's neighbour, grew up in the 19th century as an elegant seaside resort, with fine houses and terraces, an esplanade, and an extensive seafront common made by draining the marshes. Still a pleasant resort, Southsea is now part of the City of Portsmouth, as is Eastney, which grew up on its outskirts in the 19th century. Also 18th- and 19th-century developments are the 'villages' of Portsea, where many of the shipwrights and craftsmen employed in the docks had their homes, and Landport, now the commercial and administrative centre of the modern city. Charles Dickens was born in this area in 1812 in a house on Old Commercial Road. In 1892 Sir Arthur Conan Doyle established a surgery in Portsea; it was here that Sherlock Holmes was created.

Ten miles north east of Portsmouth, on the outskirts of Havant is Rowlands Castle, home of the Bexboroughs. The 9th earl was Governor-General of Canada in the 1930s. Troops from Canada were stationed close to the castle in World War II.

Twelve miles north west of Portsmouth is the village of Swanmore. The Canadian academic and humorist, Stephen Leacock, was born here in 1869. The family emigrated in 1876 and the family house, just west of the church, has a plaque.

PLACES TO SEE

Charles Dickens Birthplace Museum The modest family home is now a Dickens shrine.

HMS *Victory* and Royal Naval Museum Admiral Lord Nelson's flagship is the only surviving First Rate Ship of the Line of its period. The adjacent museum houses other relics of Trafalgar.

Tower House and the Round Tower

The Round Tower (OACT) is the earliest of Portsmouth's permanent defences.

City Museum and Art Gallery Housed in part of the old Pembroke Barracks.

Southsea Castle (OACT) Built in 1545, the castle houses a museum of historical and archaeological interest.

John Mason was captain of Southsea in 1634.

Cumberland House Museum Natural history exhibits, and an aquarium are housed here.

Royal Marine Museum, Eastney The museum is housed in the original Victorian Officers' Mess. It has many items relating to Canada and America, including a recruitment poster for the American War of Independence.

Eastney Pumping Station (OACT) Two Boulton and Watt engines can be seen working on most summer weekends.

Fort Widley (OACT) Built in the 1860s this fort and others like it were the last defensive structures to be built on the principles of a medieval castle.

PRESTWICH
Gtr Manchester *14 SD80*
An industrial town, now inextricably part of **Manchester**, Prestwich boasts, in Heaton Hall (OACT), one of the finest late 18th-century houses in Lancashire, designed by James Wyatt for the Earl of Wilton.

PRINCETOWN
Devon *2 SX57*
The largest and bleakest Dartmoor town. Standing at 1400ft above sea-level, Princetown is dominated by its famous prison. Originally built in 1806 to hold French prisoners during the Napoleonic wars, Princetown also housed more than 2000 American soldiers captured in 1812. The church of St Michael in the town was built by French and American prisoners. The east window was given by American women in memory of 200 of their men who died at Princetown. The moor surrounding the town is rich in prehistoric remains. Notable among these are the Bronze Age hut circles at Merrivale, 2 miles away. Conan Doyle used the bleakness of the moor as a setting for Sherlock Holmes' adventures in *The Hound of the Baskervilles* (1902).

PUDDLETOWN
Dorset *3 SY79*
As charming as its name suggests, Puddletown stands at the foot of the Piddle Valley, and only changed its old name of Piddletown in the 1950s. Hardy called it Weatherby in *Far from the Madding Crowd* and the open country between the village and Wareham features in several of his novels as Egdon Heath. A mile-long avenue of rhododendrons leads through Puddletown Forest. Nearby is Athelhampton Manor Hall (OACT).

PULBOROUGH
W Sussex *5 TQ01*
Three miles south is Parham House, an Elizabethan mansion begun by Sir Thomas Palmer who sailed with Drake to Cadiz; the house is set in beautiful gardens (OACT). 3 miles east of Pulborough is Thakeham Friends Meeting House (OACT) where William Penn and his family worshipped when they lived on the Warminghurst Estate. In 1672 Penn married Gulielma Springettt of Ringmer, near **Lewes**; she inherited the estate, and the family moved here in 1676. Edmund Freeman, one of the original Pilgrims, was born in Pulborough.

Q   R

QUANTOCK HILLS, THE
Somerset *2 ST13*
The Visitor Centre for the Quantocks is at Fyne Court, Broomfield, and is worth visiting for information about this lovely range of hills. The slopes are heavily wooded, and the tops are clothed with attractive heathland. Red deer run wild, and there are regular hunts at the appropriate seasons. Crowcombe, East Quantoxhead, Spaxton and Enmore are among the most attractive villages, and there are some beautiful wooded valleys, particularly in the north east.

QUEENSFERRY, SOUTH
Lothian *23 NT17*
The old ferry that used to ply across the Firth of Forth departed from Hawes Pier, where there is an old inn featured both by Sir Walter Scott, in *The Antiquary* and by Robert Louis Stevenson in *Kidnapped*. The ferry stopped in 1964 when the Forth Road Bridge was opened. This 2000yd-long bridge is as impressive a piece of engineering as the 2765yd-long railway bridge that was built at the end of the 19th century. Dalmeny House (OACT), home of the Earl of Rosebery, commands magnificent views of the Firth of Forth. The house contains the Rothschild Collection of 18th-century French furniture, porcelain and tapestries. 2 miles west, Hopetoun House (OACT) is Scotland's most distinguished Adam mansion, home of the Marquis of Linlithgow. Deer and St Kilda sheep coexist peacefully in the grounds, and the house contains interesting furnishings.

RAGLAN
Gwent *9 SO40*
On a knoll just outside the village are the impressive ruins of 15th-century Raglan Castle (AM). One of the latest examples of medieval fortification in Britain, it was a Royalist centre during the Civil War, holding out against Fairfax for 11 weeks in 1646. One side of the moated five-storey Great Tower was blown up and the rest of the castle slighted.

Raglan Castle

RANWORTH
Norfolk *12 TG31*
Particularly fine treasures in the parish church of this village between Ranworth and South Walsham Broads include a 14th- or 15th-century painted screen and the Ranworth (or Sarum) Antiphones, an illuminated 15th-century choir book of great beauty. From the church tower there are lovely views over Ranworth Broad. The Broadland Conservation Centre, on Ranworth Inner Broad, can be reached by a nature trail.

RAVENGLASS
Cumbria *18 SD09*
Once a port, this unspoilt fishing village stands on the estuary of the Rivers Esk, Mite and Irt. It is best known for the 7-mile long Ravenglass and Eskdale railway which runs to Dalegarth through the beautiful Eskdale Valley. Established in 1875 to carry iron ore, this 15-inch narrow gauge railway, affectionately known as 'L'aal Ratty', now carries passengers using both steam and diesel locomotives. There is a Railway Museum here. Also near Ravenglass, at Walls Castle, are some preserved Roman ruins.

READING
Berkshire *4 SU77*
Reading, now a large university town and shopping and market centre, has lost much of its impressive past. Henry I was buried in the 12th-century abbey, which was later 'dissolved' by Henry VIII, and is now no more than a few insubstantial remains. Archbishop Laud was baptized in St Lawrence's Church. William and Thomas Penn, sons of William Penn, founded Reading, Pennsylvania, naming it after Reading, England. The family had connections with the town, and worshipped at the Quaker Meeting House. At **Twyford**, 5 miles north east, Penn died in 1718 at Southcombe Farm. Reading Castle, and a palace built by Henry VIII have also been destroyed; however, Roman remains from the nearby town of Silchester are preserved in the Reading Museum and Art Gallery. The Museum of English Rural Life, in the university, has an interesting collection of agricultural, domestic and craft exhibits. Reading's prison was made famous by Oscar Wilde in *The Ballad of Reading Gaol* (1898); it was while he was imprisoned here that Wilde wrote *De Profundis*. The academic and controversialist Goldwin Smith, who settled in Toronto and left his considerable wealth to Cornell University, New York, where he had taught, was born in 1823 at 15 Friar Street which is marked with a plaque. There is a portrait in Reading Museum.

Across the Thames, 3 miles north west of Caversham, is Mapledurham House.

REAY
Highland *30 NC96*
Sand dunes separate the village from the sandy beach of Sandside Bay: in the 18th century they engulfed an earlier settlement. 2 miles north east a farm contains the remains of Dounreay Castle, including a 16th-century tower. A 135ft sphere marks the site of the United Kingdom Atomic Energy Authority. There is an exhibition relating to fast reactors and nuclear energy.

RECULVER
Kent *6 TR26*
Two towers of a Norman church destroyed in 1809 are preserved to serve as a navigational guide for Thames shipping. They stand on the site of a 7th-century Saxon church, and walls also remain of a Roman fort (AM) built in about AD 200.

REDCAR
Cleveland *20 NZ62*
Miles of firm, sandy beaches stretch from here to the Tees estuary and the town has become a lively resort, with a wide range of leisure and entertainment facilities, including Coatham Amusement Park, the largest indoor funfair in the north east. There is also a well-known racecourse. The oldest lifeboat in the world, built in 1800, can be seen in the Zetland Museum on the Promenade. Nathaniel Hawthorne lived here for a time.

REDMIRE
N Yorkshire *20 SE09*
Pale stone cottages are scattered round the large green of this peaceful, isolated Wensleydale village. To the north are limestone hills; to the south, the wooded valley of the River Ure, with its waterfall, Redmire Force, 1 mile south west. Mary Queen of Scots was imprisoned for a time in 14th-century Bolton Castle (OACT) which stands to the north east of the village.

REEDHAM
Norfolk *12 TG40*
Those interested in the art of taxidermy can visit the museum at Pettitts Rural Industries, where there are often craft demonstrations too. The buildings are set in gardens where pheasants, peacocks and all sorts of waterfowl and game birds are on show. There are several disused windmills in the vicinity; 19th-century Berney Arms Windmill (AM), in Havergate Marshes, 3 miles north east, is in full working order. It can be reached by boat from **Great Yarmouth**.

REEPHAM
Norfolk *12 TG12*
The centre of a barley growing and brewing region in the 18th century, Reepham has an attractive market square and many fine buildings as evidence of its past prosperity. Three churches once shared a common churchyard, although only two still stand. The nearby manor house contains a portrait of the Indian princess Pocahontas, who married John Rolfe, whose family built Booton church. 2 miles south of Reepham, the 50-acre Norfolk Wildlife Park has an extensive collection of European mammals and birds of prey in natural surroundings.

REIGATE
Surrey *5 TQ24*
Situated on the edge of the **North Downs**, Reigate's open spaces include the 130-acre Reigate Heath, where church services are held in a converted 220-year old windmill. The town retains some interesting old buildings. The priory, founded in 1235, was converted into a Tudor mansion and now houses a school and a museum (OACT). Reigate's large parish church contains the grave of Lord Howard of Effingham, who commanded the English fleet which defeated the Armada. Only the mound remains of the Norman castle; beneath is a cave and medieval tunnels, used as air raid shelters in World War II. On Reigate Hill there is a memorial to 9 United States airmen who died in the crash of Flying Fortress No 339035.

REPTON
Derbyshire *10 SK32*
This little village, whose broad main street is lined by attractive timber-framed and Georgian red brick houses, was the 7th-century capital of the Saxon kingdom of Mercia. The tiny 10th-century crypt of the medieval church is a treasured example of Anglo Saxon architecture. Ruins of a 12th-century priory are incorporated into Repton School, founded in 1557.

RHONDDA
Mid Glamorgan *8 SS99*
A chain of towns in two valleys, Rhondda Fawr ('large'), and Rhondda Fach ('small'), make up the densely populated Rhondda borough. The valleys are separated by the Cefu Rhondda ridge, which reaches 2000ft in places. In the 19th century these pleasant rural valleys were transformed by coalmines and miners' cottages, but the Rhondda's industries have been decimated. The hardships of life in the Rhondda have been vividly

described in Richard Llewellyn's poignant novel *How Green was my Valley* and in the film *Proud Valley*, in which Paul Robeson starred – having spent several months living as a miner in the area.

In Clydach, just south of Rhondda, is a statue of the chemist Ludwig Mond, whose technique for refining nickel formed the basis of the Mond Industrial fortunes, including ICI and the International Nickel Company of Canada.

RHUDDLAN
Clwyd *13 SJ07*
The majestic ruins of Rhuddlan Castle lie on a mound above the banks of the River Clwyd. Begun in 1277 by Edward I, the castle (AM) was built on a diamond plan, and the remains of towers, gatehouses and 9ft-thick curtain walls can be seen. A Royalist stronghold in the Civil War, the castle was slighted by the Roundheads after it surrendered to them in 1648. Bodrhddan Hall (OACT), 1½ miles east, stands in fine grounds and contains armour, furniture and notable pictures.

Rhuddlan Castle

RHYL
Clwyd *13 SJ08*
With 3 miles of sandy beaches and a good sunshine record, Rhyl has become the most popular resort on the North Wales coast. It offers numerous leisure facilities, with funfair, boating lake, amusement park, roller-skating rink, cycle track, bandstands and indoor swimming pool. There are two theatres and a golf links, and pleasant gardens include the Botanical Gardens, and Royal Floral Hall with sub-tropical plants.

RHYNIE
Grampian *27 NJ42*
The 1851ft Tap o' Noth, rising from the Clashindarroch Forest, dominates this village, set around an attractive green which serves as a market square. There is an ancient Crow Stone in a field near the church, displaying various Pictish symbols. Leith Hall (NTS) 3½ miles north east, dates in part from 1650. Built round a courtyard, it contains Jacobean relics and has a fine rock garden; it is the home of the Leith and Hay families.

RIBCHESTER
Lancashire *14 SD63*
Green hills encircle this village on the River Ribble, crossed here by an 18th-century bridge. A great Roman fort, built in about AD 80, covered 6 acres of ground. There are some exposed remains of the granary, and a museum contains many interesting finds, including coins, pottery and jewellery and a unique collection of Celtic heads. Stones and possibly even pillars from the fort were used to build the 13th-century church.

RICHBOROUGH
Kent *6 TR36*
Some of the best-preserved Roman walls in England, 12ft thick and up to 24ft high, can be found here. They are part of the ruins of a 3rd-century fort (AM) which defended *Rutupiae*, the chief port of entry for Roman legions. From here Watling Street led to London and on to Chester. A museum houses an interesting collection of finds from the site.

RICHMOND
N Yorkshire *20 NZ10*
There are beautiful views over the town and surrounding dales from the tower of Richmond's splendid 11th-century castle. Every evening a curfew is rung from the tower of the medieval church, which dominates the market square. The church now houses the excellent regimental museum of the Green Howards (OACT), who served in South Carolina during the Revolutionary Wars. The museum also has items relating to Colonel Currie, a commander commissioned by Abraham Lincoln in the Civil War. Richmond was the home of Francis Johnson, a pilgrim leader who died in Amsterdam in 1618, before the migration to the New World. The town was also the ancestral home of Smithson of the Smithsonian Institute, while Lewis Carroll received his early education at Richmond Grammar School. Nearby, south of Scorton, is Kiplin Hall, birthplace of George Calvert who, as Lord Baltimore, founded Avalon, Newfoundland, and Maryland, which he named after Henrietta Maria, wife of Charles I, who granted the charter. Calvert was a convert to Catholicism and planned the colonies as refuges for persecuted Catholics. Although Calvert visited the Avalon settlement, he died before the Maryland emigration which was led by his son Leonard. Kiplin Hall (OACT) makes special provisions for visitors from Maryland.

RICHMOND-UPON-THAMES
Gtr London *5 TQ17*
Richmond is well known for the 2400 acre Richmond Park, the largest of the royal parks. Enclosed for hunting by Charles I in 1637, it has large stretches of unspoiled pasture, heath and woodland, with herds of red and fallow deer. Royalty from Queen Victoria to the present Queen have stayed in the 18th-century White Lodge, now part of the Royal Ballet School. Little remains of the old medieval royal palace, but Thatched Cottage is the home of Princess Alexandra and Mr Angus Ogilvy.

Isabella Plantation, Richmond Park

Captain George Vancouver, navigator and explorer, died at Petersham, Richmond in 1798, and is buried in the parish churchyard. There is a memorial in the church. He sailed twice with Cook, and in 1778 put ashore in British Columbia. From 1791–5 he recorded the Canadian West Coast and then retired to Mariner's Cottage, River Lane, Petersham and wrote up his journals, published after his death as *Voyage of Discovery to the North Pacific Ocean*.

RICKMANSWORTH
Hertfordshire   *5 TQ09*
Situated at the meeting point of three rivers, this former market town is set among lakes and water meadows. The long, winding High Street of this lovely old town boasts several handsome Georgian buildings, including Basing House, an imposing, seven-bayed house, where William Penn, the Quaker leader, spent the early years of his married life with Gulielma Springett. It was here that the settlement of Pennsylvania was planned.

RIDGEWAY, THE
11 SP91–3 SU06
In 1973 an 85-mile long distance footpath was opened by the Countryside Commission. Running between Ivinghoe Beacon in Buckinghamshire and **Avebury** in Wiltshire, part of it follows the route of an ancient trackway along the Berkshire Downs above the Kennet Valley, which was in use as a trade route long before the Romans came.

RIEVAULX
N Yorkshire   *15 SE58*
In a lovely, secluded site in the Rye Valley, below the North York Moors, are the majestic and extensive ruins of Rievaulx Abbey (AM). The once-prosperous abbey was founded in 1132 by the Cistercians and at one time had 140 monks and more than 500 lay brothers. Overlooking the abbey, with beautiful views of Ryedale and the Hambleton Hills, is the ½ mile sweep of Rievaulx Terrace (NT), landscaped in the 18th century by the owner of nearby Duncombe Park.

RIPLEY
N Yorkshire   *15 SE26*
West of the village square is magnificent 16th- to late 18th-century Ripley Castle (OACT), with grounds landscaped by Capability Brown. Both James I and Cromwell stayed here.

The Ingilby family have lived at a castle here since 1350, and in 1827 the lord of the manor attempted to remodel the village on the lines of a French village.

RIPON
N Yorkshire   *15 SE37*
Situated on the River Ure, Ripon has a fine cathedral dating from the 12th century. It stands on the site of an Anglo Saxon church, of which the crypt remains, now containing an exhibition of church treasures. Inside the cathedral a tablet commemorates Robert Porteous, a cousin of George Washington. Narrow, winding streets surround the rectangular market square; at one corner of the square is the medieval Wakeman's House (OACT), now a local museum. This was the home of the town's nightwatchman, and the 1000-year-old tradition is still observed each night at 9 pm, when the present Wakeman blows his horn. This once marked the beginning of his nightly vigil.

The ruins of Cistercian **Fountains Abbey** can be seen 3 miles west, together with the extensive 650-acre Studley Royal Country Park, with deer, lake and ornamental gardens. St Mary's Church in the park is built with marble from many places, including California and Tennessee.

ROBIN HOOD'S BAY
N Yorkshire   *20 NZ90*
At the northern end of a 3-mile long bay, sheltered by rocky cliffs, the little houses of this picturesque and colourful fishing village cling precariously to the steep slopes of a ravine. The village has become a popular tourist resort. The **North York Moors National Park** lies to the south west, and there is a scenic coastal path to **Whitby**.

ROCHDALE
Gtr Manchester   *14 SD81*
This old mill town on the northern edge of Manchester, near the Pennine moors now has new industries to supplement the traditional textile industry on which its wealth was based. Although a few of the old weavers' houses, the upper storeys lined by long horizontal windows, remain, large new blocks of flats predominate. The town was the birthplace of the worldwide Co-operative movement – the Rochdale Equitable Pioneers' Society – and the original shop, opened in 1844 at 31 Toad Lane, is now a museum. 5 miles

north east, at Blackstone Edge, is one of the best preserved stretches of Roman road in Britain.

ROCHE ABBEY
S Yorkshire   *15 SK59*
Although in ruins, the walls of the north and south transepts of this 12th-century Cistercian abbey (AM) still stand to their full height. The abbey has a particularly fine setting, in a valley landscaped by Capability Brown in the 18th century.

ROCHESTER
Kent   *6 TQ76*
Strategically placed on the lower reaches of the River Medway, Rochester has been inhabited since pre-Roman times, and was developed to guard the important crossing over the river, on the route between London and Dover. The Romans built a walled city here, later refortified by the Saxons in about AD 600. The town's importance was recognized by William the Conqueror, who ordered a castle (AM) to be built to defend it: only the 113ft-high keep remains. Today the town is a busy port and industrial and commercial centre, whose older buildings are clustered round the cathedral and in the High Street. The cathedral, founded by St Augustine, was consecrated in AD 604, and became England's second bishopric. The present building is mainly Norman, dating from 1080, with a fine north-west door and impressive west front. The crypt is particularly fine, and the tombs of several medieval bishops can be seen. Ancient manuscripts in the cathedral library include a copy of Miles Coverdale's English version of the Bible, printed in 1535. The cathedral is set in peaceful open lawns, where the ruins of the chapter house, cloisters and gateways of a monastery destroyed during the Reformation can be seen.

There are a number of Canadian associations in the cathedral; a tablet to Sir Edmund Walker Head, Governor-General from 1854–61, and an early advocate of confederation between the various Canadian provinces; a memorial to three graduates of the Royal Military College of Kingston, Ontario, who met their deaths in Africa; and another to Royal Engineers who served in Canada, including Colonel John Bye (see Tunbridge Wells). There are strong Canadian connections with the Royal Engineers, who are Rochester-based.

Rochester Cathedral

Rochester has many associations with Charles Dickens, who lived at Gad's Hill Place for many years until his death in 1870. The Charles Dickens Centre at Eastgate House, a fine late Tudor house in the High Street, contains a display of Dickens' characters and makes clever use of sound and light to bring the displays to life. Many of the houses and inns in the town, including Eastgate House, feature in his novels, and a re-erected Swiss chalet from the garden of Gad's Hill can be seen in the grounds. Also of interest is the museum, housed in the red brick Guildhall, built in 1687. It contains general collections of arms and armour, ship models, Victoriana, and toys. Among the exhibits is a Staffordshire bust of George Washington.

ROCKBOURNE
Hampshire   *3 SU11*
A stream, dry in summer, runs beside the main street of this delightful village in a hollow of the Hampshire Downs. The 16th- to 18th-century houses and cottages are a blend of styles: cob wall and thatch; brick and tile; timber and stone. The 13th-century church lies on a grassy hillside. A $\frac{1}{2}$ mile south east are a large Roman villa and a museum (OACT).

ROCKINGHAM
Northamptonshire   *10 SP89*
On a hill, overlooking the thatched and slated village on its slopes, is the magnificent castle (OACT), which dates mostly from Elizabethan times. A keep was first built here on the orders of William the Conqueror, and was used by King John as a hunting lodge for Rockingham Forest, which then covered a vast area. The gardens alone are well worth a visit, and the house has many associations with Charles Dickens, who was a frequent visitor of the Watsons, the then owners, to whom he dedicated *David Copperfield*. The house served him as a model for Chesney Wold in *Bleak House*. To the east of Rockingham are Deene Park (OACT) and Kirby Hall (AM), which was altered in the 17th century by Inigo Jones, and now resembles a Renaissance palace.

ROLLRIGHTS, THE
Oxfordshire   *10 SP22*
Between the villages of Great and Little Rollright, on the edge of the Cotswolds, are the Rollright Stones. There is a Bronze Age stone circle known as the 'King's Men', a solitary standing stone, known as the 'King Stone', and at a distance, a group of stones called the 'Whispering Knights'. All date from before 1500 BC and were probably used in funeral ceremonies. The legend is more picturesque, however: a local king and his men were said to have met with a witch on this spot. She promised the king that if he could see the neighbouring village of Long Compton from the hill he would be king of all England. Of course, he was sure that he could, and went to look, but the witch had raised up a thick mist and he and his men were turned to stone. The Whispering Knights were supposed to be a group of malcontents already plotting to overthrow their leader.

ROMFORD
Essex   *5 TQ58*
Romford is the birthplace of Francis Quarles, whose hymns were used by the early Pilgrims in the churches of John Winthrop and John Cotton. Douglas Bader and other World War II pilots were based here during the War.

ROMNEY MARSH
Kent   *6 TR03*
Protected by a sea wall, this expanse of flat, sheep-grazed land, 17 miles long by 12 miles wide, has been reclaimed from the sea over centuries and lies barely above sea-level, drained by deep dykes. In the west and north, it is bounded by the Royal Military Canal, and its seaward fringe is crossed by the Romney, Hythe and Dymchurch miniature steam railway. To the south are Walland and Denge marshes. Recently, tulip growing has become important in the area, but Romney Marsh is historically associated with smuggling. The principal town of the Marsh is **New Romney**.

Romney Marsh

ROMSEY
Hampshire   4 SU32
This ancient market town stands on the River Test, noted for its trout and salmon. Broadlands (OACT), originally the home of Lord Palmerston, whose statue stands in the town's market place, is better known as the home of the late Lord Mountbatten of Burma. It is an elegant 18th-century country house surrounded by a 400-acre park, landscaped by Capability Brown. Inside is an exhibition devoted to Lord Mountbatten's life. Only the 12th-century abbey church remains of the great abbey founded in the 10th century. However this Norman building is a splendid sight and contains many treasures, including an Anglo Saxon rood and a Crucifixion, the Romsey Psalter, an illuminated manuscript of the 15th century, and several interesting monuments.

ROSEHEARTY
Grampian   27 NJ96
To the west of this peaceful, pretty fishing town is the Cave of Cowshaven, where Lord Pitsligo hid after he had been outlawed in 1745 for his part in the Jacobite Rising. He was Lord of the now-ruined Castle of Pitsligo, and already an old man when he took part in the rebellion, he spent the rest of his long life hiding from his pursuers, in caves, under bridges, and in friends' houses until his death in 1762. To the east, at the rocky beach, amid rugged cliffs, there is an open air sea-water swimming pool.

ROSS-ON-WYE
Hereford & Worcester   9 SO62
Situated on a bend of the River Wye, with views of the Welsh hills, this clifftop market town has become a tourist centre for the Wye Valley. Dominating the market place is the gabled Market Hall which dates from the 17th century, and there are many Georgian and earlier houses lining the steep streets. John Kyrle (1637–1724) did much for the town, including giving a walled public garden, the Prospect, and a water supply. He also repaired the spire of St Mary's Church, where he is buried. He is praised by Alexander Pope in his *Moral Essays* as the 'Man of Ross'.

ROTHBURY
Northumberland   24 NU00
Rothbury's stone houses are grouped on a sloping green on the bank of the River Coquet. Backed by the Simonside Hills, the town is popular with tourists, walkers and anglers. 1 mile north east is Cragside (OACT), a Victorian house in a 900-acre Country Park, which has the distinction of having been the first house in the world to be lit by electricity generated by water power.

ROTHERHAM
S Yorkshire   15 SK49
An industrial town in the Don Valley, Rotherham has coal mines and iron, steel and glass works. Its arched chantry bridge dates from the 15th century, as does Rotherham's fine Perpendicular church. The town's museum (OACT) is housed in Clifton Park built in 1782 by Carr of York. 4 miles north west is Wentworth Woodhouse, which has one of the longest frontages in England. The palatial 18th-century mansion was the home of the Marquess of Rockingham and during the American War of Independence a meeting place for the Rockingham Whigs, Liberals who supported the American cause.

ROTHES
Grampian   28 NJ24
The Glen Grant Distillery (OACT) was established in the town in 1840. It produces a fine malt whisky, and blending whiskies. Traditional methods are used and visitors are welcome. On the opposite side of the Spey Valley is the wooded viewpoint of Conerock Hill.

ROTTINGDEAN
Sussex   5 TQ30
Only 3½ miles along the coast from **Brighton**, Rottingdean maintains a village atmosphere, with a little green and pond, just off the High Street. Rudyard Kipling lived here in a house overlooking the green for several years, and a room in the Grange Museum and Art Gallery (OACT), once the home of the painter Sir William Nicholson, is devoted to the author. The museum also contains a delightful toy collection. On the South Downs nearby is a well-restored 18th-century smock mill, used by Nicholson as his design for the colophon of the publishers William Heinemann. Roedean, the famous girls' school, lies midway between Rottingdean and Brighton, while a few miles east is Lancing College, a modern public school; its fine neo-Gothic chapel rises 94ft and is one of the highest in England. Evelyn Waugh, author of *Brideshead Revisited*, was educated at the school, upon which he based another novel, *Decline and Fall*.

ROUSHAM
Oxfordshire   10 SP42
Near the grey stone village of Steeple Aston, the great Jacobean mansion of Rousham House (OACT), built in 1635, has a fine library with over 150 portraits and other paintings. A Royalist stronghold during the Civil War, the house was enlarged in the 18th century by William Kent, but it is in the 30-acre landscaped garden, through which the River Cherwell flows, that his genius can still be seen. Of particular interest, although involving an uphill walk, is the folly he built known as the 'Eye Catcher'.

Eye Catcher folly at Rousham House

ROYSTON
Hertfordshire   11 TL34
This town developed at the crossroads of the Roman Ermine Street, and the ancient Icknield Way. A cave with religious wall carvings of uncertain date was discovered beneath the crossroads in 1742. The town's attractive streets contain a variety of interesting houses and inns, and include the remains of James I's Palace. The Old Town Hall contains a local museum (OACT). To the north west is the small village of Croydon and **Wimpole Hall.** The last owner of the Hall, Mrs Elsie Bainbridge, was the daughter of Rudyard Kipling.

RUDYARD

Staffordshire *14 SJ95*
The chief attraction of this pretty
village is the 2-mile long Rudyard
Reservoir, surrounded by lovely
woods and hills. There are lakeside
walks, and boating and fishing are
permitted. Novelist and poet Rudyard
Kipling was named after the village,
where his parents became engaged.

RUFFORD

Lancashire *14 SD41*
Rufford Old Hall (NT, OACT), dates
from the 15th century, though the
wings were added in 1662 and 1821. It
is a particularly good example of a
late-medieval, timber-framed hall. The
great hall has remarkable woodwork,
with a notable hammerbeam roof, and
contains a rare 15th-century movable
screen. The hall contains 16th-century
arms and armour, 17th-century
furniture and tapestries, and in one
wing is the Philip Ashcroft folk
museum.

RUGBY

Warwickshire *10 SP57*
A manufacturing town, with
important railway and engineering
works, Rugby is the home of the
famous public school, founded in 1567.
The game of rugby football originated
here in 1823, when one William Webb
Ellis, according to school tradition,
picked up the ball during an ordinary
game of soccer and ran with it. The
pattern of education established by
headmaster Dr Thomas Arnold
between 1828 and 1842 was followed
by many other public schools, and
served as the model for Thomas
Hughes' immortal novel, *Tom
Brown's Schooldays*, published in
1857. Hughes, a pupil of the school,
was a follower of F D Maurice, and
aided him in the work of Christian
Socialism, and the founding of the
Working Mens' College. He also
established a 'World Community' at
Rugby, Tennessee.

RUSHTON

Northamptonshire *10 SP88*
Spanning the River Ise, Rushton is a
delightful country village. In a corner
of the grounds of Rushton Hall, built
around 1500 and now a school, is the
intriguing Triangular Lodge (AM),
built by Sir Thomas Tresham. Every
part of the 16th-century building –
sides, floors, windows, gables – is
based on the number three, an emblem
of the Trinity, and an ancient mystical
symbol.

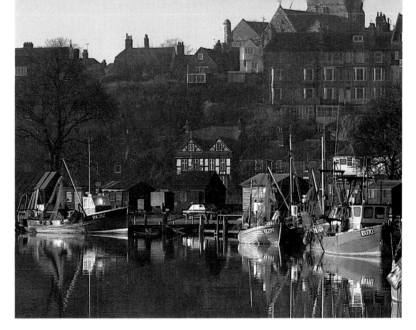

Rye; the River Rother

RUTHIN

Clwyd *13 SJ15*
An unusual feature of this old market
town on a hill in the fertile Clwyd
valley is the curfew bell, which has
been rung every night at 8 pm since the
11th century. The town has some
interesting old buildings, including
ruins of a 13th-century castle round
which a fortified town grew up. In the
19th century a Gothic castle was
grafted on to the original building and
has been turned into a hotel. Evenings
of medieval banqueting and
entertainment are now held here. A
bank is now housed in the early 15th-
century courthouse and prison in the
square. Also here is the Maen Huail
stone, on which King Arthur is said to
have beheaded Huail, a rival in love.

RUTHWELL

Dumfries & Galloway *18 NY06*
In a special apse of the parish church is
the late 7th-century carved cross for
which the town is famous: the 18ft
cross is richly carved with scenes from
the life of Christ and with Runic
characters. These relate in parts the
Dream of the Rood, an ancient poem
probably by the first Anglo Saxon
poet, Caedmon. In 1810 the first
savings bank was established here: it is
commemorated in the Henry Duncan
Museum.

RYDAL

Cumbria *18 NY30*
Situated in the Lake District National
Park, Rydal is at the east end of Rydal
Water, one of the most delightful of
the smaller lakes, sheltered by 2000ft

Rydal Fell on the north side. In 1813
William Wordsworth moved to Rydal
Mount (OACT), a house
incorporating an early 16th-century
farmer's cottage, where he died in
1850. Beautifully situated in a 4½-acre
fell garden, it overlooks Windermere
and Rydal Water. The house contains
family portraits and possessions.

• RYE

E Sussex *6 TQ92*
Once a flourishing coastal port, Rye
was one of the original Cinque Ports
but in the 16th century the harbour
silted up, and today this hilly town is
nearly 2 miles inland. Best known of
Rye's picturesque cobbled streets is
Mermaid Street, lined by 15th- to 17th-
century houses, including the Mermaid
Inn, dating from 1420, a notorious
smugglers' haunt in the 18th century.
The 13th-century Ypres Tower
(OACT) contains an interesting local
museum, and 18th-century Lamb
House (OACT) was the home of
novelist Henry James from 1898 until
his death in 1916. Henry James, born
in America, took British citizenship in
1915 and in the same year was
awarded the Order of Merit. Many
literary figures visited him at Lamb
House. John Alkin, an early Harvard
graduate, was a native of Rye, and
vicar of St Mary's Church.
  In **Winchelsea** parish church 2 miles
south west of Rye hangs the coat of
arms of General Prescott, Governor-
in-Chief of the Canadas, Nova Scotia
and New Brunswick. He fought at
Louisburg and in the American War of
Independence.

S

SAFFRON WALDEN
Essex *11 TL53*

Saffron Walden is one of the most beautiful towns in Essex: a town in which several periods of architecture coexist. Two old inns – the Sun (now an antique shop) and the Cross Keys – are worthy of attention: the former is famous for its outstanding pargeted plasterwork, the latter has associations with Shakespeare. The magnificent 15th–16th-century Perpendicular church of St Mary, has a richly carved interior and several fine brasses. Among the tombs is that of Thomas, Lord Audley, founder of Magdalene College, Cambridge, and Lord Chancellor to Henry VIII, who sanctioned Henry's divorce from Katherine of Aragon. There is evidence of an Iron Age settlement; the Romans certainly established themselves here; and, in the 12th century, a castle (now in ruins) was built. But the wealth of Saffron Walden came from the cloth trade. The common has a surviving maze, and the Town Museum many interesting items. 1 mile away, **Audley End** is a superb 17th-century mansion.

ST ABBS
Borders *24 NT96*

A picturesque fishing village, a fine sandy beach, and a splendid coastline: these are some of the features that explain why St Abbs is such a popular holiday resort. On St Abbs Head stands a lighthouse built in 1861. 3 miles north west, the ruins of Fast Castle perch 70ft up on the clifftop. This, in Sir Walter Scott's *The Bride of Lammermoor*, is 'Wolf's Crag', the tower of Edgar of Ravenswood.

ST AGNES
Cornwall *1 SW75*

Until late in the 19th century, St Agnes was a tin-mining centre, and the ruins of the old workings now add to its charm. It is a pleasant resort with a sandy beach and fine coastal scenery. You can motor to the top of 700ft St Agnes Beacon for some of the most extensive views in Cornwall. On the cliffs between St Agnes and Chapel Porth is the ruined Wheal Coates Engine House (NT).

ST ALBANS
Hertfordshire *5 TL10*

The Roman city of *Verulamium*, from which St Albans grew, was the only British city important enough in Roman times to be accorded the status of *municipium*, which meant that its inhabitants had the right to Roman citizenship. Although sacked by Boudicca in AD 61, it was rebuilt and soon regained its importance. After the Romans left, however, *Verulamium* was abandoned and eventually the remains were covered over. The old site was not excavated until the 20th century, when remains of a theatre, a hypocaust and several mosaic pavements were discovered. The Verulamium Museum houses finds from the site. On the opposite bank of the River Ver, the medieval city of St Albans grew up around the massive abbey church, now St Alban's Cathedral, which was built on the site where Alban, the first British saint, was martyred in 287. The abbey dates from the 11th century, though there have been many later additions. St Alban's shrine of Purbeck marble was destroyed, but the fragments were found and pieced together again in the 19th century. Around the town centre are several attractive old streets, centred on the 15th-century curfew tower. Among other places of interest are the City Museum; St Albans Organ Museum; the Kingsbury Water-mill Museum in the village of St Michael's; the Royal National Rose Society's Gardens, and Gorhambury House (OACT), a fine, late-Georgian mansion. The Fighting Cocks Inn is thought to be the oldest in Britain.

Eight miles south east of St Albans at Ridge, Viscount Alexander of Tunis, Governor-General of Canada 1946–52, is buried in the churchyard. He was the last British Governor.

ST ANDREWS
Fife *24 NO51*

This lovely old Royal Burgh on the east coast of Fife has a long and ancient history. A mecca for the world's golfers, it is also a distinguished university city – St Andrews University was founded in 1411 – and was for centuries the ecclesiastical centre of Scotland.

In 1759, Benjamin Franklin was among those to have an honorary degree conferred upon him by the university. According to tradition it was here that St Rule was shipwrecked, carrying the relics of St Andrew the Apostle, who was adopted

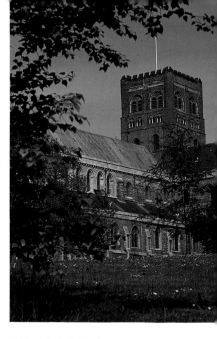

St Alban's Cathedral

as Scotland's patron saint. Little still stands of the small 12th-century church built to house the relics but the massive bell tower and the sacred remains were soon installed in St Andrew's Cathedral, in its day the largest and finest of all Scotland's churches, built in the 12th and 13th centuries. In 1559, however, it fell victim to the iconoclasm of John Knox. He preached one of his most eloquent and fiery sermons from the cathedral pulpit and this inspired the mob to destroy much of the rich interior. Over the years, it gradually fell in ruins and only fragments have survived. St Andrew's Castle (AM), also in ruins, stands in grim isolation on a rock overlooking the North Sea.

James Wilson, an early proponent of American Independence and spokesman for the state of Pennsylvania, was born just outside St Andrews. However, St Andrew's international reputation derives from its status in the golfing world. The town has four courses: the Old, the New, the Eden and the Jubilee. Written records of the Old Course date back at least to the 15th century, when James II protested that the sport was distracting his men from archery practice. Mary Queen of Scots played golf here, and James VI had his own course at Blackheath, in London, when he became sovereign of England and moved to London with his court. The 'R&A', as the Royal and Ancient Golf Club is familiarly known, had its origins in the Society of St Andrew's Golfers, founded in 1764. King

William IV consented to the title 'Royal and Ancient' in 1834, and by 1897 the game had become so popular that a governing body was felt to be desirable. The Royal and Ancient took over this role, which it still fulfils today. For a modest fee, anyone may play the Old Course, and Scotland, being the home of golf, has many other championship courses.

ST ASAPH
Clwyd *13 SJ07*
Surprisingly and despite competition from **Rhuddlan** and **Denbigh**, St Asaph is a cathedral city, with the smallest cathedral in the country and one of the oldest in Wales. Henry Morton Stanley, the reporter and African explorer was born in Denbigh, but spent his early years in a workhouse in St Asaph. Benjamin Franklin's friend, Jonathan Shipley, was Bishop of St Asaph.

ST AUSTELL
Cornwall *1 SX05*
St Austell is the centre of the china clay industry – a raw material that is used not only in porcelain but also in the manufacture of paper, cosmetics, medicines, paint and many other things. St Austell was a tin mining village until, in 1755, William Cookworthy discovered the clay and

China clay, St Austell

decided it might have industrial possibilities. Now, dispatched in ships from Fowey and Par and Charlestown (where there is a Visitor Centre (OACT) incorporating an interesting museum of shipwrecks), it is a major export. Outside the town china clay dust and waste materials appear as white mountains. The Wheal Martyn Museum (OACT) tells the history of the china clay industry.

ST CLEER
Cornwall *1 SX26*
St Cleer stands 700ft above sea-level on the edge of **Bodmin Moor**. It has a church with a 15th-century tower, a holy well, and fantastic views. A mile or two from the village, the landscape is rich in prehistoric monuments. Most famous is Trevethy Quoit, an imposing chambered tomb. The Hurlers, three stone circles said to be men turned to stone for playing a game on Sunday, the Cheesewring, a curiously shaped natural phenomenon, and King Donert's Stone, believed to commemorate a 9th-century Christian king, are all within easy reach.

ST DAVID'S
Dyfed *7 SM72*
Only 2000 people live in St David's, and yet this tiny city might reasonably be described as the Canterbury of Wales. It was here, in the 6th century, that St David – the country's patron saint – established a stronghold for Christianity in the west. The cathedral that bears his name is the third to be built on the spot – the original was destroyed by raiders. Work on the present building began in 1180 and was not completed until 1572. The interior is as rich as the exterior is plain, and there is much fine carving. Nearby stand the ruins (AM) of the medieval Bishop's Palace. On the headland at Whitesand Bay, a plaque marks the site of St Patrick's Chapel, from where the saint supposedly sailed to Ireland in the 5th century. Ramsey Island, a ½ mile offshore, is a privately owned bird sanctuary; Grassholm Island, 12 miles west of St David's Head, has one of the world's largest gannetries.

ST FAGAN'S
S Glamorgan *8 ST17*
When the second phase of the Civil War swept across South Wales, many of the people rose against Parliament, and a unit of the New Model Army crushed the revolt at St Fagan's, on the outskirts of Cardiff. Nowadays, St Fagan's has more pleasant associations

– as the home of the Welsh Folk Museum, which is accommodated in the grounds of the 16th-century castle (OACT). The exhibits include a woollen mill, several old Welsh farmhouses, a tannery, a tollgate, a chapel and a quarryman's cottage. In addition to the buildings, which have been brought here from all parts of Wales and re-erected, there are interesting galleries devoted to Welsh life, and craftsmen regularly display their skills.

ST HELENS
Merseyside *14 SJ59*
St Helens has two famous names to its credit: Pilkington, the glass manufacturers, and the late Sir Thomas Beecham – conductor extraordinary. The latter was born here in 1897. The Pilkington Glass Museum (OACT) contains many fascinating items. A former director of the firm, Major W N Pilkington, had the distinction of being the first fare-paying air passenger in the UK.

ST IVES
Cornwall *1 SW54*
During the 19th century St Ives was one of Cornwall's most prosperous pilchard ports. No fewer than 75 million were caught during one day in 1864. It was also used for the shipping of tin and copper until these industries began to decline in the late 1800s. It was at this time that artists began to move to the port, establishing a vibrant community; John Macneill Whistler and Walter Sickert were among the many who stayed here. Although it brought fame to St Ives, the presence of the artistic community has done much to preserve the beauty of the village. Evidence of St Ives' earlier history, when John Wesley was so influential in Cornwall, is seen in two streets named 'Teetotal' and 'Salubrious'. The 15th-century church has a Madonna and Child carved by Dame Barbara Hepworth; a museum of her work is in the village. Finally, the Barnes Museum of Cinematography should be seen.

ST JUST-IN-ROSELAND
Cornwall *1 SW83*
Cornwall has a reputation for sub-tropical luxuriance and the churchyard at St Just-in-Roseland is a fine example. The work was begun by a tree-loving vicar in the mid 19th century. Now you can see such rarities as an African strawberry tree, a Chilean myrtle, palms and camellias.

ST KEYNE
Cornwall *1 SX26*
Just east of the village is the remarkable Paul Corin Collection (OACT) of automatic (and, in many cases, very large) musical instruments such as the Mortier organ, which measures 27ft by 20ft, the Hoogluys fairground organ, and – an exquisite rarity – a 1929 German theatre organ. On no account should it be missed.

ST MAWES
Cornwall *1 SW83*
St Mawes on the Roseland Peninsula is magnificent and unspoiled by the tourist industry. Even the castle (AM), built by Henry VIII to defend the Fal estuary, escaped the depredations of the Roundheads in the Civil War and is well preserved. A ferry connects the town with **Falmouth.**

ST MICHAEL'S MOUNT
Cornwall *1 SW53*
This tiny island used to be joined to the mainland (tree stumps discovered under the sea prove it). In 1044, a Benedictine monastery was founded here by monks from Mont St Michel off Brittany – hence the similarity of name and appearance. After the 12th century it assumed the role of a fort and, in 1425, was acquired by the Crown. In 1657, during the Civil War, the St Aubyn family moved in and remained here until 1954, when the National Trust took over. The island can be reached by foot or by boat, depending on the tides, from Marazion.

ST NEOT
Cornwall *1 SX16*
Bodmin Moor rises behind the charming village, which nestles in a river valley. The church has remarkable stained glass windows – many of them 15th- and 16th-century. Legend, told in one of the windows, asserts that St Neot was only 15 inches high, and that he could make crows obey him. There is a well dedicated to him in the village.

ST NEWLYN EAST
Cornwall *1 SW85*
The nearby Lappa Valley Line is a 15-inch gauge steam railway that runs along part of the old GWR Newquay–Chacewater route. The train makes a round trip of 2 miles and stops at East Wheal Rose Halt – the site of a once famous silver and lead mine; now a 5 acre pleasure area.

ST OSYTH
Essex *12 TM11*
St Osyth stands on one of the many little creeks on the River Colne. Three Martello towers in the vicinity were built as defences against Napoleon. The remains of a 12th-century priory are incorporated into a 16th-century mansion. Mainly of flint construction, the building is superb.

SALCOMBE
Devon *2 SX73*
The broad and placid waters of **Kingsbridge** estuary, confined by steep, thickly wooded banks, many small sandy bays – and, 2 miles away, imposing cliffs around Bolt Head – combine to give Salcombe its splendid setting. The town clings to the hillsides, its streets bright with sub-tropical plants. Overbecks Museum and Garden (NT) is an Edwardian house set in lovely gardens 1 mile to the south. The tower of a ruined Tudor castle, Fort Charles, is all that survived a battering by the Roundhead artillery in the Civil War. A passenger ferry connects Salcombe with East Portlemouth on the opposite bank.

SALFORD
Gtr Manchester *14 SJ89*
The boundary between **Manchester** and Salford is the River Irwell. Industry came to Salford in the form of cotton mills, and it has never departed. The reconstruction of Lark Hill Place, a 19th-century North of England industrial street, in Salford Museum and Art Gallery in Peel Park recreates Salford's past. Sir Charles Hallé, founder of the orchestra, is buried in the fine, modern Roman Catholic cathedral. The ship canal and docks reflect another side of Salford's contribution to commerce – and, likewise, a replica coal mine in the Buile Hill Park Science Museum. The half-timbered Bull Inn, the partly 15th-century Ordsall Hall (OACT) and the old mansion of Kersal Cell recall a much older and rather quieter aspect of Salford. But contemporary Salford lies in the art gallery, where there is a lavish collection of Lowrys. L S Lowry knew Salford well and painted it with a sad relish.

SAMLESBURY
Lancashire *14 SD53*
Samlesbury is in the attractive Ribble Valley. The church was rebuilt in the 16th century and has 17th- and 18th-century box pews and a two-decker pulpit. Samlesbury Hall (OACT) dates

back to the 14th and 16th centuries. Among the objects on view are paintings and European and Oriental casks and cabinets.

SAMPFORD COURTENAY
Devon *2 SS60*
Whitewashed cob and thatched cottages, the imposing prospect of Cawsand Beacon (1799ft) on Dartmoor, and a 15th-century church – all these add up to one of Devonshire's many pretty villages. Trouble came to Sampford Courtenay in 1549, when Edward VI introduced his new prayer book – with the text in English. The villagers took part in the 'Prayer Book Rebellion', marching on Exeter with other Catholics from Devon and Cornwall, but they were defeated and many were hanged.

SANCREED
Cornwall *1 SW42*
The 14th-century church, with its richly carved screen and embellished crosses, and the Iron Age settlement, Carn Euny (AM), complete with a *fogou*, an ancient subterranean hiding hole characteristic of Cornwall, should be seen.

SANDRINGHAM
Norfolk *12 TF62*
Sandringham House (OACT), built in the 19th century, is the Royal Family's country residence. It was bought in 1861 by Edward, Prince of Wales (later Edward VII). The Norwich gates were, as their name suggests, manufactured in Norwich as a wedding present to the Prince from the County of Norfolk when he married Princess Alexandra in 1863. King George V and King George VI both died at Sandringham. In the Church of St Mary Magdalene, the Royal Parish Church, are a silver altar and memorials to Edward VII, Queen Alexandra, George VI and Queen Mary, some items presented by Americans. The estate includes a country park covering 300 acres. Vintage Royal Daimlers are on show in the Royal Car Museum, and there is also a Big Game Museum.

SANDTOFT
Humberside *16 SE70*
Sandtoft Transport Centre, 15 miles east of **Doncaster**, is primarily dedicated to the preservation of the trolleybus – though motorbuses and other vehicles are also on display. Over 60 vehicles have been lovingly restored.

YORKSHIRE DALES

Neither Yorkshire nor Lancashire is to be seen merely as a site of Britain's Industrial Revolution. Yorkshire boasts both the Dales and a splendid coast to the north, including Whitby, Scarborough and Flamborough Head. It has also some well-preserved abbeys, especially Rievaulx and Fountains and the Studley Royal estate, with the most spectacular water garden in England.

The splendour and grace of the abbey ruins indicate the wealth that sheep brought – the Cistercians built their churches and abbeys mainly in the north, in rural and isolated country, and the flocks were looked after by lay brothers. At its zenith, Rievaulx had 150 monks and over 500 lay brothers. Fountains Abbey, near Ripon is the most complete – and magnificent – of the Cistercian houses in Britain; the view from its west door, down the long nave ending in the Chapel of the Nine Altars and the fifteenth-century east window, is hard to surpass.

Haworth Parsonage, where the three Brontë sisters lived, dreamed and wrote, has a similar haunting quality. Emily captured it for all time in *Wuthering Heights*.

High or Top Withens nearby is the probable location where Heathcliff and Catherine had their meetings. The father, Patrick, was as talented as his daughters, talented and eccentric; a lonely and tortured man, he always carried a pistol – when preaching in church, at family prayers at night, and at breakfast. Of Irish origins (the name was really Brunty, but he was given a good classical education as the protégé of the local squire!) he was gifted, but mean. The parsonage had neither curtains at the windows nor carpets on the floors – the girls suffered acutely, and none lived long. He outlived all his children.

Yorkshire is not only Brontë country. J B Priestley was born in Bradford – in the *Good Companions*, it is from 'Bruddensford' (Bradford) that Josiah Oakroyd sets off on his journey on the Great North Road. Baroness Orczy wrote *The Scarlet Pimpernel* in Wensleydale, not Paris. Sculptor Henry Moore got some of his inspiration in his youth from Brimham Rocks, near Pateley Bridge. And the sweep and beauty of the dales has been recently caught in the novels and TV films (*All

Rievaulx Abbey

Creatures Great and Small*) of James Herriot, who was and remains captivated by the beauty of the Swaledale he first saw over 40 years ago. His actual practice is in Thirsk, to the east of the dales, but his fictional surgery is in 'Darrowby', with cameras in and out of 'Skeldale House' – in the actual world, in and out of Cringley House, an Abbeyfield Home, in Askrigg in Wensleydale. The author is a familiar figure in Carperby and West Witton; he and 'Siegfried Farnon, MRCVS' roam the dales and capture in camera a land of high fells, smooth-running rivers and many 'forces' or waterfalls, of limestone escarpments, drystone walls and springy green grass.

This is, first and last, and for those with stamina, walker's country. The Pennine Way is 270 miles long, from Edale in Derbyshire to Kirk Yetholm in Scotland – probably the finest long walk in Britain. Its triumph is Pen-y-ghent (Hill of the Border), a mere 2273 feet high, but in ruggedness a mountain.

Words used in the Dales: *beck* – stream, *dale* – valley, *fell* – hill, *foss* or *force* – waterfall, *tarn* – moorland lake.

Places to Visit

Abbeys
Bolton, on the Wharfe, in use as a parish church
Fountains, near Ripon
Jervaulx, near Middleham
Rievaulx, the oldest of the Cistercian houses, with its eighteenth-century terrace above.

Castles
Bolton, where Mary Queen of Scots was imprisoned.
Knaresborough
Middleham ('The Windsor of the North' in Richard III's reign) now better known as a racehorse-training centre.
Richmond, a Norman foundation, and now a Regimental Museum of the Green Howards, who fought in the War of American Independence.
Skipton

'Forces' or Waterfalls
Aysgarth in Wensleydale
Hardraw near Howes

Further Reading

AA Yorkshire Dales Guide
Susan Cunliffe-Lister, *Days of Yore*, published by the author
The novels of James Herriot

The parlour, Haworth Parsonage

SALISBURY
Wiltshire *3 SU12*

The 'new' city of Salisbury dates back to the 13th century when Bishop Poore decided to move his clergy and cathedral from **Old Sarum**, where lack of water and quarrels with the military governor of the castle were making life difficult. There is a story that the new site for the cathedral was chosen by an arrow shot from a bow drawn at a venture, but all the evidence points to a decision taken after long and careful planning and the site, in the middle of the fertile plain and at the confluence of the rivers Avon and Nadder, was an obvious choice. The foundation stone of the cathedral was laid on 28 April 1220, and the building, one of the finest expressions of Early English architecture in the country, was completed, apart from the spire, cloisters and chapter house, by 1258.

The city grew up around the Cathedral Close, its streets laid out on the usual medieval grid plan, intersecting to form square blocks or 'chequers' where the old houses were packed tightly together. This old plan can still be seen in the streets around the Close, where many historic timbered buildings have survived. The finest of them is probably the 17th-century Joiners' Hall, with its intricately carved woodwork; and the most unusual is certainly the house of the wealthy 15th-century wool merchant, John Halle, which is now the foyer of a local cinema.

Salisbury was granted its first charter in 1227 and, thanks to its far-sighted bishops, who bridged the rivers and diverted the road to the west country to run through their new town, it became a thriving market and wool centre. There is still a twice-weekly market in the spacious market square, and the handsome stone Poultry Cross, dating from the 15th century when fowl were sold there, still stands.

In 1618, Sir Walter Raleigh managed to delay his return to London and certain punishment by staying here, following his failure to discover gold on his expedition to Guiana. Feigning illness, he appeared to eat nothing but was secretly supplied with food from the White Hart Hotel. In 1780 Henry Laurens, vice president of the American Congress, also stayed at the White Hart as a captive, having been captured off the Newfoundland coast. A year later Laurens was exchanged for Cornwallis, and then appointed with John Adams, Benjamin Franklin and John Jay as a commissioner and signatory to the peace treaty with

Britain. Henry's son was also captured by the British.

Salisbury reached the height of its prosperity in the 18th century from which era many of the most elegant houses in the beautiful, walled Close survive. Although Salisbury owed much to its bishops, in the past, relations were not harmonious, and the clergy had to protect themselves by building a wall, and fortified gateways, still the northern and eastern entrances to the Close, for protection. By the 18th century, however, behaviour was more civilized, and the Close assumed the aspect it has today, of tranquil lawns shaded by trees and ringed by handsome mansions, many of which were formerly the town houses of the wealthiest citizens.

Salisbury Cathedral has various memorials to the ancestors of American families, namely the Brighams, from whom Robert Worth Brigham, US Ambassador, claimed descent, and Sir Thomas Gorges, of the Massachusetts family. Salisbury was also the birthplace of Edward French, who emigrated to Ipswich, Massachusetts in 1630, and from whom Daniel Chester French, the sculptor, is descended: one of his best-known works is the statue of Abraham Lincoln in Washington DC. French was a close friend of Emerson and of Henry James, both of whom visited Salisbury and were moved by the beauty of the cathedral. Finally, Salisbury was the birthplace of Martha Cranmer-Oliver, an actress in the theatre in which Abraham Lincoln was assassinated.

PLACES TO SEE
The Cathedral A masterpiece of the Early English style, Salisbury is one of the most beautiful cathedrals in the country, set in an equally lovely walled Close. The graceful spire, which is such a well-known landmark, was added at the end of the 13th century. The cloisters, completed immediately after the cathedral itself, are the earliest cathedral cloisters in England. They lead to the chapter house, famous for its wealth of sculpture. The library houses many rare books and manuscripts, including one of the four contemporary copies of Magna Carta.

Mompesson House (NT) Built in the early 18th century for a wealthy merchant family, this gracious house is one of the most splendid in

Salisbury Cathedral beyond the river

the Close and is noted for its plasterwork and woodwork.

Museum of the Duke of Edinburgh's Royal Regiment Militaria and regimental memorabilia are housed in one of the Close's most attractive buildings.

St Thomas's Church Built in the 15th century, this Perpendicular church contains a magnificent 'Doom' painting.

Salisbury and South Wiltshire Museum Relics from Stonehenge and Old Sarum, of the city's medieval and later history, and the Pitt Rivers collection of archaeology, are housed in the King's House in the Close.

Salisbury Plain North of Salisbury, has played host to thousands of troops. The 33,000 Canadians camped out in the bitter winter of 1914–15 suffered great privation. Many died and are buried locally. There is a plaque at Durrington cemetery. Divisional HQ was at Ye Old Bustard, a pub 3 miles north west of **Stonehenge**.

SANDWICH
Kent *6 TR35*
One of the original Cinque Ports, Sandwich used to be an important naval base. Henry VIII built a castle (now gone) to safeguard his coastal defences. Since those days, nature – through storm and tempest – has reshaped the landscape and Sandwich is now 2 miles from the sea. It is a beautiful town with ample evidence of its former glory. The Barbican and Fishergate were both gateways to the town; St Bartholomew's Hospital guesthouse is 15th century; Marwood Court was built in 1564; and St Clement's church has a Norman tower. The 16th-century Guildhall in the Cattle Market has a museum that recalls local history. Nearby, the Royal St George is one of England's most famous and exclusive golf clubs. Edward VIII (as Prince of Wales) and the late Ian Fleming (creator of James Bond) were both members of the club.

Five miles west, Wingham has a fine row of half-timbered houses. South at Northbourne, Sir Edwin Sandys is buried in the parish church. Sandys, the son of Archbishop Sandys, became Treasurer of the Virginia Company when approached by Pilgrims Robert Cushman and John Carver in 1617. He drew up the Constitution of Virginia, which served as a model for other colonies. Later, he was suspected of trying to establish a Puritan Republic in America, and was imprisoned in the Tower of London. He died in 1629.

SANDY
Bedfordshire *11TL14*
This small but growing town was listed in the Domesday Book. St Swithin's Church (14th century) has a statue to Prime Minister Sir Robert Peel's son, Captain William Peel – one of the first men to be awarded the VC. Sandy Lodge houses the headquarters of the Royal Society for the Protection of Birds. A nature trail leads to the Bird Sanctuary (OACT). John Barnes, an early Utah senator, was born here, while Sutton, 1½ miles to the east, was the ancestral home of the Burgoynes.

SANQUHAR
Dumfries & Galloway *22 NS70*
The Covenanters' fight to defend Presbyterianism against the Stuarts is commemorated in a granite monument on the site of the old Town Cross where their famous Declarations in 1680 and 1685 were read out. A tolbooth, erected in 1735, has withstood the erosion of time: a castle owned by the Crichtons and, later, by the Douglases, has fared less well and is now in ruins. To the east of the town stand the Lowther Hills where, in the late 17th century, persecuted Covenanters hid out.

SAWREY
Cumbria *18 SD39*
Hill Top Farm (NT) at Near Sawrey is a 17th-century house – still without electric light – in which Beatrix Potter lived, and in which she wrote and illustrated many of her books (a picture of the Tower Bank Arms at Sawrey appears in *The Tale of Jemima Puddle-Duck*). Several of her drawings, pieces of furniture, china, etc are on display. Owing to the size of the house, it is necessary to restrict the number of visitors at any one time.

SAXMUNDHAM
Suffolk *12 TM36*
This village stretches out along the main road, and has many fine buildings. The church of St John the Baptist has a hammerbeam roof and interesting monuments. Bruisyard Winery and Vineyard (OACT) lies just outside the village main street at Bruisyard, 4 miles north west of Saxmundham. Immediately west of Saxmundham is Sternfield, where the little parish church contains a Benjamin West.

SCARBOROUGH
N Yorkshire *20 TA08*
Scarborough has a harbour, a fishing village, stately hotels, towering cliffs and, of course, the required amusements that make a seaside place 'popular'. The Romans built a signal station here, and the Normans built an imposing castle on the headland, of which the large square keep (AM) survives; the rest was reduced to rubble by Roundhead artillery in the Civil War.

The town's career as a spa began in the 17th century. A Mrs Farrow noticed that the water that ran over certain russet-coloured rocks had an acid tang. She found that it was good for her, and believed that it might be a cure for scurvy, jaundice, depression – even leprosy. Before very long, the sick, and those who believed themselves to be ill, came flocking, especially when, nearly a century later, sea bathing became so popular a pastime. Anne Brontë was among the visitors to Scarborough; she died here in 1849 and is buried in St Mary's churchyard.

Donkey rides at Scarborough

SCONE
Tayside *23 NO12*
Scone (pronounced 'Skoon') was the capital of the Pictish kingdom. The Stone of Destiny, reputed to be Jacob's pillow, was brought here from Iona in AD 843. In 1296 it was captured by Edward I of England and forms part of the Coronation Chair in Westminster Abbey. The abbey and palace at Scone were founded by Alexander I in about 1114. The early kings of Scotland – until the time of James I – were crowned here. But in 1559 an angry mob from Perth, drunk with the rhetoric of that religious pedagogue John Knox, destroyed them. The palace was rebuilt in the 16th century, and Charles II was the last king to be crowned in it. In 1950 the Stone of Destiny was stolen from Westminster, and later discovered beneath the high altar in the ruins of Arbroath Abbey. The present Scone Palace (OACT) was built in the early 19th century as the home of the Earl of Mansfield. Inside are fine collections of furniture, china and ivory. The grounds contain a pinetum planted with Douglas fir seeds sent from America in 1834 by David Douglas. Douglas the famous botanist was born here and worked on the estate.

SCROOBY
Nottinghamshire *15 SK69*
Scrooby became the birthplace of the Pilgrim Church in 1606 when the Reverend Richard Clyfton brought his Separatist followers from the divided congregation at **Gainsborough**. Meetings were held in the manor house, the home of William Brewster.

The manor has an interesting history: it was owned by the Archbishop of York and the family acted as his agents. In 1582 the Archbishop was Edwin Sandys, whose son was a founder of Virginia. It was he who ensured that the Brewsters kept the house when Queen Elizabeth I wanted to use it as a hunting lodge. After Brewster's departure with the Pilgrims, the house fell into decay. However, remaining walls were incorporated into the present farmhouse which is marked by a plaque. The Pilgrims left Scrooby for Holland, but were captured and imprisoned at **Boston**, Lincolnshire. Eventually the group reached Leyden in Holland where they planned the emigration to New England. The English Government attempted to trace Brewster but his name did not appear on the *Mayflower* List. However it is probable that he travelled using an alias. Among Brewster's descendants were Longfellow, President Zachary Taylor and President Ulysses Grant. Scrooby Church is a place of pilgrimage for those interested in the history of New England and Puritanism. It dates from about 1380, and is built of limestone from the Roche Abbey quarries. In 1864 the church was 'restored' and many of its finest features were sold.

SEATHWAITE
Cumbria *18 NY29*
Seathwaite is very remote. Tucked away in the Dunnerdale valley, it is overshadowed by Harter Fell (2143ft) – with precipitous Wrynose Pass away to the north east at the head of the valley. In the village churchyard 'Wonderful Walker', born in 1709 and for 67 years vicar of the parish, is buried. He figures in Wordsworth's poem *The Excursion*.

SEATOLLER
Cumbria *18 NY21*
Seatoller is in the beautiful but rainy valley of Borrowdale. At Sprinkling Tarn, the average yearly rainfall is over 185 inches. Seathwaite Farm, 2 miles away, is one of the wettest inhabited places in England. In the 17th and 18th centuries, they used to mine plumbago (a kind of graphite) at Seatoller.

SEATON DELAVAL
Northumberland *20 NZ37*
Sir John Vanbrugh designed the great 18th-century mansion of Seaton Delaval Hall (OACT) for Admiral George Delaval and it was constructed between 1718 and 1728. Built in the Palladian style and set in exquisite gardens, the hall is considered to be Vanbrugh's masterpiece and contains paintings, documents and statuary.

SEDBERGH
Cumbria *18 SD69*
This is a fell-town. The boys' public school was founded in 1525 by a Canon of Windsor and Provost of Eton. A new school – built in 1716 – now serves as library and museum to the present establishment, which was erected in the late 19th century. Sedbergh itself is a busy market centre with a mainly 13th-century parish church. The Quaker Meeting House, 1 mile to the south west, dates back to 1675. George Fox once preached a sermon under a yew tree – part of which is preserved. There is a National Park Centre (OACT) in the town.

SEDGEMOOR
Somerset *3 ST33*
Sedgemoor is an expanse of fenland, much of which was once covered by the sea. Now it provides valuable grazing for cattle, and its pollarded willow trees are used to provide canes for basket-making. Historically, Sedgemoor was the scene of the Duke of Monmouth's defeat in 1685.

SELBORNE
Hampshire *4 SU73*
Gilbert White, born in 1720 and at one time curate of the parish, recorded the natural history of Selborne in a fascinating book of that name published in 1788, and in print ever since. Most of his observations were made in the steep beechwood 'hangers' that climb the slopes of the hills above the village, and he and his brother constructed a walk, 'the Zig-Zag' that leads up through the woods to Selborne Common (NT), a sheltered grassy space on top of the hill. Gilbert White's house and garden, The Wakes, is now a museum, devoted partly to his work and partly to an exhibition relating to Captain Oates (who died heroically on Scott's last expedition to the Antarctic), who also had connections with Selborne.

SELBY
N Yorkshire *15 SE63*
The abbey was founded in 1069 by Benedict of Auxerre on the assumption that three swans landing on the River Ouse amounted to a 'sign from heaven'. Perhaps it was, though, for despite the fact that Benedict was trespassing on royal property, William I gave his consent, and some say his son, later Henry I, was born here. The magnificent abbey church survives. One of the two main branches of the Washington family lived near Selby, and the family shield appears in the stained glass of the abbey church, considered to be the earliest representation of the stars and stripes in glass.

SELKIRK
Borders *24 NT42*
Selkirk, once a royal burgh, stands on a hill overlooking Ettrick Water and is an excellent touring centre. A statue to Sir Walter Scott in the market place is a reminder that he was sheriff of the county from 1799 until 1832. His chair and some of his letters are preserved in the Sheriff Court House. At the other end of the High Street, there is a statue

Sedgemoor

Selworthy, Vale of Porlock

to Mungo Park, the African missionary and explorer, who was born at nearby Foulshiels in 1771. A third monument, erected in 1913, recalls the burning of Selkirk by the English after their victory at Flodden in 1513. Bowhill (OACT) is the ancestral home of the Dukes of Buccleuch. It contains outstanding collections of paintings, porcelain and furniture, and relics of Montrose, Sir Walter Scott and Queen Victoria.

SELWORTHY
Somerset   2 SS94
Selworthy is probably the prettiest village in the lovely Vale of Porlock. There are old cottages, a 15th-century tithe barn, and thatched almshouses. The mainly 16th-century church has, unusually, a white exterior. Selworthy Beacon (1013ft) provides some fine views and Dunkery Beacon stands on the far side of the vale.

SEVENOAKS
Kent   5 TQ55
Sevenoaks is a London commuter town said to derive its name from a group of seven oak trees which once grew here, now replaced by a group of younger trees. Sevenoaks public school was founded in the 15th century by Sir William Sevenoke, a foundling who assumed the name of the town and rose to become Lord Mayor of London. Cricket has been played on The Vine since the 18th century. John Donne was rector of Sevenoaks, while the 19th-century poet Edward Thomas lived 3 miles to the south at Sevenoaks Weald, and it was here that

W H Davies wrote his *Autobiography of a Supertramp*. Sevenoaks parish church contains the Amherst family vault. Lord Jeffrey Amherst lived at Montreal near here, now marked by an obelisk. In 1760 Amherst became Governor-General of British North America, having captured Ticonderoga from the French. He also negotiated the terms of surrender after the fall of Montreal. Amherst commanded the King's Royal Rifle Corps, who wore green rather than the conspicuous red uniforms usually worn by the British. Based at **Winchester**, the regiment has special links with America. Lord Amherst was Governor of Virginia and Amherst College, Massachusetts, is named after him.

SHAFTESBURY
Dorset   3 ST82
Shaftesbury, the only hilltop town in the county, is where King Cnut (Canute) died in 1035. It is situated on top of a 700ft-high plateau overlooking Blackmore Vale. Its old name was Shaston and that is how Thomas Hardy refers to it in his Wessex novels. The abbey (AM), of which only fragments remain, was founded in AD 981, and it was here that King Edward the Martyr was brought after being murdered by his stepmother at **Corfe Castle**. The town has an excellent museum (OACT) which stands at the top of the picturesque, cobbled Gold Hill and contains a fascinating collection of locally made buttons, needlework, toys, agricultural and domestic items, fans, pottery and finds from local excavations.

SHALLOWFORD
Staffordshire   9 SJ82
Izaak Walton, author of the 'fisherman's bible', *The Compleat Angler*, lived in a cottage here which has been restored and a small museum (OACT) and a period garden established. Before he took up writing and fishing, Walton was an eminent ironmonger in London.

SHAP
Cumbria   18 NY51
At 1300ft above sea-level, Shap Fell is the highest point on the A6, and the village stands at nearly 1000ft. 1 mile to the west are the ruins of a 14th-century abbey (AM) and a sulphur well. The village was built using stone from Shap Abbey. In the grounds of Shap Wells Hotel, 3 miles south, is an interesting statue of Queen Victoria as a young girl. 5 miles south east, Orton was the birthplace of George Whitehead in 1636, a leader and co-founder of the Quakers. High Borrow Bridge, halfway between Shap and Kendal, was the site of a battle in 1745 between the Duke of Cumberland and the followers of Bonnie Prince Charlie.

SHARDLOW
Derbyshire   10 SK43
Shardlow stands beside the Trent and Mersey Canal. It used to be an inland port; now the narrow boats have been replaced by pleasure craft. The 200-year-old Clock Warehouse (OACT) contains an exhibition showing – in words, pictures, models, and artefacts – how England's waterway system was created.

SHEBBEAR
Devon   2 SS40
The Alscott Farm Agricultural Museum (OACT) contains a collection of vintage tractors, ploughs and dairy and household implements – plus photographs. It adds up to a fascinating picture of north Devon's agricultural past. A traction engine and a scale model of an Edwardian travelling fairground add to the interest. Shebbear itself is remote, peaceful and beautiful. The Devil's Stone, outside the churchyard, is identical to those brought from South Wales for the building of Stonehenge: suggesting that (despite its name) this has always been a sacred place.

SHEERNESS
Kent   6 TQ97
Sheerness stands on the north-western tip of the Isle of Sheppey at the point

where the Medway meets the Thames. The dockyard, which Samuel Pepys helped to plan, was founded by Charles II, who also built the fort here. With the arrival of steam, Sheerness became a base where naval vessels could take on coal without continuing upriver to Chatham. Sheerness continues to be an important commercial port. South east, on the island at Leysdown on Sea, the Wright brothers, Wilbur and Orville, met with British counterparts, including C S Rolls of Rolls-Royce, before World War I.

SHEFFIELD
S Yorkshire *15 SK38*
Nature provided Sheffield with all the requirements of a steel-manufacturing centre: the hills upon which it stands contained iron ore; there were trees to provide charcoal and the River Don to generate power; finally, there was coal in the vicinity. There had, in fact, been a settlement here back in the Iron Age. The city's cutlery business is almost as old as the Norman castle, of which only fragments remain. Chaucer mentions a Sheffield knife in *The Canterbury Tales* – the miller carries one in the Reeve's Tale. By the accession of Elizabeth I, scissors, scythes and shears had been added to the output. During the reign of James I, the Company of Cutlers in Hallamshire was established. The Master Cutler yields only to the Lord Mayor in precedence. In the 20th century Henry Brearley of Sheffield invented stainless steel. Unable to obtain a patent in Britain he successfully obtained one in the United States in 1915. Thomas Hollis was an early benefactor of Harvard.

Mary Queen of Scots spent a year in Sheffield Castle as a prisoner and 13 more in a Tudor house which has long been demolished. The site of the castle is now occupied by the Castle Market, which was opened in 1959. This roofed shopping centre, like the Crucible Theatre, is a good example of modern city planning and design. Dark satanic mills there may be, but the centre is neither dark nor satanic, and the modern buildings of the university are architecturally interesting. The City Museum houses a remarkable collection of cutlery dating back to the 16th century. The Bishop's Palace, a 15th-century timbered house, is also a museum – portraying life in Tudor times. The city boasts two art galleries: the Mappin and the Graves. The York and Lancashire Museum has

an above-average collection of militaria; and the Abbeydale Industrial hamlet, on the outskirts, should certainly be seen. Using waterwheels turned by the River Sheaf, it produced scythes and other agricultural tools from 1712 until 1933. On certain days the furnaces are lit. Abbeydale has associations with William Morris. The Shepherd Wheel, in nearby Whiteley Woods, is an even earlier water-powered grindery.

North east of Sheffield are **Rotherham** and Wentworth Woodhouse. On the northern outskirts of the city is Ecclesfield where Joseph Hunter, who first researched the names of the Pilgrim Fathers, is buried. 4 miles south east of Sheffield, Eckington parish church contains a Sitwell monument which dates from 1625. Nearby Renishaw Hall (OACT) was originally built by George Sitwell in the same year – this was the early home of Edith Sitwell.

SHEFFIELD PARK
E Sussex *5 TQ42*
Sheffield Park station was built in 1882 and retains its Victorian atmosphere. The line – part of British Rail's Lewes to East Grinstead track – was closed in 1960. Almost immediately, a group of enthusiasts set about resurrecting the section between Sheffield Park and Horsted Keynes, and called it the Bluebell Line; vintage steam trains run most weekends and daily in the summer season. There is a railway museum at the station. Sheffield Park (NT) was laid out between 1769 and 1794 by the 1st Earl of Sheffield. It is always beautiful, particularly in spring, when the rhododendrons and azaleas are in bloom. The house (OACT) dates back to the Tudor period, but was remodelled in the 18th century.

SHELDON
W Midlands *10 SP18*
In the parish church is a memorial to Thomas Bray, who founded a mission to Maryland in 1699, which led to the organization of the Society for the Propagation of the Gospel in Foreign Parts.

SHEPTON MALLET
Somerset *3 ST64*
Shepton Mallet is an agricultural town and the permanent site of the Bath and West Show. Cider and brewing, glove- and shoe-making, the manufacture of agricultural machinery are its industries and it originally derived its

prosperity from the medieval wool trade. The church, with its beautifully carved barrel ceiling and fine stone pulpit, dates from this era. Shepton Mallet Museum contains discoveries from the Mendip caves.

SHERBORNE
Dorset *3 ST61*
Sherborne is one of Dorset's most architecturally consistent towns, with many medieval buildings in golden Ham stone. The focus of the town is its 15th-century abbey church, which has beautiful fan vaulting in the Lady Chapel, and a glass reredos engraved by Sir Lawrence Whistler in 1958. Great Tom, the church bell, was a gift from Cardinal Wolsey. Part of the original abbey buildings are incorporated into Sherborne School, one of the town's well-known public schools. Among Sherborne's famous pupils were C Day-Lewis and the brothers John Cowper and Llewelyn Powys. Sherborne has two castles; the Old (AM), built in the 12th century by Bishop Roger, Chancellor to Henry I, was besieged and slighted during the Civil War. The New Castle (OACT) was begun in 1594 by Sir Walter Raleigh, who lived in the town for 15 years. Queen Elizabeth had leased him the Old Castle in 1592. The castle stands in the 20-acre park landscaped by Capability Brown, and it was here that Sir Walter was 'extinguished' when his servant first saw him smoking the tobacco he brought back from the New World. In 1688, William of Orange probably printed his *Proclamation to The English People* in the castle. The owners of Sherborne Castle are said to have been cursed by an early Bishop of Sarum; indeed, three were executed, two died in prison and one was poisoned. Sherborne Castle is the ancestral home of the Digbys. One of them, Robert Digby, was in New York as Commander-in-Chief of the British Fleet in 1781. In 1783 he visited Nova Scotia, carrying some Loyalists there. Digby, Nova Scotia is named after him. There is a portrait in Sherborne Castle. $2\frac{1}{2}$ miles north is the Lullingstone Silk Farm and Worldwide Butterfly Farm (OACT).

SHERBORNE ST JOHN
Hampshire *4 SU65*
Near the village of Sherborne St John stands the Vyne (NT), a fine Tudor house built by Henry VIII's Lord Chamberlain, William Sandys. Of a later date are the elegant rococo

plaster ceilings and beautiful furnishings. Especially interesting are the Gothic chapel and tomb chamber of Chaloner Chute, Speaker of the House of Commons in the Cromwellian era, who had bought the house from Lord Sandys. Sherborne St John's old church contains several interesting features – notably the 15th-century brasses in the Brocas Chapel.

SHERINGHAM
Norfolk *12 TG14*
There are really two Sheringhams: Lower Sheringham, which is an attractive resort largely developed at the end of the last century, and Upper Sheringham – the village. The beach is shingle, though sandy at low tide. Sheringham Hall, a Regency house built between 1812 and 1817, stands in beautiful parkland: the gardens are occasionally open, the house by arrangement only. The ruins of 13th-century Beeston Abbey are nearby. The North Norfolk Railway Company has a display of steam locomotives and rolling stock at Sheringham station and trains are in operation at certain times in the summer season.

SHERWOOD FOREST
Nottinghamshire *15*
Sherwood was the domain of Robin Hood and his Merry Men, who 'robbed the rich to feed the poor'. The forest is greatly diminished but tracts of beautiful oak woodland survive. However, Major Oak, supposed meeting place of the band in which they were all able to hide, stands 1 mile south of Edwinstowe, where Robin is said to have married Marion in the small church. (Incidentally, several early emigrants to America came from Edwinstowe.) Little John is buried at **Hathersage. Thoresby Park** (OACT) near Ollerton and Chamber Park (NT) incorporated parts of the ancient woodland.

SHETLAND ISLANDS, THE
Highland *28*
The Shetlands comprise more than 100 islands, some little more than isolated rocks, but only 17 are inhabited. Muckle Flugga, an islet off Unst, is the most northerly point in the British Isles and lies 170 miles north of John o'Groats and only 300 miles from the Arctic Circle. Mainland, the largest of the Shetlands, has the islands' capital, Lerwick, a bustling little place of distinctly Scandinavian character. Ferries run from Aberdeen on the mainland, and there is an airport at

Major Oak, Sherwood Forest

Sumburgh, in the south of Mainland. The most powerful presence on the island nowadays is the gigantic North Sea Oil terminal at Sullom Voe, although now, having radically changed the islanders' traditional crofting and fishing way of life, North Sea Oil is offering less and less employment.

The first settlers were probably Picts – followed in the 9th century by the Norsemen. The Shetlands remained part of Scandinavia until the marriage of the king's daughter Margaret to James III of Scotland in 1469 when Christian I ceded them as part of her dowry. Norse influence remained strong and the old Norn dialect survived for centuries. Remains of medieval, Viking, and earlier Pictish settlements can be seen at Jarlshof (AM) sear Sumburgh. Near Scalloway are the Tingwall Agricultural Museum, and ruined Scalloway Castle (AM). Remains of Pictish brochs are common, but the best example is on Mousa, an attractive little island off the south east coast of Mainland. Other islands to visit are Bressay, not far from Lerwick; East and West Burra, and Trodra, linked by bridges to each other and to Mainland; Muckle Roe is also linked by bridge to Mainland; Unst, the northernmost of the inhabited islands; Whalsay, and Yell. Fetlar and Foula are noted for their birdlife; Papa Stour is honeycombed with spectacular caves. Remote from the main group of islands are the Out Skerries. **Fair Isle,** halfway between the Orkneys and the Shetlands, is famous not only for its knitwear but also for the richness of the birdlife: the island is run by the National Trust for Scotland. Wild life also abounds on the Shetlands; seals and otters are a familiar sight, in some parts almost as familiar as the small,

sturdy Shetland ponies, once the mainstay of the crofters, which are now so highly prized as pets.

SHIELDAIG
Highland *25 NG85*
The journey to this pleasant crofting and fishing village on an inlet of Loch Torridon is well worthwhile. The road linking it with Torridon provides some fantastic views of 3456ft Liathach; 3232ft Ben Alligin, and 2995ft Beinn Dearg. A newly built road west of the village to Applecross has opened up a panorama over the Inner Sound to the islands of Raasay and Skye. Many of the rocks in the vicinity have characteristic horizontal red bands of Torridon sandstone.

SHREWSBURY
Shropshire *9 SJ41*
Shrewsbury, situated on a bend of the River Severn, has ten bridges spanning the river. The town may have been founded by Britons who fled from the Roman city of *Vicoconium* (now Wroxford) 5 miles south east, and there are relics of the Roman occupation in Rowley's House Museum, one of Shrewsbury's many half-timbered buildings. In the old part of the city are winding streets such as Wyle Cop, Grope Lane, and Gullet Passage, and Bear Steps (OACT), a restored 14th-century cottage, with old shops and a meeting hall, is well worth a visit. The Norman castle (OACT), built high above the river, was much enlarged by Edward I, and in the 18th century was converted into a house by the architect and engineer Thomas Telford for Sir William Pulteney. St Mary's Church, with its lofty spire, dates from the 12th century. The nave has a 15th-century carved roof and some fine stained glass, particularly in the Jesse Window. St Chad's Church is notable for its circular nave. Shrewsbury has several monuments to its famous sons: Charles Darwin attended Shrewsbury School and is commemorated by a bronze statue. Clive (of India), MP for the town from 1761 until his death in 1774, is similarly remembered. A column 134ft high, only just shorter than Nelson's Column in Trafalgar Square, is a memorial to Lord Hill, who commanded a brigade at Waterloo. Shrewsbury's largest park, the Quarry, is the work of the famous gardener, Percy Thrower. At its centre are formal gardens known as the Dingle. The town was the birthplace of Edward Hopkins, Governor of

Shrewsbury

Connecticut in alternate years from 1640–52. Later he was made a Naval Commissioner by Cromwell. Nathaniel Hawthorne stayed in Shrewsbury with his family. The Shropshire and Hertfordshire Regimental Museum has 2 American flags captured in the Revolutionary War. Just outside Shrewsbury is Attingham Park, Atcham. 6 miles north at Harmer Hill, Lea Hall was the earliest home of the Lee family.

SHUGBOROUGH
Staffordshire *9 SJ92*
Shugborough Hall (OACT), home of the Earls of Lichfield, and Staffordshire County Museum, lies 5 miles east of Stafford. The mansion, which dates back to 1693, contains a fine collection of French furniture and some interesting relics of Admiral George Anson – the intrepid navigator who inherited the property in 1720 and lived there until his death in 1762. Among the features of the garden are the 'Chinese House', the Cat's Monument and the Tower of the Winds. The stable block houses the County Museum which contains exhibitions of costume, domestic life and crafts. Park Farm is an agricultural museum and raises rare breeds of animals. Lord Anson spent 9 years in Charleston as well as circumnavigating the world and exploring the South Seas. The house contains items relating to South Carolina and to Texas where three sons of a later generation lived. He is buried in Colwich parish church.

SIBLE HEDINGHAM
Essex *12 TL73*
Sible Hedingham was the birthplace of Sir John Hawkwood – a 14th-century mercenary who fought in the Black Prince's forces at Poitiers, then moved on to Italy, where he and his band of hand-picked mercenaries were almost continually in action. Sir John is one of the figures in a frieze painted by Paolo Uccello in Florence, and he died there in 1394. There is a monument to him in the south aisle of St Peter's Church. Not far from the church stand two handsome buildings, the 15th-century White Horse Inn, and the rectory, which dates from the 18th century.

SIDMOUTH
Devon *2 SY18*
Steep wooded hills guard Sidmouth, a select coastal resort. Its tall Regency houses, with their wrought-iron balconies, recall Sidmouth's standing in the early 19th century. The pleasant beach is flanked by spectacular red cliffs and the town began life as a fishing village. During the Napoleonic Wars, the well-to-do, unable to visit Europe, went to Sidmouth instead. The Old Manor in Church Street is the museum (OACT) and is one of the town's oldest houses.

SILCHESTER
Hampshire *4 SU66*
The Romans called Silchester *Calleva Atrebatum* and it was a considerable town, with a dyeing industry. The inhabitants worshipped in 3 temples. In the 4th century, a small Christian church was built within the town walls. It is, so far as anyone can tell, the *only* one built in Britain during the years of Roman occupation. But the Romans departed and *Calleva Atrebatum* fell into total decay, except for the walls and a gateway (AM), which are still substantial. The remains of an amphitheatre can be seen outside the walls and there is a site museum, though the best finds are in Reading Museum.

SINGLETON
W Sussex *4 SU81*
Linch Down rises 818ft to the north west of this lovely Sussex village and offers splendid views. It is the perfect setting for the Weald and Downland Open Air Museum (OACT), an outstanding collection of historic buildings from all over the south country which have been re-erected on the slopes of the Downs. From time to time there are demonstrations of rural crafts.

, SISSINGHURST
Kent *6 TQ73*
Sissinghurst Castle (NT) was built during the reign of Mary Tudor. During the Seven Years War (1756–63), by then in a dilapidated condition, it was used as a prison for captured French seamen. Later the buildings served as a workhouse, then as a farmhouse; eventually falling into disrepair. In 1930, the estate was bought by the writer Victoria Sackville-West and her husband, Harold Nicolson. They restored the gatehouse, parts of two wings, and created what must surely be one of the most beautiful gardens in Britain.

Sissinghurst lies just north of Cranbrook, a particularly pretty Wealden town with several American connections. William Eddy left here in 1630 in the *Handmaid* which sailed to Plymouth, Massachusetts. In 1635 he was appointed clerk of the settlement. In the 1860s William Booth, another resident of Cranbrook, emigrated. His success in the American West enabled his son to establish a rural estate called Cranbrook near Detroit.

The house contains the printing press used by Virginia and Leonard Woolf in the early days of the Hogarth Press – among the publications was the first edition of T S Eliot's *The Wasteland* (1922).

SITTINGBOURNE
Kent *6 TG96*
Sittingbourne, on an inlet of the River Swale, used to be important to Britain's paper making industry. The New Dolphin Sailing Barge Museum (OACT) on Milton Creek has an original sail-loft and forge, and collections of riggers' tools. There are often barges being restored.

SKIPTON
N Yorkshire *14 SD95*
Skipton, set in a valley in the Airedale moors, stands at the most northerly point of the Leeds and Liverpool Canal

(opened in 1816, it runs for nearly 130 miles). Despite its textile industry, the town has a countrified look which makes it a pleasant centre for touring the Dales. The 14th-century castle (OACT) was the home of the Clifford family. After it had been partially demolished in 1649, Lady Anne Clifford rebuilt it, and added the family motto 'Desormais' (henceforth) to the gatehouse. A yew tree planted by Lady Anne stands in the grounds. The Craven Museum concentrates on local geology for its exhibits; the fascinating George Leatt Industrial and Folk Museum (OACT) is housed in the 1750 High Corn Mill.

SKOMER ISLAND
Dyfed   *7 SM70*
Skomer is littered with the relics of ancient settlements, suggesting it was heavily populated. The present inhabitants are all navigators by nature: kittiwake, cormorant, petrel, puffin, razorbill, guillemot, and shearwater. There are even some normally land-based birds such as buzzard and peregrines.

SLEDMERE
Humberside   *16 SE96*
Sledmere village and the surrounding Yorkshire Wolds owe a great deal to the Sykes family. In Tudor times, they were Leeds merchants; and then, in 1751, Richard Sykes began work on Sledmere House (OACT) – the site of which had once been that of a medieval manor. His nephew, Sir Christopher, carried on the work in

the 1780s. The house is beautifully decorated and contains many handsome pieces of furniture. Sir Christopher's most important achievement was the introduction of agriculture to the Wolds – an achievement celebrated by a classical temple beside the main gate. On top of Gaston Hill, a 120ft Gothic tower was erected in memory of Sir Tatton Sykes after his death in 1863. Sir Tatton, it seems, was renowned for his skill as a bare-knuckle fighter. Indeed, there seem to be monuments great and small to Sykes wherever you look in Sledmere. They are well deserved. Before this industrious family took the village under its protection, the inhabitants used to live in fear of raids by packs of wolves from the wilderness that surrounded them.

SLIMBRIDGE
Gloucestershire   *3 SO70*
Slimbridge, 4 miles east of Sharpness, is the home of the Severn Wildfowl Trust founded by Sir Peter Scott in 1946. It contains the largest and most comprehensive collection of wildfowl in the world: some resident, and some arriving and departing according to the seasons. Well sited observation towers are available to the public, with whom the Trust is justly very popular.

SMALLHYTHE
Kent   *6 TQ82*
In medieval times, when the River Rother was wider and deeper, Smallhythe was a prosperous port and shipbuilding centre. The harbour-master's house, now named Smallhythe Place (NT) (OACT), was the actress Ellen Terry's home from 1901 until her death in 1928. In the parish church where she worshipped, the 15th-century font is set in an ancient millstone given by the actress. Her house now contains a theatrical museum, with items relating to Ellen and to her contemporary Sir Henry Irving, as well as to earlier representatives of the acting profession such as David Garrick and Sarah Siddons.

SMARDEN
Kent   *6 TQ84*
In the days of Edward III, Smarden was a busy market town. Now, with its black and white timbered houses, it is one of the prettiest villages in the country. Reminders of its days of prosperity occur in the Dragon House (decorated with a frieze of dragons) near the village pump, and Chesenden

– a Wealden hall-house. The church is often called 'the barn of Kent' due to the height (36ft) of its wooden roof.

SMOO CAVE
Highland   *30 NC46*
Smoo Cave, which lies a mile or so to the east of Durness, is a huge cavern cut into the base of the limestone cliff. The first of the three chambers is the largest – 200ft long by 120ft high, and is entered through a 53ft-high arch. The name probably comes from *smjuga* ('a rock').

SNAPE
Suffolk   *12 TM35*
In the 19th century, Newson Garrett, father of Britain's first woman doctor, Elizabeth Garrett Anderson, established a maltings on the edge of the village. It was served by sailing barges travelling up and down the River Alde to the Maltings Quay. As a result of the **Aldeburgh** Music Festival inaugurated in 1948 by Benjamin Britten, part of the premises was transformed into a concert hall.

SNOWDONIA NATIONAL PARK
Gwynedd   *13 SH65*
The Welsh name for Snowdonia is *Eryi* – 'the haunt of the eagle', and though the eagles have gone, the grandeur remains. Snowdon itself dominates the area, at 3560ft it is the highest mountain in Wales. The Park covers 845 square miles of mountainous countryside stretching as far as the coast of Cardigan Bay. This is superb

Mt Snowdon

Castle gateway, Skipton

country for the walker and rock climber. The mixture of mountain, lake and deep valley creates some of the loveliest scenery in North Wales, and noted beauty spots such as **Betws-y-Coed** attract visitors in their thousands. Thomas Jefferson's ancestors were from Snowdonia. His father's James River farm was called Snowdon.

SOLVA
Dyfed   *7 SM82*
The creek, sheltered by steep green slopes, is not unlike a fjord, and the village of small white cottages clinging to the hillside enhances this impression. There were lime-kilns in business during the 19th century, and the quay was built in 1861 to handle stone used in the construction of Small Rocks lighthouse 15 miles offshore. Solva is now a haven for pleasure craft.

SOMERTON
Somerset   *3 ST42*
In the days of the West Saxons Somerton was the capital of Somerset. An attractive country town, there is a most pleasing uniformity about its grey stone buildings grouped round the square. The church tower is particularly interesting: it was built in stages from the 12th century to the 15th, and has a notable tiebeam roof.

SONNING
Berkshire   *4 SU77*
Sonning is one of the prettiest of the Thames-side villages. The arched bridge spanning the river is one of the oldest across the Thames. There is a lock, thatched cottages, and a mill.

SOTTERLEY
Suffolk   *12 TM48*
Sotterley Agricultural Museum (OACT), which is housed in Alexander Wood Farm, presents a splendid collection of hardware – mechanical and non-mechanical. The blacksmith's shop, the farmhouse kitchen, and agricultural implements splendidly evoke the past. There is also a collection of cars and motorbikes.

SOUTHAMPTON
Hampshire   *4 SU41*
For many years the main port of departure for the USA was Liverpool, but in 1911 the White Star Line moved its base to Southampton and the others followed. Not only was it closer to London, and had a sheltered anchorage, it also enjoyed that unique phenomenon – two high tides in every

Mayflower memorial, Southampton

24 hours. For the better part of half a century, the docks were enlivened by the massive and beautiful shapes of great ocean liners – some plying between England and New York, others (the Union Castle ships) running a service to South Africa. When air travel came into its own, however, the liners disappeared, apart from occasional appearances by the *QEII* and the *Canberra*.

Southampton had been in business as a port long before the luxury ships came to it. It was a place of embarkation for the crusades, for the Napoleonic Wars, and, indeed, during both World Wars when more than ten million Allied troops set off for France. In 1620, the *Mayflower* set sail from here – an event that is celebrated by a tall stone column near the spot where the Pilgrim Fathers walked up the gangplank. Later, bad weather forced them into Plymouth for repair. Tablets mention William Brewster, Edward Winslow, John Alden, who was from Southampton, and others. This was a major port in the Newfoundland fish trade. Another North American connection is that in 1710 a group of Iroquois chieftains disembarked here to urge Queen Anne to attack the French in Canada. A memorial, carved in white marble, in East Park, is dedicated to the engineers of the *Titanic* – the ill-starred if magnificent shipbuilding folly that foundered.

Marlands Hall is a museum devoted to the achievements of R J Mitchell, designer of the Spitfire – the first of which was built in Southampton. Among the exhibits is Mitchell's

Supermarine S6B, which won the Schneider Trophy race in 1931 with a speed of 340mph. Neither Spitfires nor Hurricanes could save Southampton from bombardment by the Luftwaffe in World War II. The damage was awesome and much of the past was smashed to rubble. As a result a good deal of the town is new. However, among the historic buildings which survived are the Bargate, which once served as Guildhall and courthouse and is now a museum; the 14th-century Wool House (now the Maritime Museum); and God's House Tower, the remains of a Norman hospital originally founded in 1185. The fine 16th-century Tudor House, set in a charming Elizabethan garden, now houses a museum of local history. Also of interest are the City Art Gallery and Southampton Zoo.

'Artemus Ward', the pen-name of the American humorist Charles Farrar Browne, is to be found on a plaque in the London Hotel, in Terminus Terrace. He died nearby in 1867. His remains were taken back to Waterford, Maine where he had been born.

Horton Heath, 5 miles north east of Southampton, was the birthplace of Samuel Sewall (1652–1730), the fellow of Harvard, jurist and publisher in Boston and New England. He wrote a very interesting diary giving many details of the times in which he lived.

SOUTH DOWNS
W and E Sussex   *5, 6*
The chalky uplands of the South Downs extend from a point near Petersfield in Hampshire to Beachy Head in Sussex, forming the southern rampart of the Weald as the **North Downs** form the northern. Woodlands clothe the western end, but in the east the Downs offer great expanses of windswept turf. A long distance footpath, the South Downs Way, crosses the length. The highest points are Butser Hill (889ft), Duncton Down (837ft) and Ditchling Beacon (813ft). Almost without exception, the views are tremendous, and there are interludes such as the intrusion of the River Cuckmere to form a valley in which nestles Alfriston, a beautiful small town. Birling Gap is within easy walking distance of the early lighthouse, Belle Tout (built in 1831); and then, over to the west and due north of **Worthing**, there is Chanctonbury Ring: a triumphant copse. Not officially haunted, though many who have been there claim to have experienced a strange sensation.

SOUTHEND-ON-SEA
Essex *6 TQ88*
London's seaside resort is best known for its pier – at 1½ miles the longest in the world. The town has 7 miles of shoreline. Among the better examples of holiday kitsch is a floral clock with a 20ft diameter and the Kursaal, crammed full of amusements. The Regency character of the town is nevertheless preserved in the Royal Terrace where the Prince Regent's Princess Caroline stayed. Porters is an early 17th-century manor house where Disraeli stayed and which is now the Mayor's Parlour. Other places of interest are the Historic Aircraft Museum and Southchurch Hall (OACT), a beautifully restored 14th-century manor house.

Five miles north is Great Stambridge. Mary Forth, mother of John Winthrop the younger and 5 other children, was born here. She married John Winthrop the elder in the parish church, where a plaque commemorates the Pilgrim leader.

SOUTH HARTING
W Sussex *4 SU71*
High on the South Downs, near the village of South Harting, stands Uppark (NT) (OACT), a late 17th-century mansion, much improved in the 18th century by the fabulously wealthy Sir Matthew Fetherstonhaugh, whose collections of paintings, porcelain and furniture can still be admired. Nearby is the Vandalia Memorial Tower, commemorating a syndicate formed to establish a colony in America – the scheme foundered at the outbreak of war in 1776.

SOUTHPORT
Merseyside *14 SD31*
Southport is a pleasant resort, with elegant shops in Lord Street, beautiful gardens, some good golf courses, a pier, and 6 miles of sandy beach (once used for motor racing). The Atkinson Art Gallery has interesting collections of 19th- and 20th-century painting and sculpture; the Botanic Gardens Museum is devoted to natural and local history; historic locomotives and other old vehicles are in the Steamport Transport Museum (OACT); on the Promenade there is a model village and model railway, and a zoo in Princes Park.

SOUTH SHIELDS
Tyne & Wear *20 NZ36*
The port at South Shields was established by the Romans as a kind of preliminary before they moved on to found Newcastle. Finds from the Roman period are displayed in the museum on the site of *Arbeia*, the excavated Roman fort. Although less important than Newcastle, industry did not pass South Shields by. Ernest Thompson Seton, America's first Chief Scout, was born here.

SOUTHWELL
Nottinghamshire *15 SK65*
Charles I gave himself up to the Scottish army at the Saracen's Head in Southwell in 1647 and they promptly sold him to Parliament. Happier memories are recalled by Burgage Manor (not open), where Byron used to spend his holidays, and by the Bramley seedling apple, which was developed in the garden of Bramley Tree Cottage. But the most imposing feature of this Nottinghamshire town is the great Norman minster, famous for the exquisite carvings in the Chapter House. In the north transept is an alabaster effigy and tomb of Archbishop Sandys; among the attendant children is the young Sir Edwin, who was to influence the early history of Virginia.

SOUTHWOLD
Suffolk *12 TM57*
Southwold is an altogether delightful little resort at the mouth of the River Blythe. Among its many pleasant features are numerous greens, which came about as the result of a fire that laid waste most of the town in 1659. The parish church of St Edmund is a beauty – with a fine tower (100ft), a medieval painted pulpit, and a Seven Sacraments font. Next to neighbouring

Southwold lighthouse

Blythburgh and **Long Melford** it is indisputably the finest church in Suffolk. The beach is a mixture of sand and shingle. Unusual but by no means unattractive features of Southwold are the lighthouse, which stands within the town, and the famous Adnams brewery. Southwold was the home of Eric Blair, better known by his pen-name, George Orwell. The town is connected with Southwold, Long Island, founded in 1640 by people from here led by the Reverend John Young.

SPALDING
Lincolnshire *11 TF22*
More than half the bulbs grown in Britain come from the area around Spalding, which suggests that the best time to visit it is late spring. The River Welland flows through the centre of the town, spanned by seven bridges. Ayscoughfee Hall (early 15th century) contains the Tourist Information Centre. Springfield Gardens (OACT) contain more than a million bulbs and thousands of roses.

The Spalding Gentleman's Society was founded in 1710, and included Sir Isaac Newton and Alexander Pope among its members. The Society now houses a library and museum (view by appointment only).

SPETCHLEY
Hereford & Worcester *9 SO85*
Spetchley Park, built in 1810, is an imposing mansion. The grounds (OACT) cover 30 acres. The partly 14th-century church contains interesting monuments. 2 miles north, the small church at Warndon has a picturesque timbered tower and a 15th-century font.

SPILSBY
Lincolnshire *16 TF46*
Spilsby is an attractive market town beyond which the flatlands of the Fens stretch out towards the North Sea. Sir William de Willoughby gave the town its charter in the 14th century, and there are memorials in the church to the family, and to the d'Eresbys with whom they inter-married, in the church. One of them, 2nd Baron Willoughby d'Eresby, fought at Crécy. Sir John Franklin, the explorer, is also commemorated by a tablet. Born in Spilsby, he died in the Arctic while leading the expedition which discovered the North-West Passage in 1847; a model of his flagship hangs in the church. The surrounding Fenland is full of Pilgrim connections – see **Alford, Tattershall** and **Boston.**

STAFFA, ISLE OF
Strathclyde *25 NM33*
Staffa is uninhabited and ships from Oban can land visitors only when the weather is calm. The island is famous for its dramatic coastline and caves – notably Fingal's, celebrated by Mendelssohn. Fingal (or Finn McCoul to be correct) was a giant who created Staffa, according to legend.

Church Lane, Stafford

STAFFORD
Staffordshire *9 NM92*
Stafford comes as a surprise to many people: rather than an industrial centre of the North Midlands, it has more the air of a country town, with several historic houses, notably High House, a four-storey timbered building where Charles I and Prince Rupert once stayed. Izaac Walton, (see Shallowford) the ultimate authority on angling, was born in Stafford and baptized at the Norman font in the Church of St Mary. Richard Brinsley Sheridan, playwright and onetime owner of Drury Lane Theatre in London, was Stafford's MP from 1790 until 1806. He lived at Chetwynd House (1745), which now, rather quaintly, serves as the post office. Stafford used to have two castles: the one built by William I has vanished without trace; the other (Robert de Stafford's) was rebuilt in the 19th century, and is now virtually a ruin once more.

Four miles east is Blithfield Hall (OACT) which was the ancestral home of Sir Charles Bagot, Governor of Canada 1842–3, in the difficult period following the Act of Union between Upper and Lower Canada (1840). He died in Kingston, Ontario in 1843 but is buried with his wife in the Blithfield church. Bagot goats, a rare species of which fewer than a 100 survive, live in the park.

STAINDROP
Co Durham *20 NZ12*
Staindrop's church, St Mary's, is understandably rich with monuments to the Neville family, who owned Raby Castle (OACT) for three centuries. The castle passed from the Nevilles to the Vanes in the early 17th century. Its historical associations are numerous and its octagonal drawing-room is probably the best example of a Victorian drawing-room in the country.

STAITHES
North Yorkshire *20 NZ71*
In the 18th century, 400 fishing boats would sail from this beautiful village and return laden with mackerel and cod. The port declined as trade moved to **Whitby**. Captain Cook, the famous navigator of the Pacific and masterly surveyor of the Newfoundland coast, was apprenticed to a local grocer before running away to Whitby to join his first ship.

STAMFORD
Lincolnshire *11 TF00*
Considered England's most beautiful small stone-built town, Stamford was originally the Fenland capital and a wealthy wool town. Much of the town was destroyed during the Wars of the Roses in the 15th century, but quickly recovered. Stamford has five ancient and notable churches. St Mary's has a 14th-century tower and spire, and contains the lovely 'Chapel of the Golden Choir'. In St John's Church, in 1601, Isaac Johnson, a founder of Boston and Massachusetts, was baptized. His wife was Arbella Clinton for whom John Winthrop's flagship was renamed *Arbella*. All Saints Church has a magnificent angel roof in the chancel. The impressive west window was given in 1888 by a Boston descendant of Browne, the founder of a local 16th-century almshouse. Browne's Hospital has an exquisite Tudor screen and fine stained glass in its chapel. Stamford School has a pointed arched gateway, a relic of a breakaway movement in 1333 by students of Brasenose College, Oxford. Stamford's George Hotel was frequented by Sir Walter Scott.

Outside the town stands Burghley House (OACT), ancestral home of the Cecils. Built by William Cecil, Chief Secretary of State and Lord High Treasurer to Queen Elizabeth I, the house is considered to be one of England's greatest Elizabethan mansions. Among its treasures is the 'Heaven Room' whose walls and ceiling were painted by Verrio.

In the churchyard of St Martin's Church, Daniel Lambert is buried; the fattest Englishman who ever lived, he weighed over 52 stone and his waist measured 92 inches.

STAMFORD BRIDGE
Humberside *15 SE75*
In 1066 at the Battle of Stamford Bridge, King Harald of Norway, who had sailed up the Humber and the Ouse and sacked York, was decisively beaten by King Harold of England. The battle took place on the flats above which now stands a fine 18th-century bridge. Immediately after the battle, Harold and his army went south to meet William of Normandy at Hastings, where they were defeated in a decisive battle which marked the beginning of the Norman conquest.

STANTON ST JOHN
Oxfordshire *10 SP50*
Three miles outside **Oxford**, Stanton St John was the birthplace of John White (1573–1648), Fellow of New College, Oxford and a founder of Massachusetts. White led the West Country emigration when he was Rector of Dorchester, Dorset. A stone over the door of his original home near the church records his birth. Milton's grandfather also lived here. Marston, on the northern edge of the city, was Cromwell's headquarters during the seige of Oxford in the Civil War.

STEVENAGE
Hertfordshire *11 TL22*
Anyone planning a new town could hardly do better than look at Stevenage. The new has been accomplished at no sacrifice to the old. Now Stevenage is spaciously planned, and contains several examples of good modern architecture. Old Stevenage centres on the High Street, which is attractively shaded by trees. Old cottages line the narrow streets leading off the High Street. The undercroft of St George's Church houses a museum. Stevenage was the boyhood home of E M Forster, author of *A Passage to India*.

STIRLING
Central *23 NS79*

Stirling occupies a strategic site on the River Forth, and its great castle stands high on a rocky crag commanding the approaches by sea and by land. Until the opening of the bridge at Kincardine-on-Forth in 1936, Stirling was the lowest bridging point over the river before the Firth of Forth estuary.

The castle visitors see today dates from the Renaissance period, the 15th and 16th centuries, but the rock is known to have been fortified in the 11th century, and in the 12th century the small settlement that had grown up round the castle was granted its royal charter, enabling it to hold markets and form trade guilds. Since the infant royal burgh was well placed on the only route between the Highlands and Lowlands, it became a thriving market centre, and remained so despite the turbulent wars that were fought around this area during the Middle Ages. Two of them were decisive in the history of Scotland: at the Battle of Stirling Bridge in 1297 William Wallace defeated the English armies; and at the more famous Battle of Bannockburn in 1314 Robert the Bruce inflicted such a savage defeat on Edward II of England that he not only won himself the throne but also assured Scotland's independence. After the Stuarts gained the ascendancy in 1370, the castle became a royal residence. James II and James V were born here; Mary Queen of Scots lived here for several years and also celebrated her secret marriage to Lord Darnley at the castle. The last Scottish king to live here was James VI, who on the death of Elizabeth I also became king of England, thus uniting the two crowns. After the departure of James VI, the castle became a military garrison, but has now been restored.

PLACES TO SEE

Argyll's Lodging The fine 17th-century mansion was built by the 1st Earl of Stirling in 1630 but takes its name from a later owner, the 1st Marquis of Argyll. It is now a youth hostel.

Argyll's Lodging

Old Bridge

Bannockburn 2 miles south of Stirling is the battlefield where Robert the Bruce defeated the English armies.

Cambuskenneth Abbey The ruins of the 13th-century abbey stand beside the River Forth, north east of the town.

Castle The oldest parts of the castle date from the 11th century, but most of the buildings are Renaissance. The Royal Palace was built by James V in the 16th century, and the ornate stonework was carved by French masons. There is a fascinating collection of carved oak medallions from the ceiling of the king's presence chamber, known as the Stirling Heads. The upper rooms of the palace house the Museum of the Argyll and Sutherland Highlanders. Within the castle precincts there is a Landmark Centre which tells the history of the castle.

The Guildhall Built in 1639, the Guildhall was originally Cowane's Hospital, an almshouse for members of the Merchant Guildry of Stirling. It became the Guildhall in the 18th century.

Holy Rude Church When James VI was crowned here in 1567, John Knox preached the sermon. The nave has a fine, timbered roof. The church was restored in the 1930s and a wall which had partitioned the kirk into two separate churches, east and west, due to a theological dispute in 1656, was removed.

Mar's Wark Partly ruined, the mansion was begun in the 1570s for the Earl of Mar, Keeper of Stirling Castle and Regent of Scotland during the minority of James VI.

King's Knot This elaborate knot garden was laid out in the 1620s. It is thought that the octagonal centrepiece featured in tournaments held here.

Smith Art Gallery Temporary exhibitions and local museum displays are held in this Victorian art gallery endowed by Thomas Stuart Smith.

The Tolbooth Dating from 1704, the tolbooth was formerly both town hall and jail.

STEVENTON
Hampshire *4 SU54*
For more than 40 years, Jane Austen's father was rector of the 13th-century church, which contains several monuments to the family. Miss Austen was born in the village in 1775. While living at Steventon, and in her early twenties, she wrote the first versions of *Sense and Sensibility*, *Pride and Prejudice*, and *Northanger Abbey*.

STOBO
Borders *23 NT13*
Stobo lies in the beautiful Tweed valley. The Norman church was added to in the 16th and 17th centuries, though the 13th century doorway is intact. Stobo Castle was restored in the 19th century. Across the river, Dawyck Botanic Gardens (OACT) are among the best known in Scotland. They contain some fine specimens of trees – including larch – that were imported from Sweden in the 18th century.

STOCKPORT
Gtr Manchester *14 SJ89*
Stockport has not been completely swamped by industry; there are still houses around the market place built by the landed gentry of Cheshire in the Middle Ages. It came into greater prominence in the 19th century, when soft water from the Peak District turned out to be ideal for the textile industry. Silk hats were among the local specialities. The railway viaduct, built in 1839–40 (22 arches and more than 100ft high) is a masterpiece – and so is a more recently constructed shopping precinct that spans the River Mersey. Stockport Grammar School, founded in 1487, is famous as one of the most ancient schools in the country.

STOCKTON-ON-TEES
Cleveland *20 NZ41*
On 27 September 1825, the first ever passenger-carrying train steamed into Stockton. Thereafter, the shipbuilding and engineering industries multiplied and this town on the Tees was never the same again. Nonetheless, the open air market, established in 1310, is still held in the High Street, reputed to be the widest in England. In 1827 a local chemist invented the friction match, and Thomas Sheraton, creator of great furniture, was born here in 1731. Long Newton, 4 miles west, was the home of the Vane family. Sir Henry Vane was a Governor of Massachusetts.

Gladstone Pottery Museum, Loughton, near Stoke-on-Trent

STOKE-ON-TRENT
Staffordshire *14 SJ84*
Stoke-on-Trent is made up of the Potteries – or has been since 1910 when the original 6 towns (Turnstall, Burslem, Hanley, Stoke-on-Trent, Fenton and Longton) were amalgamated. Arnold Bennett was brought up in the Potteries, describing it in *Anna of the Five Towns*. Bennett was educated at the Burslem Endowed School, which was formerly part of the Wedgwood Institute, and his family's last home is now the Arnold Bennett Museum. Many people were responsible for creating the bone china industry, though Josiah Wedgwood (1730–95) was the great pioneer, technically, artistically – and as initiator of improvements and extensions to the canal network. The smoothness of this form of transport made it the ideal form of conveyance for his fragile products, which were in great demand in the 19th century with the increasing popularity of tea and coffee. The rebuilt chapel of St Peter ad Vincula contains memorials to Wedgwood, Spode and Minton. The Spode factory can be toured and the Spode Copeland Museum has a splendid collection of ceramics nearly as good as that of the City Museum in Hanley, in which there are examples of the potter's art from Roman times to the present day. At Longton, the Gladstone Pottery Museum is a restored Victorian Pottery, with traditional bottle ovens. There is also the fascinating Chatterly Whitfield Mining Museum at Turnstall. Another distinguished son of the Potteries was Reginald Mitchell (1895–1937), who designed the Spitfire aircraft. Caverswall, 4 miles south east, provided the New World with Matthew Cradock, a founder of Massachusetts.

STOKE POGES
Buckinghamshire *5 SU98*
The poet Thomas Gray has made this little village eternally famous through his poem, *Elegy in a Country Churchyard*, and he himself is buried in the church. The churchyard is a tranquil spot, surrounded by trees; alongside it are beautiful memorial gardens, established in the 1920s, leading down to a lake with a fountain and rose garden. It is easy to forget that one is only a few miles away from Slough. Stoke Poges was bought by William Penn's son Thomas in 1789. His son, John, built the mansion, now a golf club, with money raised by the sale of his interests in Pennsylvania. A piece of the elm tree under which William Penn made his treaty with the Indians is preserved in the Club House. The church contains memorials to the Penns and the family pew. The Gray memorial (NT) was erected by John Penn.

STOKESAY
Shropshire *9 SO48*
Stokesay Castle (OACT) is one of the earliest fortified manor houses in England – the oldest parts date from the 12th century and the great hall from the 13th. It is an extraordinary structure – its massive stone towers topped with a timber-framed house – and of outstanding interest.

Stokesay Castle

THE LAKE DISTRICT

North of industrial Merseyside and north west of the Dales, lies the Lake District, an area of mountains, rocks and lakes that is England's 'Alpine' region, and its rival to Scotland's Skye or Wester Ross. It lives in the verse of the 'Lake Poets', originally a term of derision in the pages of the *Edinburgh Review* of 1817. Wordsworth, Coleridge and Southey lived and wrote in Grasmere, Keswick and Ambleside, and Ruskin lived at Brantwood on Coniston Water; Sir Hugh Walpole, the novelist and author of the *Herries Chronicles*, at Borrowdale; Arthur Ransome at Newby Bridge and Haverthwaite; and Beatrix Potter (Mrs William Heelis) at Sawrey (near Esthwaite Water).

In this small area – roughly thirty square miles – are the highest mountain in England (Scafell), the deepest lake (Wastwater), the longest lake (Windermere) and one of the best pubs in the world, the Wasdale Head Inn, a climbers' rendezvous. This is a region of cool beauty; in

places the moss can run unbroken to the sky, over rocks of slate and shale, limestone, sandstone and granite, that were formed 400 million years ago. The central climbing reaches are composed of Borrowdale volcanic rock, mainly andesite and rhyolite, legacy of volcanic lava erupting during the Ordovician and Silurian periods. The crags and fells, becks and combes, the deep lakes reflecting the changing skies, the moss and juniper, the heather and bog myrtle, and on the tops the purple saxifrage, offer scenes of ever-changing colour and contour.

Places to Visit

Ambleside, for its Roman fort; Galava at Borrans and for the Lake District Heritage Centre.
Appleby for Westmorland; some of the Washingtons were at school here.
Brougham Castle, near Penrith. Roman site (*Brovacum*) that became a Norman fortress, destroyed by the Scots in 1174; much restored by the Clifford family.

Dove Cottage, Grasmere

Carlisle Castle, built by William Rufus in 1092 on the highest point above the River Eden, as a bastion against the Scots. Headquarters of the Border Regiment.
Cartmel, for the church, for Morecambe Bay and for Holker Hall, nearby.
Castlerigg, near Keswick, for its Stone Circle.
Cockermouth, the Gallery of Costume Dolls.
Dove Cottage, Grasmere, for Wordsworth.
Furness Abbey, founded 1123

by the Order of Savigny, then a Cistercian house, with a reputation for great wealth. Suppressed in 1537.
Hardknott, for the Roman fort *Mediobogdum*.
Kendal, for Windermere; for Abbot Hall with its history, museum and Art Gallery; for Levens Hall, family home of the Bagots – Sir Charles Bagot (British Ambassador 1815–20) signed the Rush-Bagot Treaty which settled the US–Canadian boundary – now has deer park, topiary gardens and steam engines.
Lanercost Priory, founded by the Augustinians in the twelfth century; the nave is still in use as a parish church.
Penrith and the Earl of Lonsdale's fascinating game reservation at Lowther. The castle at Penrith was a royal residence for Richard III.

Further Reading

AA: The Lake District (AA Publications)
Adrian Bailey, *Lakeland Rock*, classic climbs with Chris Bonington (Weidenfeld and Nicolson 1985)
Melvyn Bragg, *Land of the Lakes* (Secker and Warburg 1984)
Norman Nicholson, *The Lakes* (Hale 1977)
Wordsworth, *The Prelude*, Book X

Bowness on Windermere

STOKESLEY
N Yorkshire *20 NZ50*

This is a charming market town on the River Leven in the Cleveland Hills, with many old houses and cobbled alleyways. The Manor House, facing the Town Hall, now serves as a library and various offices. Jane Page of Stokesley was the first white woman to settle in Victoria, Australia. A row of trees was planted in her honour along the river bank just over a century ago.

STOKE-SUB-HAMDON
Somerset *3 ST41*

Hamdon Hill (426ft) lies to the south of the village. The Britons fortified it; the Romans began quarrying it. From it comes the yellow Ham stone – from which the village has been built, and which has done much to adorn the rest of the area. The church is Norman; the Priory (NT) dates back to the 15th century and was once a chantry (endowed for priests) house. Behind the Fleur-de-Lys Inn is a fives court built about 1756. The idea was to provide an alternative to the church wall for games.

STONE
Staffordshire *14 SJ93*

Among the famous sons of Stone was Admiral John Jervis – or Earl St Vincent as he became after his victory off Cape St Vincent in 1797 (greatly helped by Nelson's initiative). The Admiral lies in a suitably elaborate mausoleum in the parish churchyard. The name of the town, some say, is derived from a cairn of stones that marked the graves of two Christian Mercian princes murdered by their pagan father. Alternatively, it may have been inspired by a local stream that petrifies plant life.

STONEHAVEN
Grampian *27 NO88*

Lovely scenery, good fishing (fresh water *and* saltwater), and enough history to intrigue the curious – these are the delights of Stonehaven. The 16th-century Tolbooth (OACT) on the quay has variously been used as a storehouse, a court and as a prison. More recently, it has been modernized and is now a museum. At the south end of Market Square, Robert William Thomson (1822–73) was born. The inventive Mr Thomson produced the first ever pneumatic tyre, the first fountain-pen, and the first dry dock. Each summer a veteran car rally is held in his memory. Near the harbour stand the Mercat Cross and an 18th-century

Stonehenge

steeple beside which, in 1715, the Old Pretender was proclaimed king.

One and a half miles south is Dunnottar Castle (OACT), the most spectacular ruin on the North Sea coast of Scotland. The ruined fortress is on a rocky headland reached by a path from the mainland. In 1645, the Earl Marischal of Scotland, a staunch Presbyterian, held the castle against the Royalist Duke of Montrose, although during the Civil War Dunnottar was the last Scottish fortress to hold out against Cromwell's troops. 'Old Mortality' of Scott's novel by the same name was based on a stonemason who tended the churchyard here.

• STONEHENGE
Wiltshire *3 SU14*

Stonehenge (AM) is one of the world's great mysteries. We know that it was built in three phases; that its construction covered a period between 2200 BC to 1300 BC – from the Neolithic to the Bronze Age; that its axis is aligned with sunrise on the longest day of the year – 21 June. What we do not know is precisely why it was built. It certainly had nothing to do with Druids: they hadn't yet arrived in Britain when work was in progress; it may have served as a sort of calendar, as well as for religious purposes, but there is no evidence that Stonehenge was ever a place of human sacrifice. The most intriguing problem of all is how those enormous stones were transported to Salisbury Plain from their points of origin on the Marlborough Downs and even further away in the Prescelly Mountains of Pembrokeshire.

STONELEIGH
Warwickshire *10 SP37*

Stoneleigh is an interesting mixture of ancient and modern. The present day appears in the form of the Royal Show, that annual event to which farmers travel from all over the country. Its permanent site is in the grounds of Stoneleigh Abbey, a magnificent 18th-century house, also with parts of the original 14th-century abbey – the gatehouse and the hospice – surviving. Other manifestations of the past can be seen on the nine-arched bridge across the river, the Norman features of St Mary's Church, and several charming timbered houses.

STONOR
Oxfordshire *4 SU78*

Stonor Park (OACT), a Tudor house with 18th-century modifications, is set in beautifully wooded parkland. Among those who worshipped in its Roman Catholic chapel was St Edmund Campion, 16th-century priest and martyr who operated a secret printing press here. Stonor has been the home of the staunchly Catholic Camoys family for over 800 years. At least three others who lived here have since been canonized.

Sturton le Steeple nearby was the birthplace of John Robinson, minister to the early pilgrims.

STOURBRIDGE
W Midlands *9 SO88*

Stourbridge is an industrial town mostly concerned with iron and, since the 17th century, glass-making. The church is 18th century; the canal is popular with inland waterway enthusiasts and the surrounding countryside is beautiful. Nearby Hagley Hall (OACT), the family home of the Lytteltons, contains fine rococo work. Samuel Johnson attended the Edward VI School for six months.

STOURHEAD
Wiltshire *3 ST73*
Stourhead (NT) is a beautiful 18th-century Palladian mansion situated in what must surely be one of the most imaginatively embellished parks in the country. Near the gates stands a 13th-century stone cross that was removed from Bristol, where it used to mark an intersection of two roads. In its niches are small statues of eight kings of England. The circumference of the lake is about a mile. Walking round it, the visitor comes across a grotto and three little temples – one of them copied from the Pantheon in Rome. But, wherever one walks, there are pleasant new vistas.

Stourhead Gardens

STOURPORT-ON-SEVERN
Hereford & Worcester *9 SO87*
Stourport has several industries – the manufacture of carpets and chains, for example – but its real interest is as an inland port. It was the creation of James Brindley, a Derbyshire farmer's son, who, in 1756, determined to build a waterway linking the Rivers Trent and Severn. The original warehouses survive, complete with a little wooden clocktower, and so does the Tontine Inn, opened 1788. The basin, carefully and sympathetically restored, is now used for pleasure craft.

STOWE
Buckinghamshire *10 SP63*
Now a famous public school, Stowe used to be the seat of the Dukes of Buckingham and Chandos. Robert Adam, Vanbrugh, William Kent and Grinling Gibbons all had a hand in the building of the house and the far from foolish follies that decorate its grounds (by Capability Brown inevitably). Among them are the Temple of Worthies (the 'worthies' are busts of Sir Francis Drake, King Alfred, Inigo Jones and Shakespeare); two other temples and the remains of 19th-century Stowe Castle. The lakes are a delight – and so, too, is the unpretentious medieval church. The obelisk is in memory of General Wolfe.

STOWMARKET
Suffolk *12 TM05*
John Milton used to visit his tutor in this small market town. George Crabbe is another poet associated with

it: he spent some of his schooldays here. An unusual feature of its Perpendicular church is a wigstand. The Victorian mock-Elizabethan railway station is not without interest. For a graphic review of East Anglian rural life, there is the Museum of East Anglian Life. Stow Lodge Hospital (late 18th century) used to be a workhouse, or 'House of Industry' as they liked to call it.

• STOW-ON-THE-WOLD
Gloucestershire *10 SP12*
Situated 800ft above sea-level, Stow-on-the-Wold is the highest town in the Cotswolds. Since it stands at the junction of eight roads, it is not surprising to learn that it was once the most prosperous wool town in England. During the 18th century, in one year alone, no fewer than 20,000 sheep were sold at Stow Fair. The market place has a fine cross and some scarcely less fine gabled houses grouped around it. Within the church – begun in Norman times and developed spasmodically over the next few centuries – Cromwell imprisoned 1000 Royalist captives during the Civil War. The Town Hall contains a collection of paintings depicting the Civil War and a statue of that saintly monarch, King Edward the Confessor.

STRATA FLORIDA
Dyfed *8 SN96*
Strata Florida was a great Cistercian abbey built in the 12th century in an isolated valley 10 miles south east of

Aberystwyth. Remains of a church and cloister, and gatehouse survive.

STRATFIELD SAYE
Hampshire *4 SU66*
Stratfield Saye House (OACT) was built in 1630, rebuilt in 1795, and, in 1817, presented by a grateful Parliament to the Duke of Wellington as a reward for his victory at Waterloo. During his long retirement from the army, the Duke divided his time between Stratfield Saye, his house in Piccadilly, and Walmer Castle – which he occupied as Lord Warden of the Cinque Ports. The Duchess, a talented water colourist despite her short sight, made several attractive paintings of the estate. Among the relics of the Iron Duke are a collection of leatherbound volumes collected during his service in India, Napoleon's Tricolour, and a brass statuette of Copenhagen – the charger he rode at Waterloo – who is buried in the grounds.

STRATHPEFFER
Highland *16 NH45*
In the days before World War I Strathpeffer was a famous spa. Even foreign royalty, tiring, perhaps, of the pleasures of Spa itself or Homburg, came here to take the waters. There are five springs in all: four sulphur and one chalybeate, discovered in the 18th century; the first pump room was built in 1820. The Station Visitor Centre (OACT) has craft workshops and an audio visual display about the area.

STRATFORD-UPON-AVON

Warwickshire *10 SP15*

Shakespeare's Birthplace

'Good friend for Jesus sake forbeare
To digg the dust enclosed heare;
Bleste be ye man yt spares thes stones,
And cursed be he yt moves my bones.'

William Shakespeare, *Epitaph on his tomb*

As the birthplace of England's greatest poet, Stratford is second only to London as a tourist attraction, but the throngs of visitors and the inevitable 'Shakespeare industries' have not quite managed to submerge the character of this thriving Midlands market town. There is no doubt that Stratford owes its state of preservation to the interest in Shakespeare and everything connected with him. His birthplace; the house where his daughter, Susanna, lived after her marriage to Dr Hall; the poet's tomb in the church, with its famous inscription; the Royal Shakespeare Theatre; are all places of pilgrimage for the enthusiast. Harvard House, the 16th-century timbered house, was owned by the grandparents of John Harvard, founder of Harvard University. Just outside the town, at Shottery and at Wilmcote, for those who are not already sated with Shakespeariana, there are the old thatched and timbered cottages where Shakespeare's wife, Anne Hathaway, and his mother, Mary Arden, spent their childhood.

William Shakespeare was born on 23 April 1564 in the fine, timbered house on Henley Street that now, restored and furnished in period, has become a museum. His own house, New Place, was demolished in the 18th century, but a garden marks the site. Shakespeare's early life is not well documented, but he is known to have attended the grammar school, an ancient foundation whose history goes back at least 200 years before his birth, and was first founded by the Guild of the Holy Cross; their chapel, rebuilt in the 15th century by Sir Hugh Clopton, a wealthy merchant who became Lord Mayor of London, contains an impressive 'Doom' painting of the Last Judgement. Clopton was a famous benefactor of the town and built, among other things, the old 14-arched bridge that spans the River Avon. Modern buildings are not prominent in the centre of Stratford, where half-timbered and Georgian brick buildings are the keynote, but the Royal Shakespeare Theatre, erected in 1932 to replace its burnt-out Victorian predecessor, dominates the river bank.

Ann Hathaway's Cottage

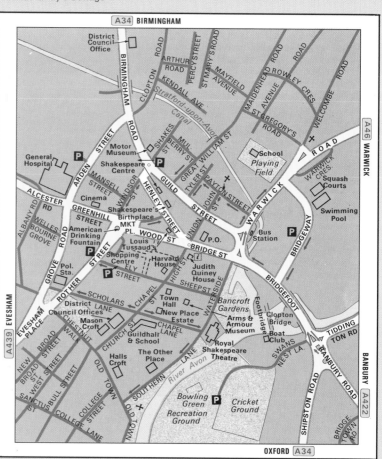

The drama festival takes place every summer and the outstanding new productions usually go on to London. This is one of the oldest of Britain's drama festivals – inaugurated some 200 years ago by the actor David Garrick.

American links and benefactions abound in Stratford. Harvard House is owned by Harvard University and is open to visitors. It bears the date 1596 and its contents include old pewter, Elizabethan furniture and American items. Americans helped to fund the Royal Shakespeare Theatre and presented a portrait of the actor Edwin Booth. The clock tower and fountain in Wood Street are more American gifts as is a window in Holy Trinity Church, where Shakespeare is buried. It includes portraits of Columbus, Amerigo Vespucci, Penn and Bishop Samuel Seabury, consecrated in Aberdeen in 1784 and the apostolic link between the Church of England and the Episcopal Church of America. One of the many distinguished American visitors in the 19th century was Washington Irving who stayed at the Red Horse Inn in Bridge Street.

Stratford has a life apart from its Shakespearian connections. It stands at the meeting point of many routes and has been a market centre for centuries. The building of the Stratford-upon-Avon canal in the early 19th century also increased trade with other Midlands centres and the town supports a number of light industries.

PLACES TO SEE
Stratford-upon-Avon
Shakespeariana is everywhere in this attractive little town: his birthplace; the ruins of New Place, where he lived after he was married; Hall's Croft, where his daughter lived, are all (OACT) preserved by the Birthplace Trust. Also of interest is Harvard House (OACT) and the 1920s Motor Museum.

Anne Hathaway's Cottage The childhood home of Shakespeare's wife is an idyllic half-timbered and thatched cottage in the hamlet of Shottery.

Abbots Morton A showplace village of black and white timbered cottages surrounding a green.

Ragley Hall (OACT) Magnificent 17th-century house with superb interior decoration and Old Master paintings.

Alcester A charming little town at the confluence of the rivers Alne and Arrow.

Pleck Gardens Three acres of roses, heathers and azaleas.

Coughton Court (NT) The family home of the Roman Catholic Throckmorton family has relics of the Gunpowder Plot.

Henley-in-Arden This lovely village has one long, broad main street.

Aston Cantlow Shakespeare's parents are believed to have married in the church of this attractive village.

Wilmcote The handsome timbered farmhouse (OACT) that was the home of Mary Arden, Shakespeare's mother, is the highlight of this peaceful village.

Hall's Croft A Tudor house, the former home of Shakespeare's daughter, Susanna, and her husband Dr John Hall. Relics of the medicine of their day make an interesting display.

Harvard House A fine timbered building, lived in by the grandparents of John Harvard, founder of Harvard University.

Louis Tussaud's Waxworks Tableaux from Shakespeare's plays are displayed here.

Model Car Museum More than 2400 miniature and scale-model cars are on display.

Motor Museum Sports cars, touring cars and other Vintage cars and motor-cycles are displayed in 1920s settings.

New Place Only foundations of Shakespeare's house remain, but there is a well-maintained knot garden and in adjacent Nash House there are many items of his day.

Shakespeare's Birthplace and Shakespeare Centre The old family home of Shakespeare's parents has been restored, furnished in period and opened as a museum. Adjacent to it is the new Shakespeare Centre, designed for study and as the headquarters of the Shakespeare Birthplace Trust.

STRATH SPEY
Grampian & Highland   *26, 27 NJ02*
Strath Spey is the wide, lower valley of the River Spey. It begins as the Upper Spey emerges from the very much narrower route it takes between the Cairngorms and the Monadhliath mountains (where it originates). An important salmon river, it is also rich in brown trout and, funnily enough, or so the story goes, pearls: according to one estimate, one out of every hundred mussels fished out of the river contains a pearl. The beautiful broad valley is the heart of Scotland's whisky country. Until the beginning of the 18th century all regions of Scotland were scattered with small whisky stills. The fine whiskies derive their exquisite taste from the peaty Highland waters. Several distilleries can be visited, including the Glenfarclas Distillery at Marypark, and the Glenfiddich Distillery at Dufftown.

STRATHYRE
Central   *22 NN51*
Strathyre is a pleasant little resort in the heart of country made famous by Sir Walter Scott in *Lady of the Lake* and *Legend of Montrose*. It is not too remote; the climbing is not too difficult; and the River Balvaig is full of brown trout. The Ben of the Fairies rises to the west.

STRATTON
Cornwall   *1 SS20*
Stratton, only a mile or two from the resort of Bude, is an altogether charming small Cornish town built on the side of a hill. Its streets are steep; some of the houses are thatched; and the church has a window by Burne-Jones and a brass commemorating Henry VIII's Vice-Admiral, Sir John Arundell. The Tree Inn, once the manor house home of the famous Grenville family, of which Sir Richard Grenville, who voyaged to the Carolinas, was a member, served as Royalist headquarters during the Civil War, on the eve of the Battle of Stamford Hill (1643); the site is about half a mile north west of the town.

STREET
Somerset   *3 ST43*
In 1820, James Clark, an apprentice in his family's sheepskin rug firm, started to use cast-off sheepskin to line slippers. This was the start of Clark's shoe company – now the largest such company in Britain. The factory can be visited and its history traced in the Shoe Museum (OACT). Street is also

the home of Millfield, the innovative public school. Outside the town on Windmill Hill is a monument to Admiral Lord Hood. 4 miles south east is the tiny village of Barton St David, from where the first member of the famous Quincy family of America emigrated.

Clarks factory, Street

STROUD
Gloucestershire   *3 SO80*
Cloth is the chief business of Stroud and especially for covering billiard tables. There is also an old-established dyeing industry, and more recently the town has turned to the manufacture of pianos. Stroud stands on the River Frome and the Stroudwater canal, closed in 1954, is now being restored. Some of the 18th-century woollen mills have survived, and there are some good examples of typical Cotswold cottages. The Stroud District Museum (OACT) has an interesting emphasis on local crafts.

STURMINSTER NEWTON
Dorset   *3 ST71*
Sturminster Newton is a singularly pretty Dorset village, locally famous for its Monday livestock market. The six-arched bridge spanning the River Stour is one of the finest medieval examples of bridgecraft in Dorset. A plaque threatens deportation as the penalty for 'injury' – which could

mean driving an overloaded cart across!

SUDBURY
Suffolk   *12 TL84*
Readers of *Pickwick Papers* will perhaps recognize this ancient borough as 'Eatanswill'. Art lovers will recall that this was the birthplace of Thomas Gainsborough (1727–88), the 18th-century artist and founder of the Royal Academy in London. His statue stands in the market place and his father's Regency-fronted Tudor house is now a museum. St Peter's Church contains the 'Sudbury Pall', a fine piece of embroidered velvet, while St Gregory's preserves the head of the Archbishop of Canterbury murdered in the Peasants' Revolt of 1381. East Anglia sent many early settlers to Massachusetts, whose first counties were Norfolk, Suffolk and Essex. Sudbury is surrounded by places of Anglo-American interest: to the south west lies the **Castle Hedingham** area; to the east is Groton. The manor at Groton was the ancestral home of the Winthrop family. The village name is also that of a famous American school. John Winthrop, who was born 1 mile away at Edwardstone, was a lawyer, educated at Trinity College, Cambridge and the Inner Temple – gradually converted to Puritanism, he signed the Cambridge Agreement in 1629; the signatories pledged to emigrate to Massachusetts. In 1630 Winthrop led the party which founded Boston, Massachusetts, sailing from England in the *Arbella*. Winthrop became the first Governor of Massachusetts and held office twelve times; he was also the first President of the Commissioners of New England. John Winthrop the younger, also born here, was a founder and Governor of Connecticut. Grandson Fitzjohn Winthrop, educated at Harvard, was also Governor of Connecticut; later he came to Britain, joining Cromwell's army in Scotland and becoming Agent for Connecticut in London. Groton parish church contains a memorial brass and window; two of Winthrop's four wives are buried here. A few miles north at Lindsey, the St James Chapel of the parish church belonged to John Winthrop. Nearby, Little Waldingfield church contains memorials to the Appleton family; the oldest house in Waldingfield, New England is said to be owned by this family. The parish church at nearby Belchamp St Paul contains a memorial window to the Golding family of America.

SULGRAVE MANOR
Northamptonshire   *10 SP54*
It was Washington Irving who first brought the attention of the Victorian public to the small 13th-century farmhouse in the Northamptonshire countryside. The Domesday Book of 1086 first mentions Souldgrave, which belonged to the Priory of St Andrew, Northampton until 1539, when they were obliged to surrender the house to the Crown during the Dissolution. It was then that Lawrence Washington, a wealthy merchant, was able to buy Sulgrave. The family lived here until financial difficulties forced them to sell in 1610. In 1914 the house was bought and restored by British subscribers to celebrate the centenary of peace between America and Britain, following the Treaty of Ghent. Maintenance of Sulgrave was undertaken by the Society of Colonial Dames of America, and is now preserved as a museum of George Washington's family, containing fascinating mementoes, including a fragment of Mrs Washington's wedding dress and many of the President's personal items. The arched doorway bears the family crest – a modified 'stars and stripes' – and the village church has the family pew and memorials to Lawrence Washington, his wife and eleven children.

Nearby, Greatworth was the home of the Pargiter family, whom several members of the Washington family married. Marston St Lawrence was the home of Reverend Charles Chauncy, a President of Harvard. North west of Sulgrave, the area around **Althorp** also has Washington connections.

SUNDERLAND
Tyne & Wear   *20 NZ45*
Sunderland is a coal port on the River Wear, and is also renowned for its shipbuilding. Its name is derived from the fact that it was 'sundered' from a monastery founded on the far bank of the river in 674. The 18th-century Wearmouth Bridge (it was replaced in 1929) was one of the first cast-iron bridges in the country. The designer was Thomas Paine, better known as the author of *The Rights of Man*; it was originally intended for Philadelphia on the far side of the Atlantic. The new Civic Centre (1970) is evidence of the town's progressive attitude to planning. Other places of interest include the Grindon Close Museum (OACT), which specializes in the Edwardian period; Monkwear-

mouth Station Museum, and the Sunderland Museum and Art Gallery.

Just west of Sunderland is Hylton, where the now ruined castle was the home of the Hylton family for centuries. The family were related to the branch of the Washingtons at nearby Washington, and a 14th-century carving on the west front bears what is believed to be the oldest Washington crest.

SUTTON COLDFIELD
W Midlands *10 SP19*
Basically, Sutton Coldfield is a residential town for its neighbour, **Birmingham**. In the early 16th century, Bishop Veysey created some fine buildings that still survive. The bishop lived in Moor Hall, which now adjoins the golf course: he founded the grammar school, designed several houses – all of them with spiral stone staircases – altered the church, and also paved the town's streets. Sutton Park, a gift from Henry VIII, covers 2400 acres. Well equipped with lakes, it is one of the largest and finest in the Midlands.

SWAFFHAM
Norfolk *12 TF80*
Swaffham's legend tells of Jack the pedlar who dreamed that if he went to London he would be told where to discover treasure. Off he went and met a stranger who said that he had had a dream of great wealth buried under a certain tree in Swaffham. Jack hurried home, discovered the hidden fortune, and used it to build the north aisle of the church of Sts Peter and Paul. His generosity is remembered in the village sign, by a monument in the market place, and by several carvings in the church. Swaffham is a most attractive market town, its wide main square graced by many mellow brick houses.

SWANAGE
Dorset *3 SZ07*
The quiet resort town of Swanage is the only place between Poole and Weymouth where the road reaches the coast. There are several old houses in the town and the oldest part is the area around the Mill Pond. The church, though rebuilt, has a 13th-century tower, and the façade of the Town Hall (erected in 1883) originally graced the Mercers' Hall in London – for which Wren designed it in 1670. Another import from London is the clock tower, which once stood near London Bridge.

SWANSEA
W Glamorgan *8 SS69*
Swansea docks were established as early as 1306. In the 17th century, they were developed for the shipping of Welsh coal, copper, and iron ore. In World War II the city was severely bombed; the damage has been replaced by an impressive new centre – spacious and with abundant greenery. Places of interest include the Glynn Vivian Art Gallery and Museum (OACT); the Maritime and Industrial Museum and the University College Museum (OACT). To the west, lie the tourist pleasures of the Mumbles and the Gower Peninsula.

SWINDON
Wiltshire *3 SU18*
The coming of the Great Western Railway did much for Swindon. In 1835, it became the site of a station on the route from London to Bristol. Four years later, Isambard Kingdom Brunel and Daniel Gooch – the visionary mechanical engineer – chose it as the location for the company's main locomotive depot. Nowadays, the GWR museum is housed in a converted Methodist chapel. The first major locomotive used by the Great Western Railway was the *North Star*, originally built for the New Orleans railway but never used in America.

SWINFORD
Leicestershire *10 SP57*
Stanford Hall (OACT), on the Leicestershire bank of the Avon, was built by Sir Roger Cave between 1697 and 1700. It is possibly the most handsome house of its period in the county. The contents include a fine collection of paintings, furniture and old family costumes. In a nearby meadow, a pillar marks the spot where P S Pilcher crashed and was killed while trying to fly in 1899. He had reached an altitude of 50ft. A replica of his machine is in the vehicle museum attached to the house.

SYON HOUSE
Gtr London *5 TQ17*
A majestic house near the River Thames at Isleworth, whose splendid interior was designed by Robert Adam for the Duke of Northumberland in the 18th century. In the park laid out by Capability Brown are rose gardens, a car museum, a butterfly house, and a large garden centre.

TADCASTER
N Yorkshire *15 SE44*
A beer-making town since the 18th century, Tadcaster is still the home of John and Samuel Smith's rival breweries. St Mary's Church, with its Perpendicular work and embattled tower, dates from the 15th century. It was moved stone by stone between 1875 and 1877 to a position 5ft higher than its original site to afford greater protection from the flood-prone River Wharfe. The river itself is spanned by an 18th-century, seven-arched bridge and, more forlornly, by the 'virgin Viaduct' – built in 1849 in anticipation of the railway that never did come.

Beningbrough Hall (NT) (OACT) 10 miles to the north is an attractive 18th-century red brick house set in a wooded park. It contains some fine examples of wood carving and beautiful Delft and oriental porcelain. Also on show are more than 100 17th- and 18th-century pictures on loan from the National Portrait Gallery.

TAIN
Highland *30 NH78*
Tain, on the Dornoch Firth, was an ancient royal burgh; a trading centre for the prosperous agricultural district and a holiday resort for golfers, fishermen and bathers, affording fine views across Dornoch Firth. The birthplace of St Duthac in AD 1000, Tain became a place of pilgrimage and sanctuary when his remains were brought home from Ireland. An Earl of Ross wore St Duthac's shirt, believed to confer immunity, at the Battle of Halidon Hill in 1333, but was fatally wounded. In 1371 the Earl and Bishop of Ross built the Collegiate Church of St Duthac. It is in Decorated style, with fine windows. James IV made regular pilgrimages to Tain along the King's Causeway – the road across Glen Aldie to Logie Easter. James V, too, came this way. Near Tain you can visit Loch Eye and the ruins of Lochslin Castle.

TALGARTH
Powys *8 SO13*
This small market town in the valley of the Afon Llynfi lies inside the **Brecon Beacons National Park**, with the Black Mountains to the east. Talgarth has a fortified tower, dating from the 11th to 13th centuries, now a shop. The church, too, has a striking 14th-century tower. 1½ miles south west, at Trefecca House, Howell Harris founded 'The Connection', a religious and trading community, commemorated in the college museum there. Llangorse Lake, 5 miles to the south, is 4 miles around, and the second biggest natural lake in Wales. It attracts water sportsmen, and also birdlife such as crested grebes and coots, and many species of duck. One island in the lake has the only evidence in Wales of prehistoric lake dwellings.

TAL-Y-CAFN
Gwynedd *13 SH77*
Here, among the woods of the Vale of Conwy, on the boundary of the **Snowdonia National Park**, is one of Britain's most beautiful gardens. Bodnant Garden (NT) slopes down over 80 acres of the Conwy valley, with the Snowdonian peaks in the background. It was planned in 1875 by Henry Pochin, a Lancashire industrialist, extended by his daughter, Lady Aberconwy, then by his grandson.

TAL-Y-LLYN
Gwynedd *13 SH71*
One of the oldest narrow-gauge railways in the world, the Tal-y-llyn runs 8 miles up the Fathew Valley from **Tywyn** to Nant Gwernol beyond Abergynolwyn. Built in 1865 to serve Bryneglwys slate quarry the line was closed in 1947 but rescued from oblivion by the first British railway preservation society in 1951. The wayside halt at Dolgoch gives access to the spectacular 125ft waterfalls nearby. 3 miles north east of Abergynolwyn is the hamlet of Tal-y-llyn situated on the shores of the magnificent Tal-y-llyn Lake which lies beneath the slopes of Cader Idris.

TARBOLTON
Strathclyde *22 NS42*
A rural village, it has strong connections with Robert Burns. The poet's family lived at Lochlea Farm 2½ miles to the north east and his father died here. Burns was a cofounder of The Bachelors' Club in the 17th-century house (NTS), now a Burns museum.

Pin Mill, Bodnant Garden, Tal-y-Cafn

TATTERSHALL
Lincolnshire *16 TA25*
Tattershall Castle (AM, NT) and its Perpendicular church were built in the mid 15th century by Ralph Cromwell, Lord Treasurer to Henry VI. He is buried in the Holy Trinity church. The splendid, moated, brick keep is all that survives of the castellated house. In 1912, Tattershall was restored by Lord Curzon, Marquess of Kedleston and Viceroy of India. He was assisted by his first wife, Mary Leiter of Chicago. The castle has fine views across the Fenlands as far as Lincoln Cathedral and the Boston Stump. Tattershall was the home of Lady Arbella Clinton, after whom John Winthrop's flagship was named. Lady Arbella married the Reverend Isaac Johnson and accompanied the Pilgrims on the journey to Massachusetts in 1630. She died soon afterwards, and Cotton Mather said of her, 'She left an earthly paradise for a wilderness, and then the wilderness for paradise, taking New England on her way to heaven.' Captain John Smith of nearby Willoughby worked here for a time as a member of the Earl of Lincoln's household. Disraeli's *Coningsby* takes its name from the village next to Tattershall. At Coningsby RAF station the Battle of Britain Memorial Flight is housed. Revesby, 6 miles east-north-east, was the home of Sir Joseph Banks (1743–1820), who explored Labrador and Newfoundland, and was a scientist on Captain James Cook's Pacific travels.

TATTON PARK
Cheshire *14 SJ78*
This exceptional mansion (NT) was rebuilt by Samuel and Lewis Wyatt for the Egerton family in the late 18th century. It is beautifully proportioned, maintained and furnished. Tatton Park's picture collection includes two Canalettos and twelve Frederick Remington lithographs of the American West. The old kitchens and servants' quarters have been restored and are exceptionally interesting. Its extensive park includes two large meres, one part of Humphry Repton's original plan for the grounds, one caused by subsidence from the mining activities of a neighbour of the Egertons. The gardens at Tatton are magnificent, and particularly appealing is the Japanese Garden, complete with a teahouse and Shinto Temple. There are also extensive glasshouses and a unique fernery.

TAUNTON
Somerset *3 ST22*
The hub of Somerset, lying between the rolling, wooded **Quantocks** and the Blackdown Hills, Taunton lies on the River Tone in the Vale of Taunton Deane, and was a major centre of the wool trade for 500 years. Today it is a lively commercial and agricultural centre whose livestock market rivals Exeter's as the most important in the West Country. Apple orchards thrive in the mild climate and fertile soil of the Vale, and cider-making is an important local industry. It is the headquarters of Somerset's cricket team, one of the country's most successful sides. It also has three public schools. Notable buildings include the castle (AM) which dates from Norman times and now houses the Somerset County and Military Museums.

Hestercombe Gardens (OACT) 3 miles north, were laid out by Sir Edwin Lutyens and Gertrude Jekyll.

At least three times in its history Taunton has supported the dissenter; in 1497 it proclaimed Perkin Warbeck king, and in the Civil War Taunton backed Parliament and many of its population were killed or wounded in the Battle of Sedgemoor fighting for the Duke of Monmouth in 1685.

Hatch Court, Hatch Beauchamp, Dorset (OACT) is a mansion 5 miles south east of Taunton. Andrew Hamilton Gault moved here in the 1920s. He had raised Princess Patricia's Canadian Light Infantry in World War I. The Patricia's fought with distinction in the two World Wars. The regimental mascot was Winnipeg the bear that A A Milne immortalized as Winnie the Pooh.

TAVISTOCK
Devon *2 SX47*
A market town traditionally regarded

as the western capital of Dartmoor. Tavistock grew up around a Benedictine abbey, founded in the 10th century and largely destroyed in the Dissolution. Some ruins can still be seen near the parish church. From the 16th century the town belonged to the Dukes of Bedford. During the 19th century its importance grew as a result of the expanding copper industry. The nearby Great Consols mine was one of the largest copper mines in the world.

TEFFONT
Wiltshire *3 ST93*
In the pretty, wooded Nadder Valley, the twin villages of Teffont Evias and Teffont Magna stand by the River Teff, which is crossed by many small stone bridges. Teffont Evias' turreted manor, Tudor and early 17th-century, and St Michael's Church (rebuilt in the early 19th century), with its graceful spire, together make a lovely sight. The cream Chilmark stone from the local quarry, now closed, was used for Salisbury Cathedral. Teffont Magna is a little more modest, with thatched cottages and a medieval church.

TEIGNMOUTH
Devon *2 SX97*
Writers have long been attracted here: Jane Austen, Keats and Fanny Burney all stayed at this elegant Regency and Victorian town situated where the Teign estuary narrows down before entering the sea. Its situation and temperate climate made it a popular holiday resort as early as the 18th century, and it remains so today. Its sandy beach, handsome esplanade, beautifully kept public gardens and golf course 800ft above sea-level are complemented by the cheerful pier. A 1700ft-long bridge across the Teign estuary links the town with the village of Shaldon, a charming holiday and

Teignmouth

yachting centre lying below the wooded headland of The Ness, through which a romantically named 'smugglers' tunnel leads to the beach.

TELFORD
Shropshire *9 SJ60*
From the wooded slopes of the Wrekin (1334ft) you can see one of Britain's newest New Towns, named after the famous 18th-century engineer and former county surveyor of Shropshire, Thomas Telford. The planners hope to weld a number of established industrialized towns and villages into a 'Forest City'. Over a million trees and shrubs are to be planted and a new city centre is planned at Randley Lake. **Ironbridge** and Coalbrookdale form part of the conurbation and are designated areas of special architectural and historical interest.

TENBY
Dyfed *7 SN10*
Tenby is finely situated on a rocky headland between two big, sandy bays. Tenby Castle on the headland overlooks the old harbour. Its 13th-century ruins, including a gatehouse and double tower, inherited the site of an ancient Welsh fort cited in a 9th-century poem: *Dinbych-y-Pysgod*, 'Little fort of the Fish'. The town clusters closely inside its medieval walls. The tower of St Mary's Church, for example, is 13th century, itself the rebuilding of an even older church, but the main structure is 15th century.

Tenby was a flourishing port from the 14th to 16th centuries. From these high days dates the gabled Tudor Merchant's House (NT), with a Flemish chimney, and fine extant frescoes. Tenby Museum, on Castle Hill, specializes in finds from Hoyle's Mouth; the cave where archaeologists have found palaeolithic flints, a human jaw and teeth, and bones of extinct animals such as the cavebear and reindeer. St Catherine's Rock, just offshore, has a Victorian fort. Giraldus Cambrensis was born 4½ miles south west at Manorbier, and was rector of the parish during the 12th century. He was the author of *Itinerary through Wales*, a historical and geographical survey of early medieval Wales. On **Caldy Island**, 2½ miles away, men have lived for thousands of years, monks for hundreds. St Margaret's Island, a bird sanctuary, can only be visited with a permit. To the north of Tenby following the Pembrokeshire Coast to Wiseman's Bridge or the coast road, near Amroth, was where Churchill,

Montgomery and Eisenhower came to watch practices for the D-Day landings.

TENTERDEN
Kent *6 TQ83*
A snug market town on the edge of the Weald, which enjoyed Cinque Port privileges, although not on the coast, through its little port at **Smallhythe** on the River Rother 2 miles south. Originally founded in the 7th century by monks from Minster Abbey in Thanet, it grew into a significant local wool-trading centre. The attractive main street contains a blend of Elizabethan, Georgian and white weatherboarded houses with bow windows and porticoed doorways, offset by wide grass verges and trees. St Mildred's Church has a particularly fine carved and panelled nave roof. William Caxton, of printing fame, was reputedly born here. Inside the Unitarian Meeting House is a painting of Benjamin Franklin attending a service here in 1774, when he and Joseph Priestley were staying in the town. The Town Station (OACT) is the principal station of the Kent and East Sussex, Britain's first Light Railway. Steam locomotives are being restored and trains now run regularly over 5 miles of line, and will eventually reach Bodiam.

TETBURY
Gloucestershire *3 ST89*
A hilltop town lying near the Wiltshire border, it has a pillared Elizabethan market hall and quietly dignified grey, stone-built houses, many of 18th-century origin. The aisled parish church, with its 19th-century tower and spire, has very fine box pews. 3 miles south west is Westonbirt, a 19th-century Italianate house set in a beautiful park. The Arboretum (open daily), one of the finest in the world, was started in 1829 and is now managed by the Forestry Commission. Chavenage (OACT), 2 miles north west, is an Elizabethan house containing furniture and tapestries.

TEWKESBURY
Gloucestershire *9 SO83*
The fine abbey church of St Mary in this attractive town on the River Avon owes its survival to the public-spiritedness of the Tewkesbury townspeople. To avoid its probable destruction in the Dissolution of the Monasteries they somehow found the money to buy it from Henry VIII and so it remains intact today. Its massive Norman tower dominates both town

and the surrounding countryside and is the largest surviving one of its type in Britain, as is the six-fold Norman arch in the west front. From the top of the tower are views of the Malvern Hills and the Welsh Mountains. Inside the abbey is more Norman work and a particularly handsome vaulted ceiling in Decorated style. The chantry chapel was endowed by the Beauchamps family of Warwick the Kingmaker. Also in the abbey are many impressive tombs and monuments, including one to Mrs Woodhull Martin (1838–1927), the only woman candidate to run for the American Presidency. Later she devoted her life to the promotion of Anglo-American friendship.

The buildings in the town itself do not fail by comparison with the abbey. There is a wealth of timberwork here, much of it medieval. Many of the attractive houses bear unusual names – 'The House of the Nodding Gables', 'The House of the Golden Key' and 'The Ancient Grudge'. The Black Bear claims to date from 1308 and the Royal Hop Pole is yet another hostelry to feature in the works of Dickens – in *The Pickwick Papers*. One of the hotels in the High Street was formerly the Old Academy founded in 1712 by the Reverend Samuel Jones of Pennsylvania. During the last war the US Army Ordnance Corps had a base in Tewkesbury. 5 miles north east near **Bredon** is Bredon's Norton, where Thomas Copley, a founder of Maryland, lived.

The Bell Hotel, Tewkesbury

THANET, ISLE OF
Kent   *6 TR36*
This flat coastal segment of north-east Kent, edged with chalk cliffs, is now an island in name only. Traditionally where the Saxons first landed, Thanet was then divided from the mainland by the Rivers Stour and Wantsum, which gave safe anchorage and access to the Thames Estuary. Thanet has three popular resorts – **Broadstairs, Margate** and Ramsgate. Minster-in-Thanet, once its leading town and trading centre, now secluded among its fruit farms, has one of Kent's best parish churches: St Mary's preserves Roman bricks, Norman work, and exemplary 15th-century choir stalls.

THAXTED
Essex   *11 TL63*
Thaxted's plastered, half-timbered, overhanging buildings represent the old Essex. The fine, early 15th-century Guildhall derives from the village's former prosperity as a centre of the cutlery and wool trades. So too does the austere magnificence of St John's Church, its endowment shared by the great Essex family of Clare. One chapel commemorates the priest John Ball, a leader of the Peasants' Revolt. The tower, with its high spire, was rebuilt in the early 19th century by Peter Platt: 'Where Peter lies, 'tis fit this tower should show, but for his skill, itself had lain as low'. Thaxted's restored windmill (1804) (OACT) houses a small museum.

THETFORD
Norfolk   *12 TL88*
Thetford stands in the centre of the ancient region of Breckland, on the edge of Thetford Chase Forest. The town was part of the Danelaw, and is alleged to have been the seat of the kings of East Anglia in 575. In the Domesday Book, Thetford was recorded as one of the fifth greatest towns in England. Its continuous history is preserved in the impressive collection of buildings from every period of British history to be found in Thetford. Its three-way bridge is an ancient crossing point of the Icknield Way, the oldest trade route in England. The most important sites are the remains of the Thetford Priory, and the motte and bailey castle. Many fine buildings of the Elizabethan and Regency eras remain.

Thetford was the home town of the political journalist and pamphleteer, Thomas Paine. A plaque commemorating his birth in 1737 was placed on Grey Gables by American servicemen stationed nearby after World War II. There is also a gilded bronze statue in honour of the writer. The local grammar school where Paine was educated is one of the oldest in the country. Paine's career as a political campaigner began when he emigrated to America on the recommendation of Benjamin Franklin. He first worked as editor of the *Pennsylvania Magazine*. During the Revolutionary War he published 16 'Crisis' papers which continued the theme of his most famous pamphlet *Common Sense* (1776), arguing for American independence from England. *The Rights of Man* (1791) was written when he returned to Europe. In England Paine was indicted for treason. He escaped to France and served on the revolutionary National Convention. Following imprisonment in France, he returned to America in 1802 in relative obscurity.

At Elveden, 3½ miles south west of Thetford, is a memorial window to the US Army Air Force, who operated from the area during the war.

THIRSK
N Yorkshire   *15 SE48*
The 'Darrowby' of James Herriot's evocative books, this thriving old market town nestles at the foot of the Hambleton Hills in the Vale of Mowbray. The Golden Fleece, a large, handsome, Georgian inn, bears witness to the town's former importance as a stagecoach posting station in the 18th and 19th centuries.

Disconsolate punters from the popular local racecourse can also drown their sorrows in the 18th-century Three Tuns or the Crown, reputedly dating from 1682. Thomas Lord, founder of Lords Cricket Ground, was born here in 1755.

THORESBY
Nottinghamshire   *15 SK67*
Thoresby Hall (OACT), built 1864–75 in the heart of **Sherwood Forest**, is one of the great ducal mansions that gave the name 'Dukeries' to this part of the countryside. Descendants of its original owners, the Earls of Manvers, still live there. It was the Duke of Kingston who built the first house on the site, in the late 17th century. His daughter, Lady Mary Wortley Montague, the famous letter writer, lived here. The Duke established Thoresby Park, with its splendid chestnut avenues and lovely lake, made by damming the River Meden.

At one end of the lake there is a model village dating from 1807 and a castellated folly named Budby Castle. 4 miles south west is Market Warsop, birthplace of the wife of the Pilgrim Reverend Clyfton of Babworth.

THORNEY
Cambridgeshire *11 TF20*
Thorney was once an island village where Hereward the Wake made his stand against William the Conqueror. Then the Fens were drained, much being done by the Dukes of Bedford. It was the Duke of Bedford who in the 17th century gave asylum to the French Protestants whose names you can read in the churchyard. The ochre coloured, mid 19th-century model village was built by the contemporary Duke. The 12th-century ruins of Thorney Abbey are part of the Abbey Church, restored by Inigo Jones. They stand on the site of a 7th-century Saxon monastery, plundered by the Danes, rebuilt by the Normans.

THORNTON DALE
N Yorkshire *16 SE88*
Thornton Beck threads through this pretty village on the edge of the North York Moors, and footbridges give access to many of the stone-built cottages and their well kept gardens. All Saints Church, rebuilt in the 14th century, has been heavily restored but the 17th-century almshouses and grammar school remain unspoiled, as does a thatched cruck-built Tudor cottage. To the north lies Newtondale, a remote and beautiful valley up which the preserved North York Moors Railway snakes, en route from **Pickering** to Grosmont.

THURSFORD GREEN
Norfolk *12 TF93*
Here you can see the result of one man's lifetime enthusiasm in the Thursford Collection of steam locomotives, traction and fairground engines, and Wurlitzer and barrel organs (OACT). The musical instruments, from all over Europe, are almost all in working order, and are played at intervals. Musical evenings, with concerts on the Wurlitzer organ, are also held.

THURSO
Highland *30 ND16*
Thurso is splendidly situated: on a broad, sandy bay in the Pentland Firth, between the towering cliffs of Holborn Head and Clardon Head. Its hinterland is the fertile Caithness plain. Scotland's northernmost mainland town affords views towards Dunnet Head, and across the Pentland Forth to the cliffs of Hoy in the Orkneys. Old St Peter's Kirk, by the once important harbour, occupies the site of a Viking church. Gilbert Murray, Bishop of Caithness, established his church here in the 13th century: the present ruins are 16th to 17th century. The medieval Bishop's Palace stands on Thurso Bay. The old fishermen's houses by the harbour have been carefully restored. From nearby Scrabster, the Orkney ferries sail; and, in both World Wars, convoys sailed for Scapa Flow. Dounreay nuclear power station 10 miles west (**see** Reay) has meant much expansion around Thurso.

The 14th-century Old Post Office, Tintagel

TICHBORNE
Hampshire *4 SU53*
This is a pretty village in the Itchen Valley, made up of 16th- and 17th-century houses, many thatched, a part-Saxon, part-Norman church on a hillock, and Tichborne Park, the Tichborne family mansion since Anglo Saxon times, rebuilt early in the 19th century. Tichborne has two claims to celebrity. First is the Tichborne Dole, an annual ceremony originated in the 12th century by Lady Mabella de Tichborne. The story is that her husband Roger decided to grant the poor the produce of as much land as the dying Mabella could walk around – she managed to crawl round 20 acres before expiring. Second is the celebrated Tichborne Claimant case: in 1871 an Australian butcher represented himself as Sir Roger Tichborne, the long-lost heir. Many people believed him, but after a long drawn out trial, his claim was disproved and he ended in gaol.

TIDESWELL
Derbyshire *15 SK17*
This small, stone-built town is finely set among the limestone hills of the **Peak District**. Miller's Dale and Chee Dale (both NT) lie within easy distance. 14th-century St John's Church is impressive enough to be known as the 'Cathedral of the Peak'. Tideswell holds an annual 'well-dressing' ceremony.

TILBURY
Essex *6 TQ67*
This ancient port in the suburbanized and industrialized Thames Estuary marshlands is the first outpost of the Port of London. Its great passenger days are over, it is now a container port. There is a ferry service to Gravesend. Purfleet is 5 miles west of Tilbury. The area's nautical past is illustrated in the Thurrock Riverside Museum at Tilbury. Tilbury Fort (AM) was one of Henry VIII's creations and the point where Queen Elizabeth I reviewed the army raised to resist invasion by the Spanish Armada.

TINTAGEL
Cornwall *1 SX08*
Legend has it that King Arthur was born here, although the castle (AM) on Tintagel Head which bears his name is Norman in origin. It was originally built in 1145 for the then Earl of Cornwall. The surviving ruins date mainly from the 13th century. Augmenting the Arthurian legend are

'Merlin's Cave' below the castle, and King Arthur's Hall, built in 1933 as the headquarters of the Fellowship of the Round Table. It has no less than 73 stained glass windows showing Arthur's Knights. The nearby coastline (much of it National Trust) is rocky, wild and romantic with stark cliffs and slate caves, particularly some 15 miles south west down the coast at Bedruthan Steps. These huge, gnarled slaty rocks, rising up 200ft from an isolated beach, are, by legend, the stepping stones of the giant Bedruthan.

TINTERN ABBEY
Gwent *9 SO50*

A beautiful ruin (AM) in an equally beautiful setting, Tintern Abbey lies in a bend on the Wye in a meadow overlooked by the wooded hills which form the boundary between England and Wales. A victim of the Dissolution, the abbey is one of the finest reminders of monasticism. It was founded in 1131, although most of the ruins date from the 13th and 14th centuries. The abbey church itself survives almost intact.

TISBURY
Wiltshire *3 ST92*

Tisbury, an ancient settlement traversed by an Anglo Saxon track, is more a town than a village. It is poised on a steep slope by the River Nadder, in the rich valley farmlands of Wiltshire. The church has a lovely panelled and carved roof, and memorials to Lady Blanche Arundel, who defended nearby Wardour Castle in the Civil War, and to Catherine Howard's sister. Rudyard Kipling and his parents are buried in the churchyard. The yew tree, 36ft in circumference, is believed to be 1000 years old. There are two Wardour Castles: the Old, a 14th-century ruin (AM), with 16th-century additions; and the New, an 18th-century house (OACT) designed by James Paine, restored for Cranborne Chase School in 1960. Pythouse (OACT), is a fine Palladian mansion.

TISSINGTON
Derbyshire *15 SK15*

A handsome village in the Peak District National Park, east of Dovedale, Tissington is distinguished by its limestone buildings, a good example being the 18th-century vicarage; triangular green; broad, grassy verges, and fine trees. In an 1830s' improvement programme, the

Well dressing, Tissington

Fitzherberts of Tissington Hall contributed many new buildings and restored the church, originally Norman and Early English in style, retaining a curiously carved Norman font. Tissington 'dresses' its five wells with an elaborate floral tapestry in an ancient annual ceremony which has survived in a number of Derbyshire Peak District villages.

TITCHFIELD
Hampshire *4 SU50*

Titchfield is 2 miles from the mouth of the River Meon, at Titchfield Haven on the Solent. This small town used to be a seaport until Dutch engineers drained the marshes in the 18th century. Titchfield has a bridge across the river built in 1625; and many 17th- and 18th-century buildings, such as the Queen's Head. Titchfield Abbey (AM), or Place House, is the splendid ruined survivor of a great 13th-century building. After the Dissolution it was converted into a house by the Earl of Southampton, Shakespeare's patron. He is buried in the parish church. When James II withdrew the Virginia Company's charter Nicholas Ferrar placed copies of the documents at Titchfield House; they are now in the Library of Congress, Washington DC.

TIVERTON
Devon *2 SS91*

Textiles and wool brought prosperity to this thriving Exe valley market town, set in the rounded hills and wooded valleys of mid Devon. The textile industry here dates from the 13th century and is evidenced today by mills and factories around the fringes

of the town. Wool merchants' money paid for the 15th- and 16th-century enlargement and alteration of the imposing St Peter's Church, with its richly carved and decorated Greenway Chapel and south porch. Tiverton Castle (OACT), former house of the Courtenay family, Earls of Devon, dates from the 12th century. Built of local pink sandstone its ruins include two towers and a 14th-century gateway, now part of a private house. Tiverton Museum, one of the best folk museums in the West Country has a large railway gallery complete with restored GWR tank locomotive, and the restored Grand Western Canal offers trips by horse-drawn barges.

TOLLARD ROYAL
Wiltshire *3 ST91*

Tollard's right to call itself Royal was granted by King John, who stayed here to hunt in Cranborne Chase. Despite disafforestation, some attractive woodlands survive, that can be surveyed from 911ft Win Green Hill (NT). Gardiner Forest, 1800 acres, was endowed by Balfour Gardiner, the composer. King John's House, originally 13th-century, was restored by the archaeologist General Pitt-Rivers. He lived in Rushmoor House, now a school, and worked on several sites in its grounds. Pitt-Rivers was responsible for the restoration of Larmer Gardens, named after the larmer tree – wych-elm – under which King John would supposedly meet his huntsmen. Here too the Court Leets were held. The old tree blew down in 1894 and was replaced by an oak tree.

TOLLESBURY
Essex *6 TL91*

Among the creeks and marshes of the Blackwater Estuary, this sizeable fishing village is the pivot of the oyster trade. Around 1900 Tollesbury had over 100 sprat catching boats. Tollesbury's square is framed by plaster and brick houses. St Mary's Church, built of pebble, stone, brick and tiles, has a Norman tower and nave. The 18th-century font is inscribed: 'Good people all pray take care, that in ye church you do not sware. As this man did.' 'This man' atoned by paying for the font.

TOLPUDDLE
Dorset *3 SY79*

In 1834, six Tolpuddle farmworkers were sentenced to transportation for uniting to resist a wage reduction. They were transported to Tasmania,

Memorial to the Tolpuddle Martyrs

but after public outcry and massive demonstrations of sympathy they were reprieved and five of the martyrs returned. Meanwhile their fellow workmen had raised funds to help them start life anew. Five of the six families emigrated to Canada, settling near London, Ontario, where their descendants still live. 100 years later the TUC built a museum of six cottages named after 'The Martyrs'. Among the village's other memorials is the Martyr's Tree (NT), a sycamore under which it is thought they met.

TOMINTOUL
Grampian *27 NJ11*
Between the River Avon and the Conglass Water, 1160ft up in the Grampian foothills, Tomintoul is the highest village in the Highlands, a centre for tourists, anglers and skiers. It is near the Glenlivet whisky country, with four inns. Its limestone houses and slate cottages are centred round the village green and main street. The Avon rises amid the high tops of the Cairngorms to the south west, flowing into Loch Avon, through Glen Avon, past 3843ft Ben Avon, and so north east to Tomintoul. One of the river's many tributaries is the Water of Ailnack, which cuts through a series of spectacular, inaccessible gorges, beneath 2692ft Geal Charn. Alongside the Conglass Water to the south east runs the famous Lecht road, built by the army in 1745.

TONBRIDGE
Kent *6 TQ54*
This prosperous market town at the navigable extremity of the River Medway, where it diverges into fordable streams, has been strategically important since Anglo Saxon and perhaps Roman times. The River Walk along the Medway, through willow-lined meadows, affords a fine view of Tonbridge Castle (AM). Its Norman to 13th-century ruins, on a site defended since 1088, are substantial: the shell of the keep, curtain walls, round-towered gatehouse. Some of Tonbridge's 18th-century houses are built of castle stone. 4 miles north at Shipbourne Sir Harry Vane the younger, Governor of Massachusetts, is buried in the church. Vane was succeeded as Governor by Winthrop largely because of his support for Anne Hutchinson and her unorthodox Puritan views which led her to found the Antinomians. Vane returned to England, becoming MP for Hull. An intimate friend of Cromwell, he was eventually executed at Tower Hill for high treason. Fairlawne, near Shipbourne, was Vane's ancestral home.

TOPSHAM
Devon *2 SX98*
From 1282 this handsome town on the Exe estuary thrived as a port, largely by courtesy of a bad-tempered gesture by an early Countess of Devon who built a weir across the Exe to deny boats passage upriver to **Exeter**. The good times ended in 1567, when the city responded by opening the first English ship canal, bypassing the Exe and allowing big ships into the cathedral city's centre. Topsham, unable to offer the same deep-water facilities, began to decline as a port although continuing as a boat-building and trading centre. Now more a genteel residential suburb of Exeter than an identifiable town in its own right, reminders of its commercial past remain in its riverside warehouses, dignified 'Dutch' merchants' houses in the Strand, and some fine old pubs.

TORPHICHEN
Lothian *23 NS97*
Torphichen is a quiet village below the Bathgate Hills, with a good view from The Knock (1017ft). Cockleroy, a local hill originally called Cuckold le Roi, is cited in an R L Stevenson poem. Cairnpapple Hill (AM) is one of Scotland's principal prehistoric sites. Originally a Neolithic sanctuary, it was enlarged in the Bronze Age, when a circular temple was built. Torphichen Preceptory (AM) was the chief seat of the Knights of St John, a church that looked like a castle. Of the original Norman church, only the chancel arch survives. The transepts are 13th century, the tower 15th century. Over the ancient nave, the 16th-century parish church stands.

TORQUAY
Devon *2 SX96*
Famous for its panoramic setting on the wooded hills above Torbay, Torquay is a superior and expansive resort, with a Continental air. This has been Devon's most popular coastline since the Napoleonic Wars drew first the naval establishment and then tourists. The Devon Riviera is distinguished by its brilliant blue sea, kind climate, and colourful and luxuriant sub-tropical vegetation, notably its palm trees. Torquay's focal point is its yachting harbour, protected by huge breakwaters. Above it rise luxury hotels and high-rise flats, fine 19th-century terraces and crescents, such as Hesketh Crescent (1846), and in the suburbs numerous guesthouses.

Torre Abbey (AM) was originally built in the 12th century. Its surviving ruins are a gateway, the abbot's tower, and two crypts. It was the monks who built the first quay on the bay. The site is shared by the 18th-century Torre Abbey Mansion (OACT), which has an art gallery, and the 12th-century Spanish Barn, made a prison for captured sailors from the Armada.

Torquay has various kinds of attractions: Aqualand, the largest aquarium in the West Country; the Natural History Museum. Ilsham Marine Drive affords fine views, as do the weathered cliffs – along which you can walk to Anstey's Cove and Babbacombe. The model village here is a showpiece; and a cliff railway runs down to the beach. Kent's Cavern (AM), on the edge of the town, was inhabited during the Ice Age, putting it among the oldest known sites in Britain. The bones of sabre-toothed tigers and bears are preserved, amid red, green and white stalagmites and stalactites, formed by the limestone in the water that drips through the rocks. Henry James used to stay at the Osborne Hotel and other literary visitors were Charles Kingsley, his wife, Elizabeth Barrett and Tennyson.

TORRIDON
Highland *25 NG85*
This village, at the head of Upper Loch Torridon, at Glen Torridon's west end, is set amid splendid Highland scenery. The National Trust for Scotland has a Visitor Centre here to guide you, and a Deer Museum (both OACT). Loch Torridon is a magnificent sea loch, opposite the north-eastern tip of Skye. It extends into Loch Shieldaig to the south, and into Upper Loch Torridon through the narrow straits to the east. On the Ploc of Torridon, a promontory in the Upper Loch, are the prehistoric stones of the Church of Ploc. The wild and beautiful Glen Torridon, with its

Corrie of a Hundred Hills, cuts through the Torridon mountains where the peaks of Ben Eighe (3309ft), form a National Nature Reserve: Liathach, the highest peak in the Torridons, is one of Scotland's finest mountains: 3456ft high, its terraces extend for 3 miles, towering above the spectacular Coire na Caime. The mountains, of stratified red sandstone, some topped in white quartzite, attract geologists and climbers and afford views from Cape Wrath to Ardnamurchan and the **Outer Hebrides**.

TOTNES
Devon *2 SX86*
The old town of Totnes stands on a steep hill above the River Dart, at its highest navigational point. The British Council of Archaeology made it one of its 40 towns of outstanding architectural and historic interest. In the great days of the medieval cloth trade, when it was an important Devon port, Totnes was a walled town, and the lines are still detectable; the 15th-century East Gate has been restored and there are remains of the 12th-century castle (AM). St Mary's Church is a remarkable relic of the 15th century, with a 120ft tower and a famous stone screen. The Elizabethan and Georgian eras contributed some fine architecture to Totnes, particularly along its steep main street. The four-storey Elizabethan House is now a museum; with a section on computers, which were pioneered by Charles Babbage (1792–1871), a one-time pupil at the King Edward VI Grammar School. The Guildhall, gabled and colonnaded, standing on the site of the medieval Totnes Priory, contains a smaller museum. The Seven Stars Inn is 17th century, the Butterwalk prettily arcaded. Rich and sheltered farming country enfolds the town. From Totnes you can take a boat downriver to Dartmouth; or a train steam-hauled on the Dart Valley Railway to Buckfastleigh. Totnes still builds boats and imports timber, but is not a port on its medieval scale. On the Quay is now a motor museum of vintage sports and racing cars.

The Irish playwright Sean O'Casey lived here while his children attended nearby **Dartington** Hall School. 2 miles south west, Harberton church has a finely carved rood-screen.

TOWCESTER
Northamptonshire *10 SP64*
An unassuming place, but it is one of the oldest towns in Britain. Originally a settlement on the Roman Watling Street, it later became an important coaching stop, as its surviving inns testify. The Saracen's Head features in *The Pickwick Papers* and the Talbot dates from 1440. The Post Office – one of a number of fine Georgian Buildings – dates from 1797. St Laurence's Church, with its soaring, ironstone, Perpendicular tower, houses an interesting collection of chained books. The peace of the neighbouring broad, pleasant, landscape is sometimes shattered by motor racing at the famous Silverstone circuit, 4½ miles south west. The more appropriate rural pastime of National Hunt racing takes place at the attractive course in the grounds of Easton Neston House. The Reverend Thomas Shepard was rector in Towcester, his native town. However, because of his Nonconformist views he was forbidden to preach in the diocese of York and London. In 1635, Shepard emigrated to Massachusetts, where he became a pastor of the town that was to become Cambridge. He took an interest in proselytizing the Indians, and was a founder of Harvard College.

TRANENT
Lothian *24 NT47*
Prestongrange Historical Site and the Scottish Mining Museum at Prestonpans tells the 800-year history of this mining district inland of the Firth of Forth. The centrepiece of the exhibition is the only Cornish beam engine which remains in Scotland. Tranent has a 16th-century dovecote; a 19th-century church on ancient foundations; a place in Scott's *Waverley* – Colonel Gardiner died here after the Battle of Prestonpans in 1745 and, 2 miles south west, the 15th-to 16th-century ruin of Falside Castle.

TRAQUAIR
Borders *23 NT33*
A neat and ancient village in the sheepfarming Southern Uplands, Traquair stands on Quair Water, a tributary of the River Tweed. St Bryde's Church, on a knoll that has been an ecclesiastical site since before the 12th century, is an 18th-century building and has a galleried outside staircase. Traquair House (OACT), seat of the Stuarts of Traquair, tall, turreted, elegant and austere, is a famous, château-style mansion inhabited for 1000 years, probably longer than any house in Scotland. Originally 10th century, preserving its tower, the house was largely rebuilt in

Traquair House

1642, the wings added later. Among its special contents are 13th-century glass, tapestries, embroideries, and relics of Mary Queen of Scots. Since William the Lion held court here in 1209, 26 English and Scottish monarchs have visited the house. Montrose perhaps sheltered here after the Battle of Philiphaugh, travelling by the old drovers' road that climbs to 1856ft over Winchmuir between Selkirk and Peebles. Traquair House ale is still made in the 18th-century brewery.

TRECASTLE
Powys *8 SN82*
In the **Brecon Beacons National Park**, the village stands on the site of the Park's biggest motte and bailey castle. From Trecastle you can explore the Black Mountain, at 2630ft the second highest in South Wales (except for the Beacons themselves), its north face scarred with precipices, and the great Usk Reservoir, near the wooded shores of which rises a huge standing stone.

TREEN
Cornwall *1 SW32*
Treen Castle (NT) is a fortified headland, shared by the ancient fort of Treryn Dinas and the Logan Rock, a rocking stone overturned by Oliver Goldsmith's nephew in 1824. It was promptly replaced and he was made to pay for it. Boscawen-un, a famous prehistoric stone circle, and the ancient ruined settlement of Carn Euny, to the north, are also near Treen.

TREGARON
Dyfed *8 SN65*
Tregaron is a relatively big village for its situation in the remote heartland of Wales, by the River Teifi. It is a centre for the sheep farms in the surrounding hills and for visitors, especially pony-trekkers. The Bog of Tregaron, a raised bog, 4 miles long and still spreading, on either side of the River Teifi, is a National Nature Reserve: the habitat of rare plants such as sundew, bog rosemary, bladderwort and sedges, and a refuge for pole-cats.

TREMADOG
Gwynedd *13 SH54*
Tremadog and its larger neighbour
Porthmadog lie at the coastal end of
the Glaslyn valley. William Maddocks
the rich MP for Boston, Lincolnshire,
built Tremadog in the early 19th
century on reclaimed land behind the
Cob, an embankment he had built
across the mouth of the river. He
intended it to be a key point on the
route to Ireland but Parliament voted
for Holyhead instead. Maddocks
received help from the Shelleys, who
stayed in the town. Tremadog was
designed as a model town in a classical
style, with neat stone buildings, a
broad main street and a square headed
by the former Market Hall. The sheer
cliffs behind the Hall included the
Coed Tremadog National Nature
Reserve, rich in oak trees and in plants
profiting from the exclusion of sheep.
Lawrence of Arabia (T E Lawrence)
was born here in 1888.

TRENTHAM
Staffordshire *14 SJ84*
Trentham Hall, property of the Dukes
of Sutherland, was built in the 14th
century, enlarged into a palatial
mansion in the 19th century and has
since been almost demolished. It
appears in Arnold Bennett's *The Card*.
Trentham Gardens (OACT),
landscaped principally by Sir Joseph
Paxton, are Staffordshire's largest
pleasure ground. They have been open
to the public since the early 1900s, half
a century earlier than most. The
village of Trentham is an ancient
settlement, whose history goes back to
early Saxon times when Wulfhere, the
first Christian King of Mercia, built a
palace in the area in AD 660.

TREORCHY
Mid Glamorgan *8 SS99*
The town is famous for its Royal Male
Voice Choir, the oldest in Wales, given
its title by Queen Victoria after its
Command performance at Windsor in
1885. Treorchy contributed to the
history of Rhondda's diversification,
by the establishment of the clothing
factory in 1939.

TRE'R-DDOL
Dyfed *7 SN69*
Yr Hen Gapel (OACT), a branch of
the National Museum of Wales, run by
the Welsh Folk Museum, specializes in
religious life in 19th-century Wales.
From Tre'r-ddol you can explore (with
a permit for the first two areas) the
Dyfi National Nature Reserve; the

Dyfi Estuary, haunt of wildfowl and
migrant waders – but keep an eye on
tides and mud; Borth Bog, fascinating
to botanists; and the Ynyslas Dunes.

TRERICE
Cornwall *1 SW85*
The stone Elizabethan manor house
(NT) is exemplary, especially the
aspect of its south and east façades
with their unusual curly gables.
Elaborate plaster ceilings are a feature
of the interior and the immense
latticed window of the main hall has
576 panes. A curious museum of old
lawn mowers is housed in the
outbuildings.

TREWINT
Cornwall *1 SX28*
Wesley's Cottage is a small 18th-
century building visited by the
Methodist leader on his missions to
Cornwall between 1744 and 1762.
Wesley Day celebrations are held on 24
May.

TRING
Hertfordshire *10 SP91*
The Reverend Lawrence Washington
retired to this Chiltern town in 1643,
having been rector of Purleigh, Essex
for 11 years. The parish register has
records of the baptisms of three
Washington children, and Lawrence's
widow, Amphillis, was buried here in
1654. Washington himself died in the
same year. Subsequently his sons
emigrated to Virginia, where the
family had connections with the Sandy
family. One son, John, was the great-
great-grandfather of the first President.
Tring's main claim to fame is its
Zoological Museum, founded in the
last century by Lionel Rothschild,
which houses the world's largest

collection of fleas. 3 miles north east,
Pitstone Windmill (NT) is one of the
oldest post mills in Britain; it has now
been restored to working order.

TROSSACHS, THE
Central *22 NN50*
'The Highlands in miniature', as this
famous landscape area north of
Glasgow is known, has been popular
with tourists since the early 19th
century. The combination of
mountains, lochs, rivers and woods
rich in hazel, oak, birch and mountain
ash, proved irresistible to Sir Walter
Scott. His poems *Lady of the Lake* and
Rob Roy were both inspired by the
region and were an early cause of its
popularity. Ellen Douglas was the
'Lady' and Loch Katrine – along with
Lochs Achray and Venacher one of
three in the area – was 'her' Lake.
Steamers still ply Loch Katrine in the
summer and call at Stronachlacher
from where Rob Roy's birthplace at
Glengyle can be reached. Part of the
area now lies in the 45,000 acre Queen
Elizabeth Forest Park and all of it is
dominated by Ben Venue (2393ft),
above the south east shore of Loch
Katrine.

TROUTBECK
Cumbria *18 NY40*
This Lake District village, delightfully
situated in the wild and beautiful
Troutbeck Valley, extends along the
hillside from Town Head to Town
End. To the north is the high
Kirkstone Pass; to the west is Lake
Windermere, into which the beck
flows. Most of Troutbeck's older
houses were built by its 'statesmen' –
yeomen farmers making a subsistence
living from the hillsides. The east
window of the church, rebuilt in the

Trentham Gardens

18th century is the joint work of Burne-Jones, William Morris and Ford Madox Brown. Park Farm (NT) shows visitors how a 2000-acre sheep station is run. Townend Farm (NT), previously owned by the same family for 300 years, is a characteristic yeoman's house built in about 1626. It is whitewashed, with the tall, tapering chimneys that are a feature of Lake District architecture, stone-mullioned windows, carved woodwork, and much of its original oak furniture.

TROWBRIDGE
Wiltshire *3 ST85*
Trowbridge is the administrative centre of Wiltshire; a touring centre for the Wiltshire Downs and the Cotswolds; and a centre of the weaving trade since the 14th century. West of England broadcloth is still made here. Among the legacies of Trowbridge's cloth-based prosperity is the clothiers' group of stone houses in the Parade, and it was a clothier who in 1483 endowed the Perpendicular church of St James.

TRURO
Cornwall *1 SW84*
In the Middle Ages this former Stannary town, lying on Truro River, an arm of the Fal Estuary, was an important port exporting mineral ore. It still has a small port, but is now better known as Cornwall's administrative centre. The cathedral which dominates the town is comparatively modern. Designed by J L Pearson, building began in 1879 and it was the first English Protestant cathedral to be built since St Paul's in London. Lemon Street is one of the best preserved examples in Britain of a Georgian street, and the Assembly Rooms (1770) were an important rendezvous for Cornish high society. The County Museum – arguably the best in Cornwall – houses a world-famous collection of minerals. At Lake's Pottery – one of the county's oldest – modern-day potters can be seen in action. Wheal Jane, 4 miles south west is a tin mine opened in 1971 – the first to do so in Europe for over 50 years. Admiral Edward Boscawen, whose fleet carried the army from Halifax to Louisbourg in Canada in 1758 and gave cover for the attacking landforces, is buried in St Michael Penkevil churchyard 2½ miles south east of Truro. The memorial is by Robert Adam.

TUNBRIDGE WELLS, ROYAL
Kent *6 TQ53*
This distinguished spa had its heyday among persons of fashion in the 18th century, though the waters can still be drunk. Samuel Pepys and John Evelyn both visited. Beau Nash left Bath to be master of Tunbridge Wells' ceremonies in 1735. Its waters were first popularized over a hundred years earlier, by Lord North. Charles I's wife, Henrietta Maria, came here after the birth of the future Charles II in 1630. This was when the building of the town began: until then, society had camped out, or lodged in neighbouring towns. The church of St Charles the Martyr was built between 1678 and 1696 in the baroque style, with fine ceilings and a wooden cupola. Tunbridge Wells' oldest street is the Pantiles, started in 1700, an elegant arcade enhanced by lime trees; its Italianate pillars support diverse frontages and a music balcony. The tiles were laid because Princess (later Queen) Anne threatened not to return after her son slipped on the original walk. Flagstones have replaced all but a few of the tiles. The town's life has many facets: the Museum and Art Gallery, orchestra, theatre, county cricket ground. Tunbridge Ware, mosaics of all kinds of local wood, was worked here from the end of the 17th century until the 1920s.

Royal Tunbridge Wells has plenty of parks and gardens; and a fine common with outcrops of weathered sandstone rocks. Such rocks are typical of the area, the source of its mineral waters, and an attraction for climbers: the nearby High Rocks; the Toad Rocks on Rushall Common; Bowles Rocks, Eridge; Harrison's Rocks, Groombridge; the Happy Valley.

At Frant, near Tunbridge Wells, John By, engineer of the Rideau Canal in Ottawa, lies buried in St Alban's Church. He died in 1836. There is a statue of him in Ottawa. A picture of it and a citation given by the citizens of Ottawa now hang in the parish church (see Rochester).

TURRIFF
Grampian *27 NJ85*
This ancient and thriving market town's present church is 18th century; its ruined church, originally 11th century, belonged to the Knights Templar, and has a double belfry and a bell dated from 1559. Turriff retains few other old buildings, but is encircled by castles and tower houses. Craigston Castle (OACT – with

written permission), 4 miles north east, perpetual seat of the Urquhart family, was built from 1604–7 in the grand Renaissance manner and little altered since. Delgaty Castle (OACT – by arrangement), 2 miles to the east, is the 13th-century seat of the Clan Hay.

TUTBURY
Staffordshire *10 SK22*
The castle (OACT), perched impressively on a rock, dates from the 11th century and originally belonged to Henry de Ferrers, one of William the Conqueror's barons. One of its three towers was built by John of Gaunt in the 14th century, and from it are fine views over the oak-filled former royal forest of Needwood. Mary Queen of Scots was twice imprisoned here. The village itself, large and old, spreads down the hillside. Its wide main street offers a pleasant variety of Tudor, Georgian and Regency houses. The 'Dog and Partridge', an attractive black and white, timbered inn, dates from the 15th century and was once the home of the Curzons of Kedleston Hall. St Mary's Church, originally an 11th-century priory, is one of the finest Norman churches in the Midlands and has a particularly imposing west front.

TWEEDSMUIR
Borders *23 NT02*
This pretty village in pastoral countryside encircled by the Lowland hills, such as the flat-topped 2754ft Broad Law and 2680ft Dollar Law. John Buchan, who took the title of Lord Tweedsmuir, lived here as a boy and made the countryside the background of many of his books. The rivers Annan, Tweed and Clyde all rise about 8 miles south west. Near Tweed's Well, 1500ft up, a cairn on the lonely Moffat road commemorates the death, in a snowstorm in 1831, of the driver and guard of the Edinburgh mailcoach. The Talla and Fruid Reservoirs hold Edinburgh's water; and from the former, the Games Hope Burn flows down from Molls Cleuch Dod (2571ft), forming on the way the waterfalls of Talla Linnfoots. Here the Covenanters held the secret meetings described in *The Heart of Midlothian*.

TWICKENHAM
Gtr London *5 TQ17*
More of an 'area' than a town or village; undeniably part of Greater London but with a clear identity of its own, Thames-side Twickenham has long been a haunt of the Royal and

famous. George II's mistress, Henrietta Howard, Countess of Suffolk, lived in Marble Hill House (OACT) built for her in 1728 by her royal lover. Horace Walpole had built for him Strawberry Hill, a Gothic revival villa and now a Roman Catholic teachers' training college. The poet Walter De La Mare died in 1956 in South End House, part of Montpelier Row which, with Sion Row, forms an unspoilt early 18th-century terrace. Alexander Pope lies buried in the churchyard of St Mary's, built between 1713 and 1714 by John James. Another church, All Hallows, although modern, has had a tower transplant from one of Wren's 17th-century City churches. The only surviving part of the 18th-century Orleans House – the fine Octagonal room designed by James Gibbs in 1736 – is now in use as an art gallery. York House, mainly dating from the 17th century, is now the Town Hall. The rugby ground has been the headquarters of the Rugby Union since 1907.

TWYFORD
Hampshire *4 SU42*
A pretty village famous principally for its association with two famous people. Alexander Pope received his earliest school education here, but was expelled for lampooning his tutor. Benjamin Franklin wrote part of his unfinished autobiography at Twyford House in 1771, home of Franklin's close friend Dr Jonathan Shipley, later Bishop of St Asaph.

Eight miles south east is Wickham, a small town with many Georgian houses. This was the birthplace in 1324 of William of Wykeham, Chancellor of England, founder of Winchester College and of New College, Oxford. The Chesapeake Mill, which stands by the bridge, was built of timbers from the American frigate *Chesapeake*, captured off Boston in 1813. The shot-scarred timbers can still be seen.

TYNEMOUTH
Tyne & Wear *20 NZ36*
Tynemouth is a seaside resort. It lies on the north side of the Tyne Estuary, a home of shipbuilding and other heavy coal and steel-based industries. For years north-easterners have holidayed and day-tripped here, attracted by some of the finest but least known beaches in England, such as Long Sands and Prior's Haven. The sheer cliffs and high river banks offer fine views of the River Tyne and the North Pier offers a $\frac{3}{4}$-mile long trip out

to sea without getting into a boat. The ruins of the moated castle-towers, gatehouse and keep (AM), dating mainly from the 11th and 14th centuries, stand on the cliffs overlooking the pier. Alongside are the remnants of the nave and chancel of the former priory (AM), itself built to replace the original Anglo Saxon foundation destroyed by the Danes. The main street contains some fine 18th-century houses, and the town also boasts an imposing monument to Admiral Lord Collingwood, who led the British Fleet at Trafalgar.

TYSOE
Warwickshire *10 SP34*
Tysoe is divided into three parts: Upper Tysoe, which has a 16th-century manor house; Middle Tysoe, distinguished by the splendid, late-11th-century Church of the Assumption, and cottages with Venetian-style windows and doors; and the small hamlet of Lower Tysoe. Tysoe's main claim to fame is the Great Red Horse of Tysoe, scarcely visible now, cut into Sun Rising Hill. This is the source of the ancient tradition of festivals of the Red Horse; of local legends of a giant horse; and of the name Red Horse Vale. The Institute of Archaeology's investigation of the Great Red Horse, and aerial photographs, concluded that Tysoe has had five horses at various times.

Radway, 3 miles north east, was the site of the famous battle of Edge Hill in 1642. Prince Rupert claimed victory for Charles I, but the young Oliver Cromwell learned much from his defeat under the Earl of Essex. At this time Radway Grange was owned by John Washington, one of the **Sulgrave** Washingtons.

TYWYN
Gwynedd *7 SH50*
This seaside town, with miles of sand, is on the edge of the **Snowdonia National Park**, at the foot of the Cader Idris range. The headquarters of the **Tal-y-llyn** Railway is at Wharf Station, adjoining the Railway Museum. The church of St Cadfan – founder of the Bardsey Island monastery – originally 6th century, but rebuilt in the 19th century, preserves its early Norman nave. Inside, St Cadfan's stone is inscribed with perhaps the earliest example of written Welsh. Tywyn's church, vicarage and school are the distinctive work of the Victorian architect G E Street.

UFFINGTON
Oxfordshire *4 SU38*
From Uffington the most famous of the white horses is clearly visible – the semi abstract quality of its 374ft-long figure suggests that it may have been cut by Iron Age Celts, though the theory that it commemorates King Alfred's 9th-century victory over the Danes remains popular. White Horse Hill, a well-known viewpoint overlooking five counties, retains traces of an Iron Age camp. Nearby are the earthworks of Uffington Castle (AM), standing on the line of the ancient **Ridgeway**. $1\frac{1}{2}$ miles south west of the village lies the so-called Wayland's Smithy (AM), a Stone Age barrow within a larger, later one; how the legend of Wayland the Smith, a mythical Scandinavian figure, the maker of invincible weapons, came to be associated with the much earlier barrow, is unknown. Sir Walter Scott's *Kenilworth* owes much to these legends. Uffington's church has some fine Early English work, with an octagonal tower, a set of eleven consecrated crosses and many lancet windows. Thomas Hughes the author of *Tom Brown's Schooldays* was born here.

ULLAPOOL
Highland *29 NH19*
Ullapool was founded in 1788 to expand the herring industry and it is still a traditional fishing town, though today it also attracts deep sea anglers, especially those in pursuit of shark. Its lovely setting near the mouth of Loch Broom has made it a popular resort and touring centre; the attractive Outer Loch islands can be reached by boat, and to the north the Inverpolly National Nature Reserve offers sanctuary to wildcat, pine-marten and golden eagle in a 27,000-acre expanse of unspoiled Highland countryside. One of the original buildings of Ullapool houses the Lochbroom Highland Museum.

NORTHERN IRELAND

If your name is

Wilson
Jackson
Taylor
Thompson
Simpson
Logan
Blair

read on

County Londonderry

Londonderry Stephen Foster's ancestors lived here. And John Crockett, father of Davy, sailed to America from what the locals call Derry, which is now the 'official' name. In World War II it was the largest Atlantic convoy escort base. It had been in the eighteenth century the major port of emigration for the Scotch-Irish. The Reverend James Macgregor led his Presbyterian flock to New Hampshire in 1719, where they began the settlement Londonderry, New Hampshire.

Maghera Charles Thompson, signer of the Declaration of Independence and Secretary of the Congress, was born here.

County Antrim

Dreen The Arthur House, Cullybackey, was the home of Chester Arthur's family (President of the US 1881–4). His father William was a Baptist clergyman who emigrated in 1816 from Ballymena.

Ballymena Alexander Brown (1764–1834), one of America's first millionaires, was born here.

Conagher Ancestors of President William McKinley came from here.

Ballynure Ancestors of Sam Houston lived here.

Larne Home at Ballyeaston of ancestors of President Andrew Johnson. His grandfather emigrated in 1750 from Larne.

Belfast Ancestral home of family of President Grover Cleveland.

Carrickfergus President Andrew Jackson's parents lived at Boneybefore.

County Tyrone

Dergalt Ancestral home of President Woodrow Wilson, whose grandfather went to America in 1807.

Deroran Family home of President James Buchanan.

Strabane John Dunlap (1747–1812), printer of the Declaration of Independence, learned his trade at Gray's Printing Shop in Main Street (as did Woodrow Wilson's grandfather). Adlai Stevenson claimed descent from a Strabane family. President James K Polk (an abbreviation of the Scottish Pollok) had a great-great-great grandfather from Strabane.

Auchnacloy Ancestral home at Dergina of General and President Ulysses S Grant.

Mountjoy Mellon House is the family home of the Mellons, who founded the Mellon National Bank.

Omagh Ulster-American Folk Park.

County Down

Cultra Ulster Folk and Transport Museum.

Castlewellan Hollywood star Greer Garson (*Mrs Miniver*) born here in 1908.

County Fermanagh

Belleek Pottery first made in 1857. Belleek Collectors' Society's headquarters are at Pine Brook, New Jersey.

Enniskillen Museum of Royal Inniskilling Fusiliers, who fought in the War of 1812, and whose marching tune became better known, and with new words, as *The Star-Spangled Banner*.

The Scotch-Irish (at least 250,000 Ulster people migrated in the eighteenth century alone) also include the Mississippi surgeon Ephraim McDowell, newspaperman Horace Greeley, space pioneers Neil Armstrong and (Senator) John Glenn, Secretary of War James McHenry, General 'Stonewall' Jackson, General James Shields, Cardinal McCloskey and James Logan, William Penn's secretary and a Founding Father of Pennsylvania.

Places to Visit

Castle Coole and **Florence Court** at Enniskillen.

Castle Ward on Strangford Lough.

The Giant's Causeway

Mount Stewart, at Strangford Lough, birthplace of Lord Castlereagh.

Some useful Northern Ireland Addresses

Public Record Office
66, Balmoral Avenue,
Belfast BT9 6NY

The Weaver's Cottage, Ulster American Folk Park

Watergate, Lough Erne

Ulster Historical Foundation
same as above

General Register Office
Oxford House,
49–55 Chichester Street,
Belfast BT1 41TL

Irish Genealogical
Association
164 Kingsway
Dunmurry
Belfast BT17 9AD

or DRH Associates
2255 Cedar Lane,
Vienna VA 22180

Presbyterian Historical
Society
Church House,
Fisherwick Place,
Belfast BT1 6DU

Ulster: home of Presidents

Andrew Jackson, 7th President (parents emigrated in 1765 from Carrickfergus)
James K Polk, 11th President (great-great-great-grandfather emigrated 1680; name had been contracted to Polk, while the family was in Ireland, from original (Scottish) Pollok).
James Buchanan, 15th President (origins Scotch-Irish family, home at Deboran, County Tyrone).
Ulysses Grant, 18th President (great-grandfather emigrated 1760 from Auchnacloy, Co Tyrone).

William McKinley, 25th President (great-great- grandfather emigrated 1743; family farm at Conagher, Co Antrim).
Theodore Roosevelt, 26th President (mother, Martha Bulloch, Scotch-Irish).
Woodrow Wilson, 28th President. (Grandfather emigrated 1807 from Dergalt, Co Tyrone; mother, Jessie Woodrow, born in Carlisle).
Richard Nixon's origins are both English and Scotch-Irish.

And ancestral home of

Charles Thomson, secretary of the Continental Congress 1774–89. Emigrated as orphan aged ten.
John Dunlap, printer of the Declaration of Independence. Born Co Tyrone, emigrated 1757.
Davy Crockett, who died at the Alamo.
John D Calhoun, Senator, Vice-President and Secretary of State.
Samuel Houston, Senator, Governor of Tennessee and later of Texas.
Francis Makemie, founder of American Presbyterianism,

emigrated aged twenty-five from Donegal.
Stonewall Jackson, great-grandfather emigrated 1748.
Cyrus McCormick, inventor of the reaper.
Henry Ferguson, inventor of the tractor, born Hillsborough 1884.
Greer Garson, born Castlewellan 1908.
Archbishop John Hughes of New York.
Cardinal John McCloskey, first American Cardinal, parents from County Derry.
Dr Ephraim McDowell, surgeon.
Stephen Foster, song-writer.
John Mitchell, of the United Irishmen of 1798.
Thomas Mellon, financier and Secretary of the US treasury.

Reference

Ulster-American Folk Park, Camphill Omagh, County Tyrone.
Ulster Historical Foundation, Balmoral Avenue, Belfast BT 6NY; (searching service 2255 Cedar Lane, Vienna VA 22180).
Irish Genealogical Association, Dunmurry, Belfast.

Giant's Causeway, Antrim

ULVA, ISLE OF
Highland *25 NM43*
The caves and basalt cliffs of Ulva, the island traditionally associated with the popular ballad *Lord Ullin's Daughter*, have attracted some famous visitors – Dr Johnson, Boswell, Sir Walter Scott and Livingstone among them. It is separated from Mull (**see** Inner Hebrides) only by the tiny Sound of Ulva, and a passenger ferry links the two.

ULVERSTON
Cumbria *18 SD27*
The 100ft replica of the Eddystone Lighthouse, on Hoad Hill, is a memorial to Sir John Barrow, founder of the Royal Geographical Society, and Secretary to the Admiralty, who was born in Ulverston in 1764. Swarthmoor Hall (OACT) 1 mile south was the home of George Fox's wife, Margaret Fell. The founder of the Quaker movement lived here, and built the Meeting House in 1688. Swarthmore College, Philadelphia, takes its name from here.

UNAPOOL
Highland *29 NC23*
At Unapool the waters of Loch Glencoul and Loch Glendhu come together at Kylesku, on the narrows which divide these two stretches of water from Cairnbawm. The road to the south passes the seven peaks of Quinag, and Eas Coul Aulin, Britain's highest waterfall, plunges from 2541ft Glas Bheinn, its sheer drop of well over 600ft exceeding that of Niagara Falls.

UPNOR
Kent *6 TQ77*
The ruins of a 16th-century castle (AM), probably built with stone taken from Rochester's medieval walls, face the River Medway; Queen Elizabeth I reviewed the fleet here in 1581, and the castle saw action when the Dutch sailed up the river in 1667. The training ship *Arethusa* is now moored in the Medway. The Whittington Stone, named after the one-time Lord Mayor of London, marks the boundary rights of local fishermen.

UPTON HOUSE
Warwickshire *10 SP34*
About 7 miles north west of **Banbury** stands Upton House (NT), a William and Mary mansion set in terraced gardens that rise gently to the woodland behind. The house contains interesting tapestries and furniture,
fine Sèvres porcelain and a collection of pictures which includes work by Stubbs and Brueghel.

UPTON UPON SEVERN
Hereford & Worcester *9 SO84*
This little market town of old-fashioned shops and inns is remarkably unspoiled. Many of its houses are Georgian or older and the 14th-century tower of the demolished church (surmounted by an 18th-century octagonal dome and cupola) looks out over the meadows of the River Severn. The early Baptist Church, built 1695, preserves old oak pews. Two of Upton's inns are of particular interest – The Bell, which has a real bell as its sign, and The White Lion, which features in Fielding's novel, *Tom Jones*.

USK
Gwent *8 SO30*
The old market town of Usk is an established touring centre, set as it is between the **Brecon Beacons National Park** and the Wye Valley; its situation on the River Usk also makes it popular with those seeking a fishing holiday. The town itself is built above the remains of *Burrium*, a Roman settlement 8 miles north of that at **Caerleon**. It is overlooked by the ruins of a Marcher lord's stronghold dating back to the 12th century and dismantled after its support of the Royalist cause in the Civil War. St Mary's Church, parts of which are 700 years old, was once attached to a Benedictine priory of nuns. It has a fine Tudor screen and a 17th-century pulpit.

UTTOXETER
Staffordshire *10 SK03*
Locally pronounced 'Utchettor', this market town on the River Tean had held its charter, granted by Henry III, since 1251. It was here in 1648 that the remnants of the Duke of Wellington's army surrendered. A sculpture on the market place conduit recalls how Samuel Johnson, in his 70s, did 'penance' for refusing to look after his father's bookshop as a boy, standing bareheaded in the rain, and a ceremony recalling this incident is held here each September. Later Nathaniel Hawthorne made a personal pilgrimage to the spot.

VALE OF EVESHAM
Hereford & Worcester *9, 10 SP04*
Much of the fertile land south and east of **Evesham** is given over to fruit growing and market gardening; the massed blossoms of orchards and flower fields are famous for their beauty in spring and early summer, and the area is particularly well known for its fine asparagus. Evesham itself is a town of historic significance; the Avon is navigable to small craft here, and a regatta takes place each May. Many of the surrounding villages are of interest: Offenham is one of the few places still to have a maypole; the mainly modern development of Badsey contains a timber-framed manor house which was once an infirmary for the monks of Evesham; Middle Littleton has the biggest tithe barn in the county and a perfect little village church, and Bretforton the famous 600-year-old Fleece Inn and several interesting dovecotes; Cleeve Prior is a prosperous village of broad streets and stone cottages set round a village green. Wickhamford church contains a memorial to a Penelope Washington, buried here in 1697. The area is linked with the Sandys family – Penelope's widowed mother remarried a Sandys.

VALLE CRUCIS ABBEY
Clwyd *14 SJ24*
The existing buildings of Valle Crucis Abbey (AM), set below the famous 1500ft Horseshoe Pass 2 miles north west of **Llangollen**, date mainly from the 13th century. It was founded in 1201 by Madog ap Gruffydd, Prince of Powys, for Cistercian monks. A good deal of the church survives, including the west front, restored by Sir George Gilbert Scott; four windows – one rose and three Early English in style – surmount an elaborately carved doorway. The remains of the monastic buildings, lying to the south and at one time used as a farmhouse, include a Chapter House with fine vaulting. The abbey's name means 'Vale of the Cross', referring to Eliseg's pillar (AM), which was erected in 603.

W

VERYAN
Cornwall *1 SW93*
The delightful village of Veryan lies in a sheltered position in a wooded valley and produces a wealth of sub-tropical trees and plants. It is famous for its five curious round houses – whitewashed, thatched and surmounted by a cross – standing two at each end of the village and one in the middle. Legend has it that they were built by a vicar for his five daughters; they were made round so that the devil could find no corners in which to lurk. The church of St Symphorian, named after a 3rd-century French martyr, contains a Norman font. 1 mile south west of the village is Gerrans Bay, overlooked by Nare Head. 4 miles north east Caerhays Castle (not open) was used in the television production of Daphne Du Maurier's *Rebecca* (**see** Menabilly).

VIRGINIA WATER
Surrey *17 SU96*
This 160-acre artificial lake at the south-eastern corner of Windsor Great Park, laid out by the Duke of Cumberland in 1746, offers good boating and is surrounded by pleasant picnic spots; the Valley and Heather Gardens are attractive, and Kurume Punch Bowl is a mass of different coloured azaleas. The totem pole, 106ft high, was given to the Queen in 1958 to mark British Columbia's centenary. It is carved by the Kwakiutl people and represents their clan ancestors. Nearby is an avenue of Canadian trees recalling the World War I work of the Canadian Forestry Corps. The colonnade of pillars on the south shore was brought from Leptis Magna and set up here on the instructions of George IV. Nearby is the famous Sunningdale golf course.

Virginia Water

WADDESDON
Buckinghamshire *10 SP71*
The manor (NT) of this picturesque village is a mock-Renaissance château, built in the 19th century for Baron Ferdinand de Rothschild. As well as mementoes of the family, it contains paintings by Gainsborough, Reynolds, Romney and Rubens, whilst the fine collection of furniture includes writing tables that belonged to Marie Antoinette and Louis XVI. The gardens are formal, with fountains and sculptures brought from France, Italy and the Netherlands. There are also two deer enclosures and an aviary. 3 miles south at Lower Winchendon, is **Nether Winchendon** House (OACT), the home of Sir Francis Bernard, Governor of Massachusetts.

WAKEFIELD and NORMANTON
W Yorkshire *15 SE32*
Before the rise of neighbouring cities Leeds and Bradford, Wakefield was the centre of the clothing trade. Its former prosperity is reflected in the many Georgian houses. Yorkshire's tallest spire can be seen on Wakefield's cathedral, and the medieval bridge chapel is the most beautiful of the four which survive in England. The 19th-century naturalist Charles Waterton was born and died just outside Wakefield at Walton Hall. Waterton's *Wanderings in South America* (1825) is still much loved. A few miles north east, Normanton was the birthplace of two early contributors to the history of North America: Martin Frobisher, who explored the North-West Passage in 1576 was born here c1535, as was the Reverend Richard Clyfton, the Puritan rector of Babworth, whose large congregation included William Brewster. Clyfton was among the *Mayflower* group, but died before the expedition got under way.

WALLINGFORD
Oxfordshire *4 SU68*
Settled by Romans, Saxons, Danes and Normans, the town received its charter in 1153, granted by Henry II whose right to the throne was confirmed in the Treaty of Wallingford. Its castle was one of the last Royalist castles to fall in the Civil War; used as a prison until 1652, it was then demolished. Wallingford's most illustrious resident was Sir William Blackstone (1723–80). He produced one of the finest coherent treatises on English Law, and his *Commentaries On the Law of England* was widely used in the formative years of the American legal system. Blackstone is buried in the family vault in St Peter's Church. Today Wallingford is a busy market town with many fine Georgian buildings and very popular riverside walks.

The distinguished Canadian doctor, Sir William Osler, is recalled in the parish church at Ewelme, north east of Wallingford. He came from a Cornish family, settled in Bond Head, Ontario and, in 1905, was appointed to the chair of medicine at Oxford. There is a portrait in the Radcliffe Science Library in Oxford.

WALLSEND
Tyne & Wear *20 NZ36*
This River Tyne town, standing at the eastern end of **Hadrian's Wall**, is traditionally involved in engineering and shipbuilding: *Mauretania*, the Cunard liner that held the Atlantic crossing – The Blue Riband – for 22 years, was launched here in 1907.

WALPOLE ST PETER
Norfolk *11 TF51*
This marshland village is dominated by the impressive church of St Peter, the 'Queen of the Marshes'. The interior is noted for a 17th-century screen which extends its full width and for the 15th-century carving on its stalls and benches. An unusual feature is the 'hud' (or 'hood') – a movable shelter once used at funerals which took place in bad weather.

WALSALL
W Midlands *9 SP09*
Walsall's traditional role was as a leather centre specializing in fine saddlery; now this typical Black Country town embraces 100 industries. Its oldest building is St Matthew's Church, whose crypt dates from the early 13th century and whose high altar is built above a vaulted archway that once spanned a road. Modern Rushall Church adjoins the remains of a 14th-century castle which was dismantled after the Civil War. A statue in the town centre commemorates Sister Dora (Dorothy

Pattison), who spent the last 12 years of her life nursing the sick and the poor of the area in the late 19th century. A plaque in Bradford Street marks the birthplace of Jerome K Jerome, author of *Three Men in a Boat*. The Museum and Art Gallery in the Central Library contains fine paintings and sculptures.

WALSINGHAMS, THE
Norfolk   *12 TF93*
In 1061 a shrine was built at Little Walsingham by Lady Richeld, commanded to do so in a vision. It was a major centre for pilgrimage – numbering kings among its visitors – until the Reformation; the pilgrimage was revived in the late 19th century and the building of the New Shrine was completed in 1937. The ruins of the old priory, including a 15th-century gateway, can be seen in the grounds of the modern abbey. Of the original shrine nothing remains. The restored 15th-century church of St Mary houses a Seven Sacraments font and an Epstein sculpture, 'The Risen Christ'. Picturesque old houses surround the village square, and a nearby 18th-century Court Room contains the Shirehall Museum. Great Walsingham's church contains magnificently carved bench-ends.

WALTHAM ABBEY
Essex   *5 TL30*
Waltham Abbey (AM) was founded by King Harold, and his body is believed to have been buried here after his death at the Battle of Hastings. The cloister entrance and the nave of the church date from the 12th century, displaying some of the oldest Norman workmanship in the country. A second phase of building took place in the 14th century, and Harold's Bridge and the gatehouse date from this period. Much of the abbey was destroyed at the Reformation, but the remains are magnificent, and the restored church contains fine monuments and stained glass and has an undercroft museum.

WALTON & WEYBRIDGE
Surrey   *5 TQ06*
Walton appears in the Domesday Book as 'Waletona', listed as having a church, two mills and a fishery; the same church still stands, though altered and restored over the centuries. The town has now merged with Weybridge – a similarly ancient settlement with a Norman church – which was the site of two royal residences in the Tudor period and the setting for Henry VIII's marriage to Catherine Howard. Weybridge is a town of 'firsts', having been the home of the world's first racing track, the world's first air travel booking office and Britain's first aerodrome.

WANTAGE
Oxfordshire   *4 SU48*
A quiet town with cobbled streets and 17th- and 18th-century houses, Wantage lies at the foot of the Berkshire Downs in the Vale of the White Horse. King Alfred the Great was born here in 849 and his statue stands in the market place. Parts of the church of Sts Peter and Paul date back to the 13th century; it has a 15th-century hammerbeam roof, some fine wood carvings and the tombs of members of the Fitzwaryn family, into which Dick Whittington married. In 1873 the first steam tramway in the country began operation here, the line remaining open until 1948.

WARDOUR
Wiltshire   *3 ST92*
The magnificent Palladian mansion (OACT), built by James Paine and Sir John Soane, was the home of the Catholic Arundell family (it is now a school). The beautifully decorated baroque chapel is one of the few Roman private chapels in continuous use; it contains art treasures. The house became connected with Maryland when the 2nd Lord Baltimore, Cecilius Calvert, married Anne, daughter of Lord Arundel of Wardour. Baltimore continued and financed his father's plans for a Catholic emigration to America. Maryland was named after Henrietta Maria, King Charles's wife. The chapel was restored with a gift from the Archbishop of Baltimore in return for a cape made from the robe worn by the last Lord Wardour at King George VI's Coronation in 1937. The present building replaces the original 14th-century hexagonal castle which fell into decay after the Civil War and whose ruins (AM) stand in landscaped gardens about a mile away.

WARE
Hertfordshire   *5 TL31*
The Great Bed of Ware – 10ft wide by 11ft long, and mentioned in Shakespeare's *Twelfth Night* – originally stood in the Saracen's Head Inn; it is now in the Victoria and Albert Museum in London. It was in Ware that Lady Jane Grey was proclaimed Queen in 1553, and William Cowper immortalized the town as John Gilpin's destination in his famous poem. The River Lea once carried heavy traffic connected with the local malting industry, but it is now used only by pleasure boats and anglers. The parish church has a memorial to Charles Chauncy, the second president of Harvard College. The town has several notable old buildings, including Bluecoat House with its 15th-century timbering and the early 17th-century Canons Maltings.

Two miles north at Wadesmill a monument commemorates Thomas Clarkson's dedication to the fight against slavery – he devoted his life to the Abolitionist Cause. Wadesmill was possibly the site of England's first tollgate in 1663. 1½ miles south, Great Amwell has a memorial to Sir Hugh Myddleton, who began the New River Scheme in 1609, to provide London with pure water from the springs here. Great Amwell is said by some to be the county's second prettiest village; the prettiest is only a few miles north east at **Much Hadham**.

WAREHAM
Dorset   *3 SY98*
Encircled by ancient earthworks, Wareham was a market town in Saxon times; its centre is Georgian, rebuilt after an extensive fire. Set on the River Frome, above the Frome Marshes, it is popular with fishermen and small boat enthusiasts. Extensive heathland between Wareham and Puddletown, now partly wooded as the result of an afforestation scheme, is the basis of Hardy's fictional Egdon Heath, and there are several nature reserves in the area. Lawrence of Arabia had connections with the town and St Martin's Church contains a fine sculpture of him by Eric Kennington, whilst a small town museum on St John's Hill has numerous Lawrence relics.

WARKWORTH
Northumberland   *24 NU20*
Overlooking Alnmouth Bay stand the impressive ruins of Warkworth Castle (AM), probably built by the 1st Earl of Northumberland in the 12th century, and used by Shakespeare as the setting for part of *Henry IV*. The curious 14th-century Hermitage (AM), with its small chapel hewn from solid rock, can be reached by rowing boat. An old bridge with a rare bridge tower at one end spans the River Coquet. In 1715, during the Jacobite Rising, the Old Pretender was proclaimed King James III at the old cross in the market place. There are many attractive old terraces.

WARMINSTER

Wiltshire   *3 ST84*

The beautiful houses and attractive cottages of Warminster, together with two fine inns, are a legacy of the prosperity it gained in the 18th century as a wool town and corn market. The church, though much rebuilt, retains a 14th-century nave, and the grammar school (founded in 1707) numbers Dr Arnold of Rugby and Dean Stanley among its former pupils. 2 miles to the west, 800ft Cley Hill (NT) rises on the Ridgeway, the prehistoric route which ran from South Devon to the Wash. William Cabell, who died in 1774 and came from here, was the founder of the American Cabell family, and the founder of Warminster, Virginia.

WARRINGTON

Cheshire   *14 SJ68*

The industrial town of Warrington, situated on the Manchester Ship Canal, has been designated a New Town and is developing rapidly. Its traditional industry is clockmaking, but ironworks and soap factories are the modern employers of labour. Bank Hall, originally the home of the Patten family but serving as the Town Hall since 1872, was designed in 1750 by James Gibbs, who was probably the architect of Holy Trinity Church. A few old houses remain, and the Barley Mow is a fine half-timbered inn. In 1848 Warrington became the first town to have a public library supported by the rates; it has two museums – the Municipal Museum and Art Gallery in Bold Street and the Regimental Museum of the South Lancashire Regiment. Near the bridge stands a statue of Cromwell, who entered the town in 1648 after his victory at Preston. South west of Warrington is Runcorn New Town and the remains of Norton Priory with its 12th-century carved undercroft.

WARTON

Lancashire   *14 SD42*

The tower of the restored 15th-century church bears the Washington arms. The family lived here for many generations, between leaving Washington and moving to **Sulgrave**. Thomas, the last Washington of Warton, was parson here from 1799 to 1823. Robert Kitson lived at Warton in the 15th century. His daughter Margaret married John Washington, while his son Thomas was the father-in-law of Sir John Spencer of **Althorp**, from whom both the Princess of Wales and Winston Churchill descended.

►WARWICK

Warwickshire   *10 SP26*

County Town on the River Avon

'That shire which wee the hart of England well may call, . . .

Brave Warwick; that abroad so long advance't her beare,
By her illustrious Earles renowned every where;'
  Michael Drayton, *Poly Olbion, (1612)*

Warwick, known as the 'heart of England', is a splendid town, standing on a rise above the River Avon at the meeting point of many roads. Originally founded by Ethelfleda, a daughter of Alfred the Great, in about 914, Warwick became an important borough under the Normans. It is dominated by its great medieval castle, built by the Beauchamps, the first Earls of Warwick, and enlarged and beautified by the Dudleys, descendants of Ambrose Dudley for whom Elizabeth I revived the title. In 1759 it passed to the Greville family whose descendants have held it ever since.

In 1694 the centre of Warwick was almost completely destroyed by fire. Few medieval buildings escaped. The finest of what remains are Lord Leycester's Hospital and Oken House, which incorporate Westgate, one of the two remaining medieval gateways. The other, Eastgate, stands at the opposite end of the High Street. Of the many fine buildings erected after the fire, the Court House, containing the Tourist Information Centre, and Shire Hall, home of the County Court, are the most outstanding public buildings. Beneath the octagonal courtrooms of the Shire Hall is the old main dungeon, where as many as 50 prisoners were sometimes confined, shackled, in a single small room. Northgate House and Abbotsford, now the Registrar's house, are the best of the post-fire town houses. The 174ft tower of St Mary's Church is a landmark. This, and the nave and aisles, were rebuilt after the fire, but the crypt, chancel, chapter house and the magnificent Beauchamp Chapel, containing the tombs of the Earls of Warwick and their families, display Norman and 14th-century architecture. 18th-century buildings constitute much of today's centre, particularly in Castle Street, Bridge End and Mill Street.

PLACES TO SEE

The Castle Most of the buildings of this great fortress date from the 14th century and later. The massive gatehouse is flanked by two forbidding towers: Guy's Tower

Beauchamp Chapel, St Mary's Church

and Caesar's Tower. There is an extensive collection of weaponry in the Armoury, and there are many famous paintings by European masters in the State Apartments. The spacious park was landscaped by Capability Brown.

Lord Leycester's Hospital This fine range of medieval buildings, some dating from the 14th century when they formed the Guild House of St George, was converted by Robert Dudley, a favourite of Elizabeth I, into a hospital for veteran soldiers.

Oken House An outstanding example of a timbered merchant's house, and containing the Warwick Doll Museum, a fascinating collection of old dolls.

St John's House Standing just east of the town, this 17th-century mansion houses a branch of the County Museum, displaying crafts, costume and musical instruments. On the first floor is the Museum of the Royal Warwickshire Regiment.

Warwickshire Museum The Sheldon Tapestry Map of the county is the pride of the collection of local history housed in the 17th-century Market Hall.

Warwickshire Yeomanry Museum Housed in the Court House, the museum has military exhibits and paintings dating back to 1794.

WASHINGTON
Tyne and Wear *20 NZ35*
A New Town, intended eventually to
have a population of 80,000, is
developing in the area around
Washington. In the original village is
Washington Old Hall (NT), the 12th-
century home of the family known as
the Wessingtons. Over the years their
name was corrupted to Washington,
and it was from this branch of the
family that the first American
President descended. Lawrence
Washington moved with his family to
Sulgrave, Northamptonshire, in the
16th century. Inside the house are
many relics, including a unique
portrait of George Washington on
parchment. 5 miles east is Hylton
Castle which has what is believed to be
the oldest stone carving of the Stars
and Stripes – the Washington arms.
(**See** Sunderland).

3 miles to the south east rises the
Penshaw monument (NT) built in 1844
to commemorate John George
Lambton, 1st Earl of Durham. It is a
roofless Victorian Greek Temple 70
feet in height and 100 feet long. Lord
Durham helped to draft the 1832
Reform Bill and he was Governor
General of Canada for 4 months in
1838, sent to deal with the rebellion in
Lower Canada. He mixed force with
clemency but resigned when the British
government failed to support his
methods. He then prepared the
celebrated Durham Report of 1839
suggesting Union and Confederation,
hinting at self-government and
advocating the assimilation of French
Canadians into a British-style culture.

On the north bank of the Wear the
Wildfowl Trust maintains a 103-acre
park (OACT) where a comprehensive
collection of waterfowl can be seen
against an attractive landscape.

WEALD, THE
Kent *6 TQ53*
This area of broken country between
the North and South Downs, Kipling's
'wooded, dim blue goodness of the
Weald', was once part of the Forest of
Anderida; today there are still wooded
areas in which wild deer roam, notably
the forests of St Leonards and
Ashdown. Much of the British navy
was built of oak from these
woodlands, and the wood was also
used to smelt Sussex iron, many of the
hammer ponds that turned the
waterwheels of the forges still existing.
Much of the cleared land has been
given over to orchards and to the hop
fields, with their oast houses.

WELBECK ABBEY
Nottinghamshire *15 SK57*
This interesting old house (not open)
in its magnificent park stands on the
site of a 12th-century monastery which
was granted to the Whalley family
after the Dissolution. They eventually
sold it to Bess of Hardwick, and one of
her descendants, the 1st Duke of
Newcastle, built the south wing in
about 1630. The house subsequently
passed to the Dukes of Portland and
remained their property until the 20th
century when it was taken over as an
Army College. The most fascinating
feature of the building is the labyrinth
of passages and suites of rooms that
undermine it – the brainchild of the
eccentric 5th Duke of Portland who
became a recluse with a phobia about
being seen by strangers.

WELLINGTON
Somerset *2 ST12*
The woollen industry has long
flourished in Wellington, and cloths
are still exported to all parts of the
world. Some fine Georgian houses
survive, as do two ancient inns – the
400-year-old Squirrel (now converted
into a house) and the Three Cups, first
recorded in 1694. The Perpendicular
church has a mid-side stair turret, a
stylistic feature more typical of Devon.
It also contains the ornate tomb of Sir
John Popham, the Lord Chief Justice
who presided at the trials of Sir Walter
Raleigh and Guy Fawkes. With his
brother George Popham, who was
born near **Bridgwater**, and was
instrumental in the early exploration
and settlement of the coast of Maine,
Popham also established almshouses in
Wellington. 3 miles south west of the
town, on the Blackdown Hills, stands
the 175ft high Wellington Monument
(NT), an obelisk erected in 1817 to
commemorate the famous Duke who
took his title from here.

WELLOW
Avon *3 ST75*
On Wellow's sloping village street
stand cottages of gold-coloured stone,
ancient farm buildings and a fine
manor house that was once the home
of the Hungerford family. It was Sir
Thomas Hungerford, the first recorded
Speaker of the House of Commons,
who rebuilt St Julian's Church in
about 1372; a statue over the south
porch shows St Julian – the patron
saint of ferrymen – holding an oar, and
fine wall paintings in the north chapel
date from the early 16th century. Dr
John Bull – reputed to be the composer

of the National Anthem – was born in
Wellow in 1562. ¾ mile south west of
the village lies Stoney Littleton Long
Barrow, a Neolithic burial chamber.

WELLS
Somerset *3 ST54*
This lovely cathedral city lies at the
foot of the Mendip Hills. The
cathedral, with its associated
buildings, forms England's largest
medieval ecclesiastical precinct and the
cathedral itself has a superbly adorned
west front. A favourite with visitors is
the 14th-century clock, with its moving
figures that strike the hours. The
moated Bishop's Palace (OACT) has
interesting state rooms, and the
remains of a 13th-century undercroft
and banqueting hall. A medieval
gateway, the Bishop's Eye, marks the
entrance to the grounds. On the moat
are swans that have been trained to
ring a bell for food. Wells Museum
illustrates the natural history of the
Mendips. In North Wootton, at North
Town House 3 miles from Wells, a
vineyard flourishes in the Mendips.
The 9000 vines were imported from
the Rhine and Alsace. The old farm
buildings house a winery in which a
dry white wine is produced – and one
that does credit to its Continental
origins. You can stroll through the
vineyards and buy wine from the
cellar.

WELNEY
Norfolk *11 TL59*
At Welney the Wildfowl Trust
maintains a sanctuary for native and
migratory birds which covers over 800
acres of the Ouse Washes. As well as a
winter refuge for thousands of
Bewick's swans and several species of
duck, it provides a spring nesting place
for ruff, redshank, snipe and black-
tailed godwit. The birds can be seen
from the observatory or from hides.

Wellington countryside

WELSHPOOL
Powys *14 SJ20*
The Welsh name of this low-lying Severnside town, Y Trallwng, literally means 'the marshy or sinking land'; it became known first as Pool and then as Welshpool to distinguish it from Poole in Dorset. Many fine Georgian buildings still stand in today's busy market town, and Powis Castle (NT), originally medieval, with late 16th-century plasterwork and panelling, lies 1 mile to the south. The history of the area is traced in the Powysland Museum (OACT), its most notable exhibit being an Iron Age shield.

WENDENS AMBO
Essex *11 TL53*
The name of this attractive small village commemorates the amalgamation of the parishes of Great and Little Wenden ('ambo' meaning 'both') in 1662. The church of St Mary the Virgin contains a fascinating cycle of 14th-century wall paintings, a 15th-century carved pulpit and a 16th-century domed font cover; the lane leading to it has lovely cottages on one side and the Hall Barn on the other.

WENDOVER
Buckinghamshire *10 SP80*
The old Chiltern town of Wendover stands on the edge of the ancient Icknield Way; to its west rises Coombe Hill (NT), at 852ft the highest point of the Chiltern range, said to afford a view of St Paul's Cathedral on a fine day and surmounted by a monument to Buckinghamshire men who died in the South African War. Though a busy road now runs through the town, many quaint old buildings survive, including the half-timbered Lion Hotel where Cromwell slept in 1643 and a windmill and water-mill which have been turned into houses. Bosworth House – now divided into cottage, house and Post Office – revealed 16th- and 17th-century wall paintings when alterations were being made. Two remain in the house, though the others were taken to the Victoria and Albert Museum. The church is mainly 14th century, though much restored, and contains some interesting carvings and a curious brass to William Bradshawe.

WENDRON
Cornwall *1 SW63*
A 17th-century lychgate gives access to the 14th- and 15th-century church of Wendron, and the churchyard contains a very early cross-slab with an incised cross. This was a tin-mining area, and the Poldark Mine and Wendron Forge complex is open to the public, with museums and the West Country's largest collection of working antiques, including a 40ft-high beam engine.

WESSEX
Wessex, the old West Saxon kingdom, embraced Hampshire, Wiltshire, Dorset, Somerset and Berkshire; later it also included Devon and Cornwall. The works of Thomas Hardy revived interest in Wessex, for his fictional place-names barely conceal the vividly painted communities and natural features in his books, **Sturminster Newton** showing clearly through the 'Stowcastle' of *Tess of the d'Urbervilles* and the great heath of *The Return of the Native* unmistakably Bockhampton. Wessex also figures prominently in the legends about the Round Table, for the earthwork of **Cadbury Castle** traditionally marks the site of Camelot, whilst **Glastonbury** was the resting place of the Holy Grail, Dozemary Pool, the lake from which Excalibur rose, and **Tintagel** the setting for another Arthurian castle.

WESTBURY
Wiltshire *3 ST85*
Moated Palace Green is believed at one time to have been the site of the residence of the Kings of Wessex. Georgian houses set round the market place reflect a later period of prosperity, when the town was involved in the weaving industry and was famous for its glove-making. The restored Perpendicular church has a central tower and contains a chained New Testament, 17th- and 18th-century monuments and an interesting modern screen. Above the town stands the oldest White Horse in Wiltshire, probably cut originally in the 9th century but remodelled to a more 'elegant' shape in the 18th century. Chalcot House (OACT) is a charming Palladian villa just over 2 miles away near the village of Dilton Marsh.

WESTBURY-ON-TRYM
Avon *3 ST57*
Westbury-on-Trym is divided from Bristol by the 442 acres of the Clifton and Durdham Downs. The restored 13th- to 15th-century church was once attached to Westbury College (NT), the 15th-century tower of which survives from the ancient College of Priests. A Wildlife Park has been developed in a nearby secluded valley. Picturesque Blaise Hamlet, about a

Westbury white horse

mile to the north of Westbury, has a group of Nash cottages (NT), a folk museum housed in Blaise Castle.

WESTBURY-UPON-SEVERN
Gloucestershire *9 SO71*
Westbury Court Garden (NT) is the earliest surviving example of a Dutch-style water garden, most having been destroyed by the craze for landscaping in the 18th century. This one was derelict for years, its canals silted and its vegetation wild, but meticulous restoration has brought it back to its original appearance – the colonnaded pavilion rebuilt, the flowers and shrubs mentioned in the records replanted.

WEST DEAN
W Sussex *4 SU81*
The Weald and Downland Museum (OACT), England's first organized open air crafts display which will eventually include some 40 re-erected old buildings, is sited at **Singleton**, near West Dean. West Dean itself is a charming downland village of flint and half-timbered houses standing in the valley of the River Lavant. At West Dean Gardens (OACT) old tools and implements – including antique lawnmowers – are on show in the Museum of the Garden, and the wild garden is of ecological interest.

WESTERHAM
Kent *5 TQ45*
The birthplace of General Wolfe. The
village contains two memorial statues,
one to Wolfe and one to Churchill,
who resided nearby at **Chartwell** from
1924 until his death. The parish church
has a memorial window to Wolfe.
Wolfe's two residences are open to the
public. Quebec House (OACT),
Wolfe's boyhood home, a largely 17th-
century house, contains many relics of
the family and historical exhibitions of
events such as the Battle of Quebec.
Squerryes Court (OACT) also contains
many relics and a Wolfe Cenotaph
stands in its beautiful gardens.
Chartwell (OACT), 2 miles to the
south of Westerham, has been
arranged as a museum with rooms left
exactly as they were used by Churchill.
The house contains personal
mementoes such as books,
photographs, uniforms and a studio
with many paintings by Sir Winston.
The landscaped gardens are famous
for their Australian black swans.
Churchill's honorary American
citizenship is displayed.

WEST HOATHLY
E Sussex *5 TQ33*
This village in the heart of the Weald
dates back to Saxon times and was
once the centre of the iron industry. Its
church stands on a ridge with fine
views to the south, and smugglers used
to signal down the valley from the
church tower before meeting at the
Cat Inn. They used nearby Gravetye
Manor – a fine gabled Elizabethan
house which was once the home of the
famous garden designer William
Robinson and is now a hotel – as a
store for contraband goods. The 15th-
century Priest's House (OACT)
contains an interesting folk museum.
Great-upon-Little, in the grounds of
Rockhurst, is a rock formation where
a large piece of sandstone is balanced
on a smaller one.

WEST MALLING
Kent *6 TQ65*
Norman influence is evident in West
Malling, as it is in its twin village of
East Malling also. St Leonard's Tower
(AM) is all that remains of a Norman
castle built of Kentish ragstone by
Bishop Gundulf of Rochester in about
1090. Remains of the abbey include an
11th-century tower and a
Perpendicular gateway. The church –
again, with a Norman tower – displays
the Royal Arms of James II. The half-
timbered Priest's House dates from the

14th-century, and some fine 18th-
century houses exist in the area. The
inn sign of The Startled Saint shows
Spitfires in St Leonard's halo, recalling
the use of the nearby airfield in the
Battle of Britain.

WESTONBIRT
Gloucestershire *3 ST88*
Westonbirt Arboretum was founded in
1829 by a local squire, Robert Stainer
Holford, and is now part of a 600-acre
Forestry Commission development;
the Arboretum itself covers 117 acres
and extends into Wiltshire. This
collection of trees is one of the finest in
the country and is particularly
beautiful in autumn, though the large
banks of rhododendrons also provide
a mass of colour in the late spring.

WESTON-SUPER-MARE
Avon *3 ST36*
A hundred years ago Weston-Super-
Mare was a little fishing village on the
Bristol Channel, now it is a popular
resort. Holidaymakers are attracted by
its splendid sands and good bathing,
piers, attractive parks and gardens, 2-
mile marine parade and golf course.
Worlebury Hill, 1 mile to the north
east, is topped by an Iron Age camp
(AM) and looks over the islands of
Steep Holme and Flat Holme to the
Welsh coast. Woodspring Museum
(OACT), set in the old workshops of
the Edwardian Gaslight Company, has
displays on transport and the wildlife
and minerals of the area; it also
portrays scenes from Victorian life –
the seaside holiday being particularly
appropriate. There is a nature reserve
at nearby Brean Down.

WEST WEMYSS
Fife *23 NT39*
In 1565 the first meeting between Mary
Queen of Scots and Darnley took place
at West Wemyss, a small Firth of Forth
town with a castle dating from the
15th century and a curiously inscribed
tolbooth with an outside staircase. The
caves in the rocky coastline to the
north east are famous for their Bronze
Age, Iron Age and early Christian
carvings.

WEST WYCOMBE
Buckinghamshire *4 SU89*
Much of West Wycombe is under the
protection of the National Trust.
Amongst its old buildings, many of
which date back to the 15th century, is
a fine inn. West Wycombe Park (NT)
(OACT), partly designed by Robert
Adam, was built for Sir Francis

West Wycombe church

Dashwood of Hellfire Club fame in the
18th century, and he also instigated the
rebuilding of the church, the large ball
on the tower of which is a well-known
local landmark and used to be a
meeting place for the club. West
Wycombe Caves (OACT) are also
associated with Dashwood and the
Hellfire Club. Dashwood was also a
serious scholar and a friend of
Benjamin Franklin. Their friendship
grew when Franklin was Postmaster
General and Dashwood was his
opposite number in England; their
correspondence was considerable and
included a plan of reconciliation to
prevent the War of Independence. In
1763 they produced a Nonconformist
prayer book which subsequently
formed part of the prayer book of the
American Episcopalian Church.

WETHERINGSETT
Suffolk *12 TM16*
Richard Hakluyt, the author of
*Principall Navigations, Voiages and
Discoveries of the English Nation*
(1589), was Rector of Wetheringsett
for the last 25 years of his life,
although he was not always resident.
The early geographer of the New
World was also instrumental in the
drafting of the Charter for Virginia.
The 14th-century church, with its
carved nave roof, is surrounded by
thatched cottages. 2 miles west, a
section of the USAAF was based at
Mendlesham.

WEYMOUTH
Dorset *3 SY67*
Weymouth, a dignified town of fine
Georgian houses, was favoured by
King George III who once lived at
Gloucester House (now a hotel).
Author Thomas Hardy was also well

acquainted with the resort, which appears in his novels as Budmouth. Weymouth is still popular with holidaymakers. There are picturesque alleys to explore in the Melcombe Regis quarter, and a 17th-century house in Trinity Street has been restored and refurnished in contemporary style (OACT). Weymouth is also a port, and a terminus for ferries.

Two men important to North American history were associated with Weymouth. Both are commemorated by a memorial on the pier. In 1583, Richard Clark of Weymouth sailed to join Sir Humphry Gilbert's voyage of discovery to Newfoundland. In 1628, John Endicott founded and settled Salem, Massachusetts, having purchased land from the Plymouth Company. Following the death of Governor Winthrop in 1649, Endicott assumed the office he would hold almost continually until his death in 1665. He was a popular Governor, despite his religious intolerance. At Wyke Regis, on the western outskirts of the town, Marriott Arbuthnott, the Lieutenant-Governor of Novia Scotia for 1776–88, is commemorated.

WHALTON
Northumberland *20 NZ18*
At the east end of this pretty village stands the manor, converted from four village houses by Sir Edwin Lutyens in 1909. Its grounds are occasionally open to the public, and the Whalton Gallery (inside the house entrance) specializes in 18th- to 20th-century watercolours and drawings. St Magdalene's Church, though much restored, dates back to the early 13th century, traces of the original workmanship still being visible in the chancel. The ancient ritual of the baal fire is still observed on the fourth of July, the old Midsummer Eve: cattle used to be driven through the fire to purify them, and at one time the villagers themselves leapt through the flames. Until quite recently, burning branches were carried round the village to defend the fields from blight and the houses from witchcraft.

WHERWELL
Hampshire *4 SU34*
The thatched cottages of the beautiful village of Wherwell (traditionally pronounced 'Orrell') stand beside a tributary of the River Test. The 19th-century church near the bridge contains part of an Anglo Saxon cross and two small 14th-century reliefs.

The once-famous abbey, founded by King Ethelred's mother, Queen Elfrida, in expiation of the murder of her stepson, was destroyed at the Dissolution; fragmentary remains can be seen in the grounds of the 19th-century house known as The Priory. Thomas West, Lord de la Warr, was baptized here in 1577. He became Governor of Virginia for life, and reorganized the settlement, which was on the point of collapse, when he arrived in 1610. The State and River Delaware were named in his honour.

WHIPSNADE
Bedfordshire *11 TL01*
Set in 500 acres of beautiful Chiltern countryside, Whipsnade Park Zoo was originally intended more or less as a convalescent home for sick animals from London Zoo. When it opened in 1931 the provision of large, open enclosures rather than heated cages was a revolutionary step; the experiment was successful, however, and the Zoo's breeding record is so good that about 80 per cent of its 2000 occupants were born there. The conservation of endangered species is high on Whipsnade's list of priorities; rare breeds on display include Black, White and Great Indian rhinos, North American bison and Przewalski's horses. The 'traditional' animals have not been forgotten, however; the Children's Zoo and the dolphins are particularly popular. A novel way of seeing the African Section is via the Whipsnade and Umfolozi Railway – a narrow-gauge, steam-operated line.

WHITBY
N Yorkshire *20 NZ81*
The resort and harbour of Whitby stand in a picturesque situation at the mouth of the River Esk, with the **North York Moors National Park** rising behind the town. It has been a fishing town for hundreds of years and was once a whaling port. Terraces of fishermen's cottages rise beneath East Cliff, and a fishing fleet still plies from the harbour.

It was at the Synod of Whitby in 664 that the divided church in England accepted the authority of the Roman Catholic church. The remains of Whitby Abbey (AM) on East Cliff are those of the 13th-century building; the first abbey was founded in 657 by St Hilda, and it was here that the 7th-century monk Caedmon wrote the Song which is considered to mark the beginning of English literature. A cross commemorating him stands nearby in

the churchyard of St Mary's, a Norman-towered edifice approached by the 199 Church Stairs. On West Cliff stands a statue of Captain Cook, who lived in Whitby as a young man. There are plaques from the Canadian and British Columbian governments. His house in Grape Street is also marked with a plaque. There is a museum of local history in Pannett Park, in which there is Cook's handwritten survey of Placentia Bay, Newfoundland.

WHITEHAVEN
Cumbria *18 NX91*
Whitehaven was a small village until the end of the 17th-century; the development of the collieries and the coming of industry, however, turned it into a busy coal and seaport town. Sir James Lowther, the son of the man who instigated the town's industrial development, built Whitehaven Castle (now a hospital) during the 18th century, and St James's Church also dates from this period. George Washington's grandmother was buried in St Nicholas's Church in 1701 and this is commemorated by an inscribed tablet, although the church has since been rebuilt.

Whitehaven stone was used in the courtyard at Mount Vernon, Washington's home in Virginia. In 1778 John Paul Jones, who had been an apprentice shipbuilder in Whitehaven, landed and destroyed ships and guns.

Whitehaven Quay

WHITHORN
Dumfries & Galloway *17 NX44*
Whithorn Priory (AM) stands on the
site of the first Christian church in
Scotland – St Ninian's 'Candida Casa'
or White House, part of the 4th-
century monastery he founded here.
The priory was built in the 12th
century by Fergus, Lord of Galloway,
and excavations of its ruins have
revealed traces of the earlier church.
Little remains of the 12th-century
building, but there is a fine Norman
doorway to the nave, and the ancient
crosses and tombstones contained in
the town museum include the 5th-
century Latinus Stone.

WHITSTABLE
Kent *6 TR16*
Long renowned for its oysters, the
resort of Whitstable also offers fishing
and bathing from a shingle beach and
good yachting facilities. A spit of land
known as 'the Street' juts about a mile
and a half into the sea, providing a
pleasant promenade at low tide. 'The
Castle', a crenellated building dating
mainly from the 19th century, has a
15th-century brick tower originally
used as a look-out post, and its
parkland is open to the public.
Stevenson's *Invicta* (now preserved at
Canterbury) pulled a train on the
Whitstable to Canterbury line – the
first passenger line to be opened – in
1830. The tunnel through Tyler Hill
was the first railway tunnel to be built
in Britain and the line was finally
closed in 1953.

WHITTINGHAM
Northumberland *24 NU01*
Two bridges span the river Aln at
Whittingham, an arched stone one for
motorists and an attractive footbridge
for pedestrians. The interior of St
Bartholomew's Church still shows
signs of Saxon workmanship, though
its original tower was replaced in the
19th century. On the other side of the
village the battlemented top of a
restored 15th-century pele tower
overlooks a new housing development.
Parts of Callaly Castle (OACT), 2
miles away, go back to the 14th century.

WICK
Highland *30 ND35*
The ancient settlement of Wick is an
important sea-fishing centre, its large
harbour designed originally by
Telford. The 'Old Man of Wick', a
windowless 14th-century tower (AM),
crowns a rock which juts into the sea
about a mile south of the town.

Nearby are the curious rock stacks
known as Brig o'Tram and the
Brough. The coastal scenery of the
area is dramatic with enormous rocks
topping the rugged cliffs. To the north
stands Noss Head Lighthouse; looking
across Sinclair's Bay west of the
lighthouse are the ruins of Castle
Sinclair and Castle Girnigoe, both
destroyed in 17th-century clan wars.
The Wick Heritage Centre (OACT)
near the harbour is devoted to local
history, and the Caithness Factory
(OACT) on Harrow Hill can be
visited. Glass blowing can be observed
here and there is also a shop.

WICKEN FEN
Cambridgeshire *11 TL57*
The nature reserve of Wicken Fen
(NT) consists of three main areas –
Sedge Fen, Adventurers Fen and St
Edmund's Fen – of which the first is
open to the public. Here bird and
insect life can be observed in
conditions little changed from those of
primeval fenland. The 'lodes', ancient
canals which acted both as highways
and as irrigation channels, remain, and
a derelict windmill has been restored
to pump water into the dykes.

WIDECOMBE-IN-THE-MOOR
Devon *2 SX77*
Widecombe is famed for its fair, held
on the second Tuesday in September; a
sign commemorating the well-known
song stands on the village green. The
large 14th-century church of St
Pancras – 'the Cathedral of Dartmoor'
– had its tower struck by lightning in
1638, and it is recorded that several
people were killed in the incident.
Nearby Church House (NT) is a
picturesque building. The village
stands at 800ft, surrounded by the
Dartmoor National Park and with
Hameldown Beacon rising to 1697ft in
the north west. A well-preserved group
of Bronze Age barrows lie to the west.

WIGAN
Gtr Manchester *14 SD50*
Though one of the great industrial
towns of the north, Wigan did not
spring into life in the 19th century; the
Romans had a fort here, and by the
13th century the settlement had
developed sufficiently to merit a royal
charter. The Industrial Revolution
reached the town with the
construction of the Leeds and
Liverpool Canal, and it gradually
developed ironworking, engineering
and textile industries, whilst coal –
discovered here centuries earlier –

Widecombe-in-the-Moor

continued to be mined until 1967,
when the last big colliery closed. It was
in Wigan that William Hesketh Lever
of Lever Brothers began to
manufacture soap in 1886. George
Orwell stayed in Wigan in the 1930s in
order to study life in working-class
Britain. The outcome was *Road to
Wigan Pier*.
  Four miles north west is Standish,
the original home of the Standish
family. The exact birthplace of
Captain Miles Standish is not known;
some believe he was born in **Chorley**,
others believe it was Ormskirk. The
military captain of the *Mayflower*
reinforced the dilemma, alluding to a
family inheritance he had been denied.
The family were also connected with
the **Isle of Man**.

WIGHTWICK MANOR
W Midlands *9 SO89*
Wightwick Manor (NT) (OACT),
though Jacobean in style, was not built
until 1887. Set in terraced gardens
remarkable for their Irish yews and
golden holly trees, it houses a fine
collection of Pre-Raphaelite art,
including work by Rossetti, Burne-
Jones, Ford Madox Brown, Watts,
Ruskin and Millais. Much of the
beautiful stained glass is by
C E Kempe.

WIGMORE
Hereford & Worcester *9 SO46*
Wigmore lies at the heart of the
Mortimer Forest, an area which the

Forestry Commission has been replanting since the 1920s. The hall has a two-storey gabled porch, and the church incorporates some fine Norman herringbone masonry and the Royal Arms of Queen Elizabeth I; between the two buildings runs the village street, with its delightful groups of half-timbered cottages. Nearby stand the mound of a moated 14th-century castle, the seat of the powerful Mortimer family, and the remains of a 12th-century Augustinian abbey.

WIGTOWN
Dumfries & Galloway   *17 NX45*
Wigtown's harbour is now silted up, but the town is still one of the main centres of the Machars Peninsula, an area noted for its fishing and wild-fowling. In the town square stand two crosses – one dating from the 18th century and topped with a sundial, the other from the 19th century. A post at the mouth of the river Bladnoch commemorates the death in 1685 of two women Covenanters, tied to stakes until they were drowned by the rising tide as a punishment for supposedly attending meetings of their sect. A mile to the south west of the town lie the remains of Baldoon Castle, the setting of Scott's *Bride of Lammermoor*, and a Bronze Age circle of 19 stones stands 3 miles north west.

WILLOUGHBRIDGE
Staffordshire   *14 SJ74*
The Dorothy Clive Garden (OACT) is set in a 200-year-old gravel quarry at the top of a small hill. Within the existing woodland framework a mass of azaleas and rhododendrons have been planted, and in the spring the banks are yellow with daffodils. The character of the setting has been enhanced by rock and water gardens.

WILMCOTE
Warwickshire   *10 SP15*
Wilmcote is best known for Mary Arden's Cottage, the lovely old timbered farmhouse in which Shakespeare's mother was born. It is simply furnished in the style of the period and has a huge fireplace with one of the largest ovens in England. The old-fashioned garden contains a dovecote and a cider-mill, and the stone barns house a collection of agricultural implements.

WILMINGTON
E Sussex   *5 TQ50*
The village of Wilmington lies in agricultural country at the foot of the

South Downs, near the point where the famous Long Man (AM) is carved into the chalk. The origin of the figure – about 230ft in height and carrying a staff in each hand – is obscure; though first recorded in 1779 it may date back to the 6th century, and it has been variously attributed to Romans, Saxons and medieval pilgrims. The church is part Norman and part Gothic, with stone ledges where the monks used to sit and a canopied Jacobean pulpit; in the churchyard stands an ancient yew tree, believed to be the oldest in the country, with a trunk 23ft in girth. A cloister once joined the church to a 12th-century Benedictine priory (OACT), the remains of which now house the Sussex Archaeological Society's Agricultural Museum.

WILTON
Wiltshire   *3 SU03*
Wilton is famous for the fine carpets that have been made there since the 17th century. Before that time, however, it was a town of note, the capital of Wessex, set at the point where the Rivers Wylye and Nadder meet. Wilton House (OACT), with its well-known double cube room, was originally Elizabethan; Holbein, Inigo Jones and his son-in-law, John Webb, all contributed to it and the collection of paintings is magnificent. The grounds are noted for their cedars. Nathaniel Hawthorne claimed descent from a William Hathorne of Wilton, who emigrated with Winthrop in 1630. Hathorne eventually settled in Salem, where he was a magistrate and member of the legislature. He commanded actions against the Indians, and was famous for his persecution of the Quakers.

WIMBORNE MINSTER
Dorset   *3 SZ09*
The Minster at Wimborne embraces many architectural styles from Norman to Gothic; its west tower carries an attractive quarter-jack clock, the quarter-hour bells struck by a grenadier bearing a hammer in each hand, and its chained library contains a partly damaged copy of Sir Walter Raleigh's *History of the World* (1634). The Priest's House Museum (OACT) has an interesting display of agricultural implements and a fine collection of horse brasses among its exhibits. A wide variety of birds, including many tropical species, can be seen at Merley Bird Gardens, to the south of the town.

WIMPOLE HALL
Cambridgeshire   *11 TL35*
Wimpole Hall (NT) (OACT) is a large country mansion begun in 1632 by Sir Thomas Chichele but considerably altered in the 18th century; it eventually became the property of Rudyard Kipling's daughter. Of interest are Lord Harley's library and the yellow drawing-room designed by Sir John Soane. The chapel has frescoes by Sir James Thornhill. It was approached, until the advent of Dutch elm disease, by a fine double avenue of elms some $2\frac{1}{2}$ miles long and 100 yards wide, and stands in a park landscaped by Capability Brown, Humphry Repton and Sanderson Miller.

WINCHCOMBE
Gloucestershire   *9 SP02*
This small Cotswold town is rich in interesting buildings – notably the George Inn, with its gallery, and the strangely named Corner Cupboard. The church is adorned with curious gargoyles and contains an embroidered altar cloth on which much of the work was done by Katherine of Aragon. Sudeley Castle (OACT) stands to the south east, rebuilt in the 15th century and restored in the 19th. It houses fine pictures and furniture alongside collections of toys and Victoriana; Catherine Parr, who married the owner of the castle when Henry VIII died, is buried in the chapel. The grounds contain an extensive waterfowl collection. 2 miles north east is Hailes Abbey Museum, the remains of a 13th-century Cistercian abbey. The museum contains relics found on the site.

WINCHELSEA
E Sussex   *6 TQ91*
A new town was built on high land above the River Brede marshes in the 13th century after the old one had been submerged, and it became an Ancient Port, attached to the original Cinque Ports. Winchelsea Museum, located in the restored 14th-century Court Hall, traces the history of these ports. Three of the gates of the original walled town still exist, the Strand Gate being of most interest. Fine workmanship from the Decorated period can be seen in the church, the nave of which was at one time the chancel; 13th-century monuments in the Farnecombe Chantry and the famous Alard tombs are noteworthy. Winchelsea's attractive houses are laid out in a regular pattern – perhaps providing an example of medieval town planning.

WINCHESTER

Hampshire *4 SU42*

King Alfred's Capital
'From the Hill at the Eastern extremity
you see a prospect of Streets, and old
Buildings mixed up with trees. Then
there are the most beautiful streams
about I ever saw – full of Trout.'
John Keats, *Letters*

Already a sizeable town in the Roman
period, Winchester became, under the
Anglo Saxons, the capital of their
kingdom of Wessex, and the place of
coronation and burial of their kings. In
Alfred the Great's reign its influence
grew and it became the capital of
England, a status it retained until after
the Norman Conquest. Although
gradually eclipsed by London,
Winchester retained its importance as
a regional capital and maintained close
links with the Crown until the reign of
Charles II. At the centre of the city
stands the magnificent cathedral, built
by the Normans to replace the one
erected by King Alfred. The crypt,
transepts and part of the cloisters date
from the 11th century; the choir and
Lady Chapel from the 12th century;
the nave and west front were rebuilt in
Perpendicular style in the 14th century.
The bishop at this time was William of
Wykeham, founder of Winchester
College, one of the most famous public
schools in the country, and also
founder of New College at Oxford.
Some of the college buildings can be
visited. They lie just outside the
peaceful Close, which itself contains
several buildings of outstanding
interest. Nearby are the Bishop's
Palace and remains of Wolvesley
Castle, one of Winchester's two
Norman castles. Of the other castle,
only the Great Hall survives, just
outside the Westgate, one of two of the
original five city gates still standing.
Above the other, Kingsgate, is St
Swithun's Chapel. St Swithun,
associated in the traditional rhyme
about rain, was a Saxon bishop of
Winchester, who at his death humbly
asked to be buried outside the door of
the cathedral. His wishes were not at
first carried out, and the result was a
protracted storm which caused his
monks hurriedly to inter him where he
had wished. His shrine in the Norman
cathedral was destroyed at the Reformation, but its site is marked.
  As a city Winchester has remained
compact, the small streets around the
cathedral still containing charming old
houses. In one of these, near
Winchester College, Jane Austen spent
the last months of her life: her
gravestone can be seen in the

cathedral. The main streets, Westgate
and High Street, are spacious and
attractive, lined with buildings of
different periods, and partly
colonnaded. A magnificent 17th-
century clock projects over the street
from the former Guildhall, now a
bank. A curfew bell is still rung from
the turret at 8 pm. In Broadway stands
a statue of King Alfred, near the River
Itchen. The river banks are laid out
with gardens and a pleasant walk leads
alongside the remnants of the city
walls. Here can be seen fragments of
the wall built by the Romans to defend
their settlement of *Venta Belgarum*,
from which the modern city sprang.
  Nine miles north east of Winchester,
at Old Alresford, Admiral Rodney is
buried in the parish church. In 1749
early in his career he was a popular
Governor of Newfoundland.

PLACES TO SEE

Winchester Cathedral Norman,
and all the later Gothic styles can
be seen in this magnificent building
which contains the tombs of many
Saxon kings and queens. Its
treasures include the 12th-century
Winchester Bible, the graves of
Jane Austen and Izaak Walton and
much fine carving. There is a
memorial to Sir George Prevost,
Governor-in-chief of British North
America in the War of 1812.

Pilgrims' Hall One of several fine
buildings in the Close, the hall has a
superb hammerbeam roof.

The City Museum Items of local
historical interest are displayed
here.

Westgate Museum Above the
medieval gate, in a room formerly
used as a prison, is a collection of
weaponry and weights and
measures of the Tudor period.

Serle's House This elegant 18th-
century mansion houses the
Museum of the Royal Hampshire
Regiment. There are many
Canadian associations here.

The Royal Greenjackets Museum is
housed in their barracks just
outside the city centre. Here can be
seen the only Victoria Cross given
for an act of courage in Canada, to
Irishman Timothy O'Hea, in 1866.

The Great Hall (OACT) The only
surviving part of the Norman castle

Gothic nave, Winchester Cathedral

is this austere, aisled hall. On the
wall hangs a massive circle of oak,
held to be King Arthur's legendary
Round Table. It was repainted in
Tudor times by order of Henry VIII
to impress his guest, the Emperor
Charles V. In 1603 Sir Walter
Raleigh was tried and found guilty
of conspiracy here. Sir John
Popham presided.

Winchester College Several of the
old buildings of this famous school
can be visited. Many distinguished
administrators in Canada were
educated here. Reverend John
White was also here.

St Cross Hospital The hospital was
founded in 1136 by Bishop Henry
of Blois, and the adjoining
Almshouses of the Noble Poverty in
1445 by Cardinal Beaufort. The
buildings stand beside the River
Itchen and the old tradition of the
Wayfarer's Dole of bread and beer
is still preserved.

WINDERMERE
Cumbria *18 SD49*
Windermere, the centre of the Lake District National Park, stands to the east of Lake Windermere, which is the largest expanse of fresh water in England. At Brockholes, north west of the town, is the Lake District National Park Visitor Centre. The town is one of England's busiest tourist centres. (see also Bowness).

WING
Buckinghamshire *10 SP82*
Among the modern buildings of this fast-growing village stand many 17th- and 18th-century cottages, and the Dormer Hospital dates from 1569. All Saints Church is noteworthy for its Anglo Saxon crypt, one of only eight remaining in England; of interest, too, is the rare Anglo Saxon apse, set on pilasters. Ascott (NT), on the eastern outskirts of the village, is a mansion dating mainly from the 19th century but incorporating medieval timbers and some Jacobean work. It contains the Anthony de Rothschild collection of pictures, together with fine examples of furniture and oriental porcelain, and is set in fine parkland.

WIRKSWORTH
Derbyshire *15 SK25*
An ancient town, with its steep terraces of stone houses, Wirksworth was once an important lead mining centre, and a unique 16th-century bronze dish which was used as the standard lead measure is preserved in the Moot Hall. Parts of St Mary's Church date back to the 13th century, and it has a wealth of early carving; an inscribed Anglo Saxon coffin lid is thought to be 9th century. Each May the centuries-old ceremony of well-dressing is still observed. The town of Snowfield in George Eliot's *Adam Bede* is probably based on Wirksworth.

WISBECH
Cambridgeshire *11 TF40*
Wisbech is situated in an area renowned for bulb growing and fruit cultivation, and fruit canning is an important local industry. The town stands on the River Nene, 12 miles from the sea – though at one time, before changes in river patterns altered its relation to the Wash, it was only 4 miles away. From the North and South Brinks an impressive array of Georgian houses, several with Dutch characteristics, looks across the quays and the river; the most notable is

Lake Windermere

Peckover House (NT) (OACT), built in the 1720s and displaying some fine rococo plasterwork. Near the bridge is Sir George Gilbert Scott's memorial to Thomas Clarkson, a compaigner for the abolition of slavery whose father was schoolmaster here. The church of Sts Peter and Paul is mainly Norman and Perpendicular, with a fine 16th-century tower. The Wisbech and Fenland Museum contains Clarkson relics and illustrates fenland life.

WISLEY
Surrey *5 TQ05*
The 300-acre grounds and gardens of the Royal Horticultural Society are particularly striking when the azaleas and rhododendrons are in bloom, but at all times of the year there are pleasant walks among trees or beside rock gardens of heath and alpine plants; new varieties of fruit and vegetables are tried out here, and student gardeners are trained. Wisley Pond, surrounded by fir trees, is a well-known beauty spot. A Norman church with a 17th-century timbered porch stands between the River Wey and the Wey Navigation Canal (NT).

WOBURN
Bedfordshire *11 SP93*
18th-century Woburn Abbey, the seat of the Dukes of Bedford, is one of Britain's most famous stately homes. The palatial house contains superb State apartments (where the newly married Victoria and Albert once slept in the four poster State bed) and a magnificent art collection which includes works by Gainsborough, Rembrandt, Reynolds and Van Dyck. Another attraction is the Wild Animal Kingdom and Leisure Park (OACT) surrounding the abbey. Visitors can drive through the monkey jungle and the lion and tiger reserves, take a Boat Safari round the chimpanzees' island, and visit the Dolphinarium.

WOKING
Surrey *5 TQ05*
A residential and commuter town on the restored Basingstoke Canal, Woking developed as a direct result of the coming of the railway in the 1830s. Its most distinctive feature is its large Mosque, built in 1889 and still the centre of Islamic observance in this country. Nearby is Brookwood Cemetery – one of the most extensive in the world, incorporating burial grounds for several London parishes and the graves of many Commonwealth servicemen including over 2500 Canadians. In Pirbright, west of Woking, the African explorer, Henry Morton Stanley, is buried in the churchyard. He was born in 1841 in Wales but went to America when he was 16 years old.

WOLVERHAMPTON
W Midlands *9 SO99*
Wolverhampton's coat of arms includes a cross, ascribed to the Anglo Saxon King Edgar, and a woolpack – but more obviously relevant to the 'Queen of the Black Country' are the flaming brazier and padlock which are also incorporated. Today, not only locks and keys but many kinds of iron and brass components and aircraft parts are manufactured here. The church of St Peter is basically 15th century, with a panelled tower and fine stone pulpit. It was here in 1757 that Butten Gwinnett, a signatory to the Declaration of Independence for Georgia, was married. In the churchyard an ancient carved cross shaft stands near a holed Bargain Stone. 19th-century Bantock House contains a museum of items made by Midland craftsmen. Bilston Museum and Art Gallery also has examples of craftsmanship and English enamels.

WOODBRIDGE
Suffolk *12 TM24*
Woodbridge, a market town on the River Deben, was once a busy seaport; it has a Shire Hall that dates back to the 16th century and several interesting old houses, including a half-timbered one with an old weighing machine attached in New Street. Edward Fitzgerald, translator of *The Rubaiyat of Omar Khayyam*, once lived at Little Grange. The building of the abbey in Church Street began in 1564; the Perpendicular church contains a Seven Sacraments font and part of a 15th-century screen; and the Friends' Meeting House dates from 1678. The famous 18th-century Tide Mill (OACT) on the estuary has now been restored.

WINDSOR

Berkshire *5 SU97*

Royal Stronghold on the Thames
'... and proudly doth pursue
His wood-nymph Windsors seate, her
lovely site to view.
Whose most delightful face when once
the river sees,
Which shewes her selfe attir'd in tall
and stately trees.'

Michael Drayton, *Poly Olbion*,
(15th song)

The castle, on a high chalk ridge overlooking the River Thames, guards the approaches to London and dominates the town whose centre is squeezed into the low ground between the castle walls and the river. In River Street a plaque indicates the birthplace of Robert Keaynes (1595–1655), founder of the Honorable Artillery Company of Massachusetts. The old streets, although attractive in themselves and graced with a number of fine buildings, only serve in summer to funnel the tens of thousands of visitors into the castle precinct. The original Norman round tower now stands at the centre of a multitude of towers, walls, courtyards and apartments added at different times by various kings. In the medieval period, Henry III, and later Edward III, did most to extend and strengthen the fortifications and give the castle its present shape. Edward III is particularly remembered as the instigator of the Order of the Garter, the most prestigious order of knighthood in the country, which he founded at Windsor in 1348. The best known story about the founding is that the king, while dancing with the Countess of Salisbury at Windsor, picked up the garter she had dropped, then quelled his sniggering courtiers with the words that are the motto of the Order: 'Honi soit qui mal y pense', – (evil be to him who evil of it thinks). The Tudor monarchs took over the Plantagenet links with Windsor, and Henry VIII built the impressive gateway now used as the main entrance. Elizabeth I built the North Terrace, which has magnificent views over the Thames valley, as a promenade, and also commanded Shakespeare to write a play for the court at Windsor: the result was *The Merry Wives of Windsor*, in which not only Sir John Falstaff features, but several local personages of that time, such as Master Ford and Mistress Page whose names are recorded in the parish registers. The Garter Inn stands on the site of the Harte and Garter Inn where, in the play, Falstaff and his

Changing the guard at Windsor Castle

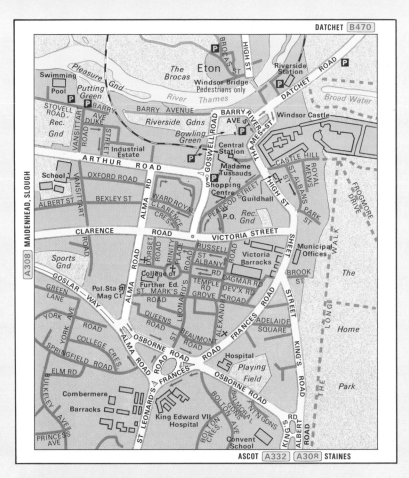

compatriots met to drink.

During the whole of the Civil War Cromwell's forces kept firm control of the castle, which therefore escaped being slighted, the fate of so many British strongholds, and it was to Windsor that his friends secretly brought the body of Charles I for burial in the vaults of St George's Chapel. Charles II often lived at Windsor, and his contribution to the castle was the Long Walk in Windsor Great Park. George IV and Queen Victoria spent much time at Windsor, and Queen Victoria and Prince Albert used the castle both as a family house, and for social occasions and State visits. Her grandson, George V, took Windsor as his family name in 1917, and this decision was ratified by Queen Elizabeth II.

PLACES TO SEE

The Castle Second only to Buckingham Palace as a royal residence, Windsor Castle dates back to Norman times. The State Apartments are magnificent, as is St George's Chapel, the resting place of eight kings, with its superb fan-vaulted ceiling. Queen Mary's Doll's House is an exquisite model house of the 1920s, complete down to the last detail. Works of art and Old Master drawings from the Royal Library are also exhibited in the castle.

The Guildhall A fine 17th-century colonnaded building by Sir Christopher Wren, which contains a small museum of local interest.

The Household Cavalry Museum is housed in Combermere Barracks. It tells the history of the regiment from 1685 to the present day.

Madame Tussaud's Royalty and Empire Exhibition is housed in the Victorian station buildings.

Savill Garden These beautiful woodland gardens occupy a part of Windsor Great Park.

Valley Gardens, famous for rhodo-dendrons and azaleas, link Windsor Great Park to Virginia Water.

Windsor Safari Park and Seaworld A drive-in zoo where animals are kept in conditions as near to a natural habitat as possible.

WOODSTOCK
Oxfordshire   *10 SP41*
Woodstock's 18th-century elegance made this one of the most beautiful small towns in England. Woodstock continues to draw visitors because of its proximity to Blenheim Palace, Sir John Vanbrugh's grandiose masterpiece built for John Churchill, the Duke of Marlborough. The house was begun as a gift from a grateful nation to the Duke after his victory over the French and Bavarians at Blenheim in 1704. There is a Canadian connection in that the Duke had been Governor of the Hudson Bay Company 1685–92. One of its main attractions is the room where Sir Winston Churchill, grandson of the 7th Duke of Marlborough, was born on 30 November, 1874. His mother was the American Jennie Jerome. The parklands were landscaped by Capability Brown, who dammed the River Glyn to make Blenheim's fine lake. The tower of Bladon parish church can be seen through the only break in the parkland's tree-lined vista. In the churchyard are the graves of Sir Winston and his parents Lord and Lady Randolph Churchill.

WOOKEY HOLE
Somerset   *3 ST54*
The River Axe, flowing through the heart of the Mendips, has hollowed out the great caves of Wookey Hole (OACT), inhabited more than 2000 years ago; the higher caverns are crossed by steel bridges which look down on the rushing torrent below. A small museum displays pottery and coins from the Celtic and Roman British periods. The Mill (OACT), which made fine paper by hand in the 17th century, has now been restored and visitors can see the old machinery used for its original purpose. The building also houses the store room of Madame Tussaud's Waxworks, and the disembodied heads of the famous (together with the moulds from which they were made) are on display. Lady Bangor's Fairground Collection includes some beautifully carved and painted figures from the era of steam-driven fairground rides.

WOOLPIT
Suffolk   *12 TL96*
Woolpit's name derives from 'wolf-pit', a pit into which captured wolves were flung before they were killed in Saxon times. The church has a magnificent south porch, reminiscent of a castle gateway, and a fine

hammerbeam roof carved with angels; the 16th-century brass eagle lectern is said to have been a gift from Queen Elizabeth I. The waters of nearby Lady's Well were reputed in the 14th century to cure any ailment. Beside the green is an 18th-century coaching inn, and attractive timber-framed Tudor and Georgian houses are scattered throughout the village.

WOOLSTHORPE
Lincolnshire   *11 SK92*
In 1642 Sir Isaac Newton was born within the grey stone walls of Woolsthorpe Manor (NT). The orchard in front of the house is a reminder of the falling apple reputed to have prompted Newton's realization of the theory of gravitational pull – a theory that revolutionized man's understanding of astronomy.

WORCESTER
Hereford & Worcester   *9 SO75*
This county town and cathedral city stands on the banks of the Severn in an area of rich agricultural land. The cathedral, which overlooks the river and the city's county cricket ground, is mostly Early English in style although the oldest part – the crypt – was built in the 11th century. In the lofty chancel are the tombs of King John, and the elder brother of Henry VIII, Prince Arthur, who died at the age of 15. Unfortunately much of Worcester has been rebuilt over the years but there are still several buildings to note in the old city centre. These include The Commandery and Tudor House which both house museums, Greyfriars – a 15th-century Franciscan house, and the Guildhall. The latter, with its elaborate façade, is one of the finest examples of early Georgian architecture in the country. Worcester has become famous for its porcelain industry which was founded in 1751 as an alternative to the ailing cloth trade. The present factory in Severn Street is open by appointment and the Dyson Perrins Museum next door has the best collection of Worcester porcelain in the world, with pieces dating from 1751 to the present.

WORKSOP
Nottinghamshire   *15 SK57*
Set on the edge of the Midlands coalfield, Worksop is a good base for exploring Sherwood Forest and the Dukeries – the group of neighbouring estates owned by the Dukes of Kingston, Newcastle and Portland.

The twin-towered church of St Mary and St Cuthbert is part of a 12th-century priory and has a fine 13th-century Lady Chapel. The 14th-century gatehouse once housed an elementary school, founded in 1623. The town museum numbers among its exhibits two Bronze Age beakers, found in nearby Clumber Park (NT), once the estate of the Duke of Newcastle. Pilgrim Richard Bernard came from Worksop.

WORSTEAD
Norfolk   *12 TG32*
Flemish weavers settled in East Anglia in the 12th century, and one of the techniques they introduced to the wool trade was the production of a tightly twisted yarn for the manufacture of a firm, hardwearing cloth – worsted, which took its name from this village at the heart of the industry. Until the coming of the Industrial Revolution weaving was carried out in the worker's own home, and several weavers' houses still exist in and around Worstead. St Mary's Church dates from the 14th century, and its tower, rising over 100ft, reflects the prosperity of the weaving era.

WORTHING
W Sussex   *5 TQ10*
Worthing, the largest town in West Sussex, was a small fishing village until Princess Amelia, the youngest daughter of George III, holidayed there in 1798. When society followed her lead the resort expanded to accommodate the influx, and it has continued to grow as the extensive pebble-and-sand beach and attractive South Downs scenery have proved popular with successive generations. In addition to safe bathing, a pier and 4 miles of promenades, the town today offers concert halls and two good theatres. Unusual travelling stocks can be seen in the town museum, and at West Tarring, to the north west, the Museum of Sussex Folklore is housed in three 15th-century cottages belonging to the Sussex Archaeological Trust. Cissbury Ring marks the site of an Iron Age camp dating from about 800 BC.

WORTH MATRAVERS
Dorset   *3 SY97*
Worth Matravers was for centuries an important centre for the quarrying of Purbeck marble (used, notably, in the tower-supports of Salisbury Cathedral), and there are still signs of the workings in the hills around the village. In St Nicholas' churchyard is buried Benjamin Jesty, who inoculated his wife and sons against smallpox in 1774 – 4 years before Edward Jenner's famous report. 2 miles south west of the village is St Aldhelm's Head, affording wide views over a coastal area of outstanding natural beauty. The small, square 12th-century chapel of St Aldhelm was possibly built on the headland as a marker for sailors.

WRAGBY
W Yorkshire   *15 SE41*
Nostell Priory (NT) is a magnificent mansion on the site of a 12th-century Augustinian priory; it was built by James Paine in 1733 and extended by Robert Adam some 30 years later. The village church stands within its park.

WREKIN, THE
Shropshire   *9 SJ60*
The Wrekin, probably the country's oldest hill, lies two miles south of the town of Wellington. Its summit, at 1334ft, is not the highest point in Shropshire, but it offers incomparable views that take in several counties. A beacon fire on this hilltop warned of the coming of the Spanish Armada – and traces of an Iron Age camp indicate that it was recognized as a good defensive site almost 2000 years ago.

WREXHAM
Clwyd   *14 SJ34*
Wrexham lies only 6 miles inside the Welsh border; previously it was part of Mercia, separated from Wales by the Saxon administrative boundary, **Offa's Dyke.** Wrexham became a prosperous industrial centre in the 19th century, important for brickmaking and mining, and for its oldest industry, tanning, supplied with hides by the town's weekly cattle market. Wrexham has two breweries; one has been brewing a lager introduced by a naturalized German family, for over a hundred years. Industry has brought rapid changes to Wrexham, but one feature remains inviolate, the 15th-century church of St Giles. Its tower, ornamented with figures, stands 136ft high and is one of the 'seven wonders of Wales'. The north porch (restored by Yale graduates in 1901) contains the tomb of Elihu Yale, the benefactor of Yale University. The church tower is replicated at Yale; a tablet inside tells Yale's story. Elihu was born in 1649 in Boston, Massachusetts, the son of an emigrant from Wrexham; 3 years later the family returned to Wales. By 1718

The Wrekin

Yale had made his fortune as Governor of the East India Company's colony at Madras. In response to a request for finance from the Reverend Cotton Mather, an early graduate of Yale College, he made a substantial donation. Plas Grono, Yale's Wrexham house, no longer stands, but Erddig Park 2 miles away survives. It is a beautiful Jacobean mansion, with displays illustrating a country squire's life 700 years ago. 14 miles from Wrexham is Plas y Yale, the ancestral home of the family. Wrexham's most infamous resident was Judge Jeffreys, notorious for the Bloody Assizes after the Monmouth Rebellion in 1745, whose sentences resulted in hundreds hanged or transported to the colonies. 3 miles north, the peal of Gresford's 12 church bells is another of the 'Welsh wonders'. The churchyard has one of the oldest and largest yews in Britain. Gresford was Washington Irving's setting for 'the Angler' in his *Sketch Book*.

WROXETER
Shropshire   *9 SJ50*
Wroxeter, on the ancient highway of Watling Street, contains the remains of the roman settlement of *Viroconium* (AM), which was established as an army camp about the middle of the 2nd century, and when the garrison moved north a new town grew up, probably remaining inhabited until the 8th. The site was excavated in the 1920s, and finds are exhibited in the local museum and in Rowley's House in Shrewsbury. Some Roman material can be seen in the church – though the workmanship is Saxon – and the columns flanking the entrance to the churchyard are Roman.

WYE
Kent   *6 TR04*
This quaint town, rich in interesting old buildings, was the birthplace in

1640 of the Restoration dramatist Aphra Behn. Wye College is part of the University of London and specializes in research to improve the standards of British farming; some of its buildings date back to the 15th century, and an old barn houses an agricultural museum. 1 mile to the north stands Olantigh Towers – built in the 18th century, then rebuilt in the same style after being almost totally destroyed by fire in 1903, and now a summer venue for music festivals. A crown cut into the chalk of the Downs to the east commemorates the coronation of King Edward VII.

WYMONDHAM
Leicestershire *10 SK81*
Wymondham has an Early English church displaying some fine carving in the nave and containing a 14th-century effigy of a knight. The 17th-century grammar school is now used as a parish room. It is said that Stilton cheeses were originally made here and then taken to Stilton to be sold to travellers using the Great North Road.

WYMONDHAM
Norfolk *12 TG10*
The parish church of this delightful country town (pronounced 'Windham') was originally part of a Benedictine abbey; it has a tower at each end and contains a fine hammerbeam roof and terracotta sedilia. Nearby stands Sir Thomas Becket's Well, once a shrine frequented by pilgrims. The 14th-century Green Dragon in Church Street was one of the few medieval buildings to survive the great fire that swept through Wymondham in 1615 and is among the oldest inns in the country. The timbered 17th-century market cross (AM), raised on wooden pillars, stands at the centre of the town, and in the streets nearby are many old buildings.

Market cross, Wymondham market place

YAXLEY
Cambridgeshire *11 TL19*
One must turn off the main road of this large and busy village to find the interesting buildings – a thatched inn, black and white thatched cottages, 17th- and 18th-century houses – and the green with its old pump. St Peter's Church dates back to the 13th century and has a beautiful steeple supported by flying buttresses; the font is original, and a fine oak chancel screen is 15th century. To the south east lies Holme Fen Nature Reserve, in what is believed to be the lowest land in England – 8–10ft below sea-level in some places.

YEALAND CONYERS
Lancashire *18 SD57*
An attractive village of traditional stone houses, Yealand Conyers is separated from Morecambe Bay by a limestone ridge. Its Quaker Meeting House dates from 1692, the year that George Fox, the founder of the movement, first preached in this part of the country. Neo-Gothic Leighton Hall (OACT) has an interesting collection of early Gillow furniture (**see** Carnforth).

YEALMPTON
Devon *2 SX55*
The Devon Shire Horse Farm (OACT) at Dunstone recaptures the atmosphere of a bygone era, the work on its 60 acres – devoted mainly to cattle and sheep – being done by these great horses. Kitley Caves (OACT), on the banks of the Yealm, offer the chance to explore floodlit caves and lime kilns.

YELVERTON
Devon *2 SX56*
Yelverton stands on the southern boundary of **Dartmoor National Park**, between the Rivers Walkham and Meavy. The Paperweight Centre (OACT) exhibits some 800 examples, both antique and modern, many of which are for sale.

YEOVIL
Somerset *3 ST51*
Traditionally a market town serving a prosperous agricultural area, Yeovil is

now a busy industrial centre, still engaged in the 300-year-old craft of glove-making but also known as home of one of the world's foremost helicopter constructors. Much of the town is built of the honey-coloured Ham limestone which is quarried locally.

YEOVILTON
Somerset *3 ST52*
The Fleet Air Arm Museum at the Royal Naval air station illustrates the development of aviation at sea from 1903, containing over 50 restored planes and numerous engines, models and photographs. A new exhibition hall housing Concorde 002 follows the progress of passenger supersonic flight.

YORKSHIRE DALES
N Yorkshire *19 SE08*
The greater part of the Yorkshire Dales, which cover a 700-sq-mile stretch from the industrial area around Leeds to the River Tees, has been formed into a National Park. Teesdale, famous for its High Force waterfall, is the most northerly of the Dales. Swaledale and Wensleydale – known for its cheese – are linked by Buttertubs Pass. Wharfedale, wild and bare in its upper reaches, becomes exceptionally beautiful between Kilnsey Crag and **Bolton Abbey**. Nidderdale takes in several reservoirs and How Stean Gorge, whilst the spectacular scenery of Airedale includes 300ft Malham Cove and Gordale Scar.

YOXFORD
Suffolk *12 TM36*
Yoxford, surrounded by the parklands of Cockfield Hall, Rookery Park and Grove Park, is known locally as 'the garden of Suffolk'. Cockfield Hall (not open) was built during the reign of Henry VIII; the central block was rebuilt early in the 17th century and the Great Hall added in the 19th. The main street of the village contains attractively timbered, balconied and bow-windowed houses, whilst St Peter's Church has a large number of brasses. 4 miles to the east lies the National Nature Reserve of Westleton Heath.

YORK

N Yorkshire *15 SE65*

Capital of the Roman province of Lower Britain, the Roman settlement of *Eboracum*, the forerunner of present-day York, became one of the most important cities in the Roman empire. Both Hadrian and Constantine stayed at York, and when the latter died there in AD 306, his son – who became known as Constantine the Great – was proclaimed emperor from York, the only Roman emperor to be proclaimed in Britain. After the Romans departed the city suffered a decline in its fortunes, although

Saxons made it the capital of their kingdom of Deira, but when the Danes invaded and settled in the north east of England, they built it up into an important centre: from their name, *Jorvic*, is derived the modern name of York. The Danish influence has also survived in many of the old street names, such as Goodramgate, Micklegate and Walmgate, while from the Roman period only some parts of the walls, and the multangular tower still stand.

When the Normans came, they

sacked York, but it rose again as a great medieval city, encircled by massive walls, the greater part of which still stand, pierced by the medieval gateways of Micklegate Bar, Bootham Bar, Monk Bar and Walmgate. The circuit of the walls is about 3 miles, and a walk around them takes about 2 hours, but offers magnificent views of the old town and the minster. Within the old walls, the medieval street pattern was a maze of lanes and alleys, some of them so narrow that the overhanging upper

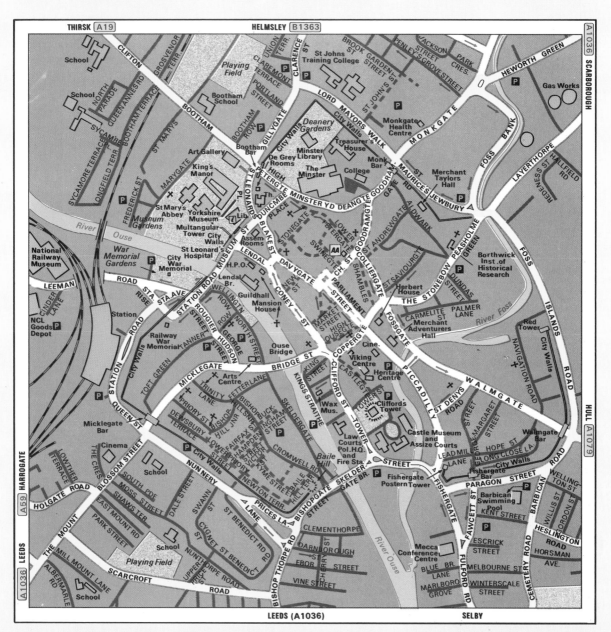

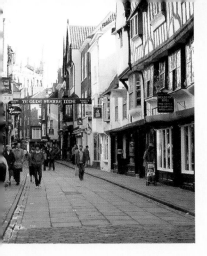

Stonegate

storeys of the buildings almost touched across the streets. A well-preserved example of such a street is the Shambles, formerly the butchers' quarter, but now colonized by antique and tourist shops.

York Minster, built between about 1220 and 1470 is one of the greatest cathedral churches in the country and, as an archbishopric, ranks second to Canterbury. The south transept is the oldest part, then came the octagonal chapter house, the nave, the choir, and the west towers. The massive crossing tower was the last part to be completed, in 1480, and was a replacement for an earlier tower that had collapsed. More than half of England's surviving medieval stained glass is contained in the windows of the minster. Eighty of them were removed for safety during World War II, and this enabled them to be cleaned and properly repaired. The great east window is almost the size of a tennis court, and the lovely west window is known as the 'Heart of Yorkshire'. Although the minster is magnificently preserved, thanks to extensive restoration work in recent times, lightning did damage it severely in 1985.

Throughout Tudor, Stuart and Georgian times, York continued to flourish and handsome buildings of all these periods can be seen in its streets. With the coming of the railway age, York became a busy railway centre and its fine Victorian railway station is a monument to the age of prosperity. In the 1960s, York became a university city; the university buildings, grouped around a lake, are attractively modern.

There are a number of American associations. In 1924, as a token of friendship, the city of New York gave a plaque which is placed in the 15th-century Guildhall. Richard Nicolls gave New York its name, after the Duke of York, later James II. John Woolman, an American Quaker and early anti-slaver, born in 1720, is buried in the Friend's Burial Ground. He died of smallpox. His journal is famous. Roger Morris, a Loyalist, who had earlier fought the French alongside Washington, is buried in St Saviour's Church, as is his wife Mary, object of Washington's attention before her marriage. The poet W H Auden, who emigrated to America in 1939, was born in York in 1907. Lindley Murray, the noted Pennsylvanian grammarian born in 1745 came to York in 1785.

PLACES TO SEE

Borthwick Institute of Historical Research (OACT) This late 15th-century Guildhall houses part of York University's collection of documents and archives.

Castle Museum An outstanding folk museum, with reconstructed streets of shops.

City Art Gallery European Old Master paintings are the nucleus of an interesting collection.

Guildhall This 15th-century building has a fine timbered roof and an underground passage.

King's Manor Once the home of the Abbot of St Mary's Abbey, this largely 17th-century building is now part of the university.

Merchant Adventurers' Hall (OACT) One of the most important of York's medieval, timber-framed houses, this once belonged to the Company of Merchant Adventurers.

National Railway Museum Displays and historic locomotives tell the history of railway engineering.

Treasurer's House (OACT) Fine paintings and furniture decorate this 17th- to 18th-century house.

York Castle Clifford's Tower is all that remains of the castle built by the Normans.

York Story An exceptionally interesting Heritage Centre, with audio-visual displays and exhibitions of crafts.

Yorkshire Museum and Gardens Roman, medieval and natural history collections are housed here. In the grounds are the ruins of St Mary's Abbey, some remains of the Roman wall and multangular tower, and St Leonard's Hospital.

Z

ZEAL MONACHORUM
Devon *2 SS70*
The unusual name of this River Yeo village was originally Sele Monacor – 'the place among the sallow (willow) trees belonging to the monks' (of Buckfast). It stands in a lonely spot 400ft above sea-level and to the north of the **Dartmoor National Park**. The twisting main street is lined with thatch-and-cob cottages, and the churchyard contains two interesting crosses.

ZENNOR
Cornwall *1 SW43*
The village, named after St Senara, stands on rock strewn uplands; the sea is less than a mile away and there is fine coastal scenery with bathing from sandy coves. On a bench-end in the 15th-century church is the famous carving of a mermaid reputed to have lured the squire's son into the sea after hearing him sing. A curious totem pole outside the Gurnard Head Hotel was carved from a telegraph pole by a Canadian sculptor. Incorporated into the design are many Cornish symbols and the carved head of Tom Hulking Horne, a famous master of Cornish wrestling. The Wayside Cottage Folk Museum (OACT) illustrates Cornish life and archaeology, displaying household, farming and mining equipment, together with a cottage kitchen and open hearth. A rare Iron Age beehive hut is $1\frac{1}{2}$ miles south west of the village at Bosporthennis, and a Neolithic dolmen known as the Zennor Quoit lies 1 mile to the south east.

Motoring Tours

Epping Forest and the Roding Valley
89 miles

From **Woodford Green** take the Epping Road A104 and in ¾ mile turn left on to A110 (SP N. Chingford). In ¾ mile turn right into Forest Side (no sign). At the end right again into Rangers Road (A1069) and pass Queen Elizabeth's Hunting Lodge. After ¾ mile turn left on to A104. In 1¼ miles at the roundabout turn left, (SP High Beach), then bear right (SP King's Oak) for High Beach. Here turn right, and in 1 mile cross a main road and M11: later turning right (SP Epping) for Upshire. On reaching B1393 turn left, and in 1 mile turn left again on to B182 (SP Roydon). In 1¼ miles turn left on to B181, then in ¾ mile left again to Epping Green and **Roydon**. Here turn left (SP Hertford) and on reaching A414 turn right (SP Chelmsford). In 3 miles keep forward for High Wych. Later turn left, A1184, and enter **Sawbridgeworth** where, turn right for **Hatfield Heath**. Here turn right on to A1060, and shortly left (SP Takeley) on to B183. At **Hatfield Broad Oak** keep left, then in 1¼ miles turn left (SP Hatfield Forest). Drive past the country park, then turn right on A120 for **Takeley**. At the traffic lights turn left (SP Broxted); in 1½ miles turn right, and in 1¼ miles right again into Molehill Green. Drive to Broxted, then join B1051 and continue to Thaxted. Here turn left on to B184 and at the end turn right to rejoin B1051 for **Great Sampford**. Turn right on to B1053 and drive to **Finchingfield** where, turn right on to B1057 for **Great Bardfield**. Here turn right (SP Dunmow). After 6¾ miles turn left on to B184 for **Great Dunmow**. Follow Chelmsford signs and in ¾ mile turn

right on to B184 (SP Ongar), through High Roding to **Leaden Roding**. Here turn right on to A1060 then in 1 mile left to rejoin B184 and continue to **Fyfield**. In 2½ miles at the roundabout go forward on to A128 for **Chipping Ongar**. At the end turn right (SP Greensted). In 1 mile pass Greensted Ch. and in ½ mile turn left (SP Stanford Rivers). After 1¼ miles at the

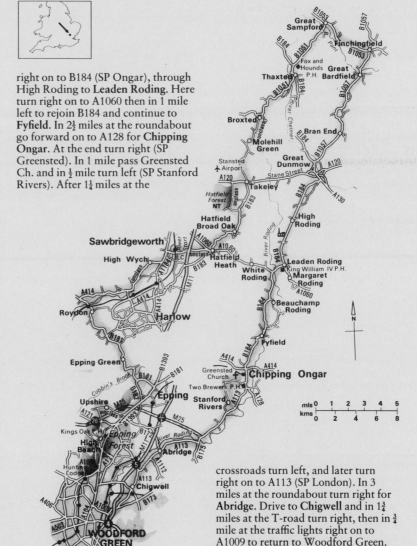

crossroads turn left, and later turn right on to A113 (SP London). In 3 miles at the roundabout turn right for **Abridge**. Drive to **Chigwell** and in 1¾ miles at the T-road turn right, then in ¾ mile at the traffic lights right on to A1009 to return to Woodford Green.

257

Riverside Towns of the Cam and Ouse
79 miles

Leave **Cambridge** following A45 Bedford signs on A1303. In 2½ miles pass the American Cemetery, then at the roundabout take the 3rd exit to **Madingley**. Continue, turning left on to the A604 and in 2 miles branch left on to B1050 SP Chatteris. At the roundabout go right to stay with B1050 to **Longstanton**, where turn left for **Willingham**. Keep forward with B1050 and then turn left on to A1123 into **Earith**. Continue through Needingworth and in 1¼ miles follow town-centre signs into **St Ives**.

Follow Cambridge signs, cross the river and in ¼ mile turn right to **Hemingford Grey**. Turn left into Braggs Lane and right, drive to Hemingford Abbots and follow signs for Huntingdon to join A604. In 1 mile branch left, then turn right at a roundabout to reach **Godmanchester**. Branch right on to B1043 and cross the river to enter **Huntingdon**.

Follow signs Kettering (A604) from the ring road to leave on A141. Pass Hinchingbrooke House and continue on A141 turning left at the roundabout to **Brampton**. Follow signs for London and in 2 miles join A1 and take the 2nd left turning to **Buckden**. At the roundabout take B661 (SP Kimbolton). Continue to **Great Staughton**, then

turn left on to the A45. Continue into **St Neots**.

Leave the town by turning right (SP Little Barford) on to the B1043. At the roundabout take the 1st exit, B1046 (SP The Gransdens), then turn next right into Potton Rd, and in a mile bear left to Abbotsley. In 1½ miles turn

right and left to **Great Gransden**, pass the Crown and Cushion PH and turn left (SP Industrial Estate). At the roundabout left again to **Caxton** and turn right then left (SP Toft, Bourn). Pass Bourn Postmill and in 1 mile turn right at a T-junction to drive through **Bourn**, then join B1046. Continue to Barton, then turn left on to A603. Cross M11 then take 3rd exit at the roundabout and continue through **Grantchester**, then cross the River Cam and drive to **Trumpington**. Here join A1309 and return to Cambridge.

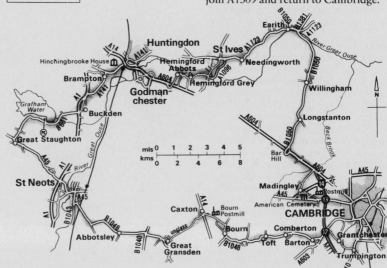

The Undiscovered Cotswolds
58 miles

Take the A361 Swindon road from **Banbury** to **Bloxham**, turning left at the end of the village on to the Adderbury road, then left again into Milton road. Skirt Milton, and in a mile turn left for **Adderbury**, where turn left on to A423 and at traffic lights right onto A41 SP Aylesbury. Three-quarters of a mile beyond **Aynho** branch right onto B4031 SP Buckingham for **Croughton**, and 2 miles beyond the village turn left on to A43 **Brackley** road. Keep on through the town and in ¾ mile turn left SP Helmdon and **Sulgrave**. At Helmdon turn left for Sulgrave. Entrance to the manor house is on the right, but continue on the Culworth road and in 1 mile turn right on to B4525, then in ½ mile left SP Culworth. At T-junction turn left again to reach **Culworth**. In 1¾ miles turn right, cross a bridge, then in ½ mile turn left for **Chipping Warden**. Join the Banbury road, A361, to **Wardington** and 1 mile further turn right for **Cropredy**. At the Brasenose Arms turn right and in ¼ mile turn left SP Mollington. Cross a staggered crossroads to reach **Mollington** and

carry on to **Warmington**. Bear left to cross the green and on reaching the top of the hill, turn left on to A41, then sharp right past the church on to B4086 SP Kineton. After 2 miles turn left at T-junction SP Edge Hill. In 1¼ miles reach A422 and turn right SP Stratford (a short detour to the left on A422 leads to Upton House). Take the next left, SP Compton Wynyates, and after 3½ miles at crossroads turn left SP Banbury. One mile further turn left on

to B4035 through Swalcliffe and Tadmarton to **Broughton**. Turn left SP North Newington and bear right to pass the entrance to Broughton Castle. Bear right again and in ½ mile turn left for **North Newington**. At the end of the village turn right SP Wroxton, then in 1¼ miles turn right on to A422 to skirt the village. Continue through Drayton for the return journey to Banbury.

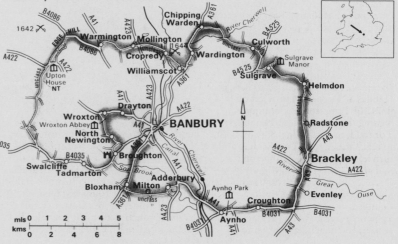

258

Land's End and Penwith
43 miles

From **Penzance**, take A3077 (SP Newlyn, Mousehole) and drive to **Newlyn**, cross the bridge and turn left (unclassified) on to the coast road to **Mousehole**. Turn left for the harbour, then right and right again (SP Paul). At **Paul**, pass the church and in ½ mile turn left on to B3315. In 2½ miles pass a road (left) to Lamorna Cove, and in 3¼ miles turn left and descend (hairpin bend) then ascend to **Treen**. Stay on B3315 and in ¾ mile pass the turning (left) for Porthcurno and Minack Theatre. After another ½ mile turn right, and 2¼ miles further turn left on to A30 to reach Land's End. Return along A30 and carry on to **Sennen**. In 1¾ miles turn left on to B3306 (SP St Just) then in 3 miles turn left again on to A3071 and drive to St Just (Cape Cornwall can be reached from here). Continue on B3306, the St Ives road, and drive through Pendeen and Morvah, skirting Zennor, to **St Ives**. Leave the village on A3074, pass through Carbis Bay, and at **Lelant** turn right, then in ½ mile at the mini-roundabout go forward (SP Penzance). At the main road turn right on to A30 and drive to Crowlas. Continue on A30 and in 1 mile at the roundabout take the 2nd exit (SP Marazion). Cross the railway bridge

for **Marazion**, from where St Michael's Mount can be visited. (A detour can be made to Goldsithney and the Wonderful World of Mechanical

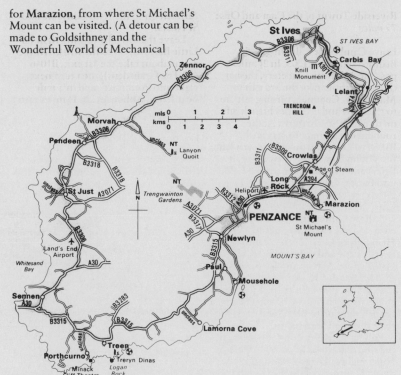

Music by continuing on the Helston road, then on B3280.) Return and cross the railway. Bear left (SP Penzance). At Long Rock, turn left on to A30 and follow the coastline of Mounts Bay for the return to Penzance.

Dartmoor's Eastern Edge
48 miles

Leave **Ashburton** on an unclassified road (SP Buckland). From **Buckland-in-the-Moor** follow signs to Widecombe. Cross the river and at the T-junction turn right. In 1 mile enter **Widecombe-in-the-Moor**. Take the Bovey Tracey road, bearing right past the green. Descend the Bovey Valley and in 3 miles at cross-roads by Edgemoor Hotel turn left and in ½ mile left again onto B3344, SP Manaton. Continue to **Manaton**. Pass the church and in ¾ mile at a T-junction, turn right on to North Bovey road and in 1½ miles cross the river into **North Bovey**. Turn left to leave the village and in ¼ mile bear right (SP Princetown). Recross the river, climb sharply and bear right. In 1¼ miles at T-junction turn left on to B3212 SP Princetown. Continue, passing the Grimspound/Hameldown Tor road, to **Postbridge**. Stay on B3212 to reach the edge of **Two Bridges** and turn left on to B3357 Ashburton road and after 4¼ miles descend sharply to Dartmeet bridge, then climb steeply to Sharp Tor and continue to **Poundsgate**. Descend to cross the river at New Bridge and enter Holne Chase woods. In ½ mile turn right on to

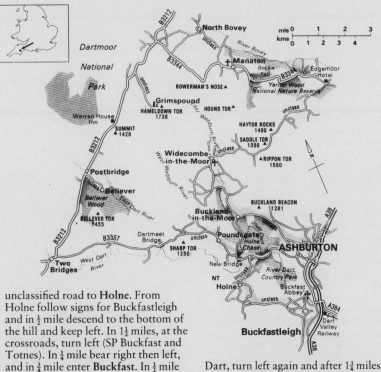

unclassified road to **Holne**. From Holne follow signs for Buckfastleigh and in ½ mile descend to the bottom of the hill and keep left. In 1½ miles, at the crossroads, turn left (SP Buckfast and Totnes). In ¼ mile bear right then left, and in ¾ mile enter **Buckfast**. In ½ mile at the T-junction turn left (right leads to Buckfastleigh). Cross the River

Dart, turn left again and after 1¾ miles at T-junction turn left on to B3357, then right to return to Ashburton.

The Eastern Weald of Kent
70 miles

Leave **Hastings** on A21 following 'London' signs and in 1½ miles at the traffic lights join B2159 (SP Battle). After 2 miles, at the junction with A2100, bear left for **Battle**, pass the square, then turn right on an unclassified road to **Whatlington**. Beyond the village join A21 (SP Hurst Green). In ½ mile turn right on to B2090 (SP Tenterden, Northiam), then right again on to B2089. At **Cripp's Corner** turn left on to B2165 (SP Staplecross). Here go forward on to the unclassified Bodiam road. Leave **Bodiam** by the Hawkhurst road and in about 1 mile turn right on to A229. At **Hawkhurst** traffic lights turn left on to A268 and drive to **Flimwell**, then turn right on to A21 London road and in about ¾ mile turn right again on to B2079 to **Goudhurst**. From here follow A262 Ashford road for 1¾ miles, then turn right on to B2085 (SP Hawkhurst) and in another 1¾ miles turn left (SP Cranbrook). Reach the main road and turn left and right for the town centre. Drive through **Cranbrook** and join A229 for ¼ mile, then turn right on to A262 (SP Ashford) and drive to **Sissinghurst**, then **Biddenden**. At the end of the village turn right and in ¾ mile branch right for **Benenden** and **Iden Green**. Two miles past Iden Green turn left on to A268 for **Sandhurst**, then **Newenden** where the route joins A28. After the level crossing bear right (SP Hastings), drive to **Northiam**, then branch left for **Beckley** and then turn right on to B1268 for Rye. Leave **Rye** by A259 Hastings road and in 2 miles bear right then turn left for **Winchelsea**. Return through the town's Strandgate and turn right on to A259 and right again for **Winchelsea Beach**. Follow the coast to **Fairlight**, and past the turning for Fire Hills Country Park rejoin A259 to return to Hastings.

Shakespeare Country
47 miles

Leave **Stratford** on A439 (SP Evesham); presently cross over a level-crossing and pass Shottery Road, right, to Anne Hathaway's cottage. Continue on A439 and later skirt Bidford-on-Avon. Pass through Salford Priors, then in 1¼ miles turn right (unclassified) to **Harvington**. Here turn right (SP The Lenches), then cross the main road and drive through part of the Vale of Evesham to **Church Lench**. Here turn right to reach Rous Lench, and continue towards Inkberrow for 1 mile then at the T-junction turn right (SP Alcester) and after 1½ miles left for Abbots Morton. Bear right through **Abbots Morton**, then in ¾ mile at the T-junction, turn left and in 1½ miles, right, on to A441 for ½ mile, then left (SP Birmingham) on to A435. Pass (left) the entrance to Ragley Hall and continue to **Alcester**. Leave by the Birmingham road (shortly, a detour along the Droitwich road, B4090, can be made to Pleck Gardens). Remain on A435 through Coughton and **Studley**. Here, at the end of the town, go forward at the roundabout then in 2 miles at the next roundabout turn right on to B4095 for **Henley-in-Arden**. At Henley turn right on to A34, the Stratford road, and drive to **Wootton Wawen**. Here take the Alcester road, B4089 (right), then in 2 miles branch left (SP Aston Cantlow), cross the river and turn right for **Aston Cantlow**. Drive through the village, then turn left (SP Wilmcote) and a mile further, again left and continue into **Wilmcote**. Here turn left (SP Stratford) and on reaching the junction with A34 turn right for the return to Stratford-upon-Avon.

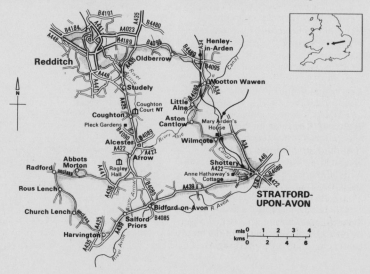

In the Lee of the Cheviot Hills
55 miles

Follow signs Morpeth then **Bamburgh**, to leave Alnwick by the B1340. Through **Denwick**, turn right SP Longhoughton. On reaching B1339 turn left to reach **Longhoughton**. One mile further turn right and in ½ mile go forward on unclassified road SP Howick. By Howick Hall entrance turn right and in ¼ mile keep on for Craster, later bearing left to reach coast. In 1½ miles, at crossroads, turn right and pass through an archway. At T-junction turn right for **Craster**. Return for ½ mile on same road, then follow SP Embleton. In ½ mile turn right and right again at T-junction. At **Embleton** keep left, then right at church onto B1339 SP Beadnell. In 1¼ miles go forward onto B1340 and in 1½ miles turn right. At crossroads turn right again to **Beadnell** and follow coast to **Seahouses**. Here turn right then left at war memorial for **Bamburgh**. Here branch right with B1342 SP Belford. In 2½ miles turn left at T-junction, cross level crossing and 1 mile further turn right onto A1 for

Belford. Here turn left onto unclassified road. In 3 miles turn right at T-junction onto B6348 SP Chatton. At end of village turn left SP Chillingham (and left at Post Office for castle). Return to road, joining B6346 to **Eglingham**. On village outskirts turn right SP Powburn, then branch left SP Glanton. Turn right and 1st left for **Whittingham**. Cross River Aln and turn right for Callaly Castle, skirting the grounds, and keeping left for Thropton and Rothbury. 2½ miles further turn left; outside **Thropton** turn left (SP Rothbury) at T-junction onto B6341. Keep on through town then bear right SP Morpeth onto B6334. In 3½ miles detour to Brinkburn Priory Church. 1½ miles further on, turn left SP Coldstream to join A697. At Longframlington turn right onto B6354 to **Felton**. Here turn right SP Morpeth, cross the Coquet and in ¼ mile turn left for Acklington and **Broomhill**, then left onto A1068, SP Alnwick for **Amble**. Turn left and follow signs Alnwick. After 1½ miles turn right at T-junction into **Warkworth**. In 3½ miles at roundabout go forward for Alnwick.

Dumfries and Galloway
88 miles

Leave **Kirkcudbright** on A755 via Bridge Street, and cross the River Dee, following signs for Gatehouse of Fleet. In 4½ miles turn left on to A75 (SP Stranraer). Continue through **Gatehouse of Fleet** and past Cardoness Castle. Continue on A75 passing Carsluith Castle on the left, and enter **Creetown**. Leave on A75 and in 3½ miles reach Palnure. (On the right, the dead-end road leads to Bargaly Glen and part of Galloway Forest Park.) Drive on for 3 miles, and at the roundabout, take the third exit, A714, to enter **Newton Stewart**. Leave Newton Stewart following signs for New Galloway, cross the Cree Bridge, and enter **Minnigaff**. Drive for 1 mile beyond the village and turn left on to A712 (SP New Galloway). Continue for 6 miles and pass Murray's Monument and in 4½ miles pass Clatteringshaws Loch, then in 6 miles turn right on to A762 into **New Galloway**. Continue on A762 (SP Kirkcudbright) pass Loch Ken and continue through Laurieston to Ringford. At **Ringford** turn left on to A75 (SP Dumfries). In 3½ miles, cross the River Dee, and a mile further, pass a track that leads left to Threave Castle. In another ½ mile a detour can be made by taking an unclassified right turn to Threave Gardens. On the main route, continue to **Castle Douglas**.

Leave on A745 (SP Dalbeattie), and in 5 miles join the Auchencairn road, A711. To the left is the market town of **Dalbeattie**. Continue along A711 passing through Palnackie, Auchencairn and Dundrennan to complete the return journey to Kirkcudbright.

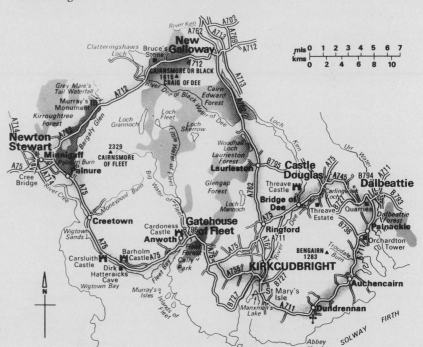

Stirling and the Trossachs
88 miles

Leave **Stirling** by the Crianlarich road, A84, and at the M9 roundabouts take the 2nd and then 3rd exits. Cross the River Forth, and after 3 miles pass the road (right) to Blair Drummond Safari Park. In 2½ miles, turn left on to B8032 (SP Deanston), then bear left (SP Callander). After 6¼ miles turn right on to B822 and right again (no signs) on to A81 and proceed to **Callander**. From here follow Crianlarich signs, A84, pass through the hamlet of **Kilmahog**, then turn left on to A821 (SP Aberfoyle, the Trossachs). Drive alongside Loch Venachar to **Brig o'Turk** and then continue into the Queen Elizabeth Forest Park. Pass the Trossachs Hotel (in ¼ mile a detour can be made by keeping forward to the pier on the eastern end of Loch Katrine where pleasure-steamer trips run during summer). The main drive turns left on the Aberfoyle road through the forest to **Aberfoyle** (where a detour can be taken along B829 to Inversnaid on Loch Lomond – 28 miles round trip). The main drive continues on the Stirling road, A821, then after a mile branches left on to A81, SP Callander. Pass the Lake of Menteith and in 1 mile turn right, SP Arnprior, on B8034. (By Menteith Church there is a passenger ferry to Inchmaholme Priory on an island in the lake.) At **Arnprior**

turn right on to A811, then left on to an unclassified road, SP Fintry. At **Fintry** turn right (no sign) on to B818, then in 5½ miles join the Glasgow road, A875, and pass through Killearn. Two miles further turn left on to A81 and drive through Blanefield to the edge of **Strathblane**, then turn left on to A891 (SP Lennoxtown). At **Lennoxtown** turn left (SP Fintry) on to B822, and start the ascent on to the Campsie

Fells. The road crosses the moors, then descends to the valley of Endrick Water, where the drive turns right on to B818 (SP Denny). Continue along the valley, then in 7¾ miles at the Carron Bridge Inn turn left (unclassified, SP Stirling), and after about 4 miles turn left and later cross the M9. In ¾ mile turn right and left on to A872 at Bannockburn, then join A9 for the return to Stirling.

Inverness and the Moray Firth
89 miles

Leave **Inverness** on the Perth road (A9) and in 1½ miles at the roundabout take the 3rd exit on to B9006 (SP Croy) to reach Culloden Moor. Shortly after the Information Centre turn right (SP Clava Cairns), go over the next crossroads, cross the River Nairn and turn right. One mile after the Cairns turn right (SP Daviot) and in 3¼ miles turn left on to B9154 for **Moy**. Drive on past Loch Moy and later turn left on to A9. In 9 miles turn left on to A938 for **Carrbridge**. Leave by the Grantown road and in 1¾ miles turn left on to B9007 (SP Forres). Drive across the moors for 6¼ miles then turn right (SP Lochindorb) to reach the shore of the loch, with its ruined castle on an island. Carry on to the junction with A939, then turn left (SP Forres) then right on to A940 and continue to **Forres**. Leave by the Inverness road (A96) and drive through **Brodie** to **Auldearn** and then to **Nairn**. Leave by B9090 (SP Cawdor) and continue to **Cawdor**. Beyond the village, in 1¼ miles turn right then cross the River Nairn, go over the next crossroads (SP

Ardersier) and keep on with B9006 and cross the main road to reach **Ardersier**. From here, B9096 leads to Fort George. From Ardersier turn left with B9039 to

follow the Moray Firth coast. On reaching the junction with A96 turn right to return to Inverness.

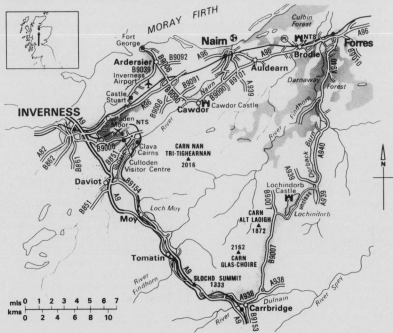

USEFUL INFORMATION

Travel in the UK

Car Hire: Can be arranged through your travel agent with the larger, nationwide car hire firms. The travel agent will be able to obtain the best budget deals, as well as arranging the most convenient pick up point, and one-way drop off – you leave the car where you want rather than bringing it back to where you started. But for spontaneous decisions when you are in the UK there are plenty of local car hire firms in any city or town, even some villages. Major car hire companies have offices in some airports and railway stations too. For an arrangement made in this country, an average (1986) price for a small saloon with unlimited mileage, all inclusive and plus VAT is @£16 per day/£89 per week. For an automatic on the same terms @ £25 per day/£135 per week.

* The American driving license is acceptable.
* Car insurance for third party fire and theft is included in the cost. Fully comprehensive insurance can be arranged for a little extra.
* Many of the larger car hire firms offer breakdown service coverage through the AA or RAC in the price. If the car hire firm does not have this coverage, both the AA, and RAC have a reciprocal coverage agreement with members of Triple A, on presentation of your membership card.
* Road signs are uniform throughout the UK, are mostly pictorial, and plentiful. A copy of the Highway Code can be obtained for about £1 from any sizeable newsagent, and this lists road signs as well as outlining UK road usage.

British Rail: Operates a network of regular intercity services on high speed trains, as well as local services. There are many bargain price tickets, and your American travel agent should be able to arrange these for you.

Coaches: National Express offer nationwide intercity services in up-to-date coaches, many with air-conditioning, hostess service and toilets. Travel can only be arranged in the UK, either at the coach station for immediate travel, or by phone allowing six working days before travelling. National Express offers a Tourist Trail ticket for overseas visitors: 15 days unlimited travel for £75 (1986 price).

By Air: As well as from London's Gatwick and Heathrow airports, many of the other smaller airports have scheduled internal flights, for example Bristol, Cardiff, East Midlands, Edinburgh, Exeter, Glasgow, Luton, Manchester, Newcastle, including to the Scilly Isles and the Channel Islands.

By Water: Coastal ferry services run to and from the Continent and Ireland and the islands around the coast. Another pleasant and peaceful way to see the backwaters and byways, however, is by canal. You can hire traditional long boats or other pleasure boats. For further information contact your travel agent.

Public Transport: Is gradually going private, particularly in rural areas. Buses and, in London, Newcastle and Glasgow, an underground (tube) system, are the best way to avoid parking problems in big cities. Most buses operate on pay (the driver) as you enter, and ticket machines for the undergrounds save queuing, so plenty of loose change can be helpful.

Accommodation in the UK

Hotels are rated on a star system, usually awarded by a recognized body, such as the AA; one star being the lowest rating. There are some motels in the UK, usually situated in busy areas and near motorways. For the roving traveller, however, Bed and (English) Breakfast provides the flexible choice. It could be in anything from a near hotel, to a spare bedroom in someone's home, and in any type of building from a farmhouse, an old manor, a converted mill, to a modern bungalow. Prices range from £6 to £20 + per person sharing a double room per night, the average being £10–£15. Many Bed & Breakfast establishments also offer an evening meal which, in some, can be of a very high standard. In the high season of July and August, and around public holidays, it is advisable, but not essential, to book ahead. You can usually find somewhere.

Money in the UK

Currency: £1 = 100 pence (which are referred to as 'pee'). Banknotes in common usages are: £5, £10, £20 and £50. Scotland has the same denomination banknotes, but issued by the Bank of Scotland, and these are legal tender both sides of the border. The coins are: £1, 50p (large, 7 sides), 20p (small, 7 sides), 10p, 5p, and the 'coppers' 2p and 1p.

Banks: Opening hours 9.30–15.30, Monday–Friday. A few branches of Barclays Bank open on Saturday mornings. It is possible to change traveller's cheques and, usually, currency at all banks for a small fixed charge. Bureaux de Change can also be found in big cities, at Gatwick and Heathrow airports and some of London's mainline railway stations, such as Victoria. Also look out for branches of Thomas Cook and the Trustee Savings Bank (TSB) for changing facilities.

Tipping: Taxi drivers, waiters, porters, hairdressers, a customary 10–15%. Some restaurants state on the menu that the Service Charge will be automatically included on the bill, and therefore you pay it, otherwise it is up to the discretion of the customer to tip.

Licensing Hours in the UK

Public houses (pubs) in England and Wales are usually open between 10.30–14.30, 17.30–23.00, but these may vary by half an hour to an hour, and hotel bars generally open later in the morning and evening. Pubs open later on Sundays, about 18.30–19.00. In Scotland the licensing hours have been extended to cover most of the day.

Health Care in the UK

For light ailments, such as a cold, a stomach upset, a graze or stings, the pharmacist at any dispensing chemist (pharmacy) will be able and happy to advise on proprietary brands of medicaments. Dispensing chemists display a sign in the window to declare that they have a dispensary inside. Some stores which only sell toiletries and related goods, and which are sometimes referred to in the UK as chemists, now call themselves drugstores to distinguish themselves from pharmacies.

To see a National Health Service doctor, either telephone or go along to the nearest surgery where you may either wait or an appointment will be made. There is no fee.

In the case of an emergency, telephone 999 and ask for the ambulance service. If you are able to get there yourself, go to the nearest hospital casualty department, where you will get help, again free of charge.
* There is a fee for medicines on prescription, payable in the pharmacy/chemist's.

Time in the UK

The 24-hour or Continental clock is used on all official documents and timetables, but is not used in general conversation.

Further Information

British Telecom's Yellow Pages telephone directory is an area by area directory of all the local services, and there should be one by any public phone. Thomson Local Directories also list local services, and may be available in hotels and places of accommodation.

There are many guidebooks now published each year on accommodation, places to eat, places where children are especially welcome, activities. Any large bookshop or newsagent should carry them.

American/English Glossary

Most American people are familiar with English terms these days, from watching films and television.
cab – taxi
elevator – lift
faucet – tap
gas(oline) – petrol
hood – bonnet
in back of – behind
tube – underground
windshield – windscreen
trunk – boot
license plate – number plate

ATLAS

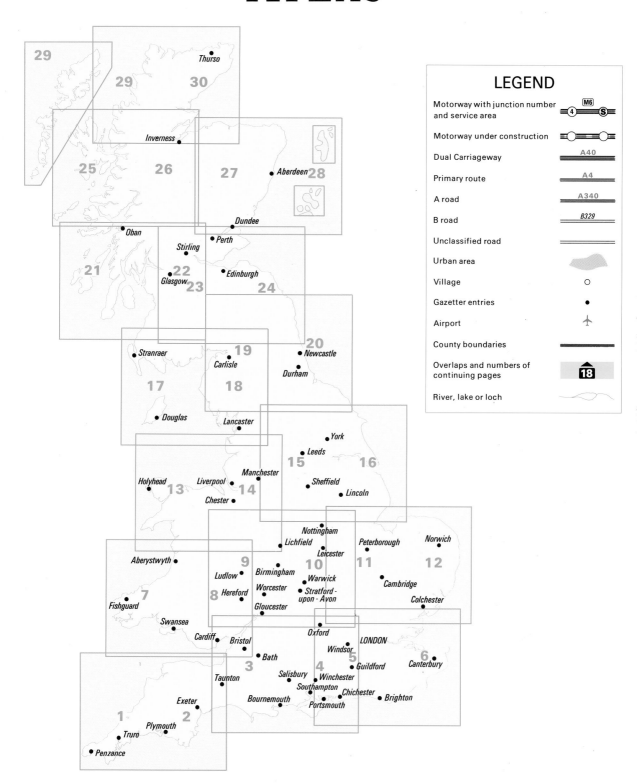

LEGEND

Motorway with junction number and service area	
Motorway under construction	
Dual Carriageway	A40
Primary route	A4
A road	A340
B road	B329
Unclassified road	
Urban area	
Village	○
Gazetter entries	●
Airport	✈
County boundaries	
Overlaps and numbers of continuing pages	18
River, lake or loch	

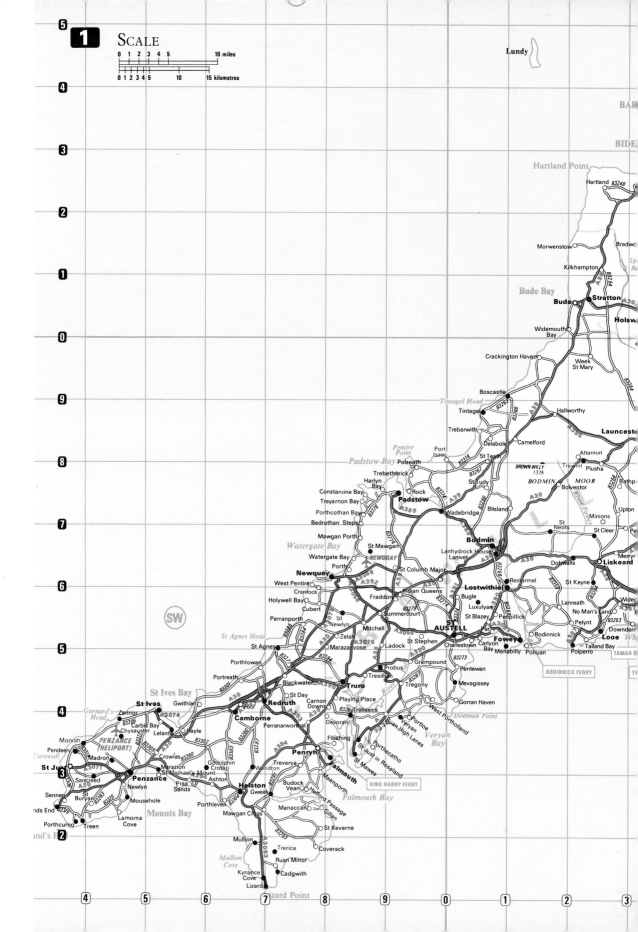

SCALE

0 1 2 3 4 5   10 miles

0 1 2 3 4 5   10   15 kilometres

Lundy

Hartland Point

Hartland B3248

BIDE

BAR

Morwenstow

Bradwo

Kilkhampton

B3254

Bude Bay

Bude

Stratton

A30

Holsw

Widemouth Bay

Crackington Haven

Week St Mary

B3254

Boscastle

Tintagel Head

Tintagel

B3263

B3266

A39

Hallworthy

Launcest

A395

Trebarwith

Delabole

Camelford

Altarnun

Trewint

Plusha

B3254

Bathp

Pentire Point

Port Isaac

B3314

St Teath

BROWN WILLY 1375

Trebetherick

Polzeath

Harlyn Bay

St Tudy

BODMIN MOOR

Bolventor

A30

River Fow

Upton

Padstow Bay

Rock

B3314

Constantine Bay

Treyarnon Bay

Padstow

B3276

A389

A39

Wadebridge

B3266

Blisland

Minions

Porthcothan Bay

St Neots

St Cleer

Pe

Bedruthan Steps

A389

Bodmin

Mawgan Porth

Lanhydrock House

Lanivet

Dobwalls

Merryr

Re

Watergate Bay

St Mawgan

A30

A38

Liskeard

Watergate Bay

St Columb Major

Lostwithiel

Restormel

St Keyne

Wider

Porth

NEWQUAY

B3274

Bugle

B3269

Lanreath

Newquay

A392

Indian Queens

Luxulyan

No Man's Land

B3253

West Pentire

A3058

Fraddon

St Blazey

Penpillick

Pelynt

B3359

Crantock

A30

Summercourt

St Austell

Par

Bodinnick

Downder

Holywell Bay

St Newlyn

A3076

Mitchell

ST AUSTELL

Fowey

Looe

Wh

Cubert

Zelah

Ladock

St Stephen

Charlestown

Carlyon Bay

Polruan

Talland Bay

Perranporth

B3285

Marazanvose

B3284

A390

Menabilly

Polperro

TAMAR E

St Agnes Head

St Agnes

B3277

B3284

Probus

Grampound

Pentewan

BODINNICK FERRY

To

Porthtowan

Tresillian

Tregony

Mevagissey

Portreath

B3301

Blackwater

A390

Truro

B3273

St Day

A3058

Gorran Haven

St Ives Bay

Gwithian

Redruth

Playing Place

West Portholland

Dodman Point

St Ives

B3306

Zennor

B3074

Pool

Carnon Downs

Trelissick

Portloe

Veryan Bay

Gurnard's Head

Carbis Bay

Camborne

B3289

Veryan

Chysauster

Lelant

Perranarworthal

Devoran

St Just in Roseland

Morvah

Hayle

B3302

Flushing

Porthscatho

Pendeen

Madron

B3280

Penryn

St Mawes

PENZANCE (HELIPORT)

Crowlas

B3280

Treverva

Falmouth

Cornwall

B3311

Marazian

Godolphin Cross

Wendron

Maenporth

KING HARRY FERRY

St Just

A30

B3071

Penzance

St Michael's Mount

Ashton

Budock Vean

Helford Passage

Sancreed

Newlyn

Praa Sands

Helston

Gweek

Falmouth Bay

Sennen

St Buryan

B3283

Mousehole

Porthleven

Gillan

St Keverne

B3315

Manaccan

nds End

B3071

Lamorna Cove

Mounts Bay

Mawgan Cross

Porthcurno

Treen

Coverack

and's E

Mullion

B3293

Trerice

Ruan Minor

Cadgwith

Mullion Cove

Kynance Cove

Lizard

B3083

A3083

Lizard Point

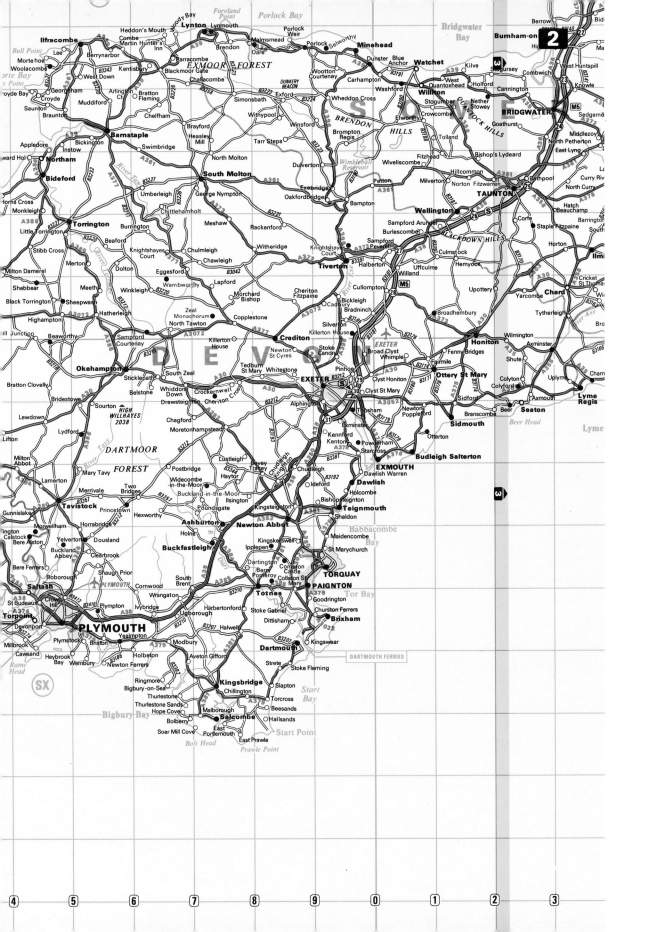

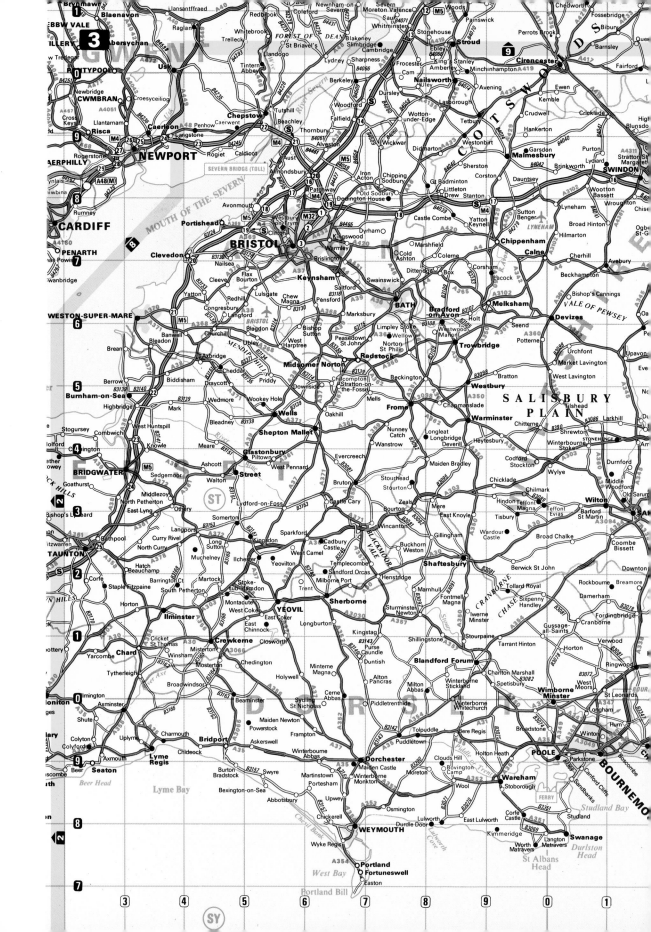

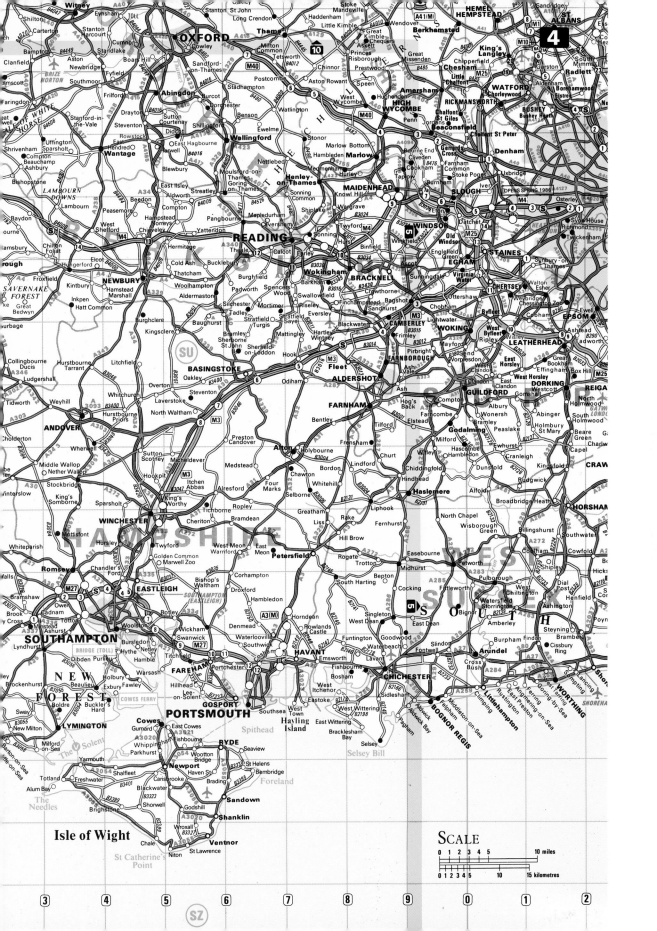

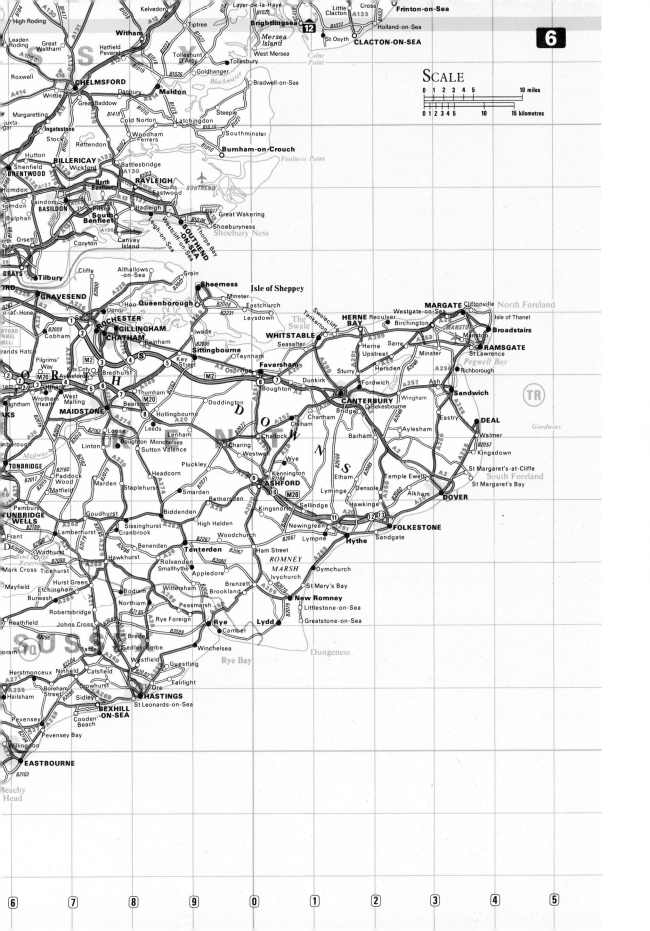

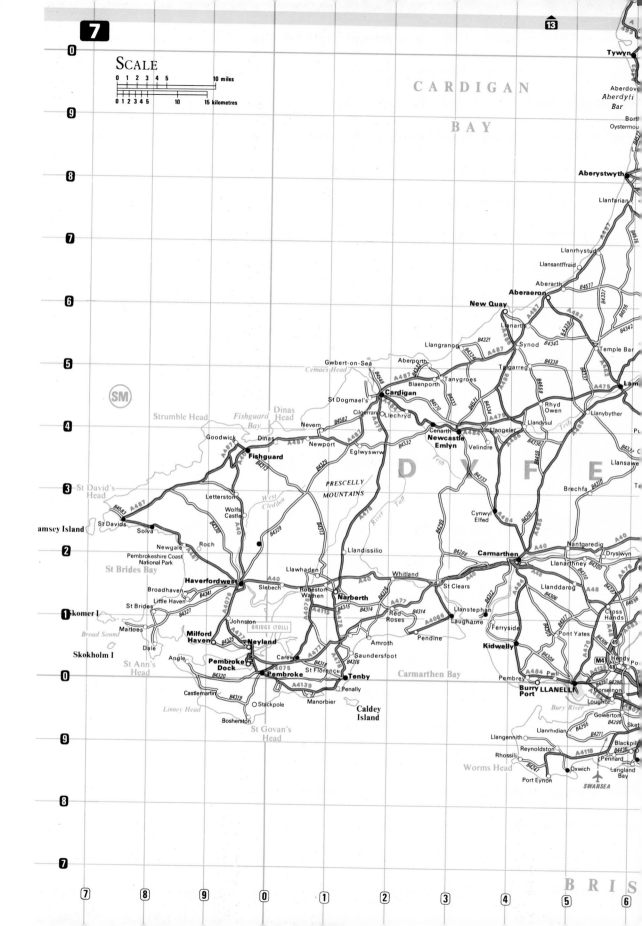

SCALE

0 1 2 3 4 5   10 miles

0 1 2 3 4 5   10   15 kilometres

CARDIGAN

BAY

Tywyn

Aberdove
*Aberdyfi
Bar*

Borth
Oystermou

Aberystwyth

Llanfarian

Llanrhystud

Llansantffraid

Aberarth
B4577

Aberaeron

New Quay

Llenarth

Synod
B4341

Temple Bar

Llangranog
B4321

Talgarreg
B4338

Aberporth

Gwbert-on-Sea

Rhyd
Owen

Lam

Blaenporth
Tanygroes

Cemaes Head

St Dogmael's

Cardigan

Llandysul

Llanybyther

Llechryd

Cilgerran

Llansawe

*Fishguard
Bay*

*Dinas
Head*

Nevern
B4582

B4570

Newcastle
Emlyn

Cenarth

Llangeler

Teifi

Goodwick

Dinas

A487

Newport

B4329

Eglwyswrw

Velindre

Brechfa

(SM)

Strumble Head

B4313

*PRESCELLY
MOUNTAINS*

River Taff

B4333

Teifi

Cynwyl
Elfed

B4299

B4298

St David's
Head

Letterston

Wolfs
Castle

*West
Cleddau*

B4329

B4313

A478

Carmarthen

Nantgaredig
Dryslwyn

amsey Island

St Davids

Solva

B4330

Llandissilio

Llanarthney
B4300

Newgale

Roch

Llawhaden

Whitland

B4310

Llanddarog

A48

Pembrokeshire Coast
National Park

St Brides Bay

Haverfordwest

Slebech

Robeston
Wathen

A40

St Clears

Llanstephan

Cross
Hands

Broadhaven

B4341

A40

Narberth

B4314

Red
Roses

B4314

Laugharne

Ferryside

Pont Yates

49

St Brides

Little Haven

B4327

A477

B4066

Pendine

Pont Yates

48

M4

Hendy
Po

Skomer I

Johnston

A477

BRIDGE (TOLL)

Amroth

Saundersfoot

Kidwelly

Pembrey

Pwll

Loughor

Marloes

Dale

Milford
Haven

B4325

Neyland

Carew

B4318

St Florence

B4316

Tenby

Carmarthen Bay

Burry
Port

LLANELLI

Gorseinon

Broad Sound

Skokholm I

Angle

Pembroke
Dock

A4075

Pembroke

B4320

A4139

Penally

Caldey
Island

Bury River

A484

Gowerton

B4296

Sket

*St Ann's
Head*

Castlemartin

B4319

Stackpole

Manorbier

Llanrhidian

B4295

Blackpill

Linney Head

Bosherston

St Govan's
Head

Langennith

Reynoldston

Rhossili

A4118

Pennard

Langland
Bay

Worms Head

Oxwich

SWANSEA

Port Eynon

B R I S

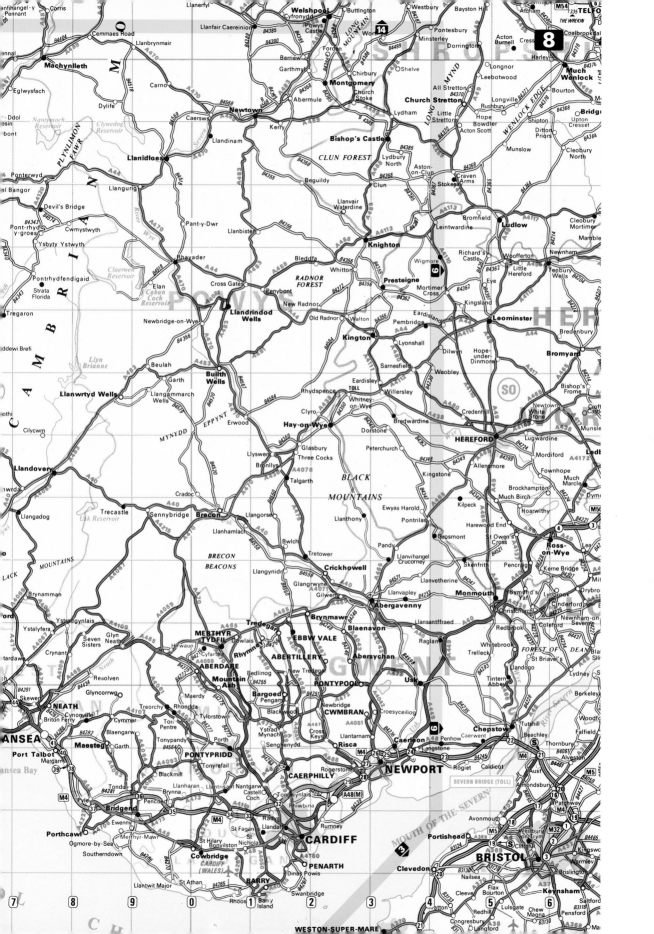

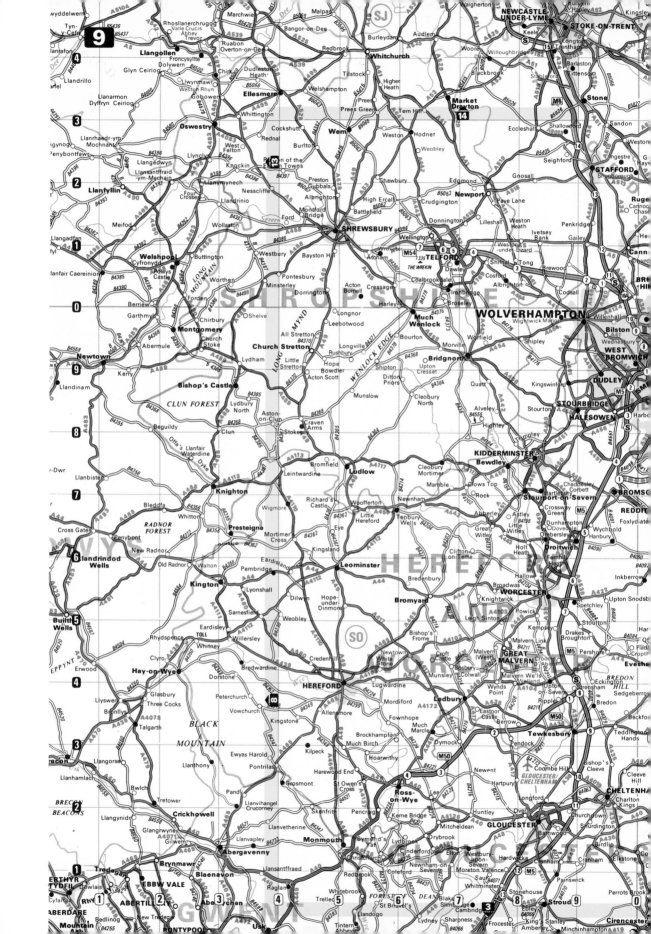

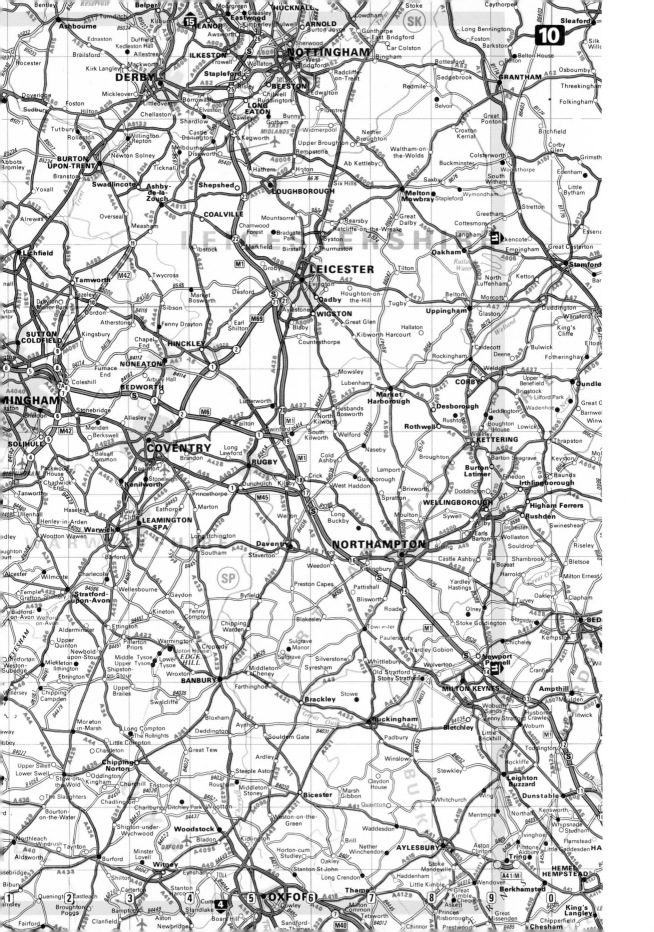

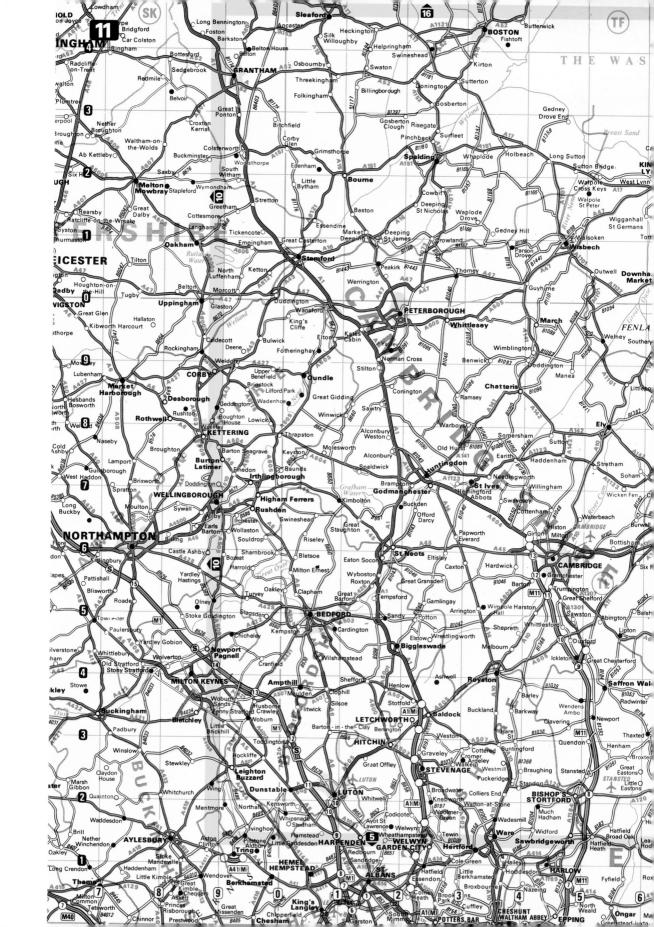

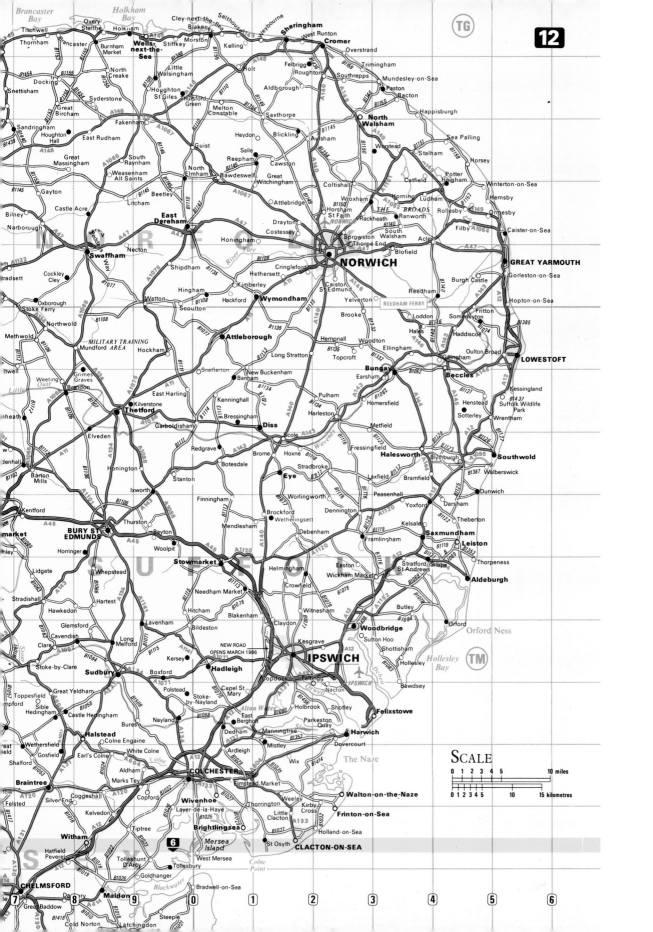

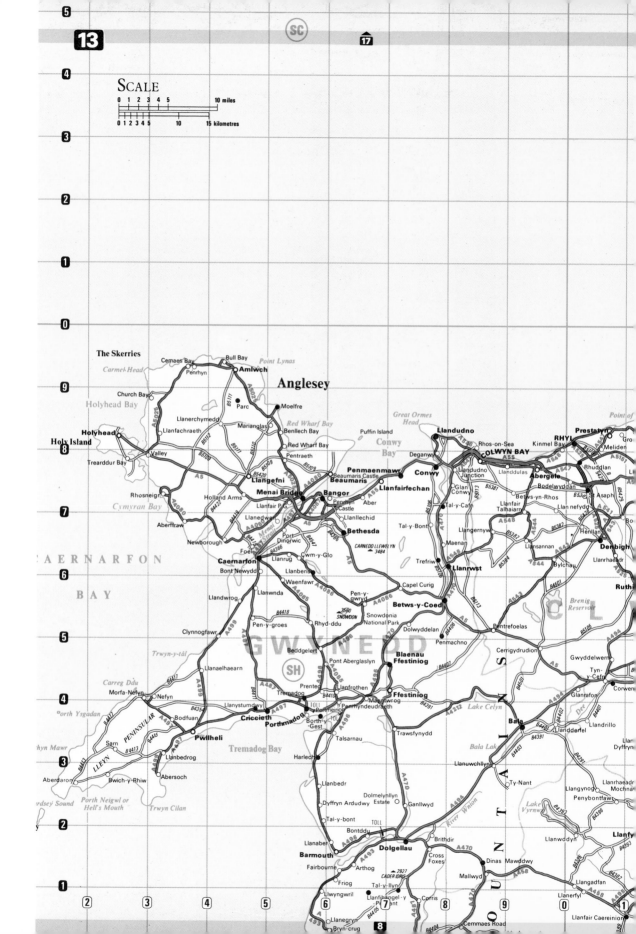

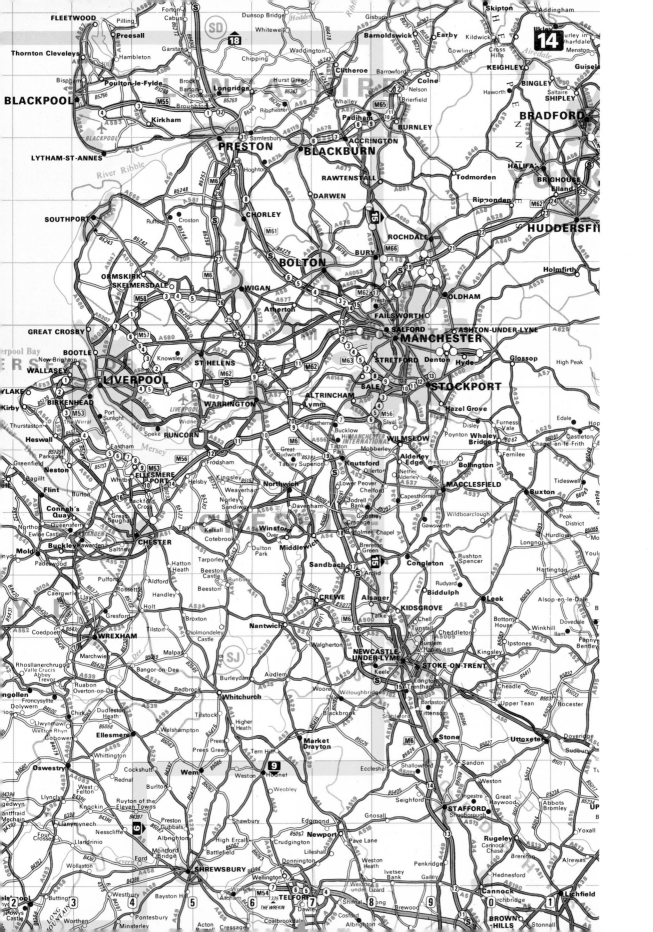

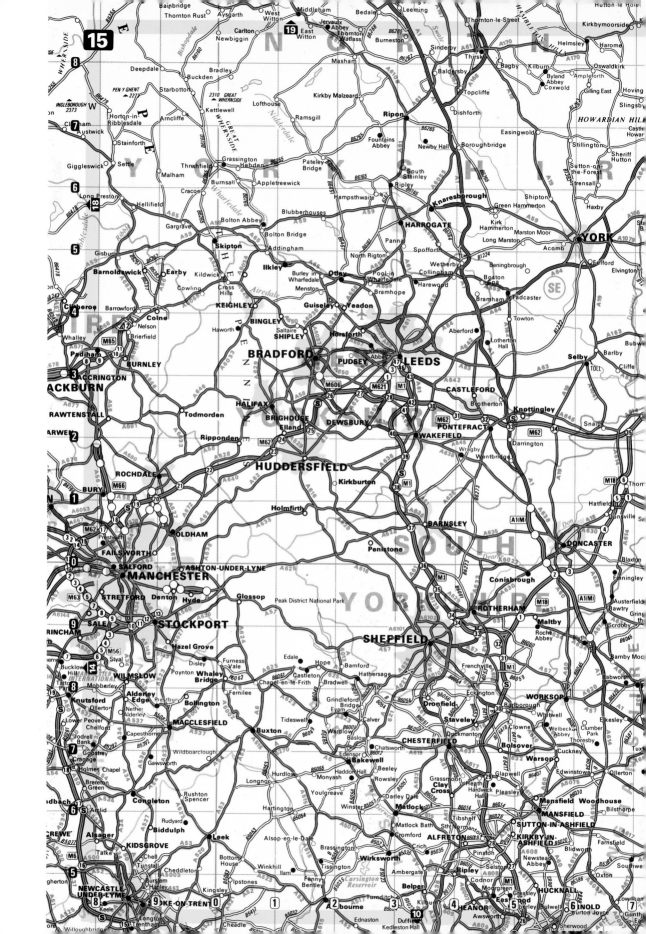

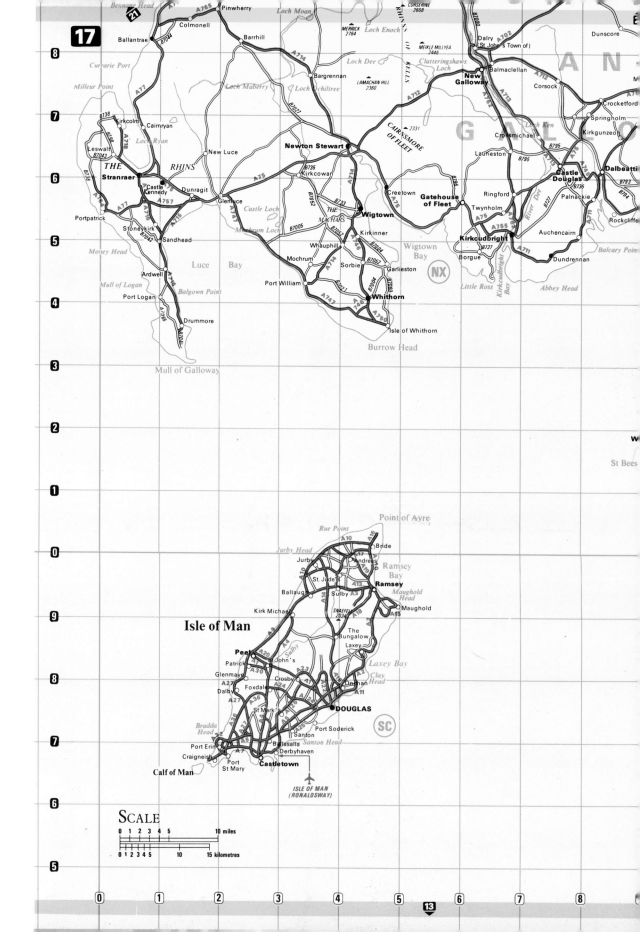

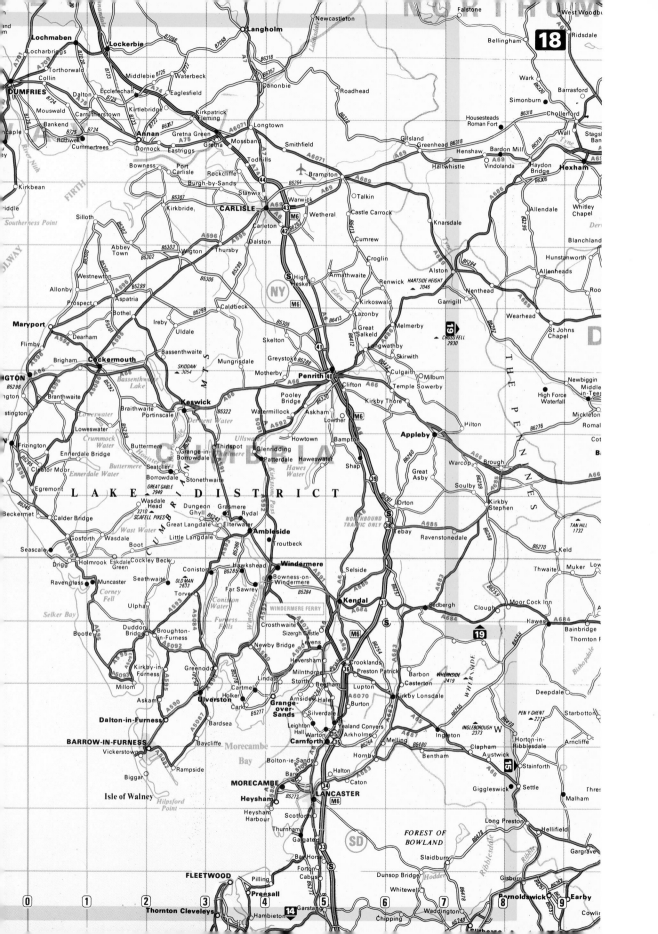

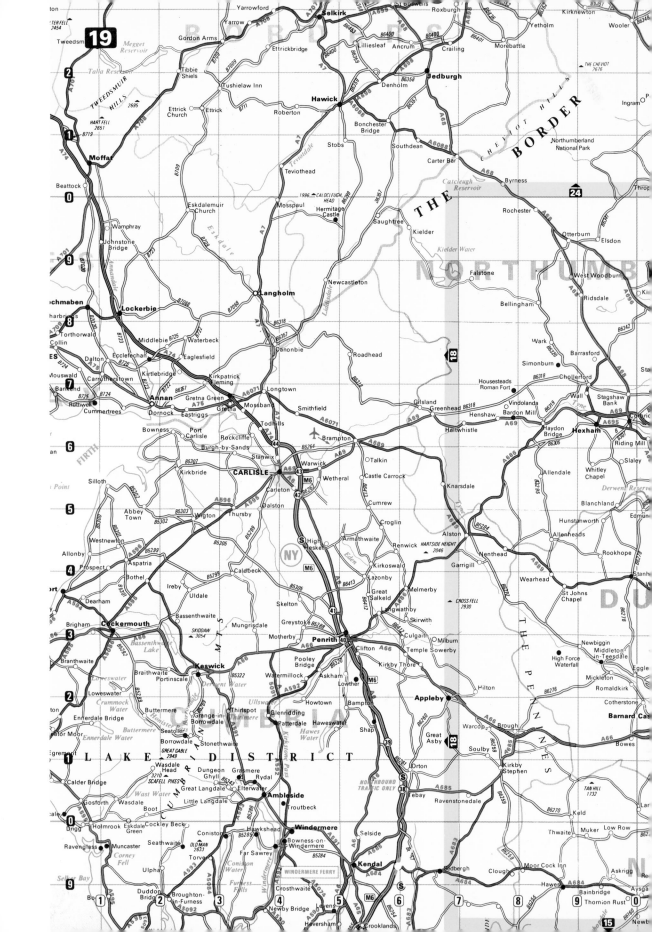

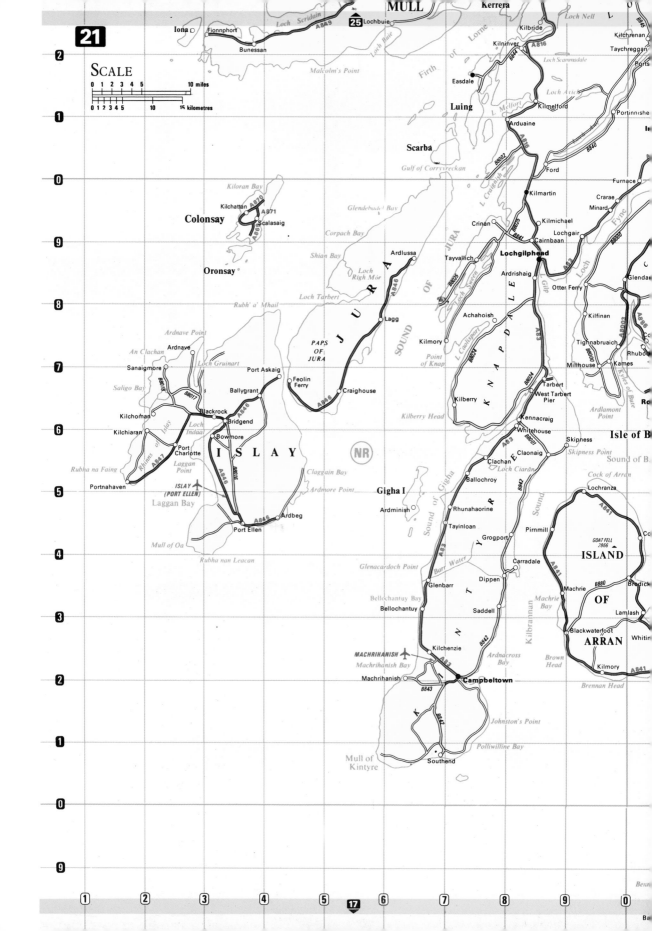

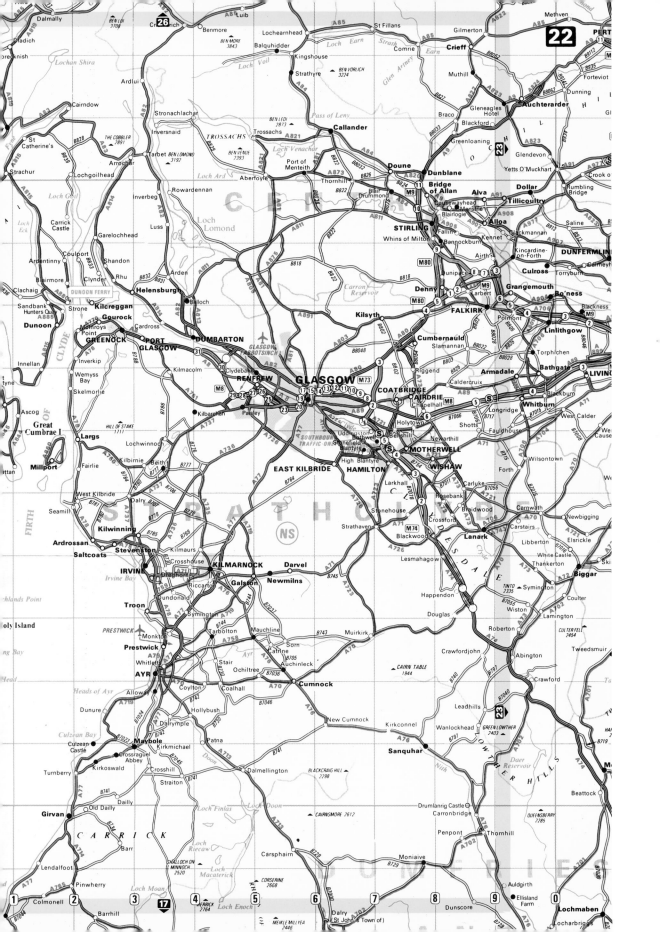

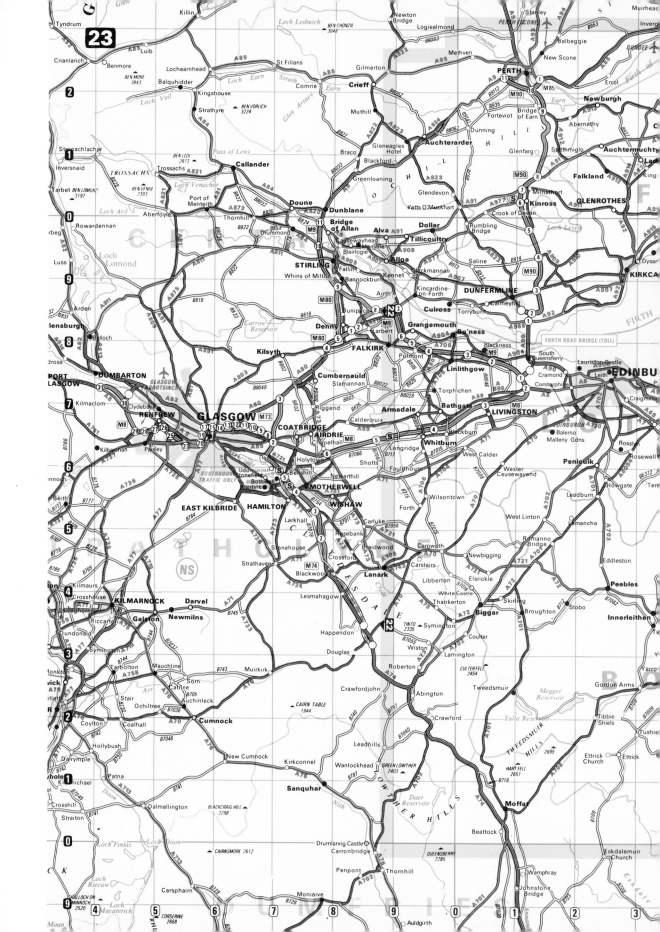

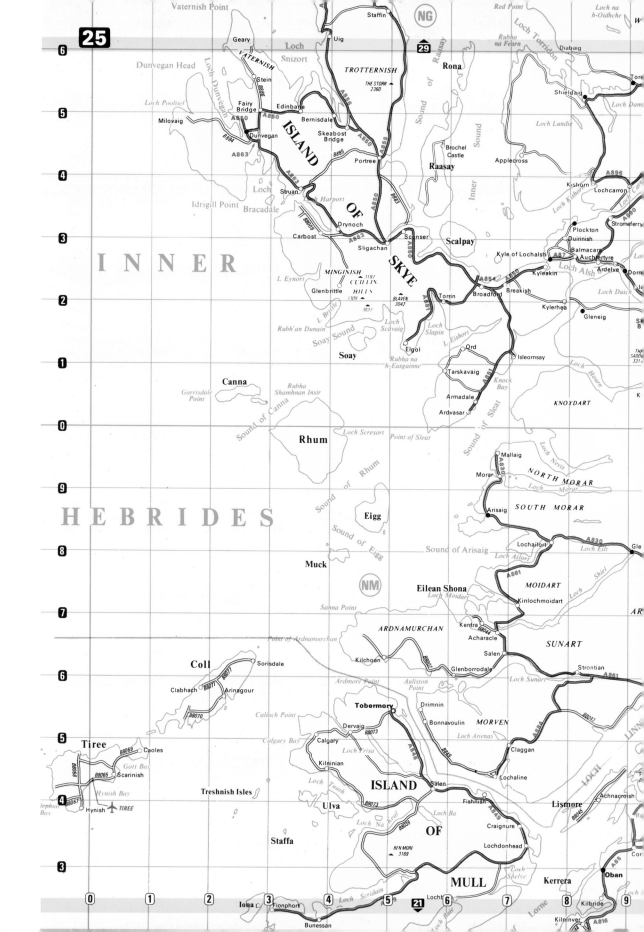

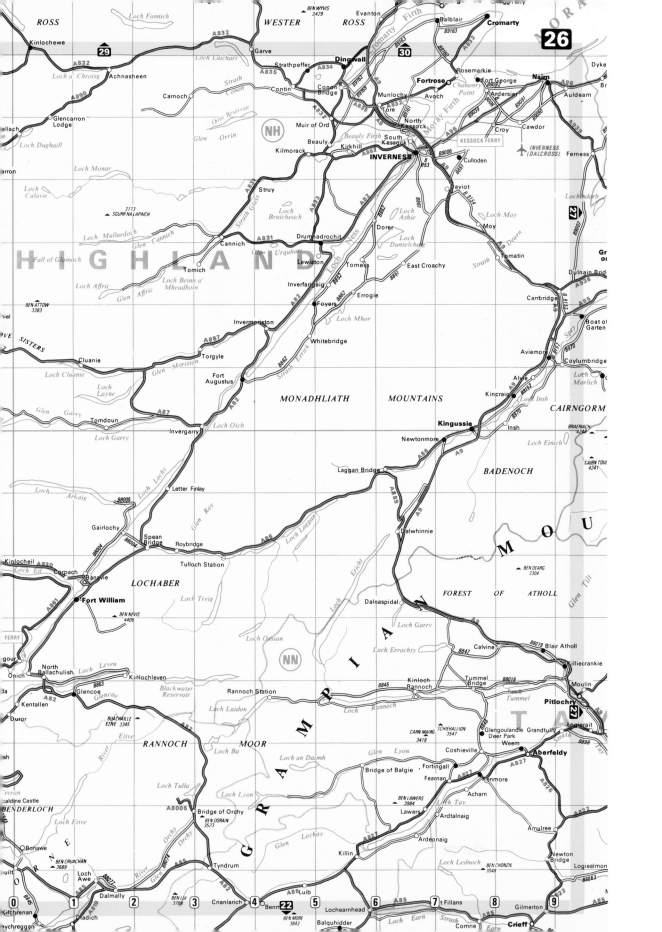

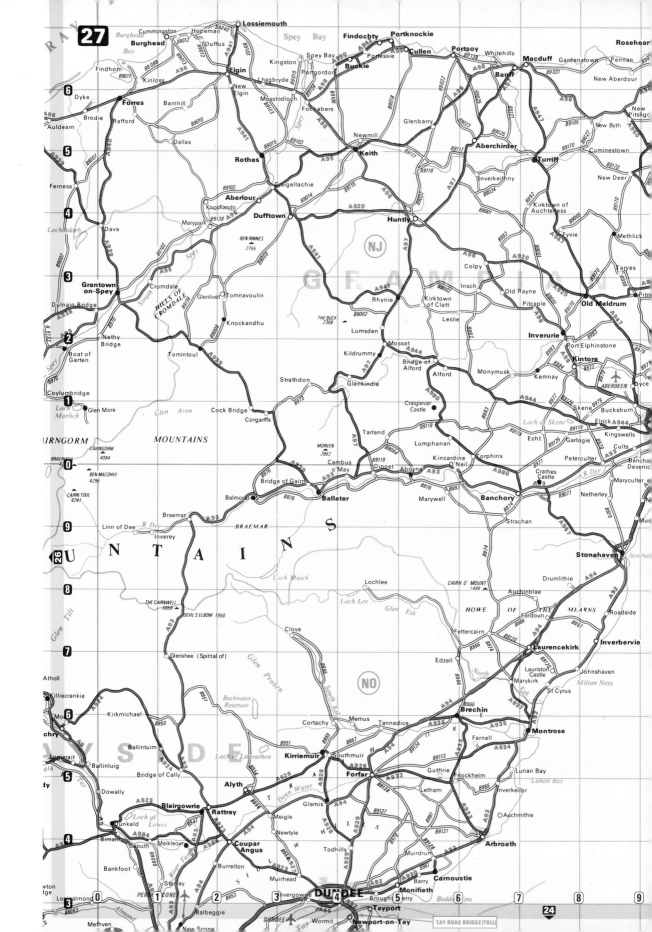

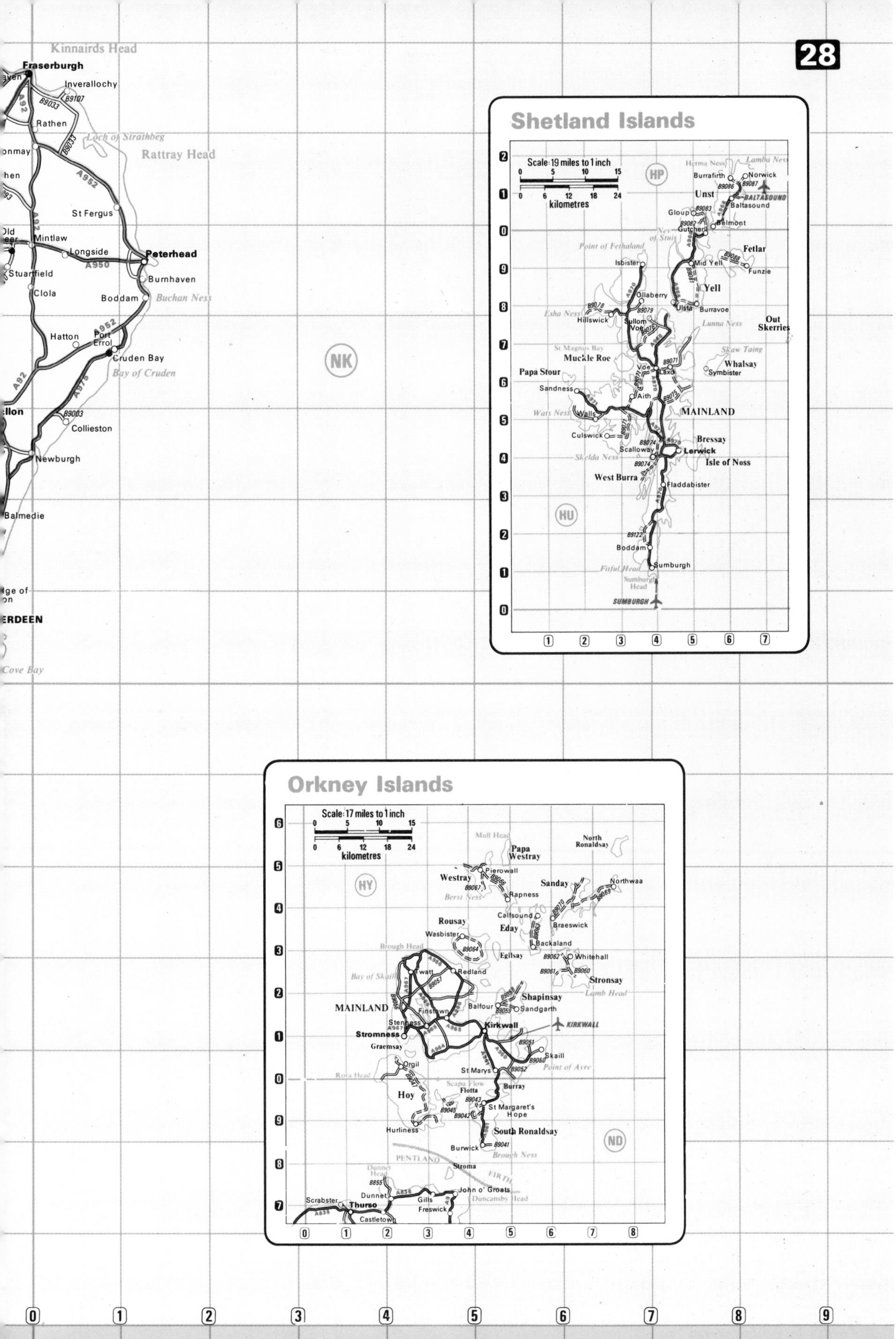

Kinnairds Head
Fraserburgh
Inverallochy
B9033
B9107
Rathen
Loch of Strathbeg
onmay
Rattray Head
A952
hen
St Fergus
Old
Mintlaw
Longside
A950
Stuarfield
Peterhead
Clola
Burnhaven
Boddam
Buchan Ness
A952
Hatton
Port
Errol
Cruden Bay
Bay of Cruden
llon
B9003
Collieston
Newburgh
Balmedie
ge of
on
ERDEEN
Cove Bay

NK

Shetland Islands

Scale: 19 miles to 1 inch
0   5   10   15
0   6   12   18   24
kilometres

HP

Herma Ness   Lamba Ness
Burrafirth   Norwick
B9086   B9087
Unst   BALTASOUND
Baltasound
Gloup   B9083
B9082   Belmont
Gutcherd
2
1   **Fetlar**
Mid Yell   B9088
Point of Fethaland   **Yell**   Funzie
Isbister   Uista
0   Oilaberry   Burravoe
9   B9078   B9079   Out
Esha Ness   Sullom   Skerries
Hillswick   Voe   Lunna Ness
8   St Magnus Bay   Skaw Taing
Muckle Roe   Whalsay
7   Voe   B9071
Papa Stour   Symbister
6   Lxsxo
Sandness   B9075
5   Walls   **MAINLAND**
Wats Ness   Aith
Culswick   **Bressay**
B9074   Scalloway   **Lerwick**
4   Skelda Ness   B9074   Isle of Noss
West Burra   Fladdabister
3
HU
2   B9122
Boddam
1   Sumburgh
Fitful Head
0   Sumburgh
Head
SUMBURGH

① ② ③ ④ ⑤ ⑥ ⑦

Orkney Islands

Scale: 17 miles to 1 inch
0   5   10   15
0   6   12   18   24
kilometres

6   Mull Head   North
Papa   Ronaldsay
Westray
5   Pierowall   HY
Westray   Sanday   Northwaa
B9067   Rapness   B9069
Berst Ness   Caltsound
4   **Rousay**   Braeswick
Wasbister   **Eday**
3   B9064   Backaland
Brough Head   Egilsay   B9062   Whitehall
Bay of Skaill   B9061   B9060
2   watt   Redland   **Stronsay**
Finstown   Lamb Head
MAINLAND   B9053   **Shapinsay**
1   Stenness   Balfour   Sandgarth   KIRKWALL
Stromness   A965   **Kirkwall**
Graemsay   B9051
0   Orgil   Skaill   Point of Ayre
Rora Head   St Marys   B9052
9   Scapa Flow   Burray   ND
Hoy   Flotta   B9043
B9045   St Margaret's
Hurliness   B9042   Hope
8   Burwick   B9041
South Ronaldsay
PENTLAND   Brough Ness
Dunnet   Stroma
7   Head   FIRTH
B855   John o' Groats
Scrabster   Dunnet   Gills   Duncansby Head
Thurso   Freswick
Castletown

⓪ ① ② ③ ④ ⑤ ⑥ ⑦ ⑧

⓪ ① ② ③ ④ ⑤ ⑥ ⑦ ⑧ ⑨

8

7

7

6

6

5

5

4

3

2

1

0

Cape Wrath

Kyle of Durness

Sandwood Loch

Sheigra

Kinlochbervie · Badcall

Loch Inchard

A838

FOINAVEN 2980

Laxford Bridge

BEN ARKLE 2582

Handa I

Loch Laxford

BEN STACK 2364

Loch Stack

Scourie

A838

Badcall

A894

Loch More

Eddrachillis Bay

Point of Stoer · *Clashnessie Bay*

Kylestrome

Loch Glendhu

Kylesku · Unapool

Drumbeg

B869

Loch Glencoul

Nedd

QUINAG 2653

Loch Merkland

Clashnessie

A894

GLASVEN 2541

Stoer

B864 · A837

Loch Assynt

Lochinver

Inchnadamph

BEN MORE ASSYNT 3273

Loch Inver

Rubha Coigeach

SULVEN 2399

CANISP 2779

Inverkirkaig

A837

Ledmore Junction

Enard Bay

Cam Loch

Reiff

Loch Veyatie

NB

Glen Oykell

Loch Ailsh

Polbain

Loch Sionascaig

Knockan

Loch Urigill

Achiltibuie

Summer Isles

Loch Lurgain

COIGACH

Oykell Br

A835

A837

Strath Kanaird

Oykell Br

Cailleach Head

Gruinard Bay

Ullapool

Loch Achall

Loch an Daimh

Leckmelm

EASTER

A835

Rubha Reidh

Cove

A832

Little Loch Broom

Laide

Loch Broom

Melvaig

Aultbea

Ardessie

Dundonnell

B8021

Loch Ewe

AN TEALLACH 3483

BEINN DEARG 3547

Midtown Brae

Loch na Sealga

North Erradale

Poolewe

Fionn Loch

Strath

Lochan Fada

Loch a' Bhraoin

Braemore Junction

Gairloch

SGURR BAN 3194

Loch Glascar

Port Henderson

B8056

A832

SGURR MOR 3637

Talladale

Aultguish

na Hunish

A832

Duntulm · Kilmaluag

Red Point

Loch na h-Oidhche

WESTER ROSS

Loch Fannich

Flodigarry

A855

SING 1779

Loch Maree

A832

Staffin

NG

Rubha na Fearn

Diabaig

EIGHE 3309

Kinlochewe

Loch Luichart

Uig

Loch Torridon

A832

Achnasheen

Loch a' Chroisg

A890

25

Rona

LIATHACH 3456

Carnoch

Strath Con

TROTTERNISH

THE STORR 2360

Sound of Raasay

Torridon

Shieldaig

A896

Glencarron Lodge

Orrin Reser

A855

Loch Damh

Achnashellach Lodge

Glen Orrin

nisdale

Skeabost Bridge

A850

A855

Loch Lundie

Loch Dughaill

Brochel

App ross

A896

Strathcarron

Loch Monar

Portree

Raasay

Kishorn

4

5

7

8

9

0

1

2

3

THE MINCH

THE LITTLE MINCH

SOUND OF THE HEBRIDES

Inset: Western Isles

ISLANDS

8 · 9 · 0 · 1 · 2 · 3 · 4 · 5 · 6 · 7

Scale 22½ miles to 1 inch

0 · 5 · 10 · 15 · 20

0 · 8 · 16 · 24 · 32

kilometres

NB

ISLE OF LEWIS

Butt of Lewis

Port of Ness

Cellar Head

Barvas

North Tolsta

NA

Carloway

A857

Tiumpan Head

Uig

Breasclete

Broad Bay

Stornoway

Eye Peninsula

STORNOWAY

A858

Balallan

B8060

Husinish

CLISHAM 2622

BEINN MHOR 1874

Husinish Point

West Loch Tarbert

Taransay

Tarbert

Scalpay

Toe Head

Harris

Pabbay

Rodel

Berneray

Boreray

iminish Point

Tigharry

Loch Langavat

A867

Lochmaddy

North Uist

BENBECULA

NF

Ronay

Balivanich

Gramsdale

NG

Creagorry

A851

Wiay

Stilligarry

B890

al Ardvule

South Uist

Loch Esmort

NB

Lochboisdale

skay

Barra

BARRA

Castlebay

Vatersay

Sandray

Mingulay

Head

NL

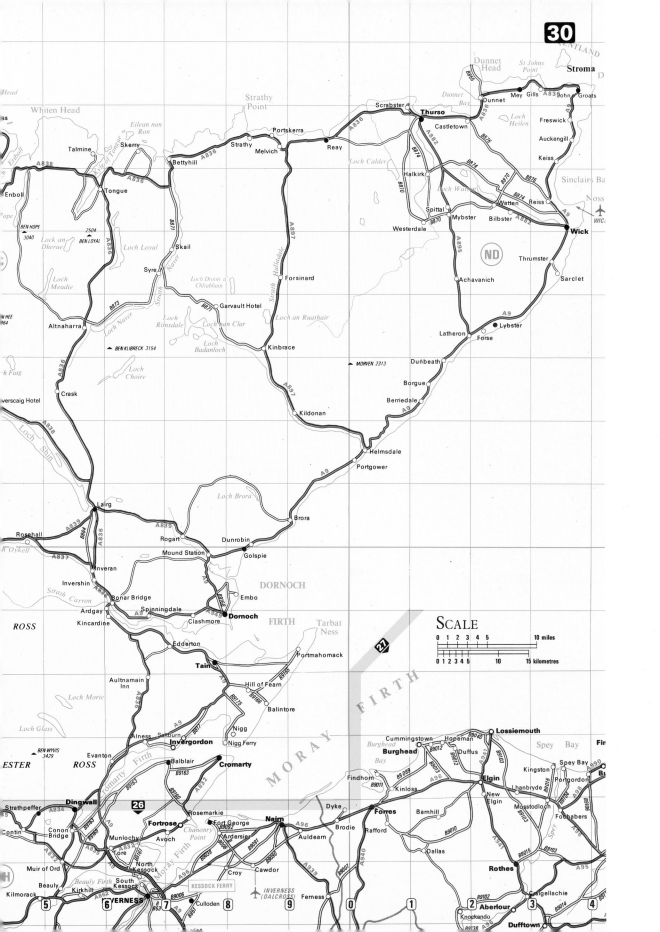

ACKNOWLEDGEMENTS

The publishers would like to thank the following for the use of their illustrative material.

Martin Adelman 47, 85, 95,110, 120, 124, 229, 246

Malcolm Aird 49

P & G Bowater 89, 90, 94, 131, 133, 174

Britain on View (British Tourist Authority) Frontispiece, 16, 112, 113, 126, 163, 204

Julia Brittain 93

Eric Carle 27

Cromwell Museum 26

Robert Eames 37, 141, 213, 216, 226

Mary Evans Picture Library 58, 254

Robin Fletcher 66, 122, 168, 231

Jarrold & Sons Ltd 129

S & O Matthews 12, 15, 18, 25, 40, 41, 46, 63, 71, 72, 75, 79, 83, 86, 93, 99, 103, 108, 115, 118, 125, 130, 132, 134, 170, 181, 189, 190, 197, 199, 203, 215, 230, 248, 252, 253

Colin Molyneux 30, 42, 64, 65, 79, 105, 140, 141, 158, 166, 176, 193

Richard Newton 66, 121, 201, 218, 233

Northern Ireland Tourist Board 236, 237

Chris Ridley 182

Scottish National Portrait Gallery 126

Scottish Tourist Board 81

L P Sports 73

Richard Surman 21, 135, 139, 222, 249, 250

Patrick Thurston 163

US Naval Academy Museum 80

Jon Wynand 15, 243